Enemies and Neighbours

IAN BLACK

Enemies and Neighbours

Arabs and Jews in Palestine and Israel,
1917–2017

ALLEN LANE
an imprint of
PENGUIN BOOKS

ALLEN LANE

UK | USA | Canada | Ireland | Australia
India | New Zealand | South Africa

Allen Lane is part of the Penguin Random House group of companies
whose addresses can be found at global.penguinrandomhouse.com

First published 2017
001

Copyright © Ian Black, 2017

The moral right of the author has been asserted

Set in 10.5/14 pt Sabon LT Std
Typeset by Jouve (UK), Milton Keynes
Printed in Great Britain by Clays Ltd, St Ives plc

A CIP catalogue record for this book is available from the British Library

ISBN: 978–0–241–00442–5

www.greenpenguin.co.uk

MIX
Paper from
responsible sources
FSC
www.fsc.org   FSC® C018179

Penguin Random House is committed to a
sustainable future for our business, our readers
and our planet. This book is made from Forest
Stewardship Council® certified paper.

Contents

CONTENTS

List of Illustrations

List of Maps

The Ottoman Empire, 1878–1914

N

RUSSIA

AUSTRO-
HUNGARIAN
EMPIRE

Black Sea

Caspian Sea

Constantinople

•Ankara

PERSIA

•Aleppo

•Tunis

Tigris

Beirut

•Baghdad

Euphrates

TUNISIA

Mediterranean Sea

CRETE

CYPRUS

•Damascus

Persian
Gulf

•Tripoli

Alexandria

•Jerusalem

TRIPOLITANIA

•Cairo

EGYPT

ARABIA

Red Sea

•Mecca

0   500 miles
0   500 km

Ottoman Empire

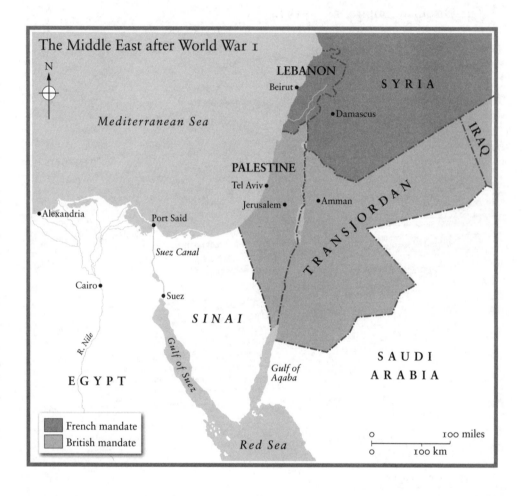

The Middle East after World War 1

N

Mediterranean Sea

LEBANON
Beirut•

SYRIA

•Damascus

IRAQ

PALESTINE
Tel Aviv•

Jerusalem• •Amman

TRANSJORDAN

•Alexandria

Port Said•

Suez Canal

Cairo•

•Suez

SINAI

Gulf of Suez

Gulf of
Aqaba

SAUDI
ARABIA

R. Nile

EGYPT

French mandate
British mandate

Red Sea

0   100 miles
0   100 km

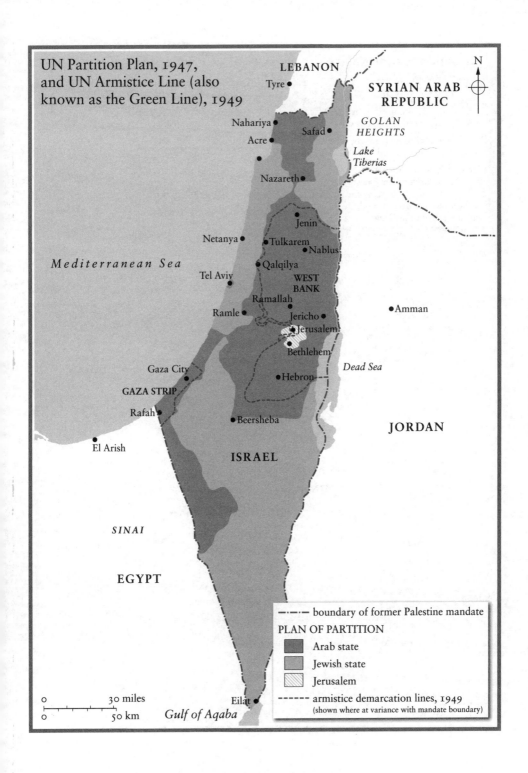

UN Partition Plan, 1947,
and UN Armistice Line (also
known as the Green Line), 1949

N

LEBANON

Tyre ●

SYRIAN ARAB
REPUBLIC

*GOLAN
HEIGHTS*

Nahariya ●

Safad ●

Acre ●

*Lake
Tiberias*

Nazareth ●

Mediterranean Sea

Jenin ●

Netanya ●

Tulkarem ●

● Nablus

Qalqilya ●

Tel Aviv ●

WEST
BANK

Ramallah ●

Ramle ●

Jericho ●

● Amman

Jerusalem ●

Bethlehem ●

Gaza City ●

Hebron ●

Dead Sea

GAZA STRIP

Rafah ●

JORDAN

● Beersheba

El Arish ●

ISRAEL

SINAI

EGYPT

0   30 miles

0   50 km

Eilat ●

Gulf of Aqaba

—·—·— boundary of former Palestine mandate

PLAN OF PARTITION

◼ Arab state

◼ Jewish state

▨ Jerusalem

- - - - - armistice demarcation lines, 1949
(shown where at variance with mandate boundary)

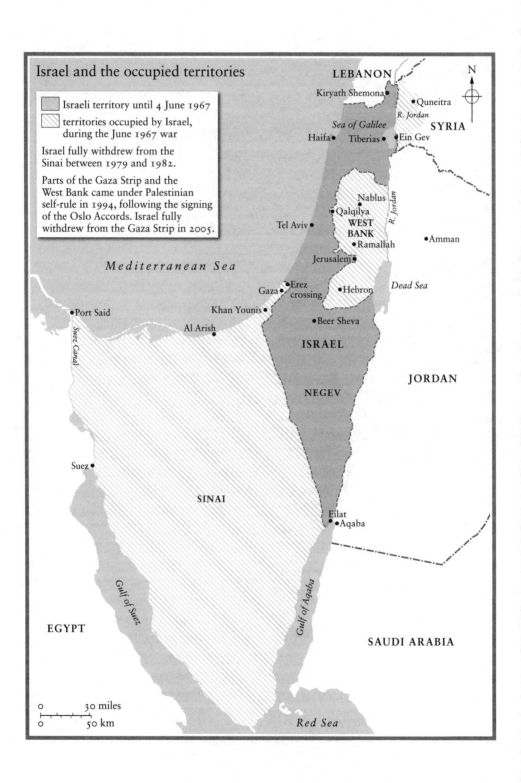

Israel and the occupied territories

Israeli territory until 4 June 1967

territories occupied by Israel,
during the June 1967 war

Israel fully withdrew from the
Sinai between 1979 and 1982.

Parts of the Gaza Strip and the
West Bank came under Palestinian
self-rule in 1994, following the signing
of the Oslo Accords. Israel fully
withdrew from the Gaza Strip in 2005.

LEBANON

N

Kiryath Shemona

Quneitra

R. Jordan

SYRIA

Sea of Galilee

Haifa   Tiberias   Ein Gev

Nablus

Qalqilya

WEST
BANK

Tel Aviv

Amman

Ramallah

Jerusalem

Mediterranean Sea

Gaza   Erez
crossing

Hebron

Dead Sea

Port Said

Khan Younis

Al Arish

Beer Sheva

Suez Canal

ISRAEL

NEGEV

JORDAN

Suez

SINAI

Eilat
Aqaba

Gulf of Suez

Gulf of Aqaba

EGYPT

SAUDI ARABIA

0   30 miles

0   50 km

Red Sea

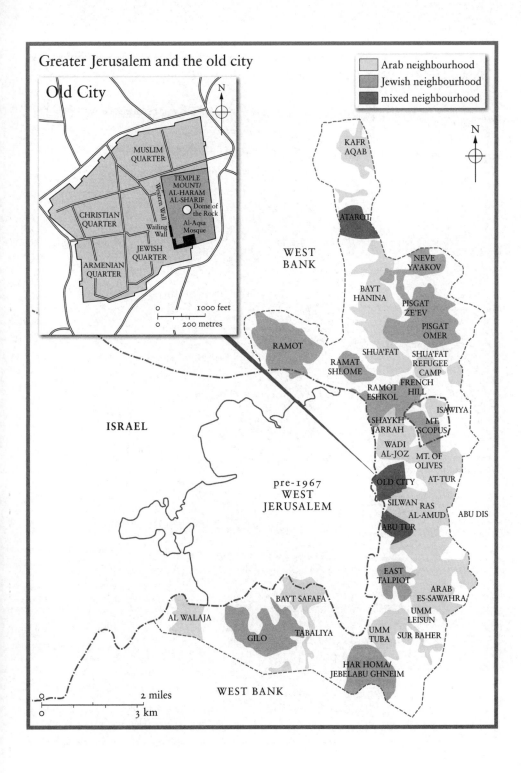

Greater Jerusalem and the old city

Arab neighbourhood
Jewish neighbourhood
mixed neighbourhood

Old City

N

MUSLIM
QUARTER

TEMPLE
MOUNT/
AL-HARAM
AL-SHARIF
Dome of
the Rock
Al-Aqsa
Mosque

Western Wall

CHRISTIAN
QUARTER

Wailing
Wall

JEWISH
QUARTER

ARMENIAN
QUARTER

0   1000 feet
0   200 metres

N

KAFR
AQAB

WEST
BANK

ATAROT

NEVE
YA'AKOV

BAYT
HANINA

PISGAT
ZE'EV

PISGAT
OMER

RAMOT

SHUA'FAT

SHUA'FAT
REFUGEE
CAMP

RAMAT
SHLOME

RAMOT
ESHKOL

FRENCH
HILL

ISAWIYA

ISRAEL

SHAYKH
JARRAH

MT.
SCOPUS

WADI
AL-JOZ

MT. OF
OLIVES

pre-1967
WEST
JERUSALEM

OLD CITY

AT-TUR

SILWAN

RAS
AL-AMUD

ABU DIS

ABU TUR

EAST
TALPIOT

ARAB
ES-SAWAHRA

AL WALAJA

BAYT SAFAFA

UMM
LEISUN

GILO

TABALIYA

UMM
TUBA

SUR BAHER

HAR HOMA/
JEBELABU GHNEIM

WEST BANK

0   2 miles
0   3 km

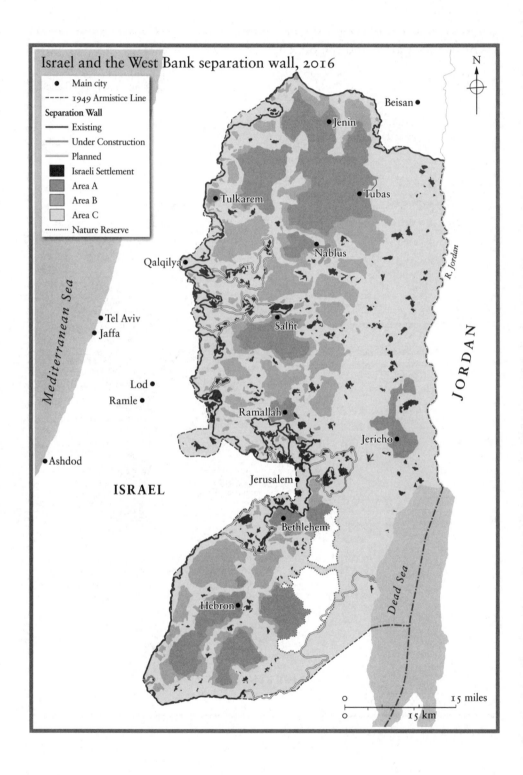

Israel and the West Bank separation wall, 2016

Legend:
- Main city
- 1949 Armistice Line
- Separation Wall
  - Existing
  - Under Construction
  - Planned
- Israeli Settlement
- Area A
- Area B
- Area C
- Nature Reserve

N

Mediterranean Sea

Beisan

Jenin

Tulkarem

Tubas

Nablus

Qalqilya

Tel Aviv

Jaffa

Salfit

R. Jordan

JORDAN

Lod

Ramle

Ramallah

Jericho

Ashdod

Jerusalem

ISRAEL

Bethlehem

Dead Sea

Hebron

15 miles

15 km

Language Matters

A Note on Terminology and Transliteration

The terminology used in this book generally reflects contemporary usage. In Ottoman times it was common to refer in Arabic, Hebrew and English to Muslims, Christians and Jews, reflecting the primary identity of the communities living under the imperial *millet* system of religious autonomy. The term 'Arab' became more widely used in Palestine and beyond in the first years of the twentieth century. The word 'Zionist' first appeared in the late nineteenth century but only became common currency during the British Mandate era. Before 1948 the term 'Palestinian' was far less widely employed than it is today and it made no distinction between Arabs and Jews. 'In those days people didn't use the word "Palestinian" so much', as the economist Yusif Sayigh explained. 'There were many things that were called Palestinian, but official names usually had the word "Arab" – for instance al-Hay'a al-Arabiya al-'Ulya, the Arab Higher Committee, not the Palestinian Higher Committee. Because the Jews were Palestinian too.'[1] The country's leading English-language newspaper was the (Zionist) *Palestine Post*, founded in 1932. (It was renamed the *Jerusalem Post* when Palestine ceased to exist.) Its leading Zionist institution was named The Jewish Agency for Palestine but in Hebrew the country was always referred to as *Eretz-Yisrael*. The use of the words 'Israel' and 'Israelis' followed the creation of the state in 1948, but the word 'Jews' (*Yahud*) continued to be commonly used, especially in colloquial Arabic. The refugees who were driven out, fled and dispersed in the *Nakba* (catastrophe) were widely referred to as 'Arabs' in the 1950s and 1960s. In English the term 'Palestine Arabs' was common. Usage changed gradually after the creation of the Palestine Liberation Organization in 1964, while Arab recognition of the PLO as the 'sole legitimate representative' of the Palestinian people in 1974 reinforced that trend. Israel's post-1948 Arab minority were usually described in Hebrew as 'Israeli Arabs', though this term was later rejected by many in favour of the modern phrase 'Palestinian Israelis' in line with the growing salience of a Palestinian national identity. The Palestinian National Authority was set up after the Oslo agreement in 1993. By the 2000s even right-wing Israelis referred routinely to Palestinians, which was not the case twenty years earlier. Arabic-language Palestinian media in the West Bank and Gaza Strip nowadays often describe Israel simply as *al-ihtilal* – the occupation.

TRANSLITERATION

Arabic and Hebrew names have been transliterated in line with standard practice but without diacritical marks, and usually following the way a person chose or chooses to spell their name in English. Place names also reflect common English usage: Jerusalem, not al-Quds or Yerushalayim; Nablus rather than Shechem; Acre, not 'Akka or 'Akko; and Gaza, not Ghaza or 'Aza.

Preface

Anniversaries are occasions for celebration, mourning, commemoration, re-telling – and reflection. This book was planned to mark key events in the history of the Israel–Palestine conflict in the centenary year of the British government's Balfour Declaration of November 1917 and the half-century since the Middle East ('Six Days') war of June 1967. Other significant events, described in the pages that follow, took place (by coincidence, unless perhaps the seventh year of nearly every decade has some mysterious, occult quality) in 1897, 1937, 1947, 1977, 1987 and 2007. *Enemies and Neighbours* looks back to the establishment of the first Zionist settlements in Palestine, then made up of several provinces of the Ottoman Empire, in the early 1880s, and proceeds chronologically, with thematic diversions, up to the present day. My hope is that this long overview, based on up-to-date research, will bring the big picture of what is widely considered to be the world's most intractable and divisive conflict into sharper focus. It tries to tell the story of, and from, *both* sides, and of the fateful interactions between them.

Unrest, violence and peace initiatives are its inevitable milestones. But to concentrate too narrowly on wars, diplomacy or terrorism is to overlook the ordinary Arabs and Jews, Israelis and Palestinians, who have encountered and confronted each other on the ground – on front lines, at refugee camps, at checkpoints and in daily life, language and culture. Politicians, strategists and soldiers in London and Washington, as well as in Amman, Beirut, Cairo and Damascus, have all played roles in this drama, but closer attention is paid here to Jerusalem, Jaffa, Ramallah, Tel Aviv, Haifa, Nablus, Hebron and Gaza and the bitterly disputed landscape around them.

Underlying structures, attitudes and routines matter as much as the endless 'newsworthy' events that erupt from them – a conclusion I have reached in my work both as a journalist and historian. Important themes include the creation of a separate, autonomous Jewish society and economy before 1948 and, especially, the extent to which the Zionists were aware of Arab opposition – which was evident far earlier, in my view, than is often understood. Other big themes are Palestinian flight, expulsion and dispossession – and the subsequent yearning to return home; the massive impact of the 1967 war; the steady expansion of Jewish settlements in the territories occupied that year; the driving forces behind two *intifadas* (uprisings), the shift to the right in Israel, the rise of Islamist views among Palestinians, the vast asymmetry between the sides, and the slow demise of the two-state solution to the conflict – and what that may mean for the future.

Israel's Palestinian minority, too often overlooked or treated as an afterthought, receives close attention because its unique circumstances from 1948 to the present day offer important insights, and because it forms a slender human link between two peoples who have all too often simply ignored each other. The main thread running through this book, from the reign of the Ottoman Sultan Abdulhamid II to the Donald Trump era, is the troubled relations between them.

The Israel–Palestine issue has a strong claim to be the most closely studied conflict on Earth. 'Voluminous' does not even begin to capture the sheer quantity of the material about it. The range and depth reflect its importance, complexity and contentiousness. Back in the mid-1970s, when I began studying the British Mandate period, it was already a well-ploughed field. Now the topsoil has gone and battalions of researchers are hacking away at the bare rock underneath.

This book is intended for the general reader. Keeping it to a manageable length has meant that choices have had to be made throughout about what to include and what to leave out. It is based on a synthesis of existing scholarship and secondary sources: primary research covering the entire 135-year history is far beyond the capability of any one author. Specialized publications like the *Journal of Palestine Studies, Israel Studies* and the *Jerusalem Quarterly* are vital resources. Nowadays material originally published in Arabic and Hebrew often finds its way quickly into English, but important older material has not.

Academic interest has grown enormously and is closely related to political positions. Several universities in the US and Britain now have dedicated (and separate) centres for Palestine and Israel studies. In the last decade or so the fundamentals of the conflict have been illuminated by the paradigm of settler colonialism – based on the experience of the US, Australia, Canada and South Africa – when native populations are *replaced* rather than *exploited* by Europeans. That approach struggles, though, to encompass the Jewish religious– national connection to *Eretz-Yisrael* that is so central to Zionist ideology and Israeli identity. And Mizrahi (Eastern or oriental) Jews who came to Israel from Iraq, Morocco and elsewhere in the Arab and Muslim worlds are another specific element with no exact parallel elsewhere. In a way this heated contemporary debate reflects a familiar truth about how the conflict is perceived: Zionists have tended to focus on their *intentions* in immigrating to Palestine; Arabs on the *results*, and especially, in the words of Edward Said, of 'having their territory settled by foreigners'.[1]

Anthropological and ethnographic research – conveying the texture of remembered *experience* – can be very valuable. Political science, sociology, geography and cultural studies have all enriched understanding too, though the terminology used can often be dense. I greatly enjoyed an article entitled 'The ingathering of (non-human) exiles: the creation of the Tel Aviv Zoological Garden animal collection, 1938– 1948' – an unusual angle on cultural aspects of state formation.[2]

Journalism remains an indispensable 'first rough draft of history' that can sometimes turn out to be impressively close to later, more polished versions. Arguably I learned as much reporting from the streets of Nablus and Gaza during the first *intifada* as from poring over declassified files or old newspapers in archives in Jerusalem and London – as well as from simply talking to people on both sides of an often impassable national divide. Working out how to cross that divide, back and forth, had its lessons too. Palestinian and Israeli journalists covering the occupied territories face special challenges and dangers, sometimes from their own society as much as from the other.

In recent years journalists, social scientists and historians have all had to take account of the immense amount of material published on social media. Facebook, YouTube and Twitter have become rich sources of facts, opinion, propaganda and disinformation about the conflict. Hashtags now matter as much as – if not more than – learned journals. The ephemeral has become both permanent and easily retrievable. 'Passing the test of time' is an outdated notion in a digital age when students of the US presidency are reduced to instantly analysing global policy pronouncements in hastily composed messages of 140 characters. Palestinians and Israelis fight their wars in cyberspace these days, as well as on the soil of their contested homeland.

Introduction

NARRATIVES AND HISTORY

In June 2013 the popular television competition *Arab Idol* was won by a Palestinian named Mohammed Assaf, a handsome twenty-three-year-old with carefully gelled jet-black hair, a shy smile and a beautifully modulated voice who belted out old favourites to an audience of thousands who voted for him by text message. Assaf was born in Libya but raised in Khan Yunis in the Gaza Strip, the densely populated coastal enclave sandwiched uncomfortably between Israel and Egypt and a permanent, festering – and often violent – reminder of the unresolved conflict between Arabs and Jews in the Holy Land.

Assaf's grandparents were among the hundreds of thousands of Palestinians who became refugees during the 1948 war, when the State of Israel gained its independence and Palestine experienced its *Nakba* (catastrophe). His winning performance – beating an Egyptian and a Syrian – was at the cutting edge of contemporary mass entertainment, courtesy of the Beirut-based MBC, which had adapted the concept pioneered by the British series *Pop Idol*. The show was streamed live to millions of viewers across the Arab world, including in Gaza and the West Bank town of Ramallah, which erupted in ecstasy when the result was announced. 'Revolution is not just about the rifle,' Assaf told an interviewer afterwards, his dinner jacket draped festively in the green, red and white colours of the Palestinian flag.[1] 'Raise the Keffiyeh' – Assaf's signature song – centres on the eponymous Palestinian headscarf, the instantly recognizable emblem of the country and its cause.[2]

Another of Assaf's popular songs commemorated an event that had taken place over eighty years earlier. 'From Acre Gaol' ('*Min Sijn*

Akka') is a ballad of patriotism and sacrifice[3] recalling Mohammed Jamjoum, Fuad Hijazi and Ata al-Zir, who were tried and hanged by the British for their part in the violent unrest that shook Palestine in 1929. That episode was described by the Mandatory authorities as the 'Wailing Wall riots'. Palestinians called it the '*al-Buraq*' revolution – an Arabic reference to the winged steed which carried the Prophet Muhammad from Mecca to Jerusalem. In Zionist and Israeli memory (terminology for the same events is usually different for both sides), the violence is referred to as 'the 1929 disturbances' in which 133 Jews were killed by Arabs, mostly in cold blood. Jamjoum, Hijazi and al-Zir were convicted of killing Jews in Hebron and Safed. 'From Acre Gaol', written and sung in colloquial Arabic, tells their story.

In 2012 a writer in Gaza hailed the trio as 'three of the most important martyrs in the history of the Palestinian struggle' who 'were publicly executed by the British mandate forces for protesting against Zionist infiltration into Palestine' – a description which clearly stretched the conventional meaning of protest and skirted over significant details.[4] Palestinian Authority TV characterized the hangings as a 'beacon in the history of our people', prompting a swift complaint about 'glorifying terrorism' from an Israeli monitoring organization called Palestinian Media Watch.[5] Later that year stamps were issued by the Palestinian Authority to commemorate them – portrayed with obligatory rifles and *keffiyehs* – on the anniversary of their execution.[6] It was one of many examples of the way in which history is an extension of the battleground on which Israelis and Palestinians still fight – and perhaps more equally than on any other front.

Assaf's song is of course a classic illustration of the saying that 'one man's terrorist is another man's freedom fighter'. But there are many others. Jews who were executed as terrorists by the British in the 1930s and 1940s – some of them on the same gallows in Acre Prison – are still officially commemorated by the State of Israel. In February 2017 the country's president, Reuven Rivlin, used his Facebook page to mark the seventy-fifth anniversary of the killing of Avraham 'Yair' Stern, leader of the group known in Hebrew as Lehi (*Lohamei Herut Yisrael*, the Fighters for the Freedom of Israel) or the Stern Gang in

English. Stern was shot dead by a British policeman who tracked him down to his hiding place in Tel Aviv in 1942. In the same vein, Israel's National Library refers to the *Irgun* (*Irgun Zvai Leumi*, the National Military Organization), which first launched attacks on Arab civilians in 1938 and killed ninety-one people when it blew up Jerusalem's King David Hotel in 1946, as a 'Jewish resistance group'.[7] The full name of Hamas, the Palestinian group that carried out numerous suicide bombings against civilian targets and fired primitive rockets from the Gaza Strip into Israel, is the Islamic Resistance Movement (*Harakat al-muqawama al-islamiyya*). For those who are resisting their own people's worst enemies, terminology is always loaded and the ends invariably justify the means they use.

Palestinian and Israeli narratives diverge over far more than the words that are commonly used for their respective national heroes, not least over the nature of the long and unresolved struggle between them over the same small territory on the eastern shore of the Mediterranean. Both are reflected throughout this book. Each is authentic, even if dismissed by the other side as propaganda or lies. Neither can be ignored. The conflict between these two peoples can only be understood by paying attention to how they see *themselves* and their history as well as each other. Narrative, in its simplest definition, is 'the story a nation tells itself about itself'.[8]

Israelis describe a quest for freedom and self-determination after centuries of anti-Semitic persecution, and the 'ingathering of the exiles' who 'return' from the Diaspora to Zion to build a sovereign and independent Jewish state in their ancient homeland, finally achieved in the wake of the extermination of 6 million Jews by the Nazis during the Second World War. That story of national liberation is succinctly captured in the Hebrew phrase '*miShoah leTekuma*' – 'from Holocaust to rebirth'. Self-respect and dignity are restored after centuries of powerlessness, suffering and humiliation. The presence of another people in that homeland (however that people and land are defined) is rarely noted beyond its violent opposition to Zionism. Land is 'redeemed' and the desert made to bloom. Israel's dominant narrative emphasizes its own readiness to compromise and to make peace while the other side has repeatedly missed opportunities to do so. The 'dove' is forced to fight. Unrelenting and pervasive

Palestinian, Arab and Muslim hostility is blamed far more than Israel's own actions – whether in 1947 and 1948, or over decades of settlement in the territories it conquered in 1967 and the military occupation it has maintained in 'Judaea and Samaria' (the West Bank) and its unilateral annexation of East Jerusalem, now part of the country's 'united and eternal capital'. (Under international law Israel remains responsible for the Gaza Strip despite its 2005 withdrawal, as it does for the West Bank partially controlled by the Palestinian Authority.) It is common for Israelis to claim that they have no Palestinian 'partner' for peace and that their enemies are motivated by hatred and prejudice, not a quest for justice and an end to conflict. Terror continues.

Palestinians describe themselves as the country's indigenous inhabitants who lived peacefully for centuries as a Muslim majority alongside Christian and Jewish minorities. Theirs is a story of resistance to foreign intruders, starting in Ottoman times but since 1917 under a perfidious British Empire that betrayed the cause of Arab independence and put its own interests first. Three decades of Mandatory rule, which promoted Jewish immigration and land purchases, were followed after the crimes of the Nazi era (for which they were in no way responsible) by an unjust UN partition plan that Palestinians rejected and fought. Then came war and ethnic cleansing in 1948 and, nineteen years later, the occupation of the rump of the country between the Mediterranean and the river Jordan. Israel's independence was the Palestinians' catastrophe. The right of Palestinian refugees to return to their homes was recognized by the UN but never by Israel. 'The essence of the encounter', in the words of the Palestinian scholar Nadim Rouhana, 'took place between a group of people living in their homeland and a group of people who arrived from other parts of the world guided by an ideology that claimed the same homeland as exclusively theirs.'[9] Yet Palestinian leaders still agreed to accept a state on only 22 per cent of the territory – a historic compromise described as 'unreasonably reasonable'.[10] The *Nakba* continues as memory and 'present history'. That is marked by ongoing occupation, land confiscation, expanding Jewish settlements, the threat of annexation, house demolitions and an 'apartheid wall' built to protect Israel's security – a disaster without end.[11] *Sumoud* (steadfastness), the preservation of national identity – and resistance – carry on in the service of a struggle for freedom, dignity and human rights.

These master-narratives are not so much competing as diametrically opposed – and utterly irreconcilable: justice and triumph for the Zionist cause meant injustice, defeat, exile and humiliation for Palestinians. They have developed and been reinforced over the decades by selectivity, repetition and unshakeable self-belief. Sir Alan Cunningham, Britain's last high commissioner for Palestine, made the point well just weeks after the Mandate's inglorious end. 'One of the most remarkable phenomena in the handling of policy in Palestine was that neither Jew nor Arab in their approach to the problem . . . would ever refer to the other,' he recalled. 'And it would seem as if they ignored each other's very existence.'[12] Common ground has been hard to find since the beginning. Textbooks that attempt to reconcile or to integrate the rival narratives have to print them on alternate pages.[13] An Israeli–Palestinian debate about an innovative project ambitiously entitled 'Shared Histories' quickly concluded that the two sides' versions in fact had very little in common – and that was before they had even reached the twentieth century![14] Efforts by Palestinian and Israeli educators to compose a 'bridging narrative' acceptable to both had to be abandoned after the second *intifada* because 'the mutual suspicion, hatred and poisoning of minds among both peoples in relation to the "other" [had] become so intense'.[15]

CONVERGING FACTS

Nevertheless, in recent decades there has been growing agreement about the *facts* of what happened in significant periods. Starting in the late 1980s, Israel's self-styled 'new historians' drew on newly opened official archives to rewrite the history of the 1948 war in a way that was closer – though not identical – to traditional Palestinian accounts that had previously been dismissed by Israel as propaganda. In different ways Benny Morris, Ilan Pappé, Tom Segev and Avi Shlaim slaughtered the sacred cows of an earlier national consensus when the heroic period of Israel's 'state-in-the-making' was no longer a taboo and controversy was raging over the 1982 war in Lebanon and the first *intifada* five years later. Palestinian scholars, handicapped by a dearth of Arab documentary sources, a lack of access to Israeli archives, and by their own statelessness, began to examine their history more assertively, although with less dramatic results.[16] In the 1990s Walid Khalidi's encyclopaedic study, *All That Remains*, laid the foundation for recording the Palestine that was eradicated by Israel.[17] Yezid Sayigh's meticulously documented account of the Palestine national movement and its search for a state is still unsurpassed, two decades after publication.[18] It is also hard to improve on the penetratingly honest insight of the Palestinian-American historian Rashid Khalidi that Zionism was not just another European colonial enterprise but was *simultaneously* the national movement of the Jewish people *and* one that achieved its goals at the expense of his own people.[19]

No one now seriously disputes, for example, how many Palestinians died in the Deir Yassin massacre in April 1948, or how many Arab villages were depopulated or destroyed during or after that year's war. Very few accept the old Israeli claim that a 'miracle' or orders from invading Arab armies triggered the Palestinian exodus. Oral testimony, once dismissed as unreliable, has greatly enriched understanding of the *Nakba*. So have autobiographical accounts of the period, motivated by the urge to bear witness to traumatic events and avoid the erasure of memory. In that spirit Palestinian genealogy, folklore and cultural studies have blossomed as data is collected on old houses and scattered communities and published online. Satellite TV channels have promoted and maintained interest. Palestine's future may be profoundly uncertain. But its past is being studied and celebrated as never before.

Academic research has penetrated popular consciousness. Ari Shavit, a prominent Israeli journalist, made waves in 2014 – especially in the US – when he published an unvarnished account of a massacre and the expulsion of thousands of Palestinians from Lydda in 1948, based on interviews with Israeli veterans. He called it candidly (and controversially) 'the price of Zionism', but argued that there had been no alternative and gave no evidence of any contrition. 'If Zionism was to be, Lydda could not be', Shavit wrote. 'If Lydda was to be, Zionism could not be.'[20] In recent years Israeli leaders have periodically expressed public sympathy for Palestinian suffering, though, crucially, they have refused to admit responsibility for it. Historical revisionism, however honest, has strict limits in the real world.

Shifting perspectives have meant that closer attention is now paid to the irreducible Arab–Jewish core of the conflict. This is partly because of Israel's peace treaties with Egypt and Jordan, the (apparent) end of inter-state wars (since 1973), discreet 'normalization' of relations with the conservative Arab Gulf states and, since 2011, the upheavals and bloody distractions of the 'Arab Spring'. It has also happened because, by the crude but significant yardstick of body counts, the Israel–Palestine conflict has escalated, despite (or perhaps because of) efforts to 'manage' rather than resolve it. In the twenty years between 1967 and the start of the first *intifada*, 650 Palestinians were killed by Israel in the West Bank and Gaza Strip. From late 1987 to September 2000, the death toll was 1,491. From the second *intifada* to the end of 2006, the figure was 4,046 Palestinians and 1,019 Israelis.[21] The Gaza Strip, now home to 2 million Palestinians, has seen four fully-fledged military campaigns since 2006. In the 2014 war, up to 2,300 Palestinians died. The conflict remains an issue of global and regional concern, a source of instability, misery, hatred and violence.

Understanding of the past always changes over time. For years after 1948 Israel's version, the victor's version, did dominate – though never entirely. In its aftermath the Palestinians were traumatized, leaderless, dispersed – and, indeed, often nameless too. They largely disappeared from public view in the West and in Israel, where if they were remembered at all it was as 'Arab refugees', 'Israeli Arabs', Jordanians or simply 'terrorists'. Wider Arab solidarity with the Palestinian cause was accompanied by discrimination and intolerance. It was only after 1967 that the Palestinians began to 'reappear', although two years later Golda Meir, then Israel's prime minister, still insisted, notoriously, that there was no such thing as a Palestinian people. By 1974, however, Yasser Arafat, the leader of the Palestine Liberation Organization (PLO), was addressing the world in their name from the podium of the United Nations – one side's terrorist, the other's freedom fighter. In 1988 Arafat declared Palestinian independence, implicitly recognizing Israel. And just five years after that, in the Oslo accord, the PLO and Israel formally and explicitly recognized each other, though that pragmatic landmark said nothing about Palestinian rights or statehood and did not lead to a final peace settlement. Indeed, it did not mark any kind of genuine reconciliation, and it came in time to be seen by many on both sides as an abject failure. The subsequent collapse of negotiations and unprecedented violence deepened the chasm between them and their sense of mutual grievance and alienation.

VICTIMS . . . AND VICTIMS

Agreement on some aspects of the past does not mean that the overarching narratives or the arguments that flow from them have moved any closer together. On the contrary, when Binyamin Netanyahu, Israel's prime minister since 2009, described demands to evacuate illegal West Bank settlements as supporting the 'ethnic cleansing' of Jews, Palestinians accused him of cynically appropriating 'their' narrative,[22] reinforcing the impression that both sides are clinging to their own sense of victimhood. Netanyahu and supporters complain that Israel is the object of anti-Semitic hatred. Official Palestinian spokesmen reject such criticism and insist they are fighting for their legitimate rights and self-determination and are protesting about breaches of international law. In 2017 the formal goal of the PLO remained the end of the occupation and the establishment of an independent Palestinian state alongside Israel. The Islamist movement Hamas, by contrast, was prepared only for a long-term truce with Israel. Netanyahu was committed at best to what he called a 'state-minus' for the Palestinians. Ending the conflict still looked like a very tall order.

It has become a truism of many rounds of unsuccessful peace talks to say that history must be left to academics and cannot be dealt with on the negotiating table.[23] 'Fanciful intellectual acrobatics only added impediments to the virtually insurmountable political obstacles that already existed', as the Israeli historian Asher Susser has written.[24] Experts in conflict resolution counter that *acknowledgement* of the other's point of view, which does not constitute *acceptance* of it, can

8

help promote practical compromises and thus win popular support for peace on both sides.[25]

History and politics cannot, however, be easily separated when the conflict is so raw and oppressive, and when one party so outweighs the other, militarily, economically and in many other ways. Netanyahu is correct to say that Palestinians have not recognized the *legitimacy*, as opposed to the existence, of the Jewish state, as he and many other Israelis demand they do – and as leading Palestinians freely admit they cannot. In the words of the Palestinian intellectual Ahmad Samih Khalidi:

> For us to adopt the Zionist narrative would mean that the homes that our forefathers built, the land that they tilled for centuries, and the sanctuaries they built and prayed at were not really ours at all, and that our defence of them was morally flawed and wrongful: we had no right to any of these to begin with.[26]

Nor, crucially, has Israel recognized, in any formal or legal sense, the *right* of the Palestinian people to the sovereign, viable and independent state it desires, and so much of the world now believes it deserves, in what remains of historic Palestine. In 1993 Israel recognized the PLO as the *representative* of the Palestinians. But what it called a 'generous' offer at the Camp David summit in 2000 was rejected as inadequate by the other side. Whether that was really a 'missed opportunity' remains a contentious question. In any event, agreement on how these two peoples are to live peacefully, freely and equitably as neighbours, not enemies, has never been reached. The story so far should help explain why such an agreement is so elusive – and may provide pointers for the way ahead.

Neither party has a monopoly on truth or morality. Happily, though, neither is monolithic either. If the master-narratives still exert their paralysing hold it is nevertheless possible to hear voices and strategies that deviate from them. Portraying one side as colonialists, settlers and racists and the other as terrorists, fanatics and anti-Semites only reduces the already slight chances of reconciliation. Significant numbers on both sides are realistic enough to acknowledge the ineradicable existence of the other – that, like it or not (and many do not), they are there to stay. Joint polls show that while contact between Palestinians and Israelis in the West Bank (other than soldiers or settlers) is limited, majorities of both find their interactions 'pleasant'. Less optimistically, trust between them is extremely low and majorities of both agree that theirs is a zero-sum relationship in which 'nothing can be done that is good for both sides' and 'whatever is good for one is bad for the other'.[27] Fear, hatred, apathy and self-interest, as well as domestic, regional and international attitudes and constraints, are powerful forces too – combining to sustain what has looked for too long like an unsustainable reality. Events in East Jerusalem in July 2017 – the killings of Israeli policemen by Israeli Arab gunmen on the Temple Mount/Haram al-Sharif; Israel's security crackdown; mass Palestinian protests; the killing of Israeli settlers; high tensions and a subsequent Israeli climbdown – were a stark reminder of how very quickly and easily matters can escalate out of control.

Historians inevitably reflect the preoccupations of the present: 2017, with its resonant anniversaries, is a period of unprecedented gloom about the prospects for easing, let alone resolving the permanent crisis in the Holy Land. In recent years debates have raged about the death of the two-state solution, the desirability and likelihood of a single state emerging by agreement, or the continuation and likely deterioration of an unjust, volatile and dangerous status quo. There is no sign that this conflict is about to end, so understanding it matters more than ever. But that also means that both peoples should heed the wise words of the Palestinian-Israeli writer Odeh Bisharat: 'If there is no shared narrative for the past, then at least let us write one for the future.'[28]

I

1917

'I did not like the boy at first. He was not the one I expected.
But I knew that this was a great event.'

Chaim Weizmann

VIEWING WITH FAVOUR

Early on the cold, damp morning of 9 December 1917, two British army cooks lost their way while looking for water not far from Lifta village, its flat-roofed houses ranged on stone terraces on the south-western outskirts of Jerusalem. They encountered a group of civilians who told them that the holy city's Ottoman governor wanted to surrender. The men did not feel equal to the task and returned to their unit, the 2/20th Battalion, London Regiment, part of a force under Major-General S. F. Mott that was moving north from Bethlehem. Mott's detachment had just experienced a grim few hours. 'The troops', recorded the official history of the Palestine campaign,

> passed a wretched night in cold, driving rain. Whole teams of gun horses came down together on the slippery road to kick and flounder in the darkness and block the struggling traffic. Camels fell with their legs splayed outwards, split at the quarters and had to be bundled off the road after their loads had been taken off. Several of their Egyptian drivers died of exposure.

The next British soldiers to meet the surrender party, waving a white sheet attached to a broom handle and led by the Arab mayor of Jerusalem, Salim al-Husseini, were sergeants Frederick Hurcomb and James Sedgewick of the 2/19th Battalion. The two NCOs felt unable to accept a letter of surrender from the governor, Izzat Pasha. But according to one Jewish eyewitness, the mayor delivered the news verbally on a patch of waste ground while the sergeants tried to get hold of matches to light their cigarettes – and posed for a photographer who captured the event for posterity. In the confusion several other surrenders, to increasingly senior officers, followed in the course of the next few hours. The official surrender ceremony took place two days later with General Edmund Allenby, the commander-in-chief of the Egyptian Expeditionary Force, just inside the Jaffa Gate of Jerusalem's walled Old City.[1] The weather, happily, had improved. It was a 'perfectly glorious day, cold bright sun, and not a cloud'.[2] Allenby was under instructions to dismount and enter the city humbly, on foot. It was a deliberate contrast, deemed important for propaganda purposes, with the 'swagger' of the German Kaiser Wilhelm II, who had ridden a gorgeously decked white horse through the gate on his visit in 1898. In London, government censors warned the press not to suggest that military operations were in any way a 'holy war', a new Crusade, or a quarrel between Christianity and Islam.[3]

Britain's conquest of Jerusalem ushered in a new phase in the history of Palestine, though it would be another ten months before Allenby's army routed the last of the Turkish forces. Important changes were already in the air. The biggest was the approaching end of four centuries of Ottoman imperial rule over a land which had a powerful resonance for Muslims, Christians and Jews, in and beyond a region where Arab nationalism had been stirring as European interest grew.

Palestine – *Filastin* in Arabic and *Eretz-Yisrael* in Hebrew – owed its name to the Romans. It was imprinted on Western consciousness as the Holy Land, the place of Christ's birth, crucifixion and resurrection; and as the biblical homeland of the long-scattered Jews. To the Islamic world it was the home of Jerusalem's al-Aqsa mosque – the third most sacred site after Mecca and Medina – from where the Prophet Muhammad had ascended to heaven. David Lloyd George, Britain's Liberal prime minister, spoke of Palestine as extending 'from Dan to Beersheba' – an evocative memory from the Old Testament he knew so well.[4] Jerusalem, Nazareth and Bethlehem were household names; the Crusades, Richard the Lionheart, Saladin and the Saracens all familiar references.

Locally, Palestine was perceived simply as part of *Bilad al-Sham* (Greater Syria) – roughly today's Syria, Lebanon and the Levant. In classical times it had been known as *Jund Filastin* (a military district) but it had not been a separate administrative unit since Sultan Selim I had defeated the Mamluk rulers of Syria and Egypt in 1517. It was divided into *sanjaqs* (districts) ruled variously from the provinces (*vilayets*) of Damascus or Beirut. In 1872 Jerusalem was given a higher status and governed directly from the imperial capital, Istanbul.[5] In the late Ottoman period Jerusalem, together with the *sanjaqs* of Nablus and Acre, formed the region that was commonly referred to as Southern Syria or Palestine. The principal Christian denominations treated Palestine as a distinct entity.[6] In Arabic it was often called *al-ard al-Muqaddasah* – the Holy Land – the phrase used in the Quran. The Hebrew *Eretz haKodesh* had precisely the same meaning.

Palestine was bordered in the east by the river Jordan and the Dead Sea; in the west by the Mediterranean and, after a British–Ottoman agreement in 1906, by a marked frontier with Egypt. On the eve of the First World War the primary identity of its majority, Arabic-speaking Muslim population was still local – family names and dialect often revealing geographic origins – as well as Palestinian, though not in a manner that demanded independence from the sultan. 'Arabism' – in the sense of an Arab nation united by a common language – was the outlook of a small elite which initially advocated autonomy within the Ottoman Empire. Christians were influenced by notions of nationalism and patriotism that were disseminated in missionary schools. The small Jewish population was largely religious. The threat posed by the Zionist movement, which had been growing slowly since its first settlements were founded in the 1880s, was another factor promoting a sense of a distinct Palestinian identity.[7]

NO CONSENT

On 2 November 1917, five weeks before Allenby walked through the Jaffa Gate, the government in London had issued a document that was to have a fateful and lasting impact on the Holy Land, the

Middle East and the world. The foreign secretary, Lord Balfour, wrote to Lord Rothschild, representing the World Zionist Organization, to inform him that:

> His Majesty's government view with favour the establishment in Palestine of a national home for the Jewish people, and will use their best endeavours to facilitate the achievement of this object, it being clearly understood that nothing shall be done which may prejudice the civil and religious rights of existing non-Jewish communities in Palestine, or the rights and political status enjoyed by Jews in any other country.

The sixty-seven typewritten words of the Balfour Declaration combined considerations of imperial planning, wartime propaganda, biblical resonances and a colonial mindset, as well as evident sympathy for the Zionist idea. With them, as the writer Arthur Koestler was to quip memorably – neatly encapsulating the attendant and continuing controversy – 'one nation solemnly promised to a second nation the country of a third'.[8] Lloyd George highlighted sympathy for the Jews as his principal motivation. But the decisive calculations were political, primarily the wish to outsmart the French in post-war arrangements in the Levant[9] and the impulse to use Palestine's strategic location – its 'fatal geography' – to protect Egypt, the Suez Canal and the route to India.[10] Other judgements have placed greater emphasis on the need to mobilize Jewish public opinion behind the then flagging Allied war effort. As Balfour told the war cabinet at its final discussion of the issue on 31 October: 'If we could make a declaration favourable to such an ideal [Zionism], we should be able to carry on extremely useful propaganda both in Russia and in America.'[11] Historians have spent decades debating the connections and contradictions between Balfour's public pledge to the Zionists, the secret 1916 Sykes–Picot agreement between Britain, France and Russia about post-war spheres of influence in the Middle East, and pledges about Arab independence made by the British in 1915 to encourage Sharif Hussein of Mecca to launch his 'revolt in the desert' against the Turks. The truth, buried in imprecise definitions, misunderstandings and duplicity, remains elusive.

Arab views of British behaviour were, nevertheless, blunt from the start, with shock and dismay reported in Palestine by early 1918. The Balfour Declaration, argued George Antonius, author of the influential work *The Arab Awakening*, betrayed the earlier agreement between Sharif Hussein and Sir Henry McMahon, the British high commissioner in Egypt. And that in turn was contradicted by Sykes–Picot, under which much of Palestine was to be subject to international administration. Britain's promise, Antonius wrote in 1938, 'lacks real validity, partly because she had previously committed herself to recognising Arab independence in Palestine and partly because the promise involves an obligation which she cannot fulfil without Arab consent'.[12] If the first point – often summarized as 'the twice-promised land' – was debatable, the second was manifestly not. Arabs, and Palestinians, had not consented; they felt they had been duped and cheated.

Chaim Weizmann, the charismatic Russian-born chemist and Anglophile who led the Zionist movement in 1917, was elated if not overjoyed at the outcome of the war cabinet's deliberations, as it was not *quite* as favourable as he had hoped. 'It's a boy,' he was told on 2 November, a week before the declaration was published in the *Jewish Chronicle*, the organ of Anglo-Jewry (although the story was overshadowed by news of the Bolshevik Revolution in Russia). 'I did not like the boy at first', Weizmann recalled. 'He was not the one I expected. But I knew that this was a great event.'[13] The most powerful country in the world had formally and publicly committed itself to the Zionist cause. It was a 'towering milestone' in the movement's brief history, just twenty years since the first Zionist Congress had been held.[14] True, 'national home' was a vague phrase, especially without the definite article, and it fell short of hopes for mention of a Jewish *state*. 'Facilitate' was perhaps not a binding commitment while the phrase 'best endeavours' a trifle nebulous. But it did clearly recognize Jewish *national* rights in Palestine. The idea of a declaration had been intended, in the words of Nahum Sokolow, Weizmann's colleague, to be 'a general approval of the Zionist aims, very short and as pregnant as possible'.[15] Detailed implementation would come afterwards.

Balfour's promise did include what sounded like an important reservation: 'that nothing shall be done to prejudice the civil and religious rights of existing non-Jewish communities' – who at that time comprised some 90 per cent of Palestine's population. Jews, notably, were defined as a 'people', while others, not even identified, were referred to only as 'communities'. It was an extraordinary phrase that echoes down the decades and explains why Balfour is remembered a century later by Arabs as the architect of perfidy and disaster.[16] Zionists, for opposite reasons, revere his memory; Balfour Street in Jerusalem is still the site of the official residence of the Israeli prime minister. The reservation had been inserted in the text to meet the strong objections raised by Lord Curzon, the former British viceroy of India and, as lord president of the council, an influential member of the war cabinet. Curzon – reflecting contemporary perceptions about the map and identity of the region – had referred to the 'Syrian Arabs' who had 'occupied [Palestine] for the best part of 1,500 years', and asked what would become of them. 'They will not be content either to be expropriated for Jewish immigrants or to act merely as hewers of wood and drawers of water to the latter', he predicted with the help of another then familiar biblical reference.[17]

The declaration's second reservation – about the rights of Jews in other countries – was a response to the opposition of Edwin Montagu, the secretary of state for India, even though he was not in the war cabinet. Montagu was a Jewish grandee who feared that an official expression of sympathy for Zionism in fact masked anti-Semitic prejudice and would undermine the hard-won position of British Jews and their co-religionists elsewhere in the world. However, it did not weaken his vehement opposition, any more than the words about 'non-Jewish communities' assuaged Arab fears. Over time, Jewish attitudes to Zionism would change significantly; Arab attitudes, by and large, did not.

THE SIGNPOST OF A DESTINY

The capture of Jerusalem marked the beginning of the end of three grim years of suffering for Palestine. Ottoman reinforcements had been deployed in September 1914 under the command of Cemal Pasha, the governor of Syria. Conscription took a heavy toll, especially on the

700,000-strong Arab population. Food, animals and fuel were in short supply due to the requisitions of the Turkish military. 'Revenues accruing from the pious and the curious' had stopped. 'Starvation rations' were the norm.[18] Disease and privation were rife. In 1915 poor harvests and a devastating plague of locusts added to the impact of the Allied naval blockade of Palestinian and Syrian ports. The Jewish population, some 59,000 on the eve of war, was depleted by emigration and the deportation of enemy nationals, especially Russians, thousands of whom were shipped to Alexandria. Some took Ottoman citizenship – despite the compulsory military service that entailed. Leading Zionist officials were gaoled. In Jerusalem, as in Damascus and Beirut, Arab nationalists were hanged. The Turks also executed two members of the Jewish 'Nili' spy ring who were keeping British intelligence abreast of enemy troop movements. 'Three years of war have reduced Palestine to a deplorable condition', reported an American living in Jerusalem. Beggars roamed the streets, soup kitchens catered for the hungry and prostitution flourished. Villages were ravaged by 'military drafts, devastated by cholera, typhus and recurrent fever'.[19] The monthly salary of an Ottoman soldier was 85 piastres, barely enough to buy a regular supply of tobacco, which became a staple of survival.[20]

The Egyptian Expeditionary Force had initially protected the Suez Canal from the Turks. Its first assault on Gaza in March 1917 marked the start of an Allied invasion of enemy territory. In April the entire civilian populations of Jaffa and Tel Aviv were ordered to leave 'for their own safety'. Beersheba and then Gaza were captured after heavy fighting in late October and early November. Jaffa fell on 16 November. Australian troops who entered Tel Aviv shouted 'Europe, Europe'. Those victories paved the way for the advance on Jerusalem.

Palestine's ultimate fate was still unknown at the end of 1917, 'though the Balfour Declaration made its incorporation into a presumably French Syria less and less probable',[21] as Ronald Storrs, Jerusalem's first military governor, wrote later. The liberal *Manchester Guardian* newspaper, an enthusiastic supporter of the Zionist cause, hailed the declaration as 'the fulfilment of an aspiration, the signpost of a destiny'. Without a national home the Jews would never have security, argued the editor, C. P. Scott, citing a recent case of the fateful vulnerability of another minority in a Muslim land. 'The example of Armenia and the wiping out of a population fiftyfold that of the Jewish colonies in Palestine was a terrible warning of what might be in store for these.' Scott saw no contradiction between the declaration's central promise and the rights of the country's native Arabs – and thus reflected widely held contemporary Western views. 'The existing Arab population of Palestine is small and at a low stage of civilisation', he wrote. 'It contains within itself none of the elements of progress, but it has its rights, and these must be carefully respected.' Balfour told Curzon in 1919, in the same vein, that 'Zionism, be it right or wrong, good or bad, is rooted in age-long traditions, in present needs, in future hopes, of far profounder import than the desires and prejudices of the 700,000 Arabs who now inhabit that ancient land.'[22] This brutally candid display of partiality, 'dripping with Olympian disdain', in the words of a leading Palestinian historian,[23] would still arouse Arab anger a turbulent century later.

2

1882–1917

'If the time comes that our people's life in Eretz Yisrael will develop to a point where we are taking their place, either slightly or significantly, the natives are not going to just step aside so easily.'

Ahad haAm

LOVERS OF ZION

On the ground in Palestine, far from the corridors of power in London, Zionist-Arab tensions pre-dated the epochal events of 1917. The following year the British military administration counted a population of 512,000 Muslims, 66,000 Jews and 61,000 Christians. The Arabs were largely peasants and artisans, and, in the countryside, where Bedouin tribes still roamed, overwhelmingly illiterate. Large tracts of land were the property of absentee owners. Urban notables had played an important role in the just-departed Ottoman administration. Jerusalem, where signs of modernization were spreading beyond the walls of the Old City, was still dominated by wealthy, patrician families such as the Husseinis and Khalidis; Nablus by the Touqans and Abdel-Hadis. Jaffa, known as 'the bride of the sea', was the country's gateway to the outside world, while Haifa, further north, was also undergoing rapid development. Beyond the replacement of the Turks by the British, the most significant novelty was that by 1918 some 15,000 Jewish newcomers were living in 45 rural colonies (*moshavot*)[1] that made up the 'new' Zionist camp – and were quite distinct from the 50,000-strong 'old' *Yishuv* (Jewish community).

Palestine's Arabs were well aware of their presence, and of the differences between the two groups. Jews had been part of the landscape for as long as anyone could remember. Over the previous century Ashkenazi Jews had come to study and pray, subsisting on *halukah* or charitable contributions in the holy cities of Jerusalem, Hebron, Tiberias and Safed, where they mourned the destruction of the Temple and awaited the coming of the Messiah. Most were Russian or from other Eastern European countries. The majority had come after 1840, when the Ottomans defeated a rebellion by the Egyptian pasha Muhammad Ali. A minority were native-born Sephardi or Mizrahi Jews, whose ancestors were from Spain, North Africa, the Balkans and as far afield as Yemen and Bokhara in Central Asia. Many spoke Arabic or Ladino. Their identity was religious, not national in any sense. Most were Ottoman citizens and were referred to in Arabic as *abnaa al-balad* (sons of the country/natives) or *yahud awlaad Arab* (Jews, sons of Arabs). Relations between Muslims, Christians and Jews were largely untroubled, each community living within its own traditions under the Ottoman *millet* system of communal religious autonomy under the sultan in Istanbul. Inequalities existed in status and taxation but there was tolerance in mixed neighbourhoods. In Jerusalem, Ashkenazis formed a majority, speaking a Palestinian variety of Yiddish, the vernacular of the Russian 'Pale of Settlement' (where East European Jews were concentrated), but replete with Arabic words.[2] Sephardim were culturally closer to Muslims than to Christians.[3] In Jaffa, Jews made up a third of the population. In Haifa there was 'no more friction than is commonly found amongst neighbours'.[4]

Palestine's connections with the wider world had deepened in the mid-nineteenth century thanks to Ottoman reforms, the penetration of European capital and the expansion of trade and communications. In the years after the Crimean War (1853–56) European consulates were established in Jerusalem, Jaffa and Haifa, partly to deal with Christian pilgrims and growing missionary activity. Economic growth, driven by exports of wheat and citrus fruits, boosted the population in the coastal cities and widened the gap with the countryside. Farmers in Gaza grew barley for the breweries of Europe. It was against that background that the French *Alliance Israélite Universelle*, a philanthropic organization which ran Jewish schools across the Middle East, founded the Mikveh Yisrael agricultural school near Jaffa in 1870. In 1878 Ashkenazi Jews from Jerusalem's overcrowded Old City founded the colony of Petah Tikvah on the coastal plain near Jaffa, on lands acquired from an Arab village. Their motives combined the traditional belief in the sanctity of *Eretz-Yisrael* with a modern emphasis on the regenerative value of a productive life 'to produce a sentimental yearning for the agrarian life in a land whose soil was inherently fruitful'.[5] Conditions were harsh and the site was abandoned and only re-established later. Its Hebrew name ('gate of hope') had a biblical echo. It became known as *Emm haMoshavot* – 'Mother of the Colonies'.

The Zionist chapter proper in the country's history began in 1882, after the outbreak of large-scale pogroms in the Russian Empire (although the term was only invented a few years later). The first settlers called themselves *Hovevei Tzion* (Lovers of Zion), a network of groups which aspired to forge a Jewish national life in Palestine and, in a significant novelty, to use the reviving Hebrew language rather than Yiddish. In August that year a two-hundred-strong group from the Romanian town of Galatz landed at Jaffa, where they were locked up for weeks before enough cash could be raised to bribe the Turkish police to release them.[6] Their goal was a plot of stony land that had been purchased south of Haifa. Laurence Oliphant, an eccentric British traveller and enthusiastic philo-Semite, described the scene shortly afterwards at Zamarin, a malaria-infested hamlet on the southern spur of Mount Carmel overlooking the Mediterranean. It is a remarkably vivid portrayal of two very different sorts of people who were warily making each other's acquaintance as future neighbours – and enemies:

> It would be difficult to imagine anything more utterly incongruous than the spectacle thus presented – the stalwart fellahin [peasants], with their wild, shaggy, black beards, the brass hilts of their pistols projecting from their waistbands, their tasselled kufeihahs [*keffiyeh* headdresses] drawn tightly over their heads and girdled with coarse black cords, their loose, flowing abbas [cloaks], and sturdy bare legs and feet; and the ringleted, effeminate-looking Jews, in caftans reaching almost to their ankles, as oily as their red or sandy locks, or the expression of their countenances – the former inured to hard

labour on the burning hillsides of Palestine, the latter fresh from the Ghetto of some Roumanian town, unaccustomed to any other description of exercise than that of their wits, but already quite convinced that they knew more about agriculture than the people of the country, full of suspicion of all advice tendered to them, and animated by a pleasing self-confidence which I fear the first practical experience will rudely belie. In strange contrast with these Roumanian Jews was the Arab Jew who acted as interpreter – a stout, handsome man, in Oriental garb, as unlike his European coreligionists as the fellahin themselves.[7]

Oliphant, drawing on the full range of contemporary European Christian prejudices, was witness to the foundation of the colony that became known as Zichron Yaakov, in remembrance of the French Jewish philanthropist Baron James (Yaakov) de Rothschild, whose son Edmond became the benefactor of that and other new outposts. In the following few years half a dozen more settlements – Rishon LeZion and Gedera on the coastal plain, and Rosh Pina and Yesud haMaala in Galilee – were established. In theory the Zionists faced the opposition of the Ottoman authorities. But in reality the administration's inefficiency, corruption and the advantages of foreign nationality – especially the intervention of consuls who enjoyed extraterritorial privileges under the 'Capitulations' system – helped overcome obstacles. Bribery – *baksheesh* – was universally used. 'Turkish officials to a man are open to bribery', wrote one settler. 'Money is the oil that turns the wheels . . . and blinds everybody.'[8] The labour of Arab *fellahin* was indispensable. The Jews depended on them for transport, supplies and the manure they used for their vineyards and plantations. In July 1883 Oliphant found more Romanians and a few Russian Jews in Rosh Pina working their potato patches and living in 'perfect amity' with their Muslim neighbours. It was 'the most hopeful attempt at a colony' he had seen in Palestine. Jewish farmers used the traditional Arab nail plough drawn by oxen, and grew local crops. Overall there was a 'typical pattern of colonial plantation agriculture and the reliance on employment of a large, unskilled, seasonal Palestinian Arab labour force', similar to the experience of European settlers in French-ruled Algeria and Tunisia.[9]

Still, Zichron Yaakov and other settlements struggled to survive and were only saved by Rothschild's largesse.

These pioneers were shocked by the rough-and-ready ways of the Arabs they encountered. And Palestine was evidently not 'a land without a people, for a people without a land', in the phrase made famous by the Anglo-Jewish writer Israel Zangwill, via the millenarian Christian Lord Shaftesbury. (Zangwill, ironically, came to support the idea of Jewish settlement in Uganda rather than Palestine.) The saying is best understood as meaning not that the country was literally *empty*, but rather reflecting the contemporary European nationalist, and Zionist, perception that people without a state of their own had no *national* identity – and certainly not a specifically *Palestinian* one.[10] It also embodied the values of a colonial era when white Europeans assumed superiority over the indigenous population: mostly Muslim peasants who lived in what looked like indolence and squalor.[11] ' "Emptiness" . . . did not denote, except for the most ignorant, the physical absence of the native population', argued the Ottoman scholar Beshara Doumani. 'Rather, it meant the absence of "civilized" people, in the same sense that the Americas and Africa were portrayed as virgin territories ready for waves of pioneers.'[12] Palestine's new colonists 'knew neither the country nor the language and customs of the native Arabs while their means as well as their technical preparation were absolutely insufficient', a Jewish economist recorded a few years later. 'In many settlements malaria was endemic and menaced the health of the colonists.'[13] Many were horrified by the harsh conditions. 'I was shocked by the Arab village I saw', wrote Hemda Ben-Yehuda, who arrived from Russia in 1892. 'Houses made of mud, without windows, housing both men and animals. Piles of garbage everywhere and half naked children . . . Old blind women and dirty girls sit in front of the houses working, grinding wheat as was done a thousand years ago.'[14]

NEIGHBOURS

The colonists encountered problems over the demarcation of boundaries with former tenants dispossessed by the sale of lands they had worked for absentee owners. Disputes were common over harvesting or grazing rights.[15] In 1886 rioting erupted in Petah Tikvah after a Jewish farmer confiscated Arab-owned donkeys grazing on his land. The background was a disagreement that escalated when Arabs were asked to vacate fields to which they still claimed ownership.[16] By 1889 Zichron had 1,200 Arab agricultural workers serving 200 Jews. In Rishon LeZion 40 Jewish families attracted nearly 300 Arab families to work as migrant labourers. Colonists were quick to 'reach for the whip and beat the offender for every transgression'.[17] Arab workers were available, cheap and far hardier than Jewish immigrants who had just arrived from Europe. The Arab labourer, wrote one Jewish observer, 'is almost always a submissive servant who may be exploited without opposition and accepts lovingly the expressions of his master's power and dominion'.[18] Zionist memoirs recorded an Arab fascination with modern agricultural machinery – and laughter when the inexperienced colonists of Rishon LeZion 'tried to coax camels into pulling carts like horses'.[19]

The overall numbers of settlers were still very small – just over 2,000 by 1893 – but local problems occasionally had a wider resonance. In 1890 a group of Bedouin protested to the sultan that they had been expelled from land purchased by the agent Yehoshua Hankin for the new settlement of Rehovot. 'The farm, which was ours since the times of our fathers and grandfathers, was forcefully taken from us by the strangers who do not wish to treat us according to the accepted norms among tillers of the soil, and according to basic human norms or compassion', they wrote.[20] Nearby Gedera, founded in 1884, was known for especially bad relations with its neighbours. The Arab villagers of Qatra lost their land because of debts but continued to cultivate it as tenants until the arrival of the Jewish colonists, who had bought 3,000 dunams (1 dunam = a quarter of an acre) from a Frenchman. The villagers still perceived the land as theirs, and complained to the Ottoman authorities about building work.

Arab objections took on a more overtly political character, though some failed to distinguish between the influx of Jews and generally growing European influence, whether of Christian pilgrims, the German Templer movement or others living under the protection of foreign powers as the country developed.[21] Travel from Jaffa was made easier by a new highway to Jerusalem, just over thirty miles away, in the mid-1880s. The railway line between them opened in 1892. In June 1891 Arabs urged an end to Jewish immigration and land purchases – demands which were to remain constant for the next half century.[22] Yet Arab notables sold land to Jews – a far less sensitive issue then than it became just a few years later. Prices rose steeply in this period, driven by land speculation and poor administration.[23] In the same year the Hebrew writer and Zionist thinker Asher Ginzburg, known by his pen-name as Ahad haAm ('one of the people'), published a famous essay entitled 'The Truth from *Eretz Yisrael*'. It contained a prescient warning:

> We who live abroad are accustomed to believing that the Arabs are all wild desert people who, like donkeys, neither see nor understand what is happening around them. But this is a grave mistake. The Arab, like all the Semites, is sharp minded and shrewd. All the townships of Syria and Eretz Yisrael are full of Arab merchants who know how to exploit the masses and keep track of everyone with whom they deal – the same as in Europe. The Arabs, especially the urban elite, see and understand what we are doing and what we wish to do on the land, but they keep quiet and pretend not to notice anything. For now, they do not consider our actions as presenting a future danger to them . . . But, if the time comes that our people's life in Eretz Yisrael will develop to a point where we are taking their place, either slightly or significantly, the natives are not going to just step aside so easily.

Ahad haAm's article has often been quoted because it provided the first serious recognition that relations with the Arabs would be one of the Zionist project's hardest tests. Yet there is a risk, with hindsight, of endowing his comments with more significance than they had at the time. The article was criticized when it appeared, not because of his brief comments about Arabs but rather because of his attacks on Jewish 'charlatans', who had been promoting the holy land as 'a new California' with an easy life, producing 'a motley mixture of gold-diggers and indigent exiles'.[24] Arabs simply did not loom as large for the Zionists in those early years as they were to do only a decade or two later.

Unlike Ahad haAm, Theodor Herzl, the Viennese journalist who founded political Zionism, knew little about the reality of life in Ottoman Palestine. His quest for a Jewish homeland began in the wake of the Dreyfus Affair in France and the shocking evidence of anti-Semitism that it revealed. In 1896 he published his classic work, *Der Judenstaat* (The Jewish State), which referred to both Palestine and Argentina as countries where 'experiments in colonisation' had taken place. Argentina had 'vast open spaces and [a] temperate climate'. Palestine, however, was 'our unforgettable historic home-land'.[25] The first Zionist Congress, held in Basel in 1897, founded the Zionist Organization, whose goal was a publicly recognized, legally secured home in Palestine 'for the Jewish people'. By then, thanks to *Hovevei Tzion*, there were already eighteen new colonies in the country.[26] It was around this time that the Ottoman authorities appointed an official committee to examine land purchases, and sales were effectively halted for the next few years.[27] In August 1898, at the second Zionist Congress, one delegate, Leo Motzkin, made clear that the Arab presence could not just be ignored: 'In large stretches of land, one constantly comes across big Arab villages, and it is a well-established fact that the most fertile regions of our land are occupied by Arabs.'[28] Herzl himself visited the country for the first and only time two months later, at the same time as Kaiser Wilhelm, but his diaries contained not one reference to Arabs.

In 1899 Herzl received an impassioned message that was passed on to him via the chief rabbi of France, Zadoc Kahn. It was from Yusuf Diya al-Khalidi, the former mayor of Jerusalem. Khalidi acknowl-edged the historic rights of the Jews in Palestine but said they should look for an uninhabited land elsewhere. 'In the name of God', Kha-lidi implored, 'let Palestine be left alone.'[29] Herzl replied to Khalidi that Zionism had no intention of harming the interests of the Arab population; on the contrary, the country's non-Jews would only be enriched by Jewish wealth (an argument that was widely employed in these years, though it never convinced the other side).

Do you believe that an Arab who has a house or land in Palestine whose value is three or four thousand francs will greatly regret seeing the price of his land rise five or tenfold? For that is necessarily what will happen as the Jews come; and this is what must be explained to the inhabitants of the country. They will acquire excellent brothers, just as the Sultan will acquire loyal and good subjects, who will cause the region, their historic fatherland, to flourish.[30]

Herzl's view was at least consistent: in his 1902 novel *Altneuland* (Old New Land), Jaffa in particular – the first sight of the country for anyone arriving by sea – was described in unflattering terms:

> Though nobly situated on the blue Mediterranean, the town was in a state of extreme decay . . . The alleys were dirty, neglected, full of vile odours. Everywhere misery in bright Oriental rags. Poor Turks, dirty Arabs, timid Jews lounged about – indolent, beggarly, hopeless. A peculiar, tomblike odour of mould caught one's breath.[31]

Herzl's fictional Arabs were for the most part nameless, one exception being the token Rashid Bey, who speaks for the natives and praises the benefits brought by the Jewish pioneers.[32]

UNSEEN QUESTION?

Zionist progress was slow but Arab hostility was becoming harder to ignore by the turn of the century. The eviction of peasants from land purchased in Galilee by the Jewish Colonization Association (JCA), founded in 1901, led to attacks on Jewish surveyors. An Arab official in Tiberias ignored the orders of his Turkish superior in Beirut and opposed the transaction, against a background of mounting Arab opposition to the Ottoman authorities.[33] By 1904, some 5,500 settlers were living in 25 agricultural colonies in 3 blocs: in eastern Upper Galilee, south of Haifa and south-east of Jaffa. That year the authorities forbade the sale of land to foreign Jews, a more direct method of control than the old practice of registering transactions in the name of Ottoman Jewish citizens, like those who helped the barons Rothschild and de Hirsch (the founder of the JCA).[34] Oliphant had encountered one of them on his memorable visit to Zamarin. Still, in Zionist speeches and discussions, 'the Arabs, their presence and their settlement in Palestine are belittled and nullified, as if they did not exist', one Jewish intellectual complained in 1905. 'The Arabs . . . were viewed as one more of the many misfortunes present in Palestine, like the Ottoman authorities, the climate, difficulties of adjustment – no greater or smaller than other troubles the settlers had to grapple with.'[35] The theft of Jewish agricultural produce or livestock by Arabs was a common complaint.

In 1907, in an article in *HaShiloah*, one of the earliest modern Hebrew-language publications, the Odessa-born educationalist Yitzhak Epstein returned to, and sharpened, the point that had been made by Ahad haAm in 1891. Epstein belonged to the *Hovevei Tzion*. He had witnessed the purchase of the lands of Ras al-Zawiya and al-Metulla (known in Hebrew as Rosh Pina and Metullah) from absentee landlords several years earlier, and he remembered the anger of the dispossessed farmers from the Druze sect. 'The lament of Arab women . . . still rings in my ears', he wrote. 'The men rode on donkeys and the women followed them weeping bitterly, and the valley was filled with their lamentation. As they went they stopped to kiss the stones and the earth.' Epstein – ahead of his time – warned that relations with the Arabs were the 'unseen question' that the Zionist movement had failed to address. Only by taking care not to dispossess Arab farmers and generally sharing the benefits of Zionist progress could their enmity be avoided. But his argument attracted little response.[36]

The year Epstein's warning was published, an Ottoman official complained about the growing presence of 'foreign Jews' in Jaffa where immigrants disembarked, often shocked by their raucous reception. 'You must tell the passengers not to be impatient, not to be in a hurry to get off the ship, and not to be overawed by the shouts and cries of the Arab sailors', a Zionist official urged a colleague who arranged steamship voyages from Odessa. 'Teach the travellers to Palestine the importance of the words "*Shwaia, shwaia*" (slowly, slowly) and tell them that if they say this to the Arabs suddenly appearing on the ship, they will calm down a bit and not shout "*Yalla, Yalla!*" (hurry, hurry) – a cry that has something contemptuous about it.'[37] In March 1908 fighting broke out in the port city between young Muslims and Jews, the violence blamed by the British consul on resentment of the Jewish population.[38] The growth of prostitution and alcohol consumption caused serious problems. Arabs, warned a Jewish writer, 'regard all the "Muscovite" women as cheap and promiscuous', and behave with 'a sexual vulgarity that they would never dare to do in the case of Sephardi women, and still less, of German or English Christian women'.[39] In 1909 an Ottoman deputy demanded that the port be closed to Jewish immigrants.[40]

In April 1909 a new Jewish residential quarter, called first Ahuzat Bayit ('Homestead') and then Tel Aviv, was founded on sand dunes to the north of Jaffa. Its Hebrew name, inspired by Herzl's *Altneuland*, signified renewal, combining the old (Tel: 'hill or mound marking the remains of an ancient site') with awakening (Aviv: 'spring'). This European-style 'garden city' with wide tree-lined boulevards and modern buildings was a world away from the cramped, noisy and insanitary streets of Jaffa. It 'embodied almost in pure form the Zionist utopia of inventing a new culture and a new identity from whole cloth', in the words of a modern Israeli scholar. 'Opposed both to the Jewish *shtetls* of eastern Europe and to the Arab towns and villages around it, it perfectly encoded the double Zionist rejection of the Diaspora and the native culture – forgetfulness and separation.'[41] In Haifa the small Jewish community began to move out of the downtown area and up on to the slopes of Mount Carmel, marking the start of segregation from the Arab population.[42] Another new neighbourhood was named Herzliya, in homage to the father of Zionism, who had died in 1904.

The overall immigration and colonization effort began to be better co-ordinated from 1908, the momentous year of the Young Turk revolution in Istanbul which saw the overthrow of the Sultan's autocratic power. The Zionist Organization set up its first premises in Palestine, in Jaffa, to supplement the Zionist office in Istanbul which ran the movement's activities throughout the Ottoman lands. Under the leadership of the German Zionist official and sociologist Arthur Ruppin, the Palestine Office focused on the purchase of 'every available tract of land'. Progress was impressive, thought a young Englishman who visited Palestine to do archaeological research on the Crusaders. 'The sooner the Jews farm it all the better', T. E. Lawrence wrote in 1909. 'Their colonies are bright spots in a desert.'[43] Incidents in which Jewish settlers were attacked and their farms and livestock pillaged increased markedly that year, but these were seen as a 'natural' Arab tendency to plunder whenever possible, rather than as a sign of political or nationalist opposition.[44]

The Arabic (and Hebrew) press had been granted new freedoms under the more liberal Ottoman constitution of the previous year and this encouraged an escalation of attacks on the fledgling Zionist enterprise, as well as the cultivation of a more distinctly Palestinian identity: that was emblazoned in the name of the *Filastin* newspaper, established in Jaffa in 1911.[45] *Al-Asmai*, also based in Jaffa, and *al-Karmil* in Haifa were both owned by Greek Orthodox Arabs whom Zionists identified as more hostile to them than the majority Muslim community. In 1910 *al-Karmil* published translated extracts from Herzl's *The Jewish State* and some of the resolutions of the 1911 Zionist Congress. *Al-Karmil*'s editor, Najib Nassar, wrote a pamphlet about the aims of Zionism, warning that its goal was not just immigration but to take over Palestine, and he exhorted his fellow Arabs not to sell land to the newcomers.[46] Arabic newspaper comment on Zionism, in Palestine, Syria and Egypt, increased markedly around the turn of the decade, many papers elsewhere reprinting pieces that first appeared in *Filastin*.[47] In March 1910 Abdullah Mukhlis described in the Damascus-based journal *al-Muqtabas* how Haifa's new Atid ('future') soap factory was employing only Jewish workers, and that Jews (then about one-fifth of the city's population) were starting to interact exclusively with members of their own community. 'Establishing a Jewish state after thousands of years of decline ... we [the Arabs] fear that the new settler will expel the indigenous and we will have to leave our country en masse. We shall then be looking back over our shoulder and mourn our land as did the Muslims of Andalusia.' Mukhlis expressed the hope that Jews would remain part of Ottoman society and abandon their separatist ways. 'Palestine may be endangered', he wrote with remarkable prescience. 'In a few decades it might witness a struggle for survival.'[48]

Not all Jews were unaware of these concerns. Sephardi public figures of the old *Yishuv* were also alarmed by Zionist aspirations. 'If I was a Muslim Turkish deputy, I would take the first opportunity to agitate for restrictive measures against Jewish activity in Palestine',

Eliahu Antebi argued in 1908.[49] Nissim Malul, the Safed-born son of a Tunisian family, was one of a group of like-minded Jews who urged Zionists to embrace Arab rather than European culture. Another was Shimon Moyal, who was born in Jaffa to Moroccan parents, and who wrote a pioneering Arabic account of the Talmud – the commentary on Jewish laws – in 1909. Both expressed concern about the opposition to Zionism in the increasingly assertive Arabic newspapers. In 1911 Ruppin's Palestine Office set up a bureau to monitor the papers and Malul was employed to translate the material into Hebrew and German – an early example of Zionist efforts to 'know the enemy' – and also to publish articles on Zionism in Arabic. Otherwise, though, this group had little influence.[50]

Arab–Jewish co-operation was still possible in this period of accelerating change. David Yellin, a Jerusalem city councillor (the native-born son of an East European father and a Baghdadi mother) and an enthusiastic Zionist, was given a letter of introduction by the Arab mayor Salim al-Husseini, on the eve of a trip to Europe to study municipal services.[51] Yellin argued that Jewish immigration would benefit the Ottoman Empire, the same reasoning Zionists were to use to promote their cause when Britain ruled the country a few years later. Ruhi al-Khalidi, a prominent intellectual and member of another leading Arab family, held several meetings with the Jewish philologist Eliezer Ben-Yehuda, who was busy reviving the Hebrew language and basing many of its neologisms on Arabic words[52] – though Khalidi also became alarmed about the scale of Zionist ambitions. Patrician Sephardi Jewish families like the Antebis and Eliachars maintained cordial relations with their Muslim and Christian counterparts.

'NOT AN EMPTY LAND'

Events in Palestine began to reverberate further afield. Shukri al-Asali, the Ottoman governor of Nazareth, publicly opposed the decision of the absentee Beirut landowner Elias Sursuq to sell the al-Fuleh lands, part of the fertile Marj Ibn Amr valley between Haifa and Jenin, to the Jewish National Fund, which had been established with Herzl's support at the fifth Zionist Congress in Basel in 1901. The Jews, claimed Asali, had come to Palestine 'solely to expel the poor Arab peasants from their land and to set up their own government'.[53] In a petition sent to the sultan in Istanbul, the purchasers were referred to as 'Zionists' – one of the first times the term was recorded in this context. In the autumn of 1911 this led to angry debates in the Ottoman parliament which were widely reported in the Arabic press. Asali refused to comply with the eviction order but the *fellahin* were expelled anyway, paving the way for the establishment of the Jewish settlement of Merhavia. The land transfer was legal, but it deprived the tenant farmers of their livelihood – a frightening novelty of Jewish land purchases.[54] It was increasingly clear that controlling land was the central purpose of the Zionists. 'There are some simple truisms about Palestine, which, though obvious, require a long time to become common property', wrote Dr Elias Auerbach of Haifa in a Zionist anthology published in German and English in 1911. 'The first of these truisms is that Palestine is not an empty land. The second is that the land takes its character from the predominant element in its population . . . Palestine is an Arabic land. To make it a Jewish land the Jews must become the principal element in the population.'[55] Parts of the book were translated into Arabic in *Filastin*. In June 1913 the paper led a campaign against the sale of state lands in Beisan to the Jews. It included telegrams sent by local leaders to the sultan and the *vali* (governor) of Beirut.[56]

Arabs noticed the contradiction between Zionist words and deeds. In 1914 Nahum Sokolow, now secretary-general of the Zionist Congress, told the Cairo daily *al-Muqattam* that Jews were coming to Palestine not as foreign colonizers but as people 'returning' to their homeland, and expressed the hope that they would draw closer to the Arabs. Haqqi Bey al-Azm, leader of the new Decentralization Party, seeking autonomy for the Ottoman provinces, was not convinced. 'Quite the contrary,' he responded,

> we see the Jews excluding themselves completely from the Arabs in language, school, commerce, customs, in their entire economic life. They cut themselves off in the same way from the indigenous government, whose protection they enjoy, so that the population considers

them a foreign race. This is the reason for the grievance of the Arabs of Syria and Palestine against Jewish immigration.[57]

Undeterred, Zionists continued to emphasize the benefits that would accrue to the Arabs from an expanding Jewish presence, and used this line especially when addressing foreign audiences. 'The more our settlements grow in number and area, the greater will be the number of Arab labourers who will be able to find in them remunerative employment', one economist argued.[58] But Arab concerns deepened as it became clear that the newest settlers wanted to *avoid* their neighbours as much as possible rather than offer them work. And calls to *replace* Arab labourers by Jews, even at a higher cost to employers, increased after the start of what is known in Zionist parlance as the second *aliya* (literally 'ascent' or 'wave of immigration') in 1904. This wave of arrivals included members of socialist movements from Russia who had lived through the pogroms. David Gruen, born in Plonsk in Poland, who Hebraized his name to Ben-Gurion, was one of them. He arrived in Jaffa in 1906, aged nineteen, and made his way to Petah Tikvah – the 'mother of the colonies'. Later he described his dismay at life in the 'old' colonies of the first *aliya*. 'The first settlers became middlemen and shop-keepers who traffic in the hopes of their people, selling the aspirations of their youth for a pittance', he wrote. 'They introduced the idol of exile into the temple of national rebirth, and creation of the homeland was desecrated by alien work' – meaning Arab labour.[59] Ben-Gurion would subsequently welcome Arab 'hatred' because it forced reluctant Jewish farmers to take on more expensive Jewish workers and advance Zionist aspirations.[60] The first co-operative settlement, Degania, was established at Umm Juni, where the river Jordan flows into Lake Tiberias, in 1910.

In the same spirit, a group of Russian Jews from the Marxist *Poalei Zion* movement formed a society called *HaShomer* (The Watchman or Guard). Its goal was to replace Arab settlement guards, who were 'notorious for their collaboration with pilferers or thieves'.[61] Part of the problem settlers had was an utter lack of familiarity with the Arabic language, culture and customs. These radical youngsters became the standard bearers of a tough frontier ethos, emulating the natives and acquiring an aura of wild romanticism – part Cossack, part Bedouin. The slogan of *HaShomer* – 'in blood and fire Judaea fell; in blood and fire Judaea shall arise' – gave eloquent expression to its militant, irredentist spirit. Zionist writers were soon hailing a new breed of Jew who was 'at home in the saddle and a fair marksman, fluent in Arabic and crowned with the distinctive headgear of the countryside, as proof of the capacity of Eastern European Jews to take root in the land of their fathers'.[62] Not for the last time, the dictates of security were to have important implications for Zionist-Arab relations. In July 1913, following an incident involving Arabs from Zarnuqa and Jews from the neighbouring colony of Rehovot, the 'Palestinian cowboys' of *HaShomer* were accused of beating Arab workers and intimidating Jewish farmers to stop employing them. The guards were said to have endangered lives 'for the sake of a bunch of grapes'.[63] Other 'unpleasant' acts were omitted from the official history of the organization and later memoirs.[64] Earlier that year a well-attended sports event in Rehovot impressed an Arab observer with speeches in Hebrew, displays of Zionist flags and horse-racing in which both men and women participated, most of them wearing Bedouin clothing so 'you would have thought they were Arabian warriors on horseback'.[65]

SURVIVING HATRED

Statistical evidence underlines the rising human cost of the confrontation, though it was on a small scale. In the twenty-seven years between 1882 and 1909, thirteen Jews were killed by Arabs, but only two of them for apparently 'national' reasons. In the Jaffa riots of 1908, Jews were attacked during Purim celebrations and one Arab was stabbed to death. In 1909 alone four Jews were killed for 'nationalist' motives, and between 1909 and 1913 twelve Jewish guards were killed. In 1911, after Arab sharecroppers were evicted from the land Arthur Ruppin had purchased from the Sursuq family near al-Fuleh, an Arab villager was killed in an altercation with Jewish workers from newly established Merhavia and three Jews were gaoled by the Ottoman authorities.[66] Violence, however, was still rare. And most

Jewish immigrants lived in towns: between 1905 and 1913, 36 per cent of them wanted to settle in Jaffa, 38 per cent in Jerusalem and Hebron, and just 16 per cent in the agricultural colonies – whose novelty meant they attracted disproportionate attention.[67] Still, the 'blind spot' of Zionism was getting harder to avoid. The 'hidden question' was creating open conflict.[68]

Arab hostility was also having an effect on Jewish opinion. In 1913 the influential Hebrew writer Yosef Haim Brenner attacked as 'idealistic' and 'immoral' calls for Arab–Jewish co-operation, and made clear what he believed had to be done:

> In this small land there reside . . . no less than six hundred thousand Arabs, who despite their backwardness and lack of culture are masters of the land, in fact and in full knowledge of the fact; and we have perforce come here to enter among them and live with them. There is already hatred between us – so it must be and will continue to be. They are stronger than us in every possible way and could crush us underfoot. But we Jews are accustomed to being the weak among the strong and we must therefore be ready for the consequences of the hatred and must employ all the scant means at our disposal in order to survive here.[69]

Chaim Weizmann, the Zionist leader, continued to speak in public of the prospects for co-operation with the Arabs but in private he expressed alarm about the growth of their national movement, the weakening of central authority in Constantinople (Istanbul) and an 'intensive propaganda campaign . . . against selling lands to "Zionists", the enemies of Turkey and the usurpers of Palestine'. He predicted: 'We shall soon face a serious enemy and it won't be enough to pay just money for the land.'[70] Moshe Smilansky, one of the founders of Rehovot, admitted in 1914 that Zionists had paid too little attention to Arabs, and while he hoped that compromise could be reached, he harboured no illusions. 'We should not forget that we are dealing with a semi-savage people, with extremely primitive concepts', he wrote. 'This is their nature: if they sense that you are strong they will yield to you and repress their hatred; if they sense that you are weak, they will dominate you. They equate gentleness with impotence.'[71]

By the first years of the twentieth century, the trajectory for Jewish separatism in Palestine was firmly set. Arthur Ruppin told the 1913 Zionist Congress in Vienna – which was closely followed in Palestine's now flourishing Arabic newspapers – that it was vital to concentrate on settling Jews at a few points to 'achieve . . . the creation of a Jewish milieu and of a closed Jewish economy in which producers, consumers and middlemen shall all be Jewish'. Ruppin complained too that Jews in Jaffa were less willing to display national solidarity because they lived in mixed neighbourhoods with Arabs.[72] On the eve of the First World War Arab critics of Zionism were well aware of these arguments, though they often exaggerated the numbers of Jews in the country and the amount of land they had purchased.[73] Khalil al-Sakakini, an influential Jerusalemite, confided in his diary in February 1914:

> What I despise is this principle which [the Zionist] movement has set up, which is that it should subjugate another [national movement] to make itself strong, and that it should kill an entire nation so that it might live because this is as if it is trying to steal its independence and to take it by deceit out of the hand of destiny. This independence, which is acquired by cash, whereby the opportunity of other nations' lethargy, weakness and indolence is exploited, is indeed a feeble independence, founded on sand. What will the Jews do if the national feeling of the Arab nation is aroused; how will they be able to stand up to [the Arabs]?[74]

Filastin echoed these fears a few months later, and made a clear distinction between Jews and Zionists:

> Ten years ago the Jews were living as Ottoman brothers loved by all the Ottoman races . . . living in the same quarters, their children going to the same schools. The Zionists put an end to all that and prevented any intermingling with the indigenous population. They boycotted the Arabic language and the Arab merchants, and declared their intention of taking over the country from its inhabitants.[75]

But the Jews at least, for the moment, felt confident enough of the way ahead. Aaron Aaronsohn, born in Romania but raised in Zichron Yaakov (the largest Jewish employer of Arab workers), boasted of their achievements as the Allied victory over the Ottoman Empire finally neared in 1917: 'We have strictly avoided Arab infiltration in our villages and we are glad of it. From national, cultural, educational, technical and . . . hygienic points of view the policy has to be strictly adhered to.'[76] The Balfour Declaration and Britain's conquest of Palestine offered the Zionists dazzling new opportunities in their promised land.

3

1917–1929

'Every native population in the world resists colonists as long as it has the slightest hope of being able to rid itself of the danger of being colonized. That is what the Arabs in Palestine are doing, and what they will persist in doing as long as there remains a solitary spark of hope that they will be able to prevent the transformation of "Palestine" into the "Land of Israel".'

Vladimir Jabotinsky

'THE USUAL PALESTINIAN TYPE'

British rule quickly revealed both the scale of Zionist ambition and the depth of Arab hostility, though the latter was muted until military operations against Turkish forces ended with the capture of Damascus in October 1918. In April Chaim Weizmann led a Zionist commission 'to investigate present conditions of the Jewish colonies' on an official trip to the country, where it demanded the use of Hebrew as an official language and the flying of the blue and white Star of David flag. When the commission visited Hebron, an accompanying Jewish journalist reflected the Zionists' hopes for the future – despite the obvious obstacles ahead. 'Some day it will be a fine city', he reported.

> But at present it is otherwise. The Arabs – there are said to be about 20,000 of them – are of the usual Palestinian type, and though many of them are quite rich, they are content to spend their days in dirty narrow streets and to go about clothed like beggars. The number of Jews is now about 850.[1]

38

In this confident mood – redolent of encounters elsewhere between European colonialists and natives – the Zionists marked the first anniversary of the Balfour Declaration with a parade in Jerusalem. That was met by Arab protests near the Jaffa Gate, demanding the withdrawal of the declaration[2] – henceforth repeated on 2 November every year – and by the creation of a new Muslim–Christian Association (MCA),[3] the first Palestinian nationalist organization, with branches across the country. 'Palestine is Arab', declared the MCA:

> Its language is Arabic. We want to see this formally recognized. It was Great Britain that rescued us from Turkish tyranny and we do not believe that it will deliver us into the claws of the Jews. We ask for fairness and justice. We ask that it protect our rights and not decide the future of Palestine without asking our opinion.[4]

It was a blunt message that heralded conflict in an atmosphere that was changing ominously. Musa al-Alami, a young Arab lawyer, noted how his old Sephardi Jewish friends in Jerusalem had severed contacts with Arabs at the behest of the 'tough and aggressive Ashkenazim'.[5]

High-level diplomacy was one response to Arab enmity. In June 1918 Weizmann travelled south to Aqaba in Transjordan to meet Emir Faisal, the third son of Sharif Hussein of Mecca and commander of the Arab forces that had swept up from the Hijaz, with British support, to fight the Turks. The Zionist leader believed he had created 'the basis of a long-term friendship' with the handsome and intelligent Hashemite prince; his admiration for 'the greatest of all the Arabs', which never dimmed,[6] contrasted sharply with his contempt for the truculent Palestinian variety. 'It is in our interest,' Weizmann explained to colleagues, 'to localize the Arab question, to take it from Jerusalem to Damascus. To take Palestine out of Pan-Arabia and to get them to concentrate on Bagdad, Mecca and Damascus.'[7] Faisal believed that Jewish money and influence in America would help the cause of Arab nationalism and secure him the throne of Syria in the face of strong French opposition – an approach that has been dubbed an 'exchange of services'.[8] The two men met again in London before signing their agreement in January

1919, ahead of the Paris peace conference. On paper it was a remarkable achievement. Article 4 stipulated:

> All necessary measures shall be taken to encourage and stimulate immigration of Jews into Palestine on a large scale, and as quickly as possible to settle Jewish immigrants upon the land through closer settlement and intensive cultivation of the soil. In taking such measures the Arab peasant and tenant farmers shall be protected in their rights and shall be assisted in forwarding their economic development.

It stipulated too that 'the Mohammedan holy places were to be under Mohammedan control'. Faisal, however, added an important caveat in Arabic to the English text: the agreement would be null and void unless the Arabs were granted full independence. When they were not, Weizmann continued to believe the deal was valid. In reality, with the French and British in firm control across the region, the agreement was a dead letter within a few months.

It was not the last time that Zionists would seek to resolve the conflict over Palestine by subsuming the issue in a wider Arab context. Years later, Weizmann harked back to the 1919 agreement as a tragically lost opportunity for mutually beneficial co-operation. It became an enduring staple of Zionist propaganda – or self-delusion – that 'Faisal's dream was allowed to perish'.[9] That ignored the fact that neither the Hashemite prince nor any other Arab leader could, at least openly, oppose Palestinian interests. Nor was it the last time that there was a jarring disconnect between the grand ambitions of diplomacy and the reality of the confrontation taking shape on the ground. Weeks after the Paris peace conference rejected Faisal's demands for Syria, Zionist officials met to discuss relations with 'our neighbours'. Ben-Gurion, by now the leader of the *Ahdut haAvoda* (Labour Unity) movement, was the most eloquent and clear-sighted of the pessimists: 'Everybody sees a difficulty in the question of relations between Arabs and Jews,' he said.

> But not everybody sees that there is no solution to this question. No solution! There is a gulf and nothing can fill this gulf. It is not possible to resolve the conflict between Jewish and Arab interests [only] by sophistry. I do not know what Arab will agree that Palestine should

belong to the Jews – even if the Jews learn Arabic. And we must recognise this situation. If we do not acknowledge this and try to come up with 'remedies' then we risk demoralisation . . . We, as a nation, want this country to be ours; the Arabs, as a nation, want this country to be theirs.[10]

GRIEVANCES, PROPAGANDA AND INSECURITY

It had long been impossible to entertain the illusion that Palestine was an empty land. 'The land-owning and commercial classes among the Palestinian Arabs are genuinely afraid that the Zionist plan involves their land being expropriated and ousted from taking any part in the industrial and commercial development of the country', the *Zionist Review* commented in early 1920.

> They are opposed, and justifiably opposed, to an exclusive Jewish domination either in the political or in the economic sphere, and they are bound to oppose Zionism so long as they think that such domination is among the aims of Zionism. But it would be a great mistake for Zionists to conclude that this opposition is irremovable, and to base their policy on that hypothesis.[11]

That was an optimistic conclusion, and arguably a false one. It was already clear that the Arabs rejected the Balfour Declaration along with Jewish immigration and land sales, even if that genuinely meant greater prosperity for all. That latter Zionist promise was unconvincing however, and not least because of the land question: in Ottoman times, tenants had not been evicted when land ownership changed, but simply answered to a new landlord. Now they were evicted, and that 'incomprehensible innovation' naturally fuelled fears about the future.[12] At best, the Zionists continued to argue, relations with the Arabs would improve as the Jewish presence became stronger and generated economic growth. If relations did not improve, then so be it.

Ronald Storrs, the British military governor of Jerusalem and author of the most elegant memoir penned about the early years of British colonial rule, described an atmosphere that was 'always critical, frequently hostile, sometimes bitterly vindictive and even menacing'[13] as Arab resentment spread. Storrs noted how 'two hours of Arab grievances drive me into the synagogue, while after an intense course of Zionist propaganda I am prepared to embrace Islam'.[14] In March 1920, Jewish feelings of insecurity were fuelled by attacks on the settlements of Metullah and Tel Hai in northern Palestine, the result of tensions in French-controlled Lebanon and Syria. The hero's death of Joseph Trumpeldor, a Russian-born *HaShomer* member who had lost an arm fighting for the Tsar in the Russo-Japanese war of 1904–5, became the object of a cult of patriotic sacrifice: a Zionist version of *'dulce et decorum est'*. Beyond Trumpeldor's martyrdom, Tel Hai came to symbolize the link between land, labour, sweat and blood, encapsulated in the slogan: 'a place once settled is not to be abandoned'.[15]

Incidents of Jews being attacked by Arabs became more frequent.[16] Zionists complained that the British were not prepared to act, but Storrs assured Jewish representatives that security would be adequate during the Muslim Nebi Musa pilgrimage in the Judaean desert near Jericho, in April. In the event three days of violence in Jerusalem left 5 Jews dead and 200 injured; 4 Arabs were killed with 25 injured. Jewish anger focused on the British administration for not acting firmly. An official British report, unpublished at the time, focused on Arab fears of Jewish immigration and settlement, though the military's response was criticized too. 'All the carefully built relations of mutual understanding between British, Arabs and Jews seemed to flare away in an agony of fear and hatred', Storrs lamented, with the familiar exasperation of the 'man on the spot' found wanting by distant peers in the imperial capital.

> Our dispositions might perhaps have been better ... but I have often wondered whether those who criticised us ... could have had the faintest conception of the steep, narrow and winding alleys within the Old City of Jerusalem, the series of steps up or down which no horse or car can ever pass, the deadly dark corners beyond which a whole family can be murdered out of sight or sound of a police post not a hundred yards away. What did they know of the nerves of Jerusalem, where in times of anxiety the sudden clatter on the stones of an empty petrol tin will produce a panic?[17]

The Palin Report described a 'condition of affairs when the native population, disappointed of their hopes, panic-stricken as to their future, exasperated beyond endurance by the aggressive attitude of the Zionists, and despairing of redress at the hands of an Administration which seems to them powerless before the Zionist organisation, lies a ready prey for any form of agitation'.[18] The militant right-wing Russian Zionist leader Vladimir Jabotinsky, who had served in the British army during the war and who tried to lead Jewish defence efforts in Jerusalem, was sentenced to fifteen years' penal servitude. But after protests in the House of Commons his sentence was reduced to a year and his legacy of activism lived on.

A MANDATE FOR CHANGE

Among the Arab community the idea of a distinct Palestinian national identity had continued to spread since the end of the war, encouraged in part by the gradually dawning realization of Zionist ambitions and the creation of a separate British administration for the country.[19] In February 1919 the first congress of Muslim–Christian Associations declared unity with Syria, though support faded when Faisal's rule collapsed and he was expelled by the French the following summer. Questions also started to be asked in Arab circles as to exactly what Faisal had agreed with Weizmann.

In May 1920 the San Remo conference granted Britain the Mandate for Palestine under the Covenant of the League of Nations. Syria, including Lebanon, and Mesopotamia (Iraq) were to be provisionally recognized as independent but meanwhile were to be assisted and advised by France and Britain respectively. The intention was to govern these former Ottoman territories 'until such time as they are able to stand alone'. Arab leaders were to argue from then on that the British were obliged on that basis to facilitate the creation of an independent Arab state in Palestine – though that was clearly not compatible with the commitment to establish a Jewish national home. Transjordan was briefly a no-man's-land until being attached to the British Palestine Mandate, but was exempted from Balfour's pledge under the rule of Faisal's brother, the Emir Abdullah bin Hussein.

The Arabian peninsula remained a battleground between Sharif Hussein and the Al Saud.

Britain's first high commissioner for Palestine, Sir Herbert Samuel, a leading Liberal Jewish politician, arrived by cruiser in Jaffa in grand viceregal style in tropical whites, plumes and cocked hat. 'The military authorities were nervous, and had made the most formidable preparations against any possible eventuality', Samuel recalled. 'But nothing happened at all, and the leading men of all the communities joined in a courteous welcome.'[20] The terms of the Mandate incorporated the Balfour Declaration almost verbatim. Article 6, crucially, pledged to promote Jewish immigration and land settlement; English, Arabic and Hebrew were declared official languages. A 'Jewish agency' was to be recognized to advise the administration, but there was no parallel Arab agency. The word 'Arab' did not in fact appear in the text, while the word 'Palestinian' was used only with reference to the acquisition of citizenship by Jews. Arab hostility was guaranteed from the start. The feeling was reciprocated: Weizmann's colleague, the Russian-born Menachem Ussishkin, refused to shake hands with the mufti of Jerusalem, Kamal al-Husseini, at a reception Storrs organized for the high commissioner.[21]

In December 1920 the MCA's third Palestinian Congress in Haifa dropped its demand for union with Syria – and rejected the Balfour Declaration. It also elected an Arab Executive (AE) committee led by Musa Kazem al-Husseini of the eminent Jerusalem family. Palestinians began to focus more on the fate of Palestine. Arabic educational works on geography and history that were published in the 1920s reflected this clearly. And so, increasingly, did political behaviour: 'After the recent events in Damascus we must change our plans entirely,' Musa Kazem told supporters. 'Southern Syria is no more. We must defend Palestine.'[22]

If official British policy was clear, there were grave doubts about it in private. 'It is indeed difficult to see how we can keep our promises to the Jews by making the country a "national home" without inflicting injury on 9/10ths of the population', one official confided to his diary. 'But we have now got the onus of it on our shoulders, and have incurred odium from the Moslems & Christians, who are not appeased by vague promises that their interests will not be affected.'[23]

In August 1921, reviewing his first year in the post, the high commissioner referred pointedly to those Zionists 'who sometimes forget or ignore the present inhabitants of Palestine', and who suddenly 'learn with surprise and often with incredulity, that there are half-a-million people in Palestine, many of whom hold, and hold strongly, very different views'.[24]

Weizmann's diplomacy had not succeeded in defusing Arab opposition. Other less subtle methods were tried as well. In May he met a Nablus notable, Haydar Bey Touqan, a former mayor and Ottoman MP, and promised him £2,000 to conduct pro-Zionist propaganda. Touqan managed to produce petitions from ten villages in support of British rule and Jewish immigration and condemning the Jerusalem riots. In all some eighty such petitions appeared.[25] Another tack was to exploit existing divisions and encourage new ones. Chaim Kalvarisky, one of the most colourful figures in the world of Jewish-Arab relations, was tasked by the Zionist executive to promote the formation of Muslim National Associations to counter the nationalist Muslim–Christian Associations. The Polish-born, French-educated Kalvarisky, an agronomist by training, was considered the *Yishuv*'s leading 'expert' on Arabs (many others would follow). He had served as a land agent in Galilee for many years, dispossessing Arab peasants, while professing sensitivity to Arab feelings.[26] Arab 'farmers parties' were established in Nazareth and Jenin under his aegis to 'maintain and deepen the divide'[27] between the villages and the urban elite – a tactic that was to resurface decades later. Newspapers were persuaded to adopt a pro-Zionist – or at least a neutral – policy. Bribes were paid to secure the postponement of a nationalist congress until after a sensitive holiday period when trouble seemed likely.[28] Kalvarisky's boldest initiative was to 'buy' Musa Kazem, president of the Arab Executive.[29] Other plans to buy Arab support, or inaction, failed to materialize because of shortages of cash. And nor, felt some Zionist critics, were these efforts effective: 'The signature of the professional petition-monger or the temporary benevolence of a venal editor have no appreciable effect on the situation', commented one official, 'and in general little can be done by the mere distribution of casual bribes, except, perhaps, on a vastly larger scale than it is possible to contemplate.'[30]

Kalvarisky's activities were by their nature discreet, but he hardly operated under deep cover. Arab interlocutors regarded him with open contempt: Awni Abdel-Hadi of Nablus, a prominent nationalist lawyer, told Kalvarisky frankly that he preferred dealing with Zionists who did *not* claim to be seeking rapprochement:

> You always speak of a Jewish-Arab agreement or good relations between Jews and Arabs. I tell you frankly that I would rather deal with Jabotinsky or Ussishkin than you. I know that they are our declared enemies who want to crush us, take our lands and force us to leave the country – and that we have to fight them. You, Kalvarisky, seem to be our friend but in the end I can see no difference between your goal and Jabotinsky's. You also support the Balfour Declaration, the national home, unrestricted immigration and the continuous purchase of Arab lands – which for me is a matter of life and death.[31]

Abdel-Hadi would repeat his view of the inevitability of conflict in later meetings with Zionist representatives.[32]

MAY DAY

Neither bribes nor diplomacy prevented the next wave of violence to hit Palestine. In May 1921 rioting erupted in Jaffa. It was triggered by a May Day clash between rival Communist and socialist Jewish groups in the Manshiyeh quarter, bordering Tel Aviv. The main target was the hostel for new Jewish immigrants, where 'pioneer couples who walked arm in arm through the streets were for the Jaffa Arabs the most tangible demonstration of the moral and social ruin which Palestine faced from Jewish immigration'.[33] Ten thousand Jews had entered the country via Jaffa port since the previous September alone – largely East European Zionists and socialists who been born among the pogroms of Tsarist Russia and had spent their youth in the turmoil of war and revolution. Arab press reports complained of the spread of 'Bolshevik' ideas – a common theme; social mores – the provocatively immodest appearance of Jewish women – were a particular preoccupation. Mixed bathing was another.

Trouble spread across the country. Attacks on the Jewish colonies of Petah Tikvah and Hadera (founded by *Hovevei Tzion* in 1891) were repulsed only by the deployment of British cavalry and aircraft. Martial law was declared. Over six days of violence forty-one Jews and forty-four Arabs were killed.[34] Of the Jewish victims, the best known was the writer Yosef Haim Brenner, who had become profoundly pessimistic about relations with the Arabs. To Jewish fury, Sir Herbert Samuel also announced a temporary halt to Jewish immigration. Fines and other collective punishments were imposed on Arab communities. 'It was my first encounter with the experience of terror, death, the Arab as an enemy', one Jewish youngster recalled later.[35] The bloodshed was the most alarming sign yet that Arab–Zionist tensions were likely to be a serious problem for the British authorities. The Haycraft Commission, which investigated the events, dismissed the view of *Yishuv* spokesmen that the trouble was the work of 'demagogues, agitators and effendis' – anything but the expression of growing Arab political opposition. 'Feeling against the Jews was too genuine, too widespread and too intense to be accounted for in above superficial manner', it reported.[36] Samuel, echoing the commission's findings, told Weizmann: 'I have come to the conclusion that the importance of the Arab factor had been underestimated by the Zionist movement; unless there is very careful steering it is upon the Arab rock that the Zionist ship may be wrecked.'[37] The report implied, Weizmann complained, 'that the Zionist desire to dominate in Palestine might provide further ground for Arab resentment'.[38] At the high commissioner's urging Weizmann met a Palestinian Arab delegation, led by Musa Kazem al-Husseini (the intended recipient of sweeteners from Kalvarisky) in London that November to discuss future constitutional arrangements, but there was little common ground. The suspicious atmosphere was not conducive to progress. Weizmann asked a student from Haifa, David HaCohen, to book a room in the Arab delegation's hotel under an assumed name and obtain copies of their documents.[39] 'Dr Weizmann, while his speech was conciliatory, adopted an unfortunate manner in delivering it', reported a British official. 'His attitude was of the nature of a conqueror handing to beaten foes the terms of peace. Also I think he despises the members of the delegation as not worthy protagonists – that it is a little derogatory [*sic*] to him to expect him to meet them on the same ground.'[40] In private, Weizmann was even harsher, telling a colleague that the Arab delegation was 'fifth-rate'.[41]

Like the more limited trouble in Jerusalem the previous year, the unrest was a powerful fillip to plans for Jewish self-defence: another answer to worries about how to 'deal with' Arab opposition to Zionism, or 'the Arab question' as it was now routinely called by the Jews. In December 1920 the newly established *Histadrut* (General Federation of Hebrew Labour in Palestine) had resolved to set up a volunteer defence organization called the *Haganah* (Defence).[42] *HaShomer*, the Jewish settlement guards group that had been established in 1909, was abolished. Under its founder Eliahu Golomb, the *Haganah* held a first 'officers training course' in August 1921. Arms-smuggling increased, with two hundred pistols brought into the country. Intelligence-gathering, focused inevitably on Arabs, became better organized. Jabotinsky, now out of prison, campaigned in vain for the revival of the Jewish battalions of the Great War and their incorporation into the British garrison in Palestine. Not long afterwards he was to call for an 'iron wall' to protect the fledgling Jewish enterprise. That much-quoted phrase has stuck as a succinct description of how, for all its talk of co-existence, the Zionist movement really dealt with Arab opposition, despite significant differences of emphasis between rival political movements. 'Every native population in the world resists colonists as long as it has the slightest hope of being able to rid itself of the danger of being colonized', Jabotinsky wrote. 'That is what the Arabs in Palestine are doing, and what they will persist in doing as long as there remains a solitary spark of hope that they will be able to prevent the transformation of "Palestine" into the "Land of Israel".'[43] Discreet *Haganah* preparations helped avert more unrest in Jerusalem on 2 November, Balfour Day, by now a regular fixture in the secular calendar of the accelerating conflict.

The Haycraft Commission noted another important change: shifting perceptions by Arabs of their Jewish neighbours. 'During the riots all discrimination on the part of the Arabs between different categories of Jews was obliterated', the report commented. 'Old-established colonists and newly arrived immigrants, Chalukah [Haluka] Jews [living on charity handouts from abroad] and Bolshevik Jews, Algerian Jews and Russian Jews, became merged in a single identity, and former friendships gave way before the enmity now felt towards all.[44] The British, increasingly, rejected the standard Zionist narrative about the fundamentally good relations between the two communities: 'It is all very well to say that there has been peace for a generation between Arabs and Jews. It was the sort of peace that exists between two bodies of men who have little or nothing to do with each other.'[45]

BLURRING DIFFERENCES

On the surface, relative calm reigned for the next few years. In 1922 the British Mandate was confirmed by the League of Nations and the country's boundaries, based on the three Ottoman provinces of southern Syria, were fixed. Transjordan became a separate entity where Balfour's promise did not apply, to the fury of Zionists who claimed it as part of their biblical patrimony and objected to what they denounced as 'partition' – a theme which would reappear in years to come. The territory across the river was ruled by Emir Abdullah, the younger son of Sharif Hussein of Mecca, under British tutelage.

By this time the Zionist enterprise had already been under way for four decades, though it had not yet brought about a significant demographic transformation: Palestine's 757,000 inhabitants consisted of an overwhelming majority of Arabs, with a Jewish minority of 83,000 or 11 per cent of the population. But immigration continued apace. The third *aliya*, dated from 1919 to 1923, brought in 35,000 largely Russian and Polish and mostly socialist Jewish newcomers. These *halutzim* (pioneers) played an important role in establishing *kibbutzim* and other collective Zionist organizations such as *Gdud haAvoda* (the labour battalion). Its members built roads, drained swamps and undertook other public construction projects, and did much to mould the ethos of an autonomous society built by Hebrew labour – the word Hebrew (*Ivrit*) deliberately replacing the word Jewish. 'We came to this land to build it and to be rebuilt in it', went a popular song of the time, reflecting the notion that a 'new Jew' – tough, dedicated, muscular and Hebrew-speaking, who rejected the values of the Diaspora – was being created in the ancient homeland.

Arabs were not part of that exclusive nationalist vision. Employing

Arabs was frowned upon in particular: in the early 1920s a Jewish farmer from Rishon LeZion complained to a British official that he had been ordered by the Jewish Agency to dismiss the local Arabs he had grown up with and employed as herdsmen and ploughmen, and instead engage new Jewish immigrants at higher pay.

> If he dismissed the Arabs in the summary manner suggested, such bad feeling would be created that, being a vindictive people, they might well burn his crops ... The Jews who had been proposed to him as labourers knew nothing about farming and ... local conditions. The Arabs would work to all hours of the night if it were a question of getting a crop in before the rain; the Jews would down tools precisely at six o'clock, no matter what the weather.[46]

The next wave of mass Jewish immigration during the Mandate – the fourth *aliya* – is dated from 1924 to 1929. The majority of these newcomers were from Poland, hit by a severe economic crisis and a wave of anti-Semitic persecution. (They were known as the 'Grabski *aliya*', named after the Polish prime minister whose financial reforms had badly affected the country's Jews.) This influx was very different sociologically from the ideologically motivated pioneers of the past, those Weizmann admiringly called 'the men of Degania and Nahalal'. It included substantial lower- and middle-class elements who brought their savings – $2,500 was the minimum required for a new 'capitalist' immigration certificate – to invest in workshops, businesses and services. Weizmann was not best pleased. 'Some of them were little disposed to pull their weight in a new country', he wrote later. 'A few, in their struggle for existence, showed anti-social tendencies; they seemed never to have been Zionists and saw no difference between Palestine as a country of immigration and, for instance, the United States.' Too many of the newcomers smacked of the 'life of the ghetto'.[47] Large numbers settled in Tel Aviv, which was now billed as the 'white city' on the Mediterranean sands. As early as 1918, a new Hebrew geography book described it as 'a European oasis within an Asian desert' and praised its straight, paved streets planted with gardens and flowers, everything 'new and shining'.[48] An influx of capital and residents, some of them turning their backs on Jaffa after the 1921 unrest, triggered a construction boom.[49] Cultural life flourished with a theatre and orchestra, though less attractive aspects included prostitution. In the words of a 1924 police report: 'Suddenly we began to see . . . cars of wealthy Arabs and Christians from Jaffa arriv[ing] in Tel Aviv in the middle of the evenings and parked alongside the houses [of] . . . new female immigrants, [and] the wild debauchery continued until the wee hours of the night.'[50]

New newspapers and publishing houses gave a boost to the spreading Hebrew language. Tel Aviv's population grew from just 2,000 in 1920 to 34,000 by 1925, the year the Scottish town planner Patrick Geddes drew up a master plan for the city. Jaffa was still bigger, but was gradually cut off from the Arab villages in its hinterland by the creation of a contiguous zone of Jewish settlement.[51] 'We saw the Arabs as our neighbours and cousins', a Tel Aviv native recalled.

> We knew the baker and the greengrocer, the people selling strawberries, prickly pears and *bouza* [ice-cream in Arabic]. When someone in Tel Aviv said: 'I'm going into town', they meant to Jaffa. That's where you went to have fun, shop, work, and above all to go [to] the port, the centre of social life. Still there was a sense of anxiety and insecurity about wandering around in Jaffa. The [Arab] *shabab* – young guys, louts and thugs used to swear at Jews and provoke them. British officials and police often encouraged them.[52]

By the spring of 1925 Palestine's total Jewish population was 108,000.[53] This was a landmark year: the first time the number of Jews who came to Palestine exceeded the number who entered the US, after the imposition of immigrant quotas there.[54] To a visiting British journalist in 1927, Tel Aviv was

> a perfect freak in Palestine . . . rather like Alexandria but without any flavour of the East. The streets were crowded. Wide hipped German & Polish & Russian girls wheeling prams – an endless file – & men looking as though they were using Sunbronze on their fat aquiline features. Not a word of English & my questions for direction not understood.[55]

Modernity and prosperity went hand in hand. British policy under the Mandate gave open preference to Jewish development, providing 'a propitious environment for the growth of a larger and more homogeneous Zionist enclave, which in turn led to the bifurcation of Palestine's economy'.[56] In 1922 an electricity concession was granted to the Russian-Jewish industrialist Pinchas Rutenberg, who built a grid which supplied power to Jaffa, Tel Aviv, Jewish settlements and British military facilities, and later constructed a power station at Naharayim on the Jordan. Winston Churchill, the colonial secretary, told MPs that the bidding process had not been unfair since 'the Arabs of Palestine would not in a thousand years have taken effective steps towards the irrigation and electrification of Palestine'. The Palestine Potash works at Sedom on the Dead Sea was another enterprise that depended on Jewish investment and technological prowess.[57]

Politically, the question of 'relations' with the Arabs seemed less urgent to the Zionists in the mid-1920s, but it had not, of course, gone away. Kalvarisky's attempts to 'buy' Palestinian moderates yielded few positive results, and his profligate methods were discredited until he was ordered 'on no account to have any control over the expenditure of Zionist funds'. Arab work by Jewish institutions was scaled back. The 'Arab question' – never a high priority for the Jewish mainstream – faded from view. Jabotinsky was a lonely and candid voice protesting against what he saw as the illusion of Arab acquiescence in Zionism, denouncing 'Kalvarisky's bribes and Weizmann's peace-lies'.[58] In 1925 he went on to found the New Zionist Organization, better known as the 'Revisionist movement' because it wanted to 'revise' the terms of the Mandate to include Transjordan within its scope. 'There are two banks to the Jordan' went its famous slogan. 'One is ours, and so is the other.'

On the Arab side, a more pro-British mood was encouraged for a while by concessions over land and the creation of a powerful Supreme Muslim Council headed by Haj Amin al-Husseini, the mufti of Jerusalem, who had been given the brand new title of Grand Mufti.[59] In 1923, however, British proposals for a legislative council met with the firm rejection of the fifth Palestine Arab Congress, which opposed anything that was based on the hated Balfour Declaration. The *Yishuv* was unhappy with the idea of any representative institutions, given the still small number of Jews. The Zionists agreed reluctantly to take part in council elections, but an Arab boycott and subsequent low turnout meant that the results were declared null and void. High Commissioner Samuel's efforts foundered on the irreconcilable clash between Britain's support for a Jewish national home and the refusal of the Zionists to accept minority status. It was another example of the way that Arab actions and divisions often ended up inadvertently helping the Zionist cause.

'NO COMMON LANGUAGE'

If the economic prosperity of the mid-1920s boosted the self-confidence of the *Yishuv*, there was still little sign that benefits were trickling down to the Arab population, as Zionist propaganda always claimed was happening. Land purchases expanded, notably in the Marj Ibn Amr (Jezreel or Esdraelon) valley where sales by the absentee Sursuq family of Beirut attracted notoriety but also distracted attention, misleadingly, from numerous smaller sales by Palestinian Arabs.[60] More Jewish settlements were established on the coastal plain. Land sales peaked in 1925. In late 1924, the annual conference of *Ahdut haAvoda*, held at Ein Harod – one of the first *kibbutzim* – provided an opportunity to debate the question of Zionist 'relations' with the Arabs. Its conclusion was that the answer lay in the joint organization of Jewish and Arab workers, and that there was no Arab 'national movement worthy of the name and that, at the current stage of development of the national home, a political agreement with the Arabs of Palestine was neither practical nor desirable'.[61] Looking back at the debates over the proposed legislative council, the *Ahdut haAvoda* leader Ben-Gurion spoke out forcefully against representative government: 'We must not be afraid to proclaim openly that between us, the Jewish workers, and the leaders of today's Arab movement, the effendis, there is no common language', he argued. Ben-Gurion did not deny the right of the Arab community to *self-rule* – but he would not, and clearly could not, concede their right to rule the country. Zionism was an authentic and progressive national movement, in his view, and Arab nationalism, the plaything of self-interested, reactionary leaders who wanted only to keep the ignorant masses under their control, was not.[62]

Even then, however, some leading Zionists were aware of a nagging sense of false security. 'What continually worries me is the relationship between Jews and Arabs in Palestine', fretted Arthur

Ruppin, the lawyer who had opened the Palestine Office in Jaffa back in 1908. 'Superficially it has improved inasmuch as there is no danger of pogroms, but the two peoples have become much more estranged in their thinking. Neither has any understanding of the other.' Arab views reflected this pessimism in a bleak mirror image: 'It is a gross error to believe that Arab and Jew may come to an understanding if only each of them exchanges his coat of extremism for another of moderation', the Palestinian Arab Congress reported to the League of Nations in 1924. 'When the principles underlying two movements do clash, it is futile to expect their meeting halfway.'[63]

In 1925 Ruppin helped found a new organization – *Brit Shalom* (Covenant of Peace). It was designed to foster Arab–Jewish understanding and promote the idea of a 'bi-national' state. Dominated by Central European, largely German-born Jewish intellectuals and pacifists – 'all these Arthurs, Hugos and Hans', in the dismissive words of one critic[64] – *Brit Shalom* met considerable hostility from the Zionist establishment, which saw it at best as idealistic and naïve, and at worst dangerously out of touch with the harsh realities of life in Palestine. Other well-known members included Martin Buber, the charismatic philosopher, the historian Gershom Scholem, and a number of Jewish professors of oriental studies at the newly founded Hebrew University of Jerusalem.

Arab hostility was unmistakable when Lord Balfour, accompanied by Weizmann and Field Marshal Allenby, attended the inauguration of the new institution on Mount Scopus, on 1 April that year, and a general strike was declared. Hundreds of telegrams of protest arrived at Government House but he drew no conclusions from driving through nearly empty streets.[65] By contrast, he was warmly welcomed by Jews in Jerusalem and Tel Aviv, and especially in Balfouriya, a settlement founded near Afula by American Zionists in honour of this 'new Cyrus' (the Persian king who had liberated the Jews from their Babylonian exile). Later the same day, in Nazareth, Balfour and his entourage were pelted with stones and had to be rescued by British soldiers.[66] Balfour also faced mass demonstrations on an ill-advised visit to Damascus, where French troops guarding him killed three protestors. Co-existence remained a noble aspiration: *Brit Shalom* promoted private discussions, published a magazine and launched a programme of Arabic evening classes for Jews as part of an effort to encourage friendly relations between the two peoples. Kalvarisky and a handful of Sephardi notables also joined. *Brit Shalom*'s appearance was seen by many Arabs as a welcome sign of weakness in the mainstream Zionist movement.[67] Politically, however, it got nowhere.

Arab rivalries helped the Zionists. Ragheb al-Nashashibi, the scion of another powerful Jerusalem family – Ronald Storrs called him 'unquestionably the ablest Arab in Palestine' – led opposition to the grand mufti. Nashashibi's Palestinian Arab National Party favoured co-operation with the British administration and was denounced as treacherous by the Arab Executive. The Zionists did whatever they could to encourage this mutual vilification, providing financial support even as their own resources dwindled.[68] Many prominent Arab families, including nationalist activists, continued to sell land to Jews – an embarrassing issue that has been little addressed in Palestinian historical literature.[69] Beyond their local impact, land transfers affected the wider Arab economy. After the Marj Ibn Amr valley was sold, modern production methods and stockbreeding replaced traditional cereal cultivation and herding; nearby Nazareth and Jenin, market towns for the grain trade, suffered, while Haifa, which was better placed to service farm machinery and sell cash crops, benefitted.[70]

In 1926 there was little organized Arab political activity at all, with even the now-traditional strikes on Balfour Day temporarily forgotten. Against the background of a deepening local economic crisis, marked by unemployment, labour protests and even net Jewish *emigration* in 1927, Zionism seemed less threatening than before. The Husseinis and Nashashibis set aside their differences to seek a measure of self-government. The seventh (and last) Palestinian Arab Congress in 1928 did not even demand the abrogation of the Mandate or express opposition to Zionism.[71] Its sessions, Kalvarisky reported, had been 'practical and moderate', though he did observe the loss of influence of the aristocratic feudal families and the rising strength of the 'extremist and chauvinist' intelligentsia, with whom it was far harder for the Jews to come to terms.[72] Arab interest in co-operating with the government attracted support because of the progress achieved by neighbouring countries under Mandatory regimes (Iraq, Syria and Lebanon) towards establishing self-governing and representative institutions – institutions which were so conspicuously absent in Palestine.

GOING TO THE WALL

If economic depression bred political quiescence, the rumbling of a new crisis ensured that the confrontation between Arabs and Jews was soon back on everyone's minds – and with an especially volatile element. It began with a dispute over arrangements at the western ('wailing') wall of the Herodian temple compound in Jerusalem's Old City, which Jews believed was the site of the Temple of Solomon. It is also the western wall of the Haram al-Sharif ('Noble Sanctuary' or Temple Mount), known to Muslims as *al-Buraq* – named for the horse the Prophet Muhammad had tethered there before completing his 'night journey' to heaven. Muslims had long feared that the Haram, site of the Dome of the Rock and the al-Aqsa mosque (Islam's third holiest site after Mecca and Medina), might be threatened. Jews had prayed at the wall's massive stones for centuries. In Ottoman times they were not permitted to place benches, screens or Torah scrolls on the site, or do anything that might be interpreted as a claim to possession. In reality, these restrictions were not always observed, custom and practice proving laxer than the letter of the law. Little changed under the British, who had pledged to respect the status quo. In 1922, the Supreme Muslim Council (SMC) opposed any attempt to enhance Jewish access and Haj Amin, the grand mufti, raised large sums of money from Muslims to renovate the Haram. Now propaganda about an alleged Zionist threat began to circulate in the Muslim world. (It may have been based on a photomontage or drawing of the Haram in Zionist propaganda leaflets and postcards that were intended to attract Jewish funding.) Occasional inflammatory speeches fuelled suspicions. Modern research has unearthed sketchy evidence of a plot by a Jewish extremist to blow up the mosque – and his execution by the *Haganah* defence organization.[73] But there was no official Zionist plan to take over the Muslim holy places. Even Weizmann's agreement with Emir Faisal had stipulated that they would remain under Muslim control. In such a tense atmosphere, however, rumour, propaganda and exaggeration mattered more than facts.

This highly charged dispute escalated on Yom Kippur (the Jewish Day of Atonement) 1928, when Jews brought a screen to the wall to separate male and female worshippers. It was removed by police. When the British reaffirmed the status quo, the SMC began a campaign to impose restrictions. 'The Muslims of Palestine are determined to sacrifice body and soul in order to safeguard their religious rights', warned a newspaper loyal to the mufti. 'It is enough that their national rights have been stolen from them.'[74] Zionist pressure brought Arab counter-pressure. Months of rising tensions, a provocative flag-waving demonstration by the Jabotinsky-inspired Beitar Revisionist movement and mutual denunciations came to a head in the summer heat of 1929.[75] Tit-for-tat attacks in Jerusalem, and more protests, were the prelude to the worst violence since 1917. On 16 August a Kurdish Jewish teenager was stabbed to death by Arabs on the border between two neighbourhoods. Contemporary accounts differ as to whether Avraham Mizrahi had kicked a football into an Arab garden or stolen a courgette. In normal times a trivial local dispute of this kind could have been easily settled. But these were far from normal times.[76]

The violence began on the Haram al-Sharif after Friday prayers on 23 August. Several Jews were killed in Jerusalem, where there were complaints that the British police failed to use force or even to fire warning shots to deter the attackers. *Haganah* men rebuffed assaults from Lifta and Deir Yassin, on the western edge of the city, on the nearby newly built Jewish suburb of Beit Hakerem with its modest stone houses and red-tiled roofs. Lifta was singled out by police and the Zionists as 'as bad a village as there was round Jerusalem'.[77] Arabs from Qaluniya attacked the neighbouring Jewish village of Motza. The dead knew their killers intimately – a reminder that Palestine's neighbours and enemies were all too often interchangeable. Of the entire Maklef family, the only survivor was nine-year-old Mordechai, who survived by jumping out of a window. (In 1948 he would take part in the battle for Haifa, and in 1952 he became the second chief-of-staff of the Israeli Defence Forces.)

MASSACRE IN HEBRON

The biggest Arab attack, in response to the news from Jerusalem, took place in Hebron, home to the Tomb of the Patriarchs and the Ibrahimi mosque, a revered religious site for Muslims and Jews. The sixty-four victims from the city's Orthodox Jewish community included a dozen women and three young children who were killed in horrific circumstances. Raymond Cafferata, a British police superintendent, described what he witnessed:

> On hearing screams in a room, I went up a sort of tunnel passage and saw an Arab in the act of cutting off a child's head with a sword. He had already hit him and was having another cut, but on seeing me he tried to aim the stroke at me, but missed; he was practically on the muzzle of my rifle. I shot him low in the groin. Behind him was a Jewish woman smothered in blood with a man I recognised as a[n Arab] police constable named Issa Sheriff from Jaffa. He was standing over the woman with a dagger in his hand. He saw me and bolted into a room close by and tried to shut me out – shouting in Arabic, 'Your Honour, I am a policeman.' . . . I got into the room and shot him.[78]

In Safed, the holy city in upper Galilee, twenty-six died. Jews had lived peacefully there, as they had in Hebron, for centuries, long before the advent of Zionism, though tensions had risen in the preceding years as they had across the country. Still, the leaders of the Hebron Jewish community had rejected an offer to have *Haganah* men sent from Jerusalem to protect them. In all 133 Jews and 116 Arabs were killed, most of the Arabs by British police; 339 Jews and 232 Arabs were injured. Ben-Gurion called the Hebron massacre a pogrom, comparing it to the notorious Kishinev killings in 1903, immortalized in a famous Hebrew poem by Chaim Nahman Bialik, entitled 'The City of Slaughter'. Eastern European anti-Semitism and Arab violence in Palestine – portrayed by Arabs as legitimate resistance to Zionist expansion – were thus fused into an indissoluble whole. Hebrew newspapers filled page after page with stomach-churning descriptions of the atrocities and pictures of the innocent victims. The lesson drawn by many was that Jews must fight back when attacked. Haim Bograshov, principal of the Herzliya Gymnasium in Tel Aviv, an elite school where Zionist values were proudly inculcated, articulated the point:

> Over the course of an entire generation we educated our children and pupils that they should not hold out their necks to the slaughter, that they should not die like the dead of Safed, perish like the butchered of Hebron. It is over. The time of riots has passed for us and will not return, for we shall not let ourselves be killed without resisting.[79]

Unlike the Russian pogroms, though, the slaughter in Hebron was not organized by the authorities. Hundreds of Jews were sheltered and saved by their Arab neighbours. Yet it remained a shocking – and enduring – example of the human cost of Arab hostility, which showed no sign of abating. In October Arabs declared a general strike in protest at 'blindly pro-Zionist' British policies. In Nablus, singled out by the authorities for punishment, eighty pupils from the government school were flogged on their bare buttocks. That was ordered by a British official who was known for his contempt for Arabs, believing only one in thirty 'so endowed by nature as to merit the expenditure of public money on his secondary education'.[80] The British Commission of Inquiry under Sir Walter Shaw, however, decided that the violence was not intended to be a revolt against British authority.

The Arabs called the attacks the *'al-Buraq* rebellion' – a reference to the Prophet's winged horse. Jews would remember the events as the '1929 disturbances'. In June 1930 three Arabs, convicted of murder in Hebron and Safed, were hanged in Acre prison, a crowd of hundreds waiting silently outside as the executions were carried out on what became known as 'Red Tuesday' after the poem by Ibrahim Touqan. Vigils were held in Haifa and Nablus. 'May the blood of these Palestinian martyrs water the roots of the tree of Arab independence', ran an Arabic eulogy.[81] The song 'From Acre Gaol' (*'Min Sijn Akka'*), by the popular poet Nuh Ibrahim, remains a staple of Palestinian collective memory. By contrast, the Jewish policeman who killed an entire Arab family in Jaffa had his death sentence commuted.[82]

In time, the 1929 violence would come to be seen as an important milestone. Pan-Muslim sentiment had been aroused over the fate of the Haram al-Sharif and was to remain a significant factor in mobilizing public opinion and governments far beyond Palestine. In Palestine itself, the Arabs sensed that the old distinction between Jews and Zionists was no longer valid. In Hebron in particular, the establishment of a new *yeshiva* (religious school) in 1924 had brought in American and European Jewish students; they were not Zionist settlers but were still likely perceived as such by the local Arabs.[83] Sephardi Jews from the old *Yishuv* closed ranks with Ashkenazi newcomers and began to do what they had refrained from doing previously – joining the *Haganah* and adopting an openly Zionist ethos.[84] The Arab–Jewish confrontation, in short, was becoming a more explicitly national one.

Moreover, awareness of the significance of that change sharpened: Jewish voices from left and right compared the situation to sitting on a volcano.[85] Christopher Sykes, an astute British chronicler of the Mandate years, identified 1929 as 'a cross-roads moment when mistakes could not easily be undone'.[86] In one of several similar cases, Arabs from Lifta on the western outskirts of Jerusalem attacked the Nahalat Shiva Jewish neighbourhood in the city centre, built on land their own forebears had sold years before. Was that a reflection of a dawning understanding that it had been a terrible mistake to allow the Zionists to gain the firm foothold they now had?[87] Shmuel Yosef Agnon, the great Hebrew writer, lived through the trauma in Talpiot, a new Jewish suburb of Jerusalem, which came under attack, and described afterwards how his feelings towards Arabs had changed. 'Now my attitude is this. I do not hate them and I do not love them; I do not wish to see their faces. In my humble opinion, what we now need is to build a big ghetto of half a million Jews in Palestine. Otherwise we are lost.'[88] Yehoshua Palmon, a Jewish native of Jaffa who was to become an influential Arab 'expert', saw 1929 as a turning point in the conflict. The violence 'taught me that we had only two alternatives before us: surrender or the sword', he reflected later. 'I chose the sword.'[89]

AROUSING APPREHENSION

In what was becoming a familiar pattern under British Mandatory rule, the events of 1929 were followed by another investigation and new policy recommendations. In March 1930 the Shaw Commission concluded that 'the claims and demands which from the Zionist side have been advanced in regard to the future of Jewish immigration into Palestine have been such as to arouse among Arabs the apprehension that they will in time be deprived of their livelihood and pass under the political domination of the Jews'.[90] Ominously for the Jews, the commission pointed to the 'landless and discontented class' being formed by Zionist expansion as the main source of trouble, and urged that 'directions more explicit' should follow. Another investigation, conducted by Sir John Hope Simpson, then looked at the economic capacity of Palestine, and concluded that there was insufficient land to meet the needs of Jewish immigrants. Rural Arab areas were already experiencing an economic crisis aggravated by a poor harvest that forced peasants to sell their land and migrate to the cities and the shanty towns spreading around them. He warned:

> The principle of the persistent and deliberate boycott of Arab labour in the [Jewish] colonies is not only contrary to the Mandate, but it is in addition a constant and increasing source of danger to the country. The Arab population already regards the transfer of lands to Zionist hands with dismay and alarm. These cannot be dismissed as baseless in the light of the Zionist policy.

Zionist opinion found this accurate assessment 'patronising and hostile'.[91]

The White Paper that followed, issued under the name of the colonial secretary Lord Passfield (Sidney Webb), appeared in October 1930. It implied that future Jewish immigration to Palestine might have to be restricted. The Zionists, unhappy with what felt like their diminishing influence in London, were horrified. Chaim Weizmann resigned as president of the Zionist Organization and the Jewish Agency, its British-recognized executive arm. Passfield was attacked by pro-Zionist Labour MPs as well as by the Conservative opposition, and the White Paper was revoked after intensive lobbying that played on the weaknesses of Ramsay MacDonald's minority Labour government.[92] In February 1931 MacDonald read out to MPs a letter he had sent to Weizmann – the Arabs called it the 'Black Letter' – repudiating Passfield's policy. 'It was under MacDonald's letter to me', Weizmann wrote, 'that the change came about in the government's attitude, and in the attitude of the Palestine administration, which enabled us to make the magnificent gains of the ensuing years.'[93] In the wake of the alarming events of 1929 the Zionist movement obtained a ringing reaffirmation of Britain's commitment to the national home. But there was no reappraisal of Jewish relations with the Arabs of Palestine.

Occasionally, more critical voices were heard. Hans Kohn was a supporter of *Brit Shalom* who unusually – though appropriately for a future leading scholar of nationalism – described the Zionist–Arab confrontation against the wider background of resistance to colonialism elsewhere: 'I cannot concur with [official Zionist policy] when the Arab national movement is being portrayed as the wanton agitation of a few big landowners', he wrote.

> I know . . . that frequently the most reactionary imperialist press in England and France portrays the national movements in India, Egypt, and China in a similar fashion – in short, wherever the national movements of oppressed peoples threaten the interest of the colonial power. I know how false and hypocritical this portrayal is. We pretend to be innocent victims . . . Of course the Arabs attacked us in August. Since they have no armies they could not obey the rules of war. They perpetrated all the barbaric acts that are characteristic of a colonial revolt. But we are obliged to look into the deeper cause of this revolt. We have been in Palestine for twelve years . . . without having even once made a serious attempt at seeking through negotiations the consent of the indigenous people. We have been relying exclusively upon Great Britain's military might. We have set ourselves goals which by their very nature had to lead to conflict with Arabs . . . We ought to have recognised that these . . . would be . . . the just cause, of a national uprising against us . . . we pretended that the Arabs did not exist.[94]

Judah Magnes, the American reform rabbi and pacifist who became the first chancellor of the Hebrew University, had drawn similar conclusions in a controversial address around the same time, during which he was heckled by students. 'If we cannot find ways of peace and understanding, if the only way of establishing the Jewish National Home is upon the bayonets of some empire, our whole enterprise is not worth while; and it is better that the eternal people that has out-lived many a mighty empire should possess its soul in patience, and plan and wait.'[95] Still, these were the arguments of a tiny Jewish minority with very little ability to influence the hardening mood in the wake of the bloodshed. In 1931 Arthur Ruppin left *Brit Shalom*, and the organization ceased to exist two years later due to the deser-tion of many members and a chronic lack of funds.

Ben-Gurion, by now a powerful figure in the Labour movement, had spoken frankly about the irreconcilable aspirations of Zionists and Arabs for years, and he concluded in November 1929 that the existence of an Arab national movement was now beyond doubt. 'The Arab in *Eretz Yisrael* should not and cannot be a Zionist,' he told colleagues. 'He cannot want the Jews to become a majority. That is the source of the true confrontation between us and the Arabs. We and they both want to be the majority.'[96] Those comments were made in private. At the same time in public, however, he maintained the official line that the disturbances were the work of 'a crowd, incited and inflamed by the fire of religion and fanaticism'.[97] In October he had already emphasized the need to focus on mass immigration and to increase the physical security of the *Yishuv*, and sketched out a plan called *Bitzaron* (Fortification). Gaps between existing settle-ments would be closed – 'joining the dots', he called it – and, in future, settlements were to be planned to ensure territorial contiguity. Jeru-salem, not hitherto a priority, was to receive special attention.

On the ground, another important effect of the 1929 violence was to increase the physical separation between the country's two com-munities. Jews left Hebron completely, though three dozen Sephardi families returned in 1931. The few Jews in Gaza and other over-whelmingly Arab areas of Palestine also left. Under the pressure of a short-lived Arab boycott movement, Jewish merchants left the Old City of Jerusalem as well as Arab parts of Haifa and Jaffa and moved to predominantly Jewish neighbourhoods, or to Tel Aviv. Acre's small community of Salonika Jewish fishermen decamped to Haifa. Arabs also left Jewish-dominated areas. 'Arab drivers are afraid to go into Jewish quarters and Jews into Arab ones', recorded the wife of a British official in Jerusalem. 'And then one takes a car with Hebrew numbers, thinking one has a Jewish driver, and finds oneself with an

Arab who has put up Hebrew numbers to get custom. All the drivers take two hats, to wear a tarbush or an ordinary hat according to the district.'[98] Demarcation became sharper. 'In every respect the schism between the two people was now open and undisguised', a British report noted.[99] The trend towards economic segregation was boosted too. The aftermath of the disturbances gave a boost to the campaign for Hebrew labour, especially in the countryside. The old idea of a joint Arab–Jewish workers' organization, never very successful, suffered a near-fatal blow. In the vineyard at Motza, outside Jerusalem, where the *Histadrut* had previously campaigned in vain for Hebrew labour only, most Arab workers were dismissed.[100] The battle lines were getting clearer.

4

1929–1936

'Zionism cannot, in the given circumstances, be turned into
a reality without a transition period of the organised revolutionary rule of the Jewish minority.'

Chaim Arlosoroff

'THE WOES INFLICTED ON PALESTINE'

On 2 November 1932 the now traditional Arab protests were held
marking Balfour Day. *Filastin* illustrated its front page with an elab-
orate cartoon portraying Lord Balfour dominating a crude map of the
country, holding his 'accursed' declaration. Emanating from it – 'the
woes inflicted on Palestine' – are lines linked to different scenes illustrating the achievements of Zionism under the protection of the
British military, represented by a haughty, pipe-smoking officer in
riding boots, and by tanks, cannon and a warship off Haifa Bay.[1]
Elsewhere in the tableau Jewish immigrants stride energetically
towards Tel Aviv, passing a glum-looking Palestinian peasant family
evicted from their land, mounted on a camel plodding towards the
desert. The scenery is dotted with modern Jewish factories, mech-
anized agriculture, bustling public works and Jewish enterprises for
electricity and potash – all important economic achievements for the
Yishuv. In the corner – or on the margin – stands a group of Arab
men wearing European suits and *tarbushes* and arguing heatedly
(though presumably ineffectively) about the transformation they are
witnessing. Balfour, for good measure, appeared in yet another drawing on the back page of the paper.

The *Filastin* cartoon well captured the gloomy mood in Arab Palestine early in a decade of profound and destabilizing change, fifteen years after the declaration. Later that Wednesday 2,000 people packed the only cinema in Nablus, decked out with an Arab flag and portraits of Sharif Hussein and King Faisal, for a protest rally to mark the occasion. Other events were held in Jerusalem and Haifa.[2] The aftermath of the 1929 violence and the disastrous 'Black Letter' saw intensifying political activity that did very little to stem Zionist progress under the Mandate, though by 1931 Jews (now numbering 175,000) still constituted less than 17 per cent of the country's total population.[3] In December that year the grand mufti, Haj Amin al-Husseini, convened an Islamic conference in Jerusalem to warn of the purported Jewish threat to the Muslim holy places. Arab newspapers repeatedly warned about the fate of peasants in the light of land sales, which accelerated from 1933, and named and shamed those who speculated or traded in this precious national commodity.[4]

Prolonged legal wrangling over the sale to the Jewish National Fund of a large Arab-owned tract in Wadi Hawarith, on the plain between Haifa and Tel Aviv, highlighted this increasingly sensitive issue, especially after the Shaw Commission noted the existence of a class of embittered and landless Arabs in its report on the causes of the 1929 disturbances. In 1930 the Bedouin tenants, men and women, attacked both the British policemen who were pulling down their tents and the Jewish settlers who had begun ploughing. What became known as the Wadi Hawarith affair ended in 1933 with the eviction of 1,200 Bedouin (though some were resettled elsewhere) and by the now standard practice of renaming the area in Hebrew, as Emek Hefer (mentioned in the First Book of Kings). The purchase was the third largest during the Mandate period, a significant milestone in the Zionist effort to 'redeem' land.[5] However, an attempt to emulate the Jews and set up a national fund (*Sunduq al-Umma*) to save Arab land failed, despite a partnership with the recently established Arab Bank. It was another example of how Arab efforts were invariably unable to match the financial resources and organizational abilities of the Zionists. Traditional Arab leaders were again exposed as weak and ineffective, together with damaging though inconclusive evidence that nationalist politicians had taken bribes or been secretly involved in land sales.[6] In 1934 the newspaper *Alif Baa* reported, highly un-usually, that economic conditions were in fact better in Arab areas where land had been sold to Jews. But it later transpired that the editor had received a large payment from the Jewish Agency.[7]

Frustration with Arab shortcomings, and mounting alarm about the strength and confidence of the Zionists, led to the creation of the *Istiqlal* (Independence) Party. This Pan-Arab organization was founded by Awni Abdel-Hadi in 1932, part of a trend which saw Palestinian political life move away from the great aristocratic and merchant families to a younger generation of nationalist activists, often journalists and teachers who had enjoyed a European education and admired Mahatma Gandhi's ongoing struggle against the British in India. Akram Zuwayter and Izzat Darwaza, both from Nablus, were other leading figures in this milieu. Haifa, where Jews by now made up nearly half of the population, became a stronghold for the party.[8] The *Istiqlal* view compared the British Mandate to a tree: if it was felled then its Zionist 'branch' would fall too.[9] The *Istiqlal*, com-mented a British report, 'was calculated to appeal to the younger generation of Arab nationalists by its uncompromising concentration on the demand for national freedom'.[10] The fight for economic sover-eignty was a significant part of its platform, while the independent status enjoyed by Iraq after its 1930 treaty with Britain was a source of encouragement.[11] The party's first rally in Haifa celebrated the Battle of Hattin in 1187, where the Crusader forces had been defeated by Salah al-Din al-Ayyubi (Saladin in popular Western memory).[12]

Zuwayter had already resigned his post as a teacher at a govern-ment school in Acre. Mayors and other Arab officials now came under pressure to quit as well. Radicalization, or at least mobiliz-ation, was evident too in a new National Congress of Arab Youth, athletics and soccer clubs, and in an independent Arab scout move-ment, whose members patrolled the Mediterranean coastline to try to prevent illegal Jewish immigrants from landing – and to make the point that the Mandatory government was not enforcing its own pol-icies. Yet legal immigration was increasing every year, and more than doubled Palestine's Jewish population from 175,000 in 1931 to 380,000 in 1936 so that Jews then made up nearly a third of the country's total. The scouts – their troops often named after early Muslim heroes like Khalid bin al-Walid – led nationalist parades or forced shopkeepers to shut down on strike days.[13] They also organized protests when the *Histadrut* picketed orange groves and building sites to intimidate recalcitrant Jewish employers to stop hiring Arab workers, whose numbers increased in the prosperous late 1920s and mid-1930s.

In February 1933 a secret meeting of activists from northern Palestine heard a stark warning from Rashid al-Hajj Ibrahim, an *Istiqlal* leader and the manager of the Arab Bank in Haifa. 'The Jews are advancing on all fronts', read the report of the meeting by the *Haganah* intelligence service.

> They keep buying land, they bring in immigrants both legally and illegally ... If we cannot demonstrate to them convincingly enough that all their efforts are in vain and that we are capable of destroying them at one stroke, then we shall have to lose our holy land or resign ourselves to being wretched second-class citizens in a Jewish state.

Asked how the Jews could be made to see this point, Ibrahim answered: 'By doing what we did in 1929, but using more efficient methods.'[14] The British were also aware of what was stirring. In June a CID intelligence report remarked on 'the training of the younger generation in political agitation, under cover of national culture'.[15] Cumulating tensions led to a decision by the Arab Executive, under pressure to act, to declare a general strike to protest against British policy. The *Haganah* and the Jewish Agency were on high alert, anxious to avoid a repeat of the surprise of 1929, and kept careful tabs on Arab plans by listening to the telephone calls of key leaders.[16] On 13 October 1933 a large Arab demonstration – in defiance of an official ban – was held outside government offices in Jerusalem. It was dispersed violently though there were no fatalities. In Jaffa two weeks later police opened fire after demonstrators refused to disperse; twenty-six Arabs were killed and the nearly two hundred injured included the elderly Musa Kazem al-Husseini, who was clubbed by police and died a few months later. Protests followed in Nablus, Haifa and Gaza. Ben-Gurion, for one, was impressed by the strength and cohesion of Arab opposition, which strikingly had targeted the British, not Jews. The latest unrest represented a 'serious and worrying turning point', he told Mapai (Workers' Party) colleagues. The victims had been disciplined demonstrators, not rioters or murderers. He called them 'national heroes' who would be admired, especially by young Arabs.[17]

ZIONIST MISSION IMPOSSIBLE

Pessimism about the prospects for the Zionist project in the face of Arab hostility had been growing. It was expressed in a sensational way in 1932 by Chaim Arlosoroff, a scholarly young Labour leader who had become head of the Jewish Agency's political department. In a private letter to Weizmann, Arlosoroff concluded that

> Zionism cannot, in the given circumstances, be turned into a reality without a transition period of the organised revolutionary rule of the Jewish minority; that there is no way to a Jewish majority, or even to an equilibrium between the two races (or else a settlement sufficient to provide a basis for a cultural centre) to be established by systematic immigration and colonisation, without a period of a nationalist minority government which would usurp the state machinery, the administration and the military power in order to forestall the danger of our being swamped by numbers and endangered by a rising (which we could not face without having the state machinery at our disposal).

Arlosoroff's letter has been described as 'prophetic' because of its frank admission that Zionist goals could not be achieved by agreement with the Arabs. It may also be seen as a statement of what was by now obvious, even if not often explicitly stated. Weizmann, in any event, did not reply.[18] (When Arlosoroff was murdered on the beach in Tel Aviv in June 1933 his death was widely blamed on right-wing Revisionists, who were deeply hostile to the Labour movement – though the perpetrators were probably Arab criminals with no political motive.[19])

Arlosoroff's gloom had been prompted in part by the need to campaign against the British proposal, revived by the 1930 Passfield White Paper, for a legislative council in which Jews and Arabs would participate on the basis of their respective proportions of Palestine's population. The problem for the Zionists was the same as it had been a decade earlier: the Arab majority that would inevitably dominate any council would clearly oppose the further development of the Jewish national home. But rather than reject the idea out of hand or acquiesce in a minority role, the Zionists instead sought a 'parity' formula that would recognize the financially significant role of world Jewry. Ben-Gurion linked this to another proposal: that once the Jews had become the majority in Palestine they would offer their help in creating an Arab federation. It was a throwback to the idea behind Weizmann's much-vaunted agreement with Emir Faisal back in 1919 – a sort of political 'grand bargain' that would subsume Palestine in a pan-Arab context. In July 1934 Ben-Gurion and Moshe Shertok (the only senior Zionist official who spoke Arabic) met Awni Abdel-Hadi, the *Istiqlal* leader, and made clear that for the Jews, 'this land was everything and there was nothing else. For the Arabs, Palestine was only a small portion of the larger and numerous Arab countries.' He compared their situation to that of English people living in Scotland, who 'were not a minority because they were part of the United Kingdom, where they constituted a majority'.[20] A few weeks later Ben-Gurion raised the issue again, in the first of a series of meetings with Musa al-Alami, a member of a prominent landowning Jerusalem family and a government lawyer. Alami, in the words of his biographer, 'seems to have regarded the Zionists rather as a Kenya farmer regards elephants: dangerous creatures always liable to destroy his property and quite capable of being lethal, which he expects the government to keep under control but against which he feels no personal enmity', and was thus able to maintain relations with Jewish leaders.[21] But when Ben-Gurion suggested that the Zionists could help the Arabs develop the country, Alami responded trenchantly that he would rather wait for a hundred years and leave the land in a state of backwardness as long as the Arabs did the job themselves.[22]

Expectations were low and trust even lower. Earlier that year Leo Kohn, a senior official in the Jewish Agency political department, met George Antonius, who was then working on *The Arab Awakening*. Kohn's report oozed disdain for this 'typical Levantine' who was anxious to present himself as 'a cultured man of the 20th century'.[23]

Outside the shadowy realm of intelligence-gathering and clandestine co-operation, encounters between Palestinian Arab and Jewish officials, let alone leaders, were extremely rare. Ben-Gurion and the mufti may have both attended a formal reception given by Sir Arthur Wauchope, the high commissioner, but that was the sum total of their interaction.[24]

FIGHTING BACK

Alongside the demonstrations of October 1933, other less visible activities provided similar indications of growing Arab determination to resist the British and the Zionists. Several secret military organizations were founded, including the *Jihad al-Muqaddas* (Holy War), led by Abdul-Qader al-Husseini, the son of Musa Kazem and the mufti's nephew. By 1934 it had collected financial contributions and acquired some firearms. Other smaller groups appeared around the same time and followed a similar clandestine path, buying and smuggling weapons and undergoing military training.[25] The border between nationalist-inspired resistance and ordinary criminality was blurred, famously in the case of Abu Jilda, a publicity conscious, one-eyed bandit from a village near Nablus, known as Robin Hood or the 'Dillinger of the desert', who was executed in 1934 for killing a policeman. But the best-known group, sometimes known as the Black Hand, was led by Sheikh Izzedin al-Qassam, a charismatic Syrian-born preacher. Qassam's name first surfaced in connection with an ambush in which three members of Kibbutz Yagur, near Haifa, were killed in April 1931. Intensive inquiries by the Zionists and British failed to reach a definitive conclusion at that time.[26] Several other incidents followed, including a grenade attack on a house in Nahalal, a model settlement in the heart of the Jezreel valley. Qassam, who had fought the French in Syria and been sentenced to death *in absentia*, had been a Sharia court official and marriage registrar in Haifa and in 1928 had been elected president of the city's Young Men's Muslim Association. In his sermons in Haifa's Istitqlal Mosque and elsewhere, he encouraged Bedouin to resist the police and Jewish land purchases and called for armed struggle. In November 1935 he and a group of followers set out for the hills of the Jenin area. Arab sources suggest he was prompted by the accidental discovery in Jaffa of a shipment of Belgian weapons hidden in barrels of cement that were apparently intended for the *Haganah* – confirmation of their mounting fears of Zionist plans.

Qassam and his band killed a Jewish police sergeant near Ein Harod – and let two Arab policemen go. In the ensuing manhunt they were tracked down to a forest near Yaabed where Qassam and two associates were killed by the British, preferring death – 'martyrdom' – to surrender. Others fled into the hills near Nablus or were arrested later. The 'Qassamiyoun' were a novelty: the group's two hundred or so members – estimates vary – were peasants or marginalized urban workers recently arrived in Haifa from the countryside, drawn by work in the port and driven by the landlessness, rising debt and social dislocation that were typical of the period. 'I sell my land and property because the government forces me to pay taxes on it while I cannot even get the basic needs for my own and my family's sustenance,' one peasant complained. 'So I am forced to go to the rich people for a short-term loan at 50 per cent interest.'[27] In Haifa's 'Tin Town' alone, in 1935, over 11,000 Arab workers lived in 'hovels made out of old petrol-tins, without any water-supply or the most rudimentary sanitary arrangements'.[28] Qassam's followers were also inspired by conservative Salafi Islam to fight the British and the Jews and to eschew the compromises of the traditional Palestinian leadership: Qassam had tried and failed to persuade the mufti to back a call for rebellion. His was also the first organized attempt by Palestinian Arabs to use armed struggle to promote their cause. Qassam's funeral in Balad al-Sheikh was attended by thousands and a cult of heroism and self-sacrifice grew up around him;[29] his name lived on in the pantheon of Palestinian national heroes for many decades later. Even Ben-Gurion paid Qassam a perceptive – if self-referential – compliment, comparing him to Joseph Trumpeldor, the hero of Tel Hai. The term 'Arab question', Ben-Gurion felt, was a misnomer. 'Its real meaning was, in his view, nothing other than the question of how to fulfill the objectives of Zionism notwithstanding the reality of an Arab presence.'[30]

The mood in the *Yishuv* in the first half of the 1930s was one of pride in Jewish achievements, wariness about the strength of Arab opposition – as well as determination to carry on. Hitler's rise to power in Germany in 1933 provided a grim backdrop that was as real and menacing for Jews as it was remote for most Palestinians, and of course it boosted German-Jewish immigration. Viewed through Palestinian eyes, the persecution of European Jews was a European problem. 'Palestine needs neither fascism nor Nazism to arouse the feelings of her sons against Zionism and its designs in the Arab world', commented an article in *Filastin* in 1934.[31] Everything in Jewish Palestine was 'fair, promising and progressive', thought Shimon Persky (later Peres), an eleven-year-old when he arrived from Poland to join his parents that same year. 'Of course there were dangers', the then-seasoned politician reminisced decades later.

> We were aware of them too. Among Arabs whom we saw coming in from nearby Jaffa, and those from Zarnuga, close to Rehovot, were people who wanted to destroy this wonderful homeland we were building. They walked around with keffiyehs wound round their faces, accentuating their piercing, threatening eyes. Some wore red tarbushes and baggy pantaloons that could easily conceal a shabriya, a vicious curved blade made for murder. It was impossible to compromise with them, as everyone knew. There was no point in even trying. There was no choice for us Jews. We would have to keep up our guard and defend ourselves when need be, until the Arabs accepted our stake on the Land.[32]

5

1936–1939

'An irrepressible conflict has arisen between two national communities within the narrow bounds of one small country. There is no common ground between them. Their national aspirations are incompatible.'

Peel Commission report, 1937

REBELLION

On the evening of 15 April 1936, three armed Arabs rolled barrels onto the road near Nur Shams in the hills between Nablus and Tulkarem. They forced passing vehicles to stop and demanded money to buy weapons and ammunition. In one truck, loaded with crates of chickens, they found two Jews, Zvi Dannenberg and Yisrael Hazan. A third Jew was travelling in another vehicle. The gunmen shot them in cold blood. Hazan, a recent immigrant from Greece, died on the spot and the two others were wounded, Dannenberg dying later of his injuries. The unnamed perpetrators, who were described by the British and Jews as highwaymen or bandits, were followers of al-Qassam. The next day two members of a dissident Zionist group killed two Arab labourers, Hassan Abu Ras and Salim al-Masri, in a roadside shack near Petah Tikvah. 'If they imagined that that would put an end to the bloodshed,' commented the official *Haganah* account of the incident, 'they were soon to be disappointed.' It was the start of the pattern of attack, reprisal and counter-reprisal that was to set the country ablaze. Three years later the conflict over Palestine had passed the point of no return.[1]

Hazan's funeral in Tel Aviv on 17 April triggered assaults by Jews on passing Arabs. By nightfall on the 19th, rioting had spread to Jaffa and nine Jews had been killed with sixty injured. Curfews were imposed by police and troops. Strikes spread across Arab areas, led by local national committees, clubs and unions. Under popular pressure, the Husseini and Nashashibi families buried their rivalry and set up a new Arab Higher Committee (AHC) under the grand mufti, Haj Amin al-Husseini. It called for a general strike, civil disobedience and non-payment of taxes. Thus began what Palestinians still call their 'great rebellion' – 'al-thawra al-kubra'. Zionists referred at the time to rioting, or simply to 'events' ('meoraot' in Hebrew), which falls dismissively short of the heroic image conjured up by the Arabic terminology.[2] Semantic differences masked recognition by both sides, however, that what was happening was a significant new chapter in the Arab–Jewish struggle.

Palestine was ripe for one of its periodic outbreaks of trouble. Security had been a preoccupation for the British and Zionists since the killing of al-Qassam the previous November, while new discussions about a legislative council had gone nowhere slowly. Arabs felt a growing sense of grievance – and menace. The previous year had seen the largest single influx of Jewish immigrants since the Mandate began: 65,000 Jews had arrived, most fleeing persecution in Nazi Germany. In addition, an economic downturn had hit the vitally important citrus sector hard.[3] In the wider world, the Italian invasion of Abyssinia had been welcomed by Arab nationalists as a blow to British prestige. The Palestinians again demanded a halt to Jewish immigration and land sales, and the creation of a national – i.e. Arab – government. The British responded by announcing a one-off increase in immigration quotas.

Attacks included crop-burning, wire-cutting, sniping and grenades thrown at Jewish vehicles on main roads. Plantations of trees were cut down. Armed bands began to form. 'We made the Jews afraid', boasted Omar Shehadi, a teenage fighter from Safad. 'They couldn't work their land, or even switch their lights on at night or go about at night.'[4] Bombs exploded in Haifa and Jaffa and the railway line to Egypt was sabotaged near Gaza. It was a challenge, though hardly a formidable military threat. In the early days British soldiers described rebels carrying 'ancient muskets using rusty nails as ammo' or throwing 'home-made grenades which were beer cans stuffed with stones . . . with an explosive in it and a bit of fuse which made more noise than cause any damage'.[5] Worse was to come. By June the high commissioner, Sir Arthur Wauchope, was describing a 'state of incipient revolution'. Another British official noted: 'Nothing happens during the day, which makes the nights and the shooting seem nightmarish and unreal.'[6] Arab militancy – and unity – seemed to be paying dividends. *Filastin* invoked the memory of al-Qassam, printing a cartoon showing a worried Chaim Weizmann looking on as the dead sheikh watched the mufti and Ragheb al-Nashashibi overcoming their differences and shaking hands.[7] Ben-Gurion admitted frankly that the 'economic blessings' of Zionism had had no effect on Arab leaders. 'Even if they admit it – and not all of them do – that our immigration brings a material blessing to the land, they say – and from the Arab viewpoint rightly so: "None of your honey and none of your sting." '[8] Every day Hebrew newspapers printed black-edged death notices. In August 1936 a renowned Arab guerrilla leader, Fawzi al-Qawuqji, a Lebanese veteran of the nationalist struggle against the French, arrived in the country at the head of a five-hundred-strong band of Syrians, Iraqis and Palestinians, and tried to consolidate the rebel forces into a well-co-ordinated army. It was a 'moment of hope' that gave the revolt an air of respectability.[9] Wauchope was as gloomy as Ronald Storrs had been after the disturbances of 1920. 'I was up early this morning', he wrote to a colleague, 'and could have wept as I saw the walls of Jerusalem turn golden under the cloudless sky and thought of – what you and I think of every sorrowful day.'[10]

DEFINING REVOLT

Ben-Gurion at least grasped that this escalating violence was ominous. In private, he took issue with colleagues who questioned whether these 'events' constituted an uprising, as now seemed clear to him. 'Perhaps in some book there is a scientific definition of a revolt', he commented, but what can we do when the rebels themselves do not act according to the laws of science and revolt according to their own understanding, their ideas and their ability? The Arabs are fighting with a strike, with terror, sabotage, murder and the destruction of property ... against the government – including Jewish immigration, which depends as they see it on the government. What else do they have to do for their behaviour to be recognised as a rebellion and an uprising?[11]

Public discourse was again very different. Ben-Gurion, Weizmann and Moshe Shertok, head of the Jewish Agency's political department, urged British officials to crack down decisively on what they dismissed as mere 'rioting'. It was a familiar argument: discontent was not deep-seated and Arab peasants had been 'terrorized' by malcontents into making trouble. Jewish leaders played up the half-hearted aspects of the strike and the heterogeneous composition of what they called the 'gangs'. A book by a leading British Zionist, written in consultation with Ben-Gurion, described the Arab movement as 'led neither by a dispossessed Palestinian fellah nor by a disappointed Palestinian effendi, but by Fawzi Kawakji [sic], an ex-Turkish officer of Syrio-Turkish extraction and of Syrian citizenship. He has collected around him Druses, Syrians, Iraqis and brigands who ... flock to any place where there is chance for excitement and perhaps booty.'[12]

Deeds proved more decisive than propaganda. The Arab strike, many Jews realized, provided a golden opportunity to bolster their economic independence – getting rid of Arab workers in the Nesher quarries near Haifa and replacing Arab stevedores in the port. Shertok noted the gratifying reaction in the old settlements of Zichron Yaakov and nearby Athlit – which had stubbornly held out against the *Histadrut*'s campaign for Hebrew labour – when Jewish workers replaced the striking Arabs. 'One farmer worked out that Jewish grapes cost him only 3mils more per ton than Arab grapes, and as well as that he spares his health as he doesn't need to stand in the sun all day shouting "Yallah!" [Get on with it!] at the Arab women.'[13] Arab employees in government service were replaced by Jews. But the most eye-catching gain was the opening of a port in Tel Aviv in response to the strike in Jaffa. Attacks on the police in the alleys of Jaffa's old city, overlooking the port, were punished by the destruction of more than two hundred buildings, ostensibly to improve health and sanitation but in fact to improve access for the British military. Up to 6,000 Arabs were left homeless.[14] No longer would 'this rancid town', as an exultant Ben-Gurion called the old city, be the first sight for Jewish immigrants as they reached the shores of the homeland. 'If Jaffa went to hell, I would not count myself among the mourners', he noted.[15] The mufti's actions, it was said, had achieved what Zionist principles could not.

Critics of the Palestine government accused it of using kid gloves and making it hard for troops and police to suppress the unrest. 'On one occasion, a group of Arab women were seen seated on a rug near a village, apparently refreshing themselves during a pause in their agricultural labours', one recorded.

> Someone had the bright idea of looking under the rug. The ladies at first failed to understand, and then combined protest with loud lamentation when they saw that bluff was useless. Under the rug the earth had been newly dug. The earth was dug up again, and in a narrow trench was found a little arsenal of arms and ammunition.[16]

In mid-May, a month into the strike and disturbances, the British announced a familiar response to the Palestine conundrum: a royal commission, 'the highest form of enquiry known in the British empire, composed of people of such eminence and authority that its recommendations must necessarily carry the greatest weight',[17] would be despatched to investigate.

IRREPRESSIBLE CONFLICT, INCOMPATIBLE ASPIRATIONS

The strike ended in October 1936 when British diplomatic efforts orchestrated an appeal by the rulers of Iraq, Saudi Arabia, Transjordan and Yemen, an early example of pan-Arab involvement in the Palestine question. Economic pressures from Arab citrus growers and boat owners – the civil war in Spain had eliminated competition from that country and fruit prices were soaring – helped persuade the Arab Higher Committee to seek a face-saving way out.[18] The commission, headed by Lord Peel, a former secretary of state for India, arrived in mid-November.

Sitting in the elegant dining room of the Palace Hotel in Jerusalem, Peel and his five colleagues heard more than a hundred witnesses, chief among them the mufti and Weizmann. The Zionist effort – aided by bugging the commissioners' private meetings – was co-ordinated and strategic. Weizmann eloquently described the broad outlines of Jewish history, the scourge of anti-Semitism, the plight of the Jewish masses in Eastern Europe, as well as his own efforts to reach agreement with the Arabs: the 1919 agreement with Emir Faisal got a long mention (it had been published in June for propaganda purposes).[19] The Arab side had declared a boycott of the hearings after the government announced a new, though limited, labour immigration quota the day the commission left for Palestine. Eventually, though, it did hear testimony from the mufti, who described the 'Jews' ultimate aim' as being to reconstruct the Temple of Solomon on the site of the Haram al-Sharif. Jewish immigration must come to a complete halt, he insisted; the question of whether the newcomers would be allowed to stay in an independent Arab Palestine would, he said, have to be left for the future.

The Peel Report, published in July 1937, remains a perceptive study of the troubled history of Palestine since 1917, and it captured well how Arab–Jewish relations had changed since then:

> Arab antagonism to the National Home was never ignored by thoughtful Zionists; but, whereas they used to regard it as no more than an obstacle, however serious, to be somehow overcome, they now see it, we believe, though they do not always say so, as the danger that it is or might become. Nobody in Palestine can fail to realise how much more bitter, how much more widely spread among the people, Arab hatred of the National Home is now than it was five or ten years ago.[20]

Its conclusion was stark:

> An irrepressible conflict has arisen between two national communities within the narrow bounds of one small country. There is no common ground between them. Their national aspirations are incompatible. The Arabs desire to revive the traditions of the Arab golden age. The Jews desire to show what they can achieve when restored to the land in which the Jewish nation was born. Neither of the two national ideals permits of combination in the service of a single State.

The terms of the Mandate were unworkable and could only be enforced by repressing the Arabs. Both Arabs and Jews demanded independence. Establishing an Arab state would violate the rights of the Jewish minority, but creating a Jewish state in the whole of Palestine would both violate Arab rights and generate wider Arab and Muslim opposition. The only workable solution was the creation of two sovereign states. 'Partition', the commission argued, 'seems to offer at least a chance of ultimate peace. We can see none in any other plan.' The proposed Jewish state would cover about 25 per cent of Palestine, north from Tel Aviv along the coast including – overwhelmingly Arab – Galilee. The Arab state could encompass the mountains and the Negev desert, as well as Jaffa, and be linked to Transjordan. Britain would continue to control Jerusalem, Bethlehem and a corridor leading to the Mediterranean.

The Peel proposal provoked furious debate in the *Yishuv* and the Zionist movement, not least because it did not include historically important areas: neither Jerusalem nor Hebron, nor any part of the province of Judaea. Opponents bemoaned the idea that any part of *Eretz-Yisrael* should be surrendered. Jabotinsky called the plan absurd and insisted there was no chance the Jews would fall into the trap. Weizmann, however, had signalled flexibility to the commission, making

> a sharp distinction between the present realities and the messianic hope . . . a hope embedded in Jewish traditions and sanctified by the martyrdom of thousands of years, a hope which their nation cannot forget without ceasing to be a nation . . . God has promised Eretz Yisrael to the Jews. This was their Charter. But they were men of their own time, with limited horizons, heavily laden with responsibility toward the generations to come.[21]

He and Ben-Gurion accepted partition in principle, but argued for more generous territorial terms. Ben-Gurion called it 'not an end, but a beginning' of the redemption of the 'whole of the country'.[22]

The Arab Higher Committee dismissed any idea of carving up the land, but dissenting representatives of Ragheb al-Nashashibi's recently founded National Defence Party resigned. Nashashibi supporters were then attacked and some murdered by supporters of the mufti. Friday prayers in mosques were used to preach against the evils of partition. The AHC repeated its demands for an end to Jewish immigration and land purchases and the replacement of the Mandate by a treaty between Britain and a sovereign and independent Arab state of Palestine. Pan-Arab support for the Palestinian position was expressed at a conference in Bludan, Syria, in September 1937. Still, the solution sketched out by Peel remained – on paper if not in reality – the most likely way to resolve the conflict.

Behind the scenes unofficial attempts were made to establish contact (if not common ground) between the sides: Judah Magnes of the Hebrew University, one of the founders of *Brit Shalom*, was involved in one initiative in the summer of 1936, but the Jewish Agency was deeply suspicious and the identity of the Arab interlocutors uncertain. In 1937 another proposal – involving a ceiling of 50 per cent for the Jewish population of an independent Palestinian state – was no more successful. Its basis was that every citizen was to have 'equal and complete political and civil rights'. The formulation was scorned by the Jewish Agency. 'This sounds eminently liberal, but what does it mean in the reality of political life?' one official asked. 'That every Beduin and illiterate is to count at the polling-booth with the most advanced European Jews. The crudely majoritarian design of the agreement is very skilfully covered under that sweeping liberal phraseology.'[23] The suspicion was that the initiative was intended to torpedo implementation of the Peel partition proposal by suggesting, falsely, that Arab–Jewish agreement was in fact possible. Magnes, the former high commissioner Sir Herbert (now Lord) Samuel and the Jewish authors of other 'unauthorized' peace initiatives were condemned by the Zionist leadership and vilified as traitors and assimilationists across the Hebrew press.

REPRESSION AND RESTRAINT

Uneasy calm returned in the summer of 1937, though unrest resumed in late September when Arab gunmen killed a British district commissioner, Lewis Andrews, with his police bodyguard, outside the Anglican Church in Nazareth. Like the incident that sparked the first wave of violence in April 1936 it was blamed on al-Qassam supporters. Andrews was the highest-ranking British official to be killed so far. This time the government response was tougher. The Arab Higher Committee and national committees were proscribed and dozens arrested. Haj Amin al-Husseini was removed from the presidency of the Supreme Muslim Council and, after first taking refuge on the Haram al-Sharif, where he was besieged by the British, he slipped away, dressed as a Bedouin, to exile in Lebanon, where he remained under surveillance by the French authorities. Other Arab leaders, including Hussein Khalidi, the mayor of Jerusalem, were deported to the Seychelles on a Royal Navy destroyer.[24]

In October disorder erupted all over the country. It was far more extensive than in 1936. Now Arabs attacked buses, railways, the strategically important Iraqi oil pipeline that extended across the north of the country to Haifa, and army posts. Armed groups formed into larger regional units which competed for support from Damascus, where the AHC had established the Central Committee for Jihad under Izzat Darwaza, which collected money and sent supplies and weapons to the Palestine rebels. The French authorities, having granted the Syrians greater autonomy the previous year, declined British requests to interfere.[25]

Repression became the norm and there were many incidents of brutality by British police and troops. 'The military courts started off well', one policeman recorded in December 1937,

> but as we expected are being too lenient and want too much evidence to convict on, so any Johnny Arab who is caught by us now in suspicious circumstances is shot out of hand. There is an average of a bomb a day thrown in Haifa now but few of them do much damage. One was thrown in a Jewish bus last night and the culprit caught. We took him to his house but there was no evidence so we let him try to escape in the garden, fortunately I will not have to attend the inquest.

The same policeman described how 'running over an Arab is the same as a dog in England except we do not report it'.[26] In November the British hanged the elderly Sheikh Farhan al-Saadi, leader of the remnants of the Qassamiyoun, and added outrage to injury by carrying out the execution during the Ramadan fast – an event immortalized by Abdel Karim al-Karmi in a poem which cursed 'the Arab kings' for ignoring the blood of the martyr.[27] Sir Charles Tegart, a colonial police expert with years of service in India, was charged with reviewing security in Palestine. His recommendations, which were quickly adopted, included constructing a chain of concrete blockhouse-type forts across the country – along the frontiers and elsewhere – as well as the introduction of Doberman dogs from South Africa for use in searches, and the opening of an Arab interrogation centre in Jerusalem. Waterboarding and other forms of torture were common.[28] Nonetheless, violence resumed with greater intensity in the summer of 1938. Rebels were soon in control of mountainous areas, running their own improvised courts, collecting taxes and patrolling openly in the streets of Nablus, the centre of the struggle. Police stations were attacked.

In late August, the peak of the revolt, the British military commander, General Robert Haining, reported that 'the situation was such that civil administration and control of the country was, to all practical purposes, non-existent'.[29] The number of rebels was estimated at 9,000–10,000, with perhaps 3,000 full-time fighters. British forces consisted of two army divisions numbering some 25,000 servicemen. The British punished Arab villages for aiding the rebels by imposing collective fines and blowing up houses that were said to have sheltered guerrillas. If fines were not paid then livestock was confiscated. Orange groves and vineyards were uprooted. Arabs were made to act as human shields by sitting on inspection trolleys, which drove on the rails ahead of trains, or they were forced to ride on lorries with army convoys to prevent mine attacks. On the lorries, some soldiers would brake hard at the end of a journey and then casually drive over the Arab – 'the poor wog' – who had tumbled from the bonnet, killing or maiming him.[30] 'If there was any land mines it was them [the Arab prisoners] that hit them. Rather a dirty trick, but we enjoyed it,' said another soldier. During searches, soldiers would surround a village (usually before dawn) and hold the men in wire cages while others searched and often destroyed everything; they burned stocks of grain and poured olive oil over food and household effects. The men were screened by hooded Arab informers, who would nod when a suspect was found, or by British officials checking their papers. Massacres took place at al-Bassa, near the Lebanese frontier, and at Halhul near Hebron, but these only came to light many years later.[31] In October 1938, the army lost control of the Old City of Jerusalem for five days. By November Haining had to report: 'The rebel gangs have now acquired, by terrorist methods, such a hold over the mass of the population that it is not untrue to say that every Arab in the country is a potential enemy of the government.'[32] The atmosphere was charged and dangerous and the stories and symbols of the period left a lasting imprint.

Initially, wearing an Ottoman *tarbush* – dark-red and tasselled – was a sign of support for the rebellion. 'It was to differentiate Arabs', recalled a Palestinian from Tiberias. 'If you went bareheaded you would be like the Jews. It was a question of identity. If someone wanted to shoot a Jew, he would not shoot at you if you were wearing a tarbush. But it also meant exposure, because the Jews would know whom to shoot at.'[33] Later, rebel bands, known as *mujahideen* or *thuwwar* (holy warriors/revolutionaries), ordered people to abandon both the *tarbush* and European headgear in favour of the peasant's traditional *keffiyeh* or *hatta* and *aqal* cord to allow them to blend in with locals and frustrate the efforts of British forces to track them down. 'The transformation was like magic', recalled Khalil Totah, headmaster of the Quaker school in Ramallah. Even judges complied. Intimidation took place on a large scale.[34] 'They put a *tarbush* on a donkey and said: "only the donkey wears a *tarbush*, buy a *hatta*"', a rebel fighter from Acre remembered later.[35]

Until the winter of 1937 few instances were recorded of Jews attacking Arabs. One notable exception was the killing near Petah Tikvah in April 1936 – the work of dissidents who had broken away from the *Haganah*. The view of the *Yishuv* institutions was that a policy of self-restraint (*havlagah*), 'following the highest traditions of Zionism', as Weizmann put it, would help persuade the British to crack down hard on the Palestinian disorder as well as allow the Jews to occupy the high moral ground and gain political advantage. The lack of significant Jewish military capacity or experience was another weighty factor. Weizmann complained to Wauchope that a government account of the disturbances contained 'not a single reference to, still less a word of praise for, the restraint which the Jews have shown during the long months of violence directed against them by the Arabs'.[36] The *havlagah* policy was largely but not universally observed. In November 1937 the murder of five Jewish workers near Jerusalem triggered a wave of reprisals. A Zionist official was horrified to come across Jewish children dancing round the corpse of an Arab in the Jewish Rehavia area. Anti-Arab attacks started to be carried out by the *Irgun Tzvai Leumi* (National Military Organization), the militant group inspired by Jabotinsky and shunned by the mainstream of the *Yishuv*. In April 1938 a member of the Revisionist youth movement Beitar named Shlomo Ben-Yosef fired at an Arab bus in Galilee in retaliation for the killing of five Jews. When Ben-Yosef was hanged in Acre gaol by the British, the *Irgun* kidnapped and hanged an Arab in Haifa and, using Mizrahi Jews disguised as Arabs, began placing bombs in markets and public places: at least thirty-five Arabs were killed in one devastating attack in July. It was a reflection both of changing times and self-delusion that the Zionist press appeared unable to believe that Jews were responsible for such an atrocity, suggesting it must be the work of *agents provocateurs* intending to inflame Arab–Jewish relations. The Jewish-run *Palestine Post* commented:

> The 'revolt' is on the verge of collapse, and nothing short of a 'war' involving the whole population could give it fresh impetus. What surer way of spreading the seed of inter-racial war than to make each Arab believe that each Jew is his enemy, and what surer means can there be of creating that belief than by manufacturing the type of crime which, in its sacrifices and resultant panic, makes the credulous Arab point to the Jews as its author.[37]

But the internal Jewish debate about *havlagah* was largely about maintaining the crucial Zionist link to Britain; only a small minority – largely *Brit Shalom* supporters – were thinking in terms of future relations with the Arabs of Palestine.[38] The mood was harsh. 'As a native of the country who knew the Arabs I knew very well that *havlagah* would be interpreted as weakness and would encourage an increase of Arab attacks upon Jews', argued Elie Eliachar, a prominent Jerusalem Sephardi figure.[39]

RE-PEEL

In the heat of events, in a Europe more preoccupied by Germany and the Sudetenland crisis than faraway Palestine, Britain's calculations were changing. In April 1938 another Commission of Inquiry, headed by Sir John Woodhead, arrived in Jerusalem to examine the unrest and to review prospects for implementing partition. Zionists sardonically called it the 'Re-Peel' commission. Like the previous body, its deliberations were secretly recorded by the Jewish Agency.[40] Over the summer its direction became clearer. In November the Woodhead Commission concluded that Lord Peel's proposal was not feasible. It produced three alternative partition schemes with different boundaries and administrative arrangements – none of them acceptable to the Zionists or to the Arabs – and recommended that the future of Palestine be reviewed at a conference in London. The AHC had opposed any co-operation with the commission. Hassan Sidqi al-Dajani, an Arab member of the Jerusalem municipal council who planned to testify before it, was assassinated and was assumed to have been another victim of the mufti's men. Dajani had been warned not to co-operate. 'Those who go to the partition commission should take their shrouds with them', he was told.[41] Now Fakhri al-Nashashibi (a cousin of Ragheb), who was backed secretly by the Jewish Agency,[42] came out openly against the mufti and demanded that the cleric's opponents be allotted half the seats in the Palestinian delegation to the London talks.[43] Fakhri was then sentenced to death – luckily for him in his absence – by a 'revolutionary court'.

In late 1938 support for the *mujahideen* began to fall off and reports multiplied of villagers being coerced to support them. There was also a marked increase in the killings of suspected collaborators, informers and policemen, as well as much settling of personal scores: Fawzi, a Tiberias taxi driver, disappeared suddenly, his body was found in an irrigation canal in a Jewish area with a skewer through his head. He was condemned as 'an informer for the Zionists'.[44] Precise numbers are hard to come by and are bedevilled by problems of sources. But one authoritative estimate suggests 1,000 Arabs were killed by rebels between 1936 and 1939.[45] In 1938, the bloodiest single year, the toll was 69 Britons, 292 Jews and 486 Arab civilians or policemen. Over 1,000 rebel fighters were killed in action.[46] Arab 'peace bands' (*Fasail al-Salam*) began to fight rebel forces. Fakhri al-Nashashibi was the leading figure behind this short-lived counter-insurgency campaign. An important role was played by Fakhri

Abdel-Hadi, a former rebel commander from Arrabeh who was on the payroll of the British consul in Damascus and seemed to some British officials to be playing a double game in pursuit of personal gain, waging feuds involving murder, abduction and robbery.[47]

But British military power – not least the deployment of RAF aircraft against lightly armed fighters on the ground – was the overwhelming reason for the defeat of the rebellion.[48] Major-General Bernard Montgomery, for a few months commander of the 8th Division in northern Palestine, was described as 'blood mad' in his attitude towards the rebels.[49] Anti-rebel peasant formations sprang up in the Nablus area and among the Druze of Mount Carmel around Haifa. Nashashibi organized peace bands in the Hebron hills, gathering 3,000 villagers for a public rally in Yatta in December 1938 which was addressed by the British army commander in Jerusalem, Major-General Richard O'Connor. Working with the Jewish Agency, Pinchas Rutenberg – the influential Jewish industrialist who ran the Palestine Electric Corporation – paid for a consignment of weapons that were delivered to Nashashibi by the *Haganah*. Nashashibi also mounted a propaganda campaign that was paid for by the Jewish Agency. Its message – timed for the run-up to the St James Conference in February 1939 – was that most Arabs did not support the rebellion. 'Fakhri', a Jewish acquaintance reported, wished 'to prove to the public that there is a strong opposition to the Mufti ... and that the majority of the Arabs of Palestine really want peace, and, if they fear the Jews, they fear the Mufti more.' The Jewish Agency arranged a meeting between a British intelligence officer and Arabs from Abu Ghosh, a village on the main road west of Jerusalem that had long enjoyed collaborative relations with its Jewish neighbours. The villagers duly condemned the rebellion and urged the British to strengthen the moderates. 'Such demonstrations of divergences of opinion between the Mufti's clique and other Arabs are all to the good', a Zionist official noted.[50]

GAINS ON THE GROUND

In these turbulent times, the Zionists made more important gains. From March 1938, as the British moved to abandon partition and, as seemed likely, to impose new restrictions on the growth of the Jewish national home, there was a scramble to create new 'facts on the ground'. Hanita, on a ridge overlooking the Lebanese border, was the most famous of the 'stockade and watchtower' (*Homa ve'Migdal*) type of settlement. The point was to build on land that had been purchased but not yet settled. If a roofed structure could be erected by nightfall, it would be considered legally permanent. Hanita also lay on an infiltration route used by Arab rebels moving in and out of Palestine, so the site served a dual purpose. Moshe Dayan, a young *Haganah* man from Nahalal in the Jezreel valley, described hundreds of pioneers setting out before dawn and scrambling up a rocky hillside with loads of equipment. 'On the hilltop site we began erecting a wooden watchtower and the standard perimeter fence, a double wall of wood filled with earth and boulders', he wrote later:

> We hoped to do all this during the day so that the tented compound within would be defended by nightfall when we expected the first attack. But night came and we had not completed the fortifications. There had been too much to do and we were also hampered by a strong wind. We could not even put up the tents. At midnight we were attacked.

Arthur Koestler wrote a vivid fictionalized account of the backbreaking work in his celebrated novel, *Thieves in the Night*. Hanita was portrayed as embodying the Zionist nexus between territory, defence and identity. 'The Arabs learned once again, after the lessons of Tel Hai, Hulda and Tirat Zvi', other Jewish settlements that had been attacked and successfully defended, 'that a place where the foot of a Jewish settler has trod, where the blood of a Hebrew defender has been spilled, will not be abandoned by its builders and defenders', as the history of the *Haganah* put it.[51] These outposts were endowed with an aura of progressive pioneering; in 1937 a model of a stockade and watchtower settlement was chosen for the Palestine Pavilion at the World Exposition in Paris. In all, fifty-seven were established by 1939.[52]

Valuable military experience was acquired by the Zionists during the Arab rebellion. Three thousand Jews had been recruited into the supernumerary police by October 1936. By summer 1939 22,000 Jews were serving in it and the settlement police, the majority effectively working for the *Haganah*.[53] *Haganah* men like Dayan and Yigal Allon joined a new British unit called the Special Night Squads (SNS), set up after the Iraqi oil pipeline had been sabotaged. It was commanded by an eccentric officer named Orde Wingate, who was described by Weizmann as 'strange and brilliant'.[54] Operating under cover of darkness in Galilee, the SNS took the war to the Arab rebels in a brutal counter-insurgency campaign. Wingate was known as *haYedid* (the Friend) by the Jews. Little was said in public at the time about the harsh methods he employed, which were described as 'extreme and cruel' by one official and which included abuse, whippings, torture and executions. On 2 October 1938, nineteen Jews, including eleven children, were killed in Tiberias by the *mujahideen* in a well-planned attack that was compared to the Hebron massacre of 1929.[55] In its wake Wingate and his men rounded up ten Arabs from the nearby village of Hattin and summarily shot them.[56] Under Wingate's influence Allon and Dayan helped develop a bolder Jewish military doctrine that was referred to in Hebrew as 'going beyond the fence', i.e. moving from static defence to offensive operations against the enemy. In all, 520 Jews had been killed since 1936.[57]

MUNICH IN ST JAMES

In February 1939 the St James Conference in London was dubbed a new 'Munich' by the Zionists, who feared a change in policy even before it began. Weizmann reminded his British and Jewish audiences that Zionist efforts to come to an understanding with the Arabs were as old as the Balfour Declaration. The 1919 agreement with Emir Faisal was again given prominent mention. No direct contact took place between the two sides, though, and back in Palestine violence continued. In March the British tracked down and killed Abdul-Rahim Hajj Mohammed, one of the legendary leaders of the rebellion.[58] Like al-Qassam before him, Hajj Mohammed entered the pantheon of Palestinian heroes whose names and reputations were to be invoked in years to come. A famous saying attributed to him went: 'The shoe of the most insignificant *mujahid* is nobler than all the members of society who have indulged in pleasure while their brethren suffered in the mountains.'[59] Arif Abdel-Razzaq, another senior commander (who was renowned for his smart, British-style uniforms) surrendered to the French authorities on the Syrian border. The Jenin commander, Youssef Abu Durra, was detained on the border with Transjordan. Memories of the rebellion lived on in Palestinian popular consciousness.[60]

In May the British issued a new White Paper. It abandoned the idea of partition and sharply restricted Jewish immigration into Palestine to 75,000 over the next five years, with subsequent figures to depend on Arab consent, and placed severe restrictions on the rights of Jews to buy land. It also provided for the establishment within ten years of an independent Palestinian state and the immediate appointment, once peace was restored, of Palestinians to head certain ministries. It left no room for doubt about the magnitude of the policy shift that was taking place: 'His Majesty's Government believe that the framers of the Mandate in which the Balfour Declaration was embodied could not have intended that Palestine should be converted into a Jewish State against the will of the Arab population of the country', the paper stated.

> His Majesty's Government therefore now declare unequivocally that it is not part of their policy that Palestine should become a Jewish State. They would indeed regard it as contrary to their obligations to the Arabs under the Mandate, as well as to the assurances which have been given to the Arab people in the past, that the Arab population of Palestine should be made the subjects of a Jewish State against their will.

The White Paper's rejection by the Zionists was as unequivocal as it was predictable. It should have been a moment of rare satisfaction for the Palestinians. But the negative Arab response to such a stunning reversal by the British made little sense. According to some accounts, a majority of members of the AHC approved it but the mufti stood firm in rejecting it – on the grounds that having fled to Lebanon he was now unable to return home because of British opposition. Objections were heard too from rebel commanders who opposed any compromise.[61] 'I thought it impossible that the British government would go any further to accommodate the Arabs', wrote Awni Abdel-Hadi, the *Istiqlal* leader. 'In politics, the task is to distinguish what is possible from what is not; the policy that consists of taking what one can, even while demanding more, is preferable to sterile obstinacy.'[62] Later Palestinian scholars judged the mufti harshly. 'Zionist opposition may have doomed the White Paper from the very start', Yezid Sayigh has written, 'but the Palestinians had, through their own reactions, lost the opportunity to enter the mandatory administration at higher levels and prepare for their own postcolonial state. The price they paid was increased social dislocation and political disorientation.'[63] Rejecting the proposals was 'short-sighted and irresponsible', argued the mufti's biographer.[64]

Palestine's physical reality was changing too. The Jewish population had nearly doubled in the preceding six years, from 234,000 in 1933 to 445,000 by 1939, rising from 21 per cent of the total to 30 per cent. And by the outbreak of the Second World War Arabs and Jews lived even more separately than they had before, continuing a trend that had begun in 1921 and accelerated after 1929. In 1936 and 1938 Jews again left Arab-majority neighbourhoods, abandoning Haifa's crowded lower town for the Hadar haCarmel district, and so mixed communities were emptied of their Jewish inhabitants and social relations were severed. Jewish areas looked after their own interests with the support of the *Yishuv*'s central institutions.[65] 'We live in a mixed city. This is not the same as life in a neighbourhood', maintained David HaCohen, the Haifa labour leader.

> The home is indeed in the neighbourhood, but the business is located in the Arab street. People spend 10 hours a day there, the port is there, the market is there, that is where those children live who are liable to get illnesses and from whom my children in the Jewish neighbourhood will contract the illnesses.[66]

Tensions were especially evident in areas like Manshiyeh on the border between Jaffa and Tel Aviv. In 1936, a British visitor observed 'a contrast that shouts' between the neighbouring towns.[67] Jews in Jaffa demanded that their neighbourhoods be annexed to Tel Aviv. 'At the present moment', the Peel Report noted, 'the two races are holding rigidly apart.'[68] Chaim Sturman, a veteran of *HaShomer*, the settlement guards, founder of Ein Harod and a renowned 'Arabist', worried that he would soon forget how to speak Arabic. (Sturman was killed by a mine in September 1938.) Earlier that year Moshe Shertok had lamented the poor standard of Arabic teaching in Jewish schools; the reason was that more than ever the *Yishuv* consisted of contiguous Jewish-only areas. 'The number of Jews who need Arabic on a daily basis is becoming smaller and smaller', he noted.[69]

In November 1939 Jewish residents of Tel Aviv's Brenner neighbourhood, adjacent to Jaffa, complained that Arabs were coming back: 'the same Arabs who only yesterday aimed the barrels of rifles and pistols at us are now sauntering through the city. Who knows what our neighbours are plotting? Will we leave the city wide open [to attack]? Will we forget the recent past?'[70] The establishment of Tel Aviv port – its traffic increasing steadily at its neighbour's expense[71] – had been a direct response to the Arab strike and unrest in Jaffa. So was the creation of the new Carmel market in the Yemenite quarter of the Jewish city. Spatially, socially and psychologically, Arabs and Jews were ever more distant.

The Zionist Congress which met in Geneva in mid-August 1939 took place in an atmosphere of 'unreality and irrelevance'.[72] It was expected to be the most significant congress since the founding one had been held in Basel in 1897. Resistance to the policy of the White Paper, it declared, 'is not directed against the interests of the Arab people'. Delegates reaffirmed

> the resolve of the Jewish people to establish relations of mutual good will and cooperate with the Arabs of Palestine and of the neighbouring countries. Despite four years of bloodshed and destruction, the Congress expresses its opinion that on the basis of mutual recognition of the respective rights of both races, a way can be found to harmonise Jewish and Arab aspirations.

A few days after the congress ended Hitler invaded Poland. Palestine's two peoples were braced for the next stage of the struggle that neither side doubted lay ahead.

6

1939–1945

'Ben-Gurion's proposal completely disregards the fact that a million Arabs live here together with us – as if they did not exist at all.'

Meir Yaari

PALESTINE AT WAR

Late in the afternoon of 9 September 1940, without warning, Italian aircraft bombed Tel Aviv and killed 137 people. The CANT Z1007 medium bombers, based in the Dodecanese islands, had been heading for Haifa, with its port and naval base, oil refineries and other strategic targets, but were intercepted by RAF fighters and dumped their payload on a residential area far from any military or industrial installation. Most of the victims were Jews, but seven Arabs died when a stray bomb hit Sumail village, then in the process of being swallowed up by the rapidly developing city.[1] The Italian air raid was over in minutes, and was a rare but shocking instance of the way the Second World War – which did so much to decide both the fate of Europe's Jews and the future course of the Arab–Jewish conflict – directly affected Palestine. Initially the war threatened financial disaster, with the disruption of trade, a severe crisis in the citrus sector[2] and a sharp rise in unemployment. Overall, though, Palestine's wartime years were peaceful and, superficially at least, relatively harmonious. In time the country enjoyed real prosperity, serving as a vast camp and supply, munitions and logistics base for British forces in the Middle East. Higher food prices and demands for manual workers in Haifa and Jaffa ports were good for the Arab economy, though Jews, with their skilled labour force and industrial base, were better placed to secure government contracts.

It took time for the Arab community to recover from the bloodshed and divisions of over three years of rebellion. Five thousand Palestinians had been killed in a brutal British counter-insurgency campaign; 146 were hanged and thousands detained. Thousands of homes had been demolished. The leaders of the Arab Higher Committee were in exile or in detention – the mufti and his relative Jamal al-Husseini (founder of the Palestine Arab Party) at first in Baghdad, and then respectively in Berlin and a prison camp in the British colony of Southern Rhodesia. They had rejected the 1939 White Paper on the grounds that it did not completely halt Jewish immigration and only proposed the establishment of a Palestinian state a decade hence. Still, for the first time since the Balfour Declaration the argument about the future of the country was going the Arabs' way. Political life was largely quiescent, dominated by petty battles over prestige and influence. Occasionally Zionist pressure did bring about increased, though usually fruitless, Arab efforts to forge a common front.[3]

On the Jewish side, the war years passed in the shadow of the White Paper, with its restrictions on immigration, a ban on most land purchases, and the prospect of an independent state in which the Jews would become a permanent minority. David Ben-Gurion famously pledged to 'fight the White Paper as if there were no war and to fight the war as if there were no White Paper'. He also declared that just as the First World War had given birth to the Balfour Declaration, this new conflict should give the Jews their own state. Even before news of mass killings of Jews began to filter out of Nazi-occupied Europe, facilitating illegal immigration had become a preoccupation for Zionist institutions. Running the British blockade became a national mission. In November 1940, a rickety ship called the *Patria* sank in Haifa harbour after *Haganah* operatives miscalculated the force of a bomb they had planted. The intention had been to cripple the vessel and prevent the deportation of its Jewish passengers, but in the event three hundred drowned. Far worse was to come. In January 1942 the Wannsee Conference in Berlin secretly drew up operational plans for Hitler's 'final solution'. In February, an old cattle transport called the *Struma* was hit by a mine or torpedo and sank in the Black Sea, where it had been sent by the Turkish authorities after the British refused to transfer its Romanian Jewish refugees to Palestine. This time the death toll was 768, a grim dramatization of the plight of Jews fleeing for their lives and the impossibility of relying on British goodwill. 'The Zionists,' said Moshe Shertok, 'do not mean to exploit the horrible tragedy of the Jews of Europe but they cannot refrain from emphasising the fact that events have totally proven the Zionist position on the solution of the Jewish problem. Zionism predicted the Holocaust decades ago.'[4]

Zionist propaganda portrayed the British high commissioner as a mass murderer. In 1941 the Fighters for the Freedom of Israel (Lehi, in its Hebrew acronym), a smaller and more extreme offshoot of the *Irgun*, had already stepped up its campaign against British rule, robbing banks, planting bombs and assassinating policemen. Its leader, a Polish-born poet named Avraham Stern, had become convinced of Britain's 'treachery' by the 1939 White Paper. In February 1942 he was tracked down to a Tel Aviv safe house and shot dead by a British detective.[5] The 'unknown soldiers' of what the British called the Stern Gang continued their ruthless fight under new leaders.

This was a relatively quiet period for relations between Arabs and Jews, not least because the large and growing British and Allied military presence meant that a new rebellion was out of the question. Moshe Shertok told Mapai colleagues in August 1940 of local agreements on security between Jewish settlements and Arab villages, though he was unsure how long they would last. 'Today they are sworn enemies of the Mufti and see their salvation in links with us,' he said.[6] The early war years did see improvements, at least locally. Neighbours re-established ties in rural areas like the Beisan valley and western Galilee. Kibbutz Ginossar, on Lake Tiberias, signed an agreement with neighbouring Ghuwayr Abu Shusha.[7] In January 1940 1,000 Jewish and Arab citrus growers met in Jaffa's Alhambra cinema to discuss co-operation.[8] The city's Arab leaders publicly expressed condolences for the victims of the Italian bombing of Tel Aviv.[9] Jews returned to Jaffa and Arabs to Tel Aviv,[10] though with misgivings on both sides. Nationally, however, there was no such rapprochement. In November 1941 Fakhri al-Nashashibi, who had organized the 'peace bands' with clandestine Zionist and British support, was murdered in Baghdad, probably by supporters of the mufti. Haj Amin al-Husseini himself fled the Iraqi capital after Rashid Ali's pro-Axis coup there, and went on to Rome and then to Berlin – where, notoriously, he met Hitler and Himmler. The Baghdad assassination was part of a concerted campaign against Arab opposition figures, including those who maintained friendly relations with or sold land to Jews. In Jerusalem Ragheb al-Nashashibi, who had supported the White Paper, tried – and failed – to secure British recognition for his National Defence Party as the sole representative of the Palestinian Arabs.

TAKING SIDES

Wartime life in Palestine was marked by rationing, shortages and a black market – and profound uncertainty about the future. To foreign eyes the country looked even more exotic than before.

> To drive along the streets of Jerusalem is never boring – one sees Jewish men in flat, fur-edged hats with their uncut hair falling over their shoulders; Arab women in tall, almost mediaeval headdresses; Greek priests with buns and stove-pipe hats; officers of the Transjordan Frontier Force with high black fur headgear slashed with scarlet to match their belts; Arab Legion, Abyssinian clergy, Palestine police, Americans, Bedouin, and British uniforms – it is quite a fashion show,

recorded a British woman who began working for the government secretariat in 1941. Arab–Jewish violence was rare but the atmosphere was still heavy with suspicion. 'I am beginning to understand why one feels unhappy and apprehensive in Jerusalem. Wherever you go, for work or fun there is an unspoken mental undertow of suspicion. No-one asks, but everyone wants to know which side you are on – Arab or Jew?'[11] High society gathered in the bar of Jerusalem's opulent King David Hotel, which provided the finest hospitality in the country and perhaps the Middle East. Katie Antonius, the glamorous widow of the historian George Antonius who had died in 1942, held celebrated soirées that were frequented by British officials, Arab notables and non-Zionist Jews. 'Mrs Antonius seems to have a political salon in the true French style', recorded the British MP

Richard Crossman after attending one. 'It was a magnificent party, evening dress, Syrian food and drink, and dancing on the marble floor.'[12] (Famously, the hostess was having an affair with General Evelyn Barker, commander of British forces in Palestine.)

Over the previous two decades Jerusalem had grown and prospered as a colonial capital, but these were its final years as a relatively cosmopolitan city, with the Arab middle classes relocated from the congestion of the Old City to the newly fashionable suburbs of Qatamon, Talbiyeh – which was largely Christian – and adjacent Baqaa. Some still lived in mixed neighbourhoods, though few Jerusalem Jews, unlike their co-religionists in Hebron and Tiberias, spoke Arabic. From the start of the 1940s daily life in Arab villages west of the city, such as Ain Karim, Lifta, Deir Yassin and al-Malha, became increasingly intertwined with that of the adjacent and growing Jewish neighbourhoods of Bet Hakerem, Givat Shaul and Romema. Social intercourse, though, remained strictly limited. The new 'garden suburbs' of Rehavia and Talpiot were exclusively Jewish. In 1944 Jews made up 97,000 of Jerusalem's 157,000-strong population, with about 30,000 Muslims and a similar number of Christians.[13]

Events were driven by the course of the war. Fears mounted about what would happen if the Germans broke through British lines in North Africa, as they threatened to do, first, in the spring of 1941, and then for a few nerve-wracking weeks in the summer of 1942, when Rommel's panzer columns advanced to 150 miles from Cairo. 'The Arabs . . . would have touched their hats to any new conqueror,' commented one senior British official. 'When Rommel was very near Cairo I think a lot of the locals were getting ready with the appropriate coloured flag to say hello.'[14] Chaim Weizmann, visiting the US, was told that the Palestinian Arabs were 'preparing for a division of the spoils . . . going about the streets of Tel Aviv and the colonies marking up the houses they expected to take over'. Fearing German invasion, there was talk of younger Jews planning mass suicide while 'older ones would take to the hills to fight their last battle'.[15] Plans were drawn up by the *Haganah* for a last stand in the Haifa area. British intelligence officers approached the Jewish Agency and Arab opposition figures for help organizing resistance in the event of a Nazi invasion that (it was assumed) would bring a vengeful mufti back to rule Palestine. Planning the Palestine Post-Occupation Scheme, the *Haganah*'s Ezra Danin set up a fund to supply weapons to a group led by Fakhri Abdel-Hadi and Suleiman Touqan from Nablus. It was, Danin reflected, the only agreement ever made between Arabs and Jews to fight a common enemy.[16] Fighting that enemy saw Zionist and British interests converge to mutual advantage in May 1941, when the *Haganah* command created the Palmah (*Plugot Mahatz* – 'striking forces') – a highly trained elite unit. Several hundred fighters, based in *kibbutzim*, were trained in sabotage and communications by British instructors at Mishmar haEmek and gained experience in operations against Vichy French forces in Lebanon and Syria. It was in one of these operations, involving Australian troops, that Moshe Dayan from Nahalal, who had served in Wingate's Special Night Squads, lost his eye. Another renowned Palmahnik was Yigal Allon of Kibbutz Ginossar. Both were to play influential military and political roles in years to come.

NON-EXISTENT ARABS

In May 1942 Zionist plans for the post-war era were spelled out at an 'extraordinary conference' in New York. The Biltmore Programme, named for the Manhattan hotel where the event was held, called for unrestricted Jewish immigration to Palestine and the establishment of 'a Jewish commonwealth in the Land of Israel'. In the face of British restrictions, the Zionists worked hard to influence the US administration and to mobilize the American-Jewish establishment as reports intensified about the Nazi's mass murder of Jews.[17] Biltmore also implied a tougher Zionist line towards the country's native Arabs, of whom the programme strikingly made no mention at all. The old compromise formulas were forgotten. In the angry words of Meir Yaari, leader of the left-wing *HaShomer Hatzair* movement: 'Ben-Gurion's proposal completely disregards the fact that a million Arabs live here together with us – as if they did not exist at all.'[18] Even after Biltmore, *HaShomer Hatzair* and a small minority of other Zionists professed to believe in the possibilities of co-existence with the Palestinian Arabs. Judah Magnes, president of the Hebrew

University, the philosopher Martin Buber, the educationalist Ernest Simon and other veterans of *Brit Shalom* founded the *Ihud* (Union) movement, advocating a 'bi-national' solution to the conflict. Magnes enjoyed enormous personal prestige, but close to zero influence among his own community. In 1943, when evidence of the scale of Nazi atrocities in Europe was already familiar, Simon lectured a group of Jewish eighteen-year-olds: 'We are entering a country populated by another people and are not showing that people any consideration,' he warned. 'The Arabs are afraid we may force them out of here.' The youngsters' response was hostile, truculent and highly revealing: 'Which is more ethical?' one of them asked. 'To leave Jews to be annihilated in the diaspora or to bring them in the face of opposition to Palestine and to carry out a transfer, even by force, of Arabs to Arab countries?' It was an attitude that was increasingly prevalent among the so-called 'Sabra' generation of Jews who were born or raised in Palestine (named after the cactus-like plant that was prickly on the outside but soft inside), and who were to fight and rise to public prominence in the years to come. 'Reference to the aspiration for peace and the desire for Arab–Jewish friendship became a kind of ritualised convention, repeated without any deep conviction',[19] in the words of one mainstream Israeli historian. *Ihud* leaders held discussions with Arab leaders in Palestine and the neighbouring countries. But these efforts were 'unavailing as long as the official leadership on both sides looked on them with disdain'.[20]

The idea of 'transfer' had always been part of Zionist thinking, though the subject was treated discreetly given that it contradicted the claim that Arabs benefitted from the Jewish presence. Back in 1895 Theodor Herzl had written in his diary of 'spiriting the penniless population across the border' – though that was not repeated in his major works. In the first decade of the century Arthur Ruppin had considered a plan to buy land in Syria to resettle Palestinian Arabs. Population transfer had a recent precedent and Ben-Gurion had raised it in a meeting with Musa al-Alami in 1934. The Peel Report gave an impetus to the idea by including proposals for an exchange of population of up to 225,000 Arabs and 1,250 Jews based on the far larger numbers involved in the brutal but successful Greek and Turkish exchange in 1923–4.[21] The issue was widely discussed in Jewish Palestine in 1937. The

Woodhead Commission, which examined scenarios for implementing partition, concluded that *voluntary* transfer was not expected to work because of the Arab population's 'deep attachment to the land' and resentment of the Jews. Population transfer, however, was still on Zionist minds. In early 1939 the Syrian Druze leader Sultan al-Atrash proposed to the Jewish Agency the sale of 16 of the community's villages in Palestine and the emigration to Syria of their 10,700 inhabitants. Weizmann called it the 'greatest opportunity' Zionism had had for fifty years – and a bargain at £3 million. 'It would relieve us of a great many of our political troubles for a long time to come, and by consolidating our holdings in upper Galilee, Huleh and the coastal plain we would be able to expand further when the time comes', he wrote. 'It would also create a significant precedent if 10,000 Arabs were to emigrate peacefully of their own volition, which would no doubt be followed by others.' In the end the plan came to nothing, but the thought – as well as of a Zionist–Druze alliance – lived on.[22] In 1940, Yosef Weitz of the Jewish National Fund confided to his diary – in a subsequently much-quoted statement – that 'there is no room for both people together in this country. The only solution is a Palestine ... without Arabs. And there is no other way than to transfer the Arabs from here to the neighbouring countries, to transfer all of them. There is no other way.'[23] Weizmann discussed transfer in a meeting with the Soviet ambassador to Britain, Ivan Maisky, in 1941. In the light of subsequent events, the issue has been highlighted by Palestinian and other critics of Zionism – one perceptively described it as a 'wordless wish'.[24] Transfer has also been described as a 'primordial dream' or 'in the air'.[25] It was not an operational plan in the mid-1940s, but nor was it forgotten.

KNOWING THE ENEMY

In the course of the war military preparedness took centre-stage in *Yishuv* life. The Palmah's co-operation with the British ended after the Allied victory at El Alamein and the unit went underground. Valuable experience had been gained. Intelligence work began to be co-ordinated nationally by the Jewish Agency and the *Haganah*, drawing on all areas of contact with Arabs to glean information that might prove useful in future.[26] In Jewish settlements it fell to the *mukhtar* (village or neighbourhood headman) to oversee security and to maintain contact and promote 'neighbourly' relations with near-by Arab villages. In Kfar Menachem, a kibbutz founded near Gedera in 1939, David Karon, a Polish-born Jew who had recently returned from fighting on the Republican side in the Spanish civil war, helped resolve a conflict when a kibbutz watchman accidentally killed an Arab. Karon formed part of Ezra Danin's expanding network of operatives for the Shai (*Sherut haYediot*), the *Haganah* intelligence service, and used his Arab connections to purchase weapons stolen from British bases.[27] In Kibbutz Eilon in Galilee – one of the new 'stockade and watchtower' settlements – *mukhtar* Dov Yirmiyahu forged close links with a Bedouin family and earned their lasting gratitude, and a valuable source of information, first by laying a water pipe to their encampment and then when their son was bitten by a snake, rushing him by the kibbutz jeep to the nearest hospital.[28] Palmah squads occasionally carried out assassinations in retaliation for attacks on Jews 'to punish and to deter'. In March 1942 commanders approved the killing of Qassem Tabash, held responsible for the death of the renowned settler Alexander Zeid (a founder of the *HaShomer* guards) at the height of the rebellion in 1938. In another case, an Arab rapist from Beisan was castrated, the story finding its way into Palmah songs and folklore.[29]

In the mid-1940s *Haganah* planners came up with the idea of preparing files with comprehensive information about Arab villages, including clans, political affiliations and activity during the rebellion. Hikes – a mainstay of Zionist activity – had long been organized across the country to familiarize young Jews with Palestine's geography, topography and history, a healthy and educational way of confirming 'Jewish proprietorship over the redeemed land of the fathers'.[30] This new discipline was called in Hebrew '*yediat haaretz*' – 'knowing the country', and data collected by Shai agents was used in these 'village files'.[31] Yasser al-Askari, a native of Safad, described encountering Jewish men and women in military-type uniforms, exploring Arab villages and beauty spots, noting access routes and other features.[32] But they had less innocent purposes. Later the

Palmah and Zionist youth movements focused on the Negev region and the Judaean desert – barred to Jews under the restrictions of the 1939 White Paper. The ancient fortress of Masada, with its legend of heroic Jewish resistance and mass suicide in the face of the Roman siege, was singled out for attention in what became a kind of secular pilgrimage.[33] Another destination was Tel Hai in Galilee, where Joseph Trumpeldor had died fighting, becoming the prototype Zionist hero in 1920.[34] These educational excursions-cum-reconnaissance missions lasted a week or longer. The route from Bet haArava – the southernmost settlement in the Negev – to Sedom and onwards became a tradition. In one celebrated case, hikers from the Palmah and a socialist youth movement, including a young Shimon Peres, were detained by the British for entering a closed military area on the way to Umm Rashrash, adjacent to Aqaba. As part of their training they had hidden revolvers and grenades under the false bottoms of their water canisters.[35] The *Haganah* also stole maps from British stores. 'In May 1944', one Palmah member recalled,

> three teams of us went out . . . to prepare 'files'. For 'cover' we took with us books on botany in Hebrew, German and French . . . We were botanists . . . When we arrived at one of the villages a crowd would gather. And so we would prepare our sketches: at some interesting place, for example by the mukhtar's house, I would gather the people, bend down and pick some plant, hold it up and show it to them: 'Will you look at this plant?' . . . Then our people would go into the house, ask for water . . . At the end of the trip we would sit down and relax and while resting – we would write up the summary of what we'd seen on the way or corrections of our notes.[36]

In 1945 the project was expanded to include information of a directly military character, with files including sketches, maps and photographs of each village and its surroundings, access roads, water-sources, and so on. Aerial photography was also used, under the guise of the activities of a flying club.[37]

Detailed knowledge of Arab areas was exploited for land purchases. In 1946 Palestinians in the south were aware of a 'smooth-talking' Jew speaking Arabic and preaching co-existence accompanied by a man from Khan Yunis who was looking for land to buy.[38] Arabs helped the Jewish National Fund acquire thousands of dunams despite the restrictions of the 1939 White Paper.[39] Palestinians in the anti-mufti opposition acted as real-estate brokers as well as informants, co-operating with subterfuges such as acting as frontmen for the JNF and other buyers. Josh Palmon of the Shai explained:

> We would tell the Arab, 'We're not the ones who will buy from you. Transfer it to the name of an Arab that we will give you.' He would transfer the property into the name of the Arab. How did we manage it so that the second Arab could turn the land over to us legally? We'd say to him: 'My good man, sign here that you took a loan from us. We'll take you to court to get the loan back; you won't return it, you'll be declared bankrupt, and then we have the right to take whatever property is registered in your name, whenever. That's something the White Paper forgot about.' It forgot that loophole, and through that loophole we bought a lot of land.[40]

Information was collected on Arab landowners who were in debt and susceptible to offers they could not refuse.[41] Collaborators fomented feuds which could be exploited. So-called 'American' methods (alcohol and prostitution) sometimes played their part. 'The Zionists' hold on the land thus grew in parallel with their greater intelligence penetration of the Arab community.'[42]

In public, Jewish settlers liked to display their good relations with Arabs, especially for foreign VIPs, as Richard Crossman of the Anglo-American Commission of Inquiry discovered when he was shown the 'turfed gardens, fountains and beautifully-kept flower beds' of Mishmar haEmek in 1946 and the neighbouring Arab village – the 'stenchiest' the British MP had ever seen. The settlement was a favourite showcase: an earlier visitor had referred to the 'reality of the dirty Arab hovels and their wretched inhabitants, only a few hundred yards beyond the kibbutz's barbed-wire fence'.[43] Crossman got beyond outward appearances: 'Obviously the Jewish mukhtar and the Sheikh got on well', he wrote.

> I asked the sheikh if he wasn't envious for his children of the life in the school on the farm 100 yards away. He said 'no' in a way which showed that he couldn't comprehend the question. I was nearly convinced that

Arab–Jewish cooperation was perfect when I asked: 'What about immigration?' Suddenly the sheikh's son leapt to his feet and delivered a full-length speech containing the whole Arab case including the return of the Mufti. 'But you don't mind the Jews in this collective?' He fiercely replied that any more Jews in Palestine would ruin the country. The Jewish mukhtar then said: 'But if you had had your way we shouldn't have been here, and you like us don't you?' At this point the sheikh and his son answered nothing, and the mukhtar turned to me and said in English: 'You see, they really like us and it's all propaganda from above on the Arab side.' Actually it was quite obvious that the sheikh was far too shrewd to criticise a neighbour. The relations are perfectly OK socially when the country is quiet; but the sheikh and his son would obey the orders of the Arab Higher Committee and shoot anyone for the sake of their country. That's the real problem.[44]

In the autumn of 1943, when an Axis victory no longer seemed likely and the tide of war had turned, growing Zionist confidence helped awaken Palestinian Arab politics from its torpor. The mufti's Nazi connections had discredited him in British eyes and made him an easy target for Zionist propaganda.[45] Awni Abdel-Hadi and Rashid al-Hajj Ibrahim, the *Istiqlal* leaders, co-operated with Ahmad Hilmi Pasha to revive the Arab national fund, *Sunduq al-Umma*. It raised nearly 100,000 Palestine pounds, a large sum, and purchased nearly 15,000 dunams that otherwise would have been sold to Jews.[46] In 1946 the mufti's move from internment in France to Cairo, and Jamal al-Husseini's release from detention in Southern Rhodesia, set off a flurry of Arab activity. But factionalism persisted. 'Palestinian politics continued to be characterized by jealousy, mistrust, jockeying for power and the fruitless movement . . . of various emissaries and mediators carrying proposals and counter-proposals', according to a later study. 'All practical efforts at effective measures to challenge Zionist aims, such as in the area of land, were also riddled with factionalism. Banks, constructive schemes and national funds, initiated, organized and controlled by the dominant leaders, became the arena for political struggles, contention, and control.'[47] The consequences of this disarray were to become painfully obvious over the following few years.

7

1945–1949

'Immigrants of ours will come to this Khirbet what's-its-name, you hear me, and they'll take this land and work it, and it'll be beautiful here.'

S. Yizhar, Khirbet Khiza[1]

OPENING SHOTS

On Sunday, 30 November 1947 armed Arabs ambushed a Jewish bus at Kfar Sirkin en route from Netanya to Jerusalem, killing five passengers. This incident, just hours after the United Nations voted to partition Palestine, is generally regarded as marking the start of Israel's war of independence and the Palestinian *Nakba* or 'catastrophe'. The motives of the perpetrators were said to be clannish and criminal rather than 'national', though the distinction was either lost or ignored at the time and has been forgotten since.[2] Later that day another bus was attacked on the road from Hadera, leaving one Jew dead and several injured. Other attacks marked the descent into all-out conflict that was driven by an accelerating cycle of retaliation and revenge.

On 13 December a teenage Palestinian boy watched in horror as a black car stopped outside the Damascus Gate to Jerusalem's Old City and 'the occupants rolled two cylinders with burning wicks into the milling crowd'. Twenty people died.[3] Two weeks later, fighters of the Lehi underground – the 'Stern Gang' to the British – targeted a coffee house in Lifta, killing six. On 30 December *Irgun* men threw grenades into a crowd of Arab workers outside Haifa's oil refinery, once notable for its cross-community trade union co-operation: eleven died. In the ensuing fury thirty-nine Jewish employees were killed by Arabs wielding metal bars, knives and hammers. Six Arabs were also killed. On the first morning of 1948 *Haganah* units raided nearby Balad al-Sheikh – burial place of Sheikh Izzedin al-Qassam. Several dozen people, including women and children, lost their lives. Local incidents fuelled a country-wide crisis. Full-scale war seemed inevitable as the new year dawned.

Escalation on the ground matched the intensifying pace of international diplomacy over Palestine after the end of the Second World War. In October 1945 the *Haganah* and *Irgun* launched a co-ordinated rebellion against British rule by sabotaging the railway system. In April 1946 the Anglo-American Committee of Inquiry recommended that the country be governed under 'bi-national' principles and called for the immediate entry of 100,000 Jewish refugees. However, that failed to bring London and Washington to a common position. In June another *Haganah* operation destroyed all the bridges connecting Palestine to its neighbouring countries, 'the crowning act of the organised struggle against the White Paper administration', in the words of one Zionist official.[4] The British mounted a massive search and arrest operation ('Operation Agatha') in which 2,700 Jews were detained, including most of the Jewish Agency leaders and a large part of the *Haganah* command, on a day dubbed 'Black Sabbath'. Three weeks later the *Irgun* blew up a wing of Jerusalem's King David Hotel, headquarters of the British civil and military administration, by smuggling milk churns packed with explosives into the basement. That killed ninety-one people, nearly a third of them Jews, and was immediately condemned by the Jewish Agency. News of this spectacular atrocity echoed around the world; it fuelled growing outrage in Britain and accelerated the end of the Mandate. In December David Ben-Gurion took over the Jewish Agency's defence portfolio. It seemed clear that a peaceful solution to the Palestine conflict was not attainable.

By February 1947 the Labour government in London had effectively given up an increasingly unpopular burden that was costing the lives of British troops and police in a 'senseless, squalid war', as Winston Churchill, now in opposition, put it.[5] It decided to submit the Palestine question to the UN and in May the fledgling world body established a Special Committee on Palestine (UNSCOP). During their visit to the country the committee's members witnessed the so-called '*Exodus* affair', when 4,500 Holocaust survivors on board an old American passenger ship were detained as illegal immigrants and deported back to Europe. The favourable publicity that ensued for the Jewish cause went some way to offsetting revulsion at Jewish terrorism. That peaked the day the *Exodus* arrived in France, when two abducted British sergeants were hanged in retaliation for the execution of *Irgun* fighters. In a grisly sequel, their booby-trapped corpses were blown apart as they were being cut down in an orange grove near Netanya. The Arabs boycotted UNSCOP – their 'cold malevolence', as a Jewish official put it, in sharp contrast to the 'warm reception by the *Yishuv*'.[6]

In September, seven of the UN committee's ten members recommended partition into two states, with international status for Jerusalem. The minority (India, Iran and Yugoslavia) proposed a federal state with Jerusalem as its capital. The Arab Higher Committee expressed 'amazement and disbelief' as this was 'contrary to the UN charter and to the principles of justice and integrity'.[7] Britain announced that it would leave Palestine in six months' time if no settlement was reached. No one seriously imagined that it would be. On 29 November 1947 the UN General Assembly voted to partition Palestine into Jewish and Arab states, leaving Jerusalem under UN supervision as a '*corpus separatum*'. Intense Zionist lobbying secured a majority of thirty-three to thirteen with ten abstentions – a close-run thing since a two-thirds vote was required. UN Resolution 181 was backed, crucially, by both the US and USSR – the world's great powers in the early days of the Cold War. It was opposed by the Palestinians and by Arab and Muslim states infuriated by American susceptibility to the Zionists. The proposed Jewish state was to consist of 55 per cent of the country, including the largely unpopulated Negev desert. Its population would comprise some 500,000 Jews and 400,000 Arabs – a very substantial minority. Jews, at that point, owned just 7 per cent of Palestine's private land. The Arab state was to have 44 per cent of the land and a minority of 10,000 Jews. Greater Jerusalem was to remain under international rule. The mufti, Haj Amin al-Husseini, declared the UN vote 'null and void'.

Jamal al-Husseini, vice-president of the Arab Higher Committee, had already warned that it was 'the sacred duty of the Arabs of Palestine to defend their country against all aggression'. Now he rejected the proposed border as a 'line of blood and fire'.[8] The Palestinian view was that 'partition did not involve a compromise but was Zionist in conception and tailored to meet Zionist needs and demands'.[9]

Arab anger was matched by Jewish jubilation. Hours after the vote at Lake Success, the UN's first home, Ben-Gurion stood on the balcony of the Jewish Agency building in Jerusalem. 'He looked slowly and solemnly around him – to the roof tops crammed with people, to the throngs that stood solid in the courtyard below him', one witness recorded.

> He raised his hand: an utter silence waited for his words. '*Ashreynu sheh zachinu la yom ha zeh.*' [Blessed are we who have been privileged to witness this day.] He concluded with '*Tchi ha Medina ha Ivrith*' [Long Live the Hebrew State – it didn't have a name yet] and called for *Hatikvah.** A solemn chant rose from all sides. The moment was too big for our feelings. There were few dry eyes and few steady voices. Ben-Gurion tossed his head back proudly, tenderly touched the flag that hung from the railing and charged the air with electricity when he shouted defiantly, 'WE ARE A FREE PEOPLE.'[10]

Later that day, the Palestinian leadership proclaimed a general strike in protest while the *Haganah* called on Jews aged between seventeen and twenty-five to register for military service. The UN decision and reactions to it were replays of what had happened a decade earlier, when the Peel Commission recommended partition as a way round the 'irreconcilable aspirations' of Jews and Arabs. Again the Jews accepted the decision, though not without misgivings. The Arabs rejected it, refusing to cede sovereignty over any part of Palestine and insisting that the UN had no right to enforce its wishes in the face of the opposition of the majority of the population. Palestinians believed that 'the country was exclusively theirs and an inseparable part of the great Arab homeland. Any diminishing of this ideal was perceived as a conspiracy, *mu'amara* in Arabic, by those who would

---

* 'The Hope'. The Zionist anthem and later Israel's national anthem.

shift the Jewish problem from European shoulders to the Arabs and at their expense.'[11] But conditions were now very different from 1937. The partition decision had the weight of international opinion behind it, despite Arab legal, moral and political objections that were overlooked both then and since.[12] Even more significantly, within months the British would be leaving for good, no longer willing or able to 'hold the ring'. No other solution was on offer. The two peoples of Palestine were to be left to fight it out.

PREPARING FOR THE FIGHT

On the eve of war the Jews were far better prepared, militarily and politically, than the Arabs, in Palestine or beyond. Their leaders had a high level of confidence that they would prevail if it came to a fight, as they assumed it would.[13] The *Haganah* had a centralized command. It could field 35,000 men, including the 2,500-strong Palmah. The 'dissidents' of the *Irgun* and Stern Gang accounted for a few thousand more, in total making up an extraordinarily large percentage of the adult Jewish population. Approximately 27,000 Jews had enlisted with British forces during the war. In addition, the institutions of the *Yishuv* exercised national discipline. 'The Jewish Agency . . . is really a state within a state with its own budget, secret cabinet, army, and above all, intelligence service', observed Richard Crossman, the British Labour MP who had visited Palestine as a member of the Anglo-American Committee of Inquiry. 'It is the most efficient, dynamic, toughest organisation I have ever seen.'[14] If it came to war, he predicted, the *Haganah* would trounce the Arabs. Crossman's was an astute assessment (and at odds with the view of the British military).[15] Still, his confidence was not widely shared. 'We knew that 635,000 Jews were facing hundreds of millions of Arabs: "the few against the many"', Uri Avnery, a young German-born Jew, wrote shortly afterwards. 'We knew: if we surrender, we die.'[16] Volunteering was the norm among Jewish youth: Tikva Honig-Parnass, a seventeen-year-old Hebrew University student, enlisted in the *Haganah* in November 1947. 'It was well-known on campus who was a member', she recalled.

Most students were members and enlisting was the culmination of everything I had been brought up to believe in. We had fought to achieve what we had, it was now in danger and it was up to me to protect it. In that discourse there was no notion of attacking or being the aggressors, only defending ourselves and what we had built.[17]

In the wake of the Holocaust, which was seen by many as the ultimate moral vindication of the Zionist quest for a homeland, the Jews also enjoyed wide international sympathy – a crucial factor which many Arabs underestimated or ignored, continuing to believe 'that people entirely innocent of the crime had been forced to pay for it'.[18]

No one now doubted that the fate of Palestine was at stake from a combination of the end of British rule and growing Zionist assertiveness. Jewish determination to win was a powerful if intangible motivating factor. Independence for the neighbouring French Mandate territories of Syria and Lebanon in 1946 had underlined the painful fact that Palestine, trapped in its 'iron cage', was still nowhere near to achieving self-government under its Arab majority and that the Palestinians were still unable to develop their own national institutions and identity.[19] It was a debilitating weakness.

The Arab Higher Committee, outlawed back in 1937, had been revived under the exiled mufti's leadership. In May 1946 Haj Amin al-Husseini arrived in Egypt (after avoiding prosecution in France) under the protection of King Farouk and sent a wave of excitement through Arab Palestine. 'Men smiled, shook hands and embraced each other while the women ululated and offered songs of praise; fires of celebration burnt in every courtyard of every village. Brooding despair gave way to a desire to fight, for the Mufti, for all his colossal faults, embodied the Palestinian Arabs' will to resist.'[20] But factionalism still held sway, a legacy of old rivalries and of the events of 1936–39. The Arab National Fund had not succeeded in halting land sales. Nor had calls to boycott Jewish produce been heeded. The AHC's critics saw it as a partisan body which covered up the failings – even treacherous ones – of its own members. 'For twenty years we have heard talk against land brokers and land sellers, yet here they sit in the front rows of every national gathering', one anti-Husseini figure (himself in clandestine contact with the Jewish Agency) complained at a rally in

Jaffa – before the loudspeakers were turned off to silence him.[21] Haj Amin's pro-Axis wartime role was exploited in Zionist propaganda: photographs of him posing with Hitler or Bosnian Muslim SS volunteers were worth thousands of words and did grave damage to the Palestinian cause.[22] (In May 1947, during a UN debate, the AHC secretary, Emile Ghouri, objected to a Zionist reference to the mufti's presence in Germany: 'The Jews are questioning the record of an Arab spiritual leader,' he said. 'Does this properly come from the mouth of a people who have crucified the founder of Christianity?'[23]) The AHC was divided between Jerusalem, Beirut and Damascus, hampering effective communication, and its influence was dwarfed by that of the recently created League of Arab States, whose seven members* had their own agendas – the majority being opposed to King Abdullah of Transjordan, whose ambitions in Palestine were well known.[24] All this meant that the Palestinians were spectacularly ill-prepared for what has been called the 'bitter endgame' of the Mandate.[25]

The AHC faced 'the colossal task of building up Palestinian Arab military strength virtually from scratch, under severe handicaps'.[26] Nothing on the Palestinian side matched the resources and organization of the *Haganah*. No master plan existed for fighting the Jews, whose capabilities were simultaneously underestimated and exaggerated. The Arab effort was also beset by rivalry: it was not until January 1947 that two existing paramilitary groups, the *Futuwwa* and the *Najada*, were combined into a single Arab Youth Organization.[27] Veterans of the Arab rebellion had military experience but only a few thousand had joined the British army, and many had been discharged or had deserted.[28] In December the AHC set up the *Jaysh al-Jihad al-Muqaddas* (Army of the Holy Jihad, AHJ) under Abdul-Qader al-Husseini (the son of Musa Kazem) and 'the ablest and most courageous of the Arab commanders'.[29] National committees were formed in villages and towns as they had been during the rebellion.[30] Weapons were purchased in neighbouring countries and Europe, but it proved difficult to distribute arms and fighters as needed. Volunteering was not common; Hisham Sharabi, from a well-to-do Jaffa family, reflected later on how he and other privileged young

---

* Egypt, Jordan, Iraq, Syria, Transjordan, Saudi Arabia and Yemen.

Palestinians had gone abroad to study without thinking about the looming conflict:

> There were people, we assumed, who would fight on our behalf. They were those who had fought in [the] 1936 rebellion and would fight again in the future. They were peasants who were not in need of specialized higher education in the West. Their natural place was here, on this land; as for us intellectuals, our place was at another level. When we fought, we fought at the front of thought. We engaged in bitter battles of the mind.[31]

The initial Arab military effort focused on Jewish communications and transport, especially main roads and access routes to isolated settlements in Galilee and the Negev. Jewish quarters in the mixed towns of Haifa, Jaffa, Tiberias and Jerusalem came under attack. Leadership, though, remained essentially local. Abdul-Qader complained of a shortage of weapons, explosives and ammunition. Defence was a weak point. The lack of medical care meant that treatable wounds often ended in amputations. Non-Palestinian forces were deployed by the Arab Liberation Army (ALA or *Jaysh al-Inqadh al-Arabi*), set up by the Arab League's Damascus-based military committee. It was made up of 5,000 volunteers and seconded Syrian and Iraqi military personnel commanded by Fawzi al-Qawuqji, 'a popular Garibaldian officer of Lebanese origin',[32] in northern Palestine, where Qawuqji had also fought in 1936. It was plagued by low morale, bad discipline and poor logistics.[33] Qawuqji and the mufti were also at loggerheads.[34] Fighters from the Egyptian Muslim Brotherhood entered the country from the south as well. Overall coordination of these disparate forces was extremely poor and 'probably the most important factor in the eventual Palestinian defeat and in the Haganah's relative ease in accomplishing it'.[35] In some towns garrisons answered to the Arab League, in others to the AHC. The Arab states behaved in a 'patronising and ... contemptuous manner' towards the Palestinians. Residents of Jaffa were appalled at the conduct of fighters from Hama in Syria, who arrived in March, 'went on a rampage of robbery and looting, and then quickly left'.[36] ALA officers accused Palestinians of being 'traitors, cowards, spies and speculators in land'. Indeed, many Palestinians did not want to fight, had secret non-aggression pacts with their Jewish neighbours, opposed the Husseinis or refused to harbour foreign forces.[37]

FATEFUL YEAR

Violence intensified after the New Year's Day *Haganah* raid on Balad al-Sheikh. In Jerusalem, on the rainy night of 5 January 1948 the *Haganah* blew up the Semiramis Hotel in Qatamon, killing twenty-six civilians it mistakenly believed were Arab 'irregulars', including the Spanish consul-general. Sir Alan Cunningham, the high commissioner, called it 'an offence to civilization' and asked Ben-Gurion how the Jews 'expected to defend themselves against world opinion for the crime of blowing up innocent people'. Ben-Gurion replied that the attack was unauthorized.[38] The effect was electrifying: 'All day long you could see people carrying their belongings and moving from their houses to safer ones in Qatamon or to another quarter altogether', wrote Hala Sakakini, a local resident.

> People were simply panic-stricken. The rumour spread that leaflets had been dropped by the Jews saying that they would make out of Qatamon one heap of rubble. Whenever we saw people moving away we tried to encourage them to stay. We would tell them: 'You ought to be ashamed to leave. This is just what the Jews want you to do; you leave and they occupy your houses and then one day you will find that Qatamon has become another Jewish quarter.[39]

Everyone in the neighbourhood felt 'vulnerable and alone', recalled Ghada Karmi. 'The men decided to put up barricades at both ends of the roads and to have them manned. But only five people had guns and the rest did not know how to use weapons.' The effort lasted until Jewish gunmen shot and killed the man on duty.[40] Two days later *Irgun* fighters threw bombs at the Jaffa Gate, this time with a death toll of twenty-five. *Haganah* attacks followed on Arab areas on the western side of town – Sheikh Badr, Lifta and Romema. On 31 January Ben-Gurion ordered the *Haganah* to settle Jewish refugees who had been displaced from the Shimon haTsadik area in east Jerusalem in newly abandoned Arab homes in the west. The next day

Palestinians and British army deserters bombed the offices of the *Palestine Post*, the Zionist English-language daily newspaper, killing twenty Jewish civilians.

The situation was deteriorating everywhere. In the first week of January Lehi operatives wearing British uniforms detonated a truck bomb outside the Grand Serail in Clock Square in Jaffa, HQ of the local Arab national committee. It killed twenty-eight Arabs. On 8 January the first contingent of 330 ALA volunteers arrived in the north. The following day saw an attack on Kibbutz Kfar Szold from across the Syrian border, in retaliation for a deadly Palmah assault on the nearby village of Khisas. The second half of the month saw fighting at Gush Etzion, the Jewish settlement bloc south of Jerusalem, where the entire thirty-five-strong Palmah force sent to relieve the defenders was wiped out. It was a devastating blow, but the '*Lamed-Hay*' (Hebrew for 'thirty-five') became a byword for youthful sacrifice, which was still remembered decades later.[41] The *Haganah* attacked Salama village near Jaffa. Hundreds more ALA men crossed the frontiers from Syria, Lebanon and Transjordan.

Palestinian civilians began to flee from the start of the hostilities. In early December 1947 the *Haganah* reported that wealthy Arabs were moving temporarily to winter residences in Syria, Lebanon and Egypt.[42] Others left for inland villages. Around 15,000 Arab residents, a fifth of Jaffa's population, had left by mid-January.[43] By late January, 20,000 Haifa residents were estimated to have abandoned their homes. Residents of Arab villages adjoining Jewish areas of Jerusalem left too.[44] The Arab Higher Committee tried to stem these departures by radio broadcasts, by appealing to neighbouring governments not to grant entry to fleeing Palestinians and by ordering local commanders to stop people leaving.[45] From Cairo, the mufti urged the national committees to halt 'desertion from the field of honour and sacrifice'.[46] But the effort was confused and advice often contradictory. Fear of attack, as in any war, was the main reason for the flight of civilians, at least at this stage, and it did not go unnoticed by the Jewish leadership. In early February Ben-Gurion remarked pointedly on the departure of Arabs from West Jerusalem: 'From your entry to Jerusalem through Lifta-Romema . . . there are no strangers [Arabs],' he told Mapai colleagues. 'One hundred per cent Jewish. I do not assume that this will change. What has happened in Jerusalem ... could well happen in large parts of the country – if we hold on.'[47]

Until the end of February Jewish forces remained largely on the defensive, partly out of fear of a possible British reaction. An ALA attack on an isolated settlement near Beisan was repulsed, with the Arabs suffering heavy casualties. But there were significant exceptions. On 15 February, Palmah units attacked Sasa in northern Galilee, killing sixty villagers and destroying twenty houses. The Palmah blew up Arab homes in Caesarea and expelled their residents. In Jaffa houses were dynamited with people still inside them.[48] The degree to which these actions were authorized by the *Haganah* national command and political leadership, or were the result of initiatives on the ground, is unclear. Their outcome, however, is not in doubt.

DALET FOR DEFENCE?

On 10 March 1948, *Haganah* commanders meeting in Tel Aviv looked ahead to the next stage of the war in a document known as *Tochnit Dalet* (Plan D). The plan was designed to secure control of Jewish-held territory – within and beyond the UN partition borders – ahead of the approaching British departure. In case of resistance, Arabs were to be expelled. If there was no resistance, they could stay under military rule. Decades later opinions still differed sharply as to whether this constituted a master plan for expulsions or 'ethnic cleansing' – a term borrowed from the Yugoslav wars of the 1990s and the title of an influential work by the anti-Zionist Israeli historian Ilan Pappé.[49] Israeli and pro-Zionist scholars had traditionally described Plan D as defensive and the Palestinian exodus as unexpected. Walid Khalidi, the leading Palestinian historian, took the opposite view.[50] Benny Morris, the pioneering 'new' Israeli historian of this crucially formative period, argued that Plan D was implemented, but only in piecemeal fashion. The Palestinian refugee problem, in Morris's much-quoted assessment, was 'born out of war, not by design'.[51] Still, a predisposition to population 'transfer' and tactical military considerations in fast-moving circumstances inclined

Haganah commanders towards removing Arabs, given the opportunity. The language employed was certainly highly suggestive. The Hebrew word *'tihur'* ('purifying') was used repeatedly in internal documents. The codenames chosen for operations – *Matateh* (Broom) and *Biur Chametz* (Passover Cleaning) seemed inspired by this mindset.[52] Pappé and others have argued that the record shows that the removal of Palestinians was 'more premeditated, systematic and extensive' than Morris acknowledged – even in the face of his own evidence.[53] No high-level Jewish political discussion is known to have been held to explicitly discuss expelling Arabs, but many expulsions unquestionably took place. And the results, in the end, mattered far more than intentions – and the nuances of later historiographical controversy.

In the ebb and flow of events, each side experienced periods of crisis. On 23 March the Iraqi head of the Arab League military committee, General Ismail Safwat ('old fashioned ... extremely brave and unutterably stupid'[54]), warned that the Arab garrisons in Jaffa, Jerusalem and Haifa were on the defensive, with the initiative in the hands of Zionist forces held back 'only by their fear of the British'.[55] Indeed, by the end of the month many of the wealthy and middle-class Arab families of those three cities had gone – for good. Simultaneously, Arab attacks took a heavy toll on Jewish convoys: forty-six Jews were killed on the road to Yehiam near the Arab village of Kabri. Other losses were incurred in convoys at Hulda and Nabi Daniel.

April was the turning point of the first phase of the war. As the British departure neared and supplies of food and water ran dangerously low in Jewish areas of Jerusalem, the *Haganah* went on to the offensive, capturing more territory that was not earmarked for the Jews under the UN plan. It mounted Operation Nachshon to get relief convoys past Bab al-Wad and through to the city, taking the hill-top Arab village of Qastel – the first to be conquered by Jewish forces – expelling its inhabitants and destroying its houses. Husseini, the commander of the AHJ, was killed there on 8 April and buried the next day amid emotional scenes at the al-Aqsa mosque alongside his father and Sharif Hussein of Mecca. It was a crushing blow to Palestinian morale and a harbinger of wider defeat.[56] Husseini was and remains one of the few heroic figures of the Arab war effort.[57] Poor logistics were also an increasingly obvious disadvantage for the Arabs: in the course of the battle for Qastel a taxi arrived in Ramallah with fighters who bought bullets on the streets to re-supply their comrades at the front.[58] ALA forces suffered another serious setback with the failure of an attack on Mishmar haEmek, the kibbutz overlooking the road from Jenin to Haifa, despite using field artillery for the first time in the war. That allowed the *Haganah* to occupy several nearby Arab villages, which were razed after their inhabitants fled or were expelled to the Jenin area.

On 12 April Qaluniya, near Qastel, fell to Palmah fighters. 'Scouts went ahead and more . . . were on the hilltops', reported an accompanying journalist.

> Everyone wore green camouflaged uniforms. They carried a medley of weapons, Sten guns, rifles, machine guns and hand grenades; a few carried 'walkie talkies'. They moved like wraiths down the wadi . . . Suddenly the village seemed to erupt. Our mortars started it, and at once came a bedlam of answering fire . . . Suddenly an explosion that seems to rip the hillside; shrieks of terror. Our shock troops and sappers had reached the houses . . . Arab resistance, feeble from the start, soon crumbled. In half an hour it was over.[59]

These were fateful days. On Friday, 9 April, the day of Husseini's funeral, the massacre of Deir Yassin played a decisive role in fuelling Palestinian fear and flight. Residents of the stone-quarrying village on the western edge of Jerusalem believed they were safe because of a non-belligerency agreement their *mukhtar* had signed with the neighbouring Jewish quarter of Givat Shaul – one of several such pacts.[60] 'There was an agreement that if any of their people attacked Deir Yassin, the Jews would stop them and catch them', recalled Muhammed Arif Sammour, a teacher. 'If anyone from Deir Yassin attacked Givat Shaul, the Arabs would stop him.'[61] Deir Yassin did not directly overlook the Tel Aviv road and it had not sheltered Arab forces fighting for Qastel. It was not a priority for the *Haganah*, though the district commander gave 'reluctant approval' for the attack.[62] It was mounted by a joint 120-strong *Irgun*–Lehi force, but when the 'dissidents' encountered heavier than expected resistance a

Palmah platoon was despatched with a mortar and machine gun. Most residents fled, but survivors described executions, rapes and looting. 'The conquest of the village was carried out with great cruelty', *Haganah* intelligence reported. 'Whole families – women, old people, children – were killed . . . Some of the prisoners moved to places of detention, including women and children, were murdered viciously by their captors.'[63] Prisoners were paraded on trucks through the centre of Jerusalem before being released. For many years, based on the original Red Cross figures, the generally accepted death toll was 240–250. In the 1980s Palestinian researchers revised the number of fatalities to 107, closer to what was described in contemporary Jewish testimony.[64]

Even at the time, though, the precise figures barely mattered. Immediately afterwards Arab press and radio reported repeatedly on the massacre, fuelling panicked flight from nearby villages and echoing far beyond. As the *Irgun* commander Menachem Begin – who always denied that a massacre had taken place – wrote later: 'The legend was worth half a dozen battalions to the forces of Israel.' The psychological impact can hardly be overestimated. David Kroyanker, a young Jewish Jerusalemite, recalled the effect on the Arabs of Talbiyeh, adjacent to his home in Rehavia. 'The Arabs were scared to death. They left their meals on the tables and the Haganah requested people in our neighbourhood to clean the houses so that Jews could move into them.'[65] Deir Yassin remains a byword for Zionist brutality that has resonated down the decades and remains a rallying cry for the Palestinian cause. Shortly afterwards, news came through of another massacre, this time of twenty-two villagers in Khirbet Nasser ed-Din, south-west of Tiberias on the shore of the Sea of Galilee.[66] That was described as 'a second Deir Yassin'.[67]

Revenge was not long in coming: on 13 April Arab fighters ambushed a convoy of trucks, ambulances, buses and armoured cars heading to the Jewish enclave on Jerusalem's Mount Scopus, home of the Hebrew University. Seventy-eight lecturers, students, nurses and doctors as well as their *Haganah* escorts, were killed as British forces looked on without intervening. The attack caused disquiet among Arab doctors.[68] The fighting intensified a gathering Palestinian exodus from Jerusalem, with the evacuation of the southern suburbs of

Baqaa, Qatamon and the German Colony, the roads clogged with lorries loaded with household goods.[69] Petrol shortages meant that the cost of travel to Amman and Damascus soared so that it was manageable only for the better-off and for government employees who had received redundancy payments. Hundreds more Palestinians fled to Bethlehem, Nablus and Jericho, which were still considered safe.[70]

Over the next few weeks the war was effectively won by the Jews as *Haganah* units continued offensive operations, helped by the arrival of rifles, machine-guns and ammunition purchased from Czechoslovakia. Tiberias fell on 18 April, its 5,000-strong Arab population, which was used to relatively good relations with the Jewish residents, fleeing with people from nearby villages terrified by the fate of Khirbet Nasser ed-Din. British forces helped organize a relatively orderly evacuation.[71] *Haganah* forces then looted the Arab quarters.[72]

Haifa – home to Palestine's main port and second-largest Arab community – was taken after a sudden British withdrawal from positions between Arab and Jewish quarters; it had originally been thought that the British would remain for three months after the end of the Mandate. Sporadic fighting had taken place for two months: on consecutive days in March car-bomb attacks caused mass casualties on both sides. Wealthier Arab families had long gone. On 22 April Palestinians fled in their thousands to the port and boarded boats to take them north to Acre and Beirut. In the ensuing panic, worsened by *Haganah* mortar fire, some vessels became overcrowded and sank with their terrified passengers. 'We suddenly heard that the British Army in the harbour area was prepared to protect all who took refuge there', a local man recalled.[73]

Thus we all flooded the lanes that were still in our hands toward the harbour. It was a terrible thing to try and make a passage for oneself. Hundreds of people blocked the narrow lanes and pushed and heaved against one another, each trying to save himself and his children. Many children, women, and old men fainted and were trampled by the surging crowds. It was like Judgment Day ... A rumour spread that the Jews had cut off the roads ... We turned about in utter terror. People around me were shouting, cursing, sobbing, and praying. In an instance another rumour spread that the road was clear. Once again we began pushing in the direction of the harbour . . . At the entrance British policemen helped to carry our children. But there was a wild rush for the boats and many people were drowned in the process.

Shabtai Levy, the Jewish mayor, urged the Arab members of an emergency committee to stay put. But they declined to sign truce terms – perhaps fearing the opprobrium of surrender – and opted instead to evacuate the city. Golda Meir of the Jewish Agency, sent to Haifa to persuade Arabs to remain, found a 'dead city' with Arab women, children and the elderly waiting to leave and empty homes where coffee and bread were still on the table. She was reminded of Jewish towns in Europe during the war.[74] Inspecting abandoned apartments in Wadi Nisnas with a *Haganah* commander, she encountered an elderly Arab woman who burst into tears; Meir wept too. Ben-Gurion made clear a few weeks later, however, that he did not want the refugees to return until hostilities were over.[75]

Haifa's loss quickly swept up other nearby Arab communities. Jaffa suffered a similar fate. *Irgun* fighters led the offensive on 25 April with an attack on Manshiyeh, now surrounded by Tel Aviv. Mortar fire rained down while *Haganah* units attacked nearby villages from the east and south. Refugees fled south by road towards Gaza, and again by sea. Salah Khalaf recalled the panic he felt as a fifteen-year-old boy: 'I was overwhelmed by the sight of this huge mass of men, women, old people and children, struggling under the weight of suitcases or bundles, making their way painfully down to the wharfs of Jaffa in a sinister tumult. Cries mingled with moaning and sobs, all punctuated by deafening explosions.'[76] Another man, named Fayiz, left his home the day the *Irgun* assault began:

Everyone was wailing and weeping and there was total chaos. My brother and I ran all over the town trying to find a truck but there weren't any. They were all either full of people or burned out. There were many dead donkeys too, with their trailers still attached to them, lying in the road. Next we went to the sea but clearly there was no chance of escape there. In the end we found a truck and our family with three others climbed on. We had one suitcase with us: everything else was left at home . . . It took us seven hours to get to Majdal [nearly

30 miles away] where we slept the night. Early next morning we travelled on to Gaza. There we were: us and a suitcase.[77]

Shafiq al-Hout, a sixteen-year-old, crowded onto the deck of a Greek ship bound for Beirut. 'I remember watching Jaffa disappear from sight until there was nothing but water all around,' he reminisced. 'It never occurred to me that I would never see it again.'[78] By 14 May, when *Haganah* units entered Jaffa, only 3,000–4,000 residents remained. The city was not conquered, but rather surrendered. At first victorious *Irgun* fighters 'pillaged only dresses, blouses and ornaments for their girlfriends. But this discrimination was soon abandoned. Everything that was movable was carried from Jaffa – furniture, carpets, pictures, crockery and pottery, jewellery and cutlery. The occupied parts of Jaffa were stripped ... What could not be taken away was smashed. Windows, pianos, fittings and lamps went in an orgy of destruction.'[79] Even though Arab Jaffa had relatively strong local institutions, social tensions undermined their effectiveness in the panicky and traumatic circumstances of all-out war.[80]

Safad, in eastern Galilee, was the next 'mixed' town to go, conquered by 10 May, its Arab neighbourhoods emptied as their inhabitants were driven out in their thousands, Piper Cub planes bombing the surrounding *wadis* to hasten the exodus. The fighting there was 'an especially good example of the state of weakness, anarchy, breakdown, and collapse that generally prevailed among the Palestinians'.[81] Yigal Allon, commanding the Palmah, organized a 'whispering campaign' to frighten Palestinians into leaving the area, telling local Jewish *mukhtars* to warn their Arab contacts to flee while they still could before Jewish reinforcements arrived. The ploy worked: tens of thousands left their homes and abandoned villages were burned. In Beisan the remaining inhabitants were expelled across the Jordan or to Nazareth. Acre, besieged and demoralized by the fate of Haifa, fell too, its defenders divided between supporters and opponents of the mufti. Only 3,000 of its 13,400 residents remained, and others left after the conquest.[82] Hava Keller, a young Polish-born woman serving with the *Haganah*, went into an Arab apartment that had just been abandoned and was disturbed to see a pair of baby shoes, which made her wonder about the child's fate years later.[83]

The *Haganah* took the offensive and made other gains in areas across the country where the armies of the neighbouring Arab states were expected to invade when the British left. In the south, on 11 May, the Givati brigade raided Beit Daras and the residents fled to nearby Isdud. In an adjacent village the *mukhtar*'s house was blown up and four people were executed. 'Now it is a mass psychosis and an all-out evacuation', *Haganah* intelligence reported. 'Arabs have abandoned hamlets before the Jews took any action against them, only on the basis of the rumours that they were about to be attacked.'[84] By mid-May, 250,000–300,000 Palestinians had already fled or been expelled from their homes.

INVASION, INDEPENDENCE, CATASTROPHE

The second stage of the war began on 15 May. It was then, according to plan, that the British finally quit. High Commissioner Cunningham departed by launch from Haifa harbour, the formality of the occasion masking what was an ignominious departure after thirty years, the country already engulfed in war. The previous evening at a ceremony in the Tel Aviv museum, the sovereign state of Israel was solemnly proclaimed – the crowning achievement of the Zionist movement half a century after its founding congress – as David Ben-Gurion read out the declaration of independence on behalf of the provisional government, prompting feelings of 'elation', recalled his colleague David Horowitz, 'mingling with dread'.[85] The new Jewish state was recognized within hours by both the US and the USSR. Ben-Gurion was declared prime minister and minister of defence.

Units of four Arab armies began to invade, having waited scrupulously for the Mandate to end. The collapse of the Palestinians, the failure of the ALA and swelling refugee flows had left the Arab states little choice but the intervention by Jordan, Iraq, Syria and Egypt was chaotic in conception and execution, the gap between rhetoric and reality embarrassingly wide. Abdel-Rahman Azzam Pasha, the Egyptian head of the Arab League, had warned of a conflict that 'would be a war of extermination and momentous massacre', though his words were distorted or misquoted to occupy a prominent place in the Zionist narrative of the conflict.[86] The Syrian president, Shukri al-Quwatli, invoked the memory of the long Arab struggle against the Crusaders. Egypt announced it was acting 'to re-establish security and order and put an end to the massacres perpetrated by Zionist terrorist bands against Arabs and humanity'.[87] The Jews, with 'no real knowledge of the Arabs' true military capabilities . . . took Arab propaganda literally, preparing for the worst and reacting accordingly'.[88] In the aftermath of the Holocaust, the sense of existential threat was all too real.

Initial Arab plans focused on invading northern Palestine with a view to reaching Haifa. Lebanon had been expected to take part but opted out at the last minute. Far more significantly, King Abdullah announced that Jordanian forces would head for Ramallah, Nablus and Hebron on what later became known as the West Bank. This suggested that he was seeking to *avoid* war with the Jews by refraining from entering areas allotted to them by the UN such as Netanya and Hadera. It appeared to confirm suspicions about collusion between the Hashemites, British and Zionists and, in turn, caused a change of plan in Cairo. The Egyptians had originally planned to move forces up the coast towards Gaza, Isdud and perhaps to Tel Aviv. But now, concerned about Hashemite ambitions, they added a second invasion route that would take their forces, via Beersheba, east to the Hebron area – an obvious attempt to deny it to Abdullah. By the end of May, however, they had run out of steam on both axes. The Israelis encountered only Iraqi and Syrian forces in the Jordan Valley – also outside the area allotted the Jewish state by the UN – but no Egyptians at this stage. Iraqi units based in Qalqilya did nothing, telling puzzled Palestinians who asked why: '*maku awamir*' – Iraqi Arabic dialect for 'we have no orders'.[89] Token Saudi and Yemeni forces were also deployed.

Palestinian fighters were helped in Jerusalem by the arrival on 19 May of Jordanian Arab Legion forces, who were greeted by jubilant crowds. Armoured cars negotiated the alleys of the Old City and strengthened its defences. Following the destruction of two of the Jewish Quarter's ancient synagogues, the Jews surrendered. The *Haganah* fighters were taken as prisoners of war to Transjordan and the civilians were released. Looting ensued. 'The bombardment had destroyed the houses . . . what was left was still plundered, swarms of

Arab children and women came into the quarter, most of them from the surrounding villages and tore out window shutters, half-burned doors, railings etc. and took them away either to sell them in the Arab market or out of the city to their villages.'[90]

In Jerusalem and elsewhere the Arab invasion posed difficult challenges for Jewish forces. But it did not save the Palestinians. On the contrary, it worsened their plight because more territory was lost and more Arabs became refugees. Understanding of the war has deepened as archives have opened and old narratives have been challenged, but it is hard to better the conclusion reached by the British author Christopher Sykes in the mid-1960s: 'The unpreparedness, disunity and even mutual hostility of the Arab forces, in contrast with the single-mindedness of their enemies, ruled out the possibility of their victory.'[91] Musa al-Alami, Ben-Gurion's Palestinian interlocutor from the 1930s, put it even more succinctly: 'It was obvious that our [Arab] aims in the battle were diverse, while the aim of the Jews was solely to win it.'[92] In the words of the Palestinian scholar Bayan Nuwayhid al-Hout: 'While the Jewish forces fought, dreaming of their state, the Arab leaders ordered their armies to fight a limited war, dreaming of and praying for a ceasefire.'[93]

Israeli forces conquered more territory. In the month after 15 May the Alexandroni Brigade cleared more than sixty Arab villages on the coastal plain between Tel Aviv and Haifa.[94] In Tantura on the 22nd, fourteen Israelis and more than seventy villagers were killed.[95] Later accounts reported summary executions, with one researcher claiming that up to 225 Palestinians had been murdered.[96] On the 31st, the death of Ali Hassan Salameh, who had replaced Husseini as commander of the AHJ, was another blow to Palestinian morale.

On 10 June a four-week UN-supervised truce began.[97] The next stage of the fighting – dubbed the 'Ten Days war' – took place in mid-July. By then there were 65,000 men under arms in the newly named Israel Defence Forces (IDF), which had absorbed the *Haganah* and Palmah as well as the 'dissidents' of the *Irgun* and Lehi in the wake of the *Altalena* affair (this had involved IDF troops firing on a ship that was delivering weapons to the *Irgun* off Tel Aviv, resulting in the deaths of nineteen men). Ben-Gurion was hailed for this brief but brutal assertion of power in the very first weeks of the new state.

The Israelis made new conquests in Galilee and in the Tel Aviv–

Jerusalem 'corridor' that the UN had allocated to the Arabs. In the north, Palestinians who had fled were told they could not return to their villages. Nazareth was taken on 16 July, though its inhabitants were not expelled, probably because of Ben-Gurion's sensitivity about its Christian holy places. Saffuriyah, a large village nearby, fell the day before, its frightened population swollen by refugees who had arrived from Shafa Amr to the west. Its inhabitants were to long remember their terror when the Israelis dropped bombs from two Auster crop-dusting planes.[98] In Aylut, Israeli forces blew up houses where weapons were found and killed sixteen young men in the olive groves.[99]

The most significant event of this period was 'Operation Dani'. This was intended to capture the Arab towns of Lydda and Ramle – allotted to the Arab state – in the centre of the country, as well as to clear the last Arab-held parts of the adjacent Tel Aviv–Jerusalem road. In Lydda on 12 July, Israeli forces who had believed that the battle was over encountered a small Arab Legion force entering the town, triggering what looked like an armed uprising. During the ensuing firefight about 250 Palestinians sheltering in a mosque compound were killed by men of the IDF's Yiftah Brigade. It was 'a sign of panic, of a lack of confidence in the troops' ability to hold the town, of their inexperience in governing civilians'.[100] Later eyewitness accounts by Israeli participants ensured that the incident gained lasting notoriety.[101] It was the biggest atrocity of the war.

Equally notorious was the subsequent expulsion of 50,000 Palestinians on Ben-Gurion's orders to the Israeli commander, Yitzhak Rabin, who later described how the prime minister gestured with his hand and said brusquely: 'Remove them.'[102] Ramle's residents were bussed out, but their neighbours from Lydda were forced to walk miles in punishing summer heat, in the middle of the Ramadan fast, to the front lines, where the Arab Legion struggled to provide shelter and supplies. Unknown numbers of refugees died from exhaustion or dehydration. George Habash, a medical student from Lydda's Greek Orthodox community, never forgot what he witnessed: 'Thirty thousand people walking, crying, screaming with terror ... women carrying babies on their arms and children clinging to their [skirts], with the Israeli soldiers pointing their weapons at their backs ...

some people fell by the wayside, and some did not rise again. It was terrible.'[103] Rabin wrote in his memoirs (which were initially censored, though the original version was subsequently leaked):

> 'Driving out' is a term with a harsh ring. Psychologically, this was one of the most difficult actions we undertook. The population of Lod did not leave willingly. There was no way of avoiding the use of force and warning shots in order to make the inhabitants march the 10 to 15 miles to the point where they met up with the legion.[104]

It is estimated that a further 100,000 Palestinians became refugees in the course of those ten days alone.[105] 'The feeling was bad but we deceived ourselves, thinking we would be back next week', recalled Abu Naim, from Ijzim, south of Haifa.

> We did not feel as bad as we should have because we thought we would be back in a week or two. What happened? People imagined that this was temporary, as if it was an outcome of rain or flood. We will move for a week and then the flood will be over. This was the feeling that led to this catastrophe.[106]

Under UN pressure, a new, open-ended truce came into effect on 18 July. Israel continued to launch operations but claimed they were not violations of this truce. Several more 'clusters' of Arab population were expelled in late August. In September the Israelis faced international embarrassment when the Stern Gang – still operating independently from the IDF on the grounds that Jerusalem was not part of Israel – assassinated the UN mediator, the Swedish Count Folke Bernadotte, during a visit to the city, which under his plan, as in the original partition scheme, was to remain under international supervision.

THIRD ROUND

In a third round of fighting, from October 1948 to January 1949, Israel expelled Egyptian forces from Isdud and Majdal on the coast and in the northern Negev, and conquered more territory in Galilee. In the south Palestinians fled along with the retreating Egyptians.

Many had already left Isdud but Zarifa Atwan and her family stayed until Israeli forces arrived:

> It was so sad to see men, women, old people and children hurrying away, carrying everything they could in handcarts or cloth bundles . . . Suddenly we heard a lot of trucks coming into the village and the sound of shots being fired into the air. We could hear loudspeakers and we rushed to the village square to see what was going on. It was the Israelis and they were saying in Arabic, 'Leave your homes and go to Gaza where you will be safe. If you don't leave we will kill you.' People started to panic. Nobody knew what to do . . . Then we heard the gunshots – the Israelis had killed two men from our village at point blank range. They were lying dead on the ground in a pool of blood and their women and children were hysterical. The villagers were herded into the Israeli trucks like cattle, the killings had made them silent and obedient, everyone was in a state of complete shock. We got in the trucks too. We didn't have time to pack, all we had were the clothes we were wearing, and all around us was the sound of women wailing and the explosions of Israeli mortar fire.[107]

Israeli eyewitness accounts of expulsions of Palestinians are rare. Strikingly, one of the most vivid is in a work of fiction, *Khirbet Khiza*, by the writer S. Yizhar, who served as an IDF intelligence officer and presented an emblematic version of the capture of a village near Majdal and the expulsion of women, children and the elderly.[108] 'Two thousand years of exile,' the narrator reflects in brusque, colloquial Hebrew. 'The whole story. Jews being killed. Europe. We were the masters now.' It was a short story that left a long trail of impassioned controversy.[109] In later years, as taboos were eroded, other veterans of 1948 went public and described their own real experiences. Uri Avnery, who also fought on the southern front at this time, reflected later on how 'we moved from village to village without thinking about the people who lived there hours or days before, their lives, their past . . . Bayt Daras, Bayt Affa . . . for us they were all the same, poor, dirty alien villages.'[110]

Beersheba fell to the Israelis on 21 October, its remaining residents expelled to Gaza, which now teemed with refugees huddled under trees and sheltering in schools and mosques.[111] Villages were abandoned before any fighting or were emptied by firing a few mortar or machine-gun rounds to trigger an exodus. Expulsions took place, though written orders were rare.[112] Refugees who fled in October but returned home in November were rounded up and expelled, their villages burned and razed. At Dawamiya in the Hebron hills, Israeli forces massacred eighty to a hundred Palestinians, including women and children, at the end of October, prompting a flurry of inconclusive internal inquiries. Israeli documents leave little doubt about the fact of the atrocity, though Arab sources claimed far higher figures. It was the worst mass killing of the final stage of the war.

'Operation Hiram' saw new Israeli conquests in eastern Galilee – allotted to the Arab state by the UN – in fighting against now demoralized ALA forces. Several villages across the border in Lebanon were also occupied. In Huleh, Israeli troops killed dozens of local men. Atrocities in Eilabun, Safsaf and Jish helped precipitate the flight of about 30,000 more Palestinians, mostly to Lebanon. It may not have been formal policy to expel Arabs, but many were 'encouraged' to go, especially after a meeting between Ben-Gurion and the local IDF commander, who then instructed his units: 'Do all in your power for a quick and immediate cleansing of the conquered areas of all the hostile elements in line with the orders that have been issued. The inhabitants of the conquered areas should be assisted to leave.'[113]

Outcomes varied according to local circumstances, including the nature of relations with neighbouring Jewish settlements: Jisr al-Zarka and Faradis had long supplied workers for the vineyards of Zichron Yaakov and Binyamina and were not depopulated. Druze villages were all spared, while Christians were generally treated better than Muslims. Abu Ghosh near Jerusalem, known for links to the *Haganah*, was left largely unscathed while other nearby villages were emptied. Fassuta in Galilee surrendered without resistance. Its residents handed over their weapons to the IDF and may have been saved from expulsion by the intervention of a Jew who worked for a cigarette company and wanted to continue buying the local tobacco crop. Neighbouring Deir al-Qasi, by contrast, was completely deserted.[114] In the Nazareth district, the inhabitants of twenty out of twenty-four villages were able to stay put; around Safad and Tiberias the majority did not. Overall Palestinian casualties, complied by different sources, are estimated to have been 13,000; the Egyptians 1,400, and the Iraqis and Jordanians several hundred. Israeli fatalities were 4,000 soldiers and 2,400 civilians, around 1 per cent of the entire Jewish population.[115]

Israelis felt little regret for the departure of the Palestinians whether they were driven out or fled for their lives. Mordechai Bar-On, an IDF company commander who fought on the Egyptian front that autumn, described watching from a distance as thousands of refugees trudged across sand dunes near Gaza, out of range.

> Nevertheless, I positioned a machine gun on one of the hills and emptied a whole belt of bullets in their direction. Nobody could have been hurt, not did I intend to hurt anyone. It was a symbolic act, a message to the Palestinians: now that you have left there is no way back, you will have to stay away.[116]

The fate of the Palestinians in 1948 was a hotly disputed issue from the start, entangled in propaganda, polemics and white-hot anger. But the *facts* about the central event of the *Nakba* are less contested than ever, with figures ranging from 700,000 to 750,000 for the number of Palestinians who were expelled or fled. According to one modern study, relying largely on oral testimony, expulsions took place in 225 localities.[117] In many cases frightened residents left believing that their absence would be temporary. In the south the *mukhtar* of Kibbutz Negba advised the villagers of neighbouring Bayt Affa to fly white flags. The *mukhtar* of Bayt Affa refused and the village was then attacked and depopulated.[118] No evidence has been found to support the long-standing Israeli claim that the invading Arab states called on the Palestinians to flee, in radio broadcasts or otherwise.[119] 'In general, throughout the war, the final and decisive precipitant to flight in most places was [Jewish] . . . attack or the inhabitants' fear of imminent attack', Morris concluded.[120] Even at the time, some Jews rejected the official claim that the Palestinians were entirely responsible for their own fate, and pointed to decisions made by the Israeli government. 'Arabs remained in Nazareth and in Majdal Ashkelon because we wanted them to stay', observed Eliezer Peri, editor of *al-Hamishmar*, the newspaper of the Marxist-Zionist Mapam movement. 'And if they didn't stay put in other places, supporters of the idea of transfer played a significant role – enough said.'[121] In an important sense, though, the precise circumstances do not alter the big picture of what had become a zero-sum conflict by 1948. In Bar-On's words:

> Beyond the details on the manner in which Palestinians had to leave this or that village, one must simply acknowledge that the tragedy would not have occurred had the Zionists never arrived in Palestine. If the Jews at the end of the nineteenth century had not embarked on a project of reassembling the Jewish people in their 'promised land', all the refugees languishing in the camps would still be living in the villages from which they fled or were expelled. Second, one must realise that when people flee out of fear and terror their flight is hardly voluntary.[122]

The key decision, however, was and remains the Israeli government's flat refusal to allow the refugees to return to their homes and land. That was the defining characteristic of the 1948 war and its aftermath.

By July 1949, when Israel signed armistice agreements with Egypt, Jordan, Lebanon and Syria, it controlled 78 per cent of Mandatory Palestine – a considerable improvement on the 55 per cent it had been allocated by the UN twenty months previously. The West Bank, including East Jerusalem with its Jewish, Muslim and Christian holy places, was occupied by Jordan. The ceasefire line, marked in green ink on UN maps, became known as the 'green line'. The Gaza Strip was administered by Egypt. Palestinian political divisions and social and military weakness, at this desperately low point, were exacerbated by the increasingly open rivalry between these two Arab states: King Farouk backed the short-lived All-Palestine government run by the mufti in Gaza, while King Abdullah convened the Jericho Congress to call for the unification of the West and East banks of the Jordan. The map of the Middle East had changed. Israel was a reality. Arab Palestine was no more.

8

1949–1953

'The contemporary history of the Palestinians turns on a key date: 1948. That year a country and its people disappeared from maps and dictionaries. "The Palestinian people does not exist," said the new masters, and henceforth the Palestinians would be referred to by general, conveniently vague terms, as either "refugees" or in the case of a small minority that had managed to escape the generalised expulsion, "Israeli Arabs". A long absence was beginning.'

Elias Sanbar[1]

THE MEANING OF THE DISASTER

In the devastating aftermath of 1948, Palestinians found it hard to grasp the dimensions of the catastrophe that had befallen them, their individual plight masking the bigger picture, their voices barely heard. In the course of twenty months about half the pre-war Arab population had fled or been driven out; 350–400 villages had been depopulated, and many destroyed or settled by Jewish immigrants. In places, families were divided by the armistice lines, which left a minority of 156,000 Palestinians in the new Jewish state, 15 per cent of its population. Of these, 75,000 people were categorized as internal refugees, or, in the bizarre terminology that began to be used, 'present absentees'[2] who had lost homes and land. 'How can I not call it a *Nakba*?' asked the historian Arif al-Arif – rhetorically – on the opening pages of his monumental work on the subject, 'when we Arabs and the Palestinians in particular experienced a disaster of a kind we never faced down all the centuries: our homeland was stolen and we were expelled from our homes and we lost many of our sons.'[3] Others likened it to an earthquake or a flood. But comparisons with natural disasters only worked so far: 'After floods, the waters recede', reflected the Israeli anthropologist Efrat Ben-Zeev. 'But after war, the conquerors do not necessarily withdraw.'[4]

Outside Israeli territory, refugees were scattered in the West Bank, occupied by Jordan, in the Egyptian-administered Gaza Strip, its original population more than doubled, in makeshift camps in Lebanon and Syria as well as further afield in Egypt and Iraq. The majority were uneducated farmers. Initially they were cared for by the International Committee of the Red Cross, and from May 1950 by the United Nations Relief and Works Agency (UNRWA). In some places they ended up only a short distance from the homes they had abandoned: Palestinians from the Jerusalem area found themselves in tents in Dehaisheh, south of Bethlehem; people from central Palestine in Jalazoun, near Ramallah. 'Probably the most affecting sight in the hills is at Bir Zeit, north of Jerusalem', *The Economist* reported in October 1948,

> where about 14,000 destitutes are ranged on terrace upon terrace under the olive trees – a tree to a family – and are forced to consume the bark and burn the living wood that has meant a livelihood for generations. Here and at Nablus, there is at present so little milk for babies that abortion seems the kindest way out.[5]

Refugees from Isdud and southern villages were a few miles away in Jabaliya and Shati, on the site of former British army camps on Gaza's coast. Um Jabr Wishah, from Bayt Affa, lost her firstborn son in the harsh conditions of the Nusseirat camp.[6] 'East of Majdal many dwell in booths made of sackcloth', an Israeli agent reported in December 1948. 'Elsewhere they have erected tin huts. Some families sell their belongings but the majority has nothing to sell. Fathers try to marry off their daughters. Prices have decreased . . . and often no bride price is paid since the parents are glad to be relieved of feeding superfluous mouths. Many women and children go begging.'[7] The Egyptian government provided hundreds of tents but large numbers of refugees remained without shelter. Fuel was scarce so wood was taken from any available source, including railway sleepers.[8]

Palestinians from Galilee were in three camps near Tyre in Lebanon, fifteen miles north of the border. They lacked basic amenities – running water, electricity, sewage systems – even when the tents were replaced by simple houses of mud bricks and corrugated-iron roofs.[9] Matar Abdelrahim arrived in Syria in November 1948: 'We felt subjugated and estranged, dependent on others for everything,' he recalled. 'We had to turn to others, even for our bread, which had once been the staple of our meals and was baked daily by our families from the wheat we had grown and harvested. Nostalgia dominated our minds and longing burned in our hearts, but in the end hunger forced us to continue living.'[10]

NO RETURN

Israel had quickly made it clear that it would not allow the refugees back. As early as June 1948 Moshe Sharett (formerly Shertok), now the foreign minister, wrote that

> the most spectacular event in the contemporary history of Palestine, in a way more spectacular than the creation of the Jewish state, is the wholesale evacuation of its Arab population. The opportunities opened up ... for a lasting and radical solution of the most vexing problem of the Jewish state are so far-reaching as to take one's breath away.

Reversion to the status quo was 'unthinkable'.[11] Chaim Weizmann, who was soon to take on the largely ceremonial role of Israel's president, called it 'a miraculous simplification of our task'. In July it became official policy to oppose refugee return. Sharett told Israeli diplomats that the question could only be decided in the context of a peace settlement with the Arab states, and in conjunction with the issue of the confiscation of Jewish property in Arab countries. Shortly afterwards he explained the position to Weizmann:

> With regard to the refugees, we are determined to be adamant while the war lasts. Once the return tide starts, it will be impossible to stem it, and it will prove our undoing. As for the future, we are equally

determined – without, for the time being, formally closing the door to any eventuality – to explore all possibilities of *getting rid, once and for all, of the huge Arab minority which originally threatened us* [emphasis added]. What can be achieved in this period of storm and stress will be quite unattainable once conditions get stabilised.[12]

In September Yosef Weitz of the Jewish National Fund was appointed to chair a 'transfer committee'. Weitz, anxious to block refugee returns, had lobbied the *Haganah* to evict Arab farmers in the Beisan area and near Haifa, and had pressed for the destruction of abandoned villages unless they could be used for Jewish settlement. A second committee concluded that the refugees were responsible for their own flight and must not be allowed back, and drew up plans to resettle them in Arab countries.[13] The official Israeli narrative about the causes of the Palestinian exodus took hold quickly and was reflected by influential foreign journalists such as Kenneth Bilby of the *New York Times*.[14] In mid-September – the day before he was assassinated by the Stern Gang – Count Bernadotte described the Palestinian exodus accurately, as resulting from 'panic created by fighting . . . by rumours concerning real or alleged acts of terrorism, or expulsion'. It would, he argued, 'be an offence against the principles of elemental justice if these innocent victims of the conflict were denied the right to return to their homes while Jewish immigrants flow into Palestine, and, indeed, at least offer the threat of permanent replacement of the Arab refugees who have been rooted in the land for centuries'.[15] In December the UN General Assembly passed Resolution 194, which made the return of the refugees a prerequisite for a peace agreement and required compensation to be paid to those who opted not to exercise that right. Wrangling over refugee return led nowhere. And the argument about linking the issue to a comprehensive settlement was partly disingenuous: Israel knew that peace would not be achieved with the Arab states without some kind of resolution of the refugee problem.[16]

Refugees did manage to come back after the war but anyone who tried to enter Israel without permission was labelled an 'infiltrator' – a novel use of language to sanitize reality. In the years to come the Hebrew word *mistanenim* ('infiltrators') was used to describe

Palestinians who were now seen as an *external* threat and subsumed under the general category of unrelenting, undifferentiated Arab enmity. This perception was especially true of the large number of Jewish immigrants who arrived after the war. These newcomers were

> unfamiliar with pre-state realities and regarded Arabs as an evil presence lurking beyond the armistice lines, eager to undermine the new life they had laboriously begun to build. They did not see a struggle between two peoples, Jews and Arabs, for the same turf; they saw an Arab–Israeli conflict, a clash between Israel and the Arab states.[17]

War had hardened hearts. 'For the Arabs who had gambled on destroying our new state there could be no way back',[18] wrote Mordechai Bar-On, who served in the IDF near Gaza in late 1948. Many Palestinians who risked their lives trying to cross the ceasefire lines after 1948 were peasants trying to reach their homes and harvest crops, driven by hunger, attachment to their land and a burning sense of injustice.[19] Returning Palestinians did carry out acts of murder and sabotage, but smuggling and theft, driven by destitution and despair, were far more common. 'We came to Lebanon and life was not what we expected it to be,' as one refugee in Beirut's Shatila camp put it. 'Conditions were bad. We had nothing to live on. I became desperate and one night I decided to leave my family and go back to the village to get some money I had buried outside my house before the Jews attacked . . . But I never reached my village. I was caught by the Jews and put in jail.'[20] Late in 1948 Palestinian women were being forced to earn their livelihood in brothels in Beirut, while 'more than 400 babies' in the camps around Tyre and Sidon had died of cold.[21] The Lebanese security service arrested many Palestinians, including the Communists Emile Habibi and Emil Touma.[22] The family of the future poet Mahmoud Darwish, who fled al-Birwa in western Galilee in June 1948, managed to return a year later and relocated to nearby Deir al-Asad. By then al-Birwa had been destroyed and new settlements established on its lands. The Nasrallah family, Christians from Shafa Amr, dodged Israeli border patrols searching for 'infiltrators' and made it back safely across the border from Lebanon, where they had stayed with relatives.[23] Others returned by fishing boat from Tyre and landed at a Jewish settlement north of Acre, ironically named

Shavei Zion – the Returnees to Zion.[24] In all about 20,000 people were able to get home, particularly to Galilee, but many more failed. Several thousand Palestinians lost their lives in the attempt.[25]

'A DEFEATED MINORITY OF A DEFEATED PEOPLE'[26]

Israel's declaration of independence hailed the rebirth of the Jewish people in its ancient homeland, and promised equality for all citizens. But the state had been born in war and moulded by Arab hostility throughout the Mandate era. Security was the main prism through which the government viewed the Arab minority. Jewish immigration and economic development were its most urgent priorities. Building this new nation meant primarily the 'ingathering of the exiles' (*kibbutz galuyot*) in fulfilment of Zionist ideology. British restrictions on immigration had been lifted immediately. In July 1950 the Law of Return, a key piece of legislation, granted Jews the world over the automatic right to live in Israel, privileging their rights over native non-Jews. With the gates now wide open, the Jewish population rapidly swelled to 1.5 million by 1951, most of the first newcomers arriving from Arab countries such as Iraq and Yemen, where animosity towards Jews and levels of persecution had grown because of the Palestine disaster. The absorption of Holocaust survivors and the memory of the recent war, with over 6,000 Israeli dead and thousands injured, served as an unshakeable justification for Israel's independence and the priority and privileges given to Jews. 'There are not two waves of immigration [*aliyot*] to this country', as Ben-Gurion put it bluntly. 'There's only one, of Jews. And there's only one settlement project, of Jews, on this land.'[27] Citizenship for Arabs was emptied of much of its content.

Israel's government recognized that it was dealing with a traumatized community. 'The people who remained were like a headless body', wrote Yehoshua ('Josh') Palmon, the *Haganah* intelligence operative who became the prime minister's adviser on Arab affairs.[28] Forced exile had created more than a demographic disaster. Palestine's Arab social, political and religious elite had gone. Associations, clubs, cafes and libraries – public and private – had disappeared with the majority of the people who used them. By 1949 Israel's National Library had collected 30,000 books, newspapers and other items from the abandoned homes of Palestinians who had fled West Jerusalem; they were eventually labelled 'AP' – 'abandoned property'.[29] Five of the eleven cities that came under Israeli control – Safed, Majdal, Tiberias, Beisan and Beersheba – were emptied of Arabs. Five others – Jaffa, Haifa, Lydda, Ramle and Acre – almost completely so. It was the same story in West Jerusalem. The near total departure of the more affluent and educated urban population meant the loss of 'the intellectual core of Palestinian society'[30] and the destruction of the commercial and manufacturing bases of the Arab economy. The only Arabic newspaper to survive the *Nakba* was the Communists' *al-Ittihad*. In the words of Sabri Jiryis from Galilee, who wrote the first in-depth studies of the Palestinian citizens of Israel, 'the Arab masses who stayed behind and who had been changed overnight from a dominant majority to a minority living under the rule of an alien people suddenly found themselves without leaders or direction. The Israeli authorities exploited this situation and based their policy on it.'[31] The vast majority were illiterate villagers and agricultural workers.

Like Palmon, Israeli Jews involved in Arab affairs were often security-minded veterans of the *Haganah*, Jewish National Fund land purchasing or the Jewish Agency, ensuring continuity at a time of epochal change. Jaffa-born Ezra Danin, a key figure in the Shai intelligence service, sat on Weitz's 'transfer committee' and dismissed criticism from the left about policy towards the Arabs. 'If we had pitied the inhabitants of Lydda and Ramle and let them stay put, the [Arab] Legion might have been able to conquer Tel Aviv, and you can imagine the picture,' he said.[32] Bechor Shitrit, minister for minority affairs in the provisional government, was an Arabic speaker who had been born to Moroccan parents in Tiberias. However, his arguments were often overruled, and his ministry was quickly disbanded. Palmon described himself as a 'wolf in sheep's clothing – harsh but outwardly decent' towards Arabs, and expressed regret that more infiltrators had not been expelled in the immediate post-war period. 'I opposed the integration of Arabs into Israeli society,' he said. 'I preferred separate development.'[33] The General Security Service (Shin

Bet) was established in 1949 to handle internal security and counter-intelligence and was soon playing an important role dealing with Arabs. Yehoshua Magidov, a Shin Bet officer in Galilee, was a native of Yavniel, one of the area's oldest Jewish settlements, and famed for his knowledge of Arabic dialects and customs.[34] Colleagues included Giora Zeid and Oded Yanai, who had persuaded Druze leaders to come over to the Jewish side in 1948. It was said of Zeid – whose father had been killed by Palestinian rebels in 1938 – that for 'most of his adult life, he worked to curb the freedom of Israeli Arabs, but . . . he considered himself their friend'.[35]

The majority of Israel's Arabs – in Galilee, the central 'Triangle' area along the Jordanian border north-east of Tel Aviv, and in the Negev – lived under military rule from the summer of 1948. In October, when the military government was established, it employed two key provisions of the 1945 British Defence Emergency Regulations: the authority to declare any area closed to the public and to impose a curfew. These draconian laws had been fiercely opposed by Jewish lawyers in Mandatory times. A new regulation allowed the minister of agriculture to allocate abandoned Arab land – belonging to those defined as 'absentees' – to Jews. Other legislation followed. A new post of 'custodian' of absentee property was created. Arab movements in and out of closed areas were regulated under a system of checkpoints, travel permits, curfews and other restrictions. Each permit, printed in Hebrew – and thus illegible to the vast majority of Arabs – required the approval of the Shin Bet, which used them as leverage and a way of recruiting collaborators. In December 1948 and January 1949, the agency issued permits for under a third of 773 applicants, rejecting the rest without explanation.[36] Anton Shammas, from Fassuta, poignantly described his father 'learning Hebrew for beginners, as if he were an "Oleh Hadash", a new immigrant to his own country . . . with the aid of books which were illustrated with water towers and ploughed furrows, depicting a lifestyle in which he had no share'.[37] The ministries of education, welfare, interior and religious affairs had special sections to govern the Palestinians as a separate category. Arab teachers faced stringent security checks. Jewish education was supposed to promote 'nationalism, pioneering values, love of the country and loyalty to the state'. These requirements did not form part of the Arab curriculum.[38] Overall, the circumstances were humiliating, and options limited: 'The first priority was to survive, even if it meant bottling up existential bitterness and rage', as a modern study described the atmosphere in those years. State representatives were greeted with 'alienated courtesy, fear and contempt, all disguised in proper formal parlance. Behind closed doors different utterances reflected hopes that the need for submission to this detested fate was only temporary.'[39]

Shock and disorientation were common emotions for Palestinians on both sides of the armistice lines. Many recalled a sense of dislocation and stunned disbelief at the sheer scale of what had transpired, along with feelings of injustice, betrayal and victimization. Shame accompanied the sense of loss when refugees were accused by local people in Gaza and the West Bank of having sold their land to the Jews.[40] 'Like many of the men my father felt an overwhelming anger and frustration', wrote Abdel Bari Atwan, who grew up in Gaza's Deir al-Balah camp. 'They had been the heads of families, the providers who had status within their own community. Now ... they were reduced to living on handouts from UNRWA. Many broke down under the strain.'[41] It took time for it to sink in that the refugees were not going back. Musa al-Alami, the Jerusalem lawyer who had held talks with Ben-Gurion in the 1930s, asked a British diplomat in Beirut when the Palestinians would be able to return. 'He still remembers the shock of incredulity with which he heard the reply, given gently but decisively, that the refugees should think not of returning to their former homes, but of making a new life elsewhere', his biographer recorded. 'The Arabs had been too blind to see the truth: that the refugees would never recover their homes in what was now Israel.'[42] For Salma Khadra Jayyusi from Galilee 'the most telling feature of the 1948 debacle was the way people failed fully to apprehend its implications. Everything happened so quickly that no one believed the loss to be definitive. You cannot believe the unbelievable with ease.'[43] In later years a woman from Lifta remembered her father telling her to cover up the family's olive trees. 'It was as if we were leaving for one or two days and coming right back.'[44] Um Jabr Wishah, living in Gaza's Bureij camp, had expected to return to her village within a week after leaving it during fighting in July 1948.[45]

Life in Bureij and the other camps was hard and precarious, despite UNRWA's efforts. The agency's mission was defined as 'the repatriation, resettlement and economic and social rehabilitation of the refugees and the payment of compensation'. But conditions were overwhelming. Ordinary refugees were preoccupied with the struggle for survival.[46] And not only refugees were affected: the town of Qalqilya, self-sufficient before the war, became destitute virtually overnight, cut off from its farmlands on the coastal plain and cattle breeding and trade with Jaffa, Tel Aviv, Lydda and Ramla. People risked their lives, and occasionally lost them, stealing oranges from their own orchards, now on the other side of the barbed-wire fence that marked the border with Israel. The state of abject poverty meant there was little difference between the original townspeople and the newly arrived refugees.[47] 'Like Palestinians everywhere, people at first refused to believe what was happening to them', recalled one resident.

> People who became refugees believed that within weeks the fighting would end and they would return to their homes and their land. War always creates refugees, and refugees always go home after the war. Why should it be any different for us? Palestinians tended to think of the ordeal as a nightmare from which they expected to wake up soon.[48]

PALESTINE INTO ISRAEL

In the aftermath of the war the physical and human landscape of the country was transformed, in many places beyond recognition. The removal of 700,000-plus Arabs accelerated the long-standing trend towards segregation between the two communities. 'Henceforth the overwhelming majority of Israelis would no longer meet Arabs in the immediate vicinity of their homes', wrote Meron Benvenisti, an astute Jewish observer of the interaction between the two peoples. 'The Arabs had departed the Jewish landscape. And the violent, complex, but intimate relations between adjacent settlements or neighbourhoods had ceased to exist.'[49] In Tel Aviv there remained just one Arab village, Sheikh Muwannis, which was later swallowed up by the expanding campus of the city's university – its finest surviving house serving as the faculty staff club, along with a few rickety structures, some neglected graves 'and a few particularly robust date trees that just happened not to interfere with the parking lot'.[50] All twenty-six Arab villages in the Jaffa sub-district were depopulated or destroyed. In Jaffa itself only the Arabic names of its outlying pre-war areas – Ajami and Abu Kabir – survived. The few Arabs who had stayed put in the adjacent villages of Yazur, Beit Dajan, Yahud, Salama and Hiriyya were moved by the army into Jaffa proper, where they were resettled in a guarded compound with a few hundred native Jaffans who had not fled. Israel's first census found that altogether they numbered 3,647.[51] Most of Jaffa's old city was destroyed in 1949, paving the way for its transformation into a theme park-cum-playground for Israeli Jewish artists and bohemians.[52] On the surrounding plain, thousands of acres of Arab citrus groves were left untended in the winter of 1948 and much of the land was earmarked for construction projects or used for more lucrative field crops by Jewish farmers. Abandoned olive groves met a similar fate. The olive tree was picturesque but it was identified with the 'enemy', and seen as primitive and conservative.[53] In Acre, the remaining Arab population was moved into the old city and new housing was built on the remains of an adjacent village. The Ottoman citadel became a museum commemorating the fighters of the pre-state Jewish underground movements – with no mention of the Arabs who had been held and executed there.[54] In parallel, on a much smaller scale, the Jewish presence in Arab areas was obliterated, most strikingly in Jerusalem's Old City and in two settlements further north. The war had also seen the loss of the isolated Gush Etzion, four *kibbutzim* founded between Bethlehem and Hebron in the 1940s. In mid-May 1948 their defenders had been overrun by the Arab Legion, whose forces, with Arab irregulars, massacred those Jews who had surrendered – crying revenge, it was reported, for the Deir Yassin killings.

In Jerusalem, 30,000 Palestinian refugees took refuge in the Old City. Along with the rest of the eastern side of town, under Jordanian control, it was cut off from the western side by no-man's-land that was bordered by barbed wire, minefields and concrete anti-sniper walls, breached by one official crossing point – the Mandelbaum Gate – on the 'seam' between the two sides. Once a fortnight a convoy of Israeli armoured buses was allowed through to resupply the Israel-held enclave on Mount Scopus. Foreign diplomats, clergymen and pilgrims were able to cross but ordinary Arabs and Israelis could not. Many of the shops, clubs, cafes, schools and restaurants that had been an essential part of Arab lives in Jerusalem were out of reach. Jaffa and Haifa were now in another country – an enemy country. All but two of the forty Arab villages in the Jerusalem sub-district that remained on the Israeli side of the border after 1949 had their populations evicted. The nearest sizeable Israeli Arab community to what had been declared the country's capital was Abu Ghosh, the village off the main road to Tel Aviv which had long had a reputation for good relations – a thinly veiled euphemism for collaboration – with the Jews. Beit Safafa, on Jerusalem's southern edge, was divided between Israel and Jordan, separated by 'a shoulder-high barrier of bedraggled barbed wire'.[55] In Israeli West Jerusalem, the once-Arab neighbourhoods of Qatamon and Talbiyeh kept their original names for everyday usage – the grandiose official Hebrew replacements of Gonen and Kommemiut never catching on. Sheikh Badr was occupied by Jews and eventually surrounded by new buildings, its wheat fields transformed into a city park named for a foreign Jewish philanthropist. Its name was changed to Givat Ram and it finally disappeared without trace. Deir Yassin became Givat Shaul, despite the objections of Martin Buber and other scholars who urged Ben-Gurion to leave it desolate as a monument to the massacre that had played such an important role in triggering the Arab exodus.[56] The now separate parts of the city turned away from each other. Tourist maps printed in East Jerusalem – its importance downgraded under Jordanian rule – showed the Israeli side as a blank white space, as if there was nothing there.[57] Haifa's Arab population was reduced from 70,000 to 3,500, mostly concentrated in Wadi Nisnas.

After 1948 the majority of Israel's Arab population lived in a hundred or so homogeneous villages. In April 1950 Jaffa was incorporated into Tel Aviv municipality and formally subordinated to its larger neighbour. The following year the five still 'mixed' cities of Tel Aviv-Jaffa, Lod (formerly Lydda), Ramle, Acre and Haifa had a total Arab population of 20,000 – 12 per cent of the total, though even there Arabs and Jews tended to live in separate neighbourhoods.[58] Only Nazareth, its pre-1948 population swollen by refugees from Haifa,

Acre and Galilee, was still an exclusively Arab town. Not long afterwards a Jewish journalist observed that most Jews knew less about it
than they did about Rangoon or Saigon.[59] The two peoples lost touch.
Sarah Ozacky-Lazar, growing up in a family of Holocaust survivors
in the Tel Aviv suburb of Yad Eliahu, knew her neighbourhood by its
old Arab name of Zablawi and saw traces of orange groves, fields and
old wells hidden among clusters of prickly pears before they were
erased by new buildings and roads. She studied Arabic at school but
never met an Arab.[60] 'I never spoke to an Arab', observed another
Jewish woman of similar background.

> I didn't know any Arabs. I didn't know what they feel, what their life
> is like, their reality, their emotions. I mean I saw people, you know,
> building houses and doing all our dirty work, but I wanted to meet
> somebody on a personal, on a social basis, and no-one in my family,
> in my immediate or even wider circle – my neighbours, my acquaint-
> ances, my friends – no-one knew Arabs. And I started feeling very
> very bad – you know, you live in a country, 20 per cent of the popula-
> tion is Palestinian, and we have no contact whatsoever with them.[61]

Abandoned Arab villages were transformed into Jewish settlements, or blown up and bulldozed, like Ajur, their ruins buried under
newly planted forests – later the theme of a famous and suggestive
short story by the Israeli writer A. B. Yehoshua.[62] The systematic
destruction of remaining structures began in earnest in July 1949,
often at night and usually attracting little attention. Half a century
later all that remained were 'a few layers of weathered stone, a half-
buried arch, a broken millstone. In some places a few structures still
remain – neglected mosques, school buildings, imposing houses reno-
vated by Israelis – and seven villages completely escaped destruction
because Israelis found them picturesque enough to preserve.'[63]
Twenty-five of the twenty-seven Arab villages in the Tiberias area
were destroyed.[64] Others, like Ain Karim or Malha on the western
side of Jerusalem, or Ain Hawd near the coast, were preserved and
taken over by Jews soon after their original Palestinian residents had
fled.[65] Arab houses in Israel were to become, and remained, a byword
for stylish, spacious living – a rare compliment to a now minority
culture.

WHAT'S IN A NAME?

Between October 1948 and August 1949, 109 new Jewish settlements were established. Most were set up on the lands, and many in the actual houses, of former Arab villages. In many cases the Hebrew names they were given followed the previous Arab ones because of the belief that the Arab name had in turn preserved evidence of Jewish settlement in biblical times or later. Thus Saffuriya, near Nazareth, became the Hebrew Tzipori, its Hebrew name before the Arab conquest of Palestine in the seventh century; Suba near Jerusalem became Sova; Beit Dajan, east of Jaffa – Bet Dagan; al-Zib near the Lebanese border – Kibbutz Gesher HaZiv; Ain Karim became Ein Kerem; Ain Hawd, Ein Hod. S'as'a in northern Galilee saw its guttural double Arabic 'ayin' replaced by the softer Hebrew 'aleph' to become Kibbutz Sasa; Lubya disappeared but became Lavi; Nuris vanished, to be replaced by Nurit; and so on. Other new names were chosen by association: Moshav Eilanit ('tree' in Hebrew) was built on the lands of al-Shajara ('tree' in Arabic).[66] Jaffa's Qassam junction became the more mellifluous Kesem ('charm') in Hebrew; nearby Salama, Kfar Shalem. 'Modern Jaffa was born again in 1948 like a reformatted computer or a reset watch', one Israeli cultural commentator has written.[67] Hebraizing the names of people and places had been an important element of the Zionist project from its start six decades earlier. Now it could be done on a transformative scale that erased the country's Arab history and identity and emphasized Jewish continuity – what Palestinians in a later, more confident and politically conscious age came to describe as part of a campaign of 'memoricide'.[68] In July 1949 Ben-Gurion told the archaeologists, historians and geographers who had been appointed to the newly created Negev Names Committee: 'We are obliged to remove the Arabic names for reasons of state. Just as we do not recognise the Arabs' political proprietorship of the land, so also do we not recognise their spiritual proprietorship and their names.'[69]

From spring 1948 looting and squatting co-existed with official confiscations of Arab buildings, land and goods. 'The urge to grab has seized everyone', complained the writer Moshe Smilansky.

'Individuals, groups and communities, men, women and children, all fell on the spoils. Doors, windows, lintels, bricks, roof-tiles, floor-tiles, junk and machine parts.'[70] Hagit Shlonsky watched from the window of her home in Jerusalem's Rehavia quarter as Jews plundered abandoned homes in nearby Qatamon. Danny Rubinstein, a ten-year-old, saw Jewish neighbours move into empty Arab homes and his father being given a looted oriental rug. 'We lived in the middle of a sea of destruction', recorded a resident of Baqa.[71] Uri Pinkerfeld of Kibbutz Revadim, re-established inside the green line after the original site in Gush Etzion was destroyed during the war, was in a 'dismantling team' that collected useful material from nearby, now empty Arab villages.[72]

In Israel's first year about 120,000 new immigrants found homes in abandoned Arab accommodation.[73] Haifa's Wadi Salib was given over to new arrivals from Morocco and quickly became a byword for an impoverished slum.[74] It was a similar story in Jaffa and Acre, as well as in Ramle, Lod – and elsewhere. In nearby Aqir village, taken over by Jewish immigrants from Bulgaria, Yemen and Romania, the newcomers found jars of wheat, kitchen utensils and cans of petrol buried by the previous owners.[75] In Yazur an immigrant woman was upset to discover her children playing with toys that had been left behind by the Arab owner of the house, and pondered their fate.[76] Another new immigrant refused to be housed in an abandoned Arab home in Salama village because he had been expelled from his own home in Ukraine a few years earlier.[77] Arab parts of West Jerusalem had been partially if not completely settled by Jews by the end of May 1948. By December, all unoccupied houses in those areas had been totally vandalized.[78] In April 1949 it was decided to allocate four hundred abandoned homes, many with elegant high ceilings, wrought-iron railings and arched doorways, to government officials.

THE ONLY DEMOCRACY IN THE MIDDLE EAST

Even as they were subjected to direct military rule, the demolition of the remains of many of their homes, and with their kinfolk suffering,

Israel's Arab citizens were able to take part in a democratic political system. The dilemma for the Israeli government 'was how it could secure its wartime gains while sharing political power with the very people who – by virtue of their desire to hold on to their land and bring home their relatives, friends and compatriots – would want to reverse them'.[79] The Arabists and security experts strongly opposed enfranchising Arabs. 'They will demand restitution of property, many will return, claim freedom of movement – all these are undesirable', Josh Palmon warned. 'No one but the communists wants to vote.'[80] But they were overruled. In the first parliamentary elections in January 1949, 3 Arab MPs entered the 120-seat Knesset. Arab lists, created by the ruling Labour party, Mapai, thus formed 'a link between those Arab notables who remained in the country and the Jewish power structure'. Two MPs represented the Democratic List of Nazareth. One of them, Sayf al-Din Zoabi, had worked closely with the Jews and had been involved in land sales and intelligence before the war.[81] The system ensured the co-optation of Arab political activity and the channelling of votes to Mapai.[82] In this way, as a government memo explained, 'the party could avoid having to form a particular ideology for its Arab voters and also ensured that those lists would not consolidate into an independent Arab bloc'.[83] The third MP, Toufiq Toubi of the Communist Party, was combative and popular and did much to make the party, known by its Hebrew acronym as Maki, the only organized political force that represented Arab interests and offered 'a solid alternative to the collaborator class'.[84] Maki was also the only party in which Arabs had equal rights to Jews. In its pre-1948 configuration, echoing the position of the Soviet Union, the party had accepted the UN partition plan of 1947 – rejected by other Palestinians – and recognized Israel.

Overall, Israeli government policy towards non-Jews operated on the time-honoured colonial principle of dividing and ruling, seeking out minorities within the minority. The country's 20,000-strong Druze community, whose leaders had been cultivated by the Jews since the 1930s, was accorded a special status, having reached a non-belligerency agreement in Galilee in April 1948. Circassians (the descendants of Muslim immigrants expelled from the Caucasus in the nineteenth century) and Bedouin in the south also got preferential treatment. In January 1949 the IDF created a 'minorities unit' comprising 400 Druze, 200 Bedouin and 100 Circassians, commanded by Jewish officers, and deployed it to ambush Palestinians trying to cross the armistice lines. Druze later became subject, like Jews, to compulsory conscription, gaining a reputation for cruel behaviour in the war on infiltration. Their role was described by one Israeli official as a 'sharp knife in the back of Arab unity'. It was also deemed useful for propaganda purposes as 'a symbol of inter-ethnic brotherhood'.[85] Towards the end of the decade a government report noted with satisfaction: 'The policy of communal division bore fruit and succeeded in creating barriers, albeit somewhat artificial ones, between certain parts of the Arab community, as in the case of the mistrust between the Druze and the other Arab communities.'[86] Moshe Sharett put it frankly: 'We strive to weaken and crumble the Arabs who live in Israel as a block and as a national minority, but to improve and advance their situation as individuals . . . We would like to reduce their number but we shall not do it by unfair methods.'[87]

Sheikhs, religious judges or other 'notables', were granted privileges and special dispensations that strengthened traditional social relations and made co-optation 'a convenient, inexpensive and effective technique of gaining access to the Arab population'.[88] Collaborators were key to the control of Arab areas, and some were long-standing acquaintances of the Israeli security officials. Collaboration brought benefits and favours – work and travel permits, firearms licences, an official blind eye to criminality, financial reward and, at the higher level, even political office. Arabs in Jish, in Galilee, were not allowed to use the nearest telephone, in Safsufa less than a mile away, without written permission from the military government – whose representatives came to the village twice a week to answer petitions.[89] 'In order to get business permits, or in the beginning, to get travel permits week after week, you had to provide something in return,' explained a man from Kufr Qara.

> You had to give them information, to collaborate . . . They wanted to know who in the village still had guns and ammunition, who was politically active in a nationalist movement, who was talking against the Jews. Also, they had a problem with infiltrators coming across the Jordanian

border into Israel. Some of these people were just unfortunate souls, poor refugees trying to return to their villages. But others were armed *fedayeen* (fighters) who were trying to set up cells and attack Jewish settlements. The Jews wanted to know who they were and where they were hiding out. And for all this they needed the help of collaborators.[90]

The military government, its transactions lubricated by bribes, 'favours' and lavish Arab hospitality, acquired a reputation for being corrupt. In 1951 its manpower was drastically cut and its control removed from Acre, Haifa, Jaffa, Lod and Ramle, all with 'mixed' populations.[91]

It was hardly surprising then, that the government, as an Israeli expert commented in 1950, 'appears as a foreign regime, separated from the people and supporting a class of intermediaries – a class which is concerned with personal favours and which has no sense of public responsibility. The old local leaders – those who did not flee – remain as the primary point of connection between the government and the public.'[92] Christian clergymen and Muslim imams were used to convey pro-government and anti-nationalist messages. Palestinians on both sides of what was becoming known as the green line were recruited to work with the police, the army and Shin Bet to foil infiltration and sabotage attempts. Palmon tried to use two well-known public figures, the Greek Orthodox Archbishop Hakim, and Muhammad Nimr Hawari – who had headed the Arab Youth Organization *al-Najada* in 1947 – to oppose Communist activities. It was a Levantine version of the Don Camillo stories by Giovanni Guareschi that pitted a Catholic priest against Communists in rural Italy of the early 1950s. (Hawari returned to Israel from Jordan in 1949 but withdrew from public life.) Emile Habibi, the Communist activist and writer, described the experience of a 'suffocating embrace' by which Israel's Arab minority were simultaneously contained and excluded.

INFILTRATORS AND EXPULSIONS

Expulsions of Palestinian 'infiltrators' continued throughout 1949 but failed to stem the flow. In May Yosef Weitz warned that refugee infiltration was now common: 'Every day our people meet acquaintances who were formerly absent now walking about in complete freedom and also returning step by step to their villages', he told Sharett. 'Refugees are returning! Nor does our government offer any policy to prevent the infiltration. There appears to be no authority, neither civil nor military. The reins have been loosed, and the Arab in his cunning has already sensed this and knows how to draw the conclusions he wishes.'[93] Expulsions went on routinely until the summer of 1950 when Israel faced adverse international publicity and complaints over the way Bedouin from the northern Negev had been forced across the border as shots were fired over their heads and over thirty had died of thirst and starvation.[94] Israel exploited the infiltration issue to expel the inhabitants of some villages that had not been destroyed during the war. In January 1949, 355 residents of Majd al-Krum, including many women and children, were put on trucks and taken to Wadi Ara, then still under the control of the Iraqi army.[95] Thousands of other Galilee villagers were sent into exile in the Jenin area. Bedouin tribes deemed hostile by the IDF were expelled to Egypt and Jordan.[96] In 1950, the remaining Arab population of Majdal, some 1,600 souls, were expelled to Gaza.[97] The town became part of Israeli Ashkelon. After that the outward flow of Palestinian refugees came to an end, but infiltration did not. In fact it was so persistent that in 1952 Ben-Gurion expressed surprise in the Knesset at the continuing efforts of Arabs to reach abandoned homes and lands, 'even though we were shooting at them and killing them'. Emile Habibi, then a new MP, interrupted him, in Hebrew, to shout: 'Don't you know what the love of homeland is like?!'[98] In retrospect it is more accurate to see the flight, expulsions, returns and the infiltrations of the *Nakba* as a process that continued over three to four years, rather than as a single, sudden event, let alone a 'miraculous' one.

9

1953–1958

'Why should we complain about their burning hatred for us?
For eight years they have been sitting in the refugee camps in
Gaza, watching us transforming the lands and the villages
where they and their fathers dwelt, into our property.'

Moshe Dayan, 1956

'WE HAVE NO CHOICE BUT TO FIGHT'

Under cover of darkness on 12 October 1953, an IDF force quietly crossed the green line and entered the West Bank village of Qibya. Unit 101 was under the command of a young major named Ariel Scheinerman, who later changed his name to Sharon. The mission was mounted in retaliation for a Palestinian grenade attack that had killed an Israeli woman and her two young children in Yehud, near Lod Airport, two days earlier. The commandos, together with a larger paratroop force, perpetrated one of the most notorious atrocities of the period and of Sharon's long and controversial military career. At least sixty-nine Palestinians, two-thirds of them women and children, were killed. 'Bullet-ridden bodies near the doorways and multiple hits in the doors of the demolished homes indicated that the inhabitants had been forced to remain inside while their homes were blown up over them', UN observers reported afterwards. Sharon claimed that he did not realize that the village's stone houses were still occupied when they were dynamited by his men.[1] The raid went ahead despite an assurance from the Jordanians that they would do everything in their power to apprehend the infiltrators. Ben-Gurion, who took part in the decision, initially stated in a radio broadcast that the IDF had not been involved and that it had been carried out by enraged civilians. That unconvincing explanation brought criticism from Moshe Sharett, Israel's foreign minister, who had to deal with the diplomatic fallout. But the raid was praised by Israeli 'hawks', including Menachem Begin, the former *Irgun* chief and now leader of the right-wing opposition *Herut* (Freedom) party, who felt it had raised 'Israel's status among both the Arabs and the great powers'. In its wake Moshe Dayan, who shortly afterwards became IDF chief of staff, shifted the retaliatory strikes from civilian to military targets. Unit 101 was disbanded.[2]

Qibya was the most infamous of scores of reprisal raids that took place in the early years of Israel's independence – two hundred in the first half of 1953 alone.[3] Between June 1949 and the end of 1952, fifty-seven Israelis, mostly civilians, were killed by Palestinian infiltrators from the West Bank. The Israeli death toll for the first nine months of 1953 was thirty-two. Over the same time the UN-chaired Mixed Armistice Commission condemned Israeli incursions forty-four times. For the two months prior to the Yehud incident, conditions had been relatively quiet along the long and twisting Jordanian–Israeli border, with no casualties reported by either side since August.[4] According to one authoritative estimate, between 2,700 and 5,000 Palestinian infiltrators were killed by Israel between 1949 and 1956, the vast majority of them by 1952.[5] In the same period, 284 Israeli civilians were killed and 500 injured by Palestinians.[6] The conflict had shifted from being an inter-communal Jewish-Arab one *within* the country to one that took place mainly on Israel's frontiers and beyond. Jordan tried hard to halt infiltration – despite Israeli claims to the contrary. The issue was a highly sensitive one because so many of Jordan's own people were Palestinians after King Abdullah's annexation of the West Bank in 1950. Abdullah's assassination by a young Palestinian at the al-Aqsa mosque in July 1951 had been a shocking reminder of potential instability from that quarter. Qibya was another.[7]

Israel's attitude to the Palestinians in this period was memorably articulated by Dayan, an instantly recognizable national hero and symbol in his own right: the first-born native (*Tzabar*/Sabra) child of Kibbutz Degania who had grown up in Nahalal in the Jezreel valley and who personified the tough, can-do values of his generation of pioneers and fighters. In April 1956 he delivered the eulogy at the graveside of Roy Rotberg, from Kibbutz Nahal Oz on the border with Gaza, who had been killed by *fedayeen* and his corpse mutilated. The one-eyed general was not known for his eloquence, but he found the words – admired even by his detractors – to convey some harsh home truths about Israel and its enemies. First there was a rare moment of candour about the fate of the Palestinians, without the usual propaganda gloss. 'Let us not blame the murderers today,' Dayan said at Rotberg's graveside. 'Why should we complain about their burning hatred for us? For eight years they have been sitting in the refugee camps in Gaza, watching us transforming the lands and the villages where they and their fathers dwelt, into our property.' And Dayan was equally frank when he described the response required by Israelis: 'We have no choice but to fight,' he declared.

> This is our life's choice, to be prepared and armed, strong and determined, lest the sword be stricken from our fist and our lives cut down. We are a generation that settles the land, and without the steel helmet and the cannon's fire we will not be able to plant a tree and build a home. Let us not be deterred from seeing the loathing that is inflaming and filling the lives of the hundreds of thousands of Arabs who live around us. Let us not avert our eyes lest our arms weaken.[8]

Another passage, less frequently quoted but no less important, referred to 'millions of Jews, who were destroyed without having a homeland, watch us from the dust of Israeli [*sic*] history and command us to settle and to build a country for our people'. It was less a national security doctrine than the essence of a widely shared Israeli-Zionist worldview in the country's formative years. It has been aptly described as an Israeli version of the American doctrine of Manifest Destiny.[9]

Dayan's Nahal Oz speech was rooted in a familiar reality. Palestinian infiltration and Israeli reprisals continued after Qibya and through 1954, though on a smaller scale for the twenty-two months when the more dovish Sharett replaced Ben-Gurion as prime minister. The *fedayeen* threat was real enough, though hardly a strategic one. In September, for example, the Israelis captured a vegetable hawker who had crossed the border from Gaza, exchanged fire with Israeli guards, blew up a tractor and stole donkeys, geese and clothes off a washing line on the edge of a settlement.[10] Retaliation was the norm. In February 1955 'Operation Black Arrow', also commanded by Sharon, killed thirty-eight Egyptians in Gaza. Riots – described as an *intifada* or uprising – erupted with the backing of the Muslim Brotherhood. Egypt's assertive and popular new nationalist leader, Gamal Abdel Nasser, became more supportive of the *fedayeen*, delighting Palestinians like Khalil al-Wazir, a refugee from Ramle who had grown up in Gaza, joined the Brotherhood as a student in Cairo, and formed a group called *Katibat al-Haq* (Battalion of Justice). Statements were sent to papers in Beirut and Damascus to magnify the impact of their cross-border operations,[11] which were conducted in great secrecy for fear that the Egyptian authorities, anxious about Israeli reprisals, would get wind of them.[12]

In September 1955 an Egyptian-Soviet arms deal, a major turning point in the early years of the Cold War, fuelled a war scare in Israel. Sharett called for a national effort to purchase weapons, which led to a public campaign to raise funds to buy helicopters and tanks.[13] In November, soon after Ben-Gurion returned to power, the IDF launched another big punitive raid on Gaza, this time killing thirty-six. Protests and unrest again shook the coastal strip, with Palestinians demanding to be allowed to strike Israel. Nasser changed tack again, and the *fedayeen* carried out 180 operations – including shootings, minings and ambushes – from December 1955 to March 1956. In April a further Israeli attack left fifty-nine dead. In July, following Rotberg's grisly murder, the Israelis assassinated Mustafa Hafez, the Egyptian intelligence chief in Gaza, with a parcel bomb, and Egypt's military attaché in Amman, Salah Mustafa, was eliminated the same way the following day.[14] In Gaza new-born babies were named after Hafez. Nasser even paid tribute to him in the historic speech announcing the nationalization of the Suez Canal a few days later – heralding a major new crisis.[15]

SECOND ROUND AT SUEZ

The war that followed a few months later against Egypt was launched pre-emptively by Israel, in collusion with Britain and France, the latter fighting a bloody anti-colonial insurgency in Algeria where the National Liberation Front (FLN) was being backed by Cairo. The governments in London and Paris were infuriated by Nasser's take-over of the canal and the wild enthusiasm he inspired across the Arab world. British Prime Minister Anthony Eden's obsession with the man he called 'Hitler on the Nile' was to lead to his own downfall. Israel's principal official justification for what it called 'Operation Kadesh' was to put an end to *fedayeen* raids from Gaza. Opening the canal to Israeli shipping was another goal. The Egyptian leader called the war the 'tripartite aggression' – the Arabic phrase neatly encapsulating regional perceptions of imperialist machinations in tandem with the Zionist enemy. The battle itself was confined to the Sinai peninsula, which was captured by Israeli paratroopers and tank forces in a few days. The Israelis were also on high alert in case Jordan entered the war: that was the background to the massacre of forty-nine Israeli Arabs at the border village of Kafr Qassem on the eve of hostilities. King Hussein, though personally inclined to support Egypt, was dissuaded, ironically, by his pro-Nasser prime minister, and took dis-cretion to be the better part of valour.

Israeli forces occupied the desert peninsula for four months until heavy US pressure forced Ben-Gurion, despite having histrionically proclaimed a 'third kingdom of Israel', to order a full withdrawal and to drop any idea of annexing the conquered territory, including the Gaza Strip. That stern precedent was not followed by subsequent US administrations. Israel's occupation of Gaza during that period saw the military once more impose itself on a Palestinian civilian popula-tion, two-thirds of them refugees, now living in eight large camps. The prime minister was pleased with the IDF's victory but dismayed that the Palestinians had not fled, as they had in 1948, and he ordered Ezra Danin, now working for the foreign ministry, to explore options for resettlement.[16] Israeli troops were accused in two cases of shoot-ing a number of Palestinian men in their homes and having lined up others and executed them. On 3 November 1956 Israeli forces report-edly killed 275 Palestinians – 140 refugees and 135 local residents – during the capture of Khan Yunis. Another thirty-six youths were killed in detention on the 10th. On 12 November (after the fighting was over), Israeli forces were said to have killed 110 Palestinians in Rafah.[17] Israel rejected the accusations.[18] An Arab study estimated that between 930 and 1,200 Palestinians had been killed by the time the Israelis withdrew in March 1957 after encountering little resistance.[19] Occupying Gaza allowed the Israelis to settle some scores. Rotberg's killers, an Egyptian and a Palestinian, were tried and sentenced to life imprisonment, and the capture of Egyptian intelligence files yielded valuable information about Palestinian activists, who were detained and interrogated. Lessons from the brief experience of running a military government outside Israel's borders would be dusted off again just over a decade later.

The 'second round' that Arabs and Israelis had expected since 1948 sent shockwaves across the Middle East and the world, spelling an end, in time, to Britain's presence in the region. The Suez war also had an impact closer to home. On the eve of hostilities, on 29 October 1956, the Israeli authorities imposed a 5 p.m. curfew on villages near the border with Jordan. In Kafr Qassem border guards shot and killed forty-nine unarmed Arab citizens, including women and children, who were returning from their fields and had breached the curfew because they were unaware of when it came into effect. Eye-witnesses described police repeatedly firing rifles and machine-guns at villagers as they arrived back at the village on foot, on bicycles, by donkey or on trucks. The victims were buried that night in a mass grave. The aftermath saw the unit's commander and seven other soldiers sentenced to prison terms of between eight and seventeen years; damages paid to the families of the dead and injured; and a new IDF rule obliging soldiers to refuse to carry out any order they deemed to be 'manifestly illegal'.

The massacre left deep scars on the Palestinians, innocent victims of a conflict that overshadowed their lives. It also reflected profound divisions within Israeli society, 'a society in which Jews tend to see themselves as "Jews" over and against "Arabs" whom they see not as "Israelis" but as aliens'.[20] In the words of a recent critical appraisal, the killings were presented in Israel as a 'tragic blip' on the screen of the state's otherwise fair treatment of its Arab minority, and carried out by uneducated Moroccan immigrants who did not reflect the wider population of citizen-soldiers or the ethos and conduct of the army. But for most Arab citizens – who made up 11 per cent of the country's population in 1956 – it represented the inevitable (if most brutal) outcome of eight years of what was commonly labeled Israel's 'policies of national oppression' against them. Along with military rule and the deprivation of their civil rights, these policies were expressed in the ongoing confiscation of their land, their consistent portrayal in official discourse as a fifth column, and the cultivation of racist attitudes against them in Jewish schools.[21]

Annual commemorations of the killings served as a reminder – as did the names of the victims inscribed on a stone column in the centre of Kafr Qassem.[22]

NASSER, *NAKBA*, NAZARETH

In the years after Suez, Israel's policy towards its Palestinian minority was still based overwhelmingly on considerations of security. Not only were Arabs kith and kin with the country's enemies, but many lived on the frontiers, close to those yearning to return to their lost homes a short distance away. Two villages in the 'Triangle', Bartaa and Baqaa, were physically divided by the green line. No more than nine miles separated Qalqilya on the West Bank and the Mediterranean coast. The central Dan region was also where the bulk of Israel's Jewish population was located.[23] 'My job is not defence, that is the task of the border police and the Jewish farming villages along the border,' the IDF military governor of the Triangle area explained in 1958. 'My job is controlling the Arab population of the area as long as there is no peace. We know that the great part of the population is loyal. But we also know that another part is not loyal, and they must be checked, patrolled, and supervised.'[24] The effect was stifling, as a disgruntled Nazareth resident complained: 'They take our land. Why? For security reasons! They take our jobs. Why? For security reasons! And when we ask them how it happens that we, our lands and our jobs threaten the security of the state – they do not tell us. Why not? For security reasons!'[25] The authorities paid particular attention to expressions of sympathy for Nasser. Stories were rife of people being informed on for listening to broadcasts of the Egyptian president's electrifying speeches on *Sawt al-Arab* (The Voice of the

Arabs) from Cairo. 'We were always close to the radio when Nasser made a speech and sat in silence as though we were in a church or a mosque', recalled Fawzi al-Asmar, who had grown up in Lydda.[26] Isser Harel, head of the Shin Bet, had opposed the military government system but changed his mind in the wake of Nasser's growing popularity among the Arab minority.[27]

If Nasser was the focus of admiration for his defiance of the West and Israel, awareness of the *Nakba* was also slowly growing among Palestinians and other Arabs. Constantine Zurayek, a Syrian intellectual, had published his famous work, *The Meaning of the Disaster*, in 1949, analysing the causes of the defeat and blaming it on the 'impotence' of the Arab states and the Palestinian leadership. Very few Palestinians wrote personal memoirs in 1948, or even in the 1950s and 1960s.[28] 'The defeated ones, living in fear and insecurity within the refugee camps in a strange environment, did not want to talk about their defeat', argued a later Palestinian study. 'In addition, they were overcome by shame, guilt and torment, which only reinforced their silence.'[29] And there were good practical reasons too: in the chaotic circumstances of flight and adjustment to a harsh new reality, notes and papers would have been unlikely to survive.[30] Many Palestinians saw themselves as tragic figures who had contributed to their fate by ineptitude and passivity.[31] 'Leaving Tiberias was a great shock for my parents', wrote the economist Yusif Sayigh, 'but they rarely mentioned it. People closed up about the *Nakba*.' Sayigh's account of the defence of Qatamon in 1948 was scathing about the half-baked Palestinian effort.[32] Muhammad Milhem from Halhoul, near Hebron, later described himself disparagingly playing chess and cards in coffee houses while the fighting raged.[33] The term *Nakba* gained wider currency after 1958 when the Palestinian historian Arif al-Arif began publishing his famous six-volume work, *Nakbat Bayt al-Maqdis* (The Catastrophe of Jerusalem). Its subtitle was 'Paradise Lost'. Adel Manna, from Majd al-Krum in Galilee, heard nothing about his family's experience in 1948, including executions, until he was ten – when his father reacted strangely to the news that his delighted son had been chosen to take part in Independence Day celebrations. Israel's independence (*Istiqlal*), the boy learned for the first time in 1958, meant 'occupation' (*Istihlal*) for the Arabs.[34] Israeli Jews were sometimes reminded of the silence of parents or grandparents who had lost relatives in the Holocaust but never wanted to talk about it – out of guilt at having survived or in order to allow their children to build normal lives unburdened by an intolerably painful past.[35]

The impact of 1948, however, was present in everyday life wherever Palestinians lived. In the refugee camps, residents organized themselves according to their village or town of origin, using their place names instead of those chosen by UN administrators. In the early 1950s people from al-Zeeb and al-Bassa, neighbouring villages near Acre, occupied adjacent areas in the Ein al-Hilweh camp on the outskirts of Tyre. In Nahr al-Bared, near Tripoli, half the population was from Saffuriya.[36] In the al-Baqaa camp outside Amman there lived large numbers of Sibawis, from Beersheba. 'For my own generation . . . our last day in Palestine was the first day that we began to define our Palestinian identity', wrote Fawaz Turki, who was born in Balad al-Sheikh and grew up in Burj al-Barajneh in Beirut.

> Like the olive trees and the land and the stone houses and the sea and the dabki [sic] dances and the ululation at weddings. Everything was where it belonged. Everything coalesced into a coherent whole. It had never occurred to anyone to define it, or to endow it with any special attributes. Until we were severed from it.[37]

Families treasured the rusting keys and fading title deeds of the homes they had left behind as their most valuable possessions, 'a promise of return, a promise that history inevitably broke'.[38]

Images of olive trees, *zaatar* (wild thyme), pomegranates, wells, fields and orange groves came to dominate Palestinian poetry and art, animating what A. L. Tibawi labelled 'visions of return' in a pioneering study. 'Having so far failed to assert his right to national integrity and independence in his own homeland through political and military means, and despaired of the efficacy of international moral succour, the Palestine Arab has since 1948 been rebuilding, among other resources, emotional strength with the declared object of regaining the lost homeland.'[39] Shared memories 'of the traumatic uprooting of their society and the experiences of being dispossessed, displaced, and stateless are what have come to define "Palestinian-ness"', another scholar wrote.[40]

In Israel, the *Nakba* could not be taught in schools or mentioned in print due to the constraints of military censorship and the fear of denunciation.[41] Even the use of the word '*watan*' – 'homeland' – was banned. In the mid-1950s a teacher was sacked for writing poetry about a mulberry tree in his old village of al-Mujaydil – renamed Migdal HaEmek in Hebrew. Later in life a refugee child from Haifa recalled being rebuked by a nervous teacher for singing a nationalist song.[42] 'In those days it was dangerous to mention the word Palestine', remembered Mohammed Ali Taha, an internal refugee. 'In schools anyone who said Palestine would be kicked out. They intervened in everything, in every detail of our daily lives. There were no libraries, no intellectuals left and most of the people were peasants who could not read or write.'[43] The Israeli authorities feared that 'present absentees' would try to return to abandoned villages and rebuild their homes. 'Ben-Gurion always reminds us that we cannot be guided by the subversion that the Arab minority has not engaged in,' the prime minister's Arab affairs adviser told a journalist. 'We must be guided by what they might have done if they had been given the chance. If we cancelled the restrictions the Communist Party would invite Arab refugees to squat on their ruins, demanding their lands back . . . [and] the return of the refugees. They will form organisations, parties, fronts, anything to make trouble.'[44] In 1954 the government fretted about Communist Party (Maki) gains in municipal elections in Nazareth. Attacks on party activists by members of the Zoabi clan, which was known for its close relations with the authorities, aroused suspicions of official complicity at a time when efforts were under way to build a new Jewish quarter to dominate the Arab city.[45]

POPULAR PASSIVE RESISTANCE

Maki played an important role in reviving Arab cultural and intellectual life in the Israel of the 1950s. *Al-Ittihad* published Palestinian nationalist writers like Ibrahim Touqan and Khalil al-Sakakini as well as Arabic literature from other countries. Poetry festivals organized by the party overcame censorship, curfews and harassment to make creativity a form of 'popular passive resistance'. *Al-Jadid*, the party's literary magazine, published articles highlighting the legacy of Arab and Islamic civilization to counter European and Zionist discourses about the Arab world. In October 1953, *al-Ittihad*'s editor, Emile Touma, attacked a project by the *Histadrut* labour federation to publish Arabic translations of Hebrew texts as chauvinism 'that portrayed Zionism as a messenger of civilisation to Arab countries'.[46] Freedom, though, was constrained by the suspicious atmosphere encouraged by the efforts of the police and Shin Bet to recruit informants. If *al-Ittihad* described someone as a collaborator with the military government he would be ostracized and isolated within the local community. For some Palestinians Mapam, a left-wing Zionist party with some Arab members, was preferable to Maki as 'the only Israeli Zionist party which attempted to establish some contact between "Arab nationalism" and "Jewish nationalism" on a basis of mutual respect',[47] even though, as its critics from the left always noted, Mapam *kibbutzim* had been built on confiscated Arab land, for all their talk of solidarity and equality.[48]

Government media efforts were unimpressive: *al-Yawm*, the semi-official Arabic daily, consisted of four pages summarized from the Hebrew daily *Davar* 'minus various items judged too sensitive to bring to the notice of the Arab readers, plus a few usually dated short reports from stringers in the larger villages, reporting mainly on visits from some government official, the building of a road or school, and similar stories of a "positive" nature'. Over time, as Israel's Arab population achieved greater education and political awareness, '[it] became increasingly unpopular, and was in fact treated as a laughing-stock by the same intelligentsia that it was supposed to serve and give expression to'.[49] Israeli policy towards the Arab population emphasized the importance of the village and the clans which dominated them, reinforcing orientalist stereotypes of backwardness and under-development and encouraging relations of dependence, co-optation and control.[50] This remained the case even when most Arabs lived in towns. 'The rural nature of the Palestinians guaranteed that they were essentially different from the Jewish population and therefore would not seek to integrate with it or assimilate into it', one Israeli scholar has observed. 'Furthermore, their rural nature guaranteed that they were traditional and therefore needed paternalist government rather than democracy.'[51] Electrification in the Arab rural sector was seen as a developmental advance that would have both cultural and security implications. 'If we illuminate this darkness, we take them out of the darkness and place them under our supervision,' one official said.[52]

Language mattered too. In the mid-1950s concerns began to be expressed that knowledge of Arabic among Jews, always very limited, was in decline as it had lost much of its practical relevance after 1948. Occasional meetings between Arab and Jewish writers lapsed into embarrassed silence because although the Arabs generally learned Hebrew, the vast majority of Jews, with the exception of native-speaking immigrants from Iraq and Egypt, knew no Arabic, and showed little interest in learning it. In the Jewish school system parents generally preferred their offspring to study English, and later French, rather than a difficult language associated with a 'backward' culture and a bitter enemy. Efforts by despairing teachers to improve the situation only made headway when the issue was taken up by the prime minister's Arab affairs adviser, working with IDF intelligence and the ministry of education to address a shortage that was seen as having serious implications for national security. Promising Jewish high-school pupils were enrolled into special 'orientalist' courses which included field trips to Nazareth and Druze villages, where they were given guided tours by a military government official – though not by the locals. Students were supposed to practise colloquial Arabic – disconcertingly different from the modern standard written form – and learn about Arab customs, but they were under strict instructions not to enter into political discussions with the Arabs who were 'a subject of study and, ultimately, control'. Relations in what one participant described as a 'hostile environment' were supposed to be 'sentiment free'. The courses were typically followed by service in IDF intelligence and advanced study at the Hebrew University. The difficulties in teaching Arabic to Israeli Jews remained a long-term problem. Arabic teachers were treated 'as if we were teaching Hottentot on the moon', one complained. The perception was 'that everything that is Oriental is also Arab, and everything that is Arab is also dirty'.[53]

10

1958–1967

'The strongest feeling, vocally and bitterly expressed by the great mass of refugees, is the demand to return to their old homes.'

UNRWA, 1956

THE FIRST TEN YEARS

Ecstatic Israelis celebrated the tenth anniversary of their independence on 24 April 1958 (according to the Hebrew calendar). The military parade that was held to mark the occasion in West Jerusalem, 'almost under the sullen guns of the Jordan army ringing the Israel-held sectors of the ancient city',[1] deliberately emphasized the armed might of the Jewish state – and its defiance of international opinion. David Ben-Gurion, the prime minister, and President Yitzhak Ben-Tzvi – who had succeeded Chaim Weizmann in 1952 – took the salute in the newly built sports stadium on the Givat Ram campus of the Hebrew University, watched by a cheering crowd of 20,000 with many thousands more lining the route. French tanks and artillery, US-made Sherman tanks and British anti-aircraft guns were followed by paratroop, infantry and naval units, their flags flying in spring sunshine that was welcome after a chilly spell. Many members of the foreign diplomatic corps stayed away for fear their attendance might be interpreted as recognition of Jerusalem as the country's capital (as declared by Israel in December 1948), although some heads of mission came in their private capacity. The event took place despite protests by the United Nations, which declared that the concentration of Israeli forces in Jerusalem violated the 1949 armistice agreement with Jordan. Israel insisted there was no violation because the troops would be withdrawn immediately after the celebration. On the other side of the city, King Hussein – who maintained indirect contact with the Israelis via the US – inspected the reinforced units he had carefully deployed to counter-balance the unusually heavy Israeli presence.

Israel's conflict with its Arab enemies was nowhere near being resolved in 1958, and it was hard to see anything changing given the entrenched positions on both sides, the divisions in the Arab world and the absence of any recognized body representing the Palestinians and their interests. 'Since the death of King Abdullah [in 1951], no Arab ruler has been willing to parley with Israel', observed Walter Eytan, a senior foreign ministry official, in a book he published that year that employed standard Israeli government arguments.

> The fact that the Arab states put themselves in the wrong by refusing to negotiate with Israel has not weighed with them. They do not recognise Israel; consequently there is no one with whom to negotiate. Their whole attitude is based on the thesis that Israel has no right to exist and that to negotiate with her is out of the question because it would mean conceding her this right. Israel has shown that she could ride out ten years of unrelenting enmity from the Arab side, and she can live with it for decades and generations more if she must.[2]

Abba Eban, Israel's famously eloquent ambassador to the US, marked a decade of independence in a prime-time TV interview with Mike Wallace on ABC News, describing 'incomparable years of joyous creation, of sovereignty restored, of a people gathered in, of a land revived, of democracy established'. Yes, he admitted, there had also been 'violence imposed by the hostility of our neighbours'. However, he flatly rejected comparisons between the Arab 'refugee problem' and the Nazi Holocaust that had recently been made by the British historian Arnold Toynbee, a long-standing critic of Zionism:

> It is a monstrous blasphemy. He takes the massacre of millions of our men, women and children and he compares it to the plight of Arab refugees, alive, on their kindred soil, suffering certain anguish but of course possessed of the supreme gift of life. This equation between

massacre and temporary suffering which can easily be alleviated is a distortion of any historic perspective. But the refugee problem isn't the cause of tension. The refugee problem is the result of an Arab policy which created the problem by the invasion of Israel, which perpetuates it by refusing to accommodate them into their expanding labour market and which refuses to solve the problem which they have the full capacity to solve. There is a basic immorality in this attitude of Arab governments to their own kinsmen whose plight they could relieve immediately once the will to relieve it existed.[3]

Israel's refusal to take back Arab refugees was certainly supported by the country's Jewish citizens. The overwhelming majority subscribed to the officially promoted belief that the Arabs were entirely responsible for the 1948 war; that the refugees had fled of their own accord or at the urging of the invading Arab armies in anticipation of victory; that the Arab countries were deliberately perpetuating the problem for political reasons by failing to integrate the refugees despite ties of kinship, language, religion and national sentiment; and that repatriation was simply not an option. In February 1956, the government had released the report of an official inquiry into the military government. It heard testimony from thirty-nine Jews and fifty Arabs, one of whom was adamant that Arab citizens had *not* demonstrated loyalty to the state. The Ratner Commission highlighted fears that Arabs could constitute a fifth column as well as encroach on state land. It opposed the return of refugees for security reasons and argued that since the refugees had left the country voluntarily, they had relinquished any claims to return.[4] Another, more heavyweight commission reached similar conclusions less than three years later. Views did not change, but it was only in 1965 that the authorities quietly ordered the destruction of those abandoned Arab villages that still remained.[5]

The word 'Palestinian' was not used in either Hebrew or English discourse in the Israel of the 1950s – except on the far left.[6] In the same period, as official spokesmen always pointed out, Israel had assimilated nearly 1 million Jewish refugees, 450,000 of them from Arab countries. Selective quotations, and false, partial or misleading contemporary testimony were employed to support the case about the war of independence. Eytan, for example, described the 'astonishment' in the Jewish Agency when the Arab population of Tiberias decamped en masse in April 1948; it was not until the late 1980s that newly declassified files in the Israeli state archives allowed historians to paint an accurate picture of what had happened there (notably including the influence of *Haganah* psychological warfare and a nearby massacre), and in many other places during the war.[7]

Eban's speech to the UN General Assembly in 1958 spelled out the Israeli case on the refugees in detail. The bottom line was this:

> Repatriation would mean that hundreds of thousands of people would be introduced into a state whose existence they oppose, whose flag they despise and whose destruction they are resolved to seek. Israel, whose sovereignty and safety are already assailed by the states surrounding her, is invited to add to her perils by the influx from hostile territories of masses of people steeped in the hatred of her existence.

Of nearly a million refugees, more than half were under fifteen: thus in 1948 many of those were under five and had no 'conscious memory of Israel at all'.[8] Eban's eloquence did not make the issue disappear: in 1961 Ben-Gurion instructed the Shiloah Institute, a government-backed think tank in Tel Aviv, to report in detail on the reasons for the Palestinian exodus. The idea was to use the material for public diplomacy in the face of calls from the Kennedy administration in the US to make concessions on the refugee issue. Rony Gabbay, one of the Shiloah researchers, had already concluded from his own academic work on 1948 that in many cases 'Jewish forces took Arab villages, expelled the inhabitants and blew up places which they did not want to occupy themselves, so that they could not be reoccupied by their enemies and used as strongholds against them.'[9]

MINORITY RIGHTS, ISRAELI WRONGS

Independence Day 1958 was a good opportunity to showcase Israel's achievements in all spheres, including the sensitive issue of the Arab minority. In the preceding months, after the first anniversary of the Kafr Qassem killings, considerable efforts were made to persuade Arab citizens to take part in the festivities. The government offered to cover part of the costs of bands, fireworks, loudspeakers and exhibitions: one in Acre's old Turkish bathhouse showcased the 'folklore of the minorities', complete with traditional embroidery, Arabic coffee and sweets. It was ready to provide generators for the occasion as few villages were connected to the national grid, though local councils were expected to pay. When a boycott movement, galvanized by Maki, gathered momentum, leaflets signed by previously unknown groups called Sons of the Galilee and the Voice of the Arabs in Israel attempted to counter it – the names suggesting a clandestine effort orchestrated by the government. Pressure was brought to bear on individuals, including the young poet Rashid Hussein, who was asked to pen a verse to mark the holiday. Officials claimed a turnout of 8,000 in Nazareth on 26 April.[10]

Reality intruded a few days later on May Day. The mood in the country's only Arab city had been soured by the confiscation of a large tract of land which already housed Jewish immigrants who were mostly employed by the government. The early stages of the project were managed by an inter-departmental committee dominated by ministry of defence personnel.[11] This would eventually become the separate Jewish town of Upper Nazareth, whose purpose was described as ' "to break" Arab autonomy in the region and in this city, and later, to create a Jewish majority'.[12] More generally, there was resentment at continuing restrictions on movement – albeit lightly eased in 1957 – which still applied to the 85 per cent of Israeli Arabs who lived under the military government.[13] Communist organizers were arrested and placed in administrative detention and a planned May Day rally banned. When the ban was ignored, clashes erupted, followed by beatings and three hundred arrests, that the Hebrew media described as a 'riot', while Arabs boasted of their collective strength in the face of 'truncheons and vicious abuse'.[14] Slogans included 'Down with Ben-Gurion', 'End military rule' and 'Long live Nasser'. These events, observed a foreign visitor, were not typical of Nazareth life and politics. 'They brought out into the streets, for all to see, what had hitherto been only argued about in cafes or recorded in the files of the military government. They dramatised an obscure, all-pervading tension between government and governed.'[15] Further efforts were made to forestall trouble on 15 May, the Gregorian calendar date for Israel's independence and the Palestinian *Nakba*. Warnings of 'forceful measures to punish incitement against the state' were issued, especially to teachers, but pupils in Nazareth ignored them and followed the habit of the wider Arab world and observed five minutes' silence to mark the occasion. In one school students put up a picture of Nasser.[16]

Later that year attempts to set up a non-Communist organization led a small group of Arab intellectuals to form *al-Ard* (the Land) in the spirit of Nasserism and the wider Arab nationalist movement. It represented the first Arab challenge to the Jewish nature of the state. It called for a repeal of all discriminatory laws and recognition of the rights of the Palestinian refugees to return. These demands were articulated in a paper, edited by Salah Baransi, which was refused a licence but still managed to appear thirteen times until the group was formally outlawed. *Al-Ard*'s appearance signalled a parting of the ways between Arab nationalists and the Communists, who were still the only Arab grouping to have formally accepted the existence of Israel. It reflected the rivalry between Nasser's pan-Arabist view and the approach of the Communist-backed Iraqi leader, Abdel-Karim Qasim, who had overthrown the monarchy. It also reflected 'more than anything else the weariness with the ambiguity or the limbo imposed on the Palestinians'.[17] It did not however win automatic support from the Arab community. *Al-Ard*'s call to boycott the 1959 Knesset elections was controversial because it reduced Maki's representation from six to three seats and thus, its critics complained, weakened overall Arab representation in the Knesset. The Israeli security establishment was still alarmed. *Al-Ard* was 'accused', among other things, of helping to open independent sports clubs in Arab villages.[18] In 1960 the prime minister's adviser on Arab affairs, Shmuel Toledano – another Arabic-speaking official who had served in the Mossad (the foreign intelligence service) – warned publicly that *al-Ard* constituted a threat to the very existence of the state. Toledano described the notion of 'Israeli Arabs' as a contradiction in terms as they belonged to 'another nationality'.[19] Still, one small new group could not overcome the general quiescence of the Palestinians inside Israel, marginalized and carefully controlled as they were, as Palestinian nationalism began to revive elsewhere.[20]

AND ACROSS THE DIASPORA

Freedoms were in short supply for the majority of Palestinians who were scattered across the Arab world at a time of ferment and regional rivalry. In February 1958, Egypt and Syria had come together to announce the creation of the United Arab Republic. In May civil war broke out in Lebanon. In July the Iraqi monarchy was violently overthrown, a blow to the West and an ominous sign for its Hashemite cousins in Jordan, where the US and Britain – as well as Israel – feared a Nasserist coup. Elsewhere, the Algerian rebellion against France that had erupted in 1954 continued its bloody course, a source of inspiration and solidarity for other Arabs who saw Western imperialism as their main enemy. Palestinians in the front-line states, or further afield in the Gulf, were neither immune from nor indifferent to these developments.

Overall, Jordan treated Palestinians far better than any other Arab country, granting them citizenship and dropping the use of the term 'refugee' in official documents. Even before April 1950 King Abdullah had decreed that the territory now under his control, most of it allotted to the Palestinians under the 1947 UN partition decision, would be known henceforth as the West Bank. Use of the term 'Palestine' in any official document or correspondence was banned. Associations with an obviously Palestinian character – such as the Haifa Cultural Association in Nablus, the Jaffa Muslim Sports Club in Ramallah – were not allowed to engage in any political activity. Like Israel, Jordan offered Palestinians formal citizenship, but like Israel it also delegitimized Palestinian identity. Both countries' policies 'emphasised control and co-optation rather than partnership and equality'.[21] Palestinian separatism was presented as a blow to Arab unity.[22] That approach was maintained by King Hussein when he succeeded his father Talal in 1952. Jordan moved government offices from Jerusalem to Amman and faced complaints from Palestinians that the city, now on the front line with Israel, was being discriminated against and neglected. In 1961 the entire municipal council resigned in protest. Palestinians joked that if Hussein could have got away with demolishing the walls of the Old City, he would have done that as well.

It was Lebanon which imposed the most severe restrictions on the 100,000–130,000 Palestinians who had arrived by 1949, a reflection in part of the country's own fragile sectarian balance. Prejudice and mistreatment were common. Fawaz Turki, from the Haifa area, remembered how, as a teenage refugee, he wept with humiliation when a Beirut street entertainer ordered his pet monkey to 'show us how a Palestinian picks up his food rations'. Even Lebanese children taunted Palestinians, telling them to 'go back where you came from', and accused them of having sold their land to the Jews.[23] Samira Azzam, an Acre-born writer living in Beirut, created a hero who was frustrated because he was never allowed to forget that he is a Palestinian and who makes desperate efforts to become a naturalized Lebanese; when he finally succeeds in getting hold of the necessary passport, for a high price, he discovers it has been forged.[24] The authorities tracked down Palestinian activists, especially anyone suspected of being a Communist, to prevent them visiting refugee camps. The situation was better in neighbouring Syria, which took in 85,000–100,000 refugees, though with a far larger host population. Their affairs were administered by the General Authority for Palestine Arab Refugees, set up in 1949. By 1960, through natural increase, numbers had risen to 127,000.

The majority of the 300,000 Palestinians in Egypt lived under the military administration and emergency laws in the Gaza Strip that lasted until 1962. Most were no more able to enter the Nile valley than they were to return to their lost homes and lands inside Israel.[25] None of the refugees could go back to a now non-existent Palestine, while full integration in the host countries – with the exception of Jordan – was equally impossible. 'The strongest feeling, vocally and bitterly expressed by the great mass of refugees, is the demand to return to their old homes', UNRWA reported in the mid-1950s. 'They have remained opposed to the development of large-scale projects for self-support, which they erroneously link with permanent resettlement and the abandonment of hope for repatriation.'[26]

Nasser's popularity, at its height after the Suez war, helped galvanize the new Arab Nationalist Movement, which provided Palestinians who were pondering their fate a decade after the *Nakba* with a framework for action. George Habash, a refugee from Lydda, had founded the ANM while a medical student at the American University of

Beirut, where he had been influenced by Constantine Zurayek's emphasis on the way the Arab states had first failed in the war of 1948 and then effectively abandoned the Palestinians, their leaders making fiery speeches but doing little else. Habash went on to work in refugee camps in Jordan where he ran a clinic with another doctor, named Wadie Haddad, a native of Safad. Both were forced to flee Jordan for Syria in 1957. The ANM, in the words of an American CIA report, 'was motivated by the formation of Israel and the expulsion of the Palestinians from their homeland'. Its basic ideology 'reflected what its title implies – a desire for the union of all Arab states, a wish to exclude foreign influence from the Arab world, and the compulsion to eradicate the state of Israel'. The organization was never cohesive and its national chapters formed local alliances on an opportunistic basis.[27] In the late 1960s, Habash founded the Popular Front for the Liberation of Palestine (PFLP), which combined revolutionary Marxism with a Palestine-first strategy.

FATAH IS BORN

Other Palestinians were also thinking about how to advance their people's cause, but, crucially, without relying too much on other Arabs. Yasser Arafat, born in Egypt in 1929 to a Gazan father and a mother from a well-connected Jerusalem family – he had lived there briefly as a child – had studied at Cairo University and fought in the early stages of the 1948 war with a Muslim Brotherhood unit in southern Palestine. He complained later that he had been disarmed twice: first by the Egyptian army, and then again while serving with Abdul-Qader al-Husseini's *Jaysh al-Jihad al-Muqaddas* near Jerusalem, by the Jordanian Arab Legion.[28] According to some sources he was involved in guerrilla attacks on British forces in the canal zone in the run-up to the Suez crisis. As a student activist, Arafat promoted a strong Palestine-first awareness. By 1957 he was in the Gulf, along with a growing number of Palestinian men who endured the sort of hardships described by Ghassan Kanafani in his novel *Men Under the Sun* as they tried to make a new life and support their families. Arafat failed to get a visa to Saudi Arabia and ended up in Kuwait as an engineer with the ministry of public works. Strikingly, in the light of his subsequent career and fame, Arafat was not strictly speaking a refugee – he always spoke with a distinct Egyptian accent – but his closest friends and colleagues bore the scars of the *Nakba*; Salah Khalaf, a literature student who had fled Jaffa as a teenager in 1948, and Khalil al-Wazir, born in Ramla and expelled as a thirteen-year-old with his family to Gaza, were with him in October 1959 in Kuwait when they established the Palestine Liberation Movement. It was named Fatah – a reverse of its Arabic acronym (*Harakat al-tahrir al-filastiniyya*) – which alluded to victory or conquest in the first glorious decades of Islamic history. 'Arafat and I . . . knew what was damaging to the Palestinian cause', Khalaf wrote later. 'We were convinced, for example, that the Palestinians could expect nothing from the Arab regimes, for the most part corrupt or tied to imperialism, and that they were wrong to bank on any of the political parties in the region. We believed that the Palestinians could only rely on themselves.'[29]

Fatah was founded in conditions of great secrecy, the protagonists adopting *noms de guerre* and oaths of allegiance suitable for a clandestine organization. Funding was provided by wealthy sympathizers in the Gulf, including the Kuwaiti and Qatari ruling families, while another founder member, Khaled al-Hassan, from Haifa, used his Kuwaiti government job to obtain visas for more activists.[30] They soon began publishing a magazine, *Filastinuna* ('Our Palestine'), edited by Wazir, but did not reveal who was backing it or the names of contributors and editors, using a Beirut post office box number for correspondence. In November 1959 it set out its stall:

The youth of the *Nakba* are dispersed . . . Life in the tent has become as miserable as death . . . [T]o die for our beloved motherland is better and more honourable than life, which forces us to eat our daily bread under humiliations or to receive it as charity at the cost of our honour . . . We, the sons of the *Nakba* are no longer willing to live this dirty, despicable life, this life which has destroyed our cultural, moral and political existence and destroyed our human dignity.[31]

The front page of *Filastinuna* often carried photographs showing the harsh conditions in the refugee camps. The desire to return was evident to anyone who encountered refugees in person. 'If you go among them in the hills of Judaea, they will take you by the arm to a crest of land and point downwards, across the rusty skeins of barbed wire', reported one visitor to the West Bank. ' "Can you see it, over there, behind those trees? That is my home." '[32] In 1963 the popular British writer Ethel Mannin published *The Road to Beersheba*, a sympathetic portrayal of Palestinian refugees and a conscious effort to respond to the stunning success of *Exodus*, the 1958 novel by the American-Jewish author Leon Uris and the subsequent epic film starring Paul Newman. (Mannin's book was dedicated 'To and for THE PALESTINIAN REFUGEES, who, in all the Arab host-countries, said to me, "Why don't you write *our* story – the story of the *other* exodus – *our* exodus?" '[33]) And the feelings were not confined to those living in misery. In her comfortable house in East Jerusalem, Nuzha Nusseibeh, born to a wealthy land-owning family near Ramla, spoke to her son Sari of

> the idyllic innocence of a magical dreamland ... oranges I envisioned as the sweetest on earth growing on a plantation stretching all the way to the gently swelling waves of the Mediterranean, a sea I'd never seen because of No Man's Land but that, like the oranges, I pictured as the noblest on earth. Then came the intrusion by the foreigners, the struggle with the British, the depredations of the Zionists, and the terrorised flight on foot.[34]

In the Palestinian 'master narrative' the pre-1948 village landscape had acquired the magical aura of a golden age, of innocence and abundance – often represented by the fine quality of *baladi* (local) fruit and vegetables – before the disaster.[35] Even inside Israel, in the mid-1960s, Arab voices were growing bolder and more articulate as poets like Samih al-Qasim and Tawfiq Zayyad wrote in *al-Jadid* of *sumoud* (steadfastness/perseverance) and resistance, and Mahmoud Darwish, 'patient in a country where people are enraged', of what it meant to be a Palestinian, most famously in his 1964 poem 'Identity Card':

> Write down!
> I am an Arab
> And my identity card number is fifty thousand
> I have eight children
> And the ninth will come after a summer
> Will you be angry?[36]

The poem's curious power, as Edward Said wrote later, 'is that at the time it appeared . . . it did not represent as much as embody the Palestinian cause, whose political identity in the world had been pretty much reduced to a name on an identity card'.[37]

Fatah's goal was 'to liberate the whole of Palestine and destroy the foundations of what it terms a colonialist Zionist occupation state and society . . . and restore Palestine as it still existed in the mind of most Palestinians, the homeland that existed before 1948'. The Jewish community that pre-dated the British Mandate could remain but under Arab sovereignty.[38] The key elements of its programme were revolution, armed struggle and readiness to establish a Palestinian entity. Frantz Fanon's writings on the Algerian war, the Mau Mau fight against the British in Kenya and the Black civil rights movement in the US all influenced its thinking. But it was hard to get any traction for the cause. 'It was very difficult for us at the start because Nasser was the great attraction', al-Hassan recalled later. 'Most of those who accepted our views were teachers. And every time they went off to other Arab countries for their three-month vacation, we found ourselves having to start all over again.' By 1963, the movement still only had a few hundred members and an inner circle of fewer than twenty.[39] Still, changes in the region proved favourable to the Palestinian cause. The break-up of the Egypt–Syria union, the United Arab Republic, in September 1961 and the civil war in Yemen – the Saudis and Nasser backing opposing sides (and the Israelis secretly helping Nasser's enemies) – were blows to ambitions for Arab unity, though the victory of the FLN and Algerian independence in 1962 gave a powerful fillip to the notion of anti-colonial armed struggle. In the context of the so-called Arab 'cold war' between 'reactionary' and 'progressive' states, both camps sought to play the Palestinian card. Syria agreed to host Fatah and young men from the refugee camps were sent there for military training. Iraq also provided facilities for a while and Algeria became a loyal supporter. Israeli awareness of Fatah was limited until 1965, when it was seen by IDF intelligence as a 'nuisance' rather than a real military challenge.[40] The Israeli public paid it very little attention; newspaper commentators deployed inverted commas to describe Fatah's goal of 'liberation', refusing to see it as the representative of an authentic national movement.[41]

ENTER THE PLO

Israel was raising Arab hackles at this time by the impending completion of its project to divert water from the river Jordan, via its national
water carrier canal, to the Negev desert, which had led to armed
clashes on the Syrian border. In Arab eyes, this decade-old effort
underlined that Israel was there to stay – preparing the ground, literally, for the absorption of millions more Jewish immigrants and
settling the sparsely populated south of the country. Israel's plan to
acquire a nuclear weapon was another fear that was emphasized in
Palestinian and Arab discourse during this period. Both developments threatened to 'turn the existing status quo into a permanent
reality'.[42] Against this background, in January 1964 Nasser convened
a summit conference of Arab kings and presidents in Cairo, the first
of what was to become a regular if largely ritualistic fixture on the
Middle Eastern diplomatic scene. It declared, for the first time, that
the collective goal of the Arab states was the 'final liquidation of
Israel'.[43] It also spoke of 'organizing the Palestinian Arab people to
enable it to play its role in liberating its country and determining its
future'. That difficult task was entrusted to Ahmed al-Shuqayri, a
middle-aged, patrician Palestinian lawyer who had served as the
Syrian and then Saudi representative at the United Nations. Shuqayri,
who had a reputation for verbosity, was not a popular choice for the
new generation of Palestinian activists, who saw him as part of the
defeated and discredited old guard, 'powerless opportunists who
lacked political integrity'.[44]

The fear was that this sponsorship by rival Arab regimes would
recreate the circumstances that had led to the catastrophe of 1948.
Haj Amin al-Husseini, who was still leading the old Arab Higher
Committee from exile in Beirut, was an especially vocal critic.[45] Arafat was cautious too, fearing the consequences of a decision which
'formalised the maladies which had given rise to Fatah', as one of his
biographers noted. 'Above all it was Nasser's brainchild and had been
created to work with the Arab countries to satisfy the Palestinians
while keeping them under control.'[46] The Fatah leader conspicuously
did not join the 420 delegates at a large Palestinian assembly, wearing

'We shall return' badges, in East Jerusalem's Intercontinental Hotel on the Mount of Olives in May 1964 but instead sent Wazir, who listened to Shuqayri declare that Palestinians had experienced sixteen years of misery and that Palestine was 'unique in its catastrophe and alone in its tragedy'. King Hussein acted as a 'reluctant and suspicious host' while Jordanian intelligence agents maintained an 'intrusive and intimidating presence'.[47] Jordan had first proposed that the conference be held in Amman, then at Qalia on the shores of the Dead Sea. It flatly refused to allow it to take place in the Old City of Jerusalem. 'I embraced and kissed King Hussein', Shuqayri would write later. 'And each of us spoke with two tongues about the Palestinian entity.'[48] The meeting announced the establishment of the Palestine Liberation Organization (PLO). It then reconstituted itself as the Palestine National Council, the PLO's 'parliament'. The new organization's charter, or covenant (mithaq), called for the total liberation of Palestine and self-determination within the borders of the British Mandate. It rejected the Balfour Declaration, the Mandate system and claims of 'historic and spiritual ties' between Jews and Palestine. Judaism was a religion not a nationality, Zionism a colonialist movement, 'aggressive and expansionist . . . racist and segregationist . . . fascist in its means and aims'. On the crucial matter of Israel's current population, it stated that 'Jews of Palestinian origin' – defined as those who 'normally resided' in the country until 1947 – were to be considered Palestinians 'if they are willing to live peacefully and loyally in Palestine'.[49] It was a big moment: 'I had the feeling that we were all endowed with a spiritual, metaphysical strength which gave us the power to resist the pressures of intimidation, to overcome all obstacles and eliminate all doubts so that we could move forward', wrote Shafiq al-Hout.[50]

Anxious to maximize his independence, Arafat kept his and Fatah's distance from the new body, discreetly seeking more help and training facilities in Syria, Algeria and Jordan. This did not escape the attention of IDF military intelligence, whose agents in the West Bank were tasked to report on Fatah and another group, called the Palestine Liberation Front, which both stood out from the Lilliputian run-of-the mill 'fronts' and other organizations that sprouted in the refugee camps and issued a few defiant statements before disappearing.[51]

Towards the end of 1964 Fatah decided to launch its first military operation against Israel. It was scheduled to take place on 31 December, but the *fedayeen* squad was intercepted and arrested by Lebanese forces before crossing the border. The bombastic communiqué announcing the abortive attack was signed by *al-Asifa* ('the Storm'), a fictitious name chosen to conceal Fatah's involvement and appease members who feared the group was not yet ready to fight a vastly superior enemy. Three days later, on 3 January 1965, Fatah did manage to infiltrate fighters from the West Bank into Israel and planted an explosive charge in the national water carrier canal in the Bet Netofa valley in lower Galilee. It did not go off but the raid was still counted 'a stunning propaganda success'.[52] Tracks were found by the IDF leading to Bet Shean (Beisan) and from there to the nearby Jordanian border. Accounts differ as to whether it was then or later when Fatah claimed its first 'martyr', a young man named Ahmed Musa who was shot dead by Jordanian troops when returning from Israeli territory. In fact other Palestinian factions had already lost fighters in operations against Israel prior to his death.[53] But a significant new chapter in the conflict had begun.

COUNTDOWN TO WAR

Over the next year *al-Asifa* mounted three dozen or so attacks on Israel, which were of little military significance but were announced to the world in florid or mendacious communiqués. On 18 January, for example, the *New York Times* reported that a 'new and secret Arab fighting organization' claimed to have killed twelve Israelis and wounded nineteen. The following day the Israelis dismissed the story as 'ridiculous'. The name of Fatah first appeared in the Israeli press at that time, where it was described as a group established by the Syrians under Palestinian cover.[54] These pinprick raids were a far cry from the group's grandiloquent prediction that 'at zero hour and the moment of the emergence of the revolution, the throngs of revolutionaries shall set off to their designated targets and strike astonishing blows that will surprise the entire world'. And Fatah's activities also attracted the opposition of Shuqayri's PLO, as well as that of Nasser and other leaders who feared that military action at the wrong time would mean a loss of their control. Still, they magnified the glory of the *fedayeen* and served Arafat's purpose of keeping alive the idea of Palestinian resistance. And there was an underlying strategy: using attacks to set off 'successive detonations' that were intended to provoke an Israeli reaction and compel even reluctant Arab governments to intervene to fight the enemy. It was also a form of propaganda by deed. 'To strike at a bridge or a culvert could not be a decisive act in liberation, but we also knew that to strike a culvert could draw ten more youths to join Fatah', Salah Khalaf explained.[55] In time decrepit sabotage equipment was replaced by chemical delay fuses and electrical timers.[56] Fatah's growing confidence was apparent when it acknowledged publicly that it was behind *al-Asifa*. In June 1965 it came out of the shadows and appealed to the UN secretary general, U Thant, to demand that one of its men, Mahmoud Hijazi, a refugee from Jerusalem who was captured by the Israelis in an early raid, be considered a prisoner of war. Hijazi, who was sentenced first to death and then to life imprisonment, was released in 1971 in exchange for an Israeli who was abducted by Fatah.[57] At the Casablanca Arab summit in September Fatah also called on the Arab states to stop their 'persecution' of liberation movement forces.[58]

Palestinian raids continued in 1966, further angering Egypt, Lebanon and Jordan, which all moved to arrest fighters and prevent further attacks for fear of attracting Israeli reprisals. Tensions rose, especially on the border between Israel and Syria, now Fatah's main base and chief sponsor – despite difficulties which included Arafat spending several weeks in prison in Damascus. Jordan, where King Hussein had already warned of 'impulsive and extemporaneous activities' after suffering two Israeli raids, was the state most hostile to the Palestinians. In April the Jordanians arrested about two hundred 'subversives', including most of the staff of the PLO office in Amman. In July Jordanian forces clashed with a Palestinian commando squad on the way to Israel, killing four of them. In October, after a bombing in Jerusalem's Romema district, close to the border with Jordan – strikingly, the first such incident in the city since 1948 – Prime Minister Levi Eshkol issued a famous warning: 'The ledger is open and the hand is recording.'[59] Jordan accepted from Israel lists of West Bankers who were collaborating with the *fedayeen* groups, and arrested them.[60] But it also bore the brunt of unexpectedly heavy Israeli retaliation in November in a punitive attack on Samu, south of Hebron in the West Bank. A daytime assault by two IDF armoured columns, protected by Mirage fighter planes, left 18 dead, 130 injured and more than 120 houses destroyed. Israel had reported twelve incidents in the preceding weeks – mine explosions, the derailing of a train and attacks on water pipelines – in which seven Israelis had been killed, while the immediate trigger was provided by a Fatah mine which blew up an Israeli armoured personnel carrier and killed three soldiers in the Hebron area. The only surprise was that when retaliation came it was against Jordan, not Syria, which had been far more supportive of the guerrillas. 'Responsibility for these attacks rests not only on the relevant governments but also on the people providing shelter and aid for these gangs,' Eshkol told his cabinet.[61] Yitzhak Rabin, now the IDF chief of staff, faced criticism for the Samu raid, which exposed Jordanian military weakness and infuriated King Hussein, and offered to resign.[62] Angry demonstrations in East Jerusalem and the West Bank gave the king an alarming taste of anti-Jordanian sentiment and of a Palestinian nationalist awakening.[63]

By the early spring of 1967 a process of rapid escalation was under way between Israel and the front-line Arab states. Syria was taking the lead but Egypt and, eventually, even normally cautious Jordan competed with each other, goading each other on, to raise the stakes dangerously. Fatah and the PLO played a significant part in that process, but it was bigger than them and, ultimately, beyond their control as well – another example of the Palestinians losing control of their own destiny at a critical moment. In six extraordinary days that June, just a few months short of half a century since the British government had issued the Balfour Declaration, the Zionist-Arab conflict took another fateful turn.

11

1967

'In 1967 Zionism won one victory too many; and in the twenty years that followed, it sealed its fate by implementing the settlement project and undertaking the de facto annexation of the West Bank.'

Meron Benvenisti[1]

VICTIMS OF VICTORY

The short, sharp war that changed the Middle East ended on 11 June 1967. By then Israel had more than tripled the territory it controlled and significantly shortened its borders, from 611 to 374 miles. It was now ruling over 1.1 million Palestinians. After three weeks of tension fuelled by bellicose rhetoric from Arab capitals Israelis reacted with relief and jubilation, along with mourning for those 679 soldiers who had died. In private the country's leaders had not doubted they would be victorious if it came to a fight, but they had expected heavy losses. In Tel Aviv, braced for air raids, people stockpiled food and filled sandbags, donated blood and dug mass graves in parks while worrying about Russian secret weapons in Egypt: Nasser's use of nerve gas in Yemen in 1963 was an alarming precedent.[2] 'The only analogy I can think of,' one leading politician said afterwards, 'is if Britain had found herself in occupation of Berlin just three days after Dunkirk. The suddenness of the transformation from a situation of acute danger to an unparalleled victory is too much for any people to absorb. It will take time to get over it.'[3] In the run-up to the war there was a popular joke circulating that urged the last Israeli to leave Lod Airport to please turn off the lights.

The Israelis had performed a remarkable feat of arms. By striking pre-emptively – impatient generals urging and finally persuading a notoriously hesitant prime minister Levi Eshkol to act – they won the war within the first few hours of 5 June with the destruction of most of the Egyptian air force while it was still on the ground.[4] The meticulously planned operation began at 07.45 after the end of Egyptian dawn patrols watching for a possible Israeli attack out of the rising sun.[5] Simultaneously the Israelis launched a ground offensive into the Gaza Strip and Sinai, reaching the Suez Canal and Sharm el-Sheikh, at the peninsula's southern tip, by 8 June. On the 5th Nasser induced Syria and Jordan to launch attacks. Israel, which had urged King Hussein to stay out of the war (and was expecting him to do so), retaliated with an offensive to encircle East Jerusalem. Israeli forces initially held back from moving into the Old City for fear of sensitivities about the Muslim and Christian holy places, but on 7 June Moshe Dayan, newly installed as minister of defence, gave the order to attack. After heavy fighting, the Israelis completed the conquest of the city later that day. The words 'Har habayit beyadeinu' ('the Temple Mount is in our hands'), reported over the radio by Colonel Motta Gur, a paratroop battalion commander, acquired a mythical status. Shlomo Goren, the IDF chief rabbi, carrying a Torah scroll, sounded the shofar – the ram's horn traditionally used to mark the start of the Jewish New Year – in emotional scenes at the Western Wall. 'We have reunited the dismembered city,' declared Dayan. 'We have returned to our most holy places, returned, never to be separated from them again' – striking words from an avowed atheist.[6] Victory, relief, religious fervour, nationalism and a sense of history-in-the-making fused into a euphoric, almost messianic mood.

Later that day Israeli forces captured Nablus without a shot being fired: IDF units were mistaken for Iraqi reinforcements that were thought to be heading up from the Jordan Valley.[7] Bethlehem fell easily. When King Hussein ordered his forces to pull back across the Jordan, the Israelis occupied the rest of the West Bank unopposed. Israel's retaliation against Syria took the form of an air strike which destroyed two-thirds of the Syrian air force – commanded by General Hafez al-Assad – and gave the Israelis total air superiority. On 9 June, Dayan, although initially opposed, ordered a ground assault on the

Golan Heights. By the next day, Israeli forces had taken the strategic plateau and the Syrians had retreated eastwards to protect Damascus. On 11 June a ceasefire was agreed. Arab losses were over 20,000.[8]

In military terms, the third Arab–Israeli war was another unequal struggle. On paper, the Arab armies had looked formidable but the Israelis enjoyed qualitative superiority in almost every sphere, as US government assessments recognized. The economy had been in recession since 1965, but the country had advantages of organization, communications and, above all, motivation: people felt, as in 1948, that their backs were to the wall, their existence threatened. War had not been expected, and when it came the IDF was in the midst of several re-equipment programmes. But it was well prepared in intelligence and tactics – especially the Soviet methods used by the Egyptians.[9] Its knowledge of the weaknesses in Egyptian air defences – the 'Achilles heel' of patchy radar cover – was crucial to the whole war plan.[10] Nasser claimed that the US and Britain had plotted with Israel and sent planes to attack Egypt, as the British and French indeed had done in the notorious 'tripartite aggression' of 1956. The charge of collusion was not true this time, however. Arab disarray and shame prompted agonized debates, at least among intellectuals, famously in the work *Self-Criticism after the Defeat* by the Syrian thinker Sadiq al-Azm, much of it focusing on issues of culture, hierarchy, initiative and modernity.[11]

Israel's victory triggered international sympathy and congratulations. 'A wave of warm friendship and understanding of Israel is washing over the world,' the minister of information, Yisrael Galili, told the Knesset. *The Economist* magazine headlined its cover story: 'They Did It'.[12] But there were critical voices too, and not only in Arab countries. 'The Israelis are shrewd – but it is the wisdom of Harvard Law School, not of Solomon', was the conclusion of a US observer who watched the fighting unfold from Jordanian Jerusalem. 'For all the biblical publicity puffs, they had fought . . . in Jerusalem, as everywhere, with all the cautious, long-range planning and reliance on technology of any modern industrial state – their combat style and manner of movement, however improvised the logistics, were reminiscent of the American army.'[13] In later years senior military figures, led by General Matti Peled, would fuel a brief 'annihilation debate', in which it was argued that victory had always been certain and that Israeli leaders had deliberately exaggerated the Arab threat to justify a pre-emptive strike.[14] Israel emphasized Nasser's closure of the Straits of Tiran, the expulsion of UN peace-keepers in Sinai and Egypt's deployments. The Palestinians, who were barely recognized internationally as part of the story and had not taken part in the fighting, lacked spokesmen, let alone effective ones. Musa Mazzawi, a London-based lawyer, explained to the BBC that the Arabs

> are not going to negotiate when their nose is being rubbed in the mud; they're not going to negotiate while General Dayan and people like him say, 'Well these million people on the West Bank of Jordan are a nuisance to me and I want the Gulf of Aqaba and I want the Gaza Strip and I want this and that.' Why? 'Because my aircraft got up a bit early on Monday morning and they struck the Egyptian airfields and they blew them to smithereens and now we can dictate to these people.' Well, you can only do that for a short time. You can't do it for ever.[15]

Military victory, it was to turn out, was indeed the easy part.

FACTS ON THE GROUND

By the end of the fighting the separate parts of Mandatory Palestine had been reunited; the Jordanians and Egyptians had gone, replaced by Israeli military governors. The conquest of Sinai and the Golan added to the feeling that 'little' Israel had acquired an empire. Emotions ran highest over East Jerusalem, with its Jewish, Muslim and Christian holy places, which had been inaccessible to Israelis since the fighting ended in 1948. The IDF central front commander, General Uzi Narkis, talked of 'erasing the stain' of its loss in the war of independence.[16] 'Each of us knew in his heart that once we took the Old City we could never give it up', Teddy Kollek, the Israeli mayor of West Jerusalem, wrote later. New facts were quickly created on the ground. On the evening of 10 June the 650 Palestinian residents of the Maghariba (Moroccan) quarter, extending right up to the Western Wall, were given two hours to evacuate their homes, which were dynamited and bulldozed into rubble, along with two twelfth-century mosques, to make room for a featureless plaza that was intended to accommodate future crowds of Jewish worshippers. 'My overpowering feeling was: do it now,' as Kollek put it. 'It may be impossible to do it later, and it *must* be done.' Kollek called the buildings 'hovel-slums'.[17] But the pro-Palestinian camp lamented the loss of 'a pleasant and architecturally distinctive quarter of freshly whitewashed roof terraces, gardens and neat unattached houses built in North African style'.[18] David Ben-Gurion, still serving as an MP with the centrist Rafi faction, along with Dayan and an ambitious younger colleague named Shimon Peres, also proposed tearing down the sixteenth-century Ottoman walls surrounding the Old City. On that point wiser counsels prevailed. Ben-Gurion demanded that the street sign 'Wailing Wall Road' in English and Arabic be taken down.[19] And Rabbi Goren, it emerged later, had proposed blowing up the Dome of the Rock.[20] On 14 June, when public access was allowed, vast crowds of Israelis streamed into the Old City, marvelling at its sights and significance while Palestinian residents watched silently from their windows.

On 27 June the government voted to unite the western and eastern sides of Jerusalem, more than doubling municipal jurisdiction to include the newer Arab suburbs as well as 12 villages, incorporating 69,000 Palestinians and extending nearly to Ramallah in the north and Bethlehem in the south.[21] The next day the Knesset passed the decision into law. Engineers and demolition crews were sent out to remove the barbed wire, anti-sniper walls and the debris of two wars. The famous Mandelbaum Gate checkpoint was dismantled. The Israeli move, condemned by Palestinians as well as internationally, was officially described as 'integration' or 'municipal fusion' rather than annexation, for fear of adverse reactions and pressure to withdraw. Israeli embassies abroad were instructed to use the same terminology.[22] Separate roads, water mains, telephone and electricity networks were reconnected but the mood was anything but mundane. 'Jerusalem is beyond time, it belongs to the scriptures – that is to eternity', Eshkol's adviser, Yaakov Herzog, explained. 'We must prevent history and geography from re-dividing it like another Berlin.'[23]

CLOSE ENCOUNTERS

In Jerusalem and beyond the Israelis came face-to-face with the masses of Palestinians they had not encountered for the previous nineteen years, tens of thousands of them still living in crowded refugee camps – Balata in Nablus, al-Amari and Jalazoun around Ramallah, and others near Bethlehem and Hebron – living reminders of a conflict that had just got much more complicated. The majority of Jews under twenty-five had rarely encountered an Arab, especially if they lived in the densely populated centre of Israel. On the eve of the war only 42 per cent of the population had lived in the country before 1948.[24] In 1963, when a Jewish teenager from Ramat Aviv came back from a rare joint summer beach and hiking camp for Jewish and Arab children he was 'surprised and sobered' by what he had learned about the military government under which his Arab counterparts then still lived.[25] 'The education we had been given was nationalist, patriotic, and ethnocentric, with no space for the "other" and certainly not the Arab, who was frightening and distant, and who, along with the Germans, we had to hate', the child of Holocaust survivors recalled of her upbringing in Tel Aviv in the 1960s.[26] Academic Yaron Ezrahi remembered a childhood game in an abandoned citrus grove on the outskirts of that city in 1949, nine-year-old 'commandos' illicitly picking oranges until someone shouted: 'The Arabs are coming', and then they would run for their lives.[27] In 1967 most Israeli Jews had little idea what life was like for Arabs even inside their own borders – let alone beyond them. The nearest most Jews came to the wider Middle East was in Jerusalem, at the end of a corridor that was all but surrounded by Jordanian territory – the narrow, winding road to it flanked by the carefully preserved remains of the armoured convoys that had supplied the besieged city in the 1948 war. 'The Arab world on the other side of the border was a threatening desert,' recalled a Jewish Jerusalemite, 'both empty and occupied by a hostile population.'[28] On the train that passed through the Judaean hills from Tel Aviv passengers would peer out at the Arab villages of Battir and Bet Safafa just over the green line. In periods of tension a guard would pull down metal shutters over the carriage windows to protect the passengers from gunfire. Older Israelis, of course, included immigrants from Morocco and Iraq, who enjoyed Egyptian films – then the finest in the Arab world. Many tuned into Radio Ramallah, which played Arabic and Western music, lighter fare than that of the ponderous Hebrew state broadcaster, Kol Yisrael.[29]

Now many felt an intoxicating sense of liberation from the constraints of the old borders. 'It was an incredibly intense experience', another Israeli wrote later, recalling the crowds of Arabs gaping at the traffic lights in the centre of the western side of Jerusalem, and the Jews staring at the Jordanian policemen in smart white gloves in the east.[30] 'Now for the first time in twenty years there was a feeling of freedom of movement, of open space', observed Walter Laqueur, a Polish-born Jewish historian who had lived in Palestine as a young man and remembered the borderless pre-1948 reality.

> Weekend after weekend streams of tourists poured into the Old City of Jerusalem, into Hebron and Ramallah and even Gaza and Nablus. Israelis could not see enough of the Arab markets and the minarets, the street scenes with which the older citizens had been familiar from the Mandatory days: villagers offering grapes and figs, donkeys braying, sellers of black coffee and cold lemonade, shoeshine boys and taxi drivers soliciting customers, middle-aged Arabs sitting in the shade in front of their closed shops and viewing suspiciously the throng of curious Jews whose very appearance seemed so out of keeping with the place. There were the specific smells and noises of the market place and the commercial centre in the Arab cities which a young generation of Israelis took in for the first time. They had spent their life half a mile away and yet it had been a closed world to them. They were indefatigable souvenir hunters, if only for a Chinese ballpoint or a cheap Japanese hand mirror. And for so many months the whole of Israel seemed to be on the move and, as bus after bus rolled into Gaza and Bethlehem, the Arab man in the street must have reached the conclusion that the number of Israeli Jews was far in excess of two million.[31]

Impressions were extremely vivid, but they could be misleading too. Three days after the conquest of Hebron, Hanna Zemer, a journalist with *Davar*, found shops and cafes open and cheap cigarettes on sale. 'The people of Hebron are already prepared to take Israeli pounds', she reported. 'They don't have just a sound commercial sense but healthy political instincts as well.'[32] Israeli newspapers highlighted 'human interest' stories about Jews who were meeting old Arab friends for the first time in nineteen years: Yaakov Elsheikh was given a touchingly warm reception at his old home in Jerusalem's Old City, as was Hanan Brozitski in Hebron, where he had been a policeman in 1929. Excitement combined with wishful thinking about improved Arab–Jewish relations. Yael Dayan, the general's daughter, pondered the meaning of victory in a hastily written memoir. 'No one answer or solution could be given . . . but one thing was clear to all of us – the price we were to demand for returning the new areas, or some of them, could not be less than the one thing we were after – peace . . . "Home" now was something new, safer, larger, stronger and happier.'[33]

For Israelis, the soundtrack to these extraordinary events was provided by that year's hit song, 'Jerusalem of Gold' ('*Yerushalayim shel Zahav*'), written by Naomi Shemer, which had first been performed at the Israeli Song Festival a few weeks before the war. Its Hebrew lyrics, rich in biblical and literary allusions, described the 'solitary' Old City, with a 'wall in its heart', where the market square was 'empty', the wells dry and no one visited the Temple Mount or went down to the Dead Sea via Jericho. The Arabs who lived, worked and prayed there did not appear anywhere in this romantic, exclusivist fantasy. Later this was followed by an album named *Jerusalem of Steel*, including other victory favourites.[34] Arabs had been out of sight and largely out of mind for a generation and more. Now, however, their presence could no longer be ignored. The Arab equivalent of Shemer's song, the plangent 'Old Jerusalem' ('*Al-Quds al-Atiqa*') by the Lebanese diva Fairouz, was not released until a few years later. It mourned the empty streets, shuttered shops and 'ownerless' houses that remained of Palestine, saluting the 'waiting people' in colloquial Arabic. It made no mention of the city's new masters.[35]

RETURN TO NORMAL?

Until the last minute, hoping that Jordan would stay out of the war, the Israelis had not anticipated conquering the West Bank, although contingency plans had been drawn up in 1958 (when Hussein had faced a coup threat) and Ben-Gurion had predicted gloomily that the Arabs would not flee en masse for a second time. In 1963, against the background of new tensions in Jordan, the IDF attorney-general launched a course for reserve officers on military law in occupied territories.[36] Now handbooks about international law and civilian populations were dusted off, and officers involved in the brief occupation of the Gaza Strip after the Sinai campaign in 1956 were drafted in, along with veterans of the military government inside Israel, which had been abolished at the end of 1966. 'Improvisation was necessary', wrote Shlomo Gazit, an army intelligence officer,

> because the IDF had no pre-established command posts ... no officers trained for such functions; and no data about the new territories, the local populations or economy. Except for a very general formula calling for the 'return of life to normal' there was no Israeli government policy for the newly occupied territories, so every military commander acted according to his best judgement.[37]

Control was entirely in the hands of the military, which assumed the power to abrogate Jordanian laws and issue new ones. Banking activities were suspended and trade and financial restrictions imposed. Severe penalties were announced, including detention without trial, curfews, house demolitions and expulsion. Many of these were permitted under emergency regulations inherited from the British Mandate – an argument used to justify their use by the Israelis.

Early Israeli decisions, like the destruction of the Maghariba quarter, were made on ad hoc bases but had lasting consequences. In the Latrun salient, near the Trappist monastery where the Jordanian border had cut awkwardly into Israeli territory, three Palestinian villages, Imwas, Yalu and Beit Nuba, were destroyed a week after their inhabitants, expelled to Ramallah on 7 June, tried to return home. Held back at roadblocks, they watched as bulldozers demolished their houses and the stones from the ruins were loaded onto Israeli trucks. The site was turned into a large picnic and recreation area and named Canada Park. Amos Keinan, a well-known writer, was serving in the IDF unit deployed to secure the operation, and he wrote an account of it that reflected his horror and dismay. Initially the document remained private, in a letter to MPs, but it was published in the early 1970s and then echoed around the world. 'The chickens and the pigeons were buried under the rubble', Keinan wrote. 'The fields were turned to desolation before our eyes, and the children who dragged themselves along the road that day, weeping bitterly, will be the fedayeen of 19 years hence. That is how, that day, we lost the victory.'[38] Israel maintained that the three villages had helped in the siege of Jerusalem in 1948 and billeted Egyptian commandos in an attack on nearby Lod.[39] The decision to demolish them was apparently based on the assumption that the West Bank would have to be returned to Jordanian control; their destruction would thus prevent their being reoccupied by Jordanian forces close to the main road to Jerusalem.[40] Similar logic may have applied when two more remote villages, Bet Awwa and Beit Mirsim, on the green line near Hebron, were razed on the grounds that they had sheltered Fatah guerrillas before the war, though residents were eventually able to return to part of their lands and rebuild their homes. In Qalqilya, at the narrowest point of the old border, where many residents had fled, 850 of the town's 2,000 houses were demolished, though they were also rebuilt. In Sourif, a West Bank village near Gush Etzion, fifteen houses were dynamited in apparent retribution for the killing of thirty-five Palmah fighters, the legendary 'Lamed-Hay', in January 1948. The IDF commanders responsible were Palmah veterans.[41] It was one of many ways in which the 1967 war finished business that Israelis felt had been left undone nineteen years earlier.

On the other side, the Palestinians experienced the blow of humiliating defeat, though virtually without their participation. In Damascus Fatah leaders huddled round a radio on 9 June to hear the devastating news of Nasser's resignation offer and the victory celebrations in Israel. Events had moved at a dizzying pace. Saeb Erakat, then a twelve-year-old living in Jericho, waved at a passing Iraqi armoured column heading west from Jordan, and then saw its charred remains after an Israeli air strike a few hours later. Leaflets were dropped over the town ordering residents to stay at home and raise white flags. Erakat's mother hung sheets out of the windows. The Israelis arrived a few hours later, checking houses and looting.[42]

Palestinians were stunned for weeks after the fighting ended. The head of UNRWA described

> the overwhelming sense of bewilderment and shock felt by the inhabitants ... as the cataclysm swept over them. The disruption of the lives and careers of countless persons, the anxiety caused by the sudden loss of earnings and remittances from abroad, the personal tragedies resulting from the separation of husbands and wives, parents and children, are only some of the problems which confront so many of the former Arab inhabitants of Palestine.[43]

It was not another *Nakba* – that emotive term still marked the great catastrophe of 1948 – but a *naksa*, a setback, though a very significant and grimly familiar one. Figures differ on the number of Palestinians who were displaced in 1967. Israel estimated 150,000; Jordan 250,000; and independent agencies around 200,000.[44] Of these many were refugees for a second time, having first arrived in the West Bank after fleeing their original homes. Israel actively encouraged them to move east, providing free transport out of the West Bank.[45] In Jerusalem, where the buses could be boarded at the Damascus Gate, Arab residents were allowed to move about the city even during the strictly enforced curfew if they could prove they were preparing to leave.[46] Uri Avnery later described meeting soldiers who said their role was to expel Palestinians. No official documents have been released on this issue.

For weeks after the war, the scene at the Allenby Bridge across the Jordan, blown up by the retreating Jordanians, was a miserable one, with refugees forced to walk on half-sunken girders or wade through the shallow water. 'By the end of June, when the Arabs were still leaving in hundreds every day, the Israeli authorities were making them sign a paper that they were leaving of their own free will', one journalist reported. 'Going down to the bridge frequently you had the impression that if the Arabs did see the Israelis they did not register, they had closed their eyes to them. Here was a face to face encounter for which neither party was then ready.'[47] Still, as an Israeli described later: 'When someone refused to give me his hand [for finger-printing] they came and beat him badly. Then I was forcibly taking his thumb, and immersing it in ink and finger-printing him ... I have no doubt that tens of thousands of men were removed against their will."[48] The refugee camps of Ein as-Sultan and Aqabat Jaber in Jericho had been bombed by the Israelis, leading to an exodus of tens of thousands of refugees. In line with long-standing policy, most were not allowed back afterwards. The same was true for the 100,000 Syrians who fled the Golan Heights. Refugees in Jordan were settled in temporary camps in Amman and Jerash.[49] Israel recorded about 5,000 people a day crossing the Jordan in June, dropping to 500 in mid-July and 300 in August.[50]

Israel's conquest of the Gaza Strip provided both new and familiar challenges. Its brief occupation a decade earlier had left some traces – and fears. Gaza's most striking characteristic was the density of its population, which was mainly urban and predominantly young, 65 per cent of them refugees from 1948, many crammed into UNRWA-run camps. It was less developed and more isolated than the West Bank as the occupation of Sinai had cut it off from its hinterland so it became more dependent on the Israelis for services and general assistance. It had weaker institutions. Unlike Jordan, Egypt had not granted citizenship to Palestinians. Life was hard, especially in the summer heat when the stench of sewage in the alleyways of the camps was unbearable. Gazans, overall, had less to lose than their compatriots on the West Bank. The Israelis established their headquarters in the Serail in Gaza City, abandoned by the Egyptians. The mayor, Ragheb al-Alami, was confirmed in his position by the Israeli governor, but Egyptian officials working for UNRWA or the former administration were expelled. The UN body estimated that 40,000 to 50,000 people had fled, perhaps because they feared a repeat of the massacres of November 1956. Most went to Jordan. Killings in Rafah on 11 June may have hastened the flight. For months afterwards there was a steady exodus, helped by Israel's policy of providing free transport to the Jordan bridges. Within days of the war's end, following a mine explosion, 110 Palestine Liberation Army (PLA) men were expelled to Egypt and eight homes were blown up by the IDF.[51]

NEW PROSPECTS?

On the face of it, new political possibilities beckoned. The war, after all, had recreated the conditions of 1947 and catapulted the Palestinians back from two decades of oblivion to centre-stage, albeit in a humiliating and subordinate role. 'Defeat', one man mused later, 'had given me back my homeland.'[52] It was, a foreign observer agreed, as if 'one of the ancient bi-national plans of high-minded Mandate personalities had come to life and there had never been partition'.[53] Even before the fighting ended, the government ordered officials to explore prospects for the creation of some kind of Palestinian government in the West Bank to replace Jordanian rule. David Kimche was a junior officer in the Mossad; Dan Bavly, a reserve army officer. The report they produced called for the immediate establishment of a Palestinian state by Israel. Shin Bet security service officers were also keen.[54] But there was an obvious drawback: a survey conducted in Nablus, the most nationalist city on the West Bank, concluded that while people did support an independent Palestine, they flatly rejected the idea of its being an Israeli creation or satellite.

On 18 June Anwar Nusseibeh, the former Jordanian ambassador to Britain, who had lost a leg in the 1948 war, assembled twenty prominent Palestinians in his Jerusalem home for a meeting with General Chaim Herzog, the West Bank military governor. Herzog had arranged permits allowing the invitees to venture out during the curfew. His HQ was in the Ambassador hotel, a few minutes away. Ruhi al-Khatib, the loyalist Jordanian mayor, was in a bitter, introspective mood. 'I cannot understand how this could have happened to us,' he told the group. Another participant, a radical nationalist and no friend of the Hashemites, replied acidly: 'It happened because for 20 years we have been building up a regime and destroying a nation – the Palestinians – while on the other side [Israel] they have been building up a state, not a personal regime. Now everybody can see the results.'[55] Jordan and Syria, having got wind of these discussions, issued stern warnings against any co-operation with the Israeli enemy. 'Operation Sadducees', a clandestine Shin Bet programme to cultivate Arab notables – mayors, former ministers, religious leaders – and turn them into quislings by delivering personal favours, lasted only a few months and brought little in the way of concrete results.[56]

The Palestinian Fatah movement, which had taken no part in the fighting, sought from the start to rally support and boost flagging morale. 'Our organisation has decided to continue struggling against the Zionist conqueror', *al-Asifa* announced from Damascus on 22 June:

> We are planning to operate far from the Arab states so they will not suffer Israeli reprisals for Fedayeen actions. It will therefore be impossible to hold the Arab people responsible for our war. Our organisation is the organisation of the Palestinian people [and] we are united in our resolve to free our stolen homeland from the hands of the Zionists.

This did not mean much on the ground, although rumours did start to circulate of Fatah cells operating in secret – and in late August Fatah announced the start of combat operations in the occupied territories. In September or October Arafat and another Fatah commander, Abu Ali Shaheen, managed to enter the West Bank and set up a secret HQ in Qabatiyeh, near Jenin, recruiting fighters and smuggling them back via Jordan for training at camps in Syria. Other accounts place Arafat's headquarters in Nablus.[57] According to one version he spent three weeks sleeping in caves or under trees while moving from village to village, and once heard Israeli troops who were searching for him moving overhead when he was in a cave near Ramallah.[58] The Palestinian leader was not yet famous but his name was known to the Israelis. In September *Haaretz* reported that a captured Fatah operative had named Arafat or 'Abu Ammar' as the group's 'chief of operations'.[59] In December Arafat was nearly captured by the Shin Bet, who had traced him to a villa in Ramallah despite his using a disguise and forged documents identifying him as a 'Doctor Mustafa' from Gaza. He fled dressed as a woman. Stories of his exploits – evading patrols, visiting Tel Aviv, travelling by bus – added to 'the myth of heroism and survival' associated with him.[60] Armed actions were rare, one exception being an attack on an IDF patrol in the Gaza Strip shortly before the Khartoum Arab summit conference at the end of August.[61] Intelligence files captured from the

Jordanian *mukhabarat* (secret police) helped the Israelis identify activists from organizations that had been underground since the government crackdown of 1957.[62] The leader of one Fatah network was arrested carrying membership lists.[63] Shin Bet officers accompanied the first IDF combat units which entered the West Bank and Gaza. Fatah men returning to the West Bank failed to take the most elementary security precautions and many were easily identified and picked up.

In early August a general strike was called in East Jerusalem to protest against Israeli 'unification' measures. At the end of the month the deposed mayor, Khatib, and fellow municipal council members, spoke out:

> The inhabitants of the Arab sector of Jerusalem and those of the West Bank resolutely proclaim their opposition to all the measures which the Israeli occupation authorities have taken and which those authorities regard as constituting a fait accompli not subject to appeal or reversal, namely, the unification of the two sectors of the City of Jerusalem. They proclaim to the whole world that this annexation, even camouflaged under the cloak of administrative measures, was carried out against their will and against their wishes. In no event shall we submit to it or accept it.[64]

On 19 September a bomb exploded outside the old Fast hotel, just inside West Jerusalem. Fatah claimed responsibility and hailed the start of 'the armed popular revolution'. It envisaged a 'general insurrection' in which fighters would be supported by 'a large clandestine network . . . in conscious imitation of the 1936–39 revolt'.[65] Guerrilla bands, ten- to fifteen-strong, were scattered in the Nablus–Jenin–Tulkarem area and the Hebron hills, commanded by Fatah men who had undergone training courses in China and Algeria. But neither the West Bank nor the Gaza Strip turned into an 'Arab Hanoi' against an 'Israeli Saigon'. In September Israeli sources reported a total of thirteen guerrilla operations; in October, ten; in November eighteen; and in December twenty.[66] September and October, Dayan said later, were the most difficult months since the ceasefire.[67] By the end of the year the Israelis announced that sixty *fedayeen* had been killed and three hundred gaoled since the war. In January 1968 between 1,000 and 1,250 activists were in prison, three-quarters of them locals.[68] In February alone the Israelis arrested 115 Fatah men, killed 35 infiltrators and stopped another 10 on the border – nearly all the 200 fighters Fatah said had entered the country in January.[69] By April 1968, the number of arrests had risen to 1,900, of whom 45 were Israeli Arab citizens. More than two hundred had been killed by the IDF and border police.[70]

OPEN BRIDGES

Israeli policy on the ground in the occupied territories evolved ad hoc. In high summer, a glut of agricultural produce – cucumbers, tomatoes, watermelons – in the northern West Bank that could not be sold in Israel due to farmers' objections, risked going to waste. The IDF officer in charge took the initiative and authorized Palestinian farmers to make deliveries by truck across the Jordan. Dayan was at first alarmed but then declared what subsequently became known as the 'open bridges' policy. It helped relieve economic pressure on the Palestinians and also became a staple of Israeli propaganda, though in reality the bridges were not always open, not to everyone and not in both directions.[71] Additionally, it enabled Jordan to maintain significant though informal influence in the West Bank. The Jordanian dinar continued to circulate and the government in Amman carried on paying the salaries, and keeping the loyalty, of thousands of employees – a handy way, for Israel, of keeping costs down and of promoting competition with more nationalist Palestinians. This quiet collaboration between Jordan and Israel, masked by *pro forma* expressions of hostility from the king's men, was hugely important and a dimension of the conflict that was normally hidden from view. Hussein had been meeting Israeli emissaries since 1963. On 2 July, barely three weeks after the end of hostilities, he secretly met Yaakov Herzog, representing Eshkol, in London. If there were to be peace, it would have to be with 'dignity and honour', he insisted. 'Do not push us into a corner.'[72]

Dayan, the unchallenged viceroy of the occupied territories, wanted the military government to keep a low profile, to keep interference in daily life to a minimum while maintaining an iron grip on security. In reality though the two were inseparable: the power to grant or withhold permission for a myriad different activities – a habit honed on Israel's Arab minority over the previous nineteen years – was central to the 'pervasive and highly intrusive system of population control it maintained' supported by the Shin Bet and its network of informers and collaborators.[73] As Dayan put it in an internal debate: 'Let the individual know that he has something to lose. His home can be blown up, his bus license can be taken away, he can be deported from the region; or the contrary: he can exist with dignity, make money, exploit other Arabs, and travel in [his] bus.'[74]

Israeli leaders, conscious of international public opinion and worried about pressure to withdraw from its conquests, as had happened after the Suez war in 1957, liked to describe their occupation as liberal or enlightened. But resistance of any kind was not tolerated. In early September a school strike was declared after the Israelis banned a number of Arabic textbooks and ordered passages erased from others. Curfews, arrests and searches, focused on Nablus, broke the protest after a few weeks. The first of many prominent Palestinians to be deported from their own country was Sheikh Abdel Hamid al-Sayih, president of the Sharia court of appeal and head of a National Guidance Committee, formed to co-ordinate resistance to the occupation. Sayih was accused of 'incitement' for issuing a *fatwa* or religious ruling ordering Muslims not to abide by Israeli law and calling for a general strike to mark the opening of the UN General Assembly.

In the morning of 25 September 1967 – there was a knock on my door. When I emerged I was told, 'You have to go to see the authorities in order to answer a question, and then you can return.' I asked whether I should pack a bag, and they said no. I got a small bag, just in case, and packed pyjamas and a towel. I was then taken to the Russian compound, where an official rose to his feet to greet me respectfully and offered me coffee or tea. I declined, saying that I wished to pray, as it was time for dawn prayers. After I finished my prayers he handed me the order of deportation. Written in Hebrew, it stated that Moshe Dayan . . . has decreed my deportation in accordance with article such and such of the emergency regulations ... After they gave me the deportation order, they took it back and replaced it with an Arabic translation, saying that since I was going into enemy territory, I should not be carrying a document written in Hebrew.[75]

Sayih went on to occupy a senior position in the PLO, like many deportees, strengthening the links between those living under occupation and their leaders outside.

REUNIONS

Palestinians, like Israelis, had to adjust to the renewed contact with people they had not encountered for nearly two decades, and, in the case of young people, never before. Anwar Nusseibeh's son Sari, then a nineteen-year-old student at Oxford, described gingerly crossing the few hundred feet of what had been no-man's-land from the family home by the Mandelbaum Gate into Mea Shearim, the crowded ultra-Orthodox quarter of West Jerusalem, for the first time in his life. Driving home from Lod airport, he was stunned by his first sight of an Israeli landscape that looked to him more like southern California than the Middle East, without donkeys, camels or Arabs, until reaching Abu Ghosh on the outskirts of Jerusalem – alerting him for the first time to the fact that the *Nakba* had left some Palestinians behind in the Jewish state.[76] Musa Budeiri, who was born in West Jerusalem but grew up in the Jordanian sector, confessed to being 'blissfully ignorant of Israel and Jews'. As Israelis streamed into East Jerusalem, 'thousands of Arabs, worried but excited, went the opposite way, seeking their lost paradise'[77] – what was now Israeli Jerusalem – to see what had happened in the intervening years to their property, their homes and family graves.[78] Cars with Jordanian number plates drove slowly round looking at the houses they had abandoned in 1948.[79] Hala Sakakini, daughter of the writer Khalil, knocked on the door of the family's fine villa in Qatamon, now in a street with a Hebrew name.

Two ladies appeared – one dark young lady and the other an elderly European lady. We addressed them first in Arabic, but they seemed not to understand; so we asked them if they spoke English, but they shook their heads; so we started to talk in German and the elderly lady understood. We tried to explain: 'This is our house. We used to live here before 1948. This is the first time we see it in nineteen years . . .' The elderly lady was apparently moved, but she immediately began telling us that she too had lost a house in Poland, as though we personally or the Arabs in general were to blame for that. We saw it was no use arguing with her.[80]

Tens of thousands of refugees visited their former homes in Jerusalem, Jaffa, Haifa, Lod, Ramla, Acre, Safed and Tiberias, though the encounter usually turned into what the journalist Danny Rubinstein called 'a fantastic voyage of delusion'.[81] In late June the Israeli press reported that no compensation would be granted for property lost in 1948 'since ownership rights have lapsed'.[82] Ali al-Khalili, a Nablus-born writer, described how, when he visited Acre to see relatives, he was stunned and inexplicably moved to find that the 'Zionists' he encountered in Netanya and Haifa were not just 'brutal soldiers', but old people and children too, just like the old people and children in Nablus.[83] Travelling to the Mediterranean coast and swimming in the sea was a special pleasure. Fadwa Touqan, the poet from Nablus, was furious when she was questioned by Israeli policemen in Jaffa shortly after the war. 'We felt the intensity of our connection [to the city] and the pulsating blood of our Palestinian roots buried deep in this Arab land that had been stolen by force and by violence – land that was now held prisoner by foreigners who had no roots in it at all.'[84]

Israel's Arab citizens were initially banned from visiting kinfolk or friends on the other side of the green line. And even when blanket restrictions, for 'security reasons', were eventually lifted hundreds remained on blacklists preventing them from entering the West Bank.[85] Khawla Abu Baker, who had grown up in Acre, spent weeks with her cousins in the orchards and tobacco fields of Yaabed, where she leafed fascinated through unfamiliar Jordanian textbooks and was taken to the spot where Sheikh Izzedin al-Qassam had been killed by the British in 1935. Abu Baker heard accusations that the Arabs of the 'inside' (*dakhil*) – a neutral way of describing those who had stayed put after the *Nakba* – had been cowardly in not resisting the Israelis.[86] Sami Michael, an Iraq-born Israeli-Jewish novelist, was to fictionalize one such tense encounter in an acclaimed book, *Hasut* (Refuge), published a few years later. Palestinians saw their kinfolk inside Israel as 'the lackeys of the enemy, the defeated sector who were lorded over by their Israeli masters'.[87]

Atallah Mansour, an Israeli-Arab journalist, visited the West Bank, 'feeling joy and sorrow' as he drove on roads littered with burned-out tanks, damaged houses and refugees. Israeli citizens had been ordered not to mix with the local population, offer them lifts or accept invitations to drink coffee in their homes. Palestinians Mansour met were suspicious but concealed this behind 'voluble flattery', refusing to believe he was either a journalist or even an Arab.[88] Rafik Halabi, an Israeli Druze, tried to pay a Ramallah hotel bill by cheque and was asked: 'How long will you people be staying?'[89] Jabra Nicola, a left-wing activist from Haifa, travelled to East Jerusalem to meet old comrades he had not seen in twenty years.[90] Others took pleasure in being able to buy olive oil soap or *kanafeh* – a local delicacy of white cheese, wheat and syrup – from Nablus, despite the unpalatable fact that this had only been made possible by another crushing Israeli victory.[91] On the other hand, Palestinians in the occupied territories and beyond were pleased to discover the work of the writers of the 'inside' like Mahmoud Darwish and Samih al-Qassem. 'The challenge in their voices, the verve and the determination to fight, to look hard into the face of the enemy, was not only an inspiration but a reassurance that Palestine and its spirit were not dead', wrote Salma Khadra Jayyusi.[92]

Palestinians were happy to be reunited with family or friends, though it could be awkward. 'Well, at first, we enjoyed this,' said a woman from Abu Gosh:

> My parents especially enjoyed it. Me, I found it strange. To be honest, almost all these relatives who had been living over in Jordan seemed different from us. They seemed like strangers in everything . . . I had expected I was going to feel close to them, we were always hearing about them . . . And they had this way about them that made you feel . . . they expected things out of us. You know, one of them would say, 'We don't have this kind of cleaner, or this soap over there.' And

another would say, 'That orange juice concentrate, where do you get that?' Hinting, you see. And we were expected to go out and buy these things for them. We did, sure. We bought lots of presents, but they were always asking for more.[93]

Naila Zayyad from Nazareth also met envious West Bankers who thought 'you eat honey in Israel'. Exposure to Israel, she felt, had bred realism: 'Having lived under Israeli rule for 18 [sic] years, we knew there was no magic formula, no throwing the Jews in the sea or wiping Israel off the map.'[94]

In Bartaa, divided down the middle by the 1949 armistice agreement, post-war reunions revealed striking differences: in the colloquial Arabic mingled with Hebrew words, higher living standards and a sense of isolation from the wider Arab world on the Israeli side that brought a hunger for Arabic books and periodicals on sale in East Jerusalem and Nablus. Unification, however, was 'virtual' rather than real, with some residents living under military occupation and receiving education and health services from the Jenin district, while in homes nearby they held Israeli identification cards.[95] 'In the beginning we behaved rather condescendingly to our relatives [on the other side]', admitted Riyadh Kabha, an Israeli citizen, 'as if we were more advanced than them and we were the winning side . . . but that didn't last long.'[96] The Communist writer Emile Habibi likened Israeli Arabs to people in prison who awoke one day to find that the rest of their family, from whom they had been separated for twenty years, had suddenly been incarcerated with them.[97] Alarmed Israeli experts soon began to warn of the risks of the 'Palestinization' of a hitherto docile minority – a big theme in years to come.[98] Aziz Shehadeh, a Jaffa-born lawyer who had fled to Ramallah in 1947, held a reunion with a relative in Haifa who offered his advice on what to expect, on the basis of his experience of 1948, once a 'honeymoon' period with Israel was over. 'It will only be a short honeymoon', the relative predicted. 'Afterwards the hardship will begin. First they will impose heavy taxes, then land acquisitions will start, then what is left of the land will be rendered out of reach through land-use planning.'[99]

THE SONS RETURN

Palestinians were right to be apprehensive about what Israel would do now. Israelis remembered how Ben-Gurion had bemoaned the failure – 'a cause of lamentation for generations' (*bekhiyah le'dorot*), in his famous phrase – to capture the West Bank at the end of the war of independence. In Hebrew the territory had always been referred to as Judaea and Samaria, the ancient Jewish kingdoms that housed the Tomb of the Patriarchs in Hebron, Rachel's Tomb in Bethlehem and biblical sites near Nablus or Jericho. Israelis were drawn by Jewish history, the land and the Lord, not necessarily in that order. For many the Palestinian inhabitants were a secondary issue, and a clearly problematic one. 'We won the war and received a nice dowry of territory', as Eshkol put it with his characteristically folksy sense of humour, often expressed in piquant Yiddish. 'But it came with a bride whom we don't like.'[100]

The 1967 war was a hugely significant turning point in the Israeli–Palestinian conflict. But it was marked by continuity as well as change. Discussions in Israel ranged back in time, not only to biblical sources and archaeological remains but also to earlier debates at key moments in Zionist history. In 1937, when the Peel Commission proposed partition as a solution to the conflict, opponents objected on the ground that it surrendered historic Jewish patrimony. Similar arguments raged around the UN partition plan a decade later. Hopes of restoring the 'wholeness' (*shlaymut*) of the Land of Israel all but disappeared from Israeli political life after 1948, even if, in the absence of peace agreements with the Arab states, the ceasefire lines were not transformed into recognized borders. Irredentism was confined to the lunatic fringe.[101] Still, *Eretz-Yisrael* remained a powerful magnet, especially for the first and second generations of native-born Jews – Sabras – or those who had arrived in the country as children. Influential political and military figures had grown up in the *kibbutzim* and reached maturity in the 1940s, hiking their way across, and spying out, a then undivided land, serving in the Palmah, winning the war of independence and crushing the Arabs. Now, it seemed, with the country made 'whole' again, anything was possible. The old debate on the territorial limits of Zionism was no longer just theoretical.

Within days of the war's end newspapers were carrying large advertisements demanding the annexation of the conquered territories. Many supporters came from the right-wing of Israeli politics. The *Herut* party, led by the former *Irgun* commander Menachem Begin, still clung officially to the view that Jordan (which, as Transjordan, had been severed from the rest of Mandatory Palestine in 1921) should have been part of the promised land, as well as the rump of Palestine. (Begin had also protested at the IDF withdrawal from Sinai and Gaza in 1957.) But there were annexationist voices on the left as well. The *Ahdut haAvoda* wing of Mapai, the ruling Labour party, hankered after those lost landscapes. Yigal Allon, the former Palmah commander, minister of labour and Moshe Dayan's arch rival, was a leading figure in that camp – and the most hawkish figure in the cabinet. Religious belief played a significant role, drawing on the teachings of the influential rabbi Zvi Yehuda Kook, who had famously described the establishment of the state of Israel as 'the beginning of redemption'. Hanan Porat, one of Kook's students and a member of the Orthodox nationalist *Bnei Akiva* youth movement, lobbied Eshkol to approve a return to Gush Etzion, the settlement bloc south of Bethlehem where he had been born shortly before it was conquered by the Arab Legion, its defenders killed and buildings destroyed in the 1948 war. The outpost that was established there in September 1967 – the first of the post-war settlements in the West Bank – was seen as in keeping with mainstream Zionist tradition that land, once 'redeemed', could not be abandoned. That, it was argued, was a duty, not an option. The same month saw the establishment of the all-party Land of Israel Movement (*Eretz Yisrael hashlayma*) made up of individuals from Labour, religious and nationalist backgrounds, some of whom had shunned each other on political grounds for decades but were now enthusiastically making common cause. Uri Zvi Greenberg, a renowned Hebrew poet of far-right views, was one of its leading lights. Back in the 1930s, when controversy raged over the Peel partition plan, he had written:

And there will be a day when from the River of Egypt to the Euphrates
And from the sea to beyond Moab my young warriors will ascend
And they will call my enemies and haters to the last battle
And blood will decide who is the only ruler here.[102]

In that kind of perspective, June 1967 represented a 'return to history'. Faced with the 'pseudo-mystical arguments, fictitious "rights", patently racist theories and an assortment of irrationalities'[103] that surfaced in the post-war period, some Jewish liberals were quick to question the wisdom of depending on the legitimacy of ancient title to hold on to the newly conquered territories. 'With the sword in one hand and the Bible in the other, some of the more fervent have argued that deeds contracted in the Late Bronze Age are the legal and moral basis for present claims, whether for real-estate or political control in general', observed the *Haaretz* columnist Amos Elon.[104] Nathan Alterman, another legendary nationalist poet, declared that returning the West Bank to Jordan, even in exchange for a peace treaty, would be 'another Munich' – inflicted on Israel by the Israeli government. He called the war 'the zenith of Jewish history'.[105]

Israel's political leadership did not rise to the occasion. Eshkol, backed by Dayan, favoured a pragmatic approach that combined improving security with keeping as few Arabs as possible in the territories that were expected to remain under Israeli control. Victory could be used to create more defensible and permanent borders, with the natural barrier of the Jordan river an obvious choice in the east. On 12 June Dayan told the BBC: 'We are awaiting the Arabs' phone call. We ourselves won't make a move. We are quite happy with the current situation. If anything bothers the Arabs, they know where to find us.'[106]

Options were discussed intensively in several marathon cabinet discussions that ended on 19 June. Proposals from the IDF were based on David Kimche's report of his meetings with Palestinians; one suggestion, by Brigadier-General Rehavam Zeevi, was to name a Palestinian state 'Ishmael', after the biblical figure considered the father of the Arabs.[107] Zeevi warned that 'protracted Israeli military rule will enhance the hatred and deepen the rift between the [Palestinian] inhabitants of the West Bank and Israel, because of the

1. (*Top left*) 'If you will it, it is no dream.' Theodor Herzl on his only visit to Palestine, November 1898.

2. (*Top right*) Looking ahead: Chaim Weizmann and members of the Zionist Commission, 1918.

3. (*Bottom*) Palestinian protest meeting in Jerusalem's old city, 1929.

4. (*Top*) The Grand Mufti of Palestine, Haj Amin al-Husseini, 1930.

5. (*Bottom*) Safe shore: the Jewish Agency's chief boatman and Arab policemen onboard a ship bringing new immigrants from Germany to Jaffa port, 1933.

6. (*Top*) Jewish supernumerary police unit under the command of the young Moshe Dayan at the newly established Kibbutz Hanita in the western Galilee, 1938.

7. (*Bottom*) Neighbours: Jewish settlers from Zichron Yaakov visiting the nearby Arab village of Sabarin, 1940. Sabarin was depopulated and destroyed in the 1948 war.

8. (*Top*) The funeral of Abdul-Qader al-Husseini at Jerusalem's al-Aqsa Mosque, April 1948, with fighters of the Arab Liberation Army and its commander, Fawzi al-Qawuqji.

9. (*Bottom*) David Ben-Gurion reading Israel's Declaration of Independence at the Tel Aviv Museum, May 1948.

10. (*Top*) *Nakba*: Palestinian refugees from a village near Haifa on their way across no-man's
and heading for Tulkarem, 1948.

11. (*Bottom*) New Jewish immigrants from Bulgaria outside their homes in Jaffa, now largely
empty of Arabs, 1949.

12. Israeli soldiers pose with a photograph of the Egyptian President, Gamal Abdel Nasser, in Rafah at the southern end of the Gaza Strip. November 1956.

13. Defence Minister Moshe Dayan and generals Uzi Narkiss and Rehavam Zeevi at the Tomb of the Patriarchs (the Ibrahimi Mosque) in Hebron, in the newly occupied West Bank, 1967.

14. Occupation: Palestinians detained by Israeli forces near the centre of Nablus in 1969.

15. (*Top*) Prime Minister Golda Meir, with Defence Minister Moshe Dayan and General Yitzhak Hofi, addressing Israeli troops on the Golan Heights during the Yom Kippur war, October 1973.

16. (*Bottom*) PLO leader Yasser Arafat addressing the UN General Assembly in November 1974. He said he was dreaming of 'one democratic state where Christian, Jew and Muslim live in justice, equality and fraternity'.

17. (*Top*) Gush Emunin leaders Rabbi Moshe Levinger (*left*) and Hanan Porat (*right*) and supporters celebrate the Israeli government's decision to allow settlers to relocate to an army camp near the West Bank village of Sebastia in 1975.

18. (*Bottom*) Prime Minister Menachem Begin at the funeral of two of the victims of a Palestinian attack on Kibbutz Misgav Am on the Lebanese border, 1980.

objective steps it will be essential to adopt in order to ensure order and security.'[108] Dayan proposed autonomy for the West Bank, while Israel maintained full control over security. Allon called for a Palestinian entity in the heart of the West Bank, along with Israeli annexation of the Jordan Valley and the Hebron hills, where settlements should be built. 'We have never held territory,' he argued, 'without settling it.'[109] That was a compromise of sorts for an influential Israeli who had always regretted Ben-Gurion's failure to conquer the West Bank.[110]

Ministers who opposed annexation warned – presciently – of the risk of international opprobrium in an age of decolonization and of turning the country into a 'bi-national' state, and urged the speedy return of most of the territory to Jordan. The Gaza Strip, Eshkol suggested, should be annexed, though the hope was that its 400,000 Palestinian refugees could be resettled elsewhere. Efforts were made, in secret, to promote that.

On that basis it was decided to inform the US of Israel's peace terms to both Egypt and Syria – 'a full treaty on the basis of the international border and Israel's security needs'. Crucially, however, it was agreed to defer discussion with Jordan, meaning that the future of the West Bank and East Jerusalem remained uncertain. In practice, Israel's policy was 'to preserve the territorial status quo of 10 June at the expense of a peace settlement'.[111] It was a fateful decision – not to decide. Allon's plan was never formally adopted, and he later adjusted his thinking to propose Jordanian annexation of the heart of the West Bank, with access via a corridor through the Jericho area, while Israel retained the Jordan Valley, East Jerusalem, Gush Etzion and the Hebron foothills. Israel's 'Jordanian option' was discussed in secret in bilateral talks in the course of 1968, but in the end King Hussein rejected it – a reflection in part of the way the Palestinians had re-emerged in 1967.[112] No other option was available. 'Israel's sin in the aftermath of the war lay in her total misunderstanding of the conditions that were created by her victory', Shlomo Ben-Ami, an academic historian and future Labour party minister, would write years later. 'She developed, therefore, no reasonable strategy as to the best way to turn her military supremacy into a political tool and use her exploits [on] the battlefield in order to change the nature of her relations with the Arab world. Instead she fell back conveniently on the politics of immobilism and *faits accomplis*.'[113]

Within just a few weeks of the end of the fighting the Palestinians could see the direction of travel, at least in Jerusalem. 'The Jews are beginning to unveil their projects for the construction of great buildings in the town and its surroundings to increase the number of the Jewish inhabitants to 500,000', warned a memorandum submitted to the UN by Khatib and other former city councillors.[114] 'The Arabs are afraid that these projects may be carried out at the expense of their properties and of their possessions by confiscation or under pressure. Likewise they fear that Jews may become the majority of the inhabitants of Jerusalem, thus appropriating the city, of which the Arabs would retain only memories.'

CURSED BLESSING

Israel's victory, some realized, was just too big: a 'cursed blessing' in the words of one early chronicler,[115] a victory 'of bewilderment' in the title of a later study,[116] a victory too many that posed complicated questions.[117] Yeshayahu Leibowitz, a renowned scientist and philosopher, emphasized the moral hazards of maintaining a military occupation, with an intrinsic tendency to breed corruption and an inevitable reliance on secret police and Arab 'Quislings', as he put it. 'There is also good reason to fear that the Israel Defense Force, which has been until now a people's army, would, as a result of being transformed into an army of occupation, degenerate, and its commanders, who will have become military governors, resemble their colleagues in other nations', he wrote in a much-quoted essay.[118] Leibowitz also memorably scorned the plaza that had been cleared by bulldozing the Arab houses in front of the Western Wall as vulgar – a 'discotel' (a play on the words 'discothèque' and '*Kotel*' – wall) and devoid of spiritual significance.[119] Another stark warning, from a more conventionally political perspective, came from the tiny Marxist anti-Zionist group Matzpen: 'Our right to defend ourselves against destruction does not confer upon us the right to oppress others', it declared:

Occupation brings foreign rule; foreign rule brings resistance; resistance brings repression; repression brings terror and counter-terror; the victims of terror are usually innocent people. The retention of the occupied territories will turn us into a nation of murderers and murder victims; let us leave the occupied territories immediately.[120]

The Baghdad-born Israeli writer Nissim Rejwan lamented 'the sheer size of the victory, the humiliation it brought on the Arab world, and the certain knowledge that the Arabs would never, ever contemplate peace and reconciliation with Israel from a position of such crippling weakness'.[121] And it was not only public intellectuals or political activists who were concerned about the national mood and its implications. 'I think that in the next round the Arabs' hatred towards us will be much more serious and profound,' mused an anonymous soldier who was interviewed in the aftermath of the war, though the publication of his remarks was censored at the time. Another fretted: 'Not only did this war not solve the state's problems, but it complicated them in a way that'll be very hard to solve.'[122] In later years many Israelis looked back and identified a moment of sudden understanding of the new situation: Matti Steinberg, a young soldier, was with his IDF armoured unit in the centre of Gaza City, deserted and under curfew, reflecting on the stunning victory and the achievement of peace, when a burst of gunfire suddenly targeted their convoy. It signalled that 'one period in the Arab–Israeli conflict had ended, but another had begun, no less turbulent and demanding than its predecessors'.[123]

Reflections like these were the other side of euphoria. Amos Oz, a rising literary star, gave powerful expression to the sense of menace and foreboding generated by the post-war reality in his acclaimed novel *My Michael*, published in 1968 when the experiences of victory and occupation were still fresh. Oz's heroine, Hanna Gonen, was troubled by dreams about the demonic – and symbolically mute – Palestinian twins, Aziz and Khalil, her childhood playmates until they disappeared from her neighbourhood on the edge of Jerusalem's Qatamon quarter in 1948, and were now, perhaps, frighteningly close again in the West Bank:

Hard things plot against me every night. The twins practise throwing hand grenades before dawn amongst the ravines of the Judean desert south-east of Jericho. Their twin bodies move in unison. Submachine guns on their shoulders. Worn commando uniforms stained with grease. A blue vein stands out on Khalil's forehead. Aziz crouches, hurls his body forward. Khalil drops his head. Aziz uncurls and throws. The dry shimmer of the explosion. The hills echo and re-echo. The Dead Sea grows pale behind them like a lake of burning oil.[124]

12

1968–1972

'We have to prove to the Israeli enemy that there are people who will not flee. We are going to confront him in the same way David confronted Goliath.'

Yasser Arafat, 1968

SETTLING IN

In the space of a few weeks in the summer of 1968, Palestinians marked two gloomy anniversaries: the first of the 1967 war, and the twentieth of the *Nakba* – both landmarks which had transformed relations between Jews and Arabs. On the ground, the year began with the expropriation of 3,345 dunams of mostly private land in East Jerusalem to build the new Jewish suburb of Ramat Eshkol – named for the hesitant Labour prime minister who had presided over the extraordinary victory of the previous year. It was the first settlement built in occupied territory after the war, just beyond what had been no-man's-land. It was intended to create a land bridge to secure Mount Scopus, so it could not be cut off again, as the university enclave had been after 1948.[1] Its apartment blocks and supermarkets, clad in obligatory pale Jerusalem limestone, formed the first link in a chain of new Jewish residential areas that were to change the topography and the demography of the city beyond recognition over the coming decades.

The first – and explicit – principle of an urban masterplan drawn up that year was 'to ensure [Jerusalem's] unification . . . to build the city in a manner that would prevent the possibility of it being repartitioned'.[2] Teddy Kollek, whose mayorship had begun in 1965, saw the need to respond to the 'staggering change' of post-war realities, and justified building in former Jordanian areas on grounds of urgent housing needs. Palestinians were neither consulted nor considered. 'It is never pleasant for anyone to have his land expropriated, and although this was uncultivated land, the very fact that compensation was offered by the people the Arabs regarded as "conquerors" made for resentment', Kollek admitted.[3] Later a smaller area was confiscated to build Neve Yaakov, further north, the site of a Jewish settlement that had been established in the 1920s and abandoned in 1948. Sari Nusseibeh, an astute if unusually forgiving Palestinian observer, commented of the Israeli mayor: 'When he lobbied his government to build the neighbourhoods [of] Ramat Eshkol, Neve Yaakov and Gilo he didn't set out to harm our national rights. He simply didn't factor them into his plans.'[4] The other big project in Jerusalem was in the Jewish Quarter of the Old City, from where Arab residents, many of them refugees from 1948, were quickly evicted. In April the finance ministry issued an order expropriating 116 dunams – 20 per cent of the Old City – for 'public purposes'.[5]

Settlements were slow to expand beyond East Jerusalem, partly because of the political implications. Israel argued that the West Bank did not constitute occupied territory since Mandatory Palestine had been divided in 1949 by armistice lines that were military and temporary; furthermore, Jordan's unilateral annexation of the West Bank the following year had been recognized only by Britain and Pakistan. The terms of the armistice, it claimed, had been annulled by Arab attacks.[6] The Arab summit conference at Khartoum strengthened the hands of those Israelis who saw little or no future for peace talks. On 1 September 1967 the leaders who had assembled in the Sudanese capital issued a famous declaration of 'three noes': no to peace, no to recognition, no to negotiations. Israel's official interpretation skated over the salient fact, which was as clear to the IDF as it was to the PLO, that the Arab states had resolved to employ political and diplomatic means, not war, 'to eliminate the consequences of the aggression'. Back in 1964, the first Arab summit had called for 'the final liquidation of Israel'.[7] Still, both Israel's justice minister and the foreign ministry's legal adviser advised that implanting settlements in occupied territory would be in breach of the fourth

Geneva Convention, which was designed to protect civilians in time of war.

Nevertheless, Kfar Etzion, between Bethlehem and Hebron, was re-established and officially described as a *Nahal* (paramilitary) outpost or 'strongpoint' to circumvent legal objections. That fiction – also used for Merom Golan, the first settlement on the Golan Heights – was undermined by the fact that these pioneers included men like Hanan Porat, who had been born in Gush Etzion in 1943 and left five years later, and were exercising what they saw as their 'right of return'; a 'right of return' that was parallel to the way Palestinian refugees dreamed of going back to Jaffa or Haifa but were unable to do so. Eshkol's decision reflected nostalgia for a settlement that had been lost in 1948, lobbying by Orthodox nationalists, and uncertainty about the future status of the West Bank. Many saw it as a one-off gesture, not a precedent.[8] But even then Yosef Weitz, who had spent his life promoting Jewish settlement before and after the watershed of 1948, thought it was a bad idea that would 'anger our few friends and provide our many enemies with a stick to beat us'.[9] The US and Arab governments were indeed quick to condemn the move.

It did turn out to be a precedent. In April 1968 another group of religious nationalists, led by a rabbi named Moshe Levinger, secured permission from the IDF to celebrate Passover in a Hebron hotel (at that time permission was required if Israeli civilians wished to stay overnight in the occupied territories). The town's significance to Orthodox Jews, drawn to it by the Tomb of the Patriarchs and the powerful memory of the 1929 massacre, was as obvious as the hostility of its Muslim residents, who had a reputation for religious conservatism. The day after arriving the group announced that they had come to 'renew' the Jewish presence in Hebron. Their principal ally was Labour's Yigal Allon, who quietly arranged for them to be armed. Within a few months the government had decided to establish – or re-establish – a Jewish neighbourhood in the city. This landmark episode combined official dithering, dubious legality, sympathetic nodding and winking and, above all, determination by an ideologically motivated minority to create irreversible facts on the ground. And subterfuge became official policy. In July 1970 Dayan and other officials discussed how land would be confiscated ostensibly for security purposes, and decided that buildings on it would be falsely presented as being for military use – and thus communicated to the mayor of Hebron.[10] The pattern was to be repeated again and again in years to come. Israel may have acquired an 'accidental empire' in 1967[11] (an argument akin to John Seeley's famous notion that the British Empire was born 'in a fit of absence of mind'), but some very calculated actions were nevertheless made from its earliest days. By January 1969 there were already ten settlements on the Golan, two in Sinai and five in the West Bank. Several more were approved the same month.[12]

Israelis on the left were dismayed by these zealous right-wingers, and discomfited by the implications of their appeal. 'The Six Day war created the conditions necessary for the transformation of the cult of the homeland into a fundamentalist-religious-chauvinist mythology', observed Meron Benvenisti, a political scientist who later served as Kollek's deputy for Arab affairs in the Jerusalem municipality. 'In the name of "love for *Eretz-Yisrael*", fanatics set out to complete the journey into the past by nationalising newly-occupied territory, which necessitated the dispossession of anyone who did not belong to the Jewish collectivity.'[13] Benvenisti's liberal Zionist argument was correct, but it failed to address the large-scale dispossession and removal of Palestinians that was – certainly for the Palestinians – the central feature of Israel's independence and the *Nakba*. The difference between two types of settlers was captured in Hebrew usage that became common after 1967 – almost without anyone noticing. *Hityashvut* – an unequivocally positive word in the Israeli/Zionist lexicon – meant simply 'settlement'. That was what took place, uncontroversially, in the Negev or Galilee. But the word preferred by partisans of *Eretz-Yisrael* – *hitnahalut* – carried an additional and unmistakable connotation of 'inheritance' or 'patrimony'. *Hitnahalut* only took place in the occupied territories. Palestinians made no such distinction. It was the start of what Israeli 'doves' came to refer to as a process of 'creeping annexation'.

RESISTANCE AND RESPONSE

Israel's grip on the West Bank and Gaza was firmly established by the end of 1967, thanks to aggressive counter-measures, denunciations by collaborators and lax security by Palestinian groups. In December alone forty-two Fatah men were rounded up by the simple expedient of observing who approached a dead-letter box next to a soft drinks stall in Hebron. In February 1968 the army surrounded the Nablus casbah and paraded thousands of men in front of masked informers provided by the security service. Two arms caches were found and seventy-four people identified as belonging to guerrilla organizations. 'Our great achievement was creating a distinct barrier between the population at large and the terrorist organisations', one Shin Bet officer explained.

> People knew that anyone who helped the terrorists would have his house blown up, be deported or arrested. We also showed them that captured terrorists were the first to inform. We created the impression that those who were supposed to be liberating the people were the most likely to betray those who helped them. This was a deliberate decision. We'd go to a village, impose a curfew and put all the men in the square and then file them past one of our prisoners – a captured terrorist – sitting in a car with a hood over his head. Now, whether or not the prisoners actually identified any suspects, we'd pretend that he had done. The cumulative effect of all this was that when the terrorists came to a village the locals would say: 'get out of here. We know that you'll inform on us.' We even tested this once by sending a group of soldiers, dressed as terrorists, into a village to ask for help. And they got exactly that answer.[14]

Yaakov Perry, a Shin Bet man stationed in Nablus, recruited a sheikh whose wife was given permission to undergo gynaecological treatment in Israel. On another occasion a Palestinian informant agreed to a clandestine meeting and arranged for the Israeli contact to be ambushed by Fatah. But a second Palestinian informed on the first and the plot was foiled.[15] Salah Khalaf (Abu Iyad), Arafat's deputy, candidly attributed Palestinian setbacks to 'the efficiency of the Israeli secret services and the carelessness of our fighters'.[16] Control of the Jordanian border, protected from Tiberias to the Dead Sea by fences, mined strips, floodlights and surveillance devices, was another vital factor: 'Trying to get men and weapons across the Jordan is a waste of time and effort', concluded Wadie Haddad of the PFLP, for whose

professionalism and discipline Israeli security officials had a grudg-
ing respect: it was far tougher to penetrate than Fatah.[17]

If the Israelis proved that they were good at counter-insurgency
operations, they found it harder to deal with political and non-
violent opposition. Sheikh Sayih's deportation was followed in March
1968 by that of his successor as head of the National Guidance Committee, Ruhi al-Khatib, the deposed mayor of Jerusalem, marking 'a
further emasculation of the independent-minded leaders of the occupied Palestinians'.[18] Organizations like the Union of Palestinian
Students and the General Union of Arab Women carried on but were
eclipsed over time by PLO institutions in exile, which always seemed
anxious not to allow too much autonomous activity. Fatah's brief
period of armed resistance had effectively ended, though it had
defeated any idea of acquiescence in the occupation. Exploratory
talks on the creation of a Palestinian entity under Israeli auspices
went nowhere, in part because of threats and at least one armed
attack on the people involved.

Outside the occupied territories the Palestinians were able to inflict
one painful blow on the Israelis – in propaganda if not in conventional military terms. In March 1968 came long-threatened retaliation
in the form of an Israeli assault on Fatah and other guerrillas, backed
by the Jordanian army, at Karameh in the Jordan Valley – by coincidence its Arabic name meaning 'dignity'. Arafat ignored the advice of
the Jordanians to avoid a confrontation after an Israeli bus ran over
a mine near the border in the Negev and two civilians were killed.
The Fatah leader, by his own account, decided to make a stand. 'No,
we have to prove to the Israeli enemy that there are people who will
not flee. We are going to confront him in the same way David confronted Goliath.' The overwhelmingly superior Israeli force secured
its objectives but lost 28 dead, the Jordanians 61 and the Palestinians
120. The Israelis left behind a tank, a half-track and several trucks –
supporting the Palestinian image of triumphant resistance. Fatah
leaders and King Hussein were photographed in front of these spoils.
Fatah recruitment soared, as did weapons flows from Egypt, Iraq and
Syria, and boosted Arafat's own reputation, carefully cultivated by a
slick PR campaign. 'Unlike the propaganda effort surrounding his
infiltration of the West Bank', his biographer noted, 'the difficult

publicity task of turning defeat into victory, this time he actually had something to celebrate.'[19] The battle he called 'a second Leningrad' was 'the first victory for our Arab nation since the 1967 war'. Even the Israelis admitted that Karameh had been a 'moral victory' for the Palestinians.[20] King Faisal of Saudi Arabia granted an audience to Arafat's senior colleagues. Nizar Qabbani, the famous Syrian poet, praised Fatah for raising the Arabs 'from the mire of shame'.[21]

Four months later the Palestine National Council – the PLO's 'parliament' – allotted seats to the *fedayeen* groups for the first time, giving a harder edge to a body hitherto dominated by the rivalries of Arab states which prioritized their own interests. The PLO's national covenant also underwent significant changes in July 1968. Reflecting the post-war situation, it emphasized the nationhood of the Palestinians and highlighted the role of armed struggle as an 'overall strategy, not merely a tactical phase', as the only way to liberate Palestine. It also clarified that the only Jews who could be considered Palestinians would be those 'who had resided in Palestine until the beginning of the Zionist invasion'. On the understanding that that meant 1917 – the start of British occupation and the Balfour Declaration – the majority of the Jewish population of Israel were excluded. That was a regression compared to the 1964 version of the charter, which had used the date of 1947.[22] In December 1968 *Time* magazine chose 'Fedayeen leader Arafat' for its cover story.[23] Fatah then issued its own seven-point platform stating that its goal was an 'independent democratic Palestine' whose citizens would enjoy equal rights regardless of their religion'. Arafat explained that alongside 2,500,000 Palestinian Arabs of the Muslim and Christian faiths there were 'another 1,250,000 Arabs of the Jewish faith who live in what is now the state of Israel'.[24] Israelis, unsurprisingly, were not impressed by that definition. In February 1969 Arafat became chairman of the PLO executive committee – a position he held until his death thirty-five years later.

COSTS AND BENEFITS

Israel's control of the West Bank and Gaza depended on more than just security measures and repression. Within months of the war's end Palestinians began to cross the green line to work in Israel, where the economy was expanding. Palestinian unemployment had been severe before 1967 and was aggravated by the war, but it gradually declined in its aftermath. Initially, West Bankers travelled to farms or building sites near the green line, especially in Jerusalem, to be recruited by intermediaries and labour contractors – many of them Arab Israeli citizens who were well-placed to take advantage of a fresh supply of cheap labour. By the end of 1968 5,000 people were working in Israel, so the following year the government set up labour exchanges in the main towns. This enabled workers to obtain benefits such as holidays and health insurance, though the majority probably continued to work unofficially – to avoid paying taxes and social security contributions. Palestinians were in any case defined as day labourers, which meant they did not qualify for the same level of benefits as Israelis; nor were they permitted to join the *Histadrut*, Israel's trade union federation. Israelis also earned six times more than West Bankers, and eight times more than Gaza's inhabitants.[25] Workers were banned from staying in Israel between midnight and 6 a.m. By 1974 the number of Palestinians working in Israel had reached 68,000.[26] Two Palestinian families in five were sending one of their members to work in Israel. Most commuted daily, but a tendency grew, especially among Gazans who lived further away, to risk arrest and stay, illegally, overnight in their workplaces or makeshift quarters.[27] For the first time since 1948 Palestinians again became a familiar part of the Israeli landscape, replacing Jewish workers in agriculture, construction work, restaurant kitchens and other menial jobs. 'Arab work' acquired a negative connotation of being cheap and shoddy. The massive influx of workers into Israel and the virtual elimination of unemployment boosted growth in the West Bank by nearly 60 per cent by 1973. The exception was in East Jerusalem, where Israel's annexation and the abolition of its separate administrative status was a blow for Palestinian doctors, lawyers, civil servants and the tourist industry – because of direct competition from Jews. Between 1968 and 1972 GNP rose annually by 16 per cent in the West Bank and 20 per cent in Gaza. Private consumption also increased rapidly.[28]

Exposure to Israel's economy and society – not just to the relatively small numbers of soldiers and officials who maintained the apparatus of occupation – was highly unsettling. 'With the June war', observed Aziz Shehadeh in Ramallah, 'all previous modes of life were shattered. The whole social structure was challenged. All previous values and convictions were put to the test . . . Everyone could see the progress the Jews had been able to make. The organisation of . . . society . . . values . . . ideals were all upset.'[29] For a visiting American-Palestinian expert, the Israelis brought a 'western-style bureaucratic and legal system, rationalized by an ideology of the rule of law. The indigenous Palestinian society, on the other hand, was organized on a kin and highly personalized basis.'[30] The growing numbers of Palestinians working in Israel were sharply aware of the differences between the two sides of an increasingly porous green line. Labourers from villages or refugee camps 'left a house in the morning that had no electricity, running water, or sewage, and worked all day in an environment where these utilities were taken for granted', commented one analyst. 'Unlike other political contexts where such stark disparities also exist, the distinction between the haves and have nots was based on national identity rather than class. The disparity no doubt reminded the Palestinians that they were an occupied people. And that the situation was not normal.'[31]

The traditional West Bank political elite, Jordanian loyalists who continued to receive pensions and run their businesses from across the river while urging people not to co-operate with the Israelis,[32] gradually saw its influence decline as sympathy for the *fedayeen* grew, especially after Karameh and the boost it gave to the PLO.[33] The foundation of three universities in the West Bank in the first half of the 1970s – Bir Zeit near Ramallah, al-Najah in Nablus and Bethlehem – not only advanced higher education but also helped nurture a new generation of politically conscious activists. In later years all three required their students to do community work, combating illiteracy or volunteering in clinics and hospitals.[34] Bir Zeit in particular attracted attention as a centre of Palestinian nationalism, elections to its student body providing an informal barometer of the political mood among young people. The tone was set by a stirring quotation from George Bernard Shaw (*John Bull's Other Island*) that was posted prominently on the campus: 'If you break a nation's nationality it will think of nothing else but getting it back again. It will listen to no reformer, to no philosopher, to no preacher, until the demand of the nationalist is granted. It will attend to no business, however vital, except the business of unification and liberation.'[35]

RUTHLESS IN GAZA

It took longer for the Israelis to pacify the Gaza Strip. It was there, in the second half of 1971, that the military struggle against the *fedayeen* reached its violent peak, numbers swelled by fighters fleeing an escalating crackdown on the PLO in Jordan. 'Gaza', a foreign journalist reported that August, 'is the only place where the Palestinian resistance, at a terrible cost and with suicidal tenacity, is worthy of the name.' General Ariel Sharon of IDF southern command disagreed with Moshe Dayan, who wanted only a minimal Israeli military presence in Gaza. Killings of Palestinians accused of collaboration were routine, seventy-five in 1970 alone,[36] but a grenade attack by a Palestinian teenager that killed two Israeli children and injured their parents in January 1971 triggered a hardening of policy. Weapons stockpiled during Egyptian rule and left behind by the PLA circulated freely. Others were smuggled in from Sinai. Dense orange groves provided natural cover for guerrilla fighters. From that July Sharon led a brutal counter-insurgency campaign targeting 700–800 'terrorists' by his own account. It was gruelling work and required innovative methods and detailed local knowledge – and the collaborators needed to identify strangers and likely *fedayeen*. The Israelis imposed 24-hour curfews, interrogated all adult males and instituted a shoot-to-kill policy. Battalion commanders were ordered to deploy bulldozers in search of underground bunkers hiding fighters and weapons. Wide roads were cleared through Gaza's three biggest refugee camps: Jabaliya, Rafah and Shati. Roads were paved and street lighting introduced to allow easy access for the IDF and reduce the dangers from mines. An estimated 6,000 homes were destroyed.[37] By mid-1971 about 100,000 people had been forced to find new homes.[38] 'We used every kind of subterfuge', Sharon wrote later:

We infiltrated our own 'terrorists' into Gaza on a boat from Lebanon, then chased them with helicopters and search parties, hoping that eventually the real terrorists would make contact. And eventually they did . . . We had people selling vegetables in the market, drinking coffee in the coffeehouses, riding donkeys. Our 'terrorists' would sometimes take a suspected PLO man out of his house and accuse him of cooperating with the Jews. He would say, 'No I've never cooperated with them. Ask my commander.' So we would get the suspect and the commander too . . . At one point our fake terrorists even built bunkers and became bunker dwellers. Our imaginations worked overtime at this sort of thing. We faced the terrorists with new situations constantly, putting them off balance, bringing them out into the open.[39]

By February 1972 104 *fedayeen* had been killed and hundreds more captured. In the year up to April 1971 Israeli courts had convicted 5,620 Palestinians of committing security offences in Gaza.[40] In November the charismatic *fedayeen* commander Ziyad al-Husseini committed suicide rather than surrender in the cellar under the home of Gaza's mayor, Rashad al-Shawwa, a patrician businessman who had been appointed by the Israelis but who maintained clandestine contact with the PLO. Shawwa had had some of his orange trees destroyed because a bunker and weapons cache were discovered in one of his orchards.[41] Husseini's widow accused the Israelis of killing him.[42] The PLO, anxious about competition from Jordan in the West Bank, directed fewer financial resources to Gaza. Sharon deployed the border police, whose Druze personnel were renowned for their brutality, as well as a newly formed IDF special forces unit named *Rimon* ('pomegranate' or 'grenade'). The harsh methods they employed faced opposition from the governor and the area military commander – facts that were seized upon by the many critics of the controversial general. *Rimon*'s commander, Meir Dagan, acknowledged later that 'scores' of wanted Palestinians had been killed if they opened fire or refused to surrender. The unit worked closely with the Shin Bet.[43]

Israel's calculation from the start was that economic opportunity and the lure of 'normal' life would blunt resistance. Dr Hayder Abdel-Shafi, the nationalist president of the Gaza Red Crescent Society, recognized early on that the imperative to work in Israel was hard to square with fighting the occupation. In 1969, he recalled, Dayan complained to him that Gazans were not crossing the green line to work.

> It was just after the war, people were still enthusiastic and confident that the occupation would not last long. Because of sheer economic necessity, however, workers – in the face of physical injury – began going to Israel. It was absolutely impossible to try to preach against it when you can't support any other way. Once it started, there was no way to stop it.[44]

Dayan believed that improved living conditions would mean not only acquiescence in the status quo but the abandonment of the Palestinian dream of return. 'As long as the refugees remain in their camps . . . their children will say they come from Jaffa or Haifa', he argued. 'If they move out of the camps, the hope is they will feel an attachment to their new land.'[45] Ordinary Gazans did reap material benefits, though otherwise there was no change and no obvious prospect of change in the status quo. 'For the first inconceivable time in their whole lives they are able to bring meat, tins of food, biscuits, shoes, fresh milk, into homes where hitherto everything has been a matter of scrounging and 1,500 UNRWA calories', a visiting foreign journalist reported in 1971. 'Terrorism has failed to offer them any alternative. A few grenades exploding into queues of labourers . . . are not sufficient deterrents.'[46] In June that year thirty-four terrorist incidents were recorded; in December, just one.[47] The numbers of Gazan workers crossing into Israel more than doubled in 1972 and rose every subsequent year.[48]

CONFRONTATION IN JORDAN . . .

Military defeat, the stick of repression and the carrots of economic improvements in the West Bank and Gaza all combined to push Palestinian resistance to Israel abroad. The battle of Karameh had been a huge boost for the PLO. But subsequent Israeli attacks forced the *fedayeen* to abandon the Jordan Valley and find new sanctuaries. That increased tensions with the Jordanian authorities, alarmed by the increasingly confident *fedayeen* presence in Amman and elsewhere. Trouble erupted on 2 November 1968 during a demonstration marking the fifty-first anniversary of the Balfour Declaration – always a potentially disruptive marker and link between past and present injustice – when Palestinians attacked the US embassy in the capital. That was followed by Jordanian army shelling of Palestinian refugee camps. Over the following months the PLO presence increased to the point where King Hussein, ever suspicious of Palestinian ambitions, began to fear not only that he would never regain the lost half of his kingdom across the river but that the very future of his regime was in doubt. In 1969 Fatah was mounting two hundred operations a month from Jordanian territory and drawing harsh Israeli retaliation.[49] In February 1970, the king announced a new clampdown on the Palestinians but then backed down and agreed a *hudna* – a truce or armistice – with Arafat. In June there was further escalation when the PFLP took eighty-eight foreigners hostage in Amman hotels.[50] Israel, with the US, watched the position of the 'plucky little king' or PLK, as he was nicknamed by Western diplomats and journalists, with growing concern, stiffening Hussein's resolve to force a showdown. It began in September 1970 and attracted global attention when the PFLP hijacked three civilian airliners and landed them at a remote desert landing strip in the kingdom called Dawson's Field – renamed 'Revolution Airport' – and blew them up. 'Things cannot go on,' the king declared. 'Every day Jordan is sinking a little further.'[51] Hussein declared martial law. In fighting punctuated by feverish inter-Arab diplomacy, PLO forces were routed and driven out of the country. Between 3,000 and 5,000 Palestinians and 600 Jordanians were killed.[52] Palestinians came to refer to this period as 'Black September'. The common interests of Jordan and Israel had never been so clear. In October 1970 King Hussein met the Israeli deputy prime minister, Yigal Allon, in the desert near Eilat and promised to work to prevent further *fedayeen* raids.[53] Scores of Palestinian fighters fled from the East Bank during the final confrontation with the king's men in July 1971. An estimated 3,000–5,000 fled to Lebanon, while another 2,300 were taken prisoner. Seventy-two even surrendered to the Israelis rather than continue fighting the Jordanians.[54] It was, as the king put it, 'a cancer operation that had to be performed to save Jordan's life'.[55]

The PLO's violent expulsion from the Hashemite kingdom was to Israel's benefit since, until September 1970, most Palestinian operations against Israel originated from there. By 1972 the number of such incidents had plummeted by over 90 per cent. Hussein's announcement of a plan for a United Arab Kingdom in March 1972 was ostensibly to 'reorganize the Jordanian-Palestinian home', but in fact it appeared designed to legitimize his renewed control of the West Bank. It conspicuously made no mention of the 'Palestinian people' and met with immediate and furious rejection by the PLO, which condemned Jordan for 'offering itself as an accomplice to the Zionist enemy'. Israel's plans for municipal elections in the West Bank had already created an alarming impression of collusion with the Jordanians, the suspicions based on Allon's 1968 plan for an Israeli line of defence in the Jordan Valley and the return of densely populated Palestinian areas to Jordanian rule. In the Knesset, however, the new prime minister Golda Meir rejected the United Arab Kingdom plan. On this occasion there had in fact been no collusion. Hussein's plan was stillborn and disappeared without trace.[56]

. . . AND IN LEBANON AND BEYOND

Palestinian forces in Lebanon – 'a garden without a fence' in the words of a senior PLO official[57] – had launched raids against Israel from the end of 1969. The organization acted according to an agreement concluded in Cairo that November, and operated throughout 1970, especially from the rugged Arqoub area in the south, quickly dubbed 'Fatahland', where the PLO assumed complete control. In one cross-border attack on a passing school bus, twelve Israeli children were killed in May 1970 at Moshav Avivim. Israel retaliated with air raids and artillery barrages, which intensified after the PLO's expulsion from Jordan. Attacks on Israeli targets abroad began with the PFLP hijacking of an El Al plane (Israel's national carrier) to Algiers in 1968. In December another Israeli plane came under fire on the ground at Athens airport. Three days later, IDF commandos landed by helicopter at Beirut airport and blew up thirteen planes belonging to Middle East Airlines, Lebanon's national carrier. The

PFLP hit back by firing Katyusha rockets across the border, killing three people in Kiryat Shmona. In 1969 Leila Khaled – a refugee from Haifa – hijacked a TWA flight from Los Angeles to Tel Aviv, or, as she put it, 'expropriated an imperialist plane and returned to Palestine'.[58] Other attacks were mounted against Israeli embassies and El Al offices. The PFLP, in the assessment of Hisham Sharabi,

> upheld the principle of total war: if Israel used napalm to kill civilians, dynamited homes in retaliation for commando activity, and engaged in collective punishment, then the guerrillas were justified in refusing to distinguish between civilian and military targets or to limit themselves to a single kind or field of action.[59]

In 1971 foreign operations accounted for just over 3 per cent of all PLO military activity, rising to 12 per cent in 1972 and peaking at 30 per cent in 1973. The bare statistics, however, mask some notorious incidents that were magnified by the ensuing publicity. In May 1972 the PFLP hijacked a Belgian Sabena plane to Lod Airport where it was stormed by Israeli commandos who freed the hostages. Soon afterwards three members of the Japanese Red Army who had been recruited by the PFLP killed twenty-four people, mostly Puerto Rican nuns on a pilgrimage, at Lod Airport – in an attack that was named 'Operation Deir Yassin' after the 1948 massacre so often referenced by Palestinians. The PLO took credit for this. Kozo Okamoto and other attackers were tried and gaoled for life.

The most notorious terrorist incident was the Munich Olympic Games massacre of Israeli athletes that September, mounted by the shadowy Black September organization, a group that was created in the wake of the 1970 Jordanian crisis by Ali Hassan Salameh, an aide to Salah Khalaf and the son of the renowned 1948 martyr of the same name.[60] Eight Palestinian gunmen infiltrated the Olympic Village and took 11 athletes hostage, demanded the release of 234 prisoners held in Israel as well as the German-held founder members of the far-left Baader-Meinhof group. Meir rejected the demand. Two hostages were killed at once and the other nine in a firefight between German police and the Palestinians at a military airfield, where five of the gunmen also died; three were captured but released later.[61] Arafat and the PLO disclaimed all knowledge of it, though the Israelis and the CIA learned that the operation had used 'Fatah funds, facilities and personnel'.[62] It was named 'Operation Ikrit and Biram', after two Galilean villages depopulated in 1948. Israelis were horrified. Arafat's view after Munich was that 'violent political action in the midst of a broad popular movement cannot be termed terrorism . . . it is appropriate in certain objective conditions in a given phase'.[63] It and other attacks attracted approving comments in Fatah publications and reinforced the perception in Israel of the unremitting hostility of the PLO. Munich triggered internal debate within the organization though, with some blaming Khalaf for the harsh global and Israeli reactions.[64]

In every case Israel retaliated with attacks on Syria and Lebanon, after Munich reportedly killing up to two hundred people, many of them civilians, but never attracting the same degree of attention as spectacular terrorist incidents abroad and rarely much sympathy. 'Palestinians think that western perspectives of terrorism are absurdly distorted', commented a sympathetic foreign writer.

> They believe that the West judges the issue with much emotiveness but with little understanding of its context. Moreover, its view is almost entirely one-sided. A guerrilla with a gun is more 'newsworthy' than an air-force pilot spraying napalm over a refugee camp, but is he more of a terrorist? The eleven Israeli athletes who were killed at the Munich Olympics are remembered all over the world, but how many people recall the four hundred refugees who were killed in the Israeli vengeance raid three days later?[65]

Munich, observed Yezid Sayigh, 'marked the turning point for the Palestinian leadership as it . . . threatened any diplomatic gains made by the PLO'. In the months that followed, Israeli assassinations in the so-called 'war of the spooks' conducted by the Mossad took a heavy toll. In February 1973 the Israelis hit bases near Tripoli and killed forty Palestinians, mostly from the PFLP. In April Israel launched one of its most daring operations yet, a raid in the heart of Beirut that killed three senior PLO officials: Kamal Adwan, Kamal Nasser and Muhammad Yusuf al-Najjar. Israel named the raid 'Springtime of Youth'. The number of Palestinian operations dropped sharply, from 670 in 1971, to 351 in 1972 and 271 in 1973.[66] The international image of Palestinians suffered badly in this period, their cause all too often being seen as synonymous with terrorism. But the reasons behind their animosity to Israel were rarely addressed by Western governments or reported in the mainstream media. Naji al-Ali, a refugee from al-Shajara in Galilee who had fled to Lebanon as a child in 1948, made a lasting contribution to humanizing his much-misunderstood people: Handala (a bitter, wild gourd in Arabic), the barefoot, spiky-haired but faceless cartoon character he drew for a Kuwaiti newspaper, came to symbolize Palestinian suffering and patience. 'Handala was born ten years old, and he will always be ten years old', al-Ali explained. 'At that age, I left my homeland, and when he returns, Handala will still be ten, and then he will start growing up. The laws of nature do not apply to him. He is unique. Things will become normal again when the homeland returns.'[67]

ISRAEL ADJUSTS

In the first few years after 1967, Israelis adapted with apparent ease to the new reality of occupation, and continued to take advantage of what it had to offer long after the first post-war months of frenzied tourism and shopping. Jerusalem's Old City – now energetically promoted by the government as the heart of Israel's 'eternal' capital – remained the most popular destination, with its restaurants, colourful bazaars and historic sites. Unrestricted access to the West Bank also meant regular trips to cheap and picturesque markets in Bethlehem, Qalqilya and Nablus – what the writer Anton Shammas dubbed 'hummus and falafel-land'.[68] Hiking in the Judaean desert, especially near Wadi Qelt off the Jerusalem–Jericho road, became a favourite weekend pastime. In July 1967, when Gaza City was first open to civilians, 35,000 Israelis had streamed in for Saturday morning shopping. Numbers dropped as armed attacks increased and it became a less attractive destination with its squalid refugee camps and cramped conditions. The Hebrew media usually referred to the 'administered territories'. On the right the terminology was 'liberated territories'. Over time, the more neutral simple 'territories' (*shtahim*) became common usage. In general, prospects for political change seemed limited, with the famous three 'noes' of the Khartoum conference fixed in the minds of most Israeli Jews, along with Moshe Dayan's famous line just days after the war about 'waiting for a telephone call' from Arab leaders.[69] (The one most likely to make the call was widely assumed to be King Hussein, reflecting the long-standing Israeli preference for a 'Jordanian option' for resolving the conflict.) In August 1968 the playwright Hanoch Levin produced a satirical show, *You and I and the Next War*: 'Wherever we walk, we are three: you and I and the next war.' Among Israelis, awareness of Palestinians as a distinct national group was still limited, as crudely illustrated by Golda Meir's notorious and revealing statement in 1969 that 'There was no such thing as Palestinians ... It was not as though there was a Palestinian people in Palestine considering itself as a Palestinian people and we came and threw them out and took their country from them. They did not exist.'[70] It was not at that time a controversial remark for the majority of Israeli Jews. In October that year Meir's Labour-led coalition was returned to power with the largest number of seats ever won in an Israeli election – 56 out of 120 seats. And Meir was nothing if not consistent: she insisted there could be no return to the pre-1967 borders, but brushed aside concerns about the annexation of parts of the West Bank. 'Israel wants only a minimum of Arab population in the *Jordanian* territory it wishes to keep,' she said in September 1972, in the angry anti-Palestinian mood after the Munich Olympics killings.[71]

Unease about the future was given powerful expression in 1970 in Hanoch Levin's controversial play, *Queen of the Bathtub*. It played to packed audiences in Tel Aviv – though some who watched were so outraged that they threw stones and stink bombs during performances. It featured a dead son speaking from the grave, sarcastically thanking his father for sending him to sacrifice his life for restoring the now undivided Jewish kingdom.[72] It brought condemnation from Meir and Moshe Dayan – for giving comfort to the enemy – as well as from bereaved families. (Dayan's actor son, Assi, made waves when he called for the return of all the occupied territories, including Jerusalem, as 'the price we must pay for a true peace'.) In one scene, the eponymous queen grabbed the pompous-sounding Labour foreign minister, Abba Eban, by the crotch at a cabinet meeting to prevent him from putting forward any peace proposals. The play, Shlomo Ben-Ami wrote later, was 'the loudest and most articulate expression of the young generation's despair with a war that never ended and with the politicians and generals incapable of departing from the logic of war'.[73]

13

1973–1977

*'The Palestine Liberation Organization is the sole legitimate
representative of the Palestinian people and its struggle.'*
Rabat Arab summit conference

ISRAELI EARTHQUAKE,
PALESTINIAN ADVANCES

In the early afternoon of 6 October 1973 the wail of sirens shattered
the eerie quiet of the Yom Kippur fast, heralding the outbreak of war
to stunned Israelis. Egyptian and Syrian offensives along the Suez
Canal and Golan Heights triggered air strikes, artillery duels and
tank battles on a scale not seen since the Second World War. Israel
was caught unprepared by the breaching of its Bar-Lev defence line
east of the canal and initial Egyptian advances in Sinai. Its aura of
invincibility was dramatically shattered and Arab pride restored. In
just over a week, however, the tide was turned by the mobilization of
the IDF reserves and counter-offensives made possible by the airlift
of weapons and ammunition from the US. By 14 October, when a
UN-brokered ceasefire began, Israeli forces were fifty miles from
Cairo and twenty-five from Damascus. The entire Egyptian Third
Army was encircled by the IDF near Ismailiya on the eastern bank of
the Suez Canal – in Africa, as the Israeli press marvelled.[1]

In the course of the war a general strike paralysed life in the occupied territories. Palestine Liberation Army units were deployed in a
limited role on both fronts but the vast majority of Palestinians played
no part in the latest round of Arab–Israeli fighting. Jordan did not
join in this time either – it sent a token force to Syria but informed the

US and Israel it was doing so – and prevented the PLO from attacking from its territory. Israel's losses of 2,650 dead were the country's worst since 1948. Egypt and Syria together lost an estimated 16,000 men. Six years since the victory of 1967 Israelis were traumatized by what was immediately characterized as an 'earthquake' and focused on blunders or oversights in intelligence, which were soon the subject of angry protests and, eventually, of an official inquiry, the Agranat Commission.[2]

Anwar al-Sadat and Hafez al-Assad launched what Arabs called the Ramadan war with the limited goal of challenging the post-1967 status quo – but with mutual suspicions about each other's intentions. The Egyptian president hoped to impose a peace settlement on Israel, while Assad, who was anxious to liberate the Golan Heights, at least sounded more committed to the Palestinian cause. In narrow national terms, Egypt succeeded brilliantly, eventually regaining the territory it had lost to Israel in 1967. Syria did not. The war set in train shifts that were to have far-reaching influence on the Middle East's most intractable conflict. At the Algiers Arab summit conference in November 1973, and even more resoundingly at the Rabat summit in October 1974, all twenty-one Arab states bowed to the PLO's increasingly strident demand to be recognized as the 'sole legitimate representative of the Palestinian people'. King Hussein of Jordan was reluctant, but gave way under pressure and promises of generous cash support from the Gulf States. That in turn paved the way for Yasser Arafat's extraordinary appearance at the United Nations two weeks later, when he famously offered his Israeli enemy a choice between 'the gun and the olive branch'. His appearance was a huge boost for Palestinian morale, and for the international standing of the PLO and its *raison d'être* as a national liberation movement. 'Arafat got to the UN because he used the gun', argued the commentator Said Aburish. 'The UN didn't invite a member of the Palestinian intellectual bourgeoisie who are always writing articles pleading for understanding; they invited the head of the Palestinian armed resistance.'[3]

The US brokered disengagement of forces agreements between Israel and Egypt, and between Israel and Syria, that were signed in January and March 1974 respectively. Both reflected the Arabs' initial military achievements more than Israel's final victory. Immovable deadlock gave way to a new, if limited, readiness for give and take.[4] For the first time since 1947, diplomacy had joined armed struggle as a way of achieving Palestinian goals. 'The Yom Kippur war, more than any other event since the creation of Israel and the *Nakba*, underlined the relative unimportance of the Palestinians in the Middle East in general and in the conflict with Israel in particular', an Israeli expert commented. 'On the other hand the war created the conditions that would allow them to make the biggest political advance in their history.'[5]

Following on from the PLO's expulsion from Jordan, the outcome of the 1973 war accelerated a strategic rethink by Palestinians. The debate now, in the words of Yezid Sayigh, 'was about the historic nature and purpose of the Palestinian national movement, as the revolutionary and statist options were now brought into direct conflict'.[6] In June 1974 the Palestine National Council (PNC) met in Cairo and reaffirmed its commitment to armed struggle. Crucially, however, it also pledged 'to establish the people's national, independent and *fighting* authority on every part of Palestinian land to be liberated'. This novel formula replaced the previous goal of a 'democratic secular state', though that was not explicitly renounced.[7] It implied readiness for a partial or compromise solution, and reflected concern that the PLO could be left out in the cold if Egypt and Syria were to negotiate directly with Israel. It was explained as a tactical change but in fact it marked a broader shift; it was a compromise between those Palestinians who accepted Israel's existence and those who held on to the vision of complete liberation (thus the addition of the word '*fighting*').[8] This approach did not command universal support: within weeks the PFLP, led by George Habash, now based in Damascus, quit the PLO to form a 'rejection front'. That ultimately undermined Palestinian unity and played into Israeli hands.

Nor, crucially, was the shift enough to convince Israelis that they had a Palestinian partner for peace. Yehoshafat Harkabi, a former IDF intelligence chief, had written influential assessments of Arab attitudes to Israel. His view was that hostility was innate and unchanging and that Arabs were still bent on the state's destruction – an argument which fuelled angry recriminations in the shocked aftermath of the war. Harkabi, along with other Israeli Arabists and the security establishment – who were often the same people – interpreted the PLO's commitment to setting up a 'national authority' on any liberated territory as a 'programme of stages' or, more crudely, as evidence of 'salami tactics' designed to slice away at Israel until it had been eliminated completely. Few of them saw it as an unequivocal commitment to a two-state solution, although dissenting voices argued that Israel's own behaviour could not be ignored.[9]

The debate, however, was not just an academic one. Shortly before the PNC's decision there were two big Palestinian attacks on Israeli civilian targets: in April by Ahmed Jibril's Popular Front-General Command on the northern town of Kiryat Shmona (leaving eighteen dead, including nine children) and in May at Maalot, also on the Lebanese border. In the latter incident, three members of the Democratic Front for the Liberation of Palestine (DFLP) took hostages in a school and demanded the release of prisoners, including the Japanese Kozo Okamoto of the Lod Airport massacre. The deaths of twenty-one teenagers who were on a school outing ensured its lasting notoriety in Israel. Israeli air strikes then killed sixty Palestinians in Ein al-Hilweh and Nabatiyeh in south Lebanon. In November 1974, a three-man DFLP squad killed four residents of Bet Shean and were subsequently killed by the IDF, their bodies burned by an angry Israeli mob.

Overall, the performance of the Egyptian and Syrian armies, smashing the humiliating status quo of 1967, was a boost to Arab self-esteem. 'Our new-found strength has taken us by surprise,' said a Palestinian analyst in East Jerusalem. 'We are drunk with our triumph.'[10] Israelis observed the change with concern. A poll conducted after the war found 'extensive and alarming' support for the PLO in the West Bank and Gaza.[11] Yehuda Litani, a *Haaretz* correspondent, described a 'revolutionary change in a [Palestinian] population which . . . will no longer cooperate with a military government, no matter how liberal, unless such cooperation is imposed on them by force'.[12] That assessment was to prove premature, perhaps the result of wishful thinking by Palestinians reported uncritically by an Israeli dove. Litani and another Arabic-speaking Jerusalem journalist, Danny Rubinstein of the *Histadrut* paper *Davar*, played an important role by reporting, in Hebrew, on both ordinary life and political views in the occupied territories in a way that was independent of the military-dominated version of events. Ordinary Israelis – and the swelling foreign press corps in Israel, reading their articles in English translation – were able to learn more about the Palestinians in their backyard as they returned to the centre-stage of the conflict.

VOTING FOR CHANGE

The upbeat post-war mood was reflected in changes in the West Bank. The creation of a new Palestine National Front led by activists of the Jordanian Communist Party was intended to co-ordinate resistance to the occupation. It organized jubilant rallies during Arafat's UN appearance and accelerated the decline of the old Hashemite loyalists. Israel responded with detentions, curfews and deportations of the PNF's leaders. In early 1976 demonstrations erupted over plans to build a Jewish settlement near Nablus and proposed changes to access to Jerusalem's Haram al-Sharif. Young men burned tyres, erected roadblocks and raised Palestinian flags – sometimes drawing deadly fire from the IDF – in scenes that were repeated countless times.

Israel's next move proved to be a serious miscalculation, calling municipal elections in the West Bank in the hope that the pro-Jordanian mayors – Sheikh Muhammad Ali al-Jaabari in Hebron and Haj Maazouz al-Masri in Nablus, both elected in 1972 – would win new terms. But they refused to stand. That was a blow to Shimon Peres, now the defence minister, who had been exploring a 'self-rule' plan that Palestinians feared would be a sort of phoney autonomy under an 'alternative leadership' which would acquiesce in continued occupation. The PLO instead endorsed younger nationalist candidates – two of whom were expelled by the Israelis – who swept the board in the elections in April 1976. Voter turnout was an impressive 72 per cent. Bassam Shakaa from Nablus was a Baathist from one of the city's wealthiest families. Karim Khalaf in Ramallah and Fahd Qawasmi in Hebron also represented a desire for an end to occupation and backed the PLO as the 'sole legitimate representative' of their people – the endlessly repeated mantra of the age. Elias Freij, the incumbent Jordanian loyalist in Bethlehem, was the exception, but he was an unusually canny operator – a gravelly voiced Palestinian Vicar of Bray – who manoeuvred deftly between the pressures of Israel, Jordan and the PLO.

Recriminations followed the elections, with Yitzhak Rabin attacking Peres for an erroneous assessment of the outcome. It seemed as if the Israeli mindset was still based on a false distinction between refugees and pro-Jordanians and that policy-makers had not absorbed the meaning of the momentous Rabat summit decision and the rapid consolidation of the PLO's position.[13] The new mayors reduced their financial dependence on the occupying Israelis by soliciting donations and loans from the Gulf States.[14] Other Middle Eastern developments meant that Palestinians living under occupation could never forget that they were part of a wider community whose suffering flowed from the very fact of their being Palestinian – stateless and dispersed by the *Nakba* and too often powerless in the face of reluctant hosts, fair-weather friends and ruthless enemies. In August 1976, in the second year of the Lebanese civil war, the fall of the besieged Tel al-Zaatar refugee camp in Beirut to Christian militiamen who were backed by Syria was another catastrophic moment, leaving some 2,000 dead, many of them civilians.[15]

LAND AND HONOUR

The new Palestinian assertiveness made itself felt inside Israel in the wake of the 1973 war. 'Arab has stopped being a dirty word,' observed the journalist Attallah Mansour. Tawfiq Zayyad, the Communist activist and poet, wrote that old notions of superiority and inferiority had been destroyed overnight. Another Palestinian writer believed that the Egyptian crossing of the Suez Canal would break 'Israeli arrogance' and bring peace.[16] The restoration of Arab pride reinforced an accelerating trend: the coming together of the different elements of the divided Palestinian people. In its early years the PLO had paid little attention to Israel's Palestinian minority, though in 1971 the Palestine National Council had broken new ground by electing Israeli-Arab members – including the poet Mahmoud Darwish and writer Sabri Jiryis. Jiryis went on to head a new PLO Research Centre in Beirut and helped expand the organization's limited understanding of Israel; that, he felt, allowed PLO leaders 'to accept the Jewish state as a fait accompli, rather than as a transient Crusader state that would soon disappear'.[17] Beyond that, however, the Arab minority mattered 'only in so far as they reflected Israeli iniquity and immoral behaviour', noted one study. 'In this capacity they were not only passive sufferers but also marginal ones compared to their fellow Palestinians in the occupied territories.'[18] The Israeli authorities, always preoccupied by a potential 'fifth column', worried about security: in 1974 a group of young men from Bartaa spent a whole month under Shin Bet interrogation because a classmate who had gone to Lebanon claimed, falsely, to have recruited them to Fatah. It was an unpleasant reminder, in the poignant words of the Mapam MP Abdel-Aziz al-Zoabi, that 'my people is at war with the state that I belong to'.[19] In 1975 the PLO called publicly for support for the Communist-dominated Democratic Front in the municipal elections in Nazareth; after its victory, under Zayyad, Fadwa Touqan, the nationalist poet from Nablus, paid a visit to Israel's largest Arab city.

Palestinian confidence was expressed most forcefully on 30 March 1976 when the National Committee for the Defence of Arab Lands, formed by the Communist Party, called for a nationwide general strike for the first time. The immediate cause was a government decision to expropriate 20,000 dunams of Arab-owned or Arab-farmed land in Galilee, between Sakhnin and Arrabeh, to construct Jewish settlements and a military training area – a grave blow in its own right as well as a painful reminder of the massive land confiscations of the 1950s. Curfews were imposed and violence ensued when crowds threw stones and petrol bombs at police stations, shouting 'Fatah, Fatah'. By the end of the day there were six dead, scores of injured and hundreds arrested in an event that underlined the anger and the second-class status of the Arab minority, incensed by the ongoing policy of Judaization of the Galilee. 'When did the police in Israel ever shoot at Jewish demonstrators?' one organizer asked.[20] Israel's security establishment saw the Land Day demonstration as an alarming 'act of civil disobedience' motivated by PLO calls to emphasize the 'Arabness' of the Galilee and the Triangle, the start of a slippery slope leading to demands for autonomy or even secession. It was a sobering reminder that reality was harsher than pious declarations about promoting Jewish-Arab relations, especially on the Zionist left. Shuli Dichter, of Kibbutz Maanit, described candidly how relations with the neighbouring village of Umm al-Qutuf were strained by the confiscation of land and disputes over grazing rights – and the behaviour of the kibbutz's Arab 'experts' (*Mizrahanim*).

> Their orientalism was based on research and study. They didn't complain about the theft of lands from the adjacent Palestinian villages. They would be furious with the plantation workers or the field hands if they slapped an Arab kid who dared to come too close to the kibbutz lands. But they didn't challenge the power structure ... or demand genuine partnership or equality in the allocation of resources with the Arabs. Their sense of justice and moral obligation was limited to social, interpersonal, private relations with the Arabs. Moreover, they took it upon themselves to absorb the anger and resentment of the neighbours as a sort of flak jacket for the kibbutz and the movement. They presented the kind face of the new settlers and identified with every complaint from the Arabs about the rudeness and insensitivity of the Jewish authorities ... Many times I heard myself say to people from Umm al-Qutuf who were angry about the theft of their pastures: 'There's nothing to be done; it's the government, not us.' I didn't believe myself and they didn't believe me. They knew perfectly well that the government discriminated between us, and that I was on the side that benefited from that discrimination.[21]

Confirmation of the fears of Israel's Arab citizens was provided soon afterwards with the leak of a confidential government report. Yisrael Koenig, the senior interior ministry official for Galilee, expressed concern about control of the minority in the light of demographic, political and economic trends. He called for the intensification of Jewish settlement in the north to break up the contiguity of Arab villages; a more systematic 'reward and punishment' policy, and a smear campaign against Communist activists.* Arab intellectuals

* Maki, the old Israeli Communist Party, split in 1965, and was reconstituted as Rakah.

were to be encouraged to emigrate and student organizations undermined. The government condemned the recommendations but the report still won wide support from local Jewish leaders.[22] Over time Land Day was to transform the image of 'the Arabs of 1948', as they were often referred to by other Palestinians.[23] PLO interest in them intensified further. Ever since then Land Day, like Balfour Day, has been marked annually, a collective experience not just inside Israel but among Palestinians everywhere. The 1976 victims are commemorated in a fine stone monument, which calls for Arab–Jewish rapprochement, in the Muslim cemetery in Sakhnin. Mahmoud Darwish penned a poem in their honour.[24]

THE DAY OF THE HAWK

In May 1977, the 'earthquake' of the October 1973 war produced a massive political shift that was to have a profound and lasting impact on the course of the Israeli–Palestinian conflict. Menachem Begin's Likud, an alliance of the right-wing *Herut* party and the Liberals, emerged as the largest party in the general election. The campaign was dominated by accusations of incompetence surrounding Yitzhak Rabin's Labour government, still tainted by the failures of Yom Kippur. Begin was remembered internationally as the leader of the *Irgun*, perpetrator of the bombing of the King David Hotel and the Deir Yassin massacre. In Israel he seemed a marginal, old-fashioned figure, commander of the 'dissident' group that had initiated terrorist attacks on Arabs and challenged the authority of the new state in the *Altalena* gun-running affair. He was not even mentioned in a bestselling book about Israel that was published in 1971.[25] Begin had a reputation for rabble-rousing demagoguery, combined with courtly manners that harked back to his Polish origins. He had seemed destined to remain in opposition. But the Likud victory reflected a populist mood born of far-reaching social changes, notably the increasing weight of oriental Jewish immigrants who resented Mapai, the 'natural party of government' since 1948 and the Ashkenazi-dominated establishment. Begin's only experience in office was as minister without portfolio in the national unity government of

1967–1970. He remained a follower of the Jabotinsky school of 'revisionist' Zionism and a firm believer in 'Greater Israel'. His knowledge of Arabs was extremely limited. When he came to power 'the outcasts became the establishment', as Begin's biographer observed.[26]

Highly significant changes were to take place under Begin's rule, both domestically and vis-à-vis the Palestinians, but above all in the expansion of settlements. The settlement enterprise in the occupied territories had gathered momentum in the preceding years. In 1974 a new movement called *Gush Emunim* (Bloc of the Faithful), energized by the recent war, burst on to the scene. Its supporters protested against Henry Kissinger, the US secretary of state, as he shuttled between Jerusalem, Damascus and Cairo to negotiate the disengagement agreements with Syria and Egypt. Crowds gathered outside Jerusalem's King David Hotel whenever Kissinger was in town, carrying black umbrellas – a none-too-subtle reminder of Neville Chamberlain at Munich in 1938. In June 1974, under the Rabin government, its supporters had set up a 'wildcat' settlement at Hawara, south of Nablus. Weeks after their initial eviction they tried again, with Begin cheering them on. The Labour party sent out characteristically mixed signals. 'After all, this isn't an enemy that has come to conquer the country,' Shimon Peres – Rabin's indefatigable rival – told more dovish colleagues who opposed appeasing the settlers. 'Our visa to Judea and Samaria is that they are Judea and Samaria and we are the Jewish people,' declared Moshe Dayan, who had abandoned Labour to become an independent MP.[27] Rabin, however, would later call *Gush Emunim* 'a cancer in the body of Israeli democracy'. Ariel Sharon recalled later that Rabin had asked him around that time about *Gush Emunim*. Sharon had replied: 'They're like we were 40 years ago, only more serious.'[28]

By the end of 1975 continuous lobbying, government vacillation and rivalry between ministers had led to the establishment of a settlement housed temporarily – pending another decision – in an army camp at Kadum near Nablus. It was named Elon Moreh – mentioned in the Old Testament as the place where God promised Abraham: 'Unto thy seed I will give this land' (Genesis 12:7). Another factor, Peres explained, was the resolution passed by the UN General Assembly that November – a year after Arafat's 'gun and olive branch' appearance – defining Zionism as racism. Building settlements in response to international pressure on Israel was a pattern that was often to be repeated in the decades to come. By 1977 eight settlements around Jerusalem housed 33,000 people, though there were only 4,300 settlers elsewhere in the West Bank.[29] These included Kfar Etzion and Kiryat Arba, just outside Hebron, as well as several outposts in the Jordan Valley. There were twenty-seven in the Golan Heights and the Gaza Strip. On the north coast of Sinai, construction was under way for a city called Yamit. Labour had already announced the construction of twenty-seven of forty-nine new outposts scheduled to be built over the next fifteen years.[30]

MORE ELON MOREHS

Begin changed both Israel's discourse about settlements and the pace of implementation. Immediately after the election he travelled to Kadum, temporary home of the Elon Moreh settlers. It was, he declared in front of the TV cameras, not occupied but 'liberated Israeli land', and he promised 'many more Elon Morehs'. Within months the government had quietly given its blessing to two other previously 'unauthorized' outposts – a 'work camp' at Ofra, in the middle of a cluster of Palestinian villages in the hills near Ramallah, and workers' accommodation for an 'industrial area' at Maaleh Adumim, north-east of Jerusalem. Begin's election was a shock to many Israelis, to Palestinians and the wider world – a sentiment that was reflected in dramatic headlines like 'THE DAY OF THE HAWK' – but it ended much of the ambiguity and double-talk surrounding land and peace. His views on Arabs were neither complicated nor conflicted. He refused to use the terms 'West Bank' or 'Palestinians' and spoke only of 'Judaea and Samaria' and the historic rights of the Jewish people. 'The Likud was too absorbed in the realisation of its own vision to fret about those Israelis who could not share it – or Palestinians who opposed', one observer noted.[31] Expectations of any moves towards peace were low to non-existent. Moshe Dayan, whom Begin appointed foreign minister, suggested to King Hussein that he meet the new Likud prime minister. The Jordanian monarch refused out of hand, saying there was no point as Begin's positions were well known.

Begin's victory was greeted with jubilation by the settlers. *Gush Emunim* saw itself as 'an *avant garde* that would awaken and lead the entire nation, and was imbued with a sense of total confidence in the justice of its path'.[32] Its activists were disappointed to hear that outright annexation was not an option and that their plan for twelve new settlements would have to be debated in cabinet, rather than simply nodded through. But their dismay did not last long. Begin's choice of agriculture minister – the confident and pushy Ariel Sharon – was a natural ally. Sharon's reputation for bulldozing ahead without formal authorization went before him. During his campaign against the *fedayeen* in Gaza he had ordered the eviction of hundreds of Bedouin from the Rafah area with a view to promoting Jewish settlement. Having quit the army he had returned to fight as a reserve officer on the Egyptian front in the 1973 war, enhancing his popularity as 'Arik King of Israel' by leading the decisive IDF counter-offensive into the Nile Valley. In the mid-1970s Sharon had advised the settlers in private, and cheered them on publicly as they kept up pressure on Rabin. Having joined and then left the Likud, he ran in the 1977 election on his own independent list, his two Knesset seats a useful addition to Begin's coalition. In September he unveiled a new master plan for settlement entitled 'A Vision of Israel at Century's End' – which envisaged 2 million Jews in the occupied territories by 2000. In 1978 a shorter-term plan to settle 100,000 Jews by 1982 was drawn up by Matti Drobless, a Begin loyalist who ran the settlement department of the Jewish Agency.

Sharon looked at the big picture between the Mediterranean and the Jordan: his strategy was to build a bloc of Jewish settlements to break up the contiguity of the Arab population on both sides of the 1967 border, simply ignoring the green line. New highways would link Samaria to the coastal plain in the west and the Jordan Valley in the east. Military logic was at work too, as it had been when Jewish outposts were established in Mandatory times. 'Individual settlements were located on strategic summits, thereby allowing them to function as observation points: maintaining visual connection with each other and overlooking their surroundings, main traffic arteries, strategic road junctions and Palestinian cities, towns and villages.' Tents, caravans and pre-fabricated homes on West Bank hilltops replaced tanks as the basic battlefield unit. 'Homes, like armoured divisions, were deployed in formation across a theatre of operations to occupy hills, to encircle an enemy or to cut its communication lines.'[33] For Sharon the key was the motivation to defend a place. 'The fact that you are present, that you know every hill, every mountain, every valley, every spring, every cave; the curiosity to know what is on the other side of the hill – that's security,' he explained.[34] But all this required more than small numbers of *Gush Emunim* activists equipped with religious fervour and a few caravans. It needed ordinary Israelis taking a practical view of how to improve their standard of living, given the opportunity of moving into a house rather than a cramped apartment, benefitting from tax exemptions, cheap mortgages and other incentives. Families could move to the West Bank and enhance their quality of life and still be in short commuting distance from Tel Aviv and Jerusalem – or 'five minutes from Kfar Saba' as the cheery advertising slogan went, emphasizing ease of access and comforting familiarity. The old green line was becoming a thing of the past. And as far as Sharon was concerned there was nothing accidental about its gradual but steady erasure. 'Sharon pushed and I implemented,' said Drobless.[35]

THIS LAND IS OUR LAND

Other consequences flowed from the expansion: Palestinian land was confiscated in ever larger quantities for what was usually defined as military or public purposes. Water resources came increasingly under Israeli control. In 1979 Israeli law was extended to five regional councils where Jewish settlers were now concentrated. 'Arrangements enacted to protect and empower Jewish settlements are extraterritorial extensions of the law of one country over the territory of another', observed the Palestinian lawyer Raja Shehadeh. 'They constitute a system of apartheid in all but name, resulting as they do in the creation of two communities living side by side subject to two different and discriminatory sets of laws.'[36] Numbers of West Bank settlers rose steadily, to 12,500 by 1980. The new settlements were built by Palestinian workers, driven by the same economic necessity that sent increasing numbers to work inside Israel.[37] The government's intention was that the West Bank be carved up 'by a grid of roads, settlements and strongholds into a score of little Bantustans so that [the Palestinians] shall never coalesce again into a contiguous area that can support autonomous, let alone independent, existence', commented one Israeli analyst.[38]

At the same time the West Bank became Israel's most important trading partner.[39] Many ties bound them together in a pattern of mutual but unequal dependence. West Bank industry remained stunted, contributing progressively less to the territory's GDP. Local investment and development were stagnant. Economic growth was driven by remittances coming from Israel and the Gulf States. Within the space of a few years Palestinians had become an indispensable element of the Israeli labour force, almost without anyone noticing. Yet social intercourse between them and Israelis remained limited. 'While Arab workers in the construction sector have numerous contacts with Jewish contractors, they rarely work with Jewish workers on the same site', a Palestinian study observed.

> In fact, most of their contacts, both in going to work and on the construction site, happen to be with people from their own village, and often from their own clan. Buses transport villagers to their work site in Israel and bring them back in the evening, thus reinforcing this village identity. When they do have contacts with Jewish workers, politics are rarely discussed; social interaction is amiable but is kept at a minimum. On the Israeli side, the villager's contact is mostly with the contractor, the boss, the police, the prostitute and the border guard. Despite his deep penetration into the Israeli economy and his workable command of Hebrew, the Arab peasant-worker's conception of Jewish society remains that of a closed and undifferentiated mass.[40]

That growing presence was nevertheless unmistakable. When an Israeli sociologist embarked in the early 1980s on a project to document Palestinians employed inside the green line it opened his eyes to what he and most other Jews had long preferred not to notice:

Suddenly I see Palestinian workers everywhere in Tel Aviv, on building sites, in hospitals, at the university of Tel Aviv, in my own department, at restaurants, shops ... suddenly I see that other people, like myself before the survey, do not see all this; they do not see that at night the campus [of TAU] is like a big dormitory for Palestinian workers spending the night in TA, and so are the basements of hospitals, shops, warehouses, the food market areas of the city, the beach in summertime, the space underneath Kikar Dizengoff – Tel Aviv's central piazza; suddenly I realise that people are not only blind to all this, but that they do not want to look at it, even when their attention is drawn to it.[41]

The prevalence of Palestinian labour a decade after the watershed of 1967 gave rise to wry jokes about what this meant for Israeli society and its values: one featured an elderly Jewish man, reminiscing to his increasingly wide-eyed grandson about his youth as a pioneer, a Zionist Stakhanovite tilling the fields, toiling on construction sites, draining swamps and making the desert bloom from dawn till dusk. 'Gosh granddad, that's amazing,' replied the astonished child. 'So when you were young, were you an Arab?'

14

1977–1981

'No more war, no more bloodshed.'

Anwar al-Sadat[1]

JOURNEY TO JERUSALEM

In November 1977 Anwar Sadat flew from Cairo to Tel Aviv and then travelled on by road to Jerusalem. It was an extraordinary, controversial and electrifying moment in the conflict between Israel and the Arabs. It provoked Israeli ecstasy and Palestinian agony and outrage. The first-ever visit by an Arab head of state led, in a relatively short time, to a peace treaty between the Jewish state and its most powerful and populous enemy, removing it from the circle of hostility around Israel that had existed since 1948. Agreement worked on the principle of exchanging land for peace – the return to Egypt of all the territory it had lost to Israel in 1967 except the Gaza Strip, which was historically part of Palestine. Hopes, always very slim, that the Egyptian initiative would somehow turn into a wider or even a comprehensive Middle East peace settlement, proved short-lived. In the end it did nothing at all for the Palestinians, locked into a bleak status quo of occupation and dispersal a full decade since the Six Days war.

Israelis were delighted, though profound suspicions still had to be overcome. The IDF chief of staff, Mordechai Gur, marred the festive mood by warning of a ploy designed to catch Israel off guard, as it had been so disastrously on Yom Kippur four years earlier. On 19 November, a Saturday evening, excitement mingled with disbelief as the Egyptian president came down the steps of the gleaming white

Boeing jet that had brought him directly to Ben-Gurion airport, and stood solemnly to attention as the two countries' national anthems were played by a military band. Menachem Begin, looking stiff and nervous, waited on the red carpet with other ministers, judges and religious leaders. Sadat kissed the former prime minister, Golda Meir, the 'old lady' he had vilified in 1973 and during the war of attrition and long-range Israeli bombing raids over the Nile Valley. He even joshed with Ariel Sharon, who had mounted a daring counter-offensive back across the Suez Canal and trapped the Egyptian Third Army. He went on to visit the grim Yad Vashem Holocaust memorial in Jerusalem, as well as the al-Aqsa mosque. The psychological and emotional impact on Israel was enormous. Sadat, went the lyrics of a poignant and popular Hebrew song, had 'pyramids in his eyes and peace in his pipe'. In his speech to the Knesset the next day, broadcast live around the world, Sadat declared that he was not seeking a separate Egyptian peace with Israel. At the request of the Israelis, he omitted a planned reference to the PLO in order, as Moshe Dayan put it, not to 'infect the atmosphere',[2] but he did urge Israel to recognize the Palestinian people and their 'legitimate rights'. Begin's reply expressed appreciation for Sadat's courage and invited the rulers of Syria and Jordan and what he called 'genuine spokesmen of the Palestinian Arabs' ('Arabs of *Eretz-Yisrael'* in the Hebrew phrase) to take part in peace talks. He also ranged back into Jewish history, including the horrors of the Nazi era, referenced the fundamental tenets of Zionism and, above all, gave no sign of making any concessions. Despite the theatrics, the gap between the two leaders yawned so visibly that Israeli ministers quietly expressed alarm. 'Nothing I write about the yearning with which Sadat was received . . . can be exaggerated', noted the Likud's Yitzhak Shamir, the speaker of parliament, 'nor about the subsequent apprehension and growing chill with which I listened to him.'[3] Still, the ringing pledge of 'no more war, no more bloodshed' enunciated by Begin and echoed by Sadat, resonated throughout the forty-four-hour visit and for long afterwards.

Sadat's unilateral move was a crushing blow for the PLO, especially since, in the autumn of 1977, Yasser Arafat had felt that things were starting to go his way internationally: Jimmy Carter, the new US president, had declared his support for a 'homeland' for the Palestinians. In August the US joined the USSR in announcing plans to reconvene the Geneva peace conference with Palestinian participation, although in the end Arafat proved unable to meet the conditions by accepting UN Resolutions 242 and 338, which implied recognition of Israel. Arafat was also taken completely by surprise – and at uncomfortably close quarters: he had been invited to the Egyptian parliament in Cairo on 9 November where he heard Sadat announce his readiness to go to 'the ends of the earth', even to the Knesset, to pursue peace with Israel. He faced angry criticism afterwards for joining in the applause. 'I was on the mountaintop,' the PLO leader told Palestinian students, 'but Sadat threw me into the valley.' Eleven days later he wept in 'grief and fury' as he watched Sadat's Knesset speech on TV from his Beirut headquarters,[4] horrified that the Arab country he always held in the highest affection had suddenly taken this astonishing course. Shortly afterwards he signed a statement condemning the Egyptian leader for 'grand treason' and urging a boycott of Arab League meetings in Cairo. Privately, however, Arafat refused to join the radical Arab bloc – Syria, Algeria, South Yemen and Libya – who formed a 'steadfastness and confrontation front' and severed all links with Egypt.[5] He quietly stayed in touch with Sadat, never slamming the door, but played no part as the peace initiative developed.

Furious statements were issued by the governments in Damascus, Tripoli and Baghdad and there were attacks on Egyptian embassies as well as angry protests in Palestinian refugee camps across the Middle East. The mood in the West Bank and Gaza was a mixture of anxiety, disbelief and shock. Still, Karim Khalaf, the nationalist mayor of Ramallah, insisted that anyone who wanted to discuss the fate of the Palestinians would have to deal with Arafat. Elias Freij, his pro-Jordanian counterpart in Bethlehem, refrained from joining the welcoming party for Sadat at Tel Aviv airport, although along with Anwar al-Khatib, the former governor of Jerusalem, and Rashad al-Shawwa, the mayor of Gaza, he did quietly meet the Egyptian leader two days later. Freij then received death threats from PLO supporters.[6] President Carter complained in December that by condemning Sadat the PLO had excluded itself from the peace process. Zbigniew

Brzezinski, his national security adviser, put it more bluntly: 'Bye bye PLO' – a phrase that was to be gleefully quoted back for years to come at anyone who had dared to believe it was true. But Brzezinski, quizzing Begin about his plans, also warned that a Palestinian 'Basutoland' (later Lesotho, the autonomous Black 'homeland' in apartheid South Africa) would not be an acceptable outcome.[7]

AUTONOMY AND DIVERSIONS

On 25 December 1977 Begin reciprocated by visiting Ismailiya on the Suez Canal where he was given a low-key welcome (Cairo was deemed too hostile an environment). It was there that he unveiled the idea of granting 'autonomy' to the West Bank and Gaza. Ezer Weizman, his defence minister, recognized immediately that Begin saw this as a way of perpetuating Israeli rule.[8] The atmosphere clouded in January 1978 when Israel announced the construction of four new settlements in north-eastern Sinai, despatching bulldozers and TV crews to film them at work. Sharon had felt under pressure since Sadat's visit to establish new outposts, but this time he backed down in the face of uproar over this demonstration of duplicity and bad faith in relations with Egypt.[9] Carter, on a visit to Aswan, had called on Israel to recognize the legitimate rights of the Palestinians and resolve the Palestinian issue 'in all its aspects'. Begin countered by insisting that Israel would retain complete and indefinite control of the West Bank and Gaza and complained that Egyptian media had called him a 'Shylock'. Egypt's foreign minister then withdrew from follow-up talks in Jerusalem, which continued in Cairo between defence ministers. No progress was made.[10]

Shortly afterwards there came a bloody and headline-grabbing diversion from the small print of peace negotiations. On 11 March 1978 a thirteen-strong Fatah squad, led by an eighteen-year-old Palestinian woman named Dalal al-Mughrabi – the Beirut-born daughter of a 1948 refugee from Jaffa – landed in rubber boats on a deserted beach south of Haifa and murdered an American woman tourist who was photographing wildlife. They then hijacked a bus on the coastal road and en route to Tel Aviv took over a second bus. At the end of a lengthy chase and shootout, thirty-eight Israeli civilians, including thirteen children, were dead and seventy-six wounded. The raid was masterminded by Khalil al-Wazir, known to all as Abu Jihad, with Arafat's approval. It had, the PLO leader said, shown 'the ability of the revolution to reach wherever it wishes'.[11] And it too was named after the Deir Yassin massacre.[12] Three days later Israel sent 25,000 troops into south Lebanon and occupied it up as far as the Litani river, except for the coastal city of Tyre. The aim was to push Palestinian groups away from the border and bolster Israel's local proxy, the South Lebanon Army (SLA). Seven days of fighting ended with a ceasefire (notably the first with Israel that was endorsed by all official PLO bodies), the creation of a new UN peacekeeping force, and an Israeli withdrawal that left the SLA in the front line of the confrontation with Fatah. 'Operation Litani' served as a bloody reminder that the Palestinians could not be ignored – and that Israel's military might could be unleashed to devastating effect. An estimated 1,100 people were killed, mostly Palestinian and Lebanese. Israel said that at least half the fatalities were Palestinian fighters. Estimates for the numbers displaced by the offensive range from 100,000 to 250,000. Begin condemned a 'Nazi atrocity' that reinforced his long-standing view of the Palestinians. 'It is inconceivable that in Judaea and Samaria and in Gaza a state should be established that would be ruled by Yasser Arafat and his murderers,' he said. Not surprisingly, this shook, though it did not derail, the nascent Israeli–Egyptian peace process. And it was not the last time Lebanon would be the hapless setting for an Israeli–Palestinian war.

Sadat and Begin both visited Washington during the summer of 1978 but relations between them worsened. In early September, Carter took a high-risk gamble, against the recommendation of his advisers, and brought the two together at the Camp David presidential retreat in Maryland, amid rustic log cabins, tennis courts, bicycle tracks, a golden-brown carpet of autumn leaves – and strict instructions to dress casually in special wind-cheaters. Begin called it a 'concentration camp de luxe'.[13] Carter hoped that the enforced seclusion would avoid performances for domestic consumption but both Begin and Sadat had direct phone lines and leaked whatever suited them.[14] Over thirteen famously 'intense and discouraging' days – which later inspired a

Broadway play – Carter shuttled between leaders who were 'totally incompatible',[15] sulked, shouted, barely concealed their mutual dislike and even had to be physically separated. In the end, despite repeated threats to walk away – Carter physically blocking the door to stop Sadat leaving – they resolved all outstanding bilateral issues. Those included the evacuation of Israel's military bases and settlements in Sinai, and so it was agreed to conclude a peace treaty and launch normal relations within three months. Sadat backed down on one vital point, dropping his initial strong insistence on a link between bilateral issues and a full withdrawal from the occupied West Bank and Gaza Strip. Mohammed Ibrahim Kamel, the Egyptian foreign minister, resigned in fury. Sadat's reward was $1.3 billion in annual US aid to the Egyptian armed forces. Carter, declared Begin, had 'worked harder than did our forebears in Egypt building the Pyramids'.

Still, when the treaty was signed, it was the most significant breakthrough ever made in the history of the Arab–Israeli conflict, though a very partial one. It broke a thirty-year taboo on Arabs dealing with Israel and satisfied narrow Egyptian national interests, but nothing more.[16] A second Camp David document, dealing with the Palestinians, agreed that future negotiations would be based on UN Resolution 242 and that any solution must recognize the legitimate rights of the Palestinians, who were to enjoy 'full autonomy' during a five-year transition period. In that period a 'self-governing authority' would be elected by the inhabitants of the West Bank and Gaza. Jordan was asked to join Egypt and Israel in agreeing how the body would be established. But generally this part of Camp David was far vaguer than the first, and open to different interpretations. East Jerusalem was not mentioned at all and there was no Israeli commitment to withdraw. And as in Sadat's Knesset speech, the PLO was not mentioned either. Inevitably there was disagreement too over the length of the moratorium on settlement construction Begin had agreed to. 'The Sinai was considered by Begin as a quid pro quo for the Israeli presence in Judea and Samaria,' said a close aide to the prime minister.[17] Arafat denounced the 'Camp David plot'.

'POWER TO EXTERMINATE MOSQUITOES'

Palestinian opposition hardened further. Jordan declined to join talks on the self-governing authority, while Egyptian-Israeli negotiations on the powers of the autonomous entity dragged on for eighteen months without result. West Bank mayors – living the daily reality of Israeli occupation – were dismissive, insisting that autonomy meant no more than legitimizing the status quo. Palestinians were being offered the power to 'collect garbage and exterminate mosquitoes', complained Karim Khalaf, the mayor of Ramallah. Autonomy, in the words of the journalist Raymonda Tawil, was 'a sham, a lie, a gigantic hoax ... an attempt to bury the Palestinian cause for ever by creating the impression that the Palestinian issue has been solved – while we remain under Israel's yoke'. Fahd Qawasmi, the mayor of Hebron, underlined what autonomy would mean in practice: 'Ali will replace Shmuel as the head of the department of education. So what! Where's my identity, my future?'[18] Following an Arab summit in Baghdad – which allotted $150 million to the occupied territories, to be administered jointly by Jordan and the PLO – a new broad-based National Guidance Committee was formed in November 1978. Representing Palestinian trade unions and student bodies, voluntary organizations, the religious establishment and the press, it helped formulate a common position on the autonomy plan and co-ordinate opposition to settlements. Fatah was part of the twenty-three-member body but did not dominate it.[19] Its leading figure was an unassuming Jerusalem engineer named Ibrahim Dakkak, who was referred to as 'the mayor of mayors'. It soon showed its worth: the signing of the Egyptian-Israeli peace treaty on the White House lawn on 26 March 1979 was accompanied by the biggest protest strike in the West Bank and Gaza since 1967, with newspapers mourning 'a black day' – a deliberate echo of Begin's warning of the implications of American recognition of the PLO. Autonomy never won the backing of any significant Palestinian figures: Sheikh Hashem Khuzandar, the imam of Gaza and a prominent Muslim Brotherhood leader, was one of very few who did support it, hailing a 'new dawn'. He was stabbed to death outside his mosque in June, his assassination claimed by the DFLP. No prominent public figures attended his funeral. Other attacks on alleged collaborators followed.

Begin had no intention of retreating from the West Bank. One of his favourite maxims was that he would never again countenance a situation where Israeli women and children would die in Netanya or Petah Tikvah because there were enemy guns in Qalqilya and Tulkarem – Palestinian towns very close to the 1967 border. His view of autonomy was that it was for people but not the territory they inhabited, a vague throwback to discussions about minority rights in inter-war Poland. 'Begin wasn't interested in Arabs', recalled Avraham Shalom, a senior Shin Bet officer. 'He was interested in the Christians in Lebanon, in Sadat. Did he even know where Nablus was? He never visited an Arab village, not even in Israel.'[20] Years later Ariel Sharon gave a candid description of Begin's autonomy as nothing but a

> fig leaf to enable Egypt to sign our peace treaty. The Egyptians needed this document in order to demonstrate their 'concern' for the Palestinian cause. We for our part had the deepest interest in signing the peace treaty and precious little interest in any change of the status quo in Judea, Samaria and Gaza.[21]

The settlers, alarmed at what had happened since the arrival in Israel of the man they called 'Hitler on the Nile', remained suspicious; they neither trusted the prime minister nor believed he would be able to resist US and Arab pressure. *Gush Emunim* activists mocked up posters of Arab policemen wearing *keffiyehs* and checking the ID cards of *kippa*-wearing Jews. 'Autonomy', they warned, was 'the temporary name for a Palestinian state', while Jewish residents of the new East Jerusalem suburbs would be subject to a special pass system.[22] In one incident that March armed settlers from Ofra drove into the centre of nearby Ramallah, rounded up Palestinian residents and forced them at gunpoint to clear roadblocks. Two Palestinians were then shot dead in Halhoul while throwing rocks at an Israeli car. It was suspected that the perpetrators were from Kiryat Arba, stronghold of the most fanatical settlers. The army imposed a two-week curfew on the town and prevented the delivery of supplies by outsiders.

Among its other intoxicating effects, Sadat's initiative led to the creation of the Peace Now movement in March 1978, at a time when the Egyptian-Israeli talks looked dangerously close to collapse. Nearly 350 reserve IDF officers, motivated by 'deep anxiety', sent an open letter to Begin, urging him not to squander an historic opportunity for peace. 'A government that prefers the existence of the State of Israel within the borders of "Greater Israel" to its existence in peace with good neighbourliness, will be difficult for us to accept', they warned.

A government that prefers the existence of settlements beyond the green line to elimination of this historic conflict with [the] normalisation of relationships in our region will evoke questions regarding the wisdom of the path we are taking. A policy that will lead to a continuation of our rule over a million Arabs will harm the Jewish-democratic character of the state, and will make it difficult for us to identify with the path of the State of Israel.[23]

Sentiments like these saw tens of thousands of Israelis maintaining pressure on the government to sign an agreement, expressing solidarity with Palestinians, demonstrating against collective punishments and planting vines to replace those uprooted by settlers in Hebron.

Begin's government naturally looked to its own constituency, and under pressure from the settler lobby, tried hard to suppress pro-PLO sentiment. Activists were detained or deported, and Bir Zeit and other West Bank universities shut down for weeks on end. Any restraint worried the right wing. Ezer Weizman, Begin's defence minister, rejected a recommendation by the Shin Bet that Bassam Shakaa, the mayor of Nablus, be deported on the grounds of a leaked conversation in which he had allegedly justified the Coastal Road massacre: every other mayor in the West Bank and Gaza threatened to resign if Shakaa was banished. Following the decision, Weizman phoned his Egyptian counterpart to tell him the good news – so that the peace talks could continue. Dr Ahmed Natshe from Hebron, who had been expelled to Jordan on the eve of the 1976 municipal elections, was allowed to return. At the same time, the Israeli military began giving 'discreet support' to Islamist groups – mostly inspired by the Muslim Brotherhood – that had been encouraged by the Iranian revolution a few months earlier. Social welfare associations, charities and student groups in Gaza began to challenge secular nationalists. In January 1980 Islamists attacked the home and office of Hayder Abdel-Shafi of the Red Crescent Society and a leading PLO loyalist. In years to come these events would be identified as the first significant appearance of an Islamist trend in Palestinian politics.

Alarm spread among the settlers at the increasingly *political* direction of Palestinian resistance. 'The new Palestinian commanders no longer bedecked themselves in tiger-striped uniforms and loaded Kalashnikovs', wrote Hagai Segal, one of the founders of Ofra.

> Rather, dressed in elegant suits and half-height shoes, they clutched microphones and incited their supporters in city squares to resist the occupation. Instead of a handful of venomous terrorists lurking in underground organisations and acting only under cover of darkness, tens of thousands of local youths enlisted enthusiastically in the new campaign, which they waged (almost) without any explosives.[24]

But Fatah soon gave a spectacular demonstration of its enduring belief in the efficacy of armed action. It struck a deadly blow in May 1980, when a four-man squad gunned down six Israeli settlers at Bet Hadassah in the centre of Hebron – one of the most effective Palestinian attacks since 1967 and, given the city's emotionally freighted history, one of the most sensitive possible targets to choose. Israeli public reactions suggested a lack of sympathy with the settlement enterprise, argued one influential commentator.[25] The government retaliated by expelling Qawasmi, the Hebron mayor, and his pro-PLO colleague from Halhoul, Mohamed Milhem, an articulate and handsome Palestinian spokesman. Weizman rejected a more drastic proposal to expel all the members of the National Guidance Committee. It was in this charged atmosphere in June 1980 that settler activists bombed the cars of Shakaa and Karim Khalaf, his colleague from Ramallah. Shakaa lost both legs, Khalaf both feet, and a police sapper was blinded trying to defuse a third device planted in the car of the mayor of El Bireh, Ibrahim al-Tawil. Israeli media dubbed it the work of the 'Jewish underground', a euphemistic phrase with echoes of the 'dissidents' of the pre-state *Irgun* and Stern Gang – though its activities clearly constituted terrorism by any normal definition.

Internationally the PLO made a significant gain with the European Economic Community's Venice Declaration, which recognized the right of the Palestinians to self-determination and called for PLO involvement in negotiations – though it did not describe the group, as Arafat had hoped, as his people's 'sole legitimate representative'. That confirmed the scepticism of the PFLP's George Habash about the value of 'suave' diplomacy compared to the achievements of armed struggle. Referring to the EEC leaders, he said: 'Let Giscard [d'Estaing] and [Willy] Brandt and [Bruno] Kreisky understand that the Palestinian rifle will remain raised, to launch itself from Jericho to liberate Jaffa and from Nablus to liberate Haifa.'[26]

BEGIN, AGAIN

Menachem Begin's second term as prime minister began in August 1981, his position bolstered by the sensational bombing of the Iraqi nuclear reactor at Osirak near Baghdad. The election victory was also an endorsement of the Likud's platform of keeping control of the West Bank and Gaza Strip and the Golan Heights. (The Syrian territory was effectively annexed to Israel at the end of the year, but this unilateral move was not recognized internationally.) Illustrating the drift to the right, a small dovish party, Sheli (Peace for Israel), which had taken the radical step of advocating negotiations with the PLO, lost the two Knesset seats it had won in 1977, while the new far-right *Tehiya* (Renaissance) party won three seats with support from the settler lobby. With Ariel Sharon promoted to run the ministry of defence, changes to occupation policy reflected the new political map. The principal one was the establishment of a separate civilian administration in the West Bank and Gaza. The new body was subordinate to the military government, but the division of labour was designed to pre-empt the outcome of the autonomy talks with Egypt by implementing Israel's interpretation of Camp David unilaterally. The head of the new administration was Menachem Milson, a Hebrew

University professor whose speciality was modern Arabic literature. Milson bolstered the Israeli-backed Village Leagues, which had been established to challenge the growing strength of the PLO in the cities. The idea was that the conservative rural sector – which still accounted for 70 per cent of the West Bank population – would be easier to cultivate and influence. The scale of the ambition was demonstrated when Sharon presented the leagues' leaders to the visiting US defence secretary, Casper Weinberger. But Israeli critics complained of outdated thinking and cited the fact that West Bank villagers were in fact just as nationalist as town dwellers – as shown by the numbers in prison for security offences.[27]

The leagues, first set up in the Hebron area, were run by *mukhtars* or other individuals who were granted powers to control water, electricity and other services, and received payment as well as weapons and training from the Israeli military. They were also authorized to issue some of the many permits needed for construction, exporting goods – or visiting relatives in Jordan.[28] The intention was to 'storm the radical towns with the reactionary peasants'.[29] The reputation of many of those involved with the leagues was dubious. The figurehead was Mustafa Dudin, a former Jordanian minister. Pro-PLO figures accused him and others of being collaborators or land dealers, raising the ghosts of the 'farmers' parties' of the 1920s and the 'treacherous' Zionist-funded opposition to the mufti in the 1930s. Israel TV's Arabic channel broadcast clips of IDF officers handing cheques to Dudin to finance development projects. Others were illiterates or criminals.[30] Palestinian hostility was strong but might not have proved decisive without a decision by Jordan, now working in tandem with the PLO, to ban membership of the leagues on pain of death and confiscation of property. Within a few weeks key members had quit, while one of its leaders in the Ramallah area was assassinated by the PLO.[31]

AN EVERYDAY OCCUPATION

By the early 1980s life in the occupied territories had settled into a sort of dreary routine moulded by growing economic dependence, the patriarchal nature of Palestinian society, a deference to authority, the sophistication of Israeli control – and sheer habit. 'The carrot', in the words of the Palestinian-Israeli writer Anton Shammas, 'had become the stick.' Palestinians described their state of mind as '*sumoud*' – 'steadfastness' or 'hanging on'. The Israelis were practised at wearing people down, discouraging initiative and organization, not hesitating to intimidate and to punish. Raja Shehadeh, a perceptive chronicler of the dreary reality of Israeli rule, described how it worked on an unnamed friend:

> So far the military forces of occupation have left him alone . . . But when they come to suspect that he is being effective . . . they will begin to pursue him . . . They will begin to keep him under surveillance. They will keep him waiting for half a day until an 'expert' with a frightening face interrogates him . . . They may even instruct their agents to spread rumours to make him lose his credibility. They won't give him the permits he needs to get any of his projects started. And then, people won't have anything more to do with him, because no project associated with him will get off the ground . . . But if he persists and is perceived as a real danger, something will be found against him, and he will be taken in. No-one will be able to prove what happened to him inside, but everyone will see how much weight he has lost and how subdued and defeated he looks when he is released. And if he revives after this and takes up where he left off, they will come one night, drive him to the border in a jeep, and the number of deportees will be increased by one.[32]

Deportation was only one form of pressure. Ahmed Ajwa, an East Jerusalem journalist, was detained without trial in December 1978 for possessing leaflets opposing the autonomy plan. Ajwa was held first in the Russian Compound in Jerusalem (known to Palestinians as the Muskoubiya) where a Shin Bet officer named Uzi beat him and abused him for alleged connections with the PLO. Later he was questioned by another man who spoke Arabic with an Iraqi accent and used the name Abu Nihad. Ajwa alleged that he had been throttled and chained to a pipe with his arms pinned behind his back and a hood over his head for seventy-two hours and was told by the interrogators that his wife was seeing other men.[33] Allegations about the systematic torture and mistreatment of Palestinians in detention centres achieved wide publicity. In June 1977 a detailed report on the issue by the *Sunday Times* in London was dismissed as a 'slur' by the Israeli government. (Later revelations suggested that the allegations were broadly correct.)[34] Palestinians were not surprised by the newspaper's findings. 'Every time the PLO does something outside we suffer,' said a member of the Aburish family from Bethany.

> Israeli anger is directed at us. Israeli soldiers picked up a cousin –
> because they thought he was a PLO sympathiser and tortured him
> for three days and it took him two weeks to be able to talk again.
> Cousin — was picked up by an Israeli patrol after — and they kept
> him in jail for two days without food and water. He didn't have any
> place to hide; we can't even protect ourselves; we are helpless.[35]

Legal challenges to the occupation, however, became increasingly common in the late 1970s. Important work was done by Israeli Jewish lawyers, notably the veteran Communist Felicia Langer, who acted for Palestinians in many cases that involved land confiscation, house demolitions and torture. It was Langer who managed to save Bassam Shakaa from deportation, though she was barred by the Communist Party from representing Palestinians who were implicated in attacks on civilians.[36] Many were represented by Leah Tsemel, who was associated with the anti-Zionist group Matzpen. Israeli Arab lawyers, with their mastery of Hebrew, were well equipped to work in this area. Palestinians believed that the Israeli lawyers were less intimidated by the military and thus better able to defend their clients. 'It's a slave mentality,' one Arab lawyer said. 'People simply refuse to believe that they can be helped by another slave in a conflict with the master.'[37]

By summer 1981 it was clear that Sadat's initiative would achieve nothing on the Palestinian front. Moshe Dayan held meetings with leaders from the West Bank and Gaza, but given the absence of any Palestinian buy-in and the slow pace of talks it was obvious that any benefits of Israeli–Egyptian peace would be strictly bilateral. In March 1982 Israel outlawed the National Guidance Committee on the grounds that it was an arm of the PLO and dismissed the mayors of Nablus, Ramallah and El-Bireh – all democratically elected six years earlier. Milson tried to justify the move by claiming that the 1976

polls were not democratic but were influenced by 'terrorism, intimidation and bribery'. Bir Zeit University was shut, triggering unrest
that left at least seven Palestinians dead[38] – and sarcastic jokes about
the Israeli professor's attitude to academic freedom. Strict censorship
was imposed on newspapers published in East Jerusalem, and they
were banned from being distributed in the West Bank.

In October 1981, Anwar Sadat was assassinated by Islamist gunmen at a parade marking the Ramadan war. His murder was a
profound shock to Israel and immediately triggered worries about the
durability of the peace treaty he had signed. (When Yasser Arafat
heard of the Egyptian leader's death, his first comment was reportedly: 'This is what happens to people who betray the Palestinian
cause.'[39]) But Sadat's vice-president, Hosni Mubarak, quickly reaffirmed Egypt's commitment to peace with Israel. Viewed from Cairo,
it would have been short-sighted to do anything else: in just a few
months Israel was required not only to return Sinai to Egypt but also,
under the peace treaty, destroy the settlements it had built on Egyptian soil since 1967. In April 1982, Yamit on the north-eastern coast
of Sinai near el-Arish was evacuated as Begin asserted his authority
in the face of alarm on the Israeli right about the implications. 'In
the struggle for Yamit I saw a struggle for Judea and Samaria,' said
Yoel Bin-Nun, a *Gush Emunim* leader.[40] Begin's colleague Yitzhak
Shamir – a former leader of the Stern Gang – was filled with 'regret . . .
and foreboding'.[41] In the end, though, the promised battle was a
damp squib. In a show of resistance that some thought carefully
choreographed, residents barricaded themselves on the rooftops before being dragged into buses by Israeli soldiers, but there was no
bloodshed – despite the dramatic TV coverage. Still, a significant
precedent had been set – removing settlements for peace – even
though it would not be followed for a very long time, and even then
not where it mattered most.

15

1982–1987

'*Our stay in Beirut is a part of the struggle over the Land of Israel, a war against the main enemy that had been fighting us for over one hundred years.*'

Rafael Eitan, 1982

THE ROAD TO BEIRUT

On 6 June 1982, Ariel Sharon ordered Israeli forces into Lebanon to destroy the PLO. Sharon's grand design was intended not only to reshape the political and military map of Israel's northern neighbour but also to 'manage the conflict with the Palestinians to its own liking', as Sharon told Sam Lewis, the US ambassador to Tel Aviv.[1] The fact that the invasion's goal was 'to solve the problems of the West Bank and Gaza' was hardly a secret. Sharon had laid out his battle plans in a meeting with Lebanese Christian leaders the previous January – the relationship with them managed by the Mossad.[2] 'Behind the official excuse of "we shall not tolerate shelling or terrorist actions" lies a strategic view which holds that the physical annihilation of the PLO has to be achieved', a well-connected *Haaretz* columnist wrote three months before the war. 'That is, not only must its fingers and hands in the West Bank be amputated (as is now being done with an iron fist), but its heart and head in Beirut must be dealt with.'[3] Comments in a similar vein were heard regularly before, during and after the war. The declared initial aim of 'Operation Peace for Galilee' was to push PLO forces twenty-five miles north of the border. In a three-pronged offensive IDF tank columns, one landing on the coast north of Sidon, captured strategic positions from

Palestinian fighters, while F16 jets bombed refugee camps and other targets in Beirut. Israel also shot down Syrian aircraft.

Begin histrionically described the purpose of the campaign as preventing another 'Treblinka'. Other emotive Second World War references followed. He responded to President Ronald Reagan's request that he end the siege of Beirut by describing Arafat as 'Hitler and his henchmen hiding in his bunker' in Fakhani. 'Our stay in Beirut,' declared the IDF chief of staff, Rafael Eitan, 'is a part of the struggle over the Land of Israel, a war against the main enemy that had been fighting us for over one hundred years.'[4] Statements of this kind, combined with mounting IDF casualties, fed widespread unease on the home front for the first time in the country's short history. On 4 July a rally by Peace Now – formed to pressure the government in the wake of Sadat's initiative – drew a crowd of 100,000 in Tel Aviv, condemning what protesters described as Israel's 'war of choice' and highlighting the yawning gap between right and left. Speakers, including reserve army officers just back from active duty in Lebanon, called for Sharon's removal and an end to the fighting. 'Israel was waging war without the traditionally automatic political consensus that had been a bedrock asset of every government that had been involved in war – up to this point', noted one opponent.[5]

In fact, many were surprised that the Lebanon war had taken so long to break out. The previous summer Palestinian rocket and artillery fire forced Israeli civilians into bomb shelters and triggered a demoralizing exodus from border towns and villages. On 17 June 1981 Israel had bombed the PLO headquarters in Beirut, killing between 120 and 300 people. Since then, however, a ceasefire brokered by the US envoy Philip Habib – an Arab-American who had grown up alongside Jews in Brooklyn – had more or less held. To Israel's alarm, however, the PLO had used the intervening period to build up its military strength.[6] Warnings of impending trouble had come thick and fast in the preceding weeks, though US attention had been distracted by the war between Britain and Argentina over the Malvinas/Falkland Islands.

The immediate trigger for Israel's action was the attempted assassination of the Israeli ambassador to Britain. Israel knew that the shooting of Shlomo Argov had been carried out by the Abu Nidal faction – the Fatah Revolutionary Council, a small Iraqi-backed enemy of Arafat's PLO – since the three gunmen, as British police quickly discovered, had operated with the help of the Iraqi embassy in London.[7] (The hit-squad leader claimed during the subsequent trial to have been born in Deir Yassin, though he was in fact a Jordanian from the East Bank.) The group's most obvious motive was the wish to strike at a high-profile Israeli target. Other, more nuanced, explanations were that it was an attempt to create a crisis in Lebanon in order to justify a ceasefire in Iraq's bloody war with Iran following recent gains by the Iranians; another was that it was Saddam Hussein's retaliation for the Israeli bombing of the Osirak nuclear reactor a year earlier. Begin and Sharon's immediate interpretation was that it constituted a breach of the ceasefire with the PLO. Sharon argued that a major offensive in Lebanon that destroyed Arafat's power base would 'loosen his hold on the Arabs living under Israeli rule in the West Bank and Gaza Strip'.[8] PLO influence would then wither, allowing 'moderate' Palestinians to negotiate their own future – by accepting autonomy under Israel or finding an outlet for their nationalist aspirations in Jordan. In a scenario favoured by right-wingers, when the PLO had been crushed, Palestinians would flee en masse across the river, overthrow the Hashemite kingdom and create a Palestinian state in its place.[9] Meir Pa'il, a veteran military commentator and critic from the left, provided an astute analysis of this vision:

> The invasion carries with it a message of vital import to the Palestinians: 'Beware you Palestinians living under Israeli rule! All that we have done to the refugee camps, the cities and towns and villages of south Lebanon, on the coast of the Mediterranean between Rashidiye, Tyre and Beirut, we can do to you in Gaza, Judea, Samaria . . . and even perhaps in Umm al-Fahm and Nazareth. And we can do that now, especially, given that there is no PLO or any other legitimate body that could be seen to represent the Palestinian cause. If you would bend down and follow our rules it would be best that you accept the limited autonomy offered you as defined by Begin-Sharon-Milson. If not, your fate will be that of Rashidiye, Ein Hilweh, or Beirut.' Was that the real aim of the invasion?[10]

CHEERING FOR PALESTINE

Palestinians in the occupied territories saluted the resistance to Israel's onslaught and reaffirmed their support for the PLO. Strikes and demonstrations were held to express solidarity, not only with their 'sole legitimate representative' but with relatives who were fighting or suffering in Lebanon. In July several mayors, including Rashad al-Shawwa in Gaza, were dismissed for refusing to co-operate with the Israelis. Bir Zeit University was again ordered shut.[11] But in Nablus, Ramallah, East Jerusalem and Gaza the mood was noticeably subdued. For those living under occupation the Lebanon war was another reminder of Israel's unassailable military superiority. Its methods of control and counter-insurgency, honed over the years in the occupied territories, were applied in Lebanon, where the Shin Bet used hooded informers and intimidating interrogations to identify wanted men. In a Sidon schoolyard an Israeli journalist stumbled on a group of men with their hands bound, blindfolded and forced to sit in the hot sun. 'When summoned they were brought to the entrance of what was once a classroom. There the blindfold was removed just in time to see two Israeli soldiers dragging a corpse out of the room. The man up for questioning could not know that the same corpse was used in this exercise over and over.'[12]

In late August, after a three-month siege of Beirut, Arafat and 6,500 Fatah fighters left for exile in Tunisia and seven other Arab countries, watched by Sharon, Eitan and the senior IDF command. The PLO leader was even photographed in the sights of an Israeli sniper. Sharon claimed victory: 'The departure of the PLO from Lebanon clears the way for Israel to achieve a settlement with moderate West Bank Palestinians,' he said.[13] Arafat responded that the PLO embodied Palestinian aspirations and that the Israeli invasion had only strengthened the will of the Palestinian people to struggle and resist.[14] But the unvarnished truth was that the PLO had lost 'the territorial base of its state in exile, its headquarters and the bulk of its military infrastructure'.[15] First Jordan and then Lebanon had not been prepared to pay the price of serving as a front-line state for the Palestinian struggle. For the first time since it was founded, the PLO had no direct access to Israel's borders.

Israel's presence in Lebanon was to continue, albeit on a more limited scale, for years to come. The war of 1982 was controversial from
the start and seen by many Israeli Jews as unnecessary. It was
routinely characterized by words like 'quagmire' and 'morass', a
Middle-Eastern Vietnam, marked by deception and brutality. In September 1982, the massacre of hundreds of Palestinians in the Sabra
and Shatila refugee camps in Beirut by Israel's Phalangist allies –
while IDF forces stood by and did nothing – cast an even darker
shadow over the enterprise. Palestinians saw Sabra and Shatila as
another example of their powerlessness and suffering and compared
it to Deir Yassin, the *Nakba* and to the events of 'Black September' in
Jordan. In one small West Bank village, more than 10,000 people
turned out for the funeral of a woman who was killed by the Israeli
army during protests against the Beirut killings.[16] In Tel Aviv 400,000
people attended a Peace Now demonstration, the largest the country
had ever seen. The Kahan Commission, which investigated the events
at Sabra and Shatila, found that Sharon was to blame and in February 1983 he resigned as defence minister. It was not, however, the end
of his career.

REAGAN HAS A PLAN

Even as the summer war was coming to an end, a new diplomatic
effort was launched to address the issue at the heart of the Arab–
Israeli conflict. On 1 September 1982 President Ronald Reagan
unveiled a plan for Palestinian self-government in the West Bank
and Gaza Strip, creating an entity that would be linked to Jordan.[17]
Crucially, it ruled out both Palestinian independence and Israeli
sovereignty. Reagan's approach combined elements taken from the
Egyptian-Israeli talks on autonomy, part of the deadlocked Camp
David process, and the Israeli Labour party's long-standing attachment to a 'Jordanian option' to resolve the conflict. It also called for
a freeze on settlement and 'progressive Palestinian responsibility for
internal security based on capability and performance'. Informed in
advance by the US ambassador, Begin muttered portentously: 'The
battle for *Eretz-Yisrael* has begun.'[18] Israel's public response was

outright rejection. Camp David, it insisted, made no distinction between internal and external security. 'There can be no doubt that were internal security not to be the responsibility of Israel,' the cabinet declared, 'the terrorist organization called the PLO – even after its defeat by the IDF in Lebanon – would act to perpetrate constant bloodshed, shedding the blood of Jews and Arabs alike. For the citizens of Israel this is a question of life and death.'[19] The US proposal demonstrated, at the very least, that the Palestinian issue remained alive and unresolved. 'The Reagan plan was a timely reminder to Israel that her Lebanese adventure did not bury the Palestinian dilemma as she had hoped', observed Shlomo Ben-Ami, who served as foreign minister two decades later. 'It only focused even more international attention on the Palestinian tragedy through the Sabra and Shatila massacre, and enhanced its international prominence, as well as the urgency of finding a homeland for a displaced people.'[20]

In the aftermath of the war the Israelis made a renewed effort to cultivate pro-Hashemite figures to undermine support for the PLO, though they relied less than they previously had on the Village Leagues, which had proved a costly and unimpressive investment and were wound up when Sharon resigned in March 1983.[21] The idea of creating an alternative Palestinian leadership looked like a misplaced fantasy, not least because of what one Palestinian commentator called 'a gut nationalist reaction against a group seen as a pliable instrument of an oppressive military government'.[22] Just a few months later a poll showed that 90 per cent of West Bankers supported Arafat's leadership. Under Sharon's successor as defence minister, Moshe Arens, long prison sentences were handed down and curfews and collective punishments imposed on 'troublesome' Palestinian areas. Tensions ran high in Hebron in the summer of 1983 after a *yeshiva* student was killed by Palestinians. Settlers from nearby Kiryat Arba, by now a substantial Jewish 'suburb' that was dominated by *Gush Emunim*, attacked the city's Islamic University and killed three students in a well-planned ambush. 'Until then,' said the settler leader Benny Katzover, 'we didn't play by the rules of the desert but by the rules of the government, and the result was disastrous.'[23]

Begin resigned as prime minister, exhausted and depressed, in the autumn of 1983 and was replaced by Yitzhak Shamir. Shamir's Stern

Gang past, like Begin's in the *Irgun*, attracted pessimistic assessments about his likely policies: they proved accurate. Israel's general election in July 1984 produced a messy and unusual outcome. With deadlock between the Labour and Likud parties, the rivals came together to form a national unity government with a rotating premiership, the veteran Shimon Peres taking office that September to be followed by Shamir two years later. Labour's Yitzhak Rabin, who had briefly been prime minister in 1976, was to serve as defence minister for the entire life of the government. 'On the surface, on paper as it were, we made not a bad team', Shamir wrote later, with a rare flash of humour, 'provided one didn't look too closely.'[24] With 97 MPs out of the Knesset's total of 120, it was the largest coalition in the country's history, but the policies of what commentators dubbed a 'two-headed monster' were based on a lowest common denominator. Five seats in parliament for a new right-wing, pro-settler grouping, *Tehiya-Tzomet*, pointed to an extremist shift among Jewish voters away from the Likud.

The government was able to agree on economic reforms and an IDF withdrawal to a limited 'security zone' in south Lebanon. The pace of settlement activity slowed, and the hardline settlers also suffered a painful blow in April 1984 when twenty-five members of the 'Jewish underground' – responsible for the 1980 bombing of the West Bank mayors and other attacks – were finally arrested. The group's leader, Menachem Livni, was a disciple of Rabbi Moshe Levinger of Hebron. They were caught red-handed preparing to bomb buses in East Jerusalem and were discovered to have planned to blow up the Dome of the Rock. Amid furious public debate, supporters in *Gush Emunim* called them 'good boys who had erred', and, in another revealing phrase, had 'taken the law into their own hands' – as if Israeli law *permitted* terrorist attacks on Palestinians.[25] In 1985 only 4,800 Jews moved to the West Bank, compared to 15,000 in 1983.[26] Still, the overall tally of the Likud's seven-year rule was a source of pride for the party: seventy-nine new settlements were established in the occupied territories between 1977 and 1984, the majority of them after 1982. 'A new map of the Land of Israel had already been created', Shamir boasted.[27] Detailed monitoring of the West Bank led to a stark conclusion by the researcher Meron Benvenisti that the situation was now irreversible. Benvenisti's critics on the Israeli left complained not only that he was wrong, but that he was playing into the hands of the annexationist right.[28]

'FACTORIES FOR MEN'

Palestinians living under occupation had no general elections, and changes in their lives and views were not always easily visible. Beneath the surface though, important social, political and economic shifts were under way – the most significant being the coming of age of a new generation who had grown up under Israeli rule and had little or no memory of Jordanian or Egyptian days. By 1985, 100,000 Palestinians were crossing the green line every day to do menial jobs in Israel. In the West Bank and Gaza, Palestinian institutions and confidence were, meanwhile, growing steadily. The goal was to build 'components of future power so that when a Palestinian state arrives it will not arrive in a vacuum'.[29] Bir Zeit students played a leading role in community and volunteer work and helped bridge the gap between towns and villages, aiming to serve the national cause – and bolster resistance.[30] The PLO, complained Israel's UN ambassador (a rising star named Binyamin Netanyahu), 'mounted an all-out effort to subvert the academic purpose of the universities and turn them into centres of incitement, extremism and terror'.[31]

Prisons – known colloquially as 'factories for men' or 'people's schools' and holding thousands at any one time – provided a natural pool for mobilization to nationalist bodies, trade and student unions and women's organizations. 'Every house in the West Bank has had someone in prison,' explained a middle-aged Nablus man, watching outside the city's gaol as Israel freed 1,150 Palestinian and other prisoners (the largest such swap to date) in exchange for three soldiers who had been captured in Lebanon in 1982. 'We are all prisoners here.'[32] It was only a slight exaggeration. By the mid-1980s an estimated 250,000 Palestinians had experienced detention or interrogation – a staggering 10 per cent of the entire population of the occupied territories.[33] Ali, from Jenin, described what happened when his thirteen-year-old son was gaoled for the first time:

Someone from his class threw a stone at a passing Israeli car, so troops came, gathered together a group of ten-year-olds, and asked them to state the names of their friends. My son's name was on the 'list'. His second arrest came four years later . . . he was elected by the prisoners to be head of the committee that distributed meals and cigarettes. Imagine it! My son, in charge of 25 people. One of them was president of the teachers' union; another was an employee at Birzeit university . . . When he came out he was more calm, more deep in thought. He had lost some of his bad habits. He used to be careless. Now he is responsible. He came out more active than before. He became politicised.[34]

Every day courts sentenced Palestinian youths for stone-throwing, tyre-burning, demonstrating and raising PLO flags. They spent weeks or months in custody before they were picked up again, often guilty of nothing more than being identified as a 'troublemaker'. Many young 'graduates' of the notorious Faraa detention centre near Tubas, proud of having spent time there, went on later to serve spells in detention on the basis of secret Shin Bet evidence describing them as 'activists in hostile organizations'. Faraa, opened in 1982, was the subject of a complaint by the International Commission of Jurists on the basis of harrowing testimony gathered from former inmates.[35] 'Most kids start out in a state of fright and confusion,' said one expert. 'Then they start to see all Israelis as the enemy and end up being radicalised by the experience.'[36] Ex-prisoners were given preferential terms for university admission and examinations. Majed al-Masri, who grew up in Balata refugee camp, became a Fatah militant behind bars.[37] 'Inside they told me that prison was for men,' said Basil, a Nablus teenager in Sahar Khalifeh's novel *Wild Thorns*. 'And that those who don't go to prison, even for a day, will never become real men, even if they grow two moustaches rather than one.'[38] Jibril Rajoub, who served fifteen years for Fatah membership, wrote three books on nationalism and ideology, learned Hebrew and translated Menachem Begin's *Irgun* memoir, *The Revolt*, into Arabic. Rajoub's own *Cell Block 704* became a bestseller in the West Bank despite being banned by the Israeli military censor. Prison, observed one left-wing Israeli activist, 'is an opening in the wall that separates Palestinians and Israelis'.[39] Palestinians' knowledge of Israel was heavily influenced by whether they honed their Hebrew by reading the liberal, anti-occupation *Haaretz* or the mass-circulation, centrist *Yedioth Aharonot* while behind bars.

Palestinian newspapers like *al-Fajr* and *al-Shaab* reflected PLO priorities in their coverage and editorials. Media and research institutes, with PLO financial support, issued communiqués and briefed foreign and Israeli journalists. In Gaza the Palestinian Women's Union conducted literacy programmes and assisted needy families. Fatah's Shabiba youth movement had tens of thousands of members. East Jerusalem's al-Hakawati Theatre, which opened in 1984, provided a stage for lightly coded critiques of the occupation within the limits imposed by official harassment and censorship: one early production was *One Thousand and One Nights of the Stone Thrower. Ali the Galilean*, by François Abu Salem, starred an Israeli Arab who works at a falafel stand in Tel Aviv, changes his name to Eli to pretend he is a Jew, but ends up stubbornly clinging on to his Palestinian identity.[40] To mark the twentieth anniversary of the occupation, al-Hakawati mounted an exhibition of drawings about Jerusalem by Arab schoolchildren. 'The spirals of smoke from burning tyres caught the imagination of several children', a visitor reported. 'Others transformed Arabs and Israelis into cowboys and Indians. One child's vision was of the Dome of the Rock – the golden dome dominating the Old City – surrounded by a chain, and lifted miraculously into the heavens by an Arab Superman. For those who live under it, the occupation is all-pervasive.'[41]

Economic changes underlined the precariousness of life under occupation as job opportunities and remittances from the Gulf States fell away when oil prices slumped in the mid-1980s. Palestinians who worked in Israel continued to be subject to the vagaries of military rule, random checks and area closures, and were sharply aware of the differences between the two sides of the green line. 'Young Palestinians ... get a whiff of the democratic privileges that Israeli citizens enjoy, but they cannot share in them', observed Yoram Binur, an Arabic-speaking Jewish journalist who spent six months pretending to be a Palestinian labourer. 'Any Arab who walks in the street at a late hour can expect to be detained and questioned ... even during periods of relative calm. He sees and recognises the value of freedom,

but is accorded the sort of treatment that characterises the most backward dictatorial regimes. How can he be anything but frustrated?'
Abed, a university graduate who worked as a labourer in West Bank
settlements, admitted to venting his frustration by smashing tiles and
pouring cement into newly installed sewage pipes.[42] Maher, a twenty-
something electrician from East Jerusalem who spoke reasonable
Hebrew, often told Israeli customers his name was Meir to give the
impression that he was Jewish.

OCCUPATION AS A WAY OF LIFE

Nothing was as remarkable as the sheer routine of the situation. 'One
of the most troubling and frightening aspects of the occupation . . .
was its mundane, prosaic nature', a perceptive foreign visitor noted
in 1985:

> For Palestinians, occupation was the ordinary – a way of life that had
> to be lived defensively without recourse or appeal, without protection
> or choice, largely absent of accountability, predictability, rationality
> or control. Furthermore, the distortion of Palestinian life remained
> unquestioned by those beyond it for whom the realities of occupation
> were wholly unknown. What was for Palestinians a narrative of crisis,
> of territorial dispossession and displacement, was for others an exam-
> ple of benign and legitimate control.[43]

Palestinians invariably spoke of 'resistance'; Israelis of 'terrorism'.
In April 1984 four Palestinians from Gaza hijacked an Israeli bus near
Ashkelon, killed a passenger and forced the driver to head south. Two
of the hijackers were killed when Israeli forces stormed the vehicle;
two others were captured alive – and photographed. But, contrary
to initial reports that were subject to military censorship, they were
then killed in what was later described as an 'organised lynch' that
included Shin Bet officers. The scandal of Bus 300 involved suborn-
ing witnesses and false testimony. It went to the very top of the
organization and bubbled away until exposed by brave whistle-
blowers and dogged Israeli journalists. The killings were apparently
based on the notion of deterrence –*pour encourager les autres*. They

came to be seen, in liberal circles at least, as another manifestation of the corrupting effects of an occupation without end. Avraham Shalom, then Shin Bet chief, was eventually forced to resign, though he received a presidential pardon. In time it would be said that the affair had damaged both the morale and the effectiveness of the ubiquitous security service.

Following its expulsion from Lebanon, the PLO continued efforts to attack Israel even as Arafat faced discontent about the conduct of the war and open rebellion by Fatah rebels – led by a renegade colonel named Abu Musa – who were supported by the Syrians. Palestinians in the occupied territories cheered the losses incurred by the retreating IDF in the war that erupted in southern Lebanon, where the new enemy were the Shia Muslim fighters of the Amal militia and a new organization called Hizbullah (Party of God). 'If the Palestinians had not been in Lebanon since 1969,' said Akram Hanieh, editor of *al-Shaab*, 'then how would 10-year-old kids have learned to use Kalashnikovs and RPGs [rocket-propelled grenades]?'[44] In April 1985 the Israelis sank a Panamanian-registered ship, the *Ataviros*, with twenty-eight men on board en route for an attack on Tel Aviv on the eve of the Independence Day holiday. Fatah said the men belonged to a unit called the Martyrs of Ein al-Hilweh, the refugee camp near Tyre that had been pulverized in 1982.[45] In October Israeli air force jets flew more than 1,200 miles – the longest-range operation since the Entebbe hostage rescue in 1976 – and bombed the PLO's headquarters at Hammam al-Shatt outside Tunis. Israel claimed that some sixty PLO members were killed, including several leaders of the elite Force 17, and several of Arafat's bodyguards. That was retaliation for the killing of three alleged Israeli agents on a yacht in Cyprus; and that, in turn, came in response to Israel's abduction of a senior Fatah commander who was intercepted at sea between Larnaca and Beirut a couple of weeks earlier. Shortly afterwards an Italian cruise ship, the *Achille Lauro*, sailing from Alexandria, was hijacked by four members of the Palestine Liberation Front, a small Iraqi-backed faction that was still formally part of the PLO. The murder of Leon Klinghoffer, an elderly, wheelchair-bound American-Jewish passenger, attracted widespread international censure – and caused embarrassment to Arafat. It was claimed at the time that the mission was in retaliation for the Israeli raid on Tunis. But it emerged afterwards that the operation had been prepared long in advance and that the hijackers had intended to sail to the Israeli port of Ashdod, where they were said to be planning a suicide attack.[46]

JORDANIAN OPTION?

Violence and diplomacy, as ever, went hand in hand. In February 1985 King Hussein of Jordan launched an effort to improve relations with the PLO and to find a formula for advancing peace talks that would be acceptable to both the Palestinians and the US. The PLO had long objected to any plan based on UN Resolution 242 of 1967, which called for the recognition of all states in the region, including Israel, because it referred to Palestinians solely as 'refugees'. In the Amman accord Arafat agreed to a form of words about self-determination and relations between Jordan and a future Palestinian state, but key PLO colleagues objected because they were unhappy with Jordan's restoration of relations with Egypt (breaking the quarantine imposed by the Arab League after President Sadat's 1979 peace treaty with Israel) and fearful of a weakening of the organization's position.[47] In the summer Hussein also quietly resumed contact with the Israelis, relieved that Shamir was no longer prime minister. Shimon Peres and the king met in London for their first face-to-face encounter in nearly ten years, a few days after the Tunis raid. Hussein's impatience with Arafat deepened further after the *Achille Lauro* fiasco. Israel responded with a flurry of positive signals to Jordan, playing up the king's irritation with the PLO.

In February 1986 King Hussein publicly broke with Arafat, announcing dramatically that 'we are unable to coordinate politically with the PLO leadership until such time as their word becomes their bond, characterised by commitment, credibility and constancy'.[48] The Israelis began to accelerate steps to improve the 'quality of life' – a favourite phrase in diplomatic exchanges with the US – in the occupied territories. The most important of these was allowing Palestinians to take over from the IDF officers who had been running West Bank town halls since the elected mayors were all sacked in

1982. The natural suspicion was that this was another Israeli attempt to unilaterally implement autonomy without Palestinian agreement. 'Is our problem one of civil rights or national rights?' asked Saeb Erakat, an al-Najah University lecturer who opposed the move. 'As long as we have occupation we must expect hardship. It's not going to make any difference if we have an Arab mayor in Nablus or not.'[49] Zafer al-Masri, scion of a prominent local family, took the job, but was assassinated within weeks for dealing with 'the Zionist Jordanian reactionary plan of liquidating the Palestinian cause', as the PFLP put it, boasting of a killing that was intended to deter others from following suit. Two other West Bankers withdrew applications to take over town councils from the Israeli authorities. Masri's funeral, where he was lauded as a 'martyr to homeland and duty', became a demonstration of mass support for the PLO and Arafat.[50] Jordan's decision to close down all PLO offices in the country in July and to expel Arafat's deputy, Abu Jihad, appeared to seal the rupture. A five-year Jordanian development plan for the 'occupied Arab lands', with substantial cash help from the US, was quietly welcomed by Israel. Procedures for Palestinians to obtain exit permits – a key instrument of control – were streamlined, while new hospitals opened in Hebron and Ramallah, and smaller towns were hooked up to the Israeli electricity grid.

The Israeli crackdown that followed targeted the PLO directly. Arrests and expulsions of activists accelerated. Akram Hanieh, editor of *al-Shaab*, appealed to the Israeli High Court to prevent his deportation on the grounds that he was a 'leading Fatah functionary', though he was not accused of any terrorist activity. Hanieh lost his legal battle, was deported and went on to become a close adviser to Arafat at his distant Tunisian HQ and a key link between the PLO leadership and the occupied territories. Other Palestinian journalists, trade unionists and student leaders were deported; scores were detained without trial. In December 1986, when two students protesting against the erection of a roadblock were killed by Israeli troops at Bir Zeit, violent disturbances erupted that lasted ten days – one of the longest periods of unrest in years and a reminder that there was a high price to be paid for maintaining the status quo. 'Israeli rule today is no more acceptable to the Arabs of the administered territories than it was in 1967', commented *Haaretz*, the mainstream but critical voice of worried Jewish liberals and doves. 'We must prevent the creation of situations in which it becomes necessary to use force to restore order. The root of the problem – and here we must not delude ourselves – is in the fact of the occupation.'[51]

In the course of 1987 unrest spread across the West Bank. In February Yitzhak Rabin ordered the closure of all Palestinian universities. Faisal Husseini, the leading Fatah loyalist in East Jerusalem, was detained three times. Fuel for deepening hatred and despair was supplied at random but regular intervals, though there was little evidence of any guiding hand or strategy. In April the Palestine National Council, meeting in Algiers, gave Arafat a standing ovation, reaffirmed its commitment to armed struggle and demanded the sole right to represent its people's cause. The formal abrogation of the long-defunct Amman accord with Jordan secured the return of George Habash's PFLP to the PLO fold. Shortly afterwards a pregnant Jewish woman from the West Bank settlement of Alfei Menashe was killed and her husband and children badly burned by a petrol bomb hurled at the family car from dense orange groves by the side of the road. Settlers then rampaged through nearby Qalqilya, smashing windows and burning crops: the Palestinian town spent weeks under curfew. In May an eight-year-old settler child from Elon Moreh, the now 'authorized' settlement in the hills north-east of Nablus, was murdered, his skull crushed by a rock. Moments like these exposed the conflict's vicious, primordial nature: at funerals the relatives of the victims were drenched in sweat, wailing, in an atmosphere of tension, grief and hatred, packed together under a burning sun. The abnormal had become normal.

Not only the liberal *Haaretz*, but other Hebrew newspapers regularly carried accounts of the demoralizing experience of army duty in the occupied territories. 'Until 1973,' reminisced a middle-aged reservist, 'you could spend your army service in the West Bank sitting and drinking coffee, lean your rifle against the wall and chat to the locals. Not any more. These days the soldiers who serve in the territories are either brutalised or broken by the experience.'[52] The belated introduction of 'non-lethal' riot-control techniques – rubber bullets, snatch squads and clubs – did not reduce the number of fatalities among Palestinian demonstrators: children learned to use onions to cope with tear gas and bared their chests at soldiers, shouting abuse and daring them to shoot. Beatings were routine – tolerating them a rite of passage and a matter of pride for young men.[53] On both sides everyday language and culture came to reflect this permanent state of low-intensity warfare, and the dehumanization of the invariably anonymous 'other'. Palestinians warned each other of the arrival of the *jaysh* (army) and adopted the Hebrew word *machsom* for the checkpoints they encountered at every turn. IDF communiqués often described soldiers firing into the air – 'firing into the air of their lungs' went the cynical addition. In media reports Arab protesters, who were often described as 'youngsters', regularly 'met their deaths' rather than just got killed.[54] The concept of 'shooting and weeping' (*yorim ve'bochim*) – a sardonic encapsulation of the heartache of the humanist Israeli forced to fight Arabs in spite of himself – was revived in the 1980s to criticize the soul-searching of the well-meaning left.[55] Neither side had any reason to expect significant change to a status quo that had lasted for two decades.

16
1987

*'This is a government with a heart of plastic, a brain of lead
and a conscience of rubber. The whole world knows that the
stone of the Palestinian David is defeating the oppression of
the Israeli Goliath.'*

Muhammad Miari[1]

'THE FIRST TWENTY YEARS'

In the spring of 1987, the Israeli civil administration of Judaea and
Samaria and the Gaza District published a glossy colour brochure to
mark twenty years of its work. Its front cover was pleasantly pastoral,
a photograph of a field of golden wheat with a typical hilltop Arab
village in the background, simple stone houses clustered round a
mosque. The booklet showcased clinics, housing and schools as well
as statistics illustrating advances in employment, industry and agriculture. As Shmuel Goren, the government's co-ordinator of operations
in the territories, noted in the Introduction, Israel's policy

> was based clearly and consistently on two principles: an all-out war
> against terrorism which has been or is supported by a small minority,
> and maximal liberalisation and investment in development of living
> conditions for those members of the population who condemn terror-
> ist acts and incitement and who want to live their lives in peace and
> tranquillity until such time as a political solution can be found.

The word 'Palestinian' appeared just once in its 110 pages – and that,
tellingly, was with reference to refugee resettlement. Nablus was
referred to by its biblical Hebrew name, Shechem. Goren expressed

his 'deepest gratitude' to the civil administration staff, adding: 'I am sure the population in the areas join me in thanking them.'[2]

The twentieth anniversary of the Six Days war provoked many publications as well as more profound reflection on both sides of the old green line. In Israel there was less emphasis than usual on the grave dangers the country had faced in 1967 and its triumphant, near-miraculous victory, and more about repression in what most Israelis now referred to simply as 'the territories' (*shtahim*). Most still knew little about them or their inhabitants, beyond shopping trips on Saturdays to Tulkarem or Bethlehem, repairing their cars in cheap Palestinian garages, visiting a dentist, or employing Palestinian builders to work on their homes. Novelist David Grossman, a rising literary star, wrote a series of articles that he turned into a book, *The Yellow Wind*, which became a surprise bestseller that summer. Grossman described the lives of Palestinians he met in the West Bank: kindergarten children in a refugee camp; a mother pleading for her child's favourite doll not to be confiscated in a security check; Jewish settlers declaring their God-given right to what they unfailingly called Judaea and Samaria. Grossman's focus was the daily humiliations of Palestinian life under military rule, as well as the moral price this was exacting from his own people: without an end to occupation, the country would face the legendary burning 'yellow wind' that blows up from hell every few generations and devours all those in its path. 'Its appeal for many Israelis was that Grossman made them feel that he had undertaken the trip to the West Bank that each of them should have taken but knew they would never take', commented the philosopher Avishai Margalit. Grossman did not predict that an uprising was imminent. But he did paint an unusually detailed and bleak picture of a reality most Jews knew little about.[3] His final chapter was titled 'The first 20 years'. It was hardly an optimistic choice, but it was a prescient one.

On the Palestinian side an entire generation had grown up by 1987 without knowing anything other than life under Israeli rule. Jonathan Kuttab, a lawyer, marked the anniversary of the *naksa* in an article in *al-Fajr*: 'Palestinians count only on themselves and their fellow Palestinians in the Diaspora. Young Palestinians today make up their own minds, independently of parents and community leaders.'⁴ Yunis, a young man from East Jerusalem, explained what was different:

> My father was in his 20s in 1967. 'People benefited from the occupation, at least at first,' he told us. 'The Jordanians had put a lot of pressure on us, and wouldn't let anything happen. Then the Israelis came and let us work in Israel. Suddenly there was more money. No-one wanted to revolt. It didn't mean that we liked Israel. Things did get worse in the 1980s. When the Likud came to power, pressure built up, so the younger generation didn't see things the same way that the fathers did.'⁵

Israelis agreed: 'Palestinians had changed', said one knowledgeable observer. 'They spoke a different language than their parents, let alone their grandparents, and railed at them for their submissiveness during two decades of Israeli rule, and for shirking their national duty to rise up against the occupiers.'⁶ Economic conditions were deteriorating too: the number of jobs available locally was declining, especially for the growing number of university graduates; some 40 per cent of the total Palestinian workforce was now employed in Israel. Remittances from the Gulf had also dropped sharply in the preceding years as oil revenues went into sharp decline.⁷ The occupation was now part of ordinary Palestinian life, especially in East Jerusalem. 'Israel is not simply the Knesset', Bir Zeit professor Sari Nusseibeh argued in June 1987.

> Israel is ... the long queues of women standing in front of the post office in Jerusalem to collect their social security ... Israel is the business licences, the building permits, the identity cards. It is the value-added taxes, the income taxes, the television licences ... It is also Dedi Zucker, Meron Benvenisti, Yehuda Litani and Amnon Zichroni [Israeli peace activists, journalists and lawyers] commiserating with Palestinians at the National Palace Hotel. Israel is the Tambour [Israeli] paint used to scribble slogans attacking Hanna Siniora [a prominent Palestinian newspaper editor] on the walls.⁸

No one imagined that the conflict was over, though the preceding few months had seen a decline in the level of violence in the occupied territories. On 25 November 1987, however, an unusually serious incident occurred. A Palestinian from the Syrian-backed PFLP-General

Command, led by Ahmed Jibril, flew a motorized hang-glider to an Israeli base in Galilee, just south of the Lebanese border, and managed to kill six soldiers before he was shot down. Palestinian media praised 'a heroic operation which destroyed the myth of Israeli defences'.[9] This helped create 'the perception that the IDF was not invincible, and concomitantly, engendered an image of a new Palestinian hero'.[10] Israeli soldiers were taunted by Palestinians chanting the score: '6–1'. In Amman, however, an Arab summit conference, preoccupied with mediation efforts to end the bloody grind of the Iran–Iraq war, then in its seventh year, had little to say about the Palestinian issue. And alone among the leaders attending, Yasser Arafat had not been received by King Hussein on arrival. 'Not only, then, was the Palestine problem ignored in the international arena, it did not even command the attention of the Arab "brothers"', one analyst noted.[11]

GAZA FIRST

On 8 December, near the Erez checkpoint at the northern end of the Gaza Strip, close to Jabaliya refugee camp, an Israeli truck crashed into two taxis bringing Palestinian workers home from Israel. Four were killed and seven seriously injured. Rumours quickly spread that this was no accident but a revenge attack, that the driver of the truck was the brother of an Israeli salesman who had been stabbed to death two days earlier in Gaza City. It was not true, as the Fatah activist who deliberately spread the story admitted later.[12] In any event, during the following days the funerals of three of the victims triggered demonstrations in which IDF soldiers were met by a barrage of petrol bombs, stones and iron bars; in Jabaliya seventeen-year-old Hatem al-Sissi was killed and scores injured by live army fire.[13] Thus began the most widespread and sustained disturbances seen in twenty years of occupation.

Unrest spread quickly. Another Palestinian was killed the next day in Nablus when an army patrol was attacked by youths throwing stones and iron bars. Four more died the day after that in Balata, the area's biggest refugee camp, two of them eleven-year-old boys. Underlining the seriousness of the situation General Amram Mitzna, the West Bank military commander, rushed to the scene and conferred with senior officers and armed Israeli civilians who looked like Shin Bet officers to the journalists arriving to cover what was rapidly becoming a big story. In the city's al-Ittihad hospital, three young men with bullet wounds in their legs lay dazed and shivering, the road outside blocked by burning tyres and rubble. Others, faces masked in *keffiyehs*, grasped rocks and bottles in case the Israelis came. By the end of the first week there were seven dead; fifteen after a fortnight. Palestinians were soon talking of an *intifada*, a popular uprising against Israeli rule. The word – used to describe anti-British protests in Iraq in the 1920s – promoted the kind of semantic debate beloved of Arabists. Its root meant 'to shake off' – passivity, inertia, outmoded ideas, foreign occupation. It did not require academic expertise to see that something unusual was happening.

'One should expect such things after 20 years of miserable occupation,' said the former mayor of Gaza, Rashad al-Shawwa. 'The people have lost all hope. They are absolutely frustrated. They don't know what to do. They have lost hope that Israel will ever give them their rights. They feel that the Arab countries are unable to accomplish anything. They feel that the PLO, which they regarded as their representative, had failed to accomplish anything.'[14] Palestinians and Israelis alike were struck by the spontaneity of the outburst. 'Even the local grassroots committees, activists and leaders were caught off guard', wrote Sari Nusseibeh. The Israeli civil administration tried persuading local *mukhtars* to use their influence to end the violence, to no avail. Mass arrests failed to calm things down. In Tunis, the PLO leadership was just as surprised. Abu Jihad told Arafat that this outbreak of resistance was unplanned. 'When the intifada broke out we were afraid', Abu Iyad admitted later. 'We remembered that the 1936 uprising lasted only six months. At the start we didn't estimate that the intifada would last beyond six months.'[15] Indeed, a statement issued by the PFLP to mark the twentieth anniversary of its founding made no mention of the protests in the occupied territories several days after they began.[16] Yitzhak Rabin, the defence minister, who was visiting the US in the second week of the unrest, kept pointing out that the PLO had been taken aback by the spontaneous eruption, as if that excused Israel's surprise and discomfort. Ariel Sharon, now back in public life as minister of trade, threw a lavish housewarming party at his new home in the Muslim quarter of Jerusalem's Old City to underline the 'deteriorating security situation' – and to make a none-too-subtle bid to replace Rabin.[17]

Nameless Palestinians kept up the momentum of protests. 'We don't have a timetable, but we already have a custom, waves of people going out at 3 in the morning, at midday, early evening', related an anonymous Gazan activist.

> From the evening until 3am we sleep and organise. Sometimes . . . we even go out at 10pm because during the night the army doesn't effectively control the streets and doesn't know the local topography, so we are in control. For instance . . . in Jabaliya, there were demonstrations all night and there was not a single soldier, even though there was a curfew. The soldiers simply fled, because thousands of people formed a sort of moving human wall and nothing will work against something like that, neither an iron fist nor bullets.[18]

Israeli soldiers in Gaza described going out in armoured personnel carriers (APCs) to clear a road of burning tyres when they were suddenly stormed by hundreds of Palestinians with bricks, iron bars and petrol bombs. 'The soldiers started firing into the air and then they used gas grenades. But it didn't help. The Arabs stormed the APCs like a swarm of bees and when one of the soldiers got a rock in the face they had no choice but to fire,' said one. 'Two demonstrators were killed and several wounded.' Palestinians quickly noticed how the Israelis had been surprised. 'An old woman told me that she saw that the Israeli soldiers were afraid of demonstrators for the first time', a journalist reported. 'There's a strange joy. Those who die, people will remember for ever. We used to call this sort of thing a strike, but that word is too small. Then we would call it a demonstration but that's too small too. This is something different. It's an intifada.'[19]

GUIDING WORDS

Over the next few weeks more centralized guidance and co-ordination became evident, though it remained clandestine to avoid arrest by the Israelis and to avoid upstaging the PLO. Spontaneous actions were transformed into organized ones that sustained and expanded the scope of the uprising. On 8 January 1988, a month into the unrest, an Arabic-language leaflet appeared calling for a three-day general strike. It was signed by 'Palestinian nationalist forces' and was the work of Fatah and DFLP activists who included a journalist, a Christian priest and a university lecturer. A second followed days later, this time signed by the United National Command for the Escalation of the Uprising. The third, on 18 January, was signed by the PLO/United National Leadership of the Uprising (UNLU) – thus uniting Palestinians 'inside' and 'outside'. Using the same terminology, leaflets (*bayan/ bayanat* in Arabic) appeared at roughly ten-day intervals after that, numbered sequentially from three onwards. Typically they called for protests and strikes, an end to the occupation, boycotts of Israeli goods and the resignation of policemen and other officials employed by Israel. Many referenced famous figures in Palestinian history – Sheikh Izzedin al-Qassam, Abdul-Qader al-Husseini – or significant dates, ranging from the Balfour Declaration to the *Nakba*. 'Reactionary' peace initiatives by Israel, the US or Jordan were attacked. Forty-three more leaflets had appeared by the end of 1989. Others were issued regularly by Hamas, the Islamic Resistance Movement, a newcomer to the Palestinian political scene. The *bayanat* were composed centrally but their content transmitted by phone or fax to be typed up or printed in different places.[20] Occasionally the Israelis would raid a printing shop and confiscate its presses and leaflets or the Shin Bet would produce their own fake ones to sow doubts and confusion. Leaflets of dubious provenance that accused prominent figures of embezzling funds or involvement in personal disputes were dismissed as psychological warfare by the Israelis. Militants were warned not to issue leaflets under any name other than the UNLU to 'block the enemy's attempts ... to split ... national ranks and sow confusion and mutual suspicions'.[21] In Nablus, printers were ordered to hand over samples of their inks to help identify who was behind the leaflets.[22] Distribution, however, came to matter less, since the Israeli media took to reporting the contents of the leaflets the moment they appeared. Two leaflets were printed in Nazareth and the Triangle area with the help of Israeli-Arab sympathizers.[23]

By the first week of 1988 the IDF had doubled its forces in the West

Bank and tripled them in the Gaza Strip. Gaza City was festooned with miniature Palestinian flags that hung from electricity poles; the streets were covered in stones and the air reeked of burning tyres and the acrid residue of tear gas. It looked and felt like a war zone. Israeli efforts to defuse the violence expanded to include plans for mass expulsions of 'leading activists in terrorist organizations', starting with nine key mid-echelon figures, including Jibril Rajoub, targeted 'because of their very presence here and the effect of their views and personalities on their supporters and admirers amongst the young generation that has not yet graduated from the university of the revolution'.[24] International criticism of these moves – banned under the Geneva Conventions – was ignored by Israel. On 21 January Rabin reportedly announced a policy of 'force, might and beatings' as an alternative to using live and rubber bullets and tear gas – after angry cabinet exchanges between the Likud and Labour wings of the unity government about the continuing unrest. The justification was brutally simple: 'A detainee sent to prison will be freed in 18 days unless the authorities have enough evidence to charge him,' a military source explained. 'He may then resume stoning. But if troops break his hand he won't be able to throw stones for a month and a half.' Near Nablus an American television crew filmed four Israeli soldiers systematically beating and breaking the arms of two bound Palestinians; two of the soldiers were later sentenced to short prison terms but one of them told Israel TV that the incident was a routine one. Palestinian labourers from Gaza refused to work for a Tel Aviv wood merchant who received an order from the IDF for 10,000 lacquered boxwood batons.[25] By the end of February the Palestinians counted 80 dead and 650 injured.

CHILDREN OF THE STONES

Part of the novelty of the *intifada* was the role of Palestinian children, organized into groups with specific tasks. Small children poured petrol on tyres and set them alight, older ones placed large rocks on roads to block traffic or made and used homemade slings. Teenagers took on a command role, working with spotters to identify cars and movements of soldiers. 'To throw a stone is to be "one of the guys"; to hit an Israeli car is to become a hero; and to be arrested and not confess to having done anything is to be a man,' explained the journalist Daoud Kuttab.

> They stand at an elevated point and direct the stone throwers as to when and how far to retreat when the soldiers advance. They decide on the moment of a countercharge, which is carried out with loud screams and a shower of stones. The leaders know the range of the Israeli weapons and are able to differentiate between rubber bullets and real bullets . . . Leaders also seem to have the ability to determine whether soldiers plan to shoot in the air or at the demonstrators.[26]

These 'children of the stones' – immortalized in a work by the famous Syrian poet Nizar Qabbani – were a powerful personification of Palestinian resistance, and a neat reversal of the traditional 'David versus Goliath' image that Israel had once cultivated and enjoyed. They attracted intense international media attention, which was uncomfortable for the Israelis. In areas that were closed off to the press when the IDF imposed curfews or declared a military zone, Palestinian activists provided videotapes of Israeli actions that looked brutal on TV. 'The Palestinians', Anton Shammas said of Rabin, 'should be deeply grateful to the man who brought the conflict to its real, simple dimensions: either peace or a struggle over land (not to mention his offering the best television exposure the "Palestinian cause" has ever had).'[27] Using stones as a weapon, 'was a reversion to an Islamic stance: *rajm* or throwing stones against evil spirits is what pilgrims to Mecca do from the top of a mountain', explained another Palestinian commentator.[28] 'The stone is sacred,' exhorted *Sawt al-Quds*, a clandestine radio station that began broadcasting from southern Syria, 'use it well.'[29] Stone-throwing became 'the renowned international signifier' of the *intifada*.[30]

Comparisons were often made with the great rebellion of the second half of the 1930s, which became a touchstone for heroism and sacrifice, largely absent from the harsher memory of 1948. The appeal of the *intifada* was that it was led by an alliance of different social classes and interests, rather than a semi-feudal elite, so that it was characterized 'by greater national unity and political savvy'.[31]

Mass-mobilization was another striking element. Distinctions of gender, class and age were broken down. 'In Ramallah, a middle-aged professional woman, after watching demonstrations on television for a month, eagerly joins a group of young boys building a roadblock; in a Gaza hospital a 100-year-old woman, her hand broken by soldiers, toothlessly murmurs defiance to the applause of other beating victims in surrounding beds.'[32] Israeli prosecutors joked that it was easier to catch overweight middle-aged Palestinians, bystanders who did not take part in demonstrations, than younger ones who did.[33] After years of passivity, there was a heightened awareness of the importance of involvement, urged on by the language of resistance employed by the UNLU. 'The uprising has created a new way of daily life, economically and socially', declared leaflet No. 15 in April 1988. 'Your way of life derives from the fact that the uprising is a lengthy and protracted revolutionary process that entails hardships, victims and a reduced income. But it has produced achievements that have deepened national unity amongst all segments of our people.'[34] These morale-boosting messages were highly effective. 'Smuggling food into the refugee camps and the creation of voluntary popular committees in streets and neighbourhoods is more important than the violence', argued a leading radical. 'People have gone beyond ideology and have come down to the practical issues. They have learned that dependence is a two-way street and become much more aware of their ability to harm Israel.'[35]

STRIKING FACTS

Repeated strike days took their toll on both the Israeli and Palestinian economies. In normal times, 120,000 men from the West Bank and Gaza worked across the green line (providing 7 per cent of the entire Israeli workforce). Attacks on buses and other forms of intimidation meant problems for the kitchens, garages and building sites of the Tel Aviv area. One enterprising dishwasher salesman seized the opportunity to try to persuade a restaurant owner to finally buy a machine, since the usual Arab staff had stayed away en masse. On the eve of May Day 1988, Palestinians were urged to 'boycott completely work in Zionist settlements' and find substitutes for work inside the green line. On another occasion a leaflet warned Palestinians 'not to submit to the pressures of Zionist factories to sleep over inside the green line on the eve of strikes, ostensibly out of concern for their lives in case of revenge, as happened to three of our workers from Gaza'.[36] Underlining the importance of the issue, the IDF published daily figures on the numbers of Palestinians who were still coming to work as usual despite the drastically changed circumstances.

Attacks on collaborators were another feature of these turbulent times. Names of Palestinians suspected of working with the Israelis were broadcast on *Sawt al-Quds*, although many, especially in rural areas, were already well known, and disappeared, sometimes to be given weapons or relocated by their handlers in the Shin Bet or the military to an old Jordanian army camp near Jenin. A seedy hotel on Tel Aviv's Hayarkon Street, near the US embassy, became a temporary bolt-hole for some of the more valuable collaborators before they were relocated with new identities abroad. Late February saw the killing of Mohammed Ayad, who had a rare gun licence issued by the Israelis. He was hanged in Qabatiyeh after killing a four-year-old child and injuring thirteen others who were marching on his home.[37] The act was praised in a leaflet as 'a lesson to those who betray their country and their people'.[38] Another leaflet gave out the addresses of collaborators and urged the 'shock squads' to 'continue purging the internal front of the filth of those who sold their soul and honour to the occupation and betrayed their people and their homeland'.[39] In September a spate of killings – victims included a petty criminal involved in land deals and another man who had been an informer in prison – appeared to reflect successes by the Shin Bet, which had been caught off guard in the first months of the *intifada* but had since been able to rebuild its network of informers. Collaborator killings were one of the features of the uprising that led to comparisons with the darker side of the great rebellion of 1936–39.

By the time the *intifada* marked its hundredth day, some one hundred Palestinians had been killed. Israel suffered its first *intifada* fatality at the same time when a soldier was shot in Bethlehem. Momentum was maintained on 30 March when Palestinian Israelis came out en masse to mark the anniversary of Land Day, expressing solidarity with their kinfolk – UNLU leaflet No. 11 was dedicated to the occasion. But the police stayed away from protests inside Israel – a marked contrast between operating procedures on the different sides of the green line. In Bartaa, half in Israel, half in the West Bank, the Israeli side remained calm while the *intifada* raged a few hundred yards away.[40]

If they were disoriented by the novel challenge of mass rebellion, the Israelis found it easier to fight the more familiar clandestine war against the PLO. In February, Mossad agents planted a bomb in a car that killed three PLO officials in Limassol, Cyprus. The three were officers of the 'occupied homeland command' who were involved in planning attacks[41] and had been deported from Jordan under US pressure.[42] The next day a limpet mine disabled a Greek passenger ferry that Palestinian activists had planned to sail to Haifa in support of the *intifada* – and to echo the Jewish refugee ships that ran the British naval blockade in the late 1940s. Retaliation came quickly: in March three Palestinian gunmen who crossed the border from Egypt hijacked a bus travelling to the Dimona nuclear plant and were killed after shooting three unarmed civilians. Next month the Israelis struck again – spectacularly.

LONG ARM, LONG BURST

In a combined IDF–Mossad operation special forces were sent all the way to Tunis to assassinate Arafat's military commander, Khalil al-Wazir, universally known as Abu Jihad. Wazir was targeted because he was responsible for the occupied territories and was believed by Israel to be the key link between the organization and the *intifada*, providing it with financial and logistical support and political guidance on the basis of detailed knowledge of local conditions. 'Abu Jihad became the manager, the brain in exile, of the spontaneous movement,' commented a Palestinian admirer. 'Hard-working, methodical and selfless, he was the right choice.'[43] Israelis remembered him for planning the Coastal Road massacre of 1978.[44] 'On the strategic level', observed two well-connected Israeli experts, 'the elimination of Abu Jihad was almost incidental to the intifada and certainly did not extricate the army from the difficult pass in which it was caught in the territories.'[45] And following the killing, protests erupted in which at least sixteen Palestinians were killed by army gunfire – the *intifada*'s worst single day of violence to date – while curfews were imposed over almost the entire West Bank. It was almost twenty-five years before Israel would admit responsibility for the Abu Jihad assassination by allowing publication of a long-censored interview with the officer who 'fired a long burst' that killed him in his Tunis villa as his wife watched in horror.[46] Palestinian accounts of the aftermath suggest that Wazir's death allowed Arafat to establish closer personal control of what was happening in the occupied territories.[47] By early May, when the uprising was six months old, the toll was 180 dead and 7,500 detained, many in harsh conditions at the recently opened Ketziot detention camp in the Negev, nicknamed Ansar III after prison facilities used by the Israelis in Lebanon. But there was no sign that steam was going out of now-routine protests, or that Israeli counter-measures were proving any more effective.

Elements of the crackdown verged on the absurd: Jad Ishaq, an agronomist from Bethlehem University, was warned by the civil administration when he teamed up with colleagues to sell seeds and agricultural equipment and dispense advice on 'backyard farming'. A craze for kitchen gardening saw middle-aged Palestinian housewives hoeing barren patches of land, in line with UNLU calls for economic self-sufficiency and boycotts of Israeli goods. When a Hebrew maga-zine ran a story about it, it was headlined 'RABIN VERSUS THE CUCUMBER'. Efforts were made to produce '*intifada* milk' from eighteen cows bought from an Israeli kibbutz. But when the army tried to impound the animals they were hidden in Bet Sahour, includ-ing at the home of the local butcher. Years later the story was retold in an animated film.[48] Mubarak Awad, a Palestinian-American psy-chologist, was credited with inspiring acts of non-violent resistance to the occupation.

Palestinian spokesmen exuded pride and defiance during this period. 'If the Israelis say that the Palestinians are tired, they are not wrong', argued a leading PLO supporter.

But the Israelis are more tired than we are. I do believe that the uprising has taken on new forms. There is a deep belief we must minimise
our dependence on the Israelis. We know we can't break it. In the
popular committees, in the alternative systems we are creating more
awareness of the possibility of being under occupation. This is the
ingenuity of the intifada.

Such confidence, however, sometimes seemed exaggerated: the resignation of Palestinians serving with the Israeli police was not followed by
the departure of 18,000 others employed by the civil administration.[49]

As this war of attrition continued on the ground, the political consequences began to be apparent. In June, at an emergency summit
conference in Algiers, Arab leaders pledged 'all possible support' for
the *intifada*, as well as an additional $23 million per month, to be
exclusively controlled by the PLO, which meant a weakening of Jordan's role. It also endorsed the creation of an independent Palestinian
state. That was a striking contrast to the previous Arab summit in
Amman, when the Palestinian issue had been all but ignored. In late
July King Hussein, irritated and weary, announced his 'disengagement' from the West Bank. This involved dissolving the lower house
of the Jordanian parliament and ending representation for people living under occupation. It also halted Jordan's $1.3 billion development
plan for the West Bank (though by late 1987 it had spent only $11.7
million on projects, partly because of difficulties raising money from
Gulf donors).[50] Jordan had accepted at the 1974 Rabat summit that
the PLO was the 'sole legitimate representative' of the Palestinian
people, though its stances, not least a long history of clandestine
contacts with Israel, had long belied that formal position. Mutual
suspicions remained strong. Now, even if the king's men were deeply
sceptical about the prospects of Arafat entering negotiations in the
face of determined American and Israeli opposition, it was clear that
Jordan would not provide the Israelis with a solution. Hussein did not
consult the PLO, which was caught off guard, fearing a trap. Arafat,
however, began to think hard about how to respond.[51] But the idea of
change was in the air. Bassam Abu Sharif, one of his closest advisers –
and a man with a flair for publicity – had already floated the notion
of direct negotiations with Israel that summer.[52] In East Jerusalem,

Fatah's Faisal Husseini had been in contact with Israeli doves exploring dialogue with the PLO before and after being released from administrative detention. Husseini had drawn up a document calling for a unilateral declaration of Palestinian independence within the boundaries established by the UN in November 1947 – which was flatly rejected at the time by Palestinian leaders.

Israel's general election in October 1988 was fought against the background of continuing unrest. The *intifada* did not, however, figure prominently in the campaign because both Labour and Likud, unwilling partners in the national unity government, were jointly responsible for policy. Rabin boasted that he had killed and gaoled and expelled more Arabs than any Likud defence minister. Even the most hawkish Likud minister – Ariel Sharon – found it hard to attack Rabin on the grounds of being 'soft' on Arabs. On the eve of the poll, a young Israeli woman and her three infant children were burned to death when Palestinians threw petrol bombs at a bus on the outskirts of Jericho. It was the worst single attack on civilians since the *intifada* began. Unlike the 300 or so Palestinian deaths at the hands of the Israeli security forces, it brought home to Israeli Jews the human cost of the conflict. Likud supporters seized the opportunity. 'Hawatmeh, Habash, Arafat and Jibril and all the other PLO terrorists will be waiting in their lairs . . . wavering between hope and fear – hope for a victory after which Shimon Peres will return Israel to the 1967 borders, and fear that the Likud under Yitzhak Shamir will triumph and stand firm,' warned one candidate.[53] The election saw losses for Labour and significant gains for religious parties – and the creation of another unity coalition, this time led by the Likud. Lesser gains were also recorded by the small peace camp. Israel's Palestinian challenge remained the number one problem facing the country.

A STATE IS BORN

Even before the new Israeli government was formed, the PLO marked a great leap forward, building on the gains and the sacrifices of the *intifada*. It understood that it needed to fill the vacuum left by Jordan's disengagement and pre-empt possible annexation by Israel – as well as signal a change to the US.[54] On 15 November 1988 the Palestine National Council convened in Algiers for a meeting that was named grandly 'the session of the *intifada* and independence, the session of the martyred hero Abu Jihad'. Arafat formally announced the creation of a state of Palestine – four decades since the creation of Israel and the *Nakba*. It was a landmark moment and the document rose to the occasion, politically, legally and emotionally. Written by Mahmoud Darwish, the widely admired Palestinian 'poet laureate', the declaration referenced the UN partition resolution of November 1947. It did not explicitly recognize Israel, though an accompanying document made reference to UN Resolution 242, which had always been seen as implying recognition. It embodied the notion of independence alongside Israel, for better or worse. And for some dejected veterans it was nothing less than an act of surrender: 'Thank God my father did not live to witness this day', commented Shafiq al-Hout, a refugee from 1948. 'I do not know what I could say to him if he asked me what was to become of his home city of Jaffa in this state that we have just declared.'[55] The declaration referred too to Palestine as 'the land of three monotheistic faiths' – a tolerant nod to religious pluralism rather than excoriating the 'Zionist invasion' in the uncompromising language of the Palestine National Covenant of 1968. The Palestinians had seized the initiative and the moral high ground as well.

On the day of the declaration, thousands of Israeli troops were deployed to stop Palestinians celebrating – and to keep the press away. The West Bank was at its gorgeous early winter best: pale almond blossoms sparkling against the stony hill terraces, sacks of fat green olives waiting to be shipped out. In Hawara, south of Nablus, an old peasant shuffled along behind his donkey, oblivious to the helmeted soldiers bivouacked by the side of the road, and the green, red and white tatters of a plastic Palestinian flag overhead. Under the surface calm, a frisson of excitement was palpable. 'We have always said we wanted peace and now we hear the news from Algiers,' muttered a wizened sweet vendor near where the declaration was read out at 4.30 p.m., the time designated by the latest PLO leaflet for popular celebrations. 'A state for us and state for Israel, that's how things should be.'[56] Troops were stationed all over East Jerusalem to try to silence the chimes of Arab freedom. Later, in Abu Tor a lone firework streaked across the night sky. In Bethlehem and elsewhere, the electricity was cut off to prevent people watching the event on TV.

Israel flatly refused to recognize that any advances had been made. Official statements dismissed the declaration as 'ambiguity and double talk ... employed to obscure violence and the fact that it [the PLO] resorts to terrorism. No unilateral step can substitute for a negotiated settlement, no gimmick can mask the tragedy inflicted upon the Palestinian people time and again by the absence of a reasonable, realistic and peace-seeking leadership.' The initials PLO, gloomy Israeli officials quipped, had come to stand for 'peace-loving organisation'. But Arafat's stance was paying off, since the PLO looked moderate and Israel stubborn. Binyamin Netanyahu, Israel's highly articulate former ambassador to the UN and a recently elected Likud MP, was drafted in to help with the PR. 'We're in the middle of a PLO propaganda offensive,' Netanyahu said.

> The whole world is focused on what Arafat is going to say, but they have ignored the PLO's grand strategy, which is a staged, salami policy to liquidate Israel. They are signing declarations of peace as tools of war. They are issuing a stream of vague, circumlocutious statements that echo round the western press – statements which imply to the untrained ear that the PLO has really changed and accepted Israel, whereas if you look at these statements a little closer, you will see that they have not.[57]

Israel was resigned to the fact that most Arab and Muslim countries and many Third World ones would recognize Palestine. Its greatest concern, however, was that the US would decide that the PLO had met its conditions for recognition, thus allowing it to drop its 1975 pledge not to deal with the organization until it recognized Israel and renounced terrorism.

In Geneva a month later, Arafat went further. Under US pressure, and with European mediation, he declared explicitly at UN headquarters that he accepted 'the right of all parties concerned in the Middle East conflict to exist in peace and security ... including the state of Palestine, Israel and their neighbours, according to resolutions 242 and 338 ... we totally and absolutely renounce all forms of terrorism, including individual, group and state terrorism'.[58] Across the occupied territories, Palestinians crowded round radios to hear his speech, broadcast live. The next day – following complaints from the Americans about lingering ambiguities and after intensive consultations with colleagues – he spelled out the message even more explicitly in front of eight hundred journalists, concluding the press conference with the words: 'Enough striptease.'[59] As a result the US then declared that it was prepared to hold 'substantive dialogue' with PLO representatives.[60] The first talks got under way in Tunisia just two days later. Yitzhak Shamir's response was adamantine: there would be no Israeli recognition of, nor negotiation with, the PLO. It was, he insisted, 'a terrorist organisation aimed at undermining our national existence and bringing about the destruction of the state of Israel'.[61] The mood in Israel combined defensiveness and rancour, drawing on decades of suspicion about the 'true' intentions of the Palestinians. 'Once they talked about throwing the Jews into the sea,' Shamir said.

> And then they [the rest of the world] said the Jews were heroes. Today they don't say that any more. Now they say self-determination for the Palestinians. Now sympathy is with the Palestinians. But nothing has changed. Arabs are Arabs. They control 22 states in this region. And the Jews are the Jews. And they have one small state with a lot of problems. The sea is the same sea and the goal remains the same.[62]

It was not the last time he would use this phrase.

ENTER HAMAS

Not all Palestinians were happy with the change in the PLO's line. Even as it was counting the gains of the *intifada* and taking the historic step of recognizing Israel, it was clear that the political map was changing. The decade before the uprising had witnessed advances for the long-established Palestinian branch of the Muslim Brotherhood, known in Gaza as *al-Mujamma al-Islami*. It had been granted informal recognition by Israel in 1978 in the wake of the Sadat initiative and was led by Sheikh Ahmed Yassin, the quadriplegic, wheelchair-bound son of a widowed refugee mother. Like other Islamist movements it had been influenced by the 1979 Iranian revolution and the Muslim response to the Soviet invasion of Afghanistan. Unlike the PLO, Yassin focused not on fighting Israel, but on promoting Islam by building mosques, schools, health-care institutions, charitable bodies and kindergartens – 'seeds planted early with a view to later harvesting hearts, minds and souls'.[63] In some ways, though, this was a false distinction, as politics and religion were inextricably linked. 'When oppression increases,' Yassin liked to say in his high, reedy voice, 'people start looking for God.'[64]

Echoing the practice in Arab countries like Egypt and Jordan, the Israelis initially promoted the Islamists as a counter-weight to the PLO and the Communists, or at least turned a blind eye to their religious, social and educational activities. The founding of the Islamic University in Gaza in 1978 had been an important milestone in this respect. In periods of tension Islamists were conspicuously not arrested, or, if arrested, released first. In 1980 *Mujamma* activists had burned down the offices of the Palestine Red Crescent in Gaza, run by Dr Hayder Abdel-Shafi, the veteran left-wing nationalist. Cafes and video shops were favourite targets, and gender segregation was enforced at the Islamic University. In 1981 the Brotherhood beat Fatah in student elections in the West Bank and Gaza. Brotherhood activists were able to operate with 'relative impunity'.[65] In June 1986, when attacks took place in Jabaliya, residents reported seeing a car full of Shin Bet agents parked across the road when fundamentalists went wild in the camp. 'The Israelis say these things are a domestic matter,' complained one PLO supporter. 'Why should they bother to intervene when someone else is doing their dirty work for them?'[66] Israel did not, as has sometimes been claimed, 'create' an Islamist movement, though some Israeli officials believed it could be used to put pressure on Fatah. It was a mistake however, and they realized it. Yassin was arrested in 1984 and sentenced to thirteen years in prison for possessing weapons and explosives. But he was released a year later as part of a prisoner exchange.[67] 'The fundamentalists had indeed sapped the strength of the PLO in Gaza', noted the Israeli writers Zeev Schiff and Ehud Yaari. 'But they soon surpassed it in indoctrination towards fanatic zeal; which from Israel's standpoint was far more menacing than anything the nationalists could show for their efforts.'[68] The Islamists attracted support because of their conservative piety and social and welfare activities that created a sense of solidarity and dignity – as well as boosting resistance to occupation. The Israelis were worried about the smaller Islamic Jihad movement, founded by a Gaza-born refugee named Fathi Shikaki. It was affiliated with Fatah and espoused armed struggle to liberate all of Palestine, and it had links to Iran. It was well organized with a cell structure and secret communications. In May 1987, six Islamic Jihad prisoners staged a sensational escape from Gaza gaol and mounted several attacks before being gunned down themselves, their status as heroic martyrs blurring political differences with rival factions. 'I welcome the fact that there are fundamentalists who are making it a priority to fight the occupation,' said Abdel-Shafi, in a pointed but diplomatic reference to mutual animosity. 'Our differences can wait.'[69] In November the Israelis deported Sheikh Abdulaziz Odeh, the group's spiritual mentor.

Late 1987 saw the appearance of a new Islamic Resistance Movement (*Harakat al-muqawama al-islamiyya* or Hamas, in its Arabic acronym) led by Yassin and composed of supporters who had been radicalized by the uprising. It was in fact secretly founded earlier, according to Khaled Meshaal, later the Hamas leader, so its first communiqué, in mid-December, was 'an announcement of the birth rather than the date of birth'.[70] It specified strike days and other activities that were not co-ordinated with the UNLU. Its language, replete with Quranic references, was religious and intolerant – calling Jews monkeys and apes – and uncompromising. Throughout the *intifada*, Hamas took a harder line than the UNLU. 'The blood of our martyrs shall not be forgotten', read a leaflet in January 1988.

> Every drop of blood shall become a Molotov cocktail, a time bomb, and a roadside charge that will rip out the intestines of the Jews. Only then will their sense return. You who give the Jews lists containing the names of youngsters and spy against their families, return to the fold, repent at once. Those who die in betrayal have only themselves to blame.[71]

Hamas made clear that Muslim values were a vital component of its worldview: 'The Jews asked: will these people act without outside support?' said another leaflet:

> They expected the generation that grew up after 1967 to be wretched and cowed, a generation brought up on hashish and opium, songs and music, beaches and prostitutes, a generation of occupation, a generation of poisoners and defeatists. What happened was the awakening of the people. The Muslim people is avenging its honour and restoring its former glory. No to concessions, [not] even a grain of dust from the soil of Palestine.[72]

Sentiments like these were codified in the Hamas charter, which was published in August 1988 and designed as an alternative to the PLO covenant.[73] Its thirty-six articles defined the movement as a wing of the Muslim Brotherhood, hailed the martyr Izzedin al-Qassam, and described Palestine as a religious endowment (*waqf*), 'consecrated for Muslims until judgement day'. In the face of the 'Jews' usurpation of Palestine' no part of it could be surrendered. Its liberation was a religious duty. 'There is no solution for the Palestinian question except through Jihad. Initiatives, proposals and international conferences are all a waste of time and vain endeavours. The Palestinian people know better than to consent to having their future, rights and fate toyed with.' It referenced anti-Semitic notions about Jewish world domination, responsibility for the French and Communist revolutions, control of the media and the aspiration to expand from the Nile to the Euphrates in a plan embodied in a notorious Russian forgery, the *Protocols of the Elders of Zion*. It opposed the PLO's support – though that had never been formalized – for the creation of a 'democratic secular state in Palestine'.[74] Yassin's own view was more guarded, but there was no mistaking his vision of the future. 'It is not enough to have a state in the West Bank and Gaza,' he declared. 'The best solution is to let all – Christians, Jews and Muslims – live in Palestine, in an Islamic state.'[75] It was no surprise that Hamas – weakened by arrests and deportations of leaders and activists – was also adamantly opposed to the sort of compromises Arafat was making as a momentous year drew to a close.

17
1988–1990

'Everything is written in three languages: Hebrew, Arabic, and death.'

Yehuda Amichai[1]

STRETCHING THE ROPE

On a wintry day in January 1989 Yitzhak Shamir, Israel's famously taciturn prime minister, flew by helicopter from Jerusalem to an army camp overlooking Nablus, capital of the Palestinian *intifada* and the largest town on the West Bank. On a muddy hillside he met IDF paratroopers on reserve duty, who spoke bitterly of having to do the dirty work of crushing the uprising. 'In order to enforce order in the casbah we must be brutally violent against people who are innocent of any crime,' one soldier said. 'I violate army regulations every day – and this weakens me and strengthens them . . . Everything we do bolsters the *intifada*.' Shamir, huddled in a blue parka against the biting cold, drummed his fingers on the table in front of him as he listened impassively to the catalogue of frustration. 'We hate these PLO terrorists,' he shouted angrily afterwards, 'because they force us to kill Arab children.' General Amram Mitzna, the West Bank military commander, looked embarrassed behind his beard.[2]

The new year had not seen any let-up in the pace of events. The UNLU called for a day of escalation to mark the anniversary of Fatah's first military operation against Israel in 1965. And thirteen Palestinian militants had been expelled across the Lebanese border – an indication of Israel's determination to continue wielding the iron fist despite diplomatic gains by the PLO and demoralization at home.

Petrol bombs were thrown and curfews imposed. Around that same time, several attempted raids across the Lebanese border occurred that were the work of Syrian-backed groups opposed to Yasser Arafat's strategy. They sought to undermine his nascent relationship with the US and demonstrate that they, at least, had not abandoned the armed struggle. And it was not only Israeli soldiers who were angry with Shamir. A few days earlier the Likud leader had been heckled and called a traitor while visiting settlers at Har Bracha, also near Nablus, where he promised retribution after a Jewish taxi driver had been shot dead. Their demand was for Israel to act decisively to crush the *intifada* – and to improve security for settlers. But the new fear, in the heartland of Samaria, was that even the steely Likud leader would buckle under mounting international pressure to negotiate with the PLO.

Shamir, prodded by the Americans, did put forward a proposal for holding elections in the West Bank – to choose Palestinians with whom Israel could negotiate some form of autonomy – but he ruled out any talks with the PLO or the dismantling of settlements. Arafat rejected any elections as unacceptable as long as the occupation continued. These responses fitted a familiar pattern: 'The Israelis', recorded the US diplomat Dennis Ross, 'would try to minimize the scope of any idea, assuming correctly that we would inevitably build on the idea, even transform it, as we tried to sell it to the Arabs or the Palestinians, who constantly tried to maximize whatever we offered.'[3] Israelis on the left and centre wanted to see a more significant response to the shift on the other side. Furious controversy erupted over the leak – blamed on the Labour party – of an IDF intelligence assessment warning that Israel could not ignore the changes that had taken place in the PLO and predicting that the US would continue to press for practical Israeli steps towards direct negotiations. Shamir denied the story, and was accused of lying, which did not inspire confidence.[4] 'Israel,' joked another government minister, 'is like a man who has jumped from the 30th floor of a building, and, passing the 5th floor window, says "so far so good". But will the parachute open before it is too late?'

Shamir's offer to hold elections was conditional on an end to violence. Israel, meanwhile, looked for new ways to deal with the *intifada*. In May it imposed an indefinite ban on Gazans working inside the green line in response to the killing of collaborators and the abduction and killing of a hitchhiking soldier, with a second soldier missing and presumed killed in similar circumstances. In the event, the ban lasted just a few days but this drastic step was meant to put pressure on Palestinian workers whose pay in normal times was the largest single source of income in Gaza.[5] The ban also seemed likely to shut down a vital safety valve and worsen an already deteriorating economic situation. 'Now there will be more intifada, not less,' insisted a ragged-looking Palestinian labourer from Khan Yunis, sent packing by police from a Tel Aviv building site. 'If you stretch the rope too far it'll simply break. What do they think? That we won't help each other? No-one has died of hunger yet during our *intifada*. The Israelis say they'll manage without us, but I don't believe it.' The move led immediately to requests for non-Arab workers to replace the absent Gazans.[6] At the same time Sheikh Yassin, the founder of Hamas, was arrested, along with his close colleague, Abdelaziz al-Rantisi, and 250 supporters, on the grounds that the group was responsible for the fate of the two missing soldiers. It was testimony to the growing threat posed by the Islamist organization. Hamas and Islamic Jihad were formally outlawed shortly afterwards.

The *intifada*, international diplomacy and Israel's volatile domestic politics were all dangerously intertwined all that summer. Shamir faced more right-wing wrath in June after another settler was killed near Nablus. The prime minister was jostled and abused, cries of 'Traitor' and 'Death to the Arabs' ringing out at the funeral of the victim. Ariel Sharon expressed his personal grief – and pursued his own political ambitions – by reciting the *kaddish*, the Jewish prayer for the dead, continuing his campaign against the Palestinian election plan. Shamir warned of the risk of civil war if divisions deepened. 'It is not a question of civil war or anarchy,' Sharon retorted. 'We are fully in control and able to deal with the root of the problem. We must not just say "we will destroy". We must destroy.'[7] Days later Shamir yielded to the hawks and ended any lingering ambiguity by declaring that he would not accept US conditions for negotiation and that settlement would continue – qualifying his elections plan almost to the point of extinction. The PLO blamed Israel for undermining

efforts to achieve peace. A cartoon portrayed a tiny Shamir, triumphantly raising his manacled and padlocked hands as a giant Sharon
strides away with the key. Less than twenty-four hours later, a young
Gazan from the Nusseirat refugee camp, reportedly shouting 'Allahu
akbar' ('God is greater/greatest'), grabbed the wheel of a bus on the
Tel Aviv–Jerusalem highway and forced it off the road into a gorge,
killing fourteen passengers. The perpetrator, who survived, told
investigators he was avenging beatings of relatives by Israeli soldiers.
This chillingly novel form of attack was the worst single incident
of terrorism inside Israel since the 1978 Coastal Road massacre.[8] In
its wake, several Arabs were forced off buses and beaten in West
Jerusalem. Activists of the far-right, racist Kach movement, led by
the Brooklyn-born Rabbi Meir Kahane, the founder of the Jewish
Defense League in the US, attacked a group of left-wing Israeli
women holding a vigil against the suppression of the intifada.
Sharon, meanwhile, called openly for Arafat to be 'eliminated', while
Dan Shomron, the IDF chief of staff, was publicly criticized, along
with General Mitzna, for his handling of the intifada. It was around
this time that Shomron was reported to be reading A Savage War of
Peace, the British historian Alistair Horne's magisterial account of
the Algerian war of independence, and to have distributed copies
to his senior officers. The parallel that interested thoughtful Israelis
was that although the French army was militarily far superior to the
FLN, that advantage had not translated into victory over the anti-
colonial rebels.

BREAKING THE BARRIER OF FEAR

Palestinian defiance masked hard times. In the occupied territories
popular songs and poetry praised sacrifices and solidarity, hailing the
sense that now that the 'barrier of fear' had been crossed there was
no going back. 'Stone and Onion and a Bucket of Water' and other
tracks on the album Children of Palestine, by the Jerusalem com-
poser Mustafa al-Kurd, blared out from cassettes everywhere,
evoking the mass demonstrations that had grabbed the attention of
the world and galvanized the Palestinians in the first year of the

intifada.[9] But the human and material costs were rising steadily. Economic pressure mounted in June when Israel adjusted its closure policy, requiring anyone crossing the green line to be issued with a new magnetic ID card. They were not given to released prisoners or administrative detainees. Many cards were confiscated by militants, forcing Palestinians to boycott Israel regardless of the financial hardship it meant. In Beit Sahour, near Bethlehem, the Israelis confiscated property in lieu of unpaid taxes – attracting sympathetic American media coverage of the Palestinians because of inevitable comparisons with the Boston Tea Party.[10]

Another growing problem was the beating and killing of collaborators. It highlighted the gap between the intellectuals and ideologues who represented and spoke for PLO factions and the young militants who maintained security, using resonant, comic-book hero names like the Black Panthers, or Red Eagles: the 'Striking Forces' of the *intifada*. Others were known simply as *al-mulathamin*, 'the masked ones'. Sabah Kanaan, murdered with knives, axes and iron bars in the old casbah in Nablus, was accused of prostitution and collaborating with the enemy. The Shin Bet recruited agents among drug dealers and prostitutes who could be coerced or induced to cooperate. Palestinians often encountered this. Israelis got a rare glimpse of the sleazy side of the occupation when a Gazan pimp who had worked for the security service murdered seven people in the slums of Tel Aviv.[11]

Killings of collaborators were often extraordinarily bold, perhaps because the perpetrators knew that Palestinian witnesses would be unlikely to testify. In one case a young man with a silenced pistol sauntered casually up to the police station in the centre of Nablus and shot down a Palestinian who had worked openly with the army and the Shin Bet – and carried an Uzi submachine gun and a walkie-talkie to prove it. Later that day the same weapon was used to kill an injured collaborator lying helpless in a hospital bed. In Ramallah a young man named Subhi Abu Ghosh was gunned down by Israelis disguised as Arabs – probably from the IDF undercover *'mistaravim'* unit codenamed *Duvdevan* (Cherry) – who arrived at a cafe in cars with West Bank licence plates in the company of a known collaborator whose role was to identify the wanted man they were looking for. In

Yaabed, collaborators patrolled openly with their Israeli-issued guns.[12] They were seen as fair game. 'The political echelon has no control over what the Striking Forces do,' said an East Jerusalem activist. 'And it is clear to us that the repeated waves of arrests [by the Israelis] created vacuums in the local leadership, and this allows younger people to take the initiative in doing something they see as heroic or nationalist.'[13] In September 1989, amid growing alarm, senior Palestinian political figures intervened when four people in a small West Bank village were about to be killed for collaboration; they were spared and allowed instead to promise to mend their ways and sever contact with the Israelis. Faisal Husseini, who was seen as Arafat's personal representative, made similar efforts to stop these killings. But the phenomenon was an inevitable by-product of this low-intensity war. 'We can do our job investigating collaborators because we have learned ourselves in Israeli jails how interrogations are conducted,' one young militant explained. A Black Panther member said: 'With all my respect to Faisal Husseini, I would like to remind him that the collaborators do not inform on him, but on us . . . Husseini does not live with us here, and can therefore not decide who is a collaborator. We are the ones who know.'[14] By the second anniversary of the *intifada*, in December 1989, an estimated 150 Palestinians had been killed as suspected collaborators. Israeli spokesmen often said that only a small number were genuine informers. Fifty thousand Palestinians had also been through the prison system. By 1989 about 13,000 were imprisoned – 1,800 of them in administrative detention without trial.[15]

In the absence of any changes on the ground or concrete political gains apart from the faltering PLO dialogue with the Americans, the uprising had itself become routine. International media coverage had been extremely important in drawing attention to the plight of the Palestinians but its intensity lessened over time, not least because of the higher and more novel drama of the revolutions that were transforming the landscape of Eastern Europe throughout 1989. But the media could mislead as well as inform. The TV cameras captured repeated clashes, but rarely filmed the Palestinians who continued to work inside Israel, or the Israelis, especially in the Tel Aviv area, who were carrying on with their lives undisturbed by or oblivious to the sporadic unrest across the green line. 'The situation in the territories was shunted – or repressed – to a marginal place in terms of public interest', noted B'Tselem, the newly founded Israeli Information Centre for Human Rights in the Occupied Territories. 'The types of stories that led ... the news in the electronic media or made headlines in the written press in the past, are today noted laconically or relegated to inside pages of the newspaper.'[16] There was an economic cost to be sure, but for the Israelis this was mitigated by the import of foreign workers and a fall in unemployment among Jews who replaced absent Palestinians. In June 1989 about 90 per cent of Palestinians from Gaza were still working, though the figure was only 56 per cent from the West Bank.[17] Life went on despite the tensions. In Jerusalem, Jewish taxi drivers took to spreading *keffiyehs* on their dashboards when driving in the eastern side of town, while Arabs in West Jerusalem displayed stickers supporting Beitar, the local soccer team notorious for its racist chants. It was hard to be precise about the political impact inside Israel, though something had clearly changed. 'The achievement of the uprising', commented the *Yediot Aharonot* columnist Nahum Barnea towards the end of a momentous year, 'is that the vast majority of Israelis who were happy with the status quo are now much more unhappy with it.'[18]

PEACE NOW?

Changes in the Israeli peace camp proved the point. Peace Now had been born as a mass movement after the Sadat initiative in 1977 and had grown in importance during the Lebanon war in 1982. On the eve of the *intifada*, however, it had been languishing in limbo for some time. It supported the Labour party's hazy commitment to 'territorial compromise' but remained cautious about dealing with the PLO: the hazards of advocating that were underlined when the veteran Israeli peacenik Abie Nathan (who had famously flown a plane named *Shalom* to Egypt to try to see Nasser in 1966) was gaoled for meeting Arafat. It was not until the Palestinian Declaration of Independence in Algiers in November 1988 that Peace Now came out and called unreservedly for Israeli negotiations with the PLO.[19] Individual Jewish peace activists had forged close ties with Faisal Husseini and other Fatah supporters in Jerusalem. Now contacts went beyond the small but vocal anti-Zionist left to include Peace Now, with both sides expressing a commitment to oppose violence and end the occupation. Husseini and other Fatah members regularly took part in public meetings with Israelis.[20] Peace Now was itself challenged by smaller, more radical groups, such as *Dai laKibbush* (Enough Occupation) and *Yesh Gvul* (There is a Border), demanding an end to occupation and offering support to soldiers, usually reservists, who refused to serve in the territories – even though numbers remained small. At least forty new protest groups were created in the first few months of the *intifada*. Women in Black began weekly vigils in Jerusalem and Tel Aviv, drawing comparisons with the Argentinian mothers in the Plaza de Mayo in Buenos Aires and attracting abuse from drivers and passers-by. Other Jewish doves offered practical help, with a group of architects and engineers forming a committee to rebuild houses demolished by the army in the West Bank village of Beita after the killing of a Jewish settler girl who was out on an organized hike – the traditional Zionist way of laying claim to the land. Pickets outside prisons and detention camps became routine.[21] A Council for Peace and Security, dominated by thirty retired IDF generals and other senior officers and security officials, was formed to make the argument that occupying the West Bank was no longer a military necessity.

Tolerance of dissent, however, still had its limits. On the second anniversary of the *intifada* in December 1989, the state-run Israel Broadcasting Authority banned two popular Hebrew songs that protested about the treatment of Palestinians and Israeli indifference to the situation. And when B'Tselem expressed concern about the deaths of 120 Palestinian children, Yitzhak Rabin replied acerbically that the organization should have written to their parents instead.[22] But the Jewish death toll was barely a score – fewer than in any month of traffic accidents and fewer than a twentieth of the Arab lives lost. For most Israeli Jews, the war in their own backyard was still 'like a war on a distant continent'.[23] And politically, there had still been little significant movement by the Israeli government. Underscoring the point, on the last day of 1989, Shamir plunged the unity coalition into crisis when he sacked the ex-Likudnik Ezer Weizman, now the

Labour minister for science, for holding unauthorized contacts with the PLO. Weizman had advised the Palestinians, through Ahmed Tibi, an Israeli-Arab intermediary, to accept Israel's West Bank elections proposal. On the same day tensions rose after an unusually heavy-handed police crackdown on an orderly Peace Now rally in Jerusalem. 'For once Palestinian and Israeli demonstrators experienced without discrimination the same violent repression by the police, who were totally baffled by what was going on,' recalled one participant.[24] Mustafa Barghouti, an independent leftist, later remembered that rally as a high point for the common hopes of Palestinians and dovish Israelis for a two-state solution to their conflict.[25]

Yet for Palestinians, Sari Nusseibeh concluded, the *intifada* had created a paradoxical situation:

> Although it made Israel fully cognizant of the cost and burden of the occupation, and although it forced the international community into a more active role in the political process through which Palestinians hoped to achieve freedom and independence in their own state alongside Israel ... the overall political result was a purgatorial reality, in which the Palestinians could neither reach that sought-after independence nor fully integrate themselves into Israel. In other words, they were neither free from Israel nor equals within it.[26]

Shamir's interpretation was even starker. It suggested that compromise with the Palestinians was simply not possible. The *intifada*, in his unbending view,

> was not a demonstration; not a spontaneous venting of frustration; not civil disobedience. It was a form of warfare against Israel and against the Arabs who want to live in peace with us. Ultimately, it was continuation of the war against Israel's existence, its immediate purpose to push us back to the 1967 lines and to establish another [*sic*] Palestinian state in the areas we leave ... [It] changed nothing in our basic situation. It served instead to underscore the existential nature of the conflict.[27]

18

1990–1991

*'The intifada ... has changed everything. It has opened new
vistas, new sets of words, new horizons, new realities. It has
made it possible to believe that justice may yet be achieved.'*
Raja Shehadeh[1]

GULF OF MISUNDERSTANDING

Not for the first time, at the start of the 1990s Palestinians found themselves victims of larger geopolitical developments in the Middle East and far beyond. The fall of the Berlin Wall and the revolutions in Eastern Europe, Iraq's invasion of Kuwait and the US-led coalition to liberate the Gulf state, Yasser Arafat's embrace of Saddam Hussein and the flurry of diplomacy that followed the war, all influenced the conflict with Israel. The PLO was especially alarmed at the lifting of the last Soviet restrictions on Jewish emigration, which provided a powerful reaffirmation of Israel's Zionist *raison d'être* and a new stream of immigrants who were welcomed in that spirit. Ominously for the Palestinians, Yitzhak Shamir declared that hundreds of thousands of newcomers would require a correspondingly big Israel – implying that yet more settlements in the occupied territories would be the answer. For Shamir the Russians were 'the promise of a stronger, brighter future sooner than we could have otherwise dared to expect'.[2] Arafat declared in his traditional New Year's message that Palestinian statehood was 'only a stone's throw away'.[3] On the ground, though, the *intifada* was petering out in the face of Palestinian exhaustion and increasingly effective Israeli counter-measures. The slaughter continued, however. In January eleven Palestinians were killed by Israeli bullets, but fifteen died at the hands of other Palestinians who had identified them as collaborators. In February, the killing of nine Israeli tourists ambushed on a bus in Egypt by Islamic Jihad gunmen was a reminder that if violence could be contained in one place, it could not be eradicated everywhere – and that there were significant differences within the Palestinian camp. In March, Israel's rickety national unity government finally collapsed over the plan for Palestinian elections. Its replacement seemed certain to shift further to the right.

Yet more bloodshed followed. In May 1990, an Israeli wearing army trousers and carrying an M16 rifle arrived at the Rishon LeZion 'slave market' junction, south of Tel Aviv, and shot dead seven Palestinian construction workers in cold blood. By the end of the day eight more Palestinians had been killed in violence that erupted all over the West Bank and Gaza Strip, where most of the victims came from. The gunman, Ami Popper, had demanded to inspect the victims' identity cards before opening fire – a long-familiar ritual on both sides of the green line. Popper was not a serving soldier and did not act at the behest of the Israeli government, as many Arabs charged (itself a reminder of toxic perceptions of their enemy). Still, whereas in other countries crazed gunmen generally killed their victims at random, in Israel, it seemed, crazed Jews did only target Arabs. Popper was sentenced to multiple life terms for murder despite pleading insanity. 'I felt that this whole country stands on a thin, flaky crust, and under it there flows a lava of terrible, irreparable hatred', reflected an Israeli journalist who was dismayed to hear expressions of support for the unrepentant killer.[4] As well as briefly reigniting the flagging *intifada*, the murders stirred unaccustomed fury among Israel's Palestinian minority, triggering demonstrations in Nazareth and elsewhere. 'I was born here and educated here but I have less value than a Russian Jew who decides to come here tomorrow', complained Adel Manna, a leading historian. 'I don't feel I belong here.'[5] Mass protests took place in refugee camps in Jordan, and Arafat called on the UN to deploy forces to protect Palestinians.

Arafat's own position was seriously undermined in May when the Palestine Liberation Front – the maverick Iraqi-backed PLO group that had hijacked the *Achille Lauro* cruise liner in 1985 – launched a seaborne raid on Israel. The Palestinians set out from a base in Libya:

one unit, pursued by Israeli helicopters, landed from speedboats on a beach near Ashdod that was crowded with thousands of holidaymakers who watched as black-clad gunmen raced for the nearby sand dunes. Four heavily armed fighters were killed by Israeli forces and twelve captured in this spectacular but abortive attack. Others were captured while still at sea further north. Israel exploited the incident to argue that the PLO and all its constituent groups continued to carry out terrorist acts and to demand that the US should finally end the dialogue with it – the *intifada*'s greatest prize. Days later, after prolonged coalition negotiations, a new Likud-led government took office, again under Yitzhak Shamir. It was without any Labour party representation and with the addition of Rehavam Zeevi's far-right *Moledet* (Homeland) party, which openly advocated the 'transfer' of Palestinians out of the country as a solution to the conflict. The US dialogue with the PLO was suspended.

ENTER SADDAM

The Arab summit conference that convened in Baghdad in May 1990 was preoccupied with some of these developments, notably the swelling Russian emigration to Israel, and mounting tensions with Kuwait over the exports of cheap oil that were holding back the recovery of the battered Iraqi economy. The main focus for Palestinians was the support offered by Saddam Hussein. The Iraqi dictator had been trying to reassert Baghdad's leadership of the Arab world – and get hold of more cash – since the end of his ruinous eight-year war with Iran in 1988. In April Saddam had raised the regional temperature by warning that he would 'burn half of Israel' – a barely veiled reference to the chemical weapons he had used against Iran and the Iraqi Kurds – if it threatened any Arab country. Arafat had drawn closer to Saddam over the preceding year in part because of Iraq's generous financial support for the *intifada*, which far outstripped the contributions of other Arab states. Arafat initially got involved in Arab mediation efforts over Kuwait, but after the suspension of the PLO's dialogue with the US and the Iraqi invasion in August he sided openly with Baghdad. Saddam then smartly and cynically linked any withdrawal of his forces from the emirate to an Israeli withdrawal from the occupied territories – as well as to a Syrian pullout from neighbouring Lebanon. The swift despatch of US forces to Saudi Arabia and efforts to form a coalition – 'Operation Desert Shield' – to free Kuwait stood in striking contrast, in Arab eyes, to the toleration of Israel's twenty-three-year occupation of Palestinian lands without even the imposition of UN sanctions.

Within weeks pro-Iraqi demonstrations were being held in both Jordan and the West Bank, where Saddam was hailed as the 'symbol of Arabism', or a new 'Saladin' bravely standing up to the West. Craftsmen in Amman replaced their traditional nativity scenes and model camels with olive-wood souvenirs of Iraqi Al-Hussein missiles, while songs praising Saddam outsold the latest Madonna album. According to one poll, 84 per cent of West Bankers considered Saddam a hero, though only 58 per cent supported the invasion of Kuwait. Palestinians also protested inside Israel.

The *intifada* was thoroughly eclipsed by this crisis; cassettes of Iraqi nationalist ballads replaced the stirring Palestinian anthems normally on sale at the Damascus Gate in East Jerusalem. To some, Saddam's linkage of Kuwait and Palestine was a brilliant move that put his enemies on the spot. But others felt that Palestinian sympathy for the 'Butcher of Baghdad' played straight into the hands of the Israeli government: Palestinians, it was said, were 'showing their true colours'. It also infuriated Israelis who championed Jewish-Arab dialogue and negotiations with the PLO. 'The Palestinian position has buried the peace process', complained the dovish Labour MP Yossi Sarid. 'They've completely destroyed all their own moral arguments. If it is legitimate to support a murderer who gassed thousands of Kurds, maybe it's not so terrible to support Shamir, Sharon and Rabin. Compared to the crimes of Saddam Hussein, the Israeli government's actions are as white as the driven snow.'[6] Yet Palestinians were defiant: 'What have we got to lose?' asked a Bir Zeit lecturer. 'Most of our leaders are in jail. Those who are not in jail are refused permission to go abroad. Those who are not abroad are under house arrest. Our cities are shut by curfews. Our people cannot work. Tens of thousands on the West Bank have lost their livelihood.'[7] Saeb Erakat, a Fatah loyalist, admitted that the Palestinian cause was suffering: 'As moderates we have really had it. We have nothing left. All doors have been slammed in our faces. There was a vacuum in the Middle East and it has been filled brilliantly by Saddam Hussein. And we think that Shamir understands Saddam's language.'[8]

Shamir's defence minister, the low-key Moshe Arens, who had replaced Labour's Rabin in the new government, was credited in Israel with having promoted a calmer mood in the West Bank and Gaza by tightening up orders on opening fire, ordering the IDF to focus on guarding main roads and settlements and refraining from needlessly entering Palestinian villages and refugee camps. Predictions that the *intifada* was over, however, proved premature. Serious clashes erupted again in September when an Israeli soldier was stoned and then burned to death in a Gaza refugee camp. Houses and shops were demolished by the army, ostensibly to widen a narrow road where attacks often took place.

BLOODSHED
ON THE HARAM AL-SHARIF

In October 1990 tensions boiled over with the worst day of violence since the *intifada* began – and Jerusalem's worst ever since 1967: 21 Palestinians were killed by the Israelis and 140 injured on the Haram al-Sharif/Temple Mount, a site as sensitive as it had been back in 1929. The high death toll and furious reactions from Arab capitals threatened to inject a new and volatile element into the Gulf crisis. The incident began when Palestinians rained stones onto the heads of Jewish worshippers at the adjacent Western Wall; Palestinians said they were defending themselves against a ceremony planned by an extremist Jewish group, the Temple Mount Faithful, 'a miniscule group of Jewish fanatics and publicity hunters'[9] who had been denied permission to lay a foundation stone for a new Jewish Temple on the site but were reported to have arrived in nearby Silwan, just outside the Old City. Most of the victims were shot by live ammunition used by border policemen who panicked when they realized they were outnumbered. Faisal Husseini was arrested and curfews imposed on villages and refugee camps all over the occupied territories.[10] 'These bullets were paid for by American taxes,' raged a Palestinian surgeon in a blood-drenched gown at the Maqassed Hospital, where many of the dead and injured were taken:

> I would like to see the US Marines here, like they are in Saudi Arabia because of Kuwait. If there is oil at stake they will do anything, but Palestinian blood is cheap. The Israelis are bringing a million Jews from Russia to eat up our land like locusts. I think that the real response to this will be mustard gas from Iraq. That is the language that they understand here.

Refusing to co-operate with a UN mission, Israel launched its own internal inquiry into the killings, which blamed 'provocation by Arab extremists'.[11] Two weeks later a Palestinian plasterer from Bethlehem wielding a bayonet murdered three Jews in the tranquil West Jerusalem suburb of Baqaa in apparent revenge for the Temple Mount deaths. The neighbourhood, home to many Peace Now activists, was traumatized. Other random stabbing attacks followed in rapid succession, fuelling an ugly, suspicious mood that highlighted the all-too-real divisions of what Israel insisted was its 'united and eternal capital'. November's funeral of the Kach movement leader, Rabbi Meir Kahane – who had been murdered in New York by an Egyptian-born gunman – attracted 20,000 people. Many wore yellow Kach T-shirts, cursed 'leftist' Jewish journalists and called to avenge his death with Arab blood.[12]

On the *intifada*'s third anniversary in December 1990, the outlook for the Palestinians was still uncertain. Supporters of the PFLP and Hamas, as well as some within Fatah, were pressing hard to announce the resumption of the armed struggle. Hamas was blamed for the murder of three Jews in Jaffa and hundreds of its supporters were arrested afterwards. 'It is very tempting,' admitted Radwan Abu Ayyash, a leading Fatah loyalist,

> especially for youngsters and religious people, because they see these Israeli crimes and want to retaliate. But internationally, we have made many gains with the intifada that we would lose if we revert to armed struggle, and we are not prepared for it. If we use guns it will not be an intifada but a war. The Israelis want war. To take this decision would be to play into their hands.[13]

Raja Shehadeh asked: 'How far will the stone get us? Are we going to succeed in driving away, with stones, their entire well-equipped modern army? Doubtful.'[14] Other Palestinian moderates admitted that they were out of touch and losing influence. 'Nowadays we look like a bunch of Mickey Mouse characters,' mused a left-wing lecturer. 'It's amazing how pleased my students are with these stabbings. It's got nothing to do with politics. They simply feel that the Israelis are getting a taste of their own medicine.' The latest UNLU leaflet called for 'all forms of struggle' and praised 'martyrdom operations'. The olive branch, it seemed, had withered.[15]

Shortly afterwards, Saddam Hussein, in Arab eyes, gave the Israelis 'a taste of their own medicine' – albeit of an unfamiliar kind. 'Operation Desert Storm' began on 17 January 1991, when the UN deadline for Iraqi withdrawal from Kuwait expired, with a massive aerial bombardment of Iraq. Iraq immediately launched eight Scud missiles against Tel Aviv and Haifa – though they were armed with conventional warheads, not chemical ones. Shamir, famous for his strong nerves, was persuaded by the Americans to hold back from retaliation, because had Israel struck Iraq it would have triggered the departure of Egypt and Syria and perhaps Saudi Arabia from the anti-Saddam coalition. Earlier in the month Shamir had met secretly with King Hussein in London, where the king had said he would not let a third party use Jordan to attack Israel; Shamir in turn promised that Israel would not violate Jordanian airspace.[16] Israel's strength, went the official line in Jerusalem, was in restraint and in its long-term interest. In all, thirty-nine Scuds hit Israel. US Patriot anti-missile batteries were employed, with limited success, to intercept them. The Scuds did extensive damage to property and killed two people, though eleven others died from heart attacks or asphyxiation while wearing gas masks. By night, Tel Aviv, the city that advertised itself as 'never stopping', suddenly resembled a West Bank town under Israeli curfew.

Blanket curfews were imposed across the occupied territories for six weeks but Palestinians in Nablus and Ramallah still cheered, clapped and applauded from their rooftops when they heard the air-raid sirens wail. That attracted hostile coverage in the Israeli media, especially when a small number of gas masks were distributed in the

West Bank by order of the Israeli High Court – an ironic sideshow of the Gulf war. 'The missiles that landed in Tel Aviv and Haifa brought the Palestinians to ecstatic excitement', commented *Davar*. 'Even if, afterwards, semi-regretful statements were voiced, the damage has been done. After long years of Sisyphean efforts aimed at bringing Israelis and Palestinians to talk, the Gulf war exposed the teeth behind the smile.'[17] Sari Nusseibeh, trying to limit the damage, explained why: 'It's a great pity war broke out, though Saddam has renewed the idea that the Arabs can stand up to the US and Israel. And if Palestinians are happy when they see a missile going from east to west, figuratively speaking, they have seen missiles going the other way for the last 40 years.'[18] A week later, after prolonged efforts by the Shin Bet to implicate him in the leadership of the *intifada*, the bookish Nusseibeh was detained for six months on suspicion of passing information to Iraq about the location of its missile strikes. The accusation brought 'derision and scorn' and was widely seen as a message to Palestinian moderates to forget about negotiations with Israel.[19]

It was clear from the start of the Kuwait crisis that Arafat's support for Saddam had been a grave miscalculation. In the wake of the war some 300,000 Palestinians were expelled from Kuwait and Saudi Arabia, destroying thriving immigrant communities and causing serious financial hardship in the occupied territories, and increasing dependence on Israel as a source of livelihood. Losses to the PLO were estimated at $133 million. That brought swift spending cuts and the closure of East Jerusalem newspapers like *al-Fajr* and *al-Shaab*. The organization sold $125 million in real estate to cover salaries, pensions and welfare payments.[20] Inside Israel tensions ran high because of the Palestinians' identification with Iraq: arguments erupted about whether Palestinian workers should be allowed into gas-proofed shelters during the missile attacks. New rules were also introduced requiring all Palestinians entering Israel to have a personal exit permit.[21]

As the 'Mother of Battles' ended it was evident that Israel had benefitted politically from events; foreign ministry officials even suggested that the country was enjoying the greatest support it had seen since the heady days of 1967. 'Israel is being integrated more than ever into the Western alliance,' noted an alarmed Raja Shehadeh:

And we here are quickly being identified as 'the other'. They, the preservers of civilization; we, the savages, the bloodthirsty, the supporters of the murder of innocent civilians by chemical weapons. It makes me want to cry out: You are mistaken. This is not who we are, we never wanted innocent civilians to be killed; we have only wanted to live. How much more shall Israel deprive us of? It took our land, our future and our inheritance and now our reputation, turning us, in the eyes of the world, into bloodthirsty inhuman warmongers.[22]

But there were potentially positive longer-term effects too: 'Israel has been marginalised as a strategic asset of the US', suggested Salim Tamari. 'This will put it under immense pressure when America, the West and the Arab world come to do business again.'[23]

NEW WORLD ORDER?

Expectations were high, and probably unrealistically so. Still, immediately the Gulf war ended, a new phase of US diplomacy began. President George H. W. Bush, pursuing what he had grandiosely named a 'New World Order', renewed efforts to resolve the Palestinian issue, frozen since before the Kuwait crisis. Israel's relief at the end of the war, mixed with an unaccustomed sense of its own vulnerability and anger that Saddam was still in power with much of his huge army intact, gave way to a sense of anxiety about the likely sequel. On 6 March 1991 Bush announced to Congress that he was seeking an Arab–Israeli peace treaty. No one in Jerusalem had forgotten the previous summer's terse warning by Bush's secretary of state, James Baker, that Israel knew the telephone number of the White House switchboard if it wanted to discuss peace with the Palestinians – which echoed Moshe Dayan's comment back in 1967. Now Baker was leading a new drive for progress on the basis of 'the principle of territory for peace' – one that had never been accepted by the Likud despite its declared readiness to negotiate. The mood was hardly improved by the fact that the day before Baker arrived in Israel, in the grimly predictable choreography of such high-profile missions, a Palestinian stabbed four Israeli women to death at a bus stop in West Jerusalem. Israeli police reported that the Gazan assailant had described the killings as 'a message to Baker',[24] though he also claimed to be avenging the death of a cousin in *intifada* unrest. In any event, the incident reinforced the point to the Americans at least that ejecting Iraq from Kuwait was a lot easier than it would be to reach a peace settlement between Israelis and Palestinians. The following day, six gunmen who had infiltrated into Israel from Jordan were killed in a clash with the IDF. Faisal Husseini and other prominent Palestinians, who held a 'stormy' meeting with the US secretary of state, insisted that only the PLO could represent them. 'Baker didn't pull a magic wand out of his briefcase to end occupation with the same finesse and speed with which American troops had cleared the Iraqis out of Kuwait', Sari Nusseibeh heard in the prison cell where he was now detained without trial.[25] Outside the US consulate building in Jerusalem, Israeli right-wingers demonstrated with placards proclaiming: 'Baker, go dance on the rooftops with Husseini.'

James Baker's meeting, however, was the start of the most ambitious drive in nearly two decades to secure an Arab–Israeli peace settlement – and, crucially, one that included the Palestinians for the first time. In eight visits to the Middle East between March and October, the US envoy – 'an adept and gifted arm-twister', according to Shimon Peres[26] – laid the groundwork for the Madrid peace conference in November 1991. The main Arab obstacle was removed when Syrian President Hafez al-Assad abandoned his long-standing demand that any such conference be held under UN auspices, a concession that underlined the dramatic effect of the end of the Cold War. Egypt and Jordan followed suit. The PLO objected at first but accepted in the end that although it would not be present, due to US and Israeli objections, its voice and positions would be represented by a joint Jordanian-Palestinian delegation that would enjoy Arafat's authority. Arafat showed the strain he was under, haranguing aides, and reportedly even physically assaulting a senior adviser as, in the absence of direct telephone links between Tunisia and Israel, he was forced to keep in touch with the Palestinian negotiating team via cumbersome connections routed through the US and Cyprus.[27] Israel insisted that the delegation could not include representatives from East Jerusalem. The simple way round that was that East Jerusalemites were present as 'advisers' to the main delegation.

Palestinian opposition to this Israeli-imposed formula was keenly felt, with strong objections from the PFLP, DFLP and Hamas. On the ground an upsurge in killings of alleged collaborators underscored how political leaders appeared to be dangerously out of touch with the mood among activists. In Nablus in April a group of young men had a gang of thieves whipped publicly. 'The dream of the intifada has become a nightmare', commented Adnan Damiri, a Fatah activist and poet who had served long terms in Israeli prisons. Damiri's article in *al-Fajr* in June 1991 sparked a rare public debate on the issue and other negative aspects of the uprising. But Israel was the toughest nut for the Americans to crack as their diplomatic offensive intensified. The mood in Jerusalem, one senior official recalled, was 'cantankerous and divisive'.[28] Israel wanted only a ceremonial opening to the conference, to be followed by separate bilateral negotiations with individual Arab states, where it believed external pressure would be at a minimum. Shamir, facing opposition from Ariel Sharon and other hardline colleagues, was alarmed when the US publicly condemned the 'enhanced pace' of settlement activity. On the eve of Baker's third visit, *Gush Emunim* settlers slipped into prefabricated homes on a new West Bank site named Revava – an action compared by one Labour MP to 'planting a bomb on Baker's plane'. The move was widely blamed on Sharon, who was duly snubbed by the Bush administration on a visit to Washington.[29] The issue was then raised in an unusually troubling way when the US demanded a delay in response to Israel's request for $10 billion in loan guarantees to help the settlement of Soviet immigrants. It was the first time since the Suez crisis in 1956 that a US administration had made financial aid conditional on a change in Israeli policy.

MEETING IN MADRID

Everyone recognized that the stakes at Madrid would be high: on the eve of the conference two Israeli settlers were killed and five injured when their bus was raked with gunfire on a lonely West Bank road. The settlers were on their way to a rally in Tel Aviv to urge the government to stand firm against demands for the surrender of any territory. Bush's description of the participants as 'reluctant and uneasy players' was an understatement.[30] Preparations went smoothly, except for a tense spat over whether the Spanish hosts would agree to remove an enormous oil painting of Charles V killing Moors from the summit venue, the Palacio Real, the spectacular residence of King Juan Carlos.[31] Starting on 31 October 1991, the conference was a dramatic and ceremonial event that attracted intense media coverage and provided some arresting images over three days. Presidents Bush and Mikhail Gorbachev both made weighty speeches invoking the momentous global changes of the preceding months. 'Let no one mistake the magnitude of this challenge,' said Bush. 'The struggle we seek to end has a long and painful history. Every life lost – every outrage, every act of violence – is etched deep in the hearts and history of the people of this region.' But it was, naturally enough, Palestinians and Israelis who were the main focus of attention. Dr Hayder Abdel-Shafi, the veteran nationalist from Gaza, chaired the Jordanian-Palestinian delegation. Faisal Husseini was in overall charge. Nabil Shaath, a senior Arafat confidant, was on the scene, co-ordinating positions with Tunis and the Russians and briefing journalists. Arafat, visiting Morocco, ordered last-minute changes to Abdel-Shafi's speech.[32]

The exclusion of the PLO was a charade that was reluctantly recognized as necessary to allow the negotiations to proceed, given US and Israeli opposition. Husseini, looking hunched and stressed, complained that the 'suit the American peace team tailored for the negotiations does not fit my body'.[33] Abdel-Shafi, softly spoken and shunning histrionics, stole the show with his quiet dignity. He demanded an end to occupation, but also laid out a realistic, practical way to achieve it. 'We seek neither an admission of guilt after the fact, nor vengeance for past iniquities, but rather an act of will that would make a just peace a reality,' he declared. Palestinians would accept a 'transitional stage provided that interim arrangements are not transformed into permanent status'. He too complained about the exclusion of the PLO but kept to the ground rules by referring only to 'the symbol of our national identity and unity'. He played cleverly on the very real divisions among Israelis, telling them: 'We have seen your anguish over the transformation of your sons and daughters into instruments of a blind and violent occupation – and we are sure that at no time did you envisage such a role for the children you thought would forge your future.' It was a fascinating glimpse of the way the long years of occupation had given the Palestinians far greater understanding of their enemy. Yitzhak Shamir, by contrast, sounded uncompromising and deeply sceptical about Arab intentions. He had, after all, even abstained in the parliamentary vote on the peace treaty with Egypt in 1979. His speech was untouched by diplomatic niceties and gave no indication of change that might be induced by positive atmospherics, personal chemistry or the dynamics of negotiation. Meetings of the Israeli delegation were held in a mood of 'doubt, suspicion and even dread concerning what the future might bring'.[34] The prime minister's state of mind veered between anger and indifference; he told a colleague he had fallen asleep during Gorbachev's opening address. Israel, Shamir declared, had only ever sought peace with Arabs who had rejected it and refused to recognize the legitimacy of the Jewish state. The issue was 'not territory, but our existence,' he said. 'It will be regrettable if the talks focus primarily and exclusively on territory. It is the quickest way to an impasse.' In his response to Abdel-Shafi, quoted in his memoirs, Shamir commented that 'even to this very day, under conditions you describe as occupation, any Jew who strays into an Arab village risks his life, but tens of thousands of Palestinian Arabs walk freely in every town and village in Israel'.[35] Shamir was myopia personified. Other Israelis noticed the change that was under way. 'I could see the arrival of a jovial and excited Palestinian delegation . . . for the first time in so many years, at the Middle Eastern conference table, on an equal footing with the other participants', noted one official. 'That the PLO was there only by proxy and new authentic Palestinian leaders of the territories formed the Palestinian delegation boded well for the international image of an embattled nation in search of dignity and freedom from occupation.'[36]

Both sides exploited opportunities to score propaganda points live via the then still novel medium of satellite TV: Farouk al-Sharaa, the Syrian foreign minister, displayed a photograph of Shamir as a Stern Gang terrorist wanted by the British police in the 1940s. Saeb Erakat draped a *keffiyeh* over his smart business suit. Hanan Ashrawi, a professor of literature from Bir Zeit – as well as a Christian and a woman to boot – proved more than a match for the slick, media-smart deputy Israeli foreign minister, Binyamin Netanyahu, who was dubbed 'the Abba Eban of the CNN era'. Indeed, the main Israeli effort, one participant admitted afterwards, 'was to provide credible public-relations explanations of Israel's policies'.[37] But the Palestinians easily won: in PR terms at least, Madrid went a long way to repairing some of the damage caused by the Gulf war, nullifying the 'huge discrepancy in physical power and the asymmetry of their international standing'.[38] In Ramallah, hundreds of Palestinians demonstrated in support of their representatives in the Spanish capital. The mood in the West Bank was euphoric. And there was more to it than a positive image or media spin. In diplomatic terms, the significance of Madrid was that it laid down a twin-track framework: one was for bilateral negotiations between Israel and Jordan, Syria and Lebanon; and the other, an Israeli–Palestinian track – a genuinely historic innovation. These tracks were indeed initially 'little more than rocky, unpaved paths'.[39] Neither led anywhere at all for a long time. But both did eventually bring progress, albeit in different and unanticipated ways.

19

1992–1994

'Peace of the Brave' or 'a Palestinian Versailles'?

RABIN'S RETURN

In June 1992, Yitzhak Rabin led the Labour party to victory in Israel's general election. Subsequent events would imbue this event with great significance, but even at the time his ascendancy seemed an important milestone. Rabin's reputation, at home and abroad, was of a gruff soldier who was high on credibility but low on vision. And he was no dove. Older Palestinians remembered him as the man who had expelled thousands from Lydda and Ramle in 1948 and commanded the Israeli army in 1967. Twenty years later, as defence minister, his response to the *intifada* was to 'break the bones' of troublemakers. His first stint as prime minister had been curtailed by scandal and overshadowed by the Likud's mould-breaking election win the following year. Having beaten Shimon Peres to the party leadership he had a strong appeal to centrist voters. The 1992 campaign focused more on social and economic issues than on war and peace. Rabin moved cautiously on that front, offering Palestinian autonomy and a partial settlement freeze but still opposing what he called 'political' outposts in heavily populated parts of the occupied territories. Otherwise his strategy appeared to be to blur the difference between Labour and Likud to appeal to floating voters.

In the first half of 1992 there had been no significant movement on the tracks laid down at Madrid. Shamir's strategy was to simply stonewall. When follow-up talks were launched in Washington the Israelis initially refused to attend unless the other side was run by the

316

Jordanians, to avoid giving the PLO any independent status. The Americans took a back seat. James Baker was unwilling to invest much more in the hard slog of Arab–Israeli peacemaking in the final year of George H. W. Bush's presidency.[1] When negotiations did begin, Israeli settlement activity and expulsions of Palestinians caused inevitable tensions. 'The last time I came back to Jericho from talks in Washington they showed me a piece of land that was Palestinian when I left and is now Israel,' complained negotiator Saeb Erakat. 'If such actions continue, it won't be very long before our constituents tell us to stay at home.'[2] The Palestinian team suffered from 'virtually worthless' planning as well as micro-management from Tunis by Arafat, who assumed, probably correctly, that the Americans or the Israelis were tapping his phone conversations and wished to demonstrate to whoever was listening that no concessions would be made without his approval.[3]

Violence intruded all too often. In February 1992 Israel's helicopter-borne assassination of the Hizbullah leader, Sheikh Abbas al-Musawi, with his wife and son – after the killing of three conscripts at an IDF camp inside Israel – came as Syria and Lebanon announced their readiness to attend more talks. But four rounds with the Palestinians produced only irreconcilable drafts of what interim self-rule should look like. In the foreign ministry in Jerusalem one official made paper aeroplanes with reports of the proceedings and launched them down the corridors.[4] And when two of Shamir's far-right coalition partners bolted, the Likud leader was left without a majority: his first response as a new election loomed was to promise to continue the settlement enterprise.[5] 'The notion of territorial compromise will fade away like a bad dream,' he promised.[6] Shamir later revealed his hand: had he been re-elected he would have dragged the talks out for ten more years and worked to increase the Jewish presence in the West Bank to half a million. 'I didn't believe there was a majority in favour of a Greater Israel, but it could have been attained over time,' he said. 'Without such a basis there would be nothing to stop the establishment of a Palestinian state.'[7]

Rabin's victory was narrow but decisive, with the support of sixty-two MPs to fifty-eight for the Likud and its right-wing and religious allies. It was still the first time since 1984 that Israelis had broken the deadlock that produced unity governments which could agree only on the lowest common denominator – and fell when tough issues were on the table. The pro-settlement party *Tehiya* disappeared, and although there was a boost for the far-right anti-clerical party *Tzomet*, the 'Judaea and Samaria' lobby was not represented. The coalition Rabin put together included the newly created left-of-centre *Meretz*, with 12 seats in the 120-member Knesset, as well as the ultra-Orthodox *Shas*, which had dovish leanings. Rabin retained the defence portfolio and made his old rival Shimon Peres foreign minister. It was the most dovish and pragmatic government in Israeli history – a dream for the centre-left. The US loan guarantees to finance Soviet Jewish immigration, which had been held up under Shamir, were then released. In one of its first acts, the government said it was freezing contracts for housing in Jewish settlements, although 'natural growth' and projects already under way were allowed to continue – a significant qualification that did nothing to assuage either Palestinian suspicions or instinctive hostility from the Israeli right. When further restrictions were announced, settler leaders condemned a 'massive assault on the Zionist enterprise' by 'a malevolent and treacherous government'. The language they used was emotive and hyperbolic. The policy of approving some settlements and undermining others was even compared to 'the Nazi selection in the death camps'.[8] Shamir called the situation 'a nightmare'. Around the same time there was a peaceful end for a potentially serious crisis that erupted when Fatah gunmen were pursued on to the campus of al-Najah University in Nablus by the IDF and a tense four-day siege ended with negotiations between Faisal Husseini and Israeli military officials.

HIGH HOPES, WIDE GAP

Expectations for positive change in Israeli–Arab relations had rarely run higher. In late August 1992, when the sixth round of the Madrid-track talks resumed in Washington, even Syrian spokesmen praised a newly 'reasonable' and 'constructive' Israeli attitude. Seeking to build confidence, Rabin rescinded an order expelling eleven Palestinian activists. Strikingly, Israeli negotiators stopped using the terms 'Judaea and Samaria' and referred simply to the 'territories' or the 'West Bank and Gaza Strip'. In another subtle but significant shift, the fictitious non-presence of the PLO gave way to a far more visible one, despite the organization's formal exclusion by the US and Israel. 'Yasser Arafat can now give public instructions to the negotiators and nothing happens,' boasted Nabil Shaath, the PLO leader's adviser. 'There is no longer a cover-up of the relationship between our delegation and the organisation. Nothing can be submitted without authorisation from PLO headquarters in Tunis. We use open fax lines – not codes.'[9]

If the atmosphere was improving, the gap between the two sides was still enormous: Israel was prepared to accept a 12-member Palestinian administrative council, while the Palestinians demanded a 180-member legislative assembly to serve as the basis for full self-government and eventual independence. Arafat complained that Rabin was using 'sugar-coated words' while pursuing 'iron-fisted' policies on the ground.[10] In East Jerusalem Palestinian preparations for the next stage were co-ordinated by technical committees headed by Sari Nusseibeh. Excited volunteers churned out papers on the Palestinian economy, infrastructure, administration and future planning. They were based in the Orient House in Sheikh Jarrah, a dilapidated former hotel that had housed Faisal Husseini's Centre for Arab Studies and had been closed by Israel in 1988. It reopened in 1992 to serve as the HQ for the Palestinian delegation to Madrid and came to be seen as the seat of a shadow Palestinian government, evoking comparisons with the Jewish Agency building in Rehavia in Mandate days. 'Capturing knowledge about our emerging nation was for us like wiping away decades of powerlessness by showing ourselves what we were made of, that we, like other peoples, could govern ourselves', Nusseibeh wrote later.[11] Fairly soon there was talk of tensions between PLO officials in Tunis and home-grown experts. 'There are bound to be problems', commented the journalist Daoud Kuttab,

> for the simple reason that people who have not been here for 25 years will have a hard time dealing with issues on the ground. Those of us who live here know the Israelis and our own situation inside out. These are problems we eat, drink and sleep. In Tunis, it's just a job, not a reality.[12]

Differences between 'insiders' and 'outsiders' were becoming a significant theme in Palestinian politics. But optimism about progress under the new Israeli government was not universally shared. 'There will be autonomy', predicted an alarmed Mahmoud al-Zahar, a Hamas leader in Gaza. 'It will be a disaster and our people will discover it very quickly – within months. It is a trap.'[13] The Hamas view was that recognition of Israel was an act of treachery. But some Fatah loyalists were unhappy too. Arafat's behaviour at meetings of the PLO executive committee in Tunis was 'intolerable', complained Shafiq al-Hout, who felt 'disenfranchised' when documents about the Washington talks were withheld from him and other critics.[14] Hayder Abdel-Shafi convened a crisis meeting after the Islamist movement accused Fatah of targeting mosques. Hamas, the DFLP and PFLP formed an ad hoc anti-autonomy alliance and won a trial of strength in the West Bank when a general strike they called to revive the terminally flagging *intifada* and protest over the talks was strictly observed. In some ways this was a re-run of what had happened in 1978 as Menachem Begin went through the motions of negotiating self-rule with Sadat: the crucial difference was that now the mainstream Palestinian leadership was actively engaged, and pushing hard to secure the recognition it craved.

Arafat, surveying developments from Tunis, was said to have been 'horrified' to discover the growing strength of Hamas, which stepped up armed actions in the autumn of 1992 ahead of the fifth anniversary of the *intifada*. In just two weeks five Israeli soldiers were ambushed and killed by Hamas in Gaza and Hebron. It then kidnapped an Israeli border policeman and demanded the release of the gaoled Sheikh Yassin – who appeared on TV from his prison cell and appealed to the kidnappers not to kill their hostage. The policeman's body was found the next day near Jericho, his hands bound and throat cut. Rabin was accused by the Likud of allowing terrorism to thrive. Abdel-Shafi, from Washington, condemned the killing. In mid-December the Israelis detained 1,600 alleged Hamas and Islamic Jihad activists and deported 415 of them to south Lebanon, giving each a little food, $50 and a blanket. It was the biggest single expulsion of Palestinians in peacetime. None had been tried, charged or allowed to appeal. Ehud Barak, the IDF chief of staff, was asked to explain to the High Court why the move was necessary: he responded that although 14,000 Palestinians were currently in prison, and 100,000 had been gaoled since the *intifada* had begun, only severe measures could deal the required blow to Hamas. As the deportees remained stranded between the Israeli and Lebanese armies in a makeshift 'camp of return' run by Hizbullah at Marj al-Zuhour – reliving the Palestinian experience of forced exile in microcosm for the TV cameras – the court ruled that it could not intervene further. The PLO suspended its participation in the Washington talks. It tried to secure the return of the deportees, but relations with Hamas worsened when Arafat refused to accept the Islamists' demand for 40 per cent of the seats on the PNC.[15] Hamas denounced the expulsion and warned that while it had previously attacked only soldiers, it would now target 'every Zionist in Palestine'.

ROAD TO OSLO

It was against this tense backdrop – punctuated by reminders of the cost and difficulty of maintaining the status quo – that the first moves took place to initiate direct talks between Israel and the PLO. The seed had been sown earlier at a meeting between the Labour politician Yossi Beilin, a protégé of Peres, and Terje Rød-Larsen of the Norwegian Institute for Applied Social Research, which had worked in the occupied territories. Over lunch at an Indian restaurant in Tel Aviv, Larsen suggested that Norway – which had long had good relations with the PLO and was not a member of the European Community – could be a conduit for discreet Israeli–Palestinian contacts, and a formal offer was made by Oslo when Beilin was serving as Peres's deputy in the foreign ministry. In December the Knesset passed the first reading of a bill removing a ban on contacts with PLO representatives. Starting in January 1993 some fourteen meetings took place in Norway between Israeli academics and Palestinian officials. None of this, crucially, was known to the participants in the still-suspended Washington talks. The backchannel remained a fairly well-kept secret for nearly nine months. 'Keeping secrets', as Peres observed dryly, 'is not usually one of our national characteristics.'[16]

Initially the involvement was asymmetrical: the Israelis, Yair Hirschfeld and Ron Pundak, were university political scientists linked to Beilin, who was operating on his own initiative. Hirschfeld, a veteran of 'track-two' diplomacy, was close to Faisal Husseini and Hanan Ashrawi. The PLO, by contrast, was involved at a high level, represented by Ahmed Qurei (Abu Alaa), Arafat's adviser and head of the PLO economic department, and two colleagues. Neither the PLO Executive Committee nor the Fatah Central Committee was informed. The intention was not to circumvent the Washington talks but to overcome the obstacles they had encountered. Progress was surprisingly fast. By March, after three rounds of talks, the parties agreed a draft declaration of principles constructed around a crucial distinction between *interim* and *permanent* status issues. The former included Israeli withdrawals and the creation of Palestinian self-government. East Jerusalem was a permanent status issue, along with refugees, settlements, borders, sovereignty and security arrangements. Leaving the thorniest elements of any agreement to one side was a huge concession by the PLO. Beilin informed Peres, and Peres Rabin, of what had been happening. 'The PLO men in Oslo were more flexible, more imaginative and more authoritative than the West Bank-Gaza team negotiating in Washington,' Peres told the prime minister.[17] Rabin initially resisted, arguing that 'the Tunis group' were 'the extremist element among the Palestinians . . . and they are preventing the more moderate elements from advancing in the negotiations with us'.[18] But he then changed tack and agreed to pursue the Oslo channel. Another calculation played a significant role in this shift: the Israelis were well aware of the PLO's grave financial crisis – a disastrous legacy of Arafat's support for Saddam Hussein during the Kuwait crisis, and of internal divisions over it. No official figures were available, but the organization was believed to be effectively bankrupt. The Israelis' insights may have been enriched by the fact that an aide to Hakam Balawi, Abu Iyad's successor as the organization's security chief, had been spying for the Mossad.[19] The aide, Adnan Yassin, reportedly installed bugging devices in a chair and desk light in the office of Arafat's veteran deputy, Mahmoud Abbas (Abu Mazen), as the Oslo talks proceeded. Abbas, the surveillance revealed, was on very bad terms with the PLO leader.[20] It was clear to Israel that Arafat was weak and had few options. It made sense to try to capitalize on that.

While all this was going on behind the scenes, violence escalated. In March 1993 alone fifteen Israeli civilians and soldiers were killed by Palestinians, many in stabbing attacks. That triggered a new policy of permanent closure of the green line 'until further notice'. After that, approvals to enter not only Israel but also East Jerusalem 'were granted sparingly and according to criteria unknown to Palestinians'.[21] The country's most famous cartoonist, Dosh, deployed his iconic character Srulik – Israel's fresh-faced equivalent of the defiant Palestinian Handala, in his trademark biblical sandals, khaki shorts and *kova tembel* (dunce) hat – to peer sceptically at a map of the country, with the 1967 border clearly marked, in the shape of a fearsome-looking knife, as a genial-looking dove explains: 'Don't worry, there is a political solution to terrorism.'[22] Seventeen Palestinians were killed by Israelis in the same period, though that, as ever, attracted less attention. 'Separation from the Palestinians was meant to define once more the psychological borders within which Israeli citizens could feel safe', commented Meron Benvenisti.[23]

When the sixth round of the secret Norwegian talks began in May, Israel for the first time sent official representatives to meet the PLO – a significant commitment that meant the stakes were higher because any leak would expose the process to intense and potentially fatal scrutiny, especially at home. Uri Savir, director-general of the foreign ministry, and Joel Singer, a legal adviser, proposed that any agreement on self-rule be implemented first in the Gaza Strip. The Palestinians responded that Jericho should be added (apparently fearing that 'Gaza first' might also prove to be 'Gaza last') and the two areas linked via a 'safe corridor'. That issue and others, including a Palestinian police force, were also being discussed in the talks in Washington, and were thus the subject of public statements. 'I cannot let it be said that I sold out the West Bank for Gaza,' Arafat told *Haaretz* in mid-June.[24] Shortly afterwards, at the seventh round in Norway (coinciding with the resumption of sessions in the US capital) the Israelis introduced the notion of 'mutual recognition' between Israel and the PLO – a concept that was very attractive to Arafat. 'I believed that the PLO was keen to win Israeli recognition as a legitimate negotiating partner, and would be willing to pay a high price for this', Singer explained.[25] Beilin also spelled out how Israel saw the move: 'If there were to be mutual recognition the PLO could promise an end to the intifada and the cessation of all acts of terror on its part, the disarming of other groups – on its arrival in Gaza – and so forth.'[26] In the light of decades of animosity, this was a truly stunning change. But Rabin, for the moment, remained cautious.

By July they were discussing details of Israeli redeployments and numbers of Palestinian police. The Declaration of Principles (DOP) was signed in Oslo by Savir and Qurei on 19 August. It was not made public, and the two sides had still not recognized each other. News of a meeting in Norway between Peres and Mahmoud Abbas broke a week later and caused a sensation. When details of the agreement began to leak out, denunciation followed – first from Hamas and then by the *Yesha* (Judaea and Samaria) settlers council, which decried the DOP as 'national treason'. Qurei had expected 'concern and alarm, with fears of treachery and betrayal'.[27] He was right. Fatah did accept the accord, though there were strong misgivings in Palestine and beyond about what one observer called Arafat's 'secretive, devious, whimsical, autocratic style . . . financial mismanagement and his abuse of funds for personal and political ends'.[28] Talks, no longer secret, continued about the hyper-sensitive question of recognition.[29]

Shafiq al-Hout, who represented the PLO in Beirut, resigned from the executive committee, as did his colleague, the poet Mahmoud Darwish. 'We, the Palestinian people, have given everything to Israel in return for one concession: that Israel recognises the PLO. That recognition rescued Arafat at a very difficult juncture in his life. We should ask ourselves why Israel wanted to save him.' Criticism of Arafat and his supporters was harsh and unyielding. 'I left him', wrote al-Hout, 'in the company of the group of hypocrites who were going to build him Hong Kong and Singapore on the sands of the Gaza Strip and the hills of the West Bank.'[30] In Israel there was profound shock – especially given the demonization of Arafat over many years. Tens of thousands of right-wing Israelis protested outside Rabin's official residence on Jerusalem's Balfour Street. Binyamin ('Bibi') Netanyahu, who had succeeded Yitzhak Shamir as Likud leader, was cheered wildly as he denounced the prime minister's 'lies', and there was loud booing every time he mentioned Arafat.

HANDSHAKE ON THE LAWN

The Oslo agreement was signed on 13 September 1993 on the White House lawn. President Bill Clinton had to coax a visibly reluctant Rabin to shake Arafat's hand, a vivid display of body language that betrayed deeply held feelings to the millions watching on TV around the world. Israelis looked on in disbelief, many flocking to bars and beaches in Tel Aviv to celebrate. Palestinians were exhilarated by the prospect of an end to occupation. It meant 'no more harassment by soldiers, no more road blocks, no more random arrests, no more land confiscation, no more settlements, no more settlers with their Uzis playing feudal masters', as Sari Nusseibeh exulted. But Fatah activists were assailed by opponents from left and right.[31] The documents were signed by Peres and Abbas on the same walnut table that had been used to sign the Egyptian-Israeli peace treaty in 1979. The 'Declaration of Principles on Interim Self-Government Arrangements' comprised seventeen articles and four annexes. It was intended to install an 'elected Council for the Palestinian people in the West Bank and Gaza Strip, for a transitional period not exceeding five years, leading to a permanent settlement based on UN Security Council Resolutions 242 and 338'. The timetable was spelled out, with the five-year-period beginning with 'the withdrawal from the Gaza Strip and Jericho area'. That would be followed by negotiations on an 'interim agreement' for a 'transfer of powers and responsibilities from the Israeli military government ... to the Council'. No more than three years into the transition, negotiations were to be held on issues including Jerusalem, refugees, settlements, security arrangements, borders, relations and co-operation with other neighbours.

Alongside the DOP was an exchange of letters between Arafat and Rabin. The PLO recognized 'the right of the State of Israel to exist in peace and security' as well as committing itself to resolve 'all outstanding issues through negotiations'. It renounced the use of 'terrorism and other acts of violence' and spelled out that 'those articles of the Palestinian covenant which deny Israel's right to exist . . . are now inoperative and no longer valid'. Rabin's terse but ground-breaking response was that 'Israel has decided to recognise the PLO as the representative of the Palestinian people and commence negotiations with the PLO within the Middle East peace process'. Israel notably made no mention of either Palestinian rights or a Palestinian state. The Israelis also insisted that Arafat sign his letter to Rabin as the chairman of the PLO, and not, as he had done in his correspondence since the declaration of independence in 1988, as the president of Palestine. The Arabic word *Rais* carried both English meanings. It was an important distinction.[32]

The Oslo agreement deserved the overused adjective historic. It did not resolve the Israeli–Palestinian conflict but it set out a series of steps for doing so, with advantages to both sides along the way. Mutual recognition superseded what Arafat had announced at the UN in Geneva in 1988. It was an extraordinary step given the history of the Arab–Zionist confrontation and the hostility and mistrust that had accumulated over a century. It gave the Palestinians authority on their territory for the first time – though, crucially, not over the Israelis who were living there, nor control of its borders. It meant a return to Palestinian soil, albeit a limited one, from a base 3,000 miles away.

Yet Oslo was a fragile construct that gave innumerable hostages to fortune. It was vague and open-ended: the final goal was not spelled out. And the imbalance in power between the two sides was enormous, to the extent that the agreement's many critics were to denounce the whole exercise as a form of 'outsourcing' by Israel to the Palestinians, of 'occupation by remote control'[33] or the substitution of direct colonial rule for indirect or 'neo-colonial' rule. Each side had an unspoken fallback: the Israelis to hold on to the occupied territories; the Palestinians to return to resistance. Israel's most important gains – recognition by the Palestinians and the pledge by them to stop fighting – were immediate. But the core issues of the conflict – still the subject of enormous gaps – remained untouched. That was a fatal flaw that would be endlessly debated in the years to come. 'Because Israel had already received most of what its leaders wanted, the incentives to make further painful concessions were low, especially ones that involved huge domestic costs', one expert argued later. 'The fact that Israel had most of its gains in hand . . . meant that the Palestinians had very few levers with which they could influence Israeli negotiators.' Another serious problem was the absence of an official arbitrator in case of disagreements.[34] And the refugee question, so central to Palestinian identity and politics, was marginalized as the PLO prepared for a limited return home from its North African wilderness. For the 1948 refugees there was no answer to the poignant question posed by Mahmoud Darwish: 'Where will the birds fly after the last sky?'[35]

The scale of the challenge was clear even to the keenest Palestinian supporters of Oslo: 'This agreement,' Abbas told the PLO central council in Tunis,

> carries in its bowels either an independent state or the consecration of
> the occupation. It all depends on our mentality as we deal with it . . .
> We are an educated people. As individuals, we have built much around
> the world. Now comes the test: can we build the institutions that can
> rebuild this scorched land? The mind of the revolution is very different
> from the mind of the state. We must all put on new robes and think
> with new minds if we are to build this state.[36]

Fatah's central committee approved the declaration by twelve votes to six. Hamas and Islamic Jihad objected forcefully. For the PFLP, Oslo was 'the biggest blow to the Palestinian national struggle in its history'. Ahmed Jibril of the PFLP-General Command threatened to kill Arafat, warning that the agreement would 'trigger a civil war' and liquidate the *intifada*.[37]

In Israel, two days of debate in the Knesset ended on 23 September with sixty-one votes in favour of the accord, fifty against and eight abstentions. Arab parties, outside Rabin's coalition, supported the government. It was a small margin for such an important agreement. Labour supporters framed the issue as a strategic choice for *both* sides. 'The Palestinians understand that they are struggling not to get what they have wanted, but to save what they can,' commented the eloquent but now politically marginal Abba Eban. 'There are better things for Israelis to do than chase Palestinian stone-throwers in the squalid alleys of Gaza.'[38] Eban's Labour Zionist view captured the most positive elements of support for Oslo in Israel. But sceptics expressed grave concern that the Palestinian move was a tactical one, consistent with the PLO's

old strategy of setting up a 'national authority' on any liberated territory until the entire territory could be freed. Palestinian recognition of
Israel was thus dismissed as a ploy in the service of the 'true' long-term
goal of the elimination of the Jewish state. Yitzhak Shamir, the former
Likud prime minister, condemned the 'indecent haste' and 'total secrecy'
with which Rabin had moved to seal a 'formerly unthinkable partnership' with Arafat – who, he argued, was bankrupt, discredited and
facing the collapse of the PLO. 'For the first time ever, an Israeli government had consented to give away parts of the Land of Israel, thus helping
to pave the way to the virtually inevitable establishment of a Palestinian
state in Judea, Samaria and Gaza – though its leaders have repeatedly
pledged that this grim possibility will never be realised.'[39] In January
1994 West Bank settlers began a campaign to set up new outposts –
'Operation *Machpil*' (Double) – to ensure that territory was not surrendered. For the liberal commentator Meron Benvenisti, the true
meaning of Arafat's move was crystal clear:

> By shaking the hand of the first and only native prime minister of
> Israel, scion of the Zionist founding fathers, he committed an act of
> surrender. Out of responsibility for his vanquished people, he asked
> for terms and begged for the magnanimity of the victors. For he reck-
> oned that there was no other option but to admit defeat.[40]

Support for Oslo among Palestinians was highest in Gaza and Jericho, perhaps reflecting the local impact of the now-imminent change.[41]
Still, there too concern was expressed that the agreement included no
commitment by the Israelis to remove settlements. Even more fundamental objections were expressed by members of the Palestinian
negotiating team in Washington who had been kept in the dark.
Abdel-Shafi, stung by the discovery of the Oslo channel, noted that
the agreement was 'phrased in terms of generalities that leave room
for wide interpretations'.[42] Faisal Husseini described Oslo as 'not
peace, just a declaration aimed at achieving peace'.[43] Hanan Ashrawi
was highly critical of the failure to obtain any guarantees from Israel.
'It is not who makes the agreement, but what it is,' she told Abbas,
rejecting the suggestion that she and her colleagues felt manipulated.
'I have no ego problems about being excluded or kept in the dark. We
know the Israelis and know that they will exploit their power as

occupier to the hilt and by the time you get to permanent status, Israel will have permanently altered realities on the ground.'[44] The American-Palestinian intellectual Edward Said attacked the 'supine abjectness' of the PLO, and argued that Israel's leaders never intended to promote Palestinian self-determination and statehood, but rather to perpetuate the occupation and confine autonomy to strictly municipal matters. Oslo had been 'a Palestinian Versailles', he concluded angrily, barely a month after the signing.

> Now that some of the euphoria has lifted, it is possible to re-examine the Israeli–PLO agreement with the required common sense. What emerges from such scrutiny is a deal that is more flawed and, for most of the Palestinian people, more unfavourably weighted than many had first supposed. The fashion-show vulgarities of the White House ceremony, the degrading spectacle of Yasser Arafat thanking everyone for the suspension of most of his people's rights, and the fatuous solemnity of Bill Clinton's performance, like a 20th-century Roman emperor shepherding two vassal kings through rituals of reconciliation and obeisance: all these only temporarily obscure the truly astonishing proportions of the Palestinian capitulation.[45]

ENEMIES CO-OPERATE

Enemies of the agreement gathered on both sides, but steps towards implementation went ahead. The mood was a strange mixture of excitement and suspicion. In October Palestinian and Israeli negotiators agreed the release of a first batch of the total of 12,000 Palestinian prisoners. Officials met in Cairo and El Arish. Warren Christopher, the US secretary of state, marked a first by meeting Arafat in Tunis. Shimon Peres and Yasser Abed-Rabbo met in Paris but failed to agree on the size of the area round Jericho to be evacuated. In November Yaakov Perry, the head of the Shin Bet, and Amnon Lipkin-Shahak, the IDF deputy chief of staff, held talks with the Fatah security chiefs Mohammed Dahlan and Jibril Rajoub in Geneva and concluded an agreement on anti-terrorist co-operation.[46] The two Palestinians had spent years in Israeli gaols and spoke Hebrew peppered with the coarsest slang, helping establish 'a backslapping relationship'.[47] Perry also met Amin al-Hindi, the Fatah intelligence chief, whom the Israelis believed had been involved in planning the Munich Olympics massacre in 1972. Their first encounter, arranged by the Americans, was understandably tense – perhaps because another of the alleged Munich planners, Atef Bseiso, had been assassinated, presumably by Israeli agents, in Paris in 1992. But the two spooks stayed in touch when Hindi was allowed to return to Gaza shortly afterwards.[48] Rabin, tellingly, had been especially keen to devolve security matters to Arafat: 'The Palestinians will be better at it than we were', he argued, 'because they will allow no appeals to the supreme court and will prevent the Israeli Association of Civil Rights from criticising conditions there by denying it access to the area. They will rule by their own methods, freeing, and this is most important, Israeli army soldiers from having to do what they will do.'[49] Israeli human rights activists took this as a backhanded compliment to their effectiveness.[50]

Then, in February 1994, came a hammer-blow, wielded by a fanatical opponent of Oslo. Baruch Goldstein, an American-born settler living in Kiryat Arba, dressed in army uniform and armed with an assault rifle, mowed down twenty-nine worshippers at the Ibrahimi mosque in Hebron. In the ensuing carnage, five more Palestinians were killed in Hebron and a further six elsewhere in the occupied territories. Scores more were injured. Goldstein fired more than a hundred rounds before his gun jammed and he was overpowered and beaten to death by survivors. Goldstein's was the act of one individual, but his views were far from unique. It was the worst incident of its kind in twenty-six years of Israeli rule and one of the bloodiest in the long and bloody history of the conflict. Goldstein, a doctor, was a supporter of the Kach movement, the most extreme manifestation of anti-Arab prejudice in Israel. He was also vengeful: in December 1993 a father and son, friends of his from Kiryat Arba, had been murdered in Hebron. Rabin, in condemning the killings, was keen to emphasize Goldstein's American background. 'The process by which demonised enemies were becoming legitimate adversaries haggling over details of a historical compromise was blocked and possibly reversed', commented Amos Elon. 'The event showed how the sinister passion of one man could affect Arab–Israeli affairs.'[51] Talks in Cairo and Taba were broken off and by the time they resumed, over a month later, the death toll had risen further. Arafat called for international protection for Palestinians. Furious settlers denounced Rabin and hundreds gathered at Goldstein's tomb to honour his memory. Pressure mounted to remove the Hebron settlers, but Rabin failed to respond. That was seen later as a tragically missed opportunity.

Retribution was not long in coming. In Afula on 6 April, eight Israelis were killed and forty-four injured when a car bomb exploded at a bus stop. Hamas called it a reprisal for the Hebron massacre. It was a terrifying and highly significant novelty – the first suicide-bombing attack to be carried out by Palestinians against civilians in Israel. 'The strategy of Hamas is to increase actions against military targets and settler targets,' a spokesman said. 'We think Hamas has the right to take any action inside Palestine.' The attack, it transpired, was planned by the movement's chief bomb-maker, Yahya Ayyash, whom the Israelis nicknamed 'the engineer' and was soon being described as 'the most wanted man in Palestine'. A week later a bus bomb in Hadera killed five Israelis as well as the teenage West Banker who detonated the device. The incident was described by Hamas as the second in a series of five attacks. Fatah, apparently alarmed by the growing appeal of its rival, began to emphasize Islamic terminology in announcements and slogans. On a visit to South Africa, Arafat compared Oslo to the Treaty of Hudaibiyah that the Prophet Muhammad had signed, from a position of weakness, with the Quraysh, an Arabian tribe that had refused to accept Islam, but which he breached when his power increased. According to the interpretation favoured in Israel, his comments implied that he would breach the terms of Oslo without hesitation and return to war in the future. Gazans saw Arafat as 'going to great lengths to offer some comforting quasi-historical comparisons that would perhaps help to sweeten his people's bitter sense of impotence and frustration'.[52]

On 4 May 1994 Rabin and Arafat met in Cairo, under Hosni Mubarak's auspices, to sign the Gaza–Jericho self-rule accord. It called for a final peace agreement to be reached within five years. The size and weaponry of the Palestinian security forces and arrangements for joint patrols with the IDF were fixed. Arafat baulked, in front of the TV cameras and hundreds of VIP guests, at endorsing a map of the Jericho area. It was a show of histrionics that was simultaneously embarrassing and unconvincing. 'Not a single Palestinian . . . mistook his performance for toughness or saw anything in it beyond a piece of play-acting', noted one critic. 'They knew that he had already accepted whatever fiefdom the Israelis had ceded to him and that the all-important issue of sovereignty had been progressively eroded.'[53] Mubarak was furious at Arafat for spoiling the ceremony, audibly calling him '*kalb, ibn kalb*' (son of a dog).[54]

In the following days Gaza and Jericho were evacuated by the Israelis, who turned over army bases and police stations to Palestinian units. PLO officials, including well-known former prisoners such as Rajoub and Dahlan, arrived from Tunis and Lebanon. Nasser Youssef, a PLA general, was in overall command. Excitement mounted: 'There is palpable delight among virtually all Gazans to be rid of the occupation, and to have among them instead the men universally known as "our brothers"', one journalist reported.

> It shows in the spontaneous gifts of food, furniture, building equipment, TV sets and other comforts for the troops. It shows too in the window of the Studio Lina, a photographic shop opposite the main gate of the military headquarters, where there are scores of pictures of the new heroes posing with their relatives, friends, or simply with people who want to be seen with a Palestinian in uniform.[55]

Linked to the accord was the Paris Protocol, which regulated economic relations between Israel and the Palestinian Authority (PA) for the interim period. It preserved a Palestinian economy that was both integrated into and dependent on Israel, reflecting the disparity in power and the Palestinian need for access to Israel's labour market. Israel had sole control over external borders, the collection of import taxes and VAT, and was thus able – crucially – to withhold financial transfers as a means of pressure or punishment.

THE RETURN

Arafat, escorted by President Mubarak to the Rafah border crossing, entered the Gaza Strip on 1 July 1994, to be welcomed by cheering

crowds waiting under a scorching sun. It was the first time the PLO
leader had set foot on Palestinian soil since 1967, over a quarter of a
century earlier. On the way to Gaza City, at Kfar Darom, one of the
fifteen Jewish settlements in the enclave, his motorcade passed protesters waving blue and white Israeli flags, guarded by Israeli troops who
were sharing control of this section of the road with Palestinian police.
'Kill the murderer' one of their banners said. Another read: 'Arafat =
Hitler'. On arrival Arafat spoke from the balcony of the old legislative
council, until a few weeks earlier Israel's military headquarters, and
defended his 'peace of the brave' with Rabin. 'I want to remind you
that we have a big mission ahead of us . . . to build this homeland, to
build our institutions and to rebuild the institutions that Israeli occupation destroyed,' Arafat declared. 'We need national unity. National
unity. Unity. Unity. Unity.'[56] In that vein he demanded the release of
Sheikh Ahmed Yassin, the gaoled Hamas leader, and pledged, in the
name of the 'martyrs' of the Palestinian revolution, that Jerusalem
would be the capital of their independent state. It was a highly significant moment. Two days later he visited a school in the Jabaliya refugee
camp – the largest in the strip and the birthplace of the *intifada* in
1987 – as an Israeli helicopter hovered overhead and his guards struggled to protect him. 'I know many of you here think Oslo is a bad
agreement,' Arafat told the chanting crowd, surprisingly frankly. 'It is
a bad agreement. But it's the best we can get in the worst situation.'[57]
Arafat, it transpired, had exploited the occasion to smuggle in an
adviser, Mamdouh Nofal, who had been military commander of the
DFLP when it carried out the Maalot attack of 1974 – and was on an
Israeli blacklist: the Israelis insisted he and three others leave the territory.[58] It was a blunt reminder of where power really lay: 'Beside the
shining symbol of "the Return" walked its shadow – submission to
Israel's overwhelming might and reliance on its magnanimity and will-
ingness to assist . . . in the process of Palestinian nation-building.'[59] But
Arafat, Nofal recalled later, had been convinced that Israeli recognition would lead inevitably to a Palestinian state, and he was 'overjoyed'
by the redeployment of Israeli forces out of Jericho and Gaza.

> It was this conviction that led him – and the Oslo team – not to scru-
> tinise the text of the Oslo agreement very carefully. He had supreme

confidence in his ability to change the rules of the game after accepting them, just as he had done at Madrid when he agreed to the PLO's exclusion from the Washington talks, only to impose its participation later.[60]

Progress continued over the summer. Joint Israeli–Palestinian patrols began, though the disparity between the two sides in numbers, equipment and capability was striking. 'From the moment we entered Gaza it looked like, my God, peace has come,' reminisced Fatah's Nabil Shaath. 'We were doing things fast, we were building trust.'[61] The Shin Bet established a close relationship with Rajoub in Jericho and Dahlan in Gaza, who carried out Arafat's instructions, though without any defined legal framework. Their men arrested criminals and opposition activists, including alleged Hamas supporters, and triggered objections from a few outspoken individuals. Amnesty International counted more than eight hundred people detained by the end of 1994 on political grounds. They were not allowed to meet lawyers and most were never brought to trial. Hamas called on Palestinian security officers to 'end their collaboration with Israel against the resistance fighters and to join the Jihad'.

In October 1994 a new crisis blew up when Hamas kidnapped a young Israeli soldier, Nachshon Wachsman, and gave the government 24 hours to free 200 Palestinian prisoners, including Sheikh Yassin. Rabin phoned Arafat to say that he held him and the PA responsible for the soldier's safety. Just as this bleak drama unfolded, the two were imminently expected to be awarded the Nobel Prize for the peace agreement they had signed. The Israelis initially believed the soldier was being held in Gaza but in fact he was in a village near Jerusalem that was still under IDF control, where he was killed by his captors in a failed rescue attempt, along with an Israeli officer and three men from the Qassam Brigades, the Hamas military wing. It was believed that the kidnappers had been traced by Palestinian intelligence and the information passed to the Israelis. Hamas supporters marched on Gaza's central prison to mourn the kidnappers. Hundreds were rounded up. Rabin's cabinet – again lambasted by right-wingers – voted to resume talks with the PLO.

Then, a week later, twenty-two Israelis were killed on Dizengoff

Street in the heart of Tel Aviv during the morning rush hour when a suicide bomber targeted a No. 5 bus. It was the worst terrorist attack inside Israel since 1978. Arafat condemned the bombing and offered his condolences. But outside the defence ministry hundreds of protesters held a torchlight vigil, chanting 'Death to Rabin'. Netanyahu said the prime minister was 'personally responsible' for the attacks since Oslo. Hamas, warned Peres, wants Israelis to 'lose our heads and stop the peace process. No way on earth.' But that process, just over a year since the drama on the White House lawn, was already in trouble.

Good news intruded on this gloomy atmosphere in late October when Israel and Jordan finalized their peace treaty – the product of decades of clandestine contact and the logical outcome of King Hussein's 1988 disengagement from the West Bank, and of the Oslo accord, which was negotiated without Jordan's knowledge. Hussein, Rabin, Bill Clinton and 5,000 guests met for the signing ceremony between these 'best of enemies' on the border in the Arava desert. Arafat was conspicuously not invited; he condemned an agreement which sidelined Palestinian ambitions and grievances, and which formally recognized Jordanian custodianship of the Muslim holy places in East Jerusalem. The apparently genuine cordiality between Rabin and the Hashemite monarch also stood in stark contrast to the suspicious and troubled relations between the Israeli and Palestinian leaders – and the very great difficulties they faced. Still, continuing attacks by Hamas and Islamic Jihad forced them to work closely together.

In November, squeezed between Rabin and his own people, Arafat attended a memorial event for Hani Abed, an Islamic Jihad activist who had been assassinated by the Israelis. He was greeted with jeering and shouts of 'collaborator' and had his *keffiyeh* torn off his head. Arafat moved more decisively against the Islamists after that: a few days later fourteen Palestinians were shot dead by police in Gaza on 'Black Friday' – the worst display of internal unrest since the Israeli pullout. Now there was no missing the alarming signs that popular support for Oslo was dwindling in the face of disillusion and the absence of obvious benefits – and that the Islamists were gaining ground. The PA security forces were opened up to Fatah activists and the number of Palestinian policemen increased from 8,000 to about 18,000.[62] 'Neither Rabin nor Arafat can stop Hamas', warned Abdel-Shafi. 'Only the people can. But they must have something precious to defend.'[63] The Israeli government was under heavy pressure too. In January 1995 a double suicide bombing killed nineteen soldiers at a bus stop at Beit Lidd outside Netanya, near a coffee stand used by IDF personnel returning from weekend leave. Islamic Jihad claimed responsibility for that attack, naming the two 'martyrs' as residents of the Gaza Strip. When Rabin visited the scene of the carnage his car was attacked by a furious crowd crying 'Traitor!' and 'How much longer?'

20

1995–1999

'The only light at the end of the tunnel is the flash of the next terrorist blast.'

Nahum Barnea, 1997[1]

ASSASSIN OF PEACE

On the evening of 9 November 1995, three Palestinian VIPs were driven to the north of the Gaza Strip where they boarded an Israeli military helicopter which flew up the coast to Sdeh Dov airfield in Tel Aviv. Under heavy security they were escorted to the nearby home of Yitzhak Rabin to offer their condolences to his widow, Leah. Yasser Arafat, in olive green battledress but without his trademark *keffiyeh* – his head looking startlingly bald and wide in the lights of the cameras – sat next to the grieving woman, drinking tea against a background of flowers. It was a strange, almost hallucinatory event, Arafat showing off his very limited knowledge of Hebrew.[2] On the short flight the PLO leader had refused to look down at the twinkling lights of the Israeli landscape, even at the famous minaret of the old Hassan Bek mosque in Jaffa, instead 'bowing his head and looking neither right nor left . . . throughout that strange journey, though it was a once-in-a-lifetime chance for us to see our beloved country'. Ahmed Qurei, who had negotiated the Oslo accords, never asked Arafat why it was that he did not want to see the panorama of 'historic Palestine', but he speculated: 'Perhaps he remembered how it was and did not wish to see what it had become.'[3] It was the first time that Arafat – who was wearing a black coat and hat and was thus unrecognized by the crowds waiting outside the Rabins' apartment on Rav Ashi Street – had set foot inside Israel since his clandestine mission to rally resistance to the occupation in the wake of the 1967 war.

Rabin's assassination by a right-wing Jewish extremist five days earlier was a body blow to Oslo and the 'peace of the brave' that Arafat praised to Leah, her family and the assembled Israelis. A rickety, provisional structure that was already under heavy fire from determined enemies on both sides had just lost one of the two leaders who had had the courage to implement it. When Nabil Shaath broke the news of Rabin's murder, Arafat responded: 'Today the peace process has died.'[4]

Arafat had asked, via the US consul in Jerusalem, to attend the funeral, but Shimon Peres, who was now acting prime minister, refused, citing security concerns.[5] Instead Qurei represented the PLO as Rabin was interred in a solemn ceremony on Mount Herzl, where Bill Clinton, King Hussein and Hosni Mubarak were among the 5,000 mourners. Qurei reflected afterwards on the solicitousness of the crew of the IDF helicopter that had flown Arafat, the Fatah veteran Mahmoud Abbas and himself to Tel Aviv; it was the same type of aircraft that had often been used to hunt down and kill Palestinian fighters. Times, it seemed, really had changed.

Yigal Amir, the right-wing Jewish extremist who fired the shots that killed Rabin at a pro-peace rally in Kikar Malchei Yisrael in Tel Aviv, was a man on a mission. The law student from Herzliya had been planning the murder for two years, once taking out his Beretta pistol to kill the prime minister but aborting the mission at the last minute. The previous year he had attended the funeral of Baruch Goldstein, perpetrator of the Hebron massacre. The political mood in Israel was ugly and deeply divided. Rabin had been portrayed wearing a *keffiyeh* and in SS uniform, including at one anti-Oslo demonstration in Jerusalem where Binyamin Netanyahu had been the main speaker. 'Crowds chanted "Rabin is the son of a whore" or "murderer" or vilified him for "leading the country to the gates of Auschwitz" or making a "pact with the devil" – Arafat.'[6] Amir was a loner, but he had friends, supporters and a wider constituency. Extremist rabbis had formulated the notion that the prime minister's policies constituted treachery that justified his killing for the sake of the Jewish people. Following his detention, moments after the shooting on 4 November, the twenty-five-year-old Amir stunned investigators with his sangfroid, even asking for a glass so he could drink a toast – 'a schnapps' – to Rabin's death. 'I acted alone on God's orders and I have no regrets,' he told them.[7]

Rabin had not gone 'soft' on terrorism or indulged Arafat. Six months before his murder, when Hamas suicide bombers killed seven Israeli soldiers in the Gaza Strip, the prime minister had cracked down hard.[8] On paper Arafat remained committed to fighting the Islamists, arresting hundreds and repeatedly warning Hamas and Islamic Jihad to respect the Oslo accords. Yet whether he was unwilling or unable – or both – to crack down hard enough, every Palestinian attack boosted Israeli hardliners in a way that appeared to be following a clear strategy: a bus bombing that killed five elderly Israelis in Ramat Gan in July seemed timed to force a crisis in Israeli–PLO bargaining on the eve of a deadline for the completion of the next stage of the Oslo negotiations. In a poll conducted after that bombing, 52 per cent of Israelis said the talks should be broken off and only 37 per cent said they should continue. Fatah accused unnamed 'traitors who hide behind headlines and slogans' of sabotaging Israeli withdrawal from the West Bank and the freeing of Palestinian prisoners.[9] Each bombing brought punitive Israeli counter-measures – mass arrests, curfews and, above all, prolonged crossing closures – that caused serious hardship to ordinary Palestinians and undermined the feeling that there was any benefit from the changes that had taken place.

Still they had ploughed on. In September 1995, the Oslo II agreement was finalized in talks at Taba, just over the Egyptian border near Eilat. It regulated relations between Israel and the Palestinians during the interim period towards negotiations for a 'Permanent Status Agreement'. Its 300-plus pages and multiple annexes dealt with the entire West Bank, excluding East Jerusalem, and a plan for a progressive Israeli military withdrawal. The expanded Palestinian security forces – now 30,000 police and 6 separate branches – took on responsibility for 'combating terrorism and violence, and preventing incitement to violence'. District Co-ordination Offices were established. Border passage arrangements at the Allenby Bridge and Rafah crossing had separate wings for both parties, formal Palestinian control represented by uniformed policemen and a flag but a parallel Israeli presence that was concealed from view by one-sided mirrors.[10] The establishment of a 'Palestinian Interim Self-Government Authority' and a Palestinian parliament were the most eye-catching parts of the deal – with provision for elections to be held for the first time.

Yet the more significant part was the territorial arrangements it laid down. The occupied territories were divided into three zones: Area A consisted of Palestinian towns and urban areas and comprised 2.8 per cent of the territory; here the PA had full responsibility for law and order. Area B was made up of villages and sparsely populated areas, comprising 22.9 per cent of the West Bank: there the PA looked after public order while the Israelis retained overall security control. By far the largest part, at 74.3 per cent of the territory, was Area C, which comprised important agricultural areas and water sources and where Israel retained full responsibility for security and public order. That meant that the PA was responsible for managing *all* Palestinian residents but had full control of just 2.8 per cent of the land.[11] The West Bank and Gaza Strip were recognized as a single territorial unit, but with a highly significant and overarching reservation – 'with the exception of issues that will be negotiated in Permanent Status negotiations'. It was at this time that Palestinian support for the peace process was at its highest: 71 per cent. Even among students, typically the most hard-line group among Palestinians, support for negotiations increased from 44 per cent in January 1994 to 62 per cent in August – September 1995, with opposition to talks dropping from 47 per cent to 24 per cent over the same period.[12] Oslo II received 72 per cent approval in October 1995, the highest level of support for the peace process ever registered. In Israel, though, a hardening mood was reflected in the Knesset vote for Oslo II: it passed by a tiny margin of sixty-one votes to fifty-nine in early October. Right-wingers were unhappy, with the Likud claiming that Rabin's government had been determined to sign the agreement at any price. Eliyahu Ben-Elissar, a senior Likud MP, called it 'a black day in the history of Israel'. Shortly afterwards Netanyahu attended a ceremony reaffirming 'loyalty to *Eretz-Yisrael*' and visited the

Hebron settlers, an eloquent expression of where his sympathies lay. Exactly a month later, Rabin was dead.

SETTLING ACCOUNTS

Settlement had been a highly sensitive issue since 1967, and especially since the Likud came to power in 1977. But its significance grew enormously after Oslo as Israel sought to establish more facts on the ground pending a final peace agreement. In January 1995, a week after Rabin, Arafat and Shimon Peres received the Nobel Peace Prize, Rabin promised that Israel would stop building new settlements and would not confiscate land except what was needed for building bypass roads in the West Bank to separate Arab and Jewish traffic and reduce friction.[13] Yet within days – following the Beit Lidd bombing and the deaths of the nineteen soldiers – the cabinet approved the construction of 2,200 more housing units in the West Bank. Building in East Jerusalem – always excluded by the Israelis from any concessions or change – continued apace. The timing of these announcements appeared to be deliberate. Plans were unveiled to construct 6,500 units at Jebel Abu Ghneim – known as Har Homa in Hebrew – south of Jerusalem. The forested area, within the city's unilaterally expanded (but internationally unrecognized) post-1967 boundaries, was a popular picnic destination for Palestinian families from Bethlehem and the surrounding villages. Palestinian and Israel critics argued that it formed a natural hinterland to Beit Sahour, adjacent to Bethlehem, and that the move was provocative just weeks before the planned IDF pullout from the city. 'Only someone completely cut off from reality can believe it is possible to build a giant project like this without fatally damaging the peace process', Peace Now protested. Throughout the summer of 1995, as the second stage of Oslo approached, settlers began to speak out more forcefully, warning that they would open fire on PA security forces and fight any attempt to evict Israelis from their homes. Activists occupied new hilltop sites, setting up makeshift encampments near Jerusalem and Ramallah and bussing in supporters from inside the green line. In July a group of right-wing rabbis, including a former chief rabbi, issued a *halachic* declaration, invoking the twelfth-century scholar Maimonides that even the command of a king could be ignored if it violated the Torah: in contemporary terms that meant that troops should disobey any order to evacuate settlements. The ruling was condemned by right and left, religious and secular, but hailed by settler leaders. Yigal Amir took notice. Oslo II did not include an explicit commitment on settlements, stipulating only that 'neither side shall take initiatives or any step that will change the status of the West Bank and Gaza Strip pending the outcome of the permanent status negotiations'.[14] But the violation of the spirit of the agreement was unmistakable.

In late October Salfit, west of Nablus and within sight of the red roofs of Ariel, one of the biggest Jewish settlements in Samaria, became the first urban area to be handed over to the PA, as part of area 'A'. The Israeli army HQ was dismantled and cranes removed its concrete car-bomb barriers, a sentry box and the steel gates, complete with cement foundations. Ahmed Faris, director-general of the PA ministry of civil affairs, accepted the building from Colonel David Barel, deputy head of the military government.[15] Jenin, Qalqilya and Tulkarem followed. In December the Israelis left Nablus, Bethlehem – three days before Christmas – and finally Ramallah, on its way to becoming the interim capital of the emerging Palestinian entity, whatever it was. Israel's departure sustained the feeling that for all Oslo's flaws, significant changes were taking place. Mourid Barghouti, visiting the new Ministry of Civil Affairs in Ramallah, reflected that Palestinians were now greeted with smiles in the place where they had suffered repeated humiliations at the hands of the Israelis for so many years.[16] Nabil Qassis, a university scientist and member of the Washington talks team, described people walking 'unbelievingly' and looking at the empty cells in the Muqataa where detainees had previously been held and tortured by the Israelis.[17]

PALESTINIAN AUTHORITY, ISRAELI POWER

Under Oslo, the PA's role was limited strictly to civil affairs and internal security. As the body took shape, power shifted from the *intifada* activists to PLO functionaries returning from Tunis, usually members of Fatah's Central Committee and Revolutionary Council. PA ministers tended to be outsiders while their deputies were West Bankers or Gazans who had worked on Nusseibeh's technical committees.[18] Fatah built 'a state-like institution based upon a pact between the bureaucracy led by the authoritarian Arafat and the local elites', as one expert put it. 'These elites enjoyed what they did not receive from Israel – a share of governmental rewards and political patronage in return for their support of the administration.'[19] The Israelis were well aware of the tensions between the Tunis returnees and local people in the West Bank and Gaza.[20]

Arafat's appointments of district governors and mayors included pro-Jordanian figures who were bitter rivals of the *intifada* rank and file. In Gaza there was anger when a local 'notable' was appointed to lead Fatah. 'The leadership has shoved aside the people who have struggled, who have sacrificed for the cause', one activist complained. 'We refuse to have leaders who have lived in five-star hotels eating fish and chocolate while our people starve. The real leaders are those who are in the fields and not in hotels, those who got their education in prisons.'[21] The heads of trade unions and NGOs were replaced by Fatah loyalists 'who judged everything by how it might affect Arafat's political standing'.

The PLO leader replicated the governing style he had used in his years in Kuwait, Beirut and Tunis, receiving petitioners and supplicants like a tribal sheikh. 'Everybody was welcome – everybody, that is, except people who represented ideas, organisation or structures', commented one observer.[22] Arafat heard two hundred dignitaries complain about the collapse of the Gaza road system, problems with drains, electricity and telephones, but at the end of the meeting they all stood in line to be photographed individually shaking hands with the chairman, 'like a Hollywood star'.[23] His habit of control was most evident with financial matters. No one else could sign the cheques.[24] 'Arafat understood from the outset that security, information, and money are the major cornerstones of leadership', an adviser recalled.[25] PLO insiders joked about the 'Fakhani Rules', a reference to the methods Arafat had honed at his HQ in the Beirut suburb of that name from 1971 to 1982.[26] His specific concern was the

Palestinian Economic Council for Development and Reconstruction (PECDAR), set up by the World Bank after Oslo to channel aid to the PA. Yusuf Sayigh, the eminent economist who was its director, resigned when Arafat appointed himself chairman.[27] 'If the money didn't flow into his coffers, he would lose his ability to buy off possible challengers', as Sari Nusseibeh put it.[28]

Security was in the hands of returning Palestine Liberation Army forces – the names of personnel vetted by the Israelis[29] – which absorbed groups like the Fatah Hawks and Black Panthers, creating jobs and awarding status to the loyal foot-soldiers of the *intifada*, albeit on meagre salaries. This allowed a large number of men who had been forced to leave Lebanon for Tunis and elsewhere – and their families – to return to Palestine. Fatima Barnawi, who had spent ten years in prison for planting a bomb in a West Jerusalem cinema in late 1967, came to Gaza to command the women's units of the Palestinian police. In the Dehaisheh refugee camp dozens of former prisoners were recruited into the security forces and others into ministries and agencies as clerks, managers and directors; many were previously unemployed. The PA functioned like most Arab states, buying loyalty by providing secure jobs for a grateful people.[30] 'The effect upon Palestinian society was catastrophic', lamented Mustafa Barghouti, an opponent of Oslo from the start. 'People began to compete with one another for jobs and money, worrying about who would be the director, the sub-director, the vice-minister, and how much they would earn – because a lot of money was at stake, part outside funding, part tax revenues.'[31] The creation of competing security agencies, ministries and departments with overlapping responsibilities allowed Arafat to intervene personally to impose his own control. 'We have leaders,' said one PA minister. 'We don't have a leadership.'[32]

Elections for the eighty-eight-member Palestinian Legislative Council in January 1996, and for the position of president, were a first, limited and chaotic test of the PA's legitimacy and popularity. 'In a land where elections have never happened, effectively ruled by a man long notorious for his inability to delegate, it was always reasonable to expect a degree of muddle', reported one correspondent. 'But with the campaign under way, there is something more unpleasant in the electoral air.' Instead of a single-constituency list system, which could produce proportional representation and encourage the electorate to think in national terms, the leadership opted for sixteen constituencies in which representatives were to be elected on a first-past-the-post basis. Opponents pleaded in vain that that would encourage clan-based voting in a society in which family still outweighed ideology, and discourage pluralist and coalition politics. 'While a majority system might be suitable for stable democracies, it might not be appropriate for societies with deep political divisions and in which fundamental questions about national identity and territorial boundaries remain open', commented the political scientist Khalil Shikaki.[33]

The only candidate challenging Arafat, and only for symbolic reasons, was Samiha Khalil, a respected campaigner for women's rights as well as a forthright critic of Oslo. The race for the council was tilted in favour of Fatah. Opposition movements, including Hamas, boycotted the poll. Independent candidates included scores of disgruntled Fatah members who failed to get on the party ticket, or who were removed by Arafat.[34] Senior PLO officials who had come from Tunis, including Nabil Shaath, Ahmed Qurei and Abu Jihad's widow Intissar al-Wazir, received more votes than local people in many constituencies.[35] An army of foreign observers included former US President Jimmy Carter and teams from the European Union, Japan, Norway and Canada. The international attention did much to boost the sense of legitimacy that mattered so much to the PLO leadership. It helped that high-profile figures like Hanan Ashrawi had been elected. 'Everyone laughed', Carter recorded, 'when Arafat told me there were going to be about fifteen women on the council, adding that "Hanan counts for ten".'[36] In the end, the polls turned out to be more about consolidating power, reinforcing recognition and legitimizing peace with Israel than establishing a genuine democracy. An election-day poll found 50 per cent support for the Oslo principles with just 16 per cent opposition. Fatah commanded the support of 57 per cent.[37]

Security remained the most neuralgic issue of them all – and, as ever, Israel's overriding priority. Days before the election the Israelis finally managed to get Yahya Ayyash, the 'engineer' of Hamas bombing fame. The most wanted man in Palestine was killed in Beit Lahiya in the Gaza Strip by an explosive device planted in a mobile phone given him by a Palestinian who was working for the Israelis. Ayyash had become a legend with an 'unbelievable ability to survive ... partly because he never spent more than an hour in one place', in the words of Carmi Gillon, the Shin Bet chief who oversaw the assassination. Rabin had personally told Arafat that Ayyash had been located in Gaza but the PLO chief insisted he was in fact in Sudan. 'I know he's here and if you don't find him and hand him over to us I'm tearing up this whole agreement and putting Gaza under siege', the prime minister warned him.[38] Hundreds of thousands turned out for Ayyash's funeral in Gaza, chanting: 'We want buses, we want cars.' The hunt had begun under Rabin but the go-ahead for the killing was given by Shimon Peres. It followed in the tradition of Israel eliminating its most dangerous enemies – regardless of the consequences. The previous summer unknown gunmen, assumed to be Mossad agents, had gunned down Fathi Shikaki, the Islamic Jihad leader, who was visiting Malta on his way back from Libya to his base in Damascus.

HAMAS STRIKES BACK

Hamas took its revenge on 25 February 1996. In Jerusalem twenty-four people were killed when a powerful bomb packed with nails and ball-bearings ripped through a packed No. 18 bus near the central bus station on Jaffa Road. Another civilian was killed in an attack at a bus stop near Ashkelon. The Islamist movement said it was retaliation for the killing of Ayyash. Coincidence or not, it was also two years to the day since the Hebron massacre, when Baruch Goldstein killed twenty-nine Palestinians in the Ibrahimi mosque, an earlier test of the endurance of the Oslo agreement. Horror piled upon horror: a week later another Hamas bomber boarded another No. 18 bus near Zion Square in Jerusalem, detonating an explosive belt that killed sixteen civilians and three soldiers. The following day a bomber killed twelve in Tel Aviv:

> Crumpled corpses were scattered around the junction of Dizengoff and King George Streets, among the busiest of thoroughfares in Israel's busiest city. Debris from shattered shop fronts rained on to

mangled cars, as dazed and terrified shoppers ran helter-skelter from the scene. Within minutes the junction was crammed with police and wailing ambulances. And before any semblance of order was restored, Israel's television channels were on hand to broadcast live from the scene. In graphic detail, the cameras picked out bodies, some with their clothes blown off, and all horribly charred. There were heart-wrenching scenes of weeping children, some wearing fancy dress for the eve of the Purim festival.[39]

The unprecedented slaughter in the streets – sixty dead in eight days – cast a giant question mark over Israeli politics and over the future of Oslo. Peres was keen to step out of Rabin's shadow and win power in his own right. In early February he had announced that he was calling an early election in which, for the first time, Israelis would be voting directly for the prime minister as well as for their party of choice. The winner of the prime ministerial vote would be in pole position to form a coalition. In mid-February Peres boasted of his government's achievements, describing peace with the Palestinians as 'flourishing, unlike those in Ireland and Bosnia'. Two weeks later, now that Hamas bombers had joined the campaign, that was an unconvincing claim. Talk of a 'new Middle East' – which gave rise to cynical jokes about the 'visionary' Peres – had never sounded so hollow. The Labour leader's 20 per cent poll lead was wiped out.

Israeli troops sealed off the West Bank and Gaza, imposing a travel and trade blockade with curfews and checkpoints, cutting roads between patches of territory controlled by the PA and launching a manhunt for Hamas suspects. Hundreds of villages and towns were paralysed by strategically placed ditches and sand or stone barricades. Tanks were deployed along the green line for the first time since 1967. Scores were arrested in areas where Hamas had support, while Palestinian security forces made a similarly indiscriminate sweep and were accused of brutality to those they detained.[40] The homes of known suicide bombers were sealed prior to demolition.

Tens of thousands of Palestinians were again cut off from their jobs in Israel, the economy of the self-rule areas suffering huge losses (estimated to be roughly equivalent to what had been given or pledged by international donors in support of the PA). Hamas institutions were shut down. PA police faced stone-throwing crowds in Bir Zeit after Israeli paratroopers raided the university and surrounding villages, bursting into dormitories and apartments, rounding up students and herding them on to a football field for interrogation. Hundreds were arrested. 'We don't know who is more against us, our government or the Israelis,' complained 'Ibrahim', a twenty-year-old Gazan student who escaped the round-up. Arafat faced more abuse when he visited Ramallah shortly afterwards.[41] In the student elections a Hamas–Islamic Jihad list won twenty-three of the fifty-one seats, Fatah just seventeen. In Ramallah prison, one detainee was told by a PA security officer: 'You are here because you're divided into three types: type one are people that Israel wants arrested; type two are people that the Authority wants arrested; type three are those arrested to placate Israel, and most of you belong to that type.'[42] The Israelis were satisfied when the man who had planned the recent bus bombings, Hassan Salameh, deputy head of the Qassam Brigades, was arrested, apparently by chance, in Hebron. It was a handy boost for Peres. Peres also accused Iran, an implacable though distant enemy, of pressing 'Islamic Jihad and other subversive organisations' to attack Israel before polling day. Behind the scenes, efforts to improve security co-ordination intensified, despite what was a prickly relationship at the best of times – the Israelis patronizing and condescending in the face of nepotism, corruption and incompetence on the PA side.[43] The Palestinians blamed the growing strength of Hamas on Israel's crackdown, but Peres and Arafat still met to discuss the situation. Peres understood that there were limits to co-operation. 'Arafat', he explained,

> cannot exist as an agent. You cannot give him orders. You have to offer him incentives too. Many people have asked me if Arafat is trustworthy . . . He didn't become a Zionist, neither will he become a Zionist . . . He's the leader of the Palestinians, and that's what he will remain. We can meet as partners for peace, but we cannot make out of him an instrument to realise our policies.[44]

The Labour leader was soon embroiled in a new crisis, this time in south Lebanon, where Israel had been shelling Hizbullah positions and hitting targets as far north as Beirut during five weeks of cross-border exchanges. But when, in the course of the 18-day 'Operation

Grapes of Wrath', Israeli shells hit a UN base at Qana and killed 108 terrified civilians sheltering in a shipping container, a routine military response took on far larger dimensions. Furious responses in Lebanon and across the Arab world were vindicated when a UN report dismissed as unlikely Israeli claims that the massacre was the result of a technical error. Palestinians naturally identified with the Lebanese victims. Israeli critics noted that the explanation given by the IDF was that it was attacking Shia villages in the south to cause a flow of civilians north, towards Beirut, in order to pressure the Syrian and Lebanese governments to restrain Hizbullah.[45] Polls taken in May showed Peres ahead by 4–6 per cent, but just two days before the election on 29 May his lead was down to 2 per cent. Israeli-Arab voters – 14 per cent of the electorate – responded to a boycott call by community leaders who condemned the Labour leader as a 'child murderer' or 'war criminal'. It transpired afterwards that 72 per cent of Arab voters cast blank or spoilt ballots.[46] Nevertheless, right-wingers had highlighted Arab support for Peres as a reason to oppose him and warned that he would divide Jerusalem. Peres lost the contest by just 29,000 votes. His smooth-talking Likud rival won a mandate to form a new government after campaigning under the slogan: 'Netanyahu is good for the Jews.'

ENTER BIBI

Binyamin Netanyahu formed the most right-wing coalition in Israeli history. In his inaugural speech on 19 June 1996, he pledged to encourage 'pioneering settlement' in *Eretz-Yisrael*, including in the Negev, Galilee, Judaea, Samaria and the Golan Heights – conspicuously making no distinction between the two sides of the green line. 'The settlers,' he declared, 'are the real pioneers of our day and they deserve support and appreciation.' In August the cabinet voted unanimously to cancel restrictions on settlement, lifting the Labour government's partial freeze. Netanyahu had been hostile to Oslo from the start; the PLO's acceptance of it, he argued, was a deception because the organization remained committed to the destruction of Israel. Rafael Eitan, the former IDF chief of staff and *Tzomet* leader, who was appointed agriculture minister, said that Oslo would have to be reopened. Eitan was remembered for describing Palestinians as 'drugged cockroaches in a bottle'. Still, contrary to fears at home and abroad, Netanyahu did not abandon the peace process, instead meeting Arafat for a brief and awkward encounter at the Erez border crossing into Gaza and agreeing to continue talks. 'Oslo', in Uri Savir's optimistic view, 'had created a new reality, which obliged Netanyahu to manoeuvre in constant dissonance among his beliefs, his political support, and the reality created by the process.'[47]

Serious trouble erupted in Jerusalem that September when the prime minister approved the opening by archaeologists of a new entrance into the Hasmonean tunnel, which linked the Via Dolorosa and the Western Wall, not far from the al-Aqsa mosque. The issue had been under delicate negotiation for a decade, so the decision, made against the advice of security chiefs, looked reckless. It was presented, however, as a matter of unchallengeable Israeli sovereignty – a position backed by Teddy Kollek's successor as mayor of Jerusalem, the Likud's Ehud Olmert. The PA described any interference with the Haram al-Sharif as 'an assault on the Muslim faith and its institutions'. Netanyahu insisted he would not speak to Arafat directly. Arafat, furious at the slight, vowed to force the prime minister to contact him: he ordered demonstrations to provoke the Israelis. Netanyahu then immediately phoned him.[48] Clashes erupted around al-Aqsa and spread, leaving seven Palestinians dead. On 26 September the Israelis deployed Cobra helicopters and killed forty-four Palestinians, twenty-five of them in Gaza. Tanks were moved into the West Bank for the first time since 1967, while seven Israeli soldiers were killed during a firefight at Joseph's Tomb in Nablus, attacked by a crowd that included PA policemen. The PA, concluded the radical Palestinian-Israeli thinker Azmi Bishara, proved that even within its 'Bantustan' it was 'not prepared to play a Quisling role like the Israeli-backed militia in the South Lebanon "security zone"'.[49] In the wake of the clashes the US stepped in more forcefully, summoning Netanyahu and Arafat to meet in Washington to discuss the next stage of the peace process: the planned Israeli redeployment in Hebron, which had been excluded from Area A as defined by Oslo II.

Netanyahu's visceral opposition to Oslo gave way to a subtler policy of bargaining hard over every step, delaying implementation, taking unilateral decisions – and seeking always to blame the other side for any problems. 'Our goals are different' from those of the previous governments, he declared:

> We are using the time interval in the agreement to achieve our goals: to maintain the unity of Jerusalem, to ensure the security depth necessary for the defence of the state, to insist on the right of Jews to settle in their land, and to propose to the Palestinians a suitable arrangement for self-rule but without the sovereign powers which pose a threat to the State of Israel.

Security and reciprocity were the twin pillars of his approach. Still, he went on to sign the protocol dividing Hebron into two zones; one, constituting 20 per cent of the city, under Israeli control for the benefit of its 450 settlers. In January 1997 that long-delayed move finally took place, fog and driving rain providing Israeli troops with welcome cover as the Knesset chamber echoed to the sound of impassioned speeches. 'We are not leaving Hebron, the city of the patriarchs, we are redeploying in Hebron,' Netanyahu told MPs. 'I want to tell you, dear brothers and sisters, that we care about you.' On Shuhada (Martyrs) Street – one of the tensest spots – someone had sprayed a Hebrew slogan in black paint: 'Not Likud, not Labour, we trust only God.' Elsewhere in Hebron scores of young men milled around the office of Jibril Rajoub's Preventive Security Service, awaiting the arrival of a contingent of two hundred uniformed Palestinian policemen to be deployed in the remaining 80 per cent of the city.[50] Arafat flew in the following day in his trademark white Russian helicopter, telling the settlers he wanted 'a just peace' and describing the city as 'liberated'. The Hebron agreement was described later by a senior UN diplomat as a 'case study in political madness' – and a turning point from which Oslo never recovered.[51]

Netanyahu faced attacks and ridicule from both right and left. In the wake of the Hasmonean tunnel affair a popular TV comedy show – *Hartsufim* (an Israeli version of the British *Spitting Image*) – portrayed the prime minister with a scantily dressed young woman, who seductively urged a panting 'Bibi' to 'enter my tunnel . . . ' It also showed Netanyahu and Arafat as bloated blubbery dolls, humping and sweating under rumpled sheets as the talk show host says: 'We have here a couple who haven't reached a climax in eight months – despite maintaining full relations.' The punchline was obvious when the writhing couple finally made it. "Oh, Bibi, I adore those withdrawals of yours,' a flushed and feminine Arafat whispers to her relieved, manly partner.[52]

Under the Likud, settlement became an even more combustible flashpoint than it had been before. Ariel Sharon, whom Netanyahu appointed minister of national infrastructure, promoted key projects. The most important was a road and tunnel that allowed direct access from Jerusalem to the Gush Etzion settlements, bypassing Bethlehem and neighbouring Beit Jala and Bet Sahour, whose residents were not permitted to use this new route. This spatial separation – labelled 'apartheid' by its critics – was the harbinger of a strategy of linkage across the green line to Jewish settlements while bypassing Arab areas. The issue came to a head in February 1997 when Netanyahu decided to go ahead with the construction of 6,500 housing units for 30,000 people at Har Homa/Jebel Abu Ghneim, first proposed under Rabin. Palestinians saw the project as intended to cut off their future capital from the northern part of the West Bank and, a familiar refrain from both sides, a violation of Oslo's basic principles. Netanyahu gave his approval despite warnings from Arafat and Faisal Husseini, now the PA minister for Jerusalem, who was operating from a satellite office at the Orient House. The PLO responded by breaking off contacts. Construction began in March after Israeli troops, with sniper and helicopter cover, sealed off the area. Israeli raids on Palestinian institutions in East Jerusalem seemed designed to underscore Netanyahu's firm rejection of any role for the PLO in the city. 'The relationship between Israel and the Palestinians declined from the modest level of understanding and partial reconciliation that had been achieved into an escalating and debilitating confrontation with the Netanyahu government over the building of settlements and other issues', Ahmed Qurei recorded.[53] Marwan Barghouti, the leader of Fatah's 'young guard', warned that many Palestinians were now questioning Arafat's strategic choice of seeking peace with Israel. 'Netanyahu's policy is to strengthen Hamas and the opposition on the Palestinian street', he said.[54] Barghouti had been deported by the

Israelis during the *intifada* and allowed back after Oslo, part of that limited 'return' that was such an important part of the agreement for the Palestinians.

The impact of Har Homa was unusually powerful. Settlement activities generally attracted less attention than headline-grabbing attacks or carefully spun diplomatic manoeuvres. Israel's settlement project was by its nature slow-moving, a process rather than single events, and was obscured by complexity, bureaucracy and subterfuge. Palestinians were, however, intensely aware of it. Arabic media monitored the construction of roads, land seizures and the number of homes being built – issues that were largely taken for granted in Israel. The cumulative effect was shocking. 'Israeli leaders' tearful declarations about peace didn't tally with what they were doing with their bulldozers', wrote Sari Nusseibeh.

> By focusing on the details – a demolition order here, a new bypass road there, on thousands of new housing units on a hillside – it's easy to lose sight of the systematic nature of the expansion. Years that were supposed to build trust between the feuding parties saw a doubling of the settlement population, from one hundred thousand to two hundred thousand: hardly what we had in mind when we danced on the streets after Oslo. That settlers got away scot-free with murder and other depredations quite literally added insult to injury.[55]

PARTNER OR ENEMY?

In July 1997 two Palestinian suicide bombers struck in the busy Mahane Yehuda market in West Jerusalem, killing thirteen people and triggering yet another closure of the West Bank and Gaza. Israel suspended negotiations. Over the following weeks Israel and the PA detained hundreds of Hamas supporters. In September, another bombing on Ben-Yehuda Street killed 5 and injured 180. 'Arafat has gone from being a peace partner to a declared enemy', wrote the influential *Yediot Aharonot* columnist Nahum Barnea, whose own son had been killed in a bus bombing eighteen months earlier. 'After a year and a half in power, the government has no answer to give citizens who are asking "What now?" The only light at the end of the tunnel is the flash of the next terrorist blast.'[56] Both bombings were claimed by the Izzedin al-Qassam Brigades, which demanded the release of Sheikh Ahmed Yassin, behind bars since 1989. 'We cannot continue this way,' Netanyahu said. 'When Arafat embraces and kisses Hamas, instead of fighting it, the message is that Hamas can strike at Israel with impunity.'[57] Israeli intelligence officials claimed later that Arafat had freed Ibrahim al-Maqadmeh, a senior Qassam commander, to signal to the Islamists that he was giving them a 'green light' for attacks.[58] Netanyahu displayed no interest in an offer from Hamas, conveyed to Israel by the Jordanians, for a thirty-year *hudna* or truce.

Netanyahu faced widespread censure at home and abroad when another Israeli operation – this time to kill the Hamas political leader Khaled Meshaal – went badly wrong. Mossad agents, who used Canadian passports to enter Jordan, sprayed a deadly nerve agent into his ear. It was an assassination that was supposed to go unnoticed. Two agents were caught, however, and four others fled to the Israeli embassy in Amman. It was a hugely embarrassing incident that infuriated King Hussein, put the peace treaty at risk and required the Israelis to provide the antidote needed to save the unconscious Meshaal's life. The king ordered his special forces to surround the embassy and storm it if the Israelis did not surrender. The subsequent deal to free the bungling Mossad men also required the Israelis to release Sheikh Yassin, who returned a few days later to a hero's welcome in Gaza. Arafat and Netanyahu met shortly afterwards, stung by the realization that their common Islamist enemy had benefitted from the row.

In fact, however, for all the strains, Israeli–Palestinian co-operation was still close, and the following year it helped reduce anti-Israeli attacks to a level that continued until late 2000. The Shin Bet maintained close liaison with the PA Preventive Security Service and had 'a certain amount of understanding about the difficulties' Arafat faced – and about his frequent passive behaviour.[59] Co-operation worked well in September 1998 when the Israelis killed the brothers Adel and Imad Awadallah, senior Hamas fugitives. Imad had been held by the PA in its Jericho enclave before escaping. The two were tracked down to a remote house surrounded by orchards west of Hebron. Adel, according to Ami Ayalon, the head of the Shin Bet, was commander of the Qassam Brigades in the West Bank. The operation was approved by Netanyahu despite fears that it would lead to a repeat of the suicide-bombing campaign that had followed the assassination of Yahya Ayyash, the 'engineer', the previous year. 'Priceless' intelligence allowed them to roll up the Hamas operational network. Ayalon reported first to Netanyahu and then went on to see Arafat in Ramallah in the early hours of the morning, telling him bluntly. 'We killed him [Awadallah] and now we expect you to do everything together with us to ensure that the peace process survives – in both our interests – because it should be clear to you that if there is now a wave of terrorist attacks then there's no peace process any more.' Jibril Rajoub and Mohammed Dahlan worked – successfully – to ensure there was no significant retaliation against Israeli targets, although protests erupted across the West Bank.[60] US links with the Palestinians were also strengthened. The PA pressed the Americans to verify the seriousness of their counter-terrorist efforts, although the Israelis were unhappy with this because they felt it reduced their own leverage. The CIA trained Palestinian security officers and their experts removed booby-trapped bugging devices the Israelis had planted in the Serail compound in Gaza City before their 1994 withdrawal: one of them exploded and killed a Palestinian who was attempting to remove it.[61] By 1998 PA security forces numbered 35,000, making the 2.8 million Palestinians in the West Bank and Gaza Strip among the most highly policed people in the world.[62]

SELLING PALESTINE?

Oslo had attracted fierce opposition from Palestinians from the very start. And by the time the early excitement had faded, smooth behind-the-scenes relations with Israel did nothing to boost Arafat's flagging popularity among his own people. Critics again pointed to his autocratic style and the way his old habit of promoting competition was exploited by the Israelis. Economic incentives flowing from monopolies on imports of cement, electricity, fuel, flour and tobacco into

Gaza guaranteed a steady stream of revenues for Arafat. The price of a ton of cement was $74. Of that $17 went to the PA and $17 into Arafat's private account in a Tel Aviv bank.[63] Special Israeli-issued VIP passes for PA officials were another instrument of pressure and co-optation that reinforced the image of an elite whose interests lay with maintaining rather than challenging the status quo to preserve their own privileges.[64] Israeli officials recognized the advantages they enjoyed: 'We control electrical power, water resources, telecommunications and so on', one boasted to dubious Likud MPs. 'We control everything. There are a number of natives who serve as middlemen. What could suit our purpose better? ... The power imbalance between us and the Palestinians never served our interests better in the past, not even before the intifada.'[65]

Arbitrary arrests carried out by Palestinian police and security services, and twenty deaths in custody since 1994, reinforced the impression that the *Sulta* – as the PA was universally known in Arabic – was just another unaccountable Arab regime. Rumours spread about extra-judicial killings of Palestinians who had sold land to Israelis. PA agents were blamed.[66] Journalists, human rights activists and academics were detained, harassed or intimidated. In summer 1995 the *al-Quds* newspaper was ordered to stop its presses because it had given prominent coverage to an interview with Farouk Qaddumi, the PLO 'foreign minister', whose opposition to Oslo and closeness to the Syrians annoyed Arafat.[67] B'Tselem reported that Rajoub's Preventive Security Service was using methods learned from the Shin Bet. Heads of voluntary organizations were questioned by security officials.[68] The PA was also dogged by allegations of corruption. In July 1997 a parliamentary commission of inquiry reported that nearly half of that year's $326 million budget had been misspent, mismanaged or embezzled.[69] It singled out the civil affairs minister, Jamil al-Tarifi, the planning minister, Nabil Shaath, and the transport minister, Ali Qawasmi as the worst offenders, cataloguing millions spent on hotel rooms, restaurants and overseas travel. It raised questions about the use of about $1 billion in foreign aid received since 1994. Tarifi was accused of building Israeli settlements.

In October 1997 Hayder Abdel-Shafi resigned from parliament in protest at the dominance of the executive. Hanan Ashrawi, minister of education and then tourism, followed, accusing Arafat of failing to curb abuses: one opinion poll showed that 56 per cent of Palestinians questioned believed their political institutions were corrupt. Lifestyle questions were linked directly to political choices and the conspicuous consumption of the new 'Tunisian' elite, which stood in stark contrast to an economy ravaged by repeated Israeli closures. Arafat's critics described 'a ramshackle, nepotistic edifice of monopoly, racketeering and naked extortion which merely enriches . . . [the leadership] as it further impoverishes society at large'. It was striking that among the fancy new villas springing up in Gaza, the most ostentatious was an especially opulent one belonging to Fatah's Mahmoud Abbas (Abu Mazen), a key negotiator of the Oslo accords. 'It is not clear who paid for this $2 million-plus affair, all balconies and balustrades in gothic profusion, but the graffiti which some irreverent scoundrel scrawled on its wall proclaimed that "this is your reward for selling Palestine".'[70] The image of the ruling elite as arrogant and out of touch was not improved by the example of the Casino Oasis, built near Jericho's Aqabat Jaber refugee camp by an Austrian company with the involvement of Israeli and Palestinian investors and under the protection of PA security forces. Hamas objected forcefully, complaining of un-Islamic decadence and other risks, including the recruitment of collaborators. In late 1999 a score of prominent figures, including nine members of parliament, issued a statement accusing Arafat of tyranny, corruption and deceit. Eight of the signatories were arrested; the MPs, who enjoyed immunity, faced violent intimidation.[71]

For many Palestinians the economic situation worsened in the post-Oslo years. Between September 1995 and March 1997, unemployment in the Gaza Strip fluctuated between 24 per cent and 39 per cent. The daily wage in the winter of 1995 was $19 in the West Bank and $15 in the Gaza Strip. In winter 1997, the daily wage dropped to below $13. Travel became harder because of the failure to agree the promised 'safe passage' between the Gaza Strip and the West Bank. Security restrictions reduced exit permits, even for urgent medical treatment in Israel. Abu Aboud, who had worked in Jaffa for fifteen years, described his disappointment and frustration: 'Most of the people in our village want to be connected to Israel, [and to] have the opportunity to work in Israel,' he explained.

What good is an independent [Palestinian] state if we will be unemployed? Arafat doesn't want me to live an honourable life in his state, so I won't declare that I'm Palestinian. What does it mean to be Palestinian? Well, for example, in our village the schools close at noon; the kids spend the rest of the day on the streets. There isn't even one computer in any of the schools. So I want to know, where does all the money [from the donor countries] go? You know, when I look around and see all the people of the PA who came from abroad [primarily Tunisia] I see them as one big mafia. So you tell me, what am I going to do with this kind of a state?[72]

UNCERTAIN BENEFITS

Arafat ignored the discontent and continued to follow Oslo. In September 1998 Bill Clinton convened another summit with Arafat and Netanyahu. Shortly afterwards Ariel Sharon – finally back in a big job despite his role in Lebanon in 1982 – was appointed foreign minister in place of David Levy, giving the prime minister ample cover on his right flank. The full talks took place in October at the secluded Wye River plantation in Maryland. Netanyahu, according to Qurei, asked that Arafat 'see to' Ghazi al-Jabali, head of PA preventive security in Gaza, who was wanted by Israel for orchestrating attacks. Arafat stormed out at what appeared to be a thinly veiled request to have Jabali killed. Clinton exploded, saying: 'This is dreadful. I can't bear this dirty business!'[73] Netanyahu also tried and failed to secure the release of the convicted Israeli spy Jonathan Pollard – a longstanding irritant in US-Israeli relations. Sharon conspicuously avoided shaking Arafat's hand but agreed to three more phases of Israeli military redeployment, comprising 13 per cent of West Bank land being transferred from the Israeli-controlled Area C to Areas A and B, the release of hundreds of prisoners, as well as stringent conditions for combating terrorism and extremism. The PLO pledged to convene the Palestine National Council to ratify, as promised in Oslo, the abrogation of clauses in the National Covenant relating to Israel's right to exist. The Israeli cabinet ratified the agreement after a short delay: eight of the seventeen ministers voted yes, but five abstained and four voted against. Implementation was again delayed, with claims from the Israeli leader that the Palestinians had failed to meet the conditions that had been agreed. Sharon called on the West Bank settlers to seize more land to thwart any future Palestinian takeover. 'Move, run and grab as many hilltops as you can to enlarge settlements because everything we take now will stay ours.'[74]

Still, at the end of December, when Clinton visited Gaza, the Palestinian parliament voted to approve Arafat's letter to the American president, confirming the nullification of the offensive provisions of the National Covenant, dating back to the foundation of the PLO in 1964. It was 'an effective renunciation' by the Palestinians 'of a crucial part of their history and a virtual apology for more than half a century of struggle for national liberation',[75] wrote one Arafat foe. Clinton thanked the Palestinians

> for your rejection – fully, finally and forever – of the passages in the Palestinian Charter calling for the destruction of Israel. For they were the ideological underpinnings of a struggle renounced at Oslo. By revoking them once and for all, you have sent, I say again, a powerful message not to the government, but to the people of Israel.

Clinton also spoke frankly of the limitations of what had been achieved so far. 'I want the people of Israel to know that for many Palestinians, five years after Oslo, the benefits of this process remain remote; that for too many Palestinians lives are hard, jobs are scarce, prospects are uncertain and personal grief is great.' He referred too to settlements and land confiscations, but urged the Palestinians to carry on even if they felt there were 'a hundred good reasons to walk away'.[76] Clinton spoke with remarkable empathy[77] and could point to one example of genuine progress. Shortly before his visit, Palestinians had finally inaugurated Gaza international airport – long delayed by Israeli objections. It was an exciting moment, and a rare glimpse of something that looked like genuine sovereignty and independence. Clinton and his wife Hillary were welcomed there by Arafat and his wife Suha – surrounded by flags, protocol, guards of honour and all the trappings of statehood.[78] But, as with so much of what had been achieved since Oslo, outward appearances were deceptive. Israel continued to control the airspace and pre-approve flight schedules. It had the right to shut down operations at any time. Netanyahu, for his part, angered supporters on the right for making too many 'concessions', while Israelis further left were unhappy with the halting progress made towards a genuine peace. In late December 1998 the Knesset voted to dissolve itself and hold new elections – effectively freezing the faltering peace process. Inevitably, the fate and future of Israeli–Palestinian relations again hung in the balance.

21

1999–2000

'Israel ... was not yet ready for real peace. The colonialist, militaristic mentality – the occupier's mentality, nourished by myths – still predominated and shaped their vision of peace.'

Akram Hanieh[1]

'MR SECURITY' – MARK II

Ehud Barak became Israel's prime minister in May 1999 after winning an election by promising to continue the legacy of Yitzhak Rabin. The new resident of Balfour Street was the most decorated soldier in the country's history. Like Rabin, this latter-day 'Mr Security' was not a natural party leader. Labour was re-branded as 'One Israel' for a campaign that was designed to win over the middle ground. Supporters even chanted 'Rabin won, Rabin won' when Barak gave his victory address and proclaimed that Israel had 'returned to sanity'. Barak, a pianist, systems analyst and chess player with an unusual ability to pick locks, was famous for his analytical mind – and was sometimes described as arrogant. But his martial qualities were striking too in a country that was still impressed by them: as a young IDF officer in the elite *Sayeret Matkal* (general staff reconnaissance unit) he had taken part in a celebrated hostage rescue mission, as well as the assassination of PLO leaders in a raid on Beirut in 1973. In 1988, at the height of the *intifada*, he had commanded the operation to kill Abu Jihad in Tunis. As IDF chief of staff he was unhappy with the Oslo agreement, not least because he had not been privy to the secret negotiating channel. In his final days in uniform in 1994 he had overseen the Gaza–Jericho redeployment. In 1995, as Rabin's interior minister, he very noticeably opposed ratification of Oslo II. Still, the PLO leadership was initially cheered by Barak's victory, remembering that he had called for Palestinian statehood and warned of 'apartheid' unless separation took place. He had even once given an interview where he combined both empathy and hostility and said that if he had been a young Palestinian he would have joined 'a terrorist organization' (*irgun mehablim*). It reminded some of the speech made in the 1950s by another famous soldier-turned-politician, Moshe Dayan, showing rare understanding for Palestinians' hatred of Israel as they sat 'in the refugee camps in Gaza, watching us transforming the lands and the villages where they and their fathers dwelt, into our property'.[2] Ahmed Qurei saw 'a glimmer of hope' that the flame of Oslo could be revived after being all-but extinguished by Netanyahu. Others were dubious. Farouk Qaddumi, an opponent of Oslo who had stayed in Tunis rather than accompany Arafat back to Gaza, agreed that Labour was more 'flexible' than the Likud but predicted that nothing would unblock the peace process without US and European pressure. The Palestinian media gave blanket coverage to the Israeli election campaign. The stakes, after all, were unusually high.

Barak won 56 per cent of the vote for prime minister, against 44 per cent for Netanyahu. He put together a broad coalition of right-wing and religious parties, the Orthodox *Shas* as well as the left-wing *Meretz*, but eschewed the support of Arab political parties even though many Arabs had voted for him,[3] and thus left them feeling betrayed. Barak however also made clear that he had distinct 'red lines' that were not compatible with minimal Palestinian demands: Jerusalem would remain Israel's 'eternal capital'; there would be no withdrawal to the 1967 borders; the West Bank would have to be demilitarized while Israeli sovereignty would be extended to accommodate Jewish settlers; and no right of return could be granted to Palestinian refugees. Immediately after the election the prime minister visited Ofra and Bet-El, calling the settlers 'my dear brothers'. Palestinian hopes – tinged by a strong element of wishful thinking by the leadership – appeared to have been quickly dashed.

On the ground there was no discernible improvement: settlement building continued apace, as did blockades and other restrictions that took their toll on the Palestinian economy. Barak moved rapidly, at least going through the motions of a return to negotiations. In his first meeting with Arafat at the Erez border crossing to Gaza in July, he explained that he intended to integrate talks on the contentious *final status* issues with implementation of the 1998 Wye agreement on outstanding *interim* commitments and Israeli redeployments, prisoner releases and a safe passage between Gaza and the West Bank. Barak's fear was that by the time the parties reached permanent status negotiations, Israel would have had to surrender all its cards; his alternative was to move directly to the end point while keeping his cards off the table. Piecemeal was out; take-it-or-leave-it was in.

Arafat, who was anxious to see brisk progress after the frustrations and evasions of the Netanyahu years, was publicly polite but privately furious.[4] In September 1999 he and Barak signed yet another agreement in Sharm el-Sheikh, watched over by Hosni Mubarak of Egypt and King Abdullah II of Jordan, who had come to the throne on the death of his father Hussein a few months earlier. Madeleine Albright, the US secretary of state, helped to mediate despite the approaching end of Bill Clinton's second term in office. Both sides reaffirmed their commitment to implement all outstanding agreements, and to work to end the conflict within twelve to fifteen months. Talks got under way but they proved tense and difficult – one meeting between Arafat and Barak involving a 'painful and personal clash'.[5]

It was around this time that Barak lurched suddenly towards Syria, hoping to make peace with Israel's most hostile Arab neighbour and use that, like the treaties with Egypt and Jordan, to weaken and isolate the Palestinians – as the PLO suspected.[6] Reaching out to Hafez al-Assad, the Syrian president, formed part of the prime minister's strategy for a unilateral withdrawal from Lebanon – a popular campaign pledge. Palestinians were left reeling as Barak pursued Assad, with American help, meeting the Syrian foreign minister Farouk al-Sharaa at Shepherdstown, near Washington, in January 2000. 'Barak', Arafat warned, 'shouldn't take me for granted.'[7] Barak's background predisposed him to dealing with the Syrian president, 'a military man at the helm of an orderly state, rather than with a terrorist and guerrilla fighter at the head of a revolutionary movement like Arafat', as the internal security minister, Shlomo Ben-Ami, reflected later. To the dismay of the Palestinians, though, the focus on Syria marked a reversion to the pre-Oslo period. Arafat was 'restless, alienated and hostile'. Assad, in declining health, eventually lost interest in bargaining over the Golan Heights as the Israeli offer fell short – though by only a few hundred yards on the eastern shore of the Sea of Galilee – of a full return to the 1967 border. Barak lost his nerve due to opposition at home, where the defence establishment and most ministers advised him to forget the 'Sphinx of Damascus' and to concentrate instead on the Palestinians, the more familiar enemy in Israel's backyard.[8] In May 2000 the Israelis went ahead with the withdrawal from Lebanon. Hizbullah celebrated a great victory while Palestinian refugees flocked from their camps to the border fence to gaze at their lost homeland from close up. Most Israelis welcomed the pullout as finally drawing a line under the 'war of choice' that had been launched by Menachem Begin and Ariel Sharon to destroy the PLO eighteen years earlier.

RESISTANCE WORKS

The Palestinians' disenchantment with Barak, preoccupied with Syria, grew with every meeting. Accusations of bad faith multiplied; they felt cheated and humiliated.[9] In January the PLO declared that 13 September 2000, the seventh anniversary of the Oslo agreement and the date on which final status negotiations were scheduled to be completed, would be the date of the establishment of the Palestinian state. Israel denounced this as a provocative move. Yet that April, on the eve of another negotiating session, Barak announced plans to build 174 new housing units in Maaleh Adumim, the big settlement east of Jerusalem overlooking the road to Jericho which was by now seen by many Israelis as an ordinary suburb and a natural extension of their capital. Talks broke down, resumed, and were again suspended. In an echo of what had happened back in 1993, another Nordic 'backchannel' was established, this time in Stockholm. It was intended to provide a respite from the 'spotlight of publicity, from the scrutiny of the media and intelligence services, and from the baleful gaze of opponents of the peace process, especially on the Israeli side'. News of it leaked on the second day of talks, coinciding uncomfortably with big demonstrations in the West Bank and Gaza in solidarity with hunger-striking prisoners in Israeli gaols and around a 'day of rage' chosen to coincide with the annual commemoration of the *Nakba*. Six Palestinians were killed and hundreds wounded, the streets strewn with stones and smouldering tyres.[10] A long-delayed agreement to hand over Abu Dis and two other Arab villages on the outskirts of East Jerusalem to the PA only passed after a stormy debate in the Knesset, but Barak suspended implementation because of the violence – the worst in four years. Fatah activists led by Marwan Barghouti, head of the movement's *Tanzim* ('organization') militia, fired weapons behind demonstrators gathering at IDF checkpoints, taking the initiative on the streets in the way that the PA rarely did. Palestinian policemen, facing social pressure and accusations of collaboration with Israel, took part in the demonstrations – an ominous new development. Yasser Abed-Rabbo, chief PLO negotiator in the official talks, resigned in protest when news broke of the Swedish track. But Stockholm was unable to narrow the gaps between the parties on the extent of an Israeli withdrawal or on refugee returns. The magic of Oslo – which had in any case long lost its original sparkle – could not be repeated. And in the aftermath of Israel's withdrawal from Lebanon, its enemies, including Hamas, compared the PLO unfavourably with Hizbullah: why could the Palestinians not also defeat Israel? Resistance worked; negotiation did not. Hassan Nasrallah, Hizbullah's leader, exhorted the Palestinians to emulate the Lebanese and renew their armed struggle. The lesson was apparently not lost on Arafat. Israeli security forces quietly monitored Palestinian preparations for acts of violence.[11]

In June 2000, Clinton and Barak agreed on a new summit. Arafat was firmly opposed, and said so, suspecting a trap in which he would either be forced to accept an American-Israeli diktat or be blamed for rejecting it, but he still felt unable to refuse the invitation. Clinton, the Palestinians feared, was anxious for a foreign policy success before leaving office when his second term ended in a few months. Barak's coalition in the Knesset began to disintegrate, while Arafat faced internal dissent as well.

Camp David had been a resonant name in the annals of Israeli–Arab diplomacy since the negotiations that produced peace with

Egypt in 1978. But an ambitious encounter designed to address the hard core of the conflict was fatally ill-prepared. Palestinians, Americans and many of the Israelis involved understood that before the summit began on 11 July: most knew how wide the gaps were and how very hard it would be to bridge them. 'What you are offering is more like a guillotine hanging over our necks', Arafat warned Shlomo Ben-Ami at a preparatory meeting in Nablus.[12] It felt like watching a disaster unfold. Fifteen days in the pressure cooker of the Maryland retreat were not enough to overcome the familiar obstacles to a final and comprehensive peace settlement. It is debatable, however, whether more time and better preparation would have made any difference.

CAMP DAVID, AGAIN

The summit had to tackle the toughest, 'permanent status' issues that had been left for the end by the Oslo accords' interim structure. These had been barely touched on in earlier rounds of negotiations. Finding common ground on Jerusalem, refugees, borders and settlements was as difficult as ever, despite the fact that since 1993 Israeli and Palestinian officials had had more direct contact than ever before. Thousands of hours of meetings in committees and working groups had woven personal relations that created a strangely cordial atmosphere in the bucolic atmosphere of the presidential retreat, with its echoes of the Begin–Sadat–Carter talks two decades earlier. Madeleine Albright invited negotiators to watch a film and to take part in a basketball game, but only the Israelis turned up so they played against the Marine security detachment. The most memorable image was of Ehud Barak playfully pushing a smiling Arafat through the door of Laurel cabin – forcing him, deferentially but impatiently, to go first. Personal chemistry could help in theory, though there was precious little between the two; it could not be remotely decisive at what Albright called 'a single make-or-break summit'. As Arafat's aide Akram Hanieh put it: 'The Americans did not seem to realise that the reality of the conflict was stronger than the unreal world they had created at Camp David.'[13]

The talks began unpromisingly. The map the Israelis submitted proposed annexing 14 per cent of the West Bank, with a long-term lease on a further 10 per cent in the Jordan Valley, leaving the Palestinians with 76 per cent of the territory. That would have left 80 per cent of Israeli settlers under Israeli control, but around 50,000 would still be living in Palestinian areas. Two corridors were to run from west to east, giving the Israelis access to the Jordan river in the event of an attack from there. That would have meant the Palestinian territory being divided into three non-contiguous blocks – including Gaza. The Palestinians rejected this outright, insisting that a full return to the 1967 borders could be the only basis for negotiation: that would give them 22 per cent of historic Palestine against the 78 per cent held by Israel on the eve of the Six Days war – the grand compromise that the PLO had, in their view, already made. A later, amended offer, involving Israeli annexation of 10.5 per cent of the West Bank, was also rejected, although the Palestinians did agree to a land swap which would allow the Israelis to retain the big settlements of Maaleh Adumim, Ariel and Gush Etzion. The final Israeli offer was for 92 per cent of the West Bank.[14] Both sides rejected a US proposal for the Palestinians to have sovereignty over East Jerusalem; the Haram al-Sharif/Temple Mount was an entirely predictable sticking point.[15] Towards the end of the summit, however, Barak moved, for the first time accepting Palestinian sovereignty over some parts of East Jerusalem, and Palestinian *custodianship* of the Haram al-Sharif with Palestinian security to protect it, though crucially it would still be under Israeli sovereignty. US bridging proposals failed because they did not deal with the Palestinian claim that the holy places were the concern of all Muslims. 'I cannot concede sovereignty over East Jerusalem', Arafat told Clinton on the final day, as tension filled the air. Barak said: 'I don't know a prime minister who would be willing to sign his name to the transfer of sovereignty over the First and Second Temple, which is the basis of Zionism.'[16]

The refugee question was even tougher. Israel treated it as a humanitarian issue under which a token number would be allowed back under the rubric of family reunification. That was a far cry from the passionately held Palestinian demand for Israel's recognition of its responsibility for creating the problem in 1948 – the *Nakba*. Ben-Ami had told Arafat in Nablus: 'I am not denying the morality of your demand for the right of return. However, we must together seek a formula whereby the right of return becomes symbolic.'[17] Palestinian leaders did in fact distinguish between Israel's recognition of the right of return as a moral question and its implementation. But that did not mean it was easy to agree on practicalities, given Israel's deep-seated fears about its Jewish character, demographics and security and being 'swamped' by Palestinians. 'Israel wanted to gain a historic compromise without dealing with history, and wanted to uproot the causes of the conflict without exposing these roots', argued the Palestinian-Israeli commentator Raef Zreik.[18] Overall, Palestinians felt that Barak's offer – which was repeatedly described as 'generous' – did not constitute a viable, sovereign state, and nor did it create the conditions necessary for ending the conflict.

Unsurprisingly, the failure at Camp David generated angry claims and counter-claims about who was responsible. Little had been written down for fear of leaks that would be used by critics, especially in Israel, which made it hard to sort out the truth at the end. Barak had avoided contact with Arafat for fear of pressure from him to confirm concessions. Israel blamed him directly for intransigence and for refusing to engage. Clinton, though less directly, did the same, and helped the process of delegitimizing the Palestinian leader. 'Arafat', Barak declared,

> was single-handedly responsible for the summit's failure because he was afraid to make the historic decisions needed at this time to bring an end to the conflict. We did not find a partner prepared to make decisions. We did what we could, we left no stone unturned, we exhausted every possibility to bring about an end to conflict and a secure future for Israel.

The official view, endlessly repeated, was that Israel's 'magnanimity was being spurned by an Arafat who was psychologically incapable of making the grand historical compromise necessary'.[19] In the most extreme interpretation, the PLO leader was not objecting to the crucial *details* of the Israeli offer, but to the underlying *principle* of a two-state solution.[20] Tragically, reconciliation seemed impossible. Clinton compared the experience of the talks to having teeth extracted without painkillers.

The Palestinians complained about a 'venomous propaganda campaign' even before Barak had left Maryland.[21] They emphasized the close co-ordination between Americans and Israelis and the inadequacy of Israeli offers, though some of them did represent genuine progress. Barak's offer on Jerusalem broke a taboo, though it came late. Significantly he went beyond both his own previously declared red lines and beyond what any Israeli leader had ever proposed before, despite mounting pressure on the right at home. Israel's concessions still fell short of minimum Palestinian demands though: the contiguity of the Palestinian state, full sovereignty in Arab areas of East Jerusalem and a compromise on refugees. 'Camp David made clear that the Israeli establishment was not yet ready for real peace', Hanieh concluded. 'The colonialist, militaristic mentality – the occupier's mentality, nourished by myths – still predominated and shaped their vision of peace.'[22]

Informed outsiders blamed both sides. 'If you were Barak, offering 90 per cent was plenty risky politically, and, given Rabin's murder, even personally; if you were Arafat, accepting it would have been fatal', concluded one US official.[23] But a close and independent examination of the evidence found the Palestinian narrative of Camp David (and the subsequent Taba talks) to be 'significantly more accurate than the Israeli narrative'.[24] The disastrous results were produced by 'mutual and by then deeply entrenched suspicion', Clinton's aide Rob Malley argued afterwards.

> Barak's strategy was predicated on the idea that his firmness would lead to some Palestinian flexibility, which in turn would justify Israel's making further concessions. Instead, Barak's piecemeal negotiation style, combined with Arafat's unwillingness to budge, produced a paradoxical result. By presenting early positions as bottom lines, the Israelis provoked the Palestinians' mistrust; by subsequently shifting them, they whetted the Palestinians' appetite. By the end of the process, it was hard to tell which bottom lines were for real, and which were not.[25]

It was not quite the end of the road. In the few weeks before the date set for the promised declaration of Palestinian statehood in September, contacts intensified again, once more with close US involvement.

Arafat signalled flexibility over timing. After all, as one aide put it: 'He has many of the elements of a state. We have 36,000 military men with weapons. We have flags, radio, television, ministries, and a legislative council.'[26] Ben-Ami was appointed foreign minister instead of David Levy, who resigned as the prime minister's support faded away. Barak and Arafat met again at the United Nations' Millennium Summit in New York. In late September the two had a 'warm' meeting at Barak's private residence at Kochav Yair, just inside the green line. Further talks in Washington narrowed more gaps as the Americans considered, for the first time, setting out their own view – which they had so far refrained from doing. By now the clock was ticking loudly towards the end of Clinton's term, adding to pressure for agreement despite all the difficulties.

SHARON PAYS A VISIT

Only a few days later, the Likud leader, Ariel Sharon (he had replaced Netanyahu after Barak's election victory), requested permission to visit the Temple Mount/Haram al-Sharif. Ostensibly his purpose was to inspect archaeological sites. His real point, he would insist later, was to highlight how Ehud Barak had been prepared to negotiate Israel's sovereignty away at Camp David.[27] Ben-Ami got assurances from Jibril Rajoub that there would be no trouble as long as Sharon did not enter the mosques. The Americans were nervous too. 'I can think of a lot of bad ideas, but I can't think of a worse one', was the response of Dennis Ross, Clinton's Middle East co-ordinator. Still, the Americans told the Palestinians they did not want to feed the Israeli right's paranoia about US pressure.[28] On 28 September, guarded by more than 1,000 police, Sharon and a handful of Likud politicians spent 45 minutes on the esplanade, leaving a trail of fury as young Palestinians threw chairs, stones, rubbish bins and whatever missiles came to hand at the escorting forces, who retaliated with tear gas and rubber bullets. Protesters followed Sharon off the site, chanting 'Murderer', and only narrowly escaped clashing with Orthodox Jews who shouted 'Go back to Mecca'. No one was killed. But the symbolism of the visit – and close to the anniversary of the

1982 Sabra and Shatila massacres – was unmistakable. Arafat condemned it but Sharon was unrepentant: 'The Temple Mount is in our hands and will remain in our hands,' he declared – repeating the famous phrase from the 1967 war.

The Israelis got wind of more trouble being planned for the next day, after Friday prayers: messages were sent to Arafat but he did not respond. Four Palestinians were killed and two hundred wounded as Israeli forces switched from rubber bullets to live fire after the Jerusalem police commander was knocked unconscious by a stone. 'Sharon's visit', Ross would argue later,

> gave [Arafat] a perfect pretext to allow violence to erupt, and it also had the benefit of demonstrating that on the Haram his hands were tied – there could be no flexibility. In this sense, Arafat countenanced violence as a tactical move to gain advantage, but underestimated how uncontrollable the ensuing events might be.[29]

Popular anger was directed at the PA, and especially at security personnel, whose children were taunted at school for their fathers' failure to defend their own people. Some changed sides: at one demonstration shortly after Sharon's visit, an armed Palestinian policeman sat at the edge of a crowd of demonstrators watching passively as ambulances evacuated the wounded. But a couple of days later he was seen running alongside protesters with his rifle.[30] Arafat's confidant Mamdouh Nofal later described an internal Fatah directive calling on its men to 'use weapons sparingly, economise on munitions and preserve the clandestinity of actions'.[31] It was the beginning of what became known as the second *intifada* – the al-Aqsa *intifada*.

Unrest spread. On 30 September in the Gaza Strip attention focused on an Israeli command post at Netzarim junction on the main north–south road. Twelve-year-old Mohammed al-Durrah, who was sheltering with his father, died in what appeared to be crossfire between Israeli soldiers and Palestinian security forces, and became the subject of a long propaganda war about who was responsible. Footage of the incident showed the boy crying and the father waving, then a burst of gunfire and dust, after which the boy is seen slumped across his father. This scene was viewed by millions of people across the world on al-Jazeera TV and other channels and generated controversy to match the horror. 'All Palestinians see the Israelis as guilty in this,' as the BBC reported. 'Even if Mohammed al-Durrah was killed by a Palestinian bullet, if it hadn't been for the Israeli occupation in Gaza he would be still alive today.'[32]

Over the following few days thirteen Israeli-Arab citizens, mostly youngsters, were killed by police when protests spread across the green line. These incidents were especially shocking because they showed how, despite cautious hope of improvement in the 1990s, the Israeli authorities appeared to view the country's Palestinian minority not as citizens to be protected, but as an enemy population to be suppressed. It was the highest death toll since the Kafr Qassem massacre in 1956; it had happened under a left-wing government and it looked like a glaring example of double standards. Trouble erupted in Nazareth and Jaffa and in other places where Jews and Arabs lived in close proximity. Some incidents seemed to draw on deep reserves of animosity and prejudice: on 9 October hundreds of Jews from Kfar Shalem, a working-class neighbourhood on the edge of Tel Aviv, used metal bars and hammers to tear down the walls of a derelict mosque in the heart of the neighbourhood, a relic of what had been Salama village until 1948. The 'events of October 2000' came to be seen as a turning point in Arab–Jewish relations inside Israel, the biggest shock since Land Day in 1976, and one that underscored fundamental inequalities.[33] Budgets for the Arab sector were frozen, went one complaint, 'and the minister of education demands that our children sing . . . *Hatikvah*'.[34] Earlier that year the High Court had ruled in favour of an Israeli-Arab couple who had faced discrimination by not being allowed by buy a home in a new Jewish neighbourhood. The Kaadan case was a landmark in the quest for equality.[35] Now though, the hopeful atmosphere of the Oslo years gave way to dark fears about the future. It no longer seemed impossible to imagine that the proponents of 'transfer' – forcibly removing Palestinians from Israel en masse – would get their way.[36] The Or Commission, which investigated the events, identified a pattern of official 'prejudice and neglect' towards the minority and blamed anti-Arab discrimination for the 'combustible atmosphere' that led to the riots. No one, however, faced prosecution.

Yet more terrible images and stories were soon making the rounds.

In mid-October two Israeli soldiers who had lost their way were stopped and lynched by a mob at the police station in Ramallah, one of their killers waving his bloodstained hands from the window. Horrified Israelis heard how another Palestinian rang the wife of one of the victims on his cell phone to tell her: 'I have just killed your husband.' PA policemen were unable or unwilling to intervene. 'We are in a very complex situation where our own people are concerned,' the station commander explained. 'Our police is coming to be deeply hated. The crowd believes we are protecting the Israelis, not them.' The incident was filmed by an Italian TV crew and broadcast internationally. The Palestinian rumour mill said the soldiers were members of an IDF undercover squad, though in fact they were ordinary reservists. The lynching was often cited by Israelis as a turning point in the second *intifada*, but it did not happen in a vacuum: in the preceding two weeks IDF forces had killed eight Palestinian children under the age of sixteen, and nine between the ages of sixteen and eighteen.[37] IDF regulations for opening fire had been relaxed. 'You don't shoot at a child who is 12 or younger,' explained an army sniper, adding that '12 and up is allowed. He is not a child any more; he is already after his *bar mitzvah*.'[38] In the first three weeks of the *intifada* the IDF fired 1 million bullets in the occupied territories: 700,000 in the West Bank and 300,000 in Gaza.

AL-AQSA *INTIFADA*

US diplomatic efforts intensified as the violence escalated. Clinton brought Barak and Arafat together for another summit, this time at Sharm el-Sheikh, although the two did not hold direct talks. The only significant result was the appointment of George Mitchell, the respected former Democratic senator who had helped the Northern Ireland peace process, to investigate the causes of the unrest and get the post-Camp David talks back on track. In November 2000 the Israelis began carrying out 'targeted killings' – assassinations – using Apache helicopter gunships. 'Down with the olive branch, up with the gun,' chanted mourners at the funeral of Hussein Abayat, a Fatah activist from Beit Sahour who had died in a Hellfire missile strike on his Mitsubishi 4x4. The Israelis held Abayat responsible for killing three soldiers and for the nightly gunfire aimed at Gilo, the Jewish settlement built on confiscated land nearby, just beyond the Jerusalem district boundary.[39] Similar attacks were mounted against Psagot, a settlement close to Ramallah. *Tanzim* attacks forced the evacuation of Joseph's Tomb in Nablus. Israeli gunboats fired into Gaza after a mortar attack on a bus carrying Jewish settler children. Clashes took place every day that month, by the end of which 112 Palestinians and 22 Israelis had been killed. In December the Israelis sent tanks into Jenin and settlers occupied a Palestinian home in Hebron.

The goal of the al-Aqsa *intifada* was to achieve what Oslo had manifestly failed to do: end the occupation. Palestinians who supported Arafat refrained by and large from attacking targets inside the 1967 borders; when Islamic Jihad planted a bomb in Jerusalem's Mahane Yehuda market, Arafat condemned it – though many Israelis dismissed that as disingenuous. This was to be the longest and bloodiest phase in relations between Israelis and Palestinians since the epochal events of 1948 – a war by any other name; a Hebrew book about it was entitled *The Seventh War*.[40] Ghassan Andoni, another Beit Sahour activist, made a different point from a Palestinian perspective: if the first *intifada* had been born of hope, the second one was driven by desperation.[41]

In late November 2000, Barak had announced early general elections – his response to pressure from the right for being too soft on the Palestinians while he was being pilloried from abroad for using excessive force. He still believed it was possible to reach a peace agreement with Arafat, on an interim basis that excluded Jerusalem for the moment on the grounds that it was simply too difficult. Sharon immediately accused him of seeking to do a deal at any price. Clinton persevered. On 23 December, with just two weeks left in the White House, the president tried to bridge the gap by issuing what he called 'general parameters' for an Israeli–Palestinian peace settlement, based on everything the Americans had heard from the two sides: a 'fair and lasting agreement', he believed, would require Israel to surrender 94–96 per cent of the West Bank, with the Palestinians obtaining 1–3 per cent compensation for areas that were annexed by Israel. Eighty per cent of the settlers would be in blocs, with contiguity of territory for each side. Israel's withdrawal would be carried out in phases over three years while an international force was deployed. There would be three Israeli early warning stations on the West Bank, and liaison arrangements with the Palestinians. Agreement would be needed on access for Israeli forces in an emergency and on Israeli flights through Palestinian air space. The Palestinian state would be 'non-militarized'. In Jerusalem, sovereignty would be divided – though exactly how would need working out. Al-Quds was to be the Palestinian capital; special arrangements would be made for the Haram al-Sharif/Temple Mount. Refugees would be able to return to the Palestinian state. Israel might accept some but would not be *required* to do so. It would be asked to recognize the suffering of the Palestinian people as a result of the 1948 war and assist international efforts to address the refugee problem. This was to lead to the formal end of the conflict and to all claims anchored in a UN Security Council resolution. 'This,' said the president, 'is the best I can do ... I want to be very clear on one thing. These are my ideas. If they are not accepted now they are not just off the table. They go with me when I leave office.'[42]

Mutual tolerance was tested to destruction: one high-level meeting was delayed because Yasser Abed-Rabbo called Barak a war criminal and the Israelis demanded an apology before resuming talks. Time pressed again as a final round of negotiations began in the Egyptian resort of Taba on 21 January 2001. President George W. Bush, who was expected to be far less engaged in the peace process, had replaced Clinton in the White House and new Israeli elections were looming in just two weeks. No US officials were present. 'Just go,' Arafat ordered a reluctant Ahmed Qurei, 'take your colleagues, and do whatever you find suitable. I shall endorse anything you and your colleagues agree to.'[43] But Sharon had already threatened that he would not honour an agreement reached by Barak. Over six days the two sides returned to the final status issues as laid out by Clinton's 'parameters', though both of them had reservations. The Palestinians rejected Israeli maps – and objected to their plans for annexation. The Israelis accused the other side of wanting Israel to make all the concessions. On the third day the talks were broken off when two Israeli civilians, restaurateurs from Tel Aviv, were shot dead by masked gunmen in

Tulkarem. On the last day both sides declared that they had 'never been closer' to agreement. US diplomats were much more sceptical about how near they actually were.[44] The Palestinian delegates declined an Israeli offer to fly them back to Gaza by IDF helicopter, fearing 'adverse comment'. Qurei told one Israeli official: 'The boss does not want an agreement',[45] and then reported back to Arafat on what had been achieved and what prospects might be after the imminent Israeli election. 'Agreement may be possible if we talk to the same Israeli negotiators in the future and if we resume from where we left off', he wrote. 'Otherwise God help us.'[46] It felt like the end of a chain of events that had begun a dozen years earlier with the first *intifada*, through Madrid and Oslo, with all its flaws and disappointments. Ehud Barak's legacy, as hopes for diplomacy evaporated and violence raged, was despair, mistrust and hatred.

22

2000–2002

'The culture of peace, nurtured over the previous decade, is being shattered. In its place there is a growing sense of futility and despair, and a growing resort to violence.'

Mitchell Report[1]

'LET THE IDF WIN'

Ariel Sharon's election victory in February 2001 was understood – by Israelis, Palestinians, Arabs and the wider world – to be a fateful moment. Sharon's campaign ads presented him as a benign figure, playing with with his grandchildren or the goats on his Negev ranch, but his clearest message was: 'Let the IDF win.' He played on his reputation for being tough and decisive. 'I know the Arabs, and the Arabs know me,' Sharon repeatedly declared. 'They know my word is my word, my yes is my yes and my no is my no. They know I mean what I say and I say what I think.'[2]

Sharon took 62 per cent of the popular vote; Ehud Barak, a humiliating 38 per cent. Scare tactics by the Barak camp failed dismally: one stunt involved sending thousands of fake call-up papers in IDF-issue brown envelopes ordering reservists to report to their units the day after the election. The message was that a vote for Sharon was a vote for war. But after four months of violence in the West Bank and Gaza Strip, increasingly spilling across the green line, Israelis had lost faith not only in Barak but in seven years of negotiations since Oslo. 'The despair and anxiety that possessed the Israeli public – and the total lack of awareness of Palestinian pain and suffering – are what has put Sharon in power', commented the dovish novelist David

Grossman, admitting that he feared the worst for the future. 'It is one thing to report on a train running off the tracks from a vantage point to the side. It is another thing entirely to report it from inside the train.'[3] Yet no one was surprised at the outcome. 'The most visible effect of the peace process was the constant drift to the right of the Israeli electorate', Shlomo Ben-Ami reflected. 'Arafat was the sin. Ariel Sharon is the punishment.'[4]

Palestinians were understandably apprehensive. Yasser Abed-Rabbo, the PA information minister, called Sharon a 'rabid and dangerous' man with 'hostile intentions to reopen a wider conflict'. Sharon's notoriety went before him, from the Qibya raid in the 1950s through the Beirut massacres in 1982 and his relentless promotion of settlements to the recent provocative visit to the Haram al-Sharif. 'Sharon has chosen war against the Palestinians, and it is easier for the Palestinian people to make war against Sharon than against Ehud Barak,' declared Hussein Sheikh, a Fatah commander in Ramallah. 'The policies of Sharon show that the peace process is gone with the wind. We think he wants the occupation to go on forever, but under another name.'[5]

The atmosphere was febrile and tense. In the week after the election, the Israelis assassinated one of Arafat's bodyguards in Gaza. The next day a Gazan driver for the Egged bus company mowed down eight civilians at a bus stop near Tel Aviv. The perpetrator of this 'lone-wolf' attack was portrayed as a Palestinian everyman with no political affiliation who had snapped because of the intolerable pressure of Israel's blockade, which especially affected breadwinners who were unable to provide for their children; he was also said to be suffering from depression – yet another example of the mentally ill on both sides invariably targeting the enemy. Shortly afterwards a Hamas suicide bomber killed three Israelis in Netanya. If war weariness was growing, the killings continued, attacks triggering retaliation, protests at funerals and further attacks in a seemingly unending cycle.

In Hebron, a ten-month-old baby girl, the child of Jewish settlers, was killed by a Palestinian sniper as she sat in her pushchair. The chubby little face of Shalhevet Pass briefly challenged the terrified features of Mohammed al-Durrah for the most iconic image of suffering children. By the six-month point of the *intifada*, seventy Israelis had been killed and hundreds injured. The Palestinian toll in

the same period was 350 killed and thousands injured. Suicide bombings, shootings and helicopter-launched rocket attacks became
routine. Still, Sharon's orders for punitive action failed to quell criticism from the right: settlers dumped a bullet-riddled car outside his
office to goad him into taking an even harder line.

Sharon reflected the sense of a national emergency by putting
together a national unity coalition with unusual speed, with Labour's
Shimon Peres and Binyamin 'Fuad' Ben-Eliezer as foreign and defence
ministers respectively. The far right was represented by the leader of
the anti-Arab *Moledet* party, Rehavam Zeevi, whose innocuous job
title as minister of tourism belied his political significance. Israelis
had not fallen in love with Sharon but a majority did back him: 'They
have confidence in him only in the way a cancer patient would have
confidence in the only available doctor', one leading commentator
remarked.[6] The new prime minister had vowed not to talk to Arafat,
but he sent his son Omri to see him in Gaza with an offer of a 'temporary' Palestinian state – on 42 per cent of the West Bank – and a
ceasefire. Israeli intelligence reported in mid-February 2001 that the
PLO leader had secretly given the go-ahead for a wave of suicide
bombings.[7] Arafat insisted in a rare interview that he had 'not given
any order to open fire' while at the same time hinting that he could
stop attacks.[8] Later comments by officials who were close to him
attested to a 'double discourse' at this time. 'Arafat would condemn
operations by day while at night he would do honourable things',
recalled Mohammed Dahlan.[9]

In April 2001, Sharon ordered tanks into Gaza, sparking international condemnation and alarm at the apparent final collapse of
Oslo. In May the international Commission of Inquiry led by George
Mitchell issued its findings. It rejected both the Palestinian assertion
that Sharon's Temple Mount walkabout had caused the *intifada* and
the Israeli accusation that Arafat had instigated and masterminded
the unrest, though it did note that the PA had done little to reduce
violence. Israel also came under fire for overreacting to it. The more
nuanced Israeli and American view was that the PLO leader sought
to exploit the violence – the continuation of a pattern that had been
visible a year earlier before Clinton issued the invitation to the Camp
David summit. Ami Ayalon, the former Shin Bet chief, argued that

'once the tiger of Palestinian violence was out of its cage Arafat rode it, did little to moderate it, and in fact fed it to improve his own legitimacy'.[10] For the Palestinian analyst Yezid Sayigh, the spontaneous reactions triggered by Sharon had provided Arafat, weak and bereft of any serious strategy, 'with an escape from his predicament'.[11] The Mitchell Report provided a succinct though bland summary of the state of the conflict at a critical juncture:

> Despite their long history and close proximity, some Israelis and Palestinians seem not to fully appreciate each other's problems and concerns. Some Israelis appear not to comprehend the humiliation and frustration that Palestinians must endure every day as a result of living with the continuing effects of occupation, sustained by the presence of Israeli military forces and settlements in their midst, or the determination of the Palestinians to achieve independence and genuine self-determination. Some Palestinians appear not to comprehend the extent to which terrorism creates fear among the Israeli people and undermines their belief in the possibility of co-existence, or the determination of the GOI [government of Israel] to do whatever is necessary to protect its people. Fear, hate, anger, and frustration have risen on both sides. The greatest danger of all is that the culture of peace, nurtured over the previous decade, is being shattered. In its place there is a growing sense of futility and despair, and a growing resort to violence.[12]

Mitchell urged both sides to de-escalate tensions and return to security co-ordination, and the Israelis to freeze settlement activities. Sharon, described by a leading Palestinian as appearing 'superficially reasonable while setting impossible conditions', demanded a period of seven days' tranquillity before implementation, while the PA admitted it had no control over 'the armed factions responsible for individual incidents'.[13] Neither of Mitchell's calls was heeded.

ARMING THE *INTIFADA*

Each side experienced the war very differently. Only small numbers of Palestinians were actively involved, unlike in the first *intifada*. But weapons, many held by PA forces under the Oslo arrangements, were used on a far larger scale. And many more non-combatants faced prolonged curfews and closures which disrupted normal life and caused severe hardship, especially in areas close to Israeli settlements and army positions. Of all Israel's measures, none was so frustrating and wearing as the checkpoints and blocked roads that turned forty-minute journeys into agonizing odysseys by taxi, foot and even donkey, accompanied by frayed nerves and edgy soldiers. Palestinians needed special permits to use some 450 miles of West Bank roads.[14] Others were completely prohibited. 'Checkpoints did not stop suicide bombings but they did close down lives', noted a foreigner who commuted between Jerusalem and the West Bank, braced for random car searches. 'The worst soldiers to deal with are the new immigrants – Russians, Ethiopians,' complained Dr Samir Khalil, a Ramallah neurologist queuing to cross the teeming Qalandiya checkpoint to reach an East Jerusalem hospital. 'Can you imagine someone who has been in this country for one year, telling me I don't have the proper papers to get to work?'[15] Boredom was as much a hazard as danger. Trying to maintain everyday routines and simply 'getting by' in the face of insurmountable obstacles and time-wasting bureaucracy was an expression of *sumoud* (steadfastness).[16] Conditions in Gaza were especially harsh, with unemployment at nearly 50 per cent and thousands surviving only with food aid from UNRWA. Offshore fishing was banned for long periods, and orchards were uprooted and houses bulldozed when the Israelis said they were being used for cover by gunmen. There was international criticism and debate in Israel over the demolition of buildings in the Rafah refugee camp following one attack. Israel also withheld tax revenues due to the PA – a pressure tactic that was used many times.

In June 2001 there came a new horror, with the suicide bombing of a beachfront disco called the Dolphinarium in Tel Aviv which killed twenty-one teenagers, mostly Russian immigrant girls. Hamas claimed responsibility. The twenty-two-year-old bomber was from a refugee family living in Qalqilya, where he was hailed as a martyr. Arafat publicly condemned the attack and announced a ceasefire, while the US despatched the CIA director, George Tenet, to broker confidence-building measures and a longer truce: it was breached almost as soon as it was agreed. Tenet, who suffered from chronic back pain, surprised his interlocutors by lying on the floor during talks in Arafat's office.[17] Israeli settlers attacked Palestinians in drive-by shootings, while collaborators were blamed when Jamal Mansour and another Hamas leader – as well as two children – were killed in Nablus in an Apache attack that clearly required precise intelligence. The raid was preceded by a phone call to Mansour by someone claiming, falsely, to be from the BBC.[18] Marwan Barghouti, the *Tanzim* leader, who was being closely monitored by the Shin Bet,[19] narrowly escaped when a missile hit a car he had been supposed to be travelling in. 'An increasing number of the Palestinian population discovered that in the bombing of restaurants, cafes, buses, nightclubs and shopping malls in Israel they possessed a weapon that seemed to balance Israel's overwhelming military supremacy', Ahmed Qurei recalled.[20] In August another fifteen Israelis, including seven children, died in a suicide attack on the Sbarro pizzeria in central Jerusalem. Five victims were members of one family. Hamas claimed that attack and named the bomber as Izzedin al-Masri, twenty-three, from near Jenin, issuing a picture of him holding an M16 rifle in one hand and a Quran in the other with an explosive belt round his waist. There was a ghoulish footnote when Islamic Jihad claimed the same bombing but named a different perpetrator and then admitted it was mistaken and had inadvertently blown the cover of one of its own men: he was also en route to a suicide mission when the first explosion occurred.

Israeli F16 warplanes then bombed a police barracks in Ramallah while Orient House, the de facto PLO headquarters in East Jerusalem, was shut down. Tanks and armoured bulldozers went into Jenin, which had acquired a dark reputation in Israel as a breeding ground for Islamist bombers. The PA police fled, but men from Hamas, Islamic Jihad – as well as Fatah – stood their ground and opened fire at the Israelis. Abu Ali Mustafa, the West Bank leader of the PFLP, died at the end of August when laser-guided missiles fired from helicopters went through the window of his Ramallah office as he took a phone call that was made to locate him. The attack was so precise that it left the window frame intact. In Gaza a popular preacher, Sheikh Ibrahim Maadi, praised 'the people who strap bombs onto their bodies or those of their sons' and called for bombings in Tel Aviv and other Israeli cities. 'The Jews have bared their teeth. They have said what they have said and done what they have done. And they will not be deterred except by the colour of the blood of their filthy people. They will not be deterred unless we willingly and voluntarily blow ourselves up among them.'[21]

Fatah adopted a policy of 'mass protest accompanied by controlled violence' – the line pursued by Marwan Barghouti, who argued that Palestinians had a duty to defend themselves:

> If the Israelis continue to attack our lives, killing people on the ground, day by day, attacking with tanks and aircraft, why should the people of Tel Aviv be allowed to live a secure life? You do not respect our 'A' areas, we do not respect your 'A' areas. If you come into my home and do as you please, why should I be polite in your home?[22]

A few days later a bomber disguised as an Orthodox Jew blew himself up on a Jerusalem street lined with schools, restaurants and a hospital. The bomber's severed head landed in the yard of the city's French Lycée, where the pupils were lining up for the beginning of the school day and 'the new headmaster ... laid a cloth over the head and shreds of body to shield the children from the sight and the horror'.[23] The next suicide attack was carried out by an Israeli-Arab citizen from Galilee in the northern town of Nahariya – another grim first. On that day, 10 September 2001, seven other people were killed in three separate attacks within the space of five hours, a rapid-fire sequence of events even by the standards of the second *intifada*. Yet these were soon overshadowed by much bigger and less familiar news from far away.

'ARAFAT IS OUR BIN LADEN'

Osama Bin Laden's attacks on America on 11 September 2001 did nothing for the Palestinian cause. Brief celebrations in East Jerusalem – children handing out sweets to passers-by to celebrate a painful blow to Israel's staunchest ally and weapons supplier, a lone gunman firing celebratory rounds in the Jenin refugee camp – attracted disproportionate media attention that was exploited by Israel to conflate global jihad with Palestinian resistance to occupation. 'Everyone has his own Bin Laden,' Sharon told Colin Powell, the US secretary of state. 'Arafat is our Bin Laden.' Arafat had, in fact, been quick to offer his condolences to President Bush and posed for the TV cameras while donating blood in a Gaza hospital for those injured in New York. 'The vast majority of the Palestinian people stood firmly to condemn this act,' insisted Saeb Erakat, the PLO's chief negotiator. 'It is a very very unfair and despicable act of the Israelis to try to find a linkage to undermine the Palestinians still further. The Israelis are trying to link their military occupation of the West Bank and Gaza with the horrible carnage in New York and Washington.'

Still, Arafat clearly understood the risks of a backlash against the Palestinians as the US worked to restore calm in the occupied territories as it considered its response to 9/11. He and Shimon Peres held an awkward encounter at the end of September on the first anniversary of the uprising, but a ceasefire agreed with CIA help survived only days in the face of opposition by Palestinians (including PA police in Gaza), who demanded to continue fighting Israel. Sharon, under pressure from the right of his coalition, renounced the truce a week later – and also denounced a call by Bush for the creation of a Palestinian state, which the White House insisted had been in the works before the Twin Towers attack. 'Don't repeat the terrible mistake of 1938 when the enlightened democracies of Europe decided to sacrifice Czechoslovakia for a convenient temporary solution,' a furious Sharon told the US. 'Do not try to placate the Arabs at our expense.' The White House called the statement 'unacceptable' – a rare public rebuke.

Shortly after the start of the US invasion of Afghanistan in response to the September attacks, Arafat's PA police fired on Hamas demonstrators in Gaza who praised Bin Laden – and then faced demands from Israel to hand over the killers of Rehavam Zeevi, who was assassinated in a Jerusalem hotel in mid-October. Palestinians said the far-right minister had been singled out because he was an enthusiastic supporter of 'targeted' killings. The PFLP claimed responsibility, vengeance for the assassination of its West Bank leader. Renewed ceasefire efforts were joined by the US Marine general Anthony Zinni, but he struggled in the face of continuing violence and Israeli warnings that he did not understand the 'Palestinian mentality'.[24] The assassination of Hamas leader Mahmoud Abu Hanoud near Nablus in November was widely interpreted as an Israeli ploy to sabotage truce efforts.[25] In mid-December Arafat went on Palestinian TV and radio to warn that the PA would punish anyone who violated his orders and planned suicide bombings and the firing of mortars. This led to a period of quiet which lasted for about three weeks. But then Raed Karmi, a *Tanzim* leader who was wanted by the Israelis, and who the PA had claimed falsely was in prison, was killed in a carefully planned operation by a bomb detonated by a surveillance drone. Karmi was said to be responsible for financing arms purchases.[26] The assassination was opposed by the IDF on the grounds that it would endanger the truce. Alarmed former Shin Bet chiefs had warned the incumbent, Avi Dichter, that he should not simply do Sharon's bidding.[27] 'This event radicalised Fatah's attitude . . . and had far-reaching consequences for the continuation of the conflict and its escalation', an Israeli study concluded later. 'It was a watershed in the attitude of . . . Fatah and the various "Fronts", which now also began to carry out suicide bombings.'[28] Thousands turned out for Karmi's funeral in Tulkarem calling for revenge. And a few days later a young Palestinian walked into a *bar mitzvah* celebration in Hadera, just across the green line from Jenin, and shot dead six people before being killed himself. He was a friend of Karmi.[29] Fatah's involvement in suicide bombings put Arafat under renewed pressure.[30]

Palestinians invariably referred not to suicide but to 'martyrdom operations', and interpreted the phenomenon as a manifestation of despair and hopelessness. 'In the last uprising, children used to play a game called "intifada"', explained the Gaza psychiatrist Eyad El Sarraj.

It was a cowboys-and-Indians-type game – more specifically, Israeli soldier versus Palestinian stone thrower, with the kids trading off between the role of the soldiers armed with sticks to represent guns and the Palestinians with keffiyehs and stones. Many of the children at the time preferred to play the Jew . . . because the Jew with the guns represented power. This game has entirely disappeared. Today, the symbol of power is the martyr. If you ask a child in Gaza today what he wants to be when he grows up, he doesn't say that he wants to be a doctor or a soldier or an engineer. He says he wants to be a martyr.[31]

The bloodshed continued. Five Palestinian schoolboys were killed by an explosive device planted by the IDF to trap fighters in Khan Yunis. Ten Israelis were killed by a car bomb on Ben-Yehuda Street in central Jerusalem. 'I saw people without arms,' one eyewitness said. 'I saw a person with their stomach hanging open. I saw a ten-year-old boy breathe his last breath.' The next day fifteen more people died in a Hamas bus bombing in Haifa. The driver remembered afterwards that a Palestinian passenger had paid his fare with a large-denomination banknote and not waited for his change before moving to the rear of the vehicle to detonate his device – a chilling detail from what was becoming a frighteningly familiar phenomenon. (Police were reportedly investigating a gambling ring that was taking bets on the location of the next suicide attack.) Hamas said the Haifa attack was revenge for the assassination of its West Bank military commander. The bomber was identified as Maher Hubashi, who had sworn revenge after seeing the dismembered corpses of two Hamas leaders who had been killed in Nablus in July. Hubashi had posted photographs of Palestinian children killed by the Israelis on his bedroom wall.[32] Israeli bulldozers ploughed up the runways at Gaza airport, while Arafat's two presidential helicopters were destroyed.

'DEFENSIVE SHIELD'

The al-Aqsa *intifada* reached its bloody peak in spring 2002. In January the Israelis pulled off a propaganda coup when naval commandos captured the *Karine A*, a freighter carrying $50 millions' worth of weapons from Iran to Gaza via the Suez Canal. Arafat denied that the shipment had anything to do with the PLO. That was unconvincing given the key role played by a senior Fatah official, though there was also evidence of links to Hizbullah.[33] Sharon said in an interview that he wished Israel had liquidated Arafat before the evacuation from Beirut in 1982. In early March a lone Palestinian sniper managed to kill ten Israeli soldiers and settlers at a checkpoint near Ofra, outside Ramallah, hiding under an olive tree and firing an old rifle for twenty-five minutes. The story evoked nostalgic comparisons with the 'great rebellion' and fanciful suggestions that the sniper was a veteran *mujahid* who had remained in hiding since 1939 – like Japanese soldiers in south-east Asian jungles decades after the Second World War.[34] By 7 March 2002, the death toll since the uprising began was 1,068 Palestinians and 319 Israelis. On 8 March alone, forty Palestinians were killed by the IDF. The next day's suicide bombing of a popular West Jerusalem cafe – across the road from the prime minister's residence on Balfour Street – prompted bleak reflections about the end of normality for Israelis, including diehard peaceniks who loathed Sharon and were horrified by his policies.[35] And an appalling month culminated on the 27th when a Hamas bomber killed twenty-nine elderly Israelis who were celebrating the Passover festival in a Netanya hotel.

The Netanya bombing coincided with an Arab League summit conference in Beirut. Little of substance usually took place at these ritualistic diplomatic events, and Arafat had failed to persuade the Israelis to allow him to leave his headquarters in the Muqataa to attend. But this was the occasion for a highly significant announcement of a new Arab peace initiative that was proposed by Saudi Crown Prince Abdullah: it declared that the Arab states would recognize Israel in its 1967 borders if there was a just solution to the Palestinian issue. It was a statement of historic importance – in principle binding all twenty-one members of the League – though how it could be translated into reality was unknown. It was in effect a reversal of the famous 'three noes' of the Khartoum summit that had been held just after the Six Days war. Now was not a time for diplomacy, however. 'Our operation coincided with the Arab summit in Beirut,' Hamas declared. 'It is a clear message to our Arab rulers that our struggling people have chosen their road and know how to regain lands and rights in full, depending only on God.'[36]

The Netanya bombing was the trigger for the long-prepared 'Operation Defensive Shield', the biggest Israeli operation in the West Bank since 1967. Within hours the IDF issued emergency call-up orders for 20,000 men. Nablus and all major towns except Jericho were reoccupied in a throwback to the pre-Oslo years. Thousands of Palestinians were arrested. In Nablus bodies lay rotting in the streets and under rubble, fed on by dogs. The IDF spent three weeks 'either destroying, gutting, or looting virtually every national Palestinian institution, public and nongovernmental, security and civilian, that had been built in the last eight years'.[37] In Ramallah Israeli troops exchanged fire with Arafat's bodyguards, surrounded his HQ with tanks and bulldozers and cut off phone lines and power; a week later it resembled a scene from a Mad Max movie, a visitor reported.[38] The IDF advances met little resistance, with one notable exception. Eight days of intensive house-to-house fighting in the densely populated Jenin refugee camp, home to 13,000 people, generated headlines around the world, though Palestinian claims of a massacre were not substantiated. The UN found that twenty-three Israeli soldiers and fifty-two Palestinians were killed, of whom up to forty-seven were fighters and up to twenty-two civilians, according to different estimates. Both sides were accused of endangering civilian lives and the IDF was censured for the destruction of hundreds of houses, many of them by giant D9 armoured bulldozers. 'Filmed from above – a place the size of several football pitches where over 100 houses once stood – is rendered a blank and texture-less expanse', reported one journalist.

> Tangled mounds of concrete and reinforcing rods climb up a gentle slope. The eye alights on a shoe here, the leg of a doll, bedding, pages from the Koran, pictures and shards of broken mirror. It is, somehow, most shocking at the very edges of the devastation where the destruction is partial. Here whole walls of buildings have been peeled off to reveal the still occupied homes inside – pictures, beds and bathrooms – daily life stripped bare.[39]

PA ministries and offices, and roads, water pipes and other Palestinian infrastructure were severely damaged or destroyed to the tune of $360 million, according to the World Bank.[40] Computers and other records were systematically targeted. Casualty figures ranged from 250–500, the majority of them PA security forces, *Tanzim* and other groups. Arafat later referred to it as 'Jeningrad'.

'Operation Defensive Shield' lasted just over a month. Troops pulled out of West Bank cities but continued to encircle them, mounting regular incursions and paralysing traffic and commerce. In May the IDF seemed poised to invade Gaza, but held off. EU diplomats brokered the evacuation of thirteen wanted Palestinian fighters to Cyprus and the Gaza Strip, ending a tense six-week Israeli siege of the Church of the Nativity in Bethlehem. In early June an Islamic Jihad suicide bomber detonated a car packed with explosives next to a bus at Megiddo junction – site of the biblical Armageddon – killing seventeen soldiers and civilians. Two weeks later nineteen more Israelis died on a Jerusalem bus that was targeted by a Hamas suicide bomber. Sharon ordered another, smaller IDF operation – 'Operation Determined Path' – involving new incursions that met minimal resistance but pushed the PA to near irrelevance. President Bush's call for Arafat to go, in a speech on 24 June, seemed to many on both sides to have been scripted in Sharon's office rather than the White House. On the eve of the speech, Sharon's envoy had presented the White House with Israeli intelligence evidence of Arafat's support for terrorism.[41] Bush also spoke for the first time about what he called a 'Road Map for peace' – a phased plan, essentially based on the Mitchell Report, for reaching Palestinian statehood. The PLO leader responded by announcing new elections.

In July an Israeli jet bombed the Gaza home of the Qassam Brigades' commander Salah Shehadeh, killing him and fourteen others, including nine children. Sharon hailed the raid and ignored international condemnation. The commander of the Israeli air force dismissively described the sensation of a 'slight bump' when a one-ton bomb was released from an F16 fighter; a subsequent inquiry found intelligence failures in targeting a densely populated area but no 'premeditated intention' to kill civilians. Shehadeh's killing came against a background of talks on a ceasefire between the *Tanzim* and Hamas and it fuelled familiar speculation about an Israeli effort to sabotage an agreement.[42] Shortly afterwards Marwan Barghouti, the *Tanzim* leader, went on trial in Tel Aviv, charged with planning attacks that killed five Israelis. Barghouti, brandishing his handcuffs and speaking the Hebrew he had learned in prison, told the court that Israel would only have security when it withdrew from Palestinian lands. 'I have charges against the Israeli government!' he declared. 'I have a charge sheet with 50 clauses against Israel for the bloodshed of both peoples!'[43] Barghouti was eventually sentenced to five consecutive life sentences.

BLINDING VIOLENCE

The al-Aqsa *intifada*'s violence took a dreadful toll on mutual empathy and understanding – always in short supply – between Palestinians and Israelis. If the dominant image of the first *intifada* was Palestinian children throwing stones, the symbol of the second was the suicide bomber. 'Israeli Jews see the phenomenon as the ultimate proof of the cruel, zealous and primitive Palestinian nature and conclude that it is impossible to engage in reasonable negotiations with people who send their children to kill both themselves and innocent people', wrote the left-wing Israeli academic Baruch Kimmerling.

> This lack of understanding has blinded most of the Israeli population to the poverty, the lifelong harassment and humiliation, the hopelessness, and the perpetual violence and killing that blight so many Palestinian lives and lead so many young Palestinians to such desperate acts – acts that are not dissimilar to the kind the Bible ascribes to Samson after he was captured by the Philistines. The same lack of empathy has also blinded Palestinians to Jewish grief and anger when suicide bombers massacre innocent civilians, emotions that are intensified when many Palestinians publicly express their happiness after every successful operation.[44]

That disconnect was striking to outsiders who were in contact with both sides and sharply aware of how language was distorted by bitter enmity. 'Where we heard descriptions of families cowering in one room, their homes blasted into by squads of combat troops bursting through the walls of one house to the next, searching, arresting, looting, beating and blasting out again . . . Israelis heard that "terrorist nests" were being rooted out', wrote Emma Williams, a British doctor living in Jerusalem.

> Where we heard friends in Ramallah or Nablus tell of their dread of the nightly pounding from aircraft, tanks and helicopters, a behemoth

hauled out and wielded against a civilian population, Israelis heard that the IDF were fighting 'a tough and hardened enemy', bringing security to the Israeli people by crushing other people, something malevolent.[45]

Public debate in Israel, fuelled by fear and mistrust, focused on the need to defeat terrorism. Avigdor Lieberman, leader of the far-right *Yisrael Beitenu* party, spoke for many when he referred to 'that dog Arafat' and urged Sharon to bomb PA headquarters. Effi Eitam of the National Religious Party called for the PLO leader to be tried for mass murder, and talked of the 'transfer' – the old euphemism for mass expulsion – of Palestinians. Zeev Schiff, the respected *Haaretz* military commentator, warned: 'The day is approaching in the terrible war that is developing here when anyone who comes to destroy Israeli families, including children and babies, will have to consider that Israel will harm his family, and not only his property.'[46] The peace camp was discredited and largely silenced.

In this charged and dangerous atmosphere, the underlying causes of the crisis were too often overlooked. Israelis who lamented the loss of their normal lives often failed to recognize that that had been caused by 'Israel's transformation of the West Bank and Gaza into one large arena of confinement', argued the Palestinian sociologist Salim Tamari.[47] Still, influential Palestinian intellectuals did warn that suicide bombings, as a form of 'resistance communication', were 'not effective in delivering the intended message because they are isolated from a strategic reading of Israeli society's reaction to and understanding of the uprising and of Palestinian resistance in general'.[48] Controversy erupted over a similar appeal in an advert, paid for by the EU, when the signatories were accused of being motivated by self-interest – because they were employed by PA institutions or had links with international NGOs – rather than genuine alarm that the armed *intifada* was proving catastrophic. In late 2002, polling showed that 51 per cent of Palestinians rejected military operations 'as harmful to the Palestinian national interest'.[49] The critical mood was reflected in a new Arabic term that was coined to describe Palestinian reality – *intifawda*: it combined the word *intifada* with *fawda*, meaning 'chaos'.

SEPARATION BY WALL

Hardly surprisingly, in these highly polarized circumstances, security became the dominant theme of Israeli discourse. Yitzhak Rabin and Ehud Barak had both considered building a barrier between Israel and the West Bank, consistent with the old idea of separation between the country's neighbours and enemies, but nothing had come of it. 'Us here, them there', as Rabin had once tersely put it. Barak had famously described Israel as 'a villa in the jungle' – a revealing phrase that was at best arrogant, at worst racist. Unilateral separation, disconnected from any wider strategy, was an old idea whose time had come. 'Within Israeli thinking', noted one observer, 'the construction of the fence is really political code for shutting up shop, locking the door – and acceptance of the fact that, in the short- to medium-term, Jew and Arab simply cannot live together.'[50]

Fences and barriers could clearly work, up to a point, though only to the benefit of one side – as demonstrated by the one that had surrounded the Gaza Strip since 1996. Sharon was initially opposed to parallel action on the West Bank because it would have divided 'indivisible' Jerusalem and left Israeli settlements unprotected. But something was changing: in June 2002 the cabinet voted to begin constructing a new 'separation fence'. Polling showed massive popular support. It was in fact part fence and part concrete wall up to twenty-four feet high, and comprised barbed wire, sensors, cameras and watchtowers. Initially it was planned to run for seventy miles, on or close to the green line, but it also cut eastward beyond it to take in Jewish settlements. The first section was completed by summer 2003 and was presented by the government as an anti-terrorist measure without political implications, though it was an obvious example of creating facts on the ground.

Palestinians protested from the start, dubbing it the 'apartheid wall' – part of an increasingly frequent comparison being made between Israel and white-ruled South Africa, including by a former Israeli attorney-general, Michael Ben-Yair.[51] If it was only about security, they argued, it would have followed the green line, which was why some called it the 'annexation wall'.[52] In fact, according to the

UN, only 15 per cent of the wall followed the green line, while the remaining 85 per cent cut up to eleven miles into the West Bank, leaving some 25,000 Palestinians isolated from the rest of the territory.[53] It cut off Palestinians from land and jobs, creating severe practical and financial hardships, while Jewish settlers enjoyed unimpeded access on dedicated bypass roads that were closed to their neighbours. 'This stupid wall has nothing to do with Israel's security,' protested a Ramallah resident. 'It does not separate Israel from Palestine, it separates Palestinians from Palestine.'[54] The economist Leila Farsakh described a process of 'Bantustanization' by which the occupied territories had been transformed into a population reserve serving the Israeli economy but unable to access it or evolve into a sovereign independent entity.[55] Between 2001 and 2002 the Palestinian economy shrunk by 40 per cent, as measured by GDP per capita.[56]

Preventing suicide bombings trumped all other arguments. 'Nearly all Israelis like the promise of this fence,' noted a Jewish activist who did not. 'They have, and seek, no idea of its human cost and no understanding of its deeper purpose. They also probably have no particular compunction about taking a little more land.'[57] Voices on the left and centre protested at the government's lack of vision but there was still massive public support for an effective security response, however narrow that was. 'Israel is caught in a trap, and military operations cannot free it from this bind', warned Sharon's biographer, Uzi Benziman. 'The choice being offered by its current government is acquiescence in abominable terror, or a corrupting conquest. Nobody in the political leadership is offering a different route – separating from the West Bank and Gaza Strip.'[58] Right-wingers opposed anything that smacked of concessions in the face of Palestinian violence, or of drawing a new border across the heart of *Eretz-Yisrael*. Now Sharon endorsed what one opponent called 'a pharaonic project of concrete, a Chinese wall hundreds of kilometres long to keep at bay the new barbarians'.[59] The decision marked another significant step along the path of unilateral action that he was now pursuing.[60] Israel was again in effective control of the West Bank; Gaza was encircled; while the PA had all but ceased functioning. Oslo, to all intents and purposes, was dead. But it was not yet buried.

23

2003–2006

'The right of the Jewish people to the Land of Israel does not mean disregarding the rights of others in the land. The Palestinians will always be our neighbours. We respect them, and have no aspirations to rule over them. They are also entitled to freedom and to a national, sovereign existence in a state of their own.'

Ariel Sharon, 2004[1]

UNDER SIEGE

It was the third week of September 2002 when Israeli tanks again tightened their grip on Yasser Arafat's Ramallah headquarters, the Muqataa, one of the British 'Tegart' forts of reinforced concrete that had been built during the Arab rebellion in the late 1930s. The IDF operation was designed to force the surrender of Palestinians who were said to have been involved in planning attacks. It followed two more suicide bombings, including one that killed six people on a Tel Aviv bus, though these were claimed by Hamas and Islamic Jihad respectively, not Fatah. Israeli plans to arrest Arafat were aborted under heavy pressure from the Bush administration.[2] Thousands of Palestinians defied a curfew to show support for their president, banging on metal pots in the streets of Ramallah, Tulkarem and Nablus; five were shot dead. International volunteers were stopped from delivering medicine and bottled water to the Muqataa while cranes smashed into the third floor. The phone lines were cut and the air-conditioning units knocked off the windows.

Israeli ministers had pledged publicly neither to harm Arafat nor to

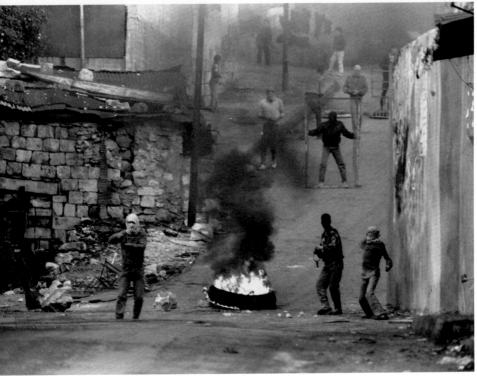

. (*Top*) Ariel ('Arik') Sharon, Israel's Minister of Defence, in helmet and flak jacket during the
vance on Beirut in the early days of the invasion of Lebanon in June 1982.

. (*Bottom*) *Intifada* days: young Palestinians confront Israeli soldiers in the market area of
blus, 1988.

21. Palestinians suspected of throwing bottles being held under detention by Israeli border policemen, Hebron, 1990.

22. Hamas leader Sheikh Ahmed Yassin flanked Israeli guards at his trial in Gaza, 1990.

23. Protests at the funerals of two Palestinians killed by Israeli forces in a West Bank village, 1990.

(*Top*) Embarrassment and irritation in Cairo as Yasser Arafat, watched by Yitzhak Rabin,
ially refuses to sign an agreement with Israel on the withdrawal from Gaza and Jericho.
y 1994.

(*Bottom*) The scene on Jaffa Road in the centre of West Jerusalem in 1996 after a Hamas
ide bomber targeted a number 18 bus.

26. (*Top*) Ehud Barak, Israel's prime minister, meeting the Palestinian Authority Chairman Yas
Arafat and security chief Mohammed Dahlan at the Erez checkpoint on the border of the Gaz
Strip, 1999.

27. (*Bottom*) Likud leader Ariel Sharon, surrounded by police, visits Jerusalem's Temple Mou
(Haram al-Sharif), September 2000.

8. IDF tanks in action
Jenin in operation
efensive shield' during
e re-occupation of the
est Bank in spring
02.

9. Marwan Barghouti,
ader of Fatah's Tanzim
ilitia, on trial in a
ilitary court in Tel Aviv
the height of the
cond *intifada* in 2002.

0. Palestinian detainees
ing taken away for
uestioning by Israeli
oops in Jenin, 2002.

31. (*Top*) Hamas fighters posing triumphantly in President Mahmoud Abbas's abandoned Gaza City office after the Islamist movement's takeover from Fatah in June 2007.

32. (*Bottom*) Palestinian President Mahmoud Abbas, Israel's Prime Minister Ehud Olmert and President George W. Bush at the Annapolis conference in November 2007.

(*Top*) View of a Palestinian town behind Israel's West Bank separation barrier, 2010.
(*Bottom*) Israeli soldiers overcome by their own tear gas at the Qalandiya checkpoint
ween Jerusalem and Ramallah, 2012.

35. (*Top*) Palestinians carrying on regardless amidst the rubble of the Gaza City neighbourhood of Shujaiya, destroyed by Israel during the 2014 war.

36. (*Bottom*) A Palestinian demonstrator throws a shoe at a poster of President Donald Trump during a protest in the occupied West Bank city of Hebron, February 2017.

expel him, though some hoped to make conditions inside so dire that he would leave and not be allowed back. The PLO leader, looking pale and unwell, had received a succession of VIP envoys in his increasingly cramped, squalid and battered surroundings during the previous five-month siege and had only left occasionally. Now the Israelis were at the gates again. Ariel Sharon's move attracted mild criticism. 'Not helpful' was the only response from Washington, where George Bush was preparing for the invasion of Iraq. Europeans spoke out more forcefully, as did the UN, which demanded the immediate lifting of the latest blockade. It ended after eleven tense days but the troops, tanks and bulldozers moved back only a few hundred yards – a redeployment the Palestinians scorned as 'cosmetic'. Arafat remained under pressure from Israel and the Americans to comply with the 'Road Map' – setting out the path to an 'independent viable, democratic, sovereign and contiguous Palestinian state living side by side in peace and security with Israel by 2005' – and to undertake internal reforms. Bush had urged Arafat to show that he was 'capable of ruling' and called on the Palestinians to 'elect new leaders . . . whose reputation was not marred by terrorism', positions that seemed to echo the constant denigration of the PLO leader by the Israelis.[3] The British government, under Tony Blair, focused on promoting PA reform, though it was not determined enough to ensure that Palestinian officials could attend a London conference on the issue in the face of Israeli objections.

Sharon faced coalition difficulties when the Labour party quit over a row about funding settlements. But the Likud then swept the board in new elections. In February 2003, after forming a government with Binyamin Netanyahu as foreign minister, Sharon set out his demands for changes in the PA. Arafat, he told Ahmed Qurei, exuding 'great personal distaste' for the PLO leader, could have only 'symbolic status'. He was to be distanced from the Palestinian security services, relinquish control over finance and appoint a prime minister. Terrorism would have to end and weapons be collected and destroyed; only then could negotiations begin. Arafat was to become 'a non-person, a ghost and an irrelevance to the supposed peace process, with which the Americans remained determined to continue despite Sharon's preference that it be quietly forgotten'.[4]

In public the tone was harsher. In the countdown to the invasion of

Iraq, Sharon's spokesman played to the American gallery by describing Arafat as 'second only to Saddam Hussein and . . . a past master in the art of duplicity'.[5] Changes did take place. Mahmoud Abbas, the Fatah veteran, became PA prime minister, although his appointment attracted little attention as he took office the day 'Operation Iraqi Freedom' began. Abbas was an uncharismatic figure whom Hamas condemned as the 'Karzai of Palestine' – a pejorative reference to the Afghan president supported by the US after the overthrow of the Taliban in 2001. Abbas soon found himself in conflict with Arafat over control of security and jobs for loyal cronies. He was replaced within months by Qurei, the speaker of the Legislative Council and a key player in the Oslo talks a decade earlier.

Palestinian suicide bombings and Israeli assassinations continued. In June 2003 a teenage Hamas bomber dressed as an Orthodox Jew killed sixteen people on a rush-hour bus in the centre of Jerusalem. It was 'a message to all the Zionist criminals that the Palestinian fighters are capable of reaching them everywhere', the Islamist movement declared. The day before Israel had tried and failed to kill a Hamas leader in Gaza. Hamas, Islamic Jihad and Fatah all announced a unilateral ceasefire at the end of the month. That was hailed by Israel as a victory, but in mid-August another Jerusalem bus was bombed by Hamas, this time leaving twenty dead. It was the worst attack of the past three years. Two bombings in September brought more Israeli strikes and an explicit threat to expel or kill Arafat. Shimon Peres, now back in opposition, condemned the idea, as did the left-wing *Meretz* Party. 'If you deport Arafat you leave the ground only for Hamas', it warned. 'That's not something the government is doing out of stupidity. It's a strategy to keep things as they are, to prevent the solution of two states.' Twenty more Israelis died in October on the eve of Yom Kippur: the target was Maxims, a joint Jewish-Arab-owned restaurant on the seafront in Haifa. The bomber was a young woman from Jenin, a trainee lawyer named Hanadi Taysser Darajat: she was avenging a brother who had been killed by the Israelis.[6] 'In the Palestinian territories there are now thousands of such people, men and women, each of them a ticking bomb', commented Uri Avnery, of the leftist *Gush Shalom* movement. 'They don't need a political motive. An Israeli who orders the killing of Palestinians must know that this may well be the result.'[7]

Unlike the West Bank, the Gaza Strip was not reoccupied during the al-Aqsa *intifada* because the Israelis had only limited control on the ground and support for Hamas was strong. The IDF instead mounted raids targeting Palestinian fighters. 'Gaza was different', mused Avi Dichter, head of the Shin Bet. 'You had to choose the right methods.'[8] In one operation in February 2003 forty tanks with helicopter support entered the centre of Gaza City, killing eleven people. In March an undercover unit used civilian taxis to prepare the way for an armoured assault in which the Israelis killed eight people, including a pregnant woman, in the Bureij refugee camp, as well as blowing up several houses. Helicopter strikes were routine amid concerns about the production of a longer range (though still home-made) rocket called the Qassam-3, which was fired across the border at the nearby Israeli town of Sderot. Internal strains showed when fighting erupted between Hamas men and PA police. Arafat, still under siege in Ramallah, was losing his ability to influence what happened in Gaza.[9] Also in March an American student, Rachel Corrie, a member of the pro-Palestinian International Solidarity Movement, which was committed to non-violent direct action, was crushed to death by an Israeli bulldozer in Rafah. Thomas Hurndall, another young ISM activist from Britain, died from an IDF gunshot wound in Rafah after months in a coma. British cameraman James Miller was killed by an Israeli sniper in May; he had been working on a documentary entitled *Death in Gaza*. All three incidents fuelled growing international criticism of Israeli actions. In June thousands of Palestinians came out to protest against 'concessions' made by Abbas at a summit in Aqaba where he denounced terrorism and promised to end the 'armed *intifada*'. In August, after the Jerusalem bus bombing, the Israelis assassinated Ismail Abu Shanab and four other Hamas leaders and bombed the home of the movement's founder, Sheikh Ahmed Yassin – who had been released from prison after the bungled attempt to murder Khaled Meshaal in 1997. Violence stalked the land.

DISENGAGEMENT

In December 2003, Sharon dropped a bombshell: addressing the annual Herzliya strategic conference, the prime minister floated the idea of withdrawing all Israeli troops and settlements from the Gaza Strip. The proposal attracted immediate opposition on the right, but it was less surprising than it initially appeared: Gaza had never had the same emotional pull as what many Israelis still called 'Judea and Samaria', and in security terms it was never less than a headache – as Sharon remembered from his time as head of IDF southern command in the early 1970s. And the financial costs were enormous: an IDF infantry company, an armoured platoon and an engineering force were assigned to guard just 26 families in one small settlement, one of 21 Gaza outposts housing 8,500–9,000 settlers in all, living in gated communities with lush lawns, swimming pools and clinics within sight of Palestinian slums, misery and deprivation.

In fact Sharon had already signalled change. A few months earlier, he had surprised Likud colleagues by for the first time using the word 'occupation' to describe the Israeli presence in the West Bank and Gaza. The idea of acting unilaterally, without agreement with the PA, reflected his profound mistrust of Arafat. It was also influenced by the withdrawal from Lebanon that Ehud Barak had carried out, to popular acclaim, in 2000. Sharon rejected a proposal drawn up by unofficial representatives of both sides for co-ordination between Israel and the PA.[10] That was a 'strategy of despair at the possibility of the joint management of the conflict with the Palestinians and at the possibility of promoting political moves'.[11] In February 2004 Sharon made clear that Israel would carrying on building the West Bank wall, just as the International Court of Justice began hearings into its legality and Israeli activists turned up in The Hague to protest with the charred remains of the No.19 bus that had been hit in a Jerusalem suicide bombing three weeks earlier.[12]

Palestinians saw Sharon's disengagement plan as a ploy to promote the idea that Israel was no longer an occupier, although under international law the West Bank and Gaza were viewed as a single entity, as Israel had recognized at Oslo. Underlying motives included shedding responsibility for 1.5 million Palestinians, and cutting Gaza off from the West Bank, where four small and isolated settlements near Jenin were also to be evacuated. Along with the construction of the separation wall it was another blow to the already fading idea that there would ever be a viable, contiguous Palestinian state in the occupied territories. 'Above all hovers the cloud of demographics', commented Ehud Olmert, Sharon's Likud colleague. Population growth projections showed that within a few years there would be roughy equal numbers of Jews and Palestinians living in Israel, the West Bank and Gaza Strip. If there was no change to the status quo an Arab majority would mean an end to Israel as 'a Jewish and democratic state'. Demographics were an essential plank of the drive for separation. 'We don't have unlimited time', Olmert warned.

> More and more Palestinians are uninterested in a negotiated two-state solution because they want to change the essence of the conflict from an Algerian paradigm to a South African one. From a struggle against 'occupation' in their parlance, to a struggle for one-man-one-vote. That is, of course, a much cleaner struggle, a much more popular struggle – and ultimately a much more powerful one. For us, it would mean the end of the Jewish state.[13]

Olmert's remarks showed an unusually perceptive understanding of shifting views on the other side.

On the immediate issue of Gaza, pro-Israeli commentators suggested that the challenge for the Palestinians was to build a 'decent mini-state, a Dubai on the Mediterranean' whose success would determine whether Israel might be prepared to surrender the West Bank at a later date. Achieving that would clearly not be easy for PA ministries that were handicapped by 'corruption, fragmentation, a lack of funds and resistance to reform', as candidly described in one US diplomatic cable.[14] Sharon's intention, his critics argued, was simply to reshape the occupation without ending it – 'slicing off Gaza is just a diplomatic nose job', quipped one.[15] US pressure was a major factor. The relationship of the disengagement plan to Bush's 'Road Map' was unclear, though both Palestinians and Israelis had their suspicions. 'Sharon has proposed his plan to bypass the Road Map and to serve as a substitute for it', Qurei joshed with Peres, 'and as you know he likes bypass roads!'[16] Dov Weissglass, the prime minister's adviser, appeared to confirm these fears when he famously explained that the aim was to preserve the peace process 'in formaldehyde' – implying that negotiations would never be pursued so that Israel would not have to make any difficult decisions 'until Palestinians became Finns'.[17]

Another reason for Sharon's decision, Weissglass revealed, was strong public support for the Geneva Accord, a two-state peace initiative signed by an unofficial group of influential Israelis and Palestinians in December 2003 that resurrected the Clinton Parameters of 2001. Sharon was also concerned by protests by former Shin Bet chiefs, IDF special forces' veterans and combat pilots, including one who had famously bombed the Iraqi nuclear reactor. For Efraim Halevy, the former Mossad chief, the Gaza disengagement plan was drawn up to escape the 'dangerous trap' of the Road Map.[18] All this meant that Sharon was proving more pragmatic than many had expected. With one eye on Washington he even commissioned a report on settlement activity. Talia Sasson, a former state attorney, produced a devastating catalogue of how government departments had, without authorization, allocated funding to dozens of 'outposts' built on private Palestinian land – even when they were acknowledged to be illegal under Israeli law.[19] 'Sharon appointed me because he needed an answer to the Americans as to why he was not evacuating the illegal outposts', Sasson recalled later. The White House was deeply suspicious of the prime minister's motives, fearing a trick. Neither Sharon nor his successors took substantial steps to dismantle those outposts or halt government funding. Indeed, plans to expand settlement in the West Bank, especially near Maaleh Adumim, just outside Jerusalem, pointed to a more familiar side.

Attacks on Hamas underlined Israel's determination to ensure that the Islamists did not claim victory once the Gaza disengagement had taken place. Sheikh Yassin was finally killed, with seven others, in a missile strike in March 2004: 200,000 people attended his funeral, along with a 21-man honour guard provided by the PA.[20] 'Sharon,' declared Ismail Hanieh of Hamas, 'has opened the gates of hell, and nothing will stop us from cutting off his head.' Yassin's successor as Hamas leader, Abdelaziz al-Rantisi, was also assassinated a few weeks later. 'Israel . . . struck a mastermind of terrorism, with blood on his hands,' the government said. 'As long as the Palestinian Authority does not lift a finger and fight terrorism, Israel will continue to have to do so itself.' Pro-Hamas demonstrators in Ramallah chanted slogans in favour of resistance and attacked those who offered compromises on behalf of the Palestinians. 'Down with the olive branch, long live the rifle', went one chant. 'Revenge, Revenge. Go, Go Hamas, you are the cannon, we are the bullets. Go Qassam, bring on the car bombs.'[21] In May 2004 nearly three hundred homes were razed in Rafah while a tank and helicopter fired on demonstrators, killing nine people. Hamas was not the only target. In June the Israelis killed a wanted *Tanzim* militant named Khalil Marshud from Balata, the big refugee camp in Nablus: he was incinerated in a taxi by a missile, probably while moving from one safe house to another. But generally the population of the West Bank's biggest city had been cowed; armed resistance had ended and Israeli 'surgical' operations had become the norm. 'The usual pattern is for soldiers to arrive unimpeded to their target areas, mostly looking for "wanted" men', reported Beshara Doumani, a Palestinian academic who was visiting from the US.

> After surrounding the area, they force their way into the highest buildings and post snipers on the roofs or at top floor windows. The residents of each apartment building are rounded up at gunpoint and stuffed into a single room on the ground floor. The scene is disconcerting: men in their pajamas ill at ease in someone else's home; children crying, whining, or peeing in their pants; women trying to be useful but hardly able even to make their way across the jam-packed room; awkward lines for a single bathroom; furtive eyes on the door locked from the outside and guarded by Israeli soldiers.[22]

DEATH OF THE PATRIARCH

In the course of the debates over Gaza it became clear that Arafat's health was in serious decline. Physical isolation and psychological pressure were taking their toll on the seventy-five-year-old. In late 2003 he suffered a mild heart attack and experienced vomiting, diarrhoea and stomach pains. In October 2004 he collapsed and lost consciousness at least once. Palestinian and Tunisian doctors monitoring him were reinforced by others from Egypt and Jordan, who diagnosed flu-like symptoms. Israel agreed that he leave for treatment in a Ramallah hospital as long as he returned to the Muqataa afterwards. But as his mysterious condition worsened he was flown out to the Percy military hospital in Paris where he fell into a coma and died, on 11 November. Chopin's 'Funeral March' was played at the Villacoublay air base before his flag-bedecked coffin was flown to Cairo for a funeral ceremony. From there his remains were returned to Ramallah for burial in the courtyard of the Muqataa. Hundreds of thousands gathered round the coffin, which was sprinkled with earth taken from al-Aqsa. Rumours spread that Arafat had been killed by the Israelis, many inevitably remembering the botched Mossad plot to assassinate Khaled Meshaal in Amman in 1997. Forensic investigations focused on the possibility that Arafat had been poisoned by the radioactive substance polonium. But after his exhumation it was eventually determined that he had died of a brain haemorrhage and an intestinal infection.[23] Arafat's widow, Suha, continued to believe that he had been the victim of Israeli foul play.

It was, in any event, truly the end of an era. His death, commented the Palestinian-American scholar Rashid Khalidi,

> was met with both sadness and relief among Palestinians, a sense of anxiety at the disappearance of the only leader most people had ever known, combined with a sense that change was imperative after so many years of going nowhere. Resentment at a father figure who had clung to power for too long was accompanied by deep insecurity at the disappearance of the icon who symbolised the Palestinian cause.[24]

The future of the cause which he had personified and with which he would always be associated had rarely looked so uncertain.

In January 2005 Mahmoud Abbas was elected to replace Arafat as president of the PA and chairman of the PLO. Abbas praised the uprising as legitimate but publicly urged his people not to use weapons. It was not an easy position to maintain: days earlier IDF tank shells had killed seven Palestinian children who were on their way to pick strawberries in northern Gaza, after mortars were fired into Israel.[25] Abbas denounced a 'bloody massacre' and demanded international intervention. In February he met Sharon in Sharm el-Sheikh for the highest-level Palestinian-Israeli encounter since the start of the al-Aqsa *intifada*. It ended in a loose ceasefire agreement: Islamic Jihad and Hamas insisted they were not bound by it but did commit to respecting a *tahdiya* (period of calm). That agreement was considered the end of the uprising – though violence carried on. The Israeli prime minister was said to trust Abbas and to enjoy 'a strong personal relationship' with him.[26]

Over the following months the political scene in Israel was dominated by preparations for the Gaza disengagement – *hitnatkut* in Hebrew. The word was chosen to avoid any sense of withdrawal under pressure. Sharon had a majority in the government, though not in the Likud, which led him to cobble together a new national unity coalition. The Knesset approved the Gaza move by fifty-nine votes to forty. But a call to submit it to a referendum was thrown out, angering the settlement lobby, which was dismayed by the spectacular defection of its most famous patron. Sharon described the decision as a 'painful step' for the nation and himself but essential for Israel's future. Tension mounted in the run-up to the evacuation, which began in mid-August 2005. Many of the Gaza settlers, wearing orange clothes (inspired by the recent revolution in Ukraine) to express their opposition, left peacefully, though some had to be forcibly removed by the IDF in an operation that was cosily named *Yad leAchim* (Helping Hand). Orthodox protesters at Neve Dekalim, the largest settlement, struggled as troops dragged them on to buses. At Kfar Darom residents barricaded themselves in the synagogue. Paint was thrown at troops and police and some evacuees coached their children to leave their homes with their hands up, or wearing a yellow star to evoke Nazi persecution.

Palestinians celebrated as the operation got under way, Israeli troops firing shots into the air to halt a march towards Gush Katif. The crowd burned a cardboard model of a settlement complete with an army watchtower. In Gaza City Hamas activists hung out banners proclaiming: 'The blood of the martyrs has led to liberation.' In the following days Israeli demolition crews razed 2,800 settler homes. The bodies in the Gush Katif cemetery were reburied inside Israel. Near Khan Yunis an abandoned synagogue was set on fire. The IDF completed its withdrawal a few days behind schedule in mid-September. It was billed as the end of an occupation that had lasted for thirty-eight years. Yet it did not end Gaza's embodiment, in the words of the *Haaretz* journalist Amira Hass, of 'the entire saga of the Israeli–Palestinian conflict . . . the central contradiction of the State of

Israel – democracy for some, dispossession for others . . . our exposed nerve'.[27] Israel retained full control of Gaza's borders – apart from the short southern stretch with Egypt – airspace and territorial waters. In international legal terms, it was still considered the occupying power. Despite the unilateral character of the disengagement, PA-Israeli security co-ordination was arranged between Mohammed Dahlan, Nasser Youssef, now the PA interior minister, and the Israeli defence minister Shaul Mofaz, who were used to working together against Hamas – and others. High-level discussions had been held that summer about the assassination of Hassan al-Madhoun, a Fatah commander with links to the rebellious al-Aqsa Martyrs Brigades, with an explicit Israeli request to the Palestinians that he be killed. Madhoun eventually died in an Israeli drone strike in November. It was a sign of changing times that the Shin Bet reported afterwards that his replacement as al-Aqsa leader was heavily influenced by Hamas.[28] Security liaison between the PA and Israel – personified by Dahlan – was portrayed by Hamas supporters as collaboration with the enemy. Hamas was doing well, noted one independent pundit, because for the last four years the lives of Palestinians had been dominated by three Gs: guns, gates and guards. Now a fourth G – God – was becoming more relevant.[29]

RESENTMENT IN RAMALLAH

The imbalance of power between the Palestinians and Israel, and troubled relations with Sharon's government, were only the most visible of the problems Abbas inherited from Arafat. Economic pressure, the lack of official transparency, the PA's dependence on EU and US aid – at over $1 billion per year the highest per capita amount in the world – rumours about corruption and efforts to control Palestinian NGOs all created resentment with the new man in the Muqataa, who so conspicuously lacked the aura of his predecessor. In the decade since Oslo, the once-sleepy town of Ramallah had experienced a boom fuelled by international assistance and the many foreign aid organizations it brought with it, creating a prosperous new elite served by smart restaurants and new hotels. Apartment blocks, office buildings and villas transformed the skyline while the underlying situation deteriorated for ordinary folk.[30] Incomes in 2005 were still 31 per cent lower than in 1999; unemployment was almost 25 per cent.[31] Public service delivery declined sharply. The aid bonanza had created a fake economy. 'It's so artificial,' argued a local businesswoman. 'It depends on foreign aid and and we've seen what happens when it stops. The government employees go without salaries.'[32] To a foreign observer

> PA corruption was very evident, and very painful for those Palestinians who were doing their best to make do with less and less just to keep their children fed and clothed. People would not complain ... about the non-payment of their salaries or about the fact that when their salaries did come through they had been cut.

An EU official returned from Gaza enraged at having seen a brand-new Cadillac being delivered to a PA minister.[33] Many believed that NGOs 'had been deliberately introduced into the Palestinian territories by pro-Israeli western agencies to siphon off the pool of available Palestinian talent and prevent it from being used to mount any resistance to Israel', reported Ghada Karmi, a 1948 refugee from Jerusalem who had come from London to work for the PA. 'Expressions like "capacity building", "sustainability", "democratisation", "empowerment", all previously unfamiliar to Palestine society, became commonplace.'[34] Consultants enjoyed monthly salaries exceeding $5,000, while the average monthly salary of a working Palestinian was $400–$500.[35] Others sneered at a 'Palestinian globalized elite' that lived in a bubble while development trumped governance and Israeli settlements and roads transformed the countryside.

Abbas had pledged to restore law and order and reorganize the security forces, as well as to remove inept or corrupt officials, but PA control of the Palestinian population was 'frequently nominal at best'.[36] And the contrast between life in the West Bank and in Gaza, where violence was far more common, could be shocking. Economic conditions were worsened by Israeli restrictions on movement caused by the separation barrier, the settlements and the network of Jewish-only roads that supported them – and by more than seven hundred checkpoints that frequently operated in an arbitrary manner. All constituted collective punishment in violation of international humanitarian law, human rights watchdogs complained. Israel's fragmentation of the Palestinian territories into disconnected parcels of land had severe practical and psychological consequences. In 2005 the West Bank was divided into ten segments (not including 'closed areas' in the 'seam' between the barrier and the green line). Passage through a checkpoint required a permit, and eligibility varied between locations. Different types of permit were issued for individuals, private vehicles, public vehicles and trucks. Blanket restrictions on movement were often imposed, preventing working-age men accessing employment. The segments were further divided into pockets between which movement was restricted by channelling access through choke points such as tunnels under 'restricted' roads used by settlers.[37] Checkpoints like the ones at Hawara and Bayt Iba near Nablus resembled permanent border crossings with security procedures to control the flow of traffic: pedestrian and car lanes, bunkers, guard towers bristling with machine guns and shrouded with camouflage netting.[38] In the words of the World Bank: 'On any given day the ability to reach work, school, shopping, healthcare facilities and agricultural is highly uncertain and subject to arbitrary restriction and delay.'[39] Raja Shehadeh, the Ramallah lawyer and writer, put it more emotionally:

> Everything has been designed by Israel to make Palestinians feel like strangers in their own country. Whether it is the huge areas of land expropriated and surrounded by barbed wire that one sees while traveling ... the many settlements, the road signs, the presence of settlers hitchhiking on roads forbidden to Palestinians, the military training areas, the danger and apprehension felt just from using the roads, or the uncertainty about being allowed to pass from one part of one's country to another. All these harsh realities conspire to make Palestinians feel that this land is no longer theirs.[40]

Nissim Levy, who spent years working in the Shin Bet, explained the effect in terms that would make sense to Israelis, who still knew so little of life beyond the green line:

> If a boy in Beersheba falls in love with a girl in Haifa, what does he do? He picks up the phone, makes a date and drives to see her. If a boy

from Bethlehem falls in love with a girl from Nablus, what does he do? He has to cross checkpoints, he needs 1,001 permits. The moment that you reach the conclusion that you have nothing to live for, you immediately find that you have something to die for.[41]

POPULAR RESISTANCE

Israel's military dominance, the failures of the PA and Arab governments and the dark mood in the aftermath of the al-Aqsa *intifada* encouraged new forms of resistance that focused on demonstrations and mobilizing civil society. The West Bank barrier was the target of regular protests at Biliin, a village between Ramallah and the green line. Biliin lost almost half its land when it was squeezed between the barrier and nearby Modiin Illit, the largest settlement in the West Bank. In 2004 the International Court of Justice issued an advisory opinion that the construction of the barrier was contrary to international law. The villagers then appealed to Israel's High Court, which eventually ruled in their favour and ordered the barrier to be rerouted. Violence erupted weekly with demonstrators ritually chanting 'No, no to the fence' in Arabic, Hebrew and English, throwing stones while Israeli soldiers fired tear gas and rubber bullets. Palestinian protests attracted left-wing Israelis as well as international activists, and were regularly filmed, reaching a wide audience in the acclaimed film *5 Broken Cameras* a few years later. 'Israeli army bulldozers had begun uprooting olive trees . . . and wiping out the place that had shaped our memories and those of our ancestors', recalled the organizer, Abdullah Abu Rahmeh.[42] Similar protests took place in Budros – captured in both a film and a graphic novel – as well as Niliin and Nabi Saleh. The barrier played a starring role in the campaign for 'Boycott, Divestment and Sanctions' (BDS), which was founded in 2005 on the first anniversary of the ICJ ruling. Earlier boycott campaigns had been launched abroad. The goal of BDS was to increase pressure on Israel 'until it fulfils its obligations under international law and ends its three basic forms of injustice – occupation and colonisation, institutionalised racial discrimination, and denial of UN-sanctioned refugee rights'.[43] The movement, said one supporter, 'recaptured and highlighted the moral core of the Palestinian claim and broadcast it widely to the world'.[44] An early target was the Jerusalem Light Railway, an ambitious project billed by Sharon as helping 'strengthen . . . expand . . . and sustain [the city] for eternity as the capital of the Jewish people and the united capital of the State of Israel'.

Leftist Israeli organizations played an important role on the ground. B'Tselem was founded during the first *intifada*. *Machsom* (Checkpoint) Watch, established by women activists in 2001, monitored 'the bureaucracy of occupation' – the closures, searches and harassment that were an everyday feature of Palestinian life. In November 2004 its members were filming as a music student on his way to give a violin lesson was stopped at the Bayt Iba checkpoint, where soldiers ordered him to play the instrument. The video of the episode attracted a huge audience and disturbing comparisons with stories of Jews made to do the same in Nazi concentration camps. 'If we allow Jewish soldiers to put an Arab violinist at a roadblock and laugh at him, we have succeeded in arriving at the lowest moral point possible', wrote the novelist Yoram Kaniuk. 'Our entire existence in this Arab region was justified, and is still justified, by our suffering; by Jewish violinists in the camps.'[45] (The retort, in the media/propaganda storm that predictably followed, was that Israel's security required vigilance and that the Palestinian who blew up the Sbarro pizza restaurant in Jerusalem in August 2001 had carried a bomb in a guitar case.[46]) *Gisha* (Access) was set up in 2005 to deal with freedom of movement issues. *Yesh Din* (There is Justice) used volunteers to improve human rights in the occupied territories. *Taayush* (Coexistence), founded at the start of the second *intifada*, worked 'to break down the walls of racism, segregation, and apartheid by constructing a true Arab–Jewish partnership' and supported Palestinians struggling to hold on to homes and lands in the South Hebron Hills. *HaMoked* (Focal Point) focused on workers' rights. Breaking the Silence (BtS) was formed by IDF soldiers to confidentially record testimonies about abuses. It began with an exhibition described as being designed to 'bring Hebron to Tel Aviv'. BtS collected 'stories of frightened boys who commanded checkpoints, enforced curfews, and patrolled streets and markets ... stories of the indifference and numbness they developed there'.[47] All these groups, often funded by European governments and charities, faced hostility and harassment from the Israeli government and its supporters at home and abroad. No more than a few hundred people were involved, angered by indifference, extreme nationalism and the mindless use of brute force against the Palestinians. All, in the eloquent words of the *Taayush* activist David Shulman, contributed to 'weaving a fine gossamer web around a raging tiger'.[48]

FORWARD TO THE FUTURE?

In November 2005 Sharon abandoned an increasingly restive Likud to found a new centrist political movement named *Kadima* (Forward) – a familiar pattern in Israeli politics since 1977. It attracted other big Likud names, including Ehud Olmert and Tzipi Livni, who had served as minister of justice, as well as Labour's Shimon Peres and Haim Ramon. *Kadima*'s creation opened up intriguing possibilities for a realignment of the middle ground of Israeli politics. In January 2006, however, Sharon suffered a massive stroke and sank into a coma, leaving a giant question mark over what he might have done next. He was replaced on an interim basis by Olmert. (Two months later Olmert led *Kadima* to election victory and became prime minister when Sharon was declared permanently incapacitated.)

Within weeks of Israel's Gaza pullout the Palestinian political scene had also undergone an equally dramatic transformation. Abbas, with the encouragement of the US, where George Bush was committed to Middle Eastern 'democracy promotion' in the wake of the overthrow of Saddam Hussein, called long-delayed elections to the Palestinian legislative council, the first since 1996. Changes to the electoral system were designed to strengthen Fatah's position. Hamas took a pragmatic decision to participate, its instinct for survival overcoming its principled opposition to the Oslo arrangements. Its campaign focused on the PA's many shortcomings: one TV advert opened with the word 'corruption' which swiftly exploded into a ball of fire, followed by a similar fate for 'nepotism', 'bribery' and 'chaos'. Only then came pictures of Palestinian gunmen battling Israeli forces in Jerusalem and Nablus. Mohammed Dahlan, for Fatah, ridiculed the Islamists. 'Hamas accused Arafat of betraying the people and destroying Palestine [by reaching the Oslo accords with Israel],' he sneered. 'But here they are taking part in elections because of what Arafat agreed. They should apologise to Fatah and admit that our plan triumphed.'[49] Polling, observed by international monitors, including the indefatigable Jimmy Carter, was orderly and with an impressively high turnout of 77 per cent. The expectation in Western capitals had been that a 'democratically legitimised and strengthened' Abbas would resume negotiations with Israel.[50] But in the weeks before polling day worried Fatah activists urged the Israelis to help postpone the elections.[51] The shock outcome was that Hamas won 42.9 per cent of the vote and 74 of the 132 seats; Fatah won 45, with independents and leftists taking the rest. It had long been clear that Abbas was making little progress with reforms and that Hamas was feeling confident, but the showing for the Islamists was still far stronger than anyone had predicted. It was a truly historic victory. Palestinians compared Abbas to the Algerian president, Chadli Benjedid, who plunged his country into a bloody civil war in 1990 by legalizing Islamist parties and allowing them to take part in elections without ever expecting them to win.[52]

Abbas, like Arafat, had broad executive powers as president but he needed parliamentary approval for his budget and legislative proposals. It was unclear how he could pursue the 'Road Map' to a two-state solution when the majority in parliament was controlled by a movement that opposed Oslo, refused to recognize Israel, had carried out multiple suicide bombings and was designated a terrorist organization by Israel and the US. The fact that Hamas had observed a *tahdiya* since March 2005 was not deemed sufficient to cancel out the other negatives. Nor were signals from Hamas that its participation in the elections could be considered de facto acceptance of Oslo, and that it might accept the 2002 Arab peace initiative (supported by all twenty-one members of the Arab League) if Israel recognized 'the rights of the Palestinian people'. Israel's unambiguous view, echoed by the so-called 'Quartet' (the US, EU, UN and Russia), despite Russian reservations, was that Hamas was a terrorist organization that refused to recognize Israel and was implacably hostile to peace moves.

The Quartet then slashed its financial support to the PA while Israel withheld customs and tax revenues it collected on its behalf. The instant result was that thousands of PA employees could no longer be paid – a hammer blow to an already rickety economy.

'Nobody seemed to have a strategy on how to deal with Gaza', a senior UN official admitted later.[53] The boycott decision became a byword for the hypocrisy of Western governments which called for democracy (while supporting their favourite Arab autocrats and selling them expensive weapons) but then ignored its results, even though, in the ever-toxic circumstances of the Israeli–Palestinian conflict, that was not the only issue at stake. The election, in any event, was a devastating verdict – a classic protest vote – on the performance of the PA (battered by allegations of corruption), impatience with infighting and, above all, continued occupation with no end in sight. 'In contrast with the decay and corruption and fecklessness of the Palestinian Authority under Fatah, which has essentially lost touch with the people, Hamas was widely seen as attentive to their needs and largely untainted by corruption', wrote the UN's special co-ordinator for the Middle East peace process, Alvaro de Soto.[54] Ismail Hanieh, the Gazan teacher who headed the Hamas list, said: 'The Americans and the Europeans say to Hamas: either you have weapons or you enter the legislative council. We say weapons *and* the legislative council. There is no contradiction between the two.'[55] Hanieh became prime minister and formed a government in March 2006. In May representatives of five factions – Fatah, Hamas, Islamic Jihad, the PFLP and DPLP – produced the so-called 'prisoners' document', which committed all to recognize the need to both resist *and* negotiate and alleviate internal tensions.[56] The consensus had little impact. Hamas MPs were banned from leaving Gaza by Israel and had to swear their constitutional oaths by video link to Ramallah. Exactly how these complicated arrangements would work was still being debated when, in June 2006, a new flare-up triggered wider escalation across an always unstable and dangerous region.

24

2006–2009

'The earthquake in the Zionist towns will start again and the aggressors will have no choice but to prepare their coffins or their luggage.'

Hamas statement

'A TIRELESS BATTLE UNTIL TERROR CEASES'[1]

On a humid afternoon in July 2006, a twelve-year-old Palestinian boy named Nadi al-Attar set off on a donkey cart with his grandmother Khayriya and two male cousins to pick figs from an orchard at their home near Beit Lahiya in the northern Gaza Strip. Without warning, an explosion killed the woman and Nadi and injured the other boys, one of them losing both legs. Eyewitnesses and subsequent investigations revealed that an artillery shell or missile had been fired by Israeli forces, apparently because Qassam rockets had been launched across the nearby border earlier. Later that afternoon an eleven-year-old girl was killed by a shell in Beit Hanoun, a mile or two further east. The IDF insisted it did not target civilians, only terrorists, and although innocent people could be hit, a spokesman admitted, the responsibility lay with the terrorists.[2] It was just one day in the bloody course of 'Operation Summer Rains', the incongruously pastoral name chosen to describe the latest assault on the volatile front line of the Israeli–Palestinian confrontation.

The 1.5 million people living in the coastal enclave had seen little benefit from the unilateral withdrawal of Israeli troops and settlers ten months earlier. On the eve of the disengagement, 65 per cent of

Gaza's population lived under the poverty line, subsisting on less than $2 per day, while 35 per cent of the workforce were unemployed. Ambitious plans by the World Bank and other international donors for industrial parks, export zones and desperately needed jobs had come to nothing. Israeli restrictions on the border crossings continued so that the number of Palestinian workers entering Israel dropped to one-third of the pre-disengagement average; Gazan exports through the Karni cargo terminal did not pick up even after the signing of an agreement on movement and access in November 2005. Life was 'miserable and dangerous', said John Ging, UNRWA's director of operations. Jan Egeland, the UN emergency relief co-ordinator, warned that Gaza had become 'a ticking time bomb'.[3] Victory for Hamas in the PA elections had boosted the movement's self-confidence and worsened tensions with Fatah. In Gaza, Fatah forces loyal to Mohammed Dahlan seized weapons to stop them being used by Hamas. Rockets fired across the border led to repeated IDF air strikes and shelling. In April 2006 Israel declared the PA 'a hostile entity'. Israel's own initiatives contributed too. On 8 June, Israel assassinated Jamal Abu Samhadana, a former Fatah official who was now leader of the Popular Resistance Committees (PRCs). Eight civilians, seven of them members of one family, were killed in an explosion at Beit Lahiya the next day. Sderot was then hit by Qassam rocket fire. Hamas ended its commitment to the unilateral *tahdiya* or period of calm that had been agreed with Fatah and other groups in Cairo in March 2005. Since then, Hamas had not taken responsibility for any attacks but had made it clear it would not prevent others from carrying them out. 'The earthquake in the Zionist towns will start again and the aggressors will have no choice but to prepare their coffins or their luggage', it warned. On 25 June Palestinian fighters tunnelled 300 yards under the border near Kibbutz Kerem Shalom, killed two members of an IDF Merkava tank crew, captured a third soldier and dragged him back into Gaza. Hamas, the PRCs and the hitherto-unknown *Jaysh al-Islam* (Army of Islam) took part in the attack. Corporal Gilad Shalit was the first IDF soldier captured by Palestinians in over a decade – a bargaining chip that might be used to free some of the thousands of Palestinians held in Israeli prisons. The goals of 'Operation Summer Rains', as approved by Ehud Olmert's cabinet, were to free Shalit, halt Qassam fire and disarm all terrorist organizations. Air strikes and artillery shells hit infrastructure and bridges linking the southern and central parts of the Gaza Strip in tandem with a series of ground incursions. The Israelis fired missiles at Gaza's only power plant, cutting off electricity to hundreds of thousands of people. By mid-August 215 Palestinians had been killed and scores of Hamas supporters arrested across the West Bank.

LEBANON, AGAIN

The crisis widened in mid-July. Inspired by the events in Gaza, and tempted to open a second front and help release its own prisoners, Lebanon's Hizbullah acted in solidarity with Hamas, its fellow-member of what both called the 'axis of resistance', and mounted a raid on Israel's northern border. Shia fighters killed three Israeli soldiers and captured two others in a well-planned operation that was a more sophisticated replay of what had happened at Kerem Shalom three weeks earlier. Five more soldiers were killed inside Lebanon in a failed rescue operation. The circumstances were different from 1982, when the PLO was Israel's target, but the Second Lebanon War took place on much of the same territory. The 34-day conflict saw an Israeli ground invasion of the south, rocket and artillery fire and air raids that killed some 1,300 Lebanese, mostly civilians, and 165 Israelis, including 44 civilians. It again saw masses of refugees fleeing the fighting, though this time that happened on both sides of the border as over 240 Hizbullah rockets hit targets inside Israel. It stoked tensions across the Arab world as well as protests and recriminations in Israel. Major-General Dan Halutz, the IDF chief of staff, faced criticism after admitting that he had sold shares on the Tel Aviv stock exchange hours after the raid, anticipating financial losses in the crisis he knew was about to start. Normal life in the metropolitan 'bubble' of Tel Aviv carried on undisturbed in other ways throughout the war. Still, the connection with what was happening on the Palestinian front was thought-provoking. For the Israelis, fighting in Lebanon was alarmingly different from Gaza, where the IDF enjoyed overwhelming superiority, its armour protecting it from Palestinian

RPGs. Hizbullah fighters, by contrast, were equipped with sophisticated anti-tank missiles that could damage even the mighty Merkava.[4] Olmert, who (as Israelis often noted) had little military experience, linked the two fronts – promising 'a tireless battle until terror ceases' – though his goals for both seemed unlikely to be achieved in either. 'We will persist until Hizbullah and Hamas comply with those basic and decent things required of them by every civilised person,' he told MPs. 'Israel will not agree to live in the shadow of missiles or rockets aimed at its residents.'[5] Both the Gaza and Lebanon attacks, it was noted, had been launched from territories from which Israel had withdrawn unilaterally. Olmert's ideas about following Sharon's Gaza disengagement with a unilateral pullback from the West Bank were quietly shelved.[6]

Palestinians in Gaza displayed pictures of Hassan Nasrallah, Hizbullah's leader, who flaunted his blows against Israel on Al-Manar TV and won plaudits across the Arab world – as well angering the conservative Sunni governments in Saudi Arabia and elsewhere that were deeply hostile to Iran and its Lebanese Shia ally. Nasrallah admitted later that he had not anticipated that full-scale war would erupt. Israeli analysts looking at Lebanon concluded that efforts to crush the Palestinian *intifada* had had a damaging effect on the country's overall military readiness – a familiar element of pragmatic 'dovish' thinking. 'The responsibility of the IDF and the other components of Israel's defence community to provide for the safety of the country's citizens in the face of suicide bombers seems to have drawn their energy, thinking, and resources away from preparations for conventional war', argued one expert. And there was likely to be a direct effect on the Palestinian question. 'Opponents of disengagement can now be expected to argue persuasively that if the reality of Gaza and Lebanon were to duplicate itself in the West Bank, Israel's vital core would be paralysed.' Hizbullah's success in marketing its narrative of victory might lead to greater polarization among the Palestinians and make it more difficult for moderates to resist the temptation to emulate the Lebanese militia. The argument that 'the only language Israel understands is force' was now likely to enjoy a field day in Palestine.[7]

HAMASTAN

Nothing had been resolved in Gaza by the time the Lebanon war ended in August 2006. The toll of 'Operation Summer Rains' was 184 Palestinians, including 42 children, killed, 650 injured and one IDF soldier killed; $15.5 millions' worth of infrastructure had been damaged by Israeli incursions, shelling and air strikes.[8] Shalit remained in captivity, moved from cellar to safe house to avoid Israeli surveillance. In September Abbas and Ismail Hanieh agreed to form a unity government but were unable to agree a common stance towards Israel. The US repeatedly urged Abbas to break with Hamas, though the Palestinian president, noted the UN envoy Alvaro de Soto, was 'philosophically as well as strategically disinclined to cross the line from brinkmanship into confrontation'.[9] US security assistance, run by Lt-General Keith Dayton with British and Canadian support, was channelled directly to Abbas's presidential guard, not the PA. The message was a dual one: reform the 'Arafat-era hotch-potch of security forces' and build up forces to take on the Islamists.[10] 'It was getting harder for the Israelis to claim that the Palestinians weren't fighting terror', wrote the US secretary of state Condoleezza Rice, 'and harder for them to claim that they had no partner for peace.'[11] Light weapons and ammunition were delivered from Egypt, with Israel's agreement.[12] Mediation by Qatar, the maverick Gulf state which was close to Hamas and other Islamist movements, failed to halt clashes, however, and Israel reacted immediately to any firing from Gaza. In November IDF shells killed nineteen Palestinians and wounded forty in Beit Hanoun because of what the Israelis said was a technical malfunction in response to Qassam rocket fire. 'Israeli policies, whether this is intended or not, seem frequently perversely designed to encourage . . . continued action by Palestinian militants', de Soto reflected.

> The occupation/resistance dynamic may be a textbook example of the chicken/egg quandary, and it is difficult to refute Israel's argument that it is obliged to hammer the Palestinians because it must protect its citizens. But I wonder if Israeli authorities realise that, season after season,

they are reaping what they sow, and are systematically pushing along the violence/repression cycle to the point where it is self-propelling.[13]

In February 2007, internecine fighting intensified. Agreement in Mecca, brokered by the Saudis, led to the formation of a new Palestinian unity government. The US and Israel, both opposed to Palestinian reconciliation, were furious as the distinction between moderates and extremists was immediately blurred – Rice called it 'a devastating blow'.[14] The UN, by contrast, believed that Hamas could become more pragmatic, but it was powerless to help. Mohammed Dahlan, seen as a 'safe pair of hands', was appointed as national security adviser to Abbas to appease the Americans. But Hamas refused to end rocket fire. Law and order broke down and conditions worsened. *Jaysh al-Islam*, which had helped capture Shalit, kidnapped the BBC's Gaza correspondent Alan Johnston, who, ironically, had described unemployed militants with time on their hands after the Israeli withdrawal. 'Gaza', Johnston mused, was 'the only place in the world where your kidnapper's one demand is that he should be allowed to become a policeman.'[15] Over the next few weeks rocket attacks increased, as did Israeli actions against Hamas. Abbas, egged on by Washington and Cairo, reinforced Fatah's security presence in Gaza, though to little effect. In mid-June the Shin Bet chief, Yuval Diskin, described Fatah as so 'desperate, disorganised and demoralised' that it had requested Israeli help to tackle Hamas.[16] The crisis peaked when the Islamists took control of the entire Gaza Strip, with at least a hundred people killed in four days of fighting, and hundreds of Fatah officials fleeing by sea to Egypt. Hamas men killed an officer of the Palestinian presidential guard by throwing him off the top of a fifteen-storey building. Fatah men did the same to a Hamas official. Hamas seized Abbas's Gaza City compound, the only institution still in its rival's hands. In a stark demonstration of the new reality, a masked, gun-toting Hamas fighter lounged in an ornate chair in the presidential office and mockingly pretended to make a phone call: 'Hello Condoleezza Rice. You have to deal with me now, there is no Abu Mazen [Mahmoud Abbas] anymore.'[17] Rice called it 'the final indignity'.[18]

Abbas declared a state of emergency and dissolved the government.

Salam Fayyad, a respected, Texas-educated economist who had worked for the International Monetary Fund and been the PA's finance minister, was appointed to replace Hanieh. Hamas presented the Gaza events as a pre-emptive action against an imminent coup by Fatah, backed by the US and Israel. 'Dahlan was trying with American help to undermine the results of the elections', insisted Mahmoud al-Zahar, who had been foreign minister in the Hanieh government. 'He was the one planning a coup.'

It was a shocking outcome that could be blamed on multiple interlinked factors: the long failure of Oslo; Hamas's electoral victory; and the international sanctions that were imposed as a result. During the 2005 debate about disengagement from Gaza, the view in the IDF was that Hamas would have an interest in maintaining calm to avoid the risk of an Israeli reoccupation. Dissenting voices had also warned, however, against the creation of what they had dubbed 'Hamastan'.[19] In the wake of the takeover, that now seemed inevitable. 'If you have two brothers put into a cage and deprive them of basic essential needs for life, they will fight,' said the Palestinian foreign minister, Ziad Abu Amr.[20] The Quartet pledged support for Abbas while the EU declared him the 'legitimate president of all Palestinians', suspended aid projects in Gaza, and lifted its boycott on the PA. The US did the same. But the occupied Palestinian territories had now been divided in two – three if East Jerusalem, under unrecognized but unshakable Israeli sovereignty, was treated separately, fragmented politically as well as geographically, with rival governments in Gaza and Ramallah claiming constitutional legitimacy. In these unpromising circumstances – in a year that marked the fortieth anniversary of Israeli occupation – another effort was launched to reach a peace settlement.

THE ROAD TO ANNAPOLIS

Ehud Olmert, described by one respected commentator as 'the most pragmatic Israeli leader since 1967',[21] hailed the Hamas takeover as an opportunity for 'dramatic change' and tried to persuade the US to treat the West Bank and Gaza Strip as separate entities – breaking the link that had been enshrined in Oslo. The response of the Bush administration was that it would do so only if Israel made concessions that would improve the 'quality of life' in the West Bank. The effect of the separation barrier on Palestinian communities, the daily grind of Israeli checkpoints slowing movement, and settler violence were all documented by the UN, US and other governments, as well as by local and international NGOs. There was certainly plenty of room for improvement.

In July 2007 President Bush announced a new effort to restart peace talks. It could 'help sustain the good guys', Rice told the president, appealing to his homespun wisdom. Bush suggested that the new gathering be described as a 'meeting' rather than a conference, to avoid raising expectations, and to assuage Israeli sensitivities about wider international involvement. The Arab invitees – unusually including both Syria and Saudi Arabia, because Bush wanted to maximize regional support – were strikingly unenthusiastic, expecting failure and fearing a new paroxysm of violence like the one that followed the Camp David debacle in 2000.[22] Abbas and Olmert held several rounds of talks in Jerusalem but there was no sign of significant movement by either side. In September the Israelis again designated Gaza a 'hostile territory'. The disconnect between these discreet exploratory talks and diplomatic manoeuvring and the harsh reality on the ground was disconcerting. In July the IDF had carried out several big incursions into Gaza. Hamas largely observed a unilateral ceasefire and most of the rockets fired in this period were launched by Islamic Jihad and the PRCs. On the eve of the meeting in Annapolis, Maryland, however, the Israelis scaled back operations in Gaza, allowed the export of strawberries and flowers at peak season and permitted a one-time shipment of lamb to enter the strip. Olmert pledged to freeze new settlement construction. But this promise, as so often, was largely meaningless as his government continued to expand a dozen existing settlements in the West Bank and, as always, it insisted that 'united' Jerusalem was exempt.

Expectations for Annapolis were kept low: the leaders on both sides were weak and unpopular compared to the illustrious if flawed giants they had replaced. Abbas had just lost half his kingdom to Hamas, with no prospect of recovering it any time soon: his presidency, went the joke in Ramallah, barely extended beyond his Muqataa headquarters. Olmert had been damaged by his conduct of the last war in Lebanon and was now facing corruption charges dating back to his time as mayor of Jerusalem. In addition, Bush's credibility was tainted by the chaos of post-Saddam Iraq.

In Gaza thousands rallied to attack Abbas for even being prepared to make concessions. He and Olmert pledged to 'immediately launch good faith, bilateral negotiations in order to conclude a peace treaty resolving all outstanding issues'. The goal was a final peace settlement to 'establish Palestine as a homeland for the Palestinian people just as Israel is the homeland for the Jewish people'. It was a reformulation of the classic principle of the two-state solution – though, of course, minus the crucial details on which, as ever, everything hung.

On the surface, the atmosphere seemed promising; unusually, Olmert's Annapolis speech contained a strikingly empathetic acknowledgement of Palestinian suffering, with even his fiercest critics wondering briefly if this marked the emergence of an Israeli De Klerk, the South African president who had released Nelson Mandela and negotiated the peaceful end of apartheid. 'Many Palestinians have been living for decades in camps, disconnected from the environment in which they grew up, wallowing in poverty, in neglect, alienation, bitterness, and a deep, unrelenting sense of humiliation,' he declared. 'I know that this pain and this humiliation are the deepest foundations which fomented the ethos of hatred toward us. We are not indifferent to this suffering. We are not oblivious to the tragedies that you have experienced.'[23] Crucially, however, he did not acknowledge any Israeli *responsibility* for what had happened in 1948. Just a few days later Olmert recalled his own earlier statement, that 'if we don't do something, we will lose the possibility of the existence of two states' and '[w]e will be an apartheid state'.[24] Abbas said that despite their differences he had noted Olmert's desire for peace. The novelty was that for the first time since 1993, both sides appeared ready to reach agreement even though the underlying gaps – on settlements, borders, Jerusalem and refugees – looked as difficult as ever to close. Abbas, in addition, now had no control over Gaza. And as always, the imbalance between them was enormous. Their declared goal was agreement on Palestinian statehood before President Bush left office in January 2009.

ABBAS–OLMERT TALKS

Hopes that Annapolis would lead to a speedy breakthrough faded quickly. Follow-up talks were overshadowed by a row over the latest plans to expand Har Homa, the 'last rampart in a wall of settlements' encircling East Jerusalem and cutting it off from Bethlehem and the rest of the West Bank. An international donor conference held in Paris in December 2007 allocated a whopping $7.2 billion to the PA but the isolation of Gaza continued unrelieved. Tony Blair, who began serving as envoy to the Quartet after stepping down as British prime minister, adopted a 'West Bank first' strategy that supported Salam Fayyad's plans for building national institutions and infrastructure, strengthening governance and, especially, security – echoing the approach of the Jewish *Yishuv* in the Mandate period. Fayyad wanted to push ahead regardless of progress in negotiations with Israel. But 'economic peace' was not enough, he insisted.[25] Palestinian critics protested that the aim was in fact to reinforce the siege of Gaza by 'increasing the fragmentation of the Palestinian people, in pumping up a ruined leadership, and in thwarting any chance of national unity for the Palestinians'.[26] Israel did ease its blockade – items as innocent as hummus, pasta, writing materials and toilet paper were all banned at different times[27] – but fuel and clean drinking water remained in short supply in Gaza. Hamas signals of readiness for a formal ceasefire were ignored by Israel. Olmert, bolstered by the Quartet, stuck by his demands for an end to violence, recognition of Israel's right to exist and abiding by existing agreements – the last stipulation implying adherence to the terms of Oslo. Israel's settlement policy, as Olmert's critics were quick to point out, was certainly in breach of the Oslo spirit.

In January 2008 Israel declared 'economic warfare' on Gaza. The UN recorded 80 Palestinians killed that month alone; in the same period 267 rockets and 256 mortars were fired across the border, injuring 9 Israelis. Israel carried out three assassinations immediately after a visit by Bush to Jerusalem and Ramallah, where demonstrators waved placards declaring 'Remove all settlements', 'It is the occupation stupid' and 'Gaza on our mind'. Bush did address the settlement issue: 'Swiss cheese isn't going to work when it comes to the territory of a state,' he said after talks with Abbas. March saw another big IDF incursion into Gaza that left at least 106 Palestinians dead. Half of them, said B'Tselem, 'did not take part in the hostilities'.[28] In June another six-month *tahdiya* was agreed with the head of Egyptian intelligence, General Omar Suleiman, who was working to broker a deal to exchange the captive soldier Shalit for 1,000 Palestinians. Suleiman always had a detailed timeline for action, noted the new UN envoy, Robert Serry, but that timeline constantly had to be extended.[29]

Negotiations continued quietly over the next few months, led by Livni for Israel and Ahmed Qurei for the Palestinians. The principle was that nothing could be agreed until everything was agreed. In May Qurei proposed that Israel annex all Jewish settlements – referred to as 'neighbourhoods' by Israel – in the Jerusalem area except for the strategically positioned Har Homa. Saeb Erakat hammered home the significance of this by telling the Israelis they would get 'the biggest *Yerushalayim* in history' – his unusual use of the Hebrew name suggesting an intimacy that rankled with Hamas and other critics, who complained of the Palestinians' 'cringing' and 'ingratiating' behaviour[30] when details of the talks were leaked to al-Jazeera and the *Guardian*.[31] (Erakat complained of a 'slander' campaign.) Livni 'appreciated' the offer but dismissed it because it did not include Har Homa or Maaleh Adumim on the road to Jericho and Ariel, the latter much deeper in the West Bank. Israel's position was fully supported by the Bush administration. The documents also showed that the Israelis would accept just 5,000 refugees, while the Palestinians proposed the return of 10,000 a year for 10 years – a total of 100,000. It was a stark reminder that no other issue was harder to deal with.[32]

In a replay of the dual negotiating tracks in Washington and Oslo in the early 1990s these talks were accompanied by a parallel private channel between Abbas and Olmert, who met dozens of times without aides, Condoleezza Rice acting as intermediary.[33] In August

Olmert offered Abbas a take-it-or-leave-it 'package deal'. It included a near-total withdrawal from the West Bank, proposing that Israel retain just 6.3 per cent of the territory in order to keep control of the major settlements. The Palestinians would be compensated with a swap of Israeli land equivalent to 5.8 per cent of the West Bank, along with a link to the Gaza Strip. The Old City of Jerusalem would be placed under international control. The two leaders met for the last time on 16 September 2008.[34] Olmert showed Abbas a map but refused to give it to him so it would not be used as an 'opening position' in future negotiations. Abbas sketched the map on a paper napkin and said he was unable to decide and needed to consult colleagues. 'No,' Olmert replied. 'Take the pen and sign now. You'll never get an offer that is more fair or more just. Don't hesitate. This is hard for me too, but we don't have an option of not resolving [the conflict].' Abbas groaned and then postponed another meeting arranged for the next day. It never took place.[35]

Olmert insisted afterwards that the Palestinian president had missed a historic opportunity – a claim that had been made by Israelis for decades. Palestinians retorted that a deal with a lame-duck Israeli prime minister – who had already announced that he would resign because of criminal charges he was facing[36] – would have been worthless, as some of Olmert's own officials also argued.[37] Israeli commentators suggested that Olmert, who was subsequently tried and gaoled, had gone far beyond his brief in order to 'save his own skin out of fear of the law',[38] or to acquire a 'get out of gaol free' card in the form of a historic peace agreement. 'Even today, after years of disappointments, a politician can gain instant and widespread popularity – in the Israeli media, at least – by promising to do everything within his power to bring the conflict with the Palestinians to a close', commented Moshe Yaalon, the former IDF chief of staff. 'On occasion, these promises can salvage even the most tainted public image.'[39] Others supported Olmert's claim that the effort genuinely represented the last chance for a two-state solution.[40] Comparisons were made with Ehud Barak's offer to Arafat at Camp David in 2000. The US envoy George Mitchell, however, believed that Abbas had good reason to doubt elements of the Israeli proposal on refugees, Jerusalem and borders. 'The vagueness that would be necessary for Olmert would be a liability for Abbas', he concluded.[41] In any event, even if Abbas had accepted the offer, fierce opposition from Hamas and other quarters would very likely have defeated it. Shortly afterwards there was another shocking reminder of the price of relying solely on military means to 'manage' rather than resolve the conflict.

CAST LEAD

Gaza's next war was a few days shorter than the 2006 Lebanese conflict, but far more destructive – and controversial. Israel's goal in 'Operation Cast Lead', so often enunciated since Sharon's unilateral disengagement, was to end Palestinian rocket fire and arms smuggling. Its eruption was shocking, but hardly surprising. Tensions had escalated sharply since 4 November 2008 – the day Barack Obama won a historic election in America – when the Israelis killed six Hamas men who were digging a tunnel near Deir al-Balah. The IDF described 'a pinpoint operation intended to prevent an immediate threat'. Another interpretation was that the attack was deliberately designed to provoke precisely *because* the Egyptian-brokered ceasefire was holding. Three months earlier Ehud Barak, back in office as Olmert's defence minister, admitted privately that Hamas was making 'a serious effort to convince the other factions not to launch rockets or mortars' and this had brought 'a large measure of peace and quiet' to Israeli border communities. But he was concerned that Hamas efforts to use the *tahdiya* to build up its strength would mean a return to military action.[42] PA security forces still worked closely with the Israelis against Hamas – and readily advertised the fact. Majid Faraj of the Palestinian *mukhabarat* (general intelligence), told his Israeli counterparts (in the presence of a journalist): 'Hamas is the enemy, and we have decided to wage an all-out war against Hamas. And I tell you there will be no dialogue with Hamas, for he who wants to kill you, kill him first. You have reached a truce with them, but we won't do so.'[43] October 2008, in fact, had been the quietest month since the outbreak of the al-Aqsa *intifada*. Now though, escalation followed quickly, with Hamas firing dozens of rockets into Israel.

Cast Lead began without warning on 27 December with air strikes that had been planned after six months of intelligence-gathering to pinpoint Hamas targets, including bases, weapon silos, training camps and the homes of senior officials. Preparations for an Israeli version of 'shock and awe' involved disinformation and deception which kept the media in the dark. And Hamas was apparently lulled into a sense of false security which allowed the initial onslaught to achieve tactical surprise.[44] Targets hit in the first devastating mid-morning strike by F16s, Apache helicopters and drones included a graduation parade of traffic policemen in Gaza City, where 15 were killed in what was denounced as a massacre: 100 targets were hit in a few minutes. 'Women were shopping at the outdoor market, and children were emerging from school', reported the New York Times.

> The centre of Gaza City was a scene of chaotic horror, with rubble everywhere, sirens wailing, and women shrieking as dozens of mutilated bodies were laid out on the pavement and in the lobby of Shifa Hospital so that family members could identify them. The dead included civilians, including construction workers and at least two children in school uniforms.[45]

TV footage showed bodies scattered on a road and dead and wounded being carried away by desperate civilians. International media coverage was intense despite a ban on foreign journalists entering the area from Israel. But al-Jazeera TV had an office in Gaza City and other news organizations had their own local Palestinian correspondents. The death toll that day alone was 230, one of the deadliest in the history of the conflict. Dozens of tunnels under the border with Egypt – used to smuggle arms as well as ordinary goods – were destroyed by Israeli bombing.

Cast Lead escalated with an Israeli ground offensive on 3 January 2009. Two days later IDF units were operating in densely populated areas as Hamas intensified rocket fire against Israeli civilian targets and managed to hit Ashdod and Beersheba for the first time. Hospitals in Gaza were overflowing with dead and wounded and facing severe shortages of medical supplies. 'There is no safe space in the Gaza Strip – no safe haven, no bomb shelters, and the borders are closed and civilians have no place to flee', said a report from the UN Office for the Co-ordination of Humanitarian Affairs.[46] Israeli Jews overwhelmingly supported the war. But the largest demonstration ever held in the Arab community took place in the Galilee town of Sakhnin, where 100,000 people carried Palestinian flags and placards declaring solidarity with Gaza. The same day, 9 January, a smaller but still largely Palestinian demonstration was also held in Tel Aviv. Dozens of Arab political activists were summoned by the Shin Bet to be warned that they would be held responsible for any trouble.[47]

In the enclave power cuts left people shivering in the winter cold in unheated homes where they learned to distinguish between the 'zzzz' of drones and the 'whoosh' that heralded an F16 air strike.[48] The operation ended on 18 January – two days before Obama entered the White House – with Israel unilaterally announcing a ceasefire and Hamas following suit a few hours later. Palestinian casualties were between 1,166 and 1,417, 431 of them children, according to figures published by the World Health Organization. In all, some 900 civilians were killed. In many cases detailed information about the circumstances of the deaths was available. Five people were killed on 4 January when Gaza's main vegetable market was hit. Two days later a UN school in Jabaliya was shelled, leaving at least thirty dead. Nearly all were children. On 14 January, Mahmoud Ezedinne Wahid Mousa, who was seriously injured, lost his parents, brother and sister in an air strike on the family home in Gaza City, where they had just finished dinner.[49] Two days later Israeli tanks shelled the Jabaliya home of Dr Izzeldin Abuelaish: three of his daughters and a niece were killed instantly and another daughter severely wounded. The IDF claimed it had been responding to sniper fire from the roof of the house, though Abuelaish and neighbours disputed this. Shortly afterwards the bereaved doctor – speaking Hebrew, and weeping – was interviewed live on Israeli TV, his grief on searing display.[50] It was a rare moment when the enemy was humanized. The old notion of 'shooting and weeping' became 'shooting, weeping and seeing', in the words of one critical scholar.[51] Other TV clips showed the funerals of Gaza's many victims, crowds chanting '*Allahu akbar*'. Israel counterposed such images with its own information warfare, applying lessons learned from the 2006 war in Lebanon. The IDF inaugurated a YouTube channel which showcased drone footage of Israeli attacks filmed from the vantage point of the bombardier, 'footage which functioned to sterilise and justify the air campaign through a video game-cum-war logic that rendered all persons and buildings seen from above as proto-targets'. Bloggers and other social media users more than filled the gap left by traditional journalistic coverage.

Israeli spokesmen insisted throughout that the IDF was defending the country's civilians. But it was doing so by killing large numbers of non-combatant Palestinians. And there was no equivalence either of suffering or between the crude, unguided projectiles of Hamas and the sheer might and technological sophistication of the IDF. Israel suffered thirteen fatalities, four of them from friendly fire. Both sides were accused of committing war crimes by a UN investigation led by the South African judge Richard Goldstone, whose 575-page report documented damning evidence of abuses. Goldstone subsequently retracted his charge against Israel but his change of position was not shared by the other members of the commission. Inside Israel, Breaking the Silence publicized testimonies of soldiers that were in line with accusations by Amnesty and other international human rights groups that the IDF had acted indiscriminately and disproportionately in civilian areas. Hamas was accused of mounting indiscriminate attacks on Israeli civilians. Shortly after the end of the fighting the UN secretary-general, Ban Ki-moon, visited Gaza and saw 'a desolate and shocking landscape uprooted by the heavy tracks of Israeli tanks and bulldozers which had levelled anything in their way – walls . . . fields, electricity poles, cars'. Some city blocks were nearly untouched but others had been reduced to rubble or buildings had had their façades blown off, exposing the interiors. Ban and his party passed a column of hundreds of men wearing green headbands and waving green flags. It was supposed to be a victory parade but they looked quiet and sullen.[52]

Cast Lead marked a bloody new low for the divided Palestinians – literally and politically. Gaza's horrors were on display to the entire world and nothing could stop them. Abbas, worried about popular unrest, begged the US to support a UN resolution calling for an immediate ceasefire but Bush ordered Rice to abstain: a veto would have been impossible in the face of domestic and international outrage about the Israeli offensive.[53] Abbas was also said to have privately urged the Israelis 'to continue the military campaign and overthrow Hamas'. In the West Bank, where people were glued to al-Jazeera's coverage of the fighting, US-trained PA security forces maintained order throughout. 'The IDF . . . felt – after the first week or so – that the Palestinians were there and they could trust them', commented General Dayton. 'As a matter of fact, a good portion of the Israeli army went off to Gaza from the West Bank – think about that for a minute – and the commander was absent for eight straight days. That shows the kind of trust they were putting in these people now.'[54] Hamas claimed victory in what it called the Battle of al-Furqan – a reference to a Quranic concept of distinguishing between good and evil. On the last full day of fighting it still managed to fire nineteen rockets into Israel. The siege remained in place, although it was briefly eased after the ceasefire even as Israel demanded Corporal Shalit's release in exchange for a full opening of the border crossings. Israeli officials argued that they had prevailed: 'Having lost the initiative with Israel's opening air raids, [Hamas] . . . was in a reactive mode throughout the fighting', argued one well-informed analysis. 'The only effective limits on the IDF were those the Israeli government imposed for operational or political purposes, or to limit Israeli military and civilian casualties. When Israel declared a ceasefire . . . Hamas was at the mercy of the IDF; Israeli decisions, not Hamas military actions, put an end to the fighting.'[55] Neither side's behaviour pointed to a way out of a volatile status quo punctuated by bouts of spectacular and destructive violence.

25

2009–2014

'*"Mowing the Grass", a new term in . . . strategic parlance,
reflects the assumption that Israel [is] in protracted intractable conflict with extremely hostile non-state entities . . . The
use of force is not intended to attain impossible political
goals, but to debilitate the capabilities of the enemy to harm
Israel.*'[1]

'ACTIVE AND AGGRESSIVE' DIPLOMACY[2]

Palestinians and Israelis alike were waiting eagerly when Barack
Obama strode briskly onto the red-curtained stage in an ornate hall
at Cairo University on 4 June 2009. Both sides were keen to hear the
new American president lay out his vision for tackling their unending
conflict, though his main focus was the wider issue of US–Muslim
relations in the wake of the wars in Iraq and Afghanistan and prospects for change across the Middle East. Expectations for Obama's
involvement were unusually high, although Arab commentators had
been disappointed by his 'deafening silence' during the latest Gaza
war as he prepared for his inauguration.[3] In his long-heralded 'new
beginning' address Obama described America's relationship with
Israel as 'unbreakable' and the situation of the Palestinians as 'intolerable'[4] – a neat and unintentionally insightful summary. He produced
no new ideas, though his emphasis was striking: the US, he spelled
out, did not accept the legitimacy of Israeli settlements, which undermined efforts to achieve peace. He appealed to Hamas to abandon
violence. 'It is a sign of neither courage nor power to shoot rockets

at sleeping children, or to blow up old women on a bus.' Mahmoud Abbas – who had been impressed by Obama when they met for the first time a few days earlier[5] – praised the speech as 'clear and frank'. The Israeli government was annoyed that Obama had not gone on to visit Jerusalem after Cairo. Ehud Barak, again serving as defence minister, called the speech 'brave'. Hamas denounced it as no different from what George W. Bush would have said. Israeli right-wingers complained that Obama had glossed over the fact that the Palestinians had not abandoned terrorism. The predictability of the responses could not mask the hope that perhaps, after all, something would now in fact change.[6]

Domestic politics on both sides were a formidable (and familiar) obstacle to the new president's determination. Tzipi Livni, Ehud Olmert's successor as leader of *Kadima*, narrowly won the February 2009 elections, but the Gaza war boosted the overall strength of the right-wing bloc and the Likud's Binyamin Netanyahu was asked to form a new government. During the campaign Netanyahu had spoken only of 'economic peace' with the Palestinians. The hardening mood in the wake of 'Operation Cast Lead' was illustrated by his choice of foreign minister, Avigdor Lieberman, a Moldovan-born ultra-nationalist who lived in a West Bank settlement and campaigned on the promise of a law requiring Israeli Arabs to swear an oath of loyalty to Israel as a Jewish state or lose their citizenship.[7] Barak led the Labour party, now reduced to just thirteen Knesset seats, two less than Lieberman's *Yisrael Beitenu* (Israel our Home), into the coalition but pledged not to be a 'fig-leaf' for extremists. Obama vowed to work 'actively and aggressively' to get the peace process moving. The seriousness of his intentions was underlined by the swift appointment of the heavyweight George Mitchell – former democratic senator, veteran of the Northern Ireland peace process and author of the report into the second *intifada* – as his Middle East envoy.

Netanyahu's response was to demand that the Palestinians formally recognize Israel as a Jewish state – the nation state of the entire Jewish people – *before* negotiating a two-state solution. In a speech at Bar-Ilan University near Tel Aviv, shortly after Obama's in Cairo, Netanyahu declared that he accepted a Palestinian state, although it was hedged about with qualifications: it would have to be fully de-militarized, with no army, missiles or control of its own airspace. Undivided Jerusalem would remain Israeli territory. That, complained one Palestinian politician, would constitute a 'ghetto', not a state.[8] 'The root of the conflict,' the prime minister declared, 'was and remains the [Palestinian] refusal to recognise the right of the Jewish people to a state of their own in their historic homeland'[9] – deftly sidestepping both the issue of that state's borders and on what terms Israel was prepared to reciprocate.

The 'Jewish state' demand was a familiar argument but a novel element in the diplomatic game. The Annapolis conference had referred to Israel as 'the homeland for the Jewish people'. Netanyahu now went a step further. The PLO had formally recognized Israel in the Oslo agreement in 1993. The Jewish question had not been mentioned in Israel's peace treaties with Egypt and Jordan or been part of any other negotiation.[10] Palestinians complained that the demand was tantamount to asking Abbas to endorse Zionism as well as undermining the position of Israel's Arab citizens. Netanyahu made clear too that it was designed to counter the Palestinian demand for the 'right of return' of refugees. The formal Palestinian response was that the issue was not for negotiation. Abbas reiterated that the PLO recognized Israel and that Israel was free to define itself however it chose.[11] The less formal position was far blunter and went straight to the heart of the matter: 'It's a preposterous precondition,' Hanan Ashrawi insisted. 'I will not be a Zionist. No Palestinian will.'[12]

AN 'INTOLERABLE' OCCUPATION

Obama's Cairo speech made no difference to Palestinian reality. The Gaza Strip's 1.7 million people remained under siege, the crossings into Israel and Egypt largely closed, restricting economic activity and hobbling reconstruction. Israel banned imports of concrete, steel rods, pipes and industrial equipment that could be used to build bunkers or weapons – along with lentils, pasta, tomato paste and other items on a constantly changing list. Initially the Israelis said they wanted to ensure that a shipment of macaroni was not destined for a Hamas charity but then clarified that it was banned as a luxury item. American pressure overturned it.[13] In mid-June Gazan militants attempted to attack a border post using horses rigged with explosives. The US and EU still refused to deal with Hamas. In Ramallah Abbas looked both impotent and complicit as PA security forces pursued a crackdown on Islamists in the West Bank.[14] In July the PLO veteran Farouq Qaddoumi accused Abbas of having plotted to kill Arafat. In August, at Fatah's congress in Bethlehem, the Palestinian president insisted that it was correct to pursue negotiations while maintaining a right to resistance, but suggested this was best done by peaceful protests against the separation wall.[15] He was accused of 'collaboration with the Zionist enemy' when he gave in to US and Israeli pressure to end efforts to secure UN Human Rights Council endorsement of the Goldstone Report.[16] Abbas strenuously denied reports that he had privately urged tougher Israeli action against Hamas during Cast Lead and was convinced, Mitchell reported, that the Netanyahu government had leaked the allegations against him.[17] PA media excoriated the Hamas government in Gaza as an 'emirate of darkness'.

Obama and Hillary Clinton, the US secretary of state, demanded a total freeze on settlements, but accepted much less. In November Netanyahu agreed to a ten-month 'moratorium' on settlement activity – he called it exercising 'restraint' – in order to relaunch peace talks. It was heavily qualified, excluding East Jerusalem, as well as construction already under way that was deemed essential for 'normal life'.[18] Days later he told his 'brothers and sisters' the settlers that building would resume as soon as the suspension was over. Abbas refused to enter negotiations.

Hamas officials occasionally signalled readiness for a *hudna* or long-term truce and hinted at de facto 'acceptance' of Israel in its 1967 borders, while refusing to formally recognize it and playing down the significance of the movement's charter, with its anti-Semitic elements, which was naturally played up by Israel.[19] But its more pragmatic side was also noticed.[20] Individual Israelis sometimes reciprocated, most notably Efraim Halevy, a former Mossad chief, who argued that in the light of the 'destructive gamesmanship' of the PA and the stagnation in Gaza, Israel needed to talk to the Islamists despite their being 'a ghastly crowd'.[21] Official determination to fight Hamas was illustrated sensationally by the assassination of Mohammed Mabhouh, who was found dead in a Dubai hotel in January 2010. Mabhouh had reportedly organized arms shipments from Iran to Gaza, which were a serious concern for Israel.[22] The UAE published photographs of his suspected killers taken from CCTV cameras. It quickly became apparent that they were Mossad agents using disguises and false or stolen British and Australian passports.[23] Israel's deadpan denials were implausible. It was more successful operationally than the bungled effort to kill Khaled Meshaal in Amman in 1997, though the impact was unclear.

Gaza's plight was highlighted spectacularly by the 'Freedom Flotilla', made up of ships carrying some six hundred activists, which sailed from Turkey. On 31 May 2010 the lead vessel, the MV *Mavi Marmara*, was boarded by Israeli commandos who killed nine Turks, reporting afterwards that they had faced a 'lynch' by 'terrorists'. Abbas condemned this as 'a massacre' while the Israelis fretted about an intelligence failure. The UN later upheld the legality of the interception but found Israel's methods 'excessive and unreasonable'. The flotilla was part of a growing international solidarity movement with the Palestinians, fuelled by the conviction that diplomacy was incapable of ending the blockade of Gaza and that the 'peace process' was a fiction masking the maintenance of the status quo and the enormous imbalance between the parties. Relations with Turkey, once Israel's only Muslim ally, were badly damaged. 'It is startling how, in its bungled effort to isolate Gaza, democratic Israel has come off worse than Hamas, which used to send suicide-bombers into restaurants', *The Economist* newspaper commented.[24] Among those on board the *Mavi Marmara* were the radical leader of the northern branch of the Islamic Movement in Israel, Sheikh Raed Salah, and Haneen Zoabi, the first Palestinian-Israeli woman member of the Knesset, illustrating the familiar way the occupation bolstered Palestinian solidarity across the green line.

Pro-Palestinian feelings brought gains for the growing movement for Boycott, Divestment and Sanctions (BDS). This campaign did not only target the occupied territories or demand the labelling of produce from illegal settlements (so that European shoppers could refuse to buy them) but *all* Israeli institutions – on the grounds that the entire state and many private bodies (banks, for example) were complicit in the occupation. It also opposed any kind of 'normalization' with Israelis, which limited the scope for joint struggle, as did the fact that influential supporters backed a one-state solution to the conflict.[25] The symbol chosen by BDS was Handala – the defiant, ageless Palestinian cartoon child drawn by Naji al-Ali. In his new role little Handala clutched the scales of justice patiently behind his back. Israel began to warn of a campaign of demonization and 'delegitimization' it claimed was motivated by the anti-Semitism of enemies who rejected its very existence. That became the dominant theme of official *hasbara* (public diplomacy or propaganda) in the Netanyahu era. The PA – still committed to Oslo, recognition of Israel and a two-state solution – did not back BDS, only the boycott of settlement produce, which was also pursued energetically by the reforming Salam Fayyad: he called it 'empowering the people' to resist occupation without resorting to violence.[26] In general Fayyad, who was garnering international plaudits for his state-building strategy, urged Palestinians to overcome their feelings of failure and loss of confidence created by decades of Israeli rule and avoid defeatism, 'passive nihilism or destructive acts of bravado'.[27] At the same time, Israeli-PA joint security operations increased by 72 per cent in 2009 – co-operation that Abbas's growing number of Palestinian critics complained was sustaining an insupportable status quo.[28]

American insistence led to the launch of a new round of Israeli–Palestinian negotiations in Washington in September 2010 after the killing of four Israeli settlers near Hebron a few days earlier. Hamas claimed responsibility for that attack and again denounced the PA's 'treachery' when its security forces arrested several suspects. It dismissed the talks as 'humiliating and degrading'. PA police broke up protests. But the talks made no progress as Netanyahu refused to extend the settlement moratorium despite tempting carrots dangled by Obama – twenty of the latest American F35 fighter aircraft and a pledge to veto anti-Israeli resolutions at the UN. The Israeli leader looked instead to his right-wing and the settlers, and the bulldozers and cement mixers roared into life again.

Economic growth, overseen by Fayyad, helped by cheap bank loans for homes and cars, brought a measure of calm and a façade of normality to the West Bank. That was a mixed blessing, some felt. In the 'bubble' of Ramallah, Raja Shehadeh complained of 'desperate hyperactivity' aimed at distracting people from resistance.[29] 'The spread of individualism means that more and more Palestinians are legitimating . . . and protecting their personal interests . . . above the collective interests and concerns of the community', commented the sociologist Jamil Hilal. 'This new middle class has an obvious interest in not rocking the boat. Any stoppage in salaries from the PA or other employers will leave this large segment of the population highly exposed.'[30] Ramallah had 'acquired the reputation of a "five-star prison", with a decided emphasis on the "five-star" rather than the "prison",' wrote a Bir Zeit academic.[31] Even Gaza saw some slight improvement: launches of rockets from the enclave were down from 2,048 in 2008 to 150 in 2010. By the end of the year, however, diplomacy had again ground to a halt. In February 2011 the US cast its veto against a UN Security Council resolution condemning Israeli settlements – the first by the Obama administration. It was drafted by Britain, France and Germany, in clear support of Abbas. Washington insisted it saw settlements as 'illegitimate', rather than 'illegal' – an unconvincing and unhelpful distinction – but it torpedoed the resolution because it risked 'hardening the positions of both sides'.[32]

ARAB SPRING, PALESTINIAN WINTER

Schism and stagnation in Palestine made for a depressing contrast with the winds of change that blew across the region in the wake of the Tunisian revolution in December 2010 – the start of what became known as the 'Arab Spring'. Israel was alarmed by the overthrow of Hosni Mubarak and fretted about the fate of its peace treaty with Egypt after the rise of the Muslim Brotherhood. Israeli officials warned of the strengthening of Hamas in Gaza and a wider 'Islamist winter' if the pattern persisted.[33] Uprisings in Libya and Bahrain were remote, but Syria loomed large. Palestinians were divided as the crisis next door escalated into full-scale war. Bashar al-Assad (who had succeeded his father Hafez in 2000) seemed to many to be a guarantor at least of stability and minority rights. Others saluted a popular uprising against a dictatorship which had always manipulated the Palestinian cause in its own interest, especially in Lebanon. Indeed, on *Nakba* day in May 2011, hundreds of unarmed Palestinian protestors poured across the normally strictly controlled Golan Heights demarcation line near Majdal Shams. It was the first time it had been breached in three decades and a sure sign that Assad was trying to divert attention from Syria's unprecedented internal unrest. Others tried to cross the border from Lebanon. Fifteen Palestinians were shot dead by the Israelis, though one enterprising Syrian-born refugee managed to reach his ancestral home in Jaffa before being detained and deported. Coupled with official *Nakba* events organized by the PA in Ramallah, it was an impressive show of Palestinian national solidarity at a time when a recent law had allowed the Israeli government to cut funding to any body commemorating the catastrophe of 1948.[34] Over the preceding few years the Tel-Aviv-based NGO *Zochrot* (Remembrance) had promoted greater knowledge of the *Nakba* – in Hebrew – by collecting testimony from Jewish veterans of the war as well as from Palestinians, and publishing detailed information about hundreds of depopulated or destroyed villages.[35] Better understanding of the past had not, however, translated into changing current mainstream Israeli attitudes towards this most sensitive of issues.

In the first few months of 2011 thousands turned out for West Bank rallies calling for national unity and new elections under the slogan 'the people want to end the split' (between Fatah and Hamas) – the Palestinian version of the Arab Spring's 'the people want to end the regime'. Abbas's original four-year presidential term had expired two years earlier but he was ruling by decree, while Fayyad's appointment as prime minister had yet to be confirmed by parliament, which had been inactive since the 2007 Gaza coup. Revelations about secret PLO talks with Israel – revealed in the leaked 'Palestine Papers' – led Saeb Erekat, the chief negotiator, to offer his resignation. Abbas, however, refused to accept it.

Gazans faced the dual problem of Israeli siege and Hamas repression. The movement's young supporters had grown up during the second *intifada* and never left the enclave, even to work in Israel, and they enforced austere social norms. Opponents called for a 'dignity revolution' in the spirit of the Arab Spring: their platform was a Facebook page named 'End the Division'.[36] In March Hamas suddenly fired dozens of mortar shells into Israel in an apparent attempt to deflect attention from domestic protests. In May Fatah and Hamas agreed on a unity government and a date for elections. Hamas was motivated by the situation in Damascus, where it was under pressure to side with Assad. Khaled Meshaal, its political chief, relocated to the Qatari capital Doha, however, and expressed solidarity with the Syrian revolution. Mubarak's overthrow was in turn a blow to Abbas. Netanyahu reacted furiously: Abbas could not make peace with Israel if he was reconciled with Hamas, he warned, ordering the withholding of tax revenues – a significant part of the PA budget. Israeli *hasbara* was inadvertently served by Ismail Hanieh, the Hamas leader in Gaza, who hailed Osama bin Laden as a *mujahid* (holy warrior) when the news broke of his killing by US special forces in Pakistan. Yet the Palestinian rivals remained at odds over who should be prime minister. Fatah nominated Salam Fayyad to reassure the US and Europe. Hamas disagreed – and demanded the PA end security co-ordination with Israel. No solution was found for paying tens of thousands of Hamas-appointed officials. Opponents of a deal included Gazans who benefitted from smuggling goods through hundreds of tunnels under the border with Egypt, a blockade-busting lifeline for the local economy. The largest of the tunnels, equipped with lighting and generators, allowed cars to be brought in as well as construction materials, medicines, drugs, cigarettes and weapons, including rocket launchers looted from Libya. On the eve of holidays, traders imported live sheep and fresh beef. Even wedding dresses came through. The traffic was worth an estimated $1 billion a year, and served to reinforce Hamas's rule. 'The siege is a blessing in disguise,' one Hamas official said. 'It is weaning us off Israel and 60 years of aid, and helping us to help ourselves.'[37]

Abbas's conclusion in the face of deadlock with both Hamas and the Israelis was to seek formal recognition of Palestinian statehood at the UN, despite the certainty that it would be blocked by the Americans. It was part of an emerging strategy of making advances internationally to try to pressure Israel; 'to legislate Palestine', in the words of one Fatah official, 'to give us the option of saying this is unlawful'.[38] A giant blue chair, symbolizing the UN seat, was placed in Ramallah's Manara Square. It was a high point for Abbas, who was greeted as a hero on his return from New York. Israel and its supporters dubbed this approach 'lawfare'.

Often, however, outside intervention could help only when narrowly focused on security issues. Thus in October 2011 Hamas released Gilad Shalit, the IDF soldier who had been captured on the Gaza border back in 2006, in a deal that was brokered by Germany and Egypt. Shalit had become a cause célèbre in Israel: his French-born father lobbied incessantly, fearing a repeat of the case of Ron Arad, an air force navigator captured when his plane was downed in Lebanon in 1986 but who died in captivity. Shalit was exchanged for 1,027 Palestinian prisoners, many serving life sentences for killing Israelis. But they did not include Fatah's Marwan Barghouti, imprisoned for organizing attacks during the al-Aqsa *intifada*, who was widely seen as a likely replacement for the ageing and increasingly unpopular Abbas. It was one of the most lop-sided of exchanges – though some of the Palestinians, monitored by the Shin Bet, were re-arrested later. Hamas trumpeted the agreement. 'Hamas is Netanyahu's sworn enemy', complained one senior Western diplomat. 'He gave them a huge morale boost and gave Abbas a kick in the teeth.' Shalit was welcomed home, not as a hero – in fact he faced criticism for not resisting capture – but as an Israeli everyman in a country where compulsory IDF service was still the norm but militarily prowess could not guarantee peace.[39] The preoccupation was reflected in the TV series *Hatufim* (known as 'Prisoners of War' in English), which drew large audiences when it was screened in Israel while Shalit was still in captivity.

TUNNEL VISION

It was hardly a surprise when Gaza erupted again in November 2012. The preceding months had seen tensions rise after Israel's assassination of the leader of the Popular Resistance Committees, Zuhair al-Qaisi, in March. Like other such 'targeted' operations, it was seen variously as a provocation or a pre-emptive strike intended to disrupt and prevent future attacks. 'A few days of fear in Sderot are a small investment that will bring a big profit in terms of punishment and deterrence', commented one Israeli analyst.[40] In May Israel released the bodies of ninety-one prisoners and suicide bombers in a 'humanitarian gesture' to the PA but that failed to calm tensions on the Gaza front. Each side blamed the other for triggering the new onslaught – the inevitable argument over sequencing impossible to resolve definitively. The Israelis counted rocket salvoes and the Palestinians pointed to the blockade of Gaza – the territory now routinely described as the world's biggest open-air prison – and the occupation of the West Bank. The underlying situation remained volatile despite modest economic growth in the enclave. The election of the Muslim Brotherhood's Mohammed Morsi as Egypt's president did not, as Hamas had hoped, make Cairo any more friendly than it had been in the Mubarak era. Hamas was accused of assisting jihadis in an incident in which eighteen Egyptian soldiers were killed in Sinai. Egypt's 'deep state', instinctively suspicious of Islamists of all stripes, had not changed.

'Operation Pillar of Defence' began on 14 November with another assassination, that of the powerful Hamas military commander Ahmed Jaabari in an Israeli drone strike which incinerated his car on a quiet side street, followed by the immediate killing of a collaborator suspected of having betrayed him. It ended eight days later with an Egyptian-brokered ceasefire that at least prevented another full-scale IDF ground invasion: 162 Gazans, including 37 children, were killed; Israel lost 3 civilians and 1 soldier. Israeli air strikes were punctuated by rocket salvoes that paralysed the south of the country and hit Tel Aviv and Jerusalem for the first time, though the US-financed Iron Dome anti-missile system proved largely effective. Gaza again suffered serious damage and much of the Hamas missile arsenal was destroyed, though the movement still claimed victory in what it named the Battle of Stones of Clay – a resonant Quranic reference.[41] 'We have come out of this battle with our heads up high', Meshaal declared. '*Allahu akbar*, dear people of Gaza, you won', mosque loudspeakers declared as the truce took effect. 'You have broken the arrogance of the Jews.' Israelis staged protests where three people were killed in the southern town of Kiryat Malachi by a rocket fired from Gaza. Netanyahu's government insisted there had been no agreement to lift the blockade by opening the crossing points but confirmed that it would no longer enforce a no-go buffer zone inside Gaza up to the border fence, which severely restricted the use of farmland. Gaza fishermen were permitted to sail out further from shore. 'The right to self-defence trumps any piece of paper', warned Ehud Barak. It would not be long before it was invoked again.

Abbas, isolated and irrelevant in Ramallah, played no part in 'proximity' ceasefire talks held in Cairo between Israeli and Hamas representatives via Egyptian intelligence. He had attracted furious accusations of surrendering the hallowed Palestinian right of return when he said on Israeli TV that he believed he had the right to visit his birthplace, Safed, in Galilee, though not to live there. In the summer of 2012 independent protests near the Muqataa – demonstrators chanting 'the people want to bring down Oslo' – were broken up violently by PA police.[42] But a year after launching his diplomatic campaign, Abbas did notch up a significant achievement, in rare and open defiance of both the US and Israel, when the UN General Assembly upgraded Palestine to a 'non-member state with observer status' – the same status as the Holy See. Lieberman had attacked this effort, without irony, as 'diplomatic terrorism'.[43] The vote was cast on 29 November 2012, the sixty-fifth anniversary of the UN's historic partition decision in 1947. Abbas had asked for a 'birth certificate' for his country. The enhanced status would give Palestine access to organizations such as the International Criminal Court, where it could file complaints of war crimes against Israel. Netanyahu, weeks before another election, responded by announcing that Israel would build thousands of new homes in the West Bank. That looked like another tactical move – but it fitted a consistent and long-standing pattern.

BARRIERS TO PEACE

Obama put settlements under a harsher spotlight than any previous US president, which was why Israeli right-wingers chanted 'Saddam

Hussein Obama' at their rallies. Netanyahu's second term as prime minister, from 2009, boosted the self-confidence of the settler lobby and the expansion of their project. Three years later, his response to the UN vote on Palestine was a plan to start building in a narrow east–west desert corridor known as E1, which separated Jerusalem from Maaleh Adumim. The significance of that was that once settled it would effectively bisect the northern and southern parts of the West Bank, already carved up by settlements and checkpoints, and break up what had been contiguous Palestinian territory, albeit under the patchwork of different areas as defined by Oslo. It was the last remaining open space that could mean a contiguous Palestinian state with its capital in East Jerusalem. In the first quarter of 2013, at the start of Netanyahu's third term, settlement construction hit a seven-year high.[44]

By September that year, the twentieth anniversary of Oslo, the number of Israelis living beyond the green line had more than doubled, from 262,500 to 520,000, including 200,000 in East Jerusalem, the latter (home to more than one-third of all settlers) ignored by government bodies on the grounds that it was not up for negotiation. The total was often cited as a damning verdict on the 1993 agreement and incontrovertible evidence that it could not lead to a resolution of the conflict. In 2013 Israel began work on 2,534 new homes in the West Bank, more than double the 1,133 built in 2012.[45] In January Palestinian activists of the Popular Resistance Committee and international supporters set up a protest camp called Bab al-Shams ('Gate of the Sun'), named after the novel by Elias Khoury, to lay claim to E1, mirroring the stealth and organization used by Israeli settlers. It was broken up by police after a few days.[46]

By the second decade of the twenty-first century the Israeli presence in the West Bank was no longer marked by clusters of caravans or mobile homes on isolated hilltops, but by rapidly growing towns. The biggest, all close to the green line, were Maaleh Adumim, Beitar Illit and Modiin Illit, each with tens of thousands of residents, some living in tower blocks. The last two were largely *Haredi* (ultra-Orthodox) settlements, with high birth rates. 'Sterile' roads leading to them, bristling with surveillance cameras, bypassed Palestinian areas using bridges and tunnels and were barred to Palestinians. The route of the separation wall encompassed them all. Ariel, dominated by Russian immigrants[47] and now with its own university, extended eleven miles east of the 1967 border.

The impact of the wall was memorably captured in Hani Abu Assad's award-winning film *Omar*, Palestine's entry for the 2013 Oscars in the best foreign film category – the eponymous young hero climbing it illicitly to woo his sweetheart on the other side. Israel's Oscar entry that year was a film called *Bethlehem*, which covered much of the same territory but was less well received. Both featured Shin Bet efforts to recruit Palestinians – a significant element of what passed for normal life. Murals by the elusive British artist Banksy, one cheekily portraying a Palestinian girl searching an Israeli soldier, added to the wall's global notoriety. In Bethlehem though, there was local unease about motives (and perhaps bad puns) when the 'Walled Off' hotel opened right next to it, advertising 'the worst view of any hotel in the world'.[48] Grafitti and portraits of Arafat and the gaoled Marwan Barghouti were painted as acts of resistance. The slogan that overlooked the big Qalandiya checkpoint, north of Jerusalem, was an inspired borrowing from computer keyboards that seemed the essence of Israeli policy towards the Palestinians: 'Control + Alt + Delete'.

The physical transformation of the West Bank landscape was underpinned by long-standing legal and administrative arrangements that entrenched the separation between Palestinians living under military rule and Israeli citizens of a democratic state. Land was confiscated, often for ostensibly military purposes, and spending concealed under innocuous headings in ministerial budgets – but carefully monitored by Israeli NGOs like Peace Now and B'Tselem. Settlers continued to enjoy significant financial benefits, including cheap loans, tax exemptions and higher spending on education per pupil than what was standard inside Israel. The government provided a subsidy of up to $28,000 for each apartment built in a settlement, one reason why many residents still explained their choice of dwelling place on financial and lifestyle grounds rather than political or ideological ones. In Ariel in 2012, for example, a four-bedroom home cost $200,000. In Tel Aviv, the same amount of money would buy only a two-room flat in a poor neighbourhood. When a spacious home in Maaleh Adumim was advertised for rent on Airbnb in January 2017, without any reference to its location across the green line, it seemed to symbolize the complete 'normalization' of the settlement enterprise. Religious or nationalist motives often mattered less than the banal considerations of ordinary life.[49]

Wider social, economic and political changes had brought the settlers closer to the mainstream of Israeli life. In 2008, 31 per cent of them defined themselves as ultra-Orthodox; 22 per cent lived in 'nationalist-religious' settlements; and 32 per cent in settlements with a variety of religious observance. Over half of the settlers who lived east of the separation barrier wanted to expand Israel's borders.[50] The settlers were also well-connected: by 2010 one-third of IDF infantry officers were drawn from the 'nationalist-religious camp'.[51] The ultra-nationalist but secular Avigdor Lieberman lived in a settlement. Dani Dayan, chairman of the *Yesha* (Judaea and Samaria) Council, was close to Netanyahu, whose coalition ally, the confident and ambitious Naftali Bennett of the far-right *HaBayit haYehudi* (Jewish Home) Party, had held the same position. Liberals protested in 2011 over the appointment to the Supreme Court of a judge who lived in Gush Etzion, and, as *Haaretz* put it, 'breaks the law every time he goes home'.[52] Hebron remained the most sensitive flashpoint because of the sheer proximity of the most hard-line settlers, armed and guarded by the IDF, and Palestinian residents, both in the city centre and in adjacent Kiryat Arba.

Settler violence against Palestinians included attacks on West Bank mosques, homes, cars and crops. Olive trees were a favourite target: 7,500 were destroyed in 2011. IDF soldiers often fired over the heads of Palestinian farmers rather than confront Jews who were stoning and harassing them. Charges were rarely brought. So-called 'price tag' attacks by extremist settlers began in 2006 after Sharon's withdrawal from Gaza and the evacuation of four small outposts in the Jenin area. Activists of *Noar haGvaot* (Hilltop Youth) – inspired by Sharon's famous 1998 call to 'grab the hilltops', and recognizable by their large skullcaps and *tzitzit* (the tasselled fringes worn by Orthodox Jewish men) – often initiated confrontations. *Hilltop*, the best-selling Hebrew novel by Assaf Gavron, portrayed life in a fictional West Bank 'outpost' where buildings were erected, water supplied and IDF protection provided, all without formal government permission, until it is eventually transformed into a 'legal' settlement.[53] In Israeli discourse, an 'outpost' was a settlement that was unauthorized but officially tolerated, although under international law it was just as illegal as all others. And there was a marked increase in evictions of Palestinians for building unlicensed structures in 'Area C' – the 60 per cent of the West Bank under direct Israeli control – prompting a strongly-worded complaint from the EU about 'forced transfer'. In the Jordan Valley, which was economically vital for a Palestinian state, Palestinians were increasingly hemmed in by settlements, IDF bases and firing zones, nature reserves and demolition orders.[54] 'If you ask a standard Israeli about it they would think it is part of Israel,' shrugged Irene Nasser, a Palestinian-Israeli activist with the 'Salt of the Earth' campaign, camped out among the date palms in the abandoned village of Ein Hijleh near Jericho – before being briskly evicted by the IDF. 'This is Palestinian land and our presence here is to reclaim it and hold on to it.'[55] Even if the separation barrier were to turn into a permanent border, with 200,000 settlers inside it, an estimated 100,000 more would still be left beyond it.

The reality of Israeli politics and life in the West Bank belied the notion that sufficient territory was likely to be surrendered for a future viable peace agreement. Facts on the ground had transformed the landscape of what remained of the 22 per cent of Palestine outside the pre-1967 borders. The land occupied by the settlements proper – numbering some 230 by 2015 – was no more than 3 per cent of the West Bank, though their areas of jurisdiction, along with the roads, tunnels and other infrastructure that supported them, took up far more. Overall, some 42 per cent of West Bank land was in Israeli hands.[56] The issue of the settlers was bigger than the settlers themselves: the enterprise was a national strategy.[57] For many Israelis, the old debate about the 'irreversibility' of occupation launched by Meron Benvenisti in the 1980s no longer seemed relevant, just like talk of a two-state solution. 'The Israeli left would like to make us believe that the green line is something solid; that everything that is on this side is good and that everything bad began with the occupation in 1967', Benvenisti argued. 'It is a false dichotomy. The green line is like a one-way mirror. It's only for the Palestinians, not for Israelis.'[58] Other

Israelis on the left and centre continued to believe that, although difficult, evacuating West Bank settlers in order to reach a permanent peace agreement with the Palestinians was a matter of political will, even as the country's mood was changing. Yet even without a definitive answer to the settlement question – crucial to any deal – Oslo's legacy was aptly described as a 'zombie' peace[59] or a 'dead solution walking'.[60]

BUILDING JERUSALEM

Nowhere was the Israeli impulse to erase the green line more determined than in East Jerusalem. The US was furious in March 2010 when Netanyahu's government announced plans for building 1,600 housing units in the ultra-Orthodox area of Ramat Shlomo during a visit by Vice-President Joe Biden. It was a 'direct and astonishing insult', felt Obama's envoy George Mitchell.[61] The overall, if unstated, goal was to increase the city's Jewish population and decrease the number of Palestinians. This was done by isolating it from its West Bank hinterland (the separation wall now snaking through its eastern edge), combined with land appropriation and discriminatory planning and budget allocation. Palestinian residents of East Jerusalem, with their blue identity cards, were worse off than Jews but did have access to a larger labour market and were generally more prosperous than their kinfolk in Nablus or Hebron, where the PA's writ ran. In 2013, 62 per cent of the city's population of 804,000 were Jews. Palestinians represented 36 per cent of residents, but only 10–13 per cent of the municipal budget was spent in their areas.[62] Efforts increased by Jewish organizations to purchase property in Arab neighbourhoods. In 2010 the Israeli peace movement – which had been largely dormant since the trauma of the second *intifada* – revived briefly to protest at the eviction of a Palestinian family from Sheikh Jarrah in favour of Israelis, one of several such cases. The property had been Jewish-owned before 1948 so the court ruling on eviction raised the question of symmetrical claims for Arab property in West Jerusalem and elsewhere in Israel. To add to both the symbolism and sensitivity of the affair the evicted family were themselves refugees from 1948.[63]

The right-wing *Elad* movement took over buildings in Silwan, south of the Old City, aiming to 'rediscover and preserve the Biblical city of David', and connect Jews to their biblical roots through tourism, archaeological excavation and generally 'Judaizing' Jerusalem. *Ateret Cohanim* (Crown of the Priests), another settler group, conducted similar activities. But municipal practice facilitated the work of the radical fringes of the settlement movement.[64] Arab houses built without hard-to-obtain permits were routinely demolished. Salah al-Din Street, the main commercial thoroughfare outside the Old City, looked frozen in time, barely changed in forty years, while West Jerusalem grew and developed. East Jerusalem's Palestinian neighbourhoods became enclaves surrounded by the post-1967 Jewish ones, with little contact with each other. In 2013 Eliezer Yaari, a Jewish journalist who lived in the Arnona district, crossed the wadi to the adjacent village of Sur Baher to try to get to know his Arab neighbours: he called his vivid book about it *Beyond the Mountains of Darkness* to try to convey just how distant and alien they seemed.[65] Shuafat refugee camp, a slum plagued by crime and drug abuse, was within the city limits but abandoned on the other side of the separation wall: 'the most dangerous place in Jerusalem, a crucible of crime, jihad and trash fires'.[66] Abu Dis and Al-Ram were divided by its thirty-foot high concrete slabs, covered in graffiti. In 2008 the Israeli interior ministry revoked the residency rights of 4,577 Arabs in East Jerusalem, the highest annual figure ever. In all, more than 14,000 Arab Jerusalemites had their status revoked since 1967. Palestinians from the West Bank who were married to Jerusalem residents encountered endless bureaucratic hurdles, which felt like deliberate harassment. Visits to the interior ministry and national insurance offices were a source of misery and humiliation.[67] Al-Quds University faced a long and unsuccessful battle for recognition by the Israeli ministry of education.

The Haram al-Sharif remained a source of permanent tension, with access regularly barred to Palestinians from the West Bank, usually men under fifty or even sixty, for security reasons. Sharon's notorious visit in September 2000 had never been forgotten and there were frequent provocative attempts by Jewish extremists such as the Temple Mount Faithful to both stake and advertise their claim, their fringe status belied by official municipal or government tolerance or even support.[68] Palestinians in Israel, especially members of the Islamic Movement, were bussed in to attend Friday prayers at al-Aqsa – another consequence of the disappearance of the pre-1967 border. The movement's leader, Sheikh Raed Salah, had been gaoled for raising money for Hamas and for incitement to violence. Prospects for finding a negotiated solution for the city, never good, appeared to be regressing. Barak and Olmert had both accepted the principle of divided sovereignty or administration and internationally supervised arrangements for the 'Holy Basin' of the Old City and Temple Mount, although such concessions were highly controversial. Natan Sharansky, the famous Soviet-era Jewish 'refusenik', who had served as minister for Jerusalem in Sharon's government in 2003, spoke for many when he cautioned then that giving up access to the Temple Mount was tantamount to betraying the very essence of Zionism. Ehud Barak had made the same point after the failure of the Camp David summit in 2000. 'Without our historical connection to Jerusalem, without the link to the past, without the feeling of continuity with the ancient kingdoms of Israel for whom the Temple Mount was the centre of existence, we really are foreign invaders and colonialists in this country', Sharansky wrote.[69] Polling showed that hardening Jewish views on the Palestinians were characterized by indifference and despair. The 'lurch to the centre' in the 2013 Knesset elections was marked by the emergence of the secular, centrist but domestic-focused *Yesh Atid* (There is a Future) movement led by the TV presenter Yair Lapid, that supported 'separation' between Israelis and Palestinians – though that did not extend to a readiness to re-divide what was still ritually described as 'united' Jerusalem. Indeed, a minister and leading settler, Uri Ariel of Jewish Home, called for the Jewish Temple to be rebuilt on the Temple Mount – breaking a taboo on officials speaking about changing the status quo. And plans to build 1,500 new homes in East Jerusalem were announced after the second batch of prisoner releases had been agreed on when the latest Israeli–Palestinian talks got under way in July 2013. The goal set by John Kerry, secretary of state in Obama's second administration, was a full peace agreement within nine months. Hamas, still isolated in its Gazan fiefdom, was excluded.

PERSIAN DIVERSION

Palestinians were the unavoidable enemy in Israel's backyard, and by far the toughest problem in what Netanyahu relished calling a 'tough neighbourhood'.[70] But after 2009 Netanyahu's sharpest regional focus was on Iran – as he made clear in his first meeting with Obama that March, an encounter so hostile that it was dubbed by officials in Jerusalem as 'The Ambush'.[71] Support for the Palestinians and hostility to Israel had been a centrepiece of Iranian policy since the 1979 revolution, when Yasser Arafat had been handed the keys to the abandoned Israeli Embassy in Tehran to use as a mission for the PLO (although during the Iran–Iraq war, Israel quietly supplied weapons to the Iranians in a classic illustration of the old axiom about befriending an enemy's enemy). Iran's ally/proxy Hizbullah was a preoccupation for Israel after the 1982 invasion of Lebanon, and Tehran also supported Hamas and Islamic Jihad. Revelations about a clandestine Iranian nuclear programme in 2002 galvanized concern in Israel about its own undeclared but widely acknowledged nuclear monopoly in the Middle East. Iran admitted to the existence of its nuclear programme in 2003 and agreed to stricter international inspections of its nuclear sites and to suspend production of enriched uranium. However, alarm deepened in 2005 with the election of the hard-line populist President Mahmoud Ahmadinejad and Iran's resumption of uranium enrichment.

In the wake of the US-led invasion of Iraq, European efforts began to negotiate a peaceful roll-back of the Iranian nuclear programme in the name of nuclear non-proliferation and regional stability. UN, US and EU sanctions were imposed to pressure Tehran while Israeli leaders repeatedly warned that they would not tolerate a nuclear Iran. In 2008 George Bush deflected a secret Israeli request for specialized bunker-busting bombs to attack Iran's nuclear sites. In 2010 Netanyahu and Barak instructed the army to prepare for pre-emptive air strikes, although they were opposed by the head of the Mossad and IDF chief of staff. Cyber-attacks and assassinations of Iranian nuclear scientists bore the hallmarks of Israeli and US covert action. Predictions of a unilateral Israeli attack in spring 2012 proved wrong, but the threat, perhaps as intended, did galvanize EU support for sanctions. That September, at the UN, Netanyahu brandished a cartoonish diagram of a bomb to represent the Iranian programme and drew a red line across it with a marker-pen to show where Israel's red line was – graphically urging Obama to heed his warning. In the wake of 'Operation Pillar of Defence' in November, Netanyahu claimed that 'virtually all the weapons' in Gaza came from Iran. Iranian-made Fajr 5 rockets were fired into Israel and billboards thanking Iran for them appeared on Gaza's streets.

The election of the pragmatic Hassan Rouhani as Iranian president in 2013 – replacing the Holocaust-denying Ahmadinejad – saw an intensification of nuclear diplomacy. By the end of the year the US, Iran and five other major powers had reached an interim agreement, under which Iran would curb its nuclear work in exchange for sanctions relief. Netanyahu, however, carried on pressing Obama on the issue as critics at home argued that his focus on Iran was 'a fig leaf' for the real danger to Israel.[72] Yuval Diskin, the former Shin Bet chief, described Netanyahu and Barak as 'messianic' in their attitude towards the Islamic Republic. In late 2013 Diskin warned publicly that the 'implications of not solving the Israeli–Palestinian conflict present a greater existential threat to Israel than the Iranian nuclear project'. The still serving head of the Mossad, Tamir Pardo, made the same point – albeit in private – a few months later.[73] (Powerful security figures like these were always guaranteed a hearing in Israel.) Netanyahu's strategy appeared to be to somehow 'manage' the Palestinian issue indefinitely, rather than try to resolve it. But it could never really be ignored for very long.

ON THE EDGE

Ariel Sharon, sunk in a coma since 2006, died in January 2014, prompting a flurry of speculation about whether, had he not been felled by illness, he would have followed through the Gaza disengagement with a further unilateral withdrawal from the West Bank. Sharon's intentions could not be proven and suggestions that he had come to believe in a genuine two-state solution, rather than another partial redeployment on Israel's terms, reflected wishful thinking rather than hard evidence. Still, the latest US-brokered peace effort had acquired surprising momentum – despite being a rough ride: Moshe Yaalon, Netanyahu's hawkish defence minister, described Kerry as 'messianic' and 'obsessive' in pursuit of a deal. It was not intended as a compliment. And the talks foundered just before the expiry of the nine-month deadline for agreement.

Netanyahu reneged on a pledge to free a fourth and final group of 104 veteran Palestinian prisoners – always a highly sensitive issue for both sides – because Naftali Bennett of Jewish Home threatened to quit the coalition if the releases went ahead. Abbas had agreed that if the prisoners were freed he would suspend his bid to join UN institutions, including the International Criminal Court.[74] But when they did not materialize, he signed applications for Palestine to join fifteen international treaties and conventions – live on Palestine TV.[75] Kerry mainly blamed Israel for the breakdown, even if he criticized the Palestinians too. 'Both sides, whether advertently or inadvertently, wound up in positions where things happened that were unhelpful,' he said. 'And so day one went by, day two went by, day three went by. And then in the afternoon, when they were about to maybe get there, 700 settlement units were announced in Jerusalem and, poof, that was sort of the moment.'[76] But it was Abbas's signature on the long-awaited reconciliation agreement with Hamas that finally killed off the negotiations.

The Palestinian Islamist movement had been badly weakened by President Morsi's overthrow by the Egyptian military in July 2013: General Abdel-Fatah al-Sisi moved quickly to shut down the tunnels into Gaza and cut off trade and revenues to the Hamas administration. Power cuts and price rises exacerbated an already precarious situation. Pressure was mounting. 'The Israelis do allow some things in, to show to the media,' Ahmed Yussef of Hamas told a visiting foreign journalist in February 2014. 'They try to keep us on a diet. They will not let us become like Somalia, but they need to keep us busy worrying about food and electricity and sewage and shortages – not about politics and the struggle with Israel, not about the refugees and our long-range objectives.'[77] When the Palestinian rivals endorsed a government of technocrats headed by an academic named Rami

Hamdallah, and without a single member of Hamas, Netanyahu suspended talks with Abbas and stopped the transfer of $100 million in customs revenues, though only after authorizing the latest payment, apparently out of fear the PA might collapse. Its continued existence, and especially its security co-operation, was, after all, still of immense value to Israel, as its Palestinian critics were only too aware.

The crisis escalated sharply in June 2014 with the kidnapping of three Israeli teenage boys who were hitchhiking home from their *yeshiva* in a West Bank settlement. Hundreds of Palestinians, including Hamas MPs and fifty former prisoners who had been freed in the Shalit prisoner exchange, were re-arrested. A strict news blackout concealed evidence that the three had probably been killed at once. The kidnapping gripped Israel, with rolling news coverage, prayer vigils and feverish social media campaigns. Pictures of the three were matched by images of Palestinian children smiling and holding up three fingers to celebrate the abduction. The #BringBackOurBoys hashtag worked for both sides. Jews chanted 'Death to Arabs!' and dragged Palestinians off the light railway that connected Jerusalem's northern Jewish and Arab neighbourhoods to the centre – a rare shared public space. Even in a city where residential segregation was normal, Jerusalem had not felt so tense and divided since the second *intifada*. Netanyahu blamed Hamas. The bodies of the three, who had been shot, were found eventually near Hebron. It appeared that the kidnapping was a local initiative; the Hamas leadership hailed the killings but denied responsibility. In any event, the episode was an embarrassment for Abbas and was exploited by Israel – though critics accused Netanyahu of deliberate deception – to drive a wedge between the PA and the Islamists and torpedo their reconciliation.[78] Rockets were fired from Gaza into Israel as the three were buried. Israeli jets and helicopters launched a wave of strikes on Gaza. Immediately afterwards a Palestinian teenager was abducted and killed in East Jerusalem, his mutilated body found burned in a nearby forest; an autopsy revealed that he had still been alive when set on fire. Three Jews, two of them teenagers, were given life sentences; a third twenty years. The father of the victim demanded that their families' homes be demolished, as often happened when Palestinians carried out acts of terrorism.

'MOWING GAZA'S LAWN'

'Operation Protective Edge', in the summer of 2014, was both the longest and and most devastating of the wars waged on Gaza since Israel's 'disengagement' nine years earlier. Over the course of fifty-one terrible days, Gaza suffered massive material and human losses. More than 20,000 homes were estimated to have been rendered uninhabitable by shelling and air strikes that the IDF claimed targeted only 'terrorist' sites. On the penultimate day of the fighting, bombs brought down the fifteen-storey Basha Tower in Gaza City. Water mains and power lines were destroyed. The Palestinians gave the death toll as 2,310, including 1,617 civilians. The UN count was 2,251 people, including 1,462 civilians, of whom 299 were women and 551 children. The Israelis put the figure at 2,125, of whom 765 were civilians. Israel's death toll stood at sixty-seven soldiers and six civilians, including a four-year-old who died when a rocket hit a house. The IDF said more than 3,700 rockets had been fired towards Israel by 20 August: one landed near Ben-Gurion airport, bringing a brief and alarming suspension of international flights. It destroyed thirty-two tunnels that were designed for attack rather than smuggling and turned out to be far more extensive than had been believed, prompting another row about inadequate intelligence. Hamas called the war 'Eaten Straw', referring to a Quranic verse about the defeat of Islam's enemies.[79]

Israel's high-tech capabilities did not spare Gazans. Automated phone calls, texts and leaflets dropped from planes announced impending attacks, but in many cases investigated by Amnesty International no prior warning was given. Journalists on the ground saw no evidence to support Israeli claims that Palestinians were used as human shields, though missiles were repeatedly fired from residential areas and there were reports of fighters being asked not to do anything to attract Israeli strikes. The head of an UNRWA school demanded the removal of a motorbike from the playground because the Israelis claimed bikes were being used to transport weapons.[80] The Shin Bet cited admissions by captured Hamas men that mosques were used for military activity and tunnels were built near kindergartens and clinics.[81] Still, critics responded, even if Hamas were violating international law on this matter, it would not justify Israel's failure to take precautionary measures to protect civilians.[82] 'Every single human being in Gaza, whether walking or on foot, riding a bicycle, steering a *toktuk* [motorbike with cart] or driving a car, is a threat to Israel now', recorded Atef Abu Saif, a local journalist. It was the stuff of nightmares but all too real. 'Occasionally turning on the TV doesn't help: the body parts; the severed hand lying at the side of the road; the stomach dangling from a limp corpse; the face covered in blood; the skull rent open . . . Destruction, rubble. Screaming. Torn bodies.'[83] Unlike in 'Operation Cast Lead' in 2008–9, access to the international media was unrestricted so coverage was intense, vivid and shocking. The level of Palestinian casualties led to charges that Israel was committing war crimes. In mid-July an Israeli air strike killed four boys playing on a beach, in full view of foreign journalists in an adjacent hotel. A *Guardian* correspondent captured the banal horror of the situation when he described a shell hole 'the size of a toaster' that killed three people, and a distraught father collecting his son's dismembered remains in a plastic bag.[84] On 24 July, thirteen Palestinians were killed in an attack on a UNRWA school.

'TELEGENICALLY DEAD'

The Gaza war was fought out in parallel in cyber-space, the IDF and the Qassam Brigades posting messages and images on social media and generating global reactions. Hamas produced a crude propaganda video of its men singing a Hebrew song, posted on YouTube, deriding Israel as weak as a 'spider's web' – the phrase made famous by Hizbullah's Hassan Nasrallah after the Israeli withdrawal from Lebanon. It became a bizarre hit in Israel and prompted mocking counter-videos. Netanyahu was on peak PR form. 'These people are the worst terrorists – genocidal terrorists,' he said. 'They call for the destruction of Israel and they call for the killing of every Jew, wherever they can find them. They want to pile up as many civilian dead as they can. They use telegenically dead Palestinians for their cause. They want the more dead, the better.'[85]

Israelis overwhelmingly supported the campaign – over 90 per cent in one poll; only 4 per cent believed excessive firepower had been used.[86] Controversy erupted over pictures of young Israelis in Sderot eating popcorn and cheering as bombs fell on nearby Gaza as if they were watching an action movie. Critical voices were muted. The Supreme Court rejected an appeal by B'Tselem against a decision not to approve a broadcast of the names of Palestinian children who had been killed during the operation. 'Compassion for the other', commented one left-wing activist, 'is seen as an act of treason.'[87] Journalists were abused simply for reporting the news. Anti-war protests were held in Nazareth and other Arab areas. Avigdor Lieberman called for a boycott of Arab businesses that went on strike in protest at the war, while Haneen Zoabi, the Arab MP, said that kidnappers of the Jewish teenagers were not 'terrorists' and described IDF soldiers as 'murderers'.

Views inside Gaza were harder to gauge. Public criticism of Hamas could be heard in normal times but not during a sustained attack, though complaints were voiced once the fighting was over. Hamas, after all, was 'the resistance'. Raja Sourani of the Palestinian Centre for Human Rights called it 'part of the Palestinian DNA'.[88] The public execution of twenty-five alleged collaborators with Israel was a reminder of the movement's ruthless side – and of Israel's extensive intelligence capabilities. That followed an Israeli bombing which targeted the Qas-sam Brigades commander, Mohammed Deif – father of the 'tunnels doctrine'. Deif escaped, but his wife and children were killed.[89] Palestin-ian analyst Mouin Rabbani suggested, though without supporting evidence, that Hamas enjoyed the backing of the majority of Gaza's population, 'because they seem to prefer death by F-16 to death by for-maldehyde',[90] a reference to the famous quip by Sharon's adviser Dov Weissglass about keeping the peace process alive but frozen until the day Palestinians turned into Finns.[91] Protests took place across the West Bank throughout the campaign. CDs of Hamas songs, toy guns and grenades and rocket-shaped balloons all sold well. Abbas, said the in-dependent leftist politician Mustafa Barghouti, was 'trying to catch up because the people are way ahead of the leadership; the people are in total support of Gaza'.[92]

Israelis felt that their government's objectives had been achieved, although Netanyahu faced criticism from Lieberman and Bennett when the ceasefire began and Hamas was still in control after the third operation of its kind in less than six years. 'Hamas needs to be punished for its aggressive behaviour and reminded of the cost it must pay for continuing the violence against Israel', argued one mainstream Israeli commentator. 'A period of calm can be achieved by destroying capabilities that are hard and expensive to rebuild. Buying time is a legitimate goal. Additionally, in the current strategic situation Hamas is isolated, making the rebuilding of its military assets a longer process.'[93] Netanyahu's opponents blamed him for the violence. 'The war in Gaza is, fundamentally, not about tunnels and not against rockets', wrote the liberal philosopher Assaf Sharon. 'It is a war over the status quo. Netanyahu's "conflict management" is a euphemism for maintaining a status quo of settlement and occupation, allowing no progress.'[94] Hamas claimed victory as well – though it was hard to see it amid the ruins, devastation and death.

26

2015–2017

'Greater Israel is being imposed on historical Palestine.'
Hanan Ashrawi

THE HUNDRED YEARS WAR

Life in downtown Ramallah looked reassuringly normal on a sunny afternoon in February 2017. Shoppers thronged the streets, cars honked in traffic jams and uniformed policemen watched as women demonstrated in Manara Square, demanding the release of their husbands or sons from Israeli prisons. Above their heads, stretched across a trio of flagpoles, was a giant metal key – the unmistakable symbol of the Palestinian vision of return. Down a road flanked by cafes, restaurants and IT specialists in what cynics nicknamed the 'green zone',* a handful of visitors were touring the Yasser Arafat Museum in the Palestinian Authority's Muqataa complex, next to the PLO leader's imposing white mausoleum. In the adjacent offices PA officials were formulating responses to a vote by the Israeli parliament the previous night to 'legalize' illegal West Bank settlements.

The museum displays the familiar milestones of the official Palestinian story: a prominent place is occupied by the Balfour Declaration, a copy mounted in a glass case alongside images of the Holy Land in the early days of the British Mandate and Zionist settlement. It is, by and large, historically accurate, but tends naturally to a mainstream nationalist narrative that omits some controversial events and spares

---

* The reference was to the heavily guarded and isolated government quarter of the Iraqi capital Baghdad after the US-led invasion and overthrow of Saddam Hussein in 2003.

neither the Israelis nor domestic opponents like Hamas. Pride of place is given to Arafat's 'gun and olive branch' appearance at the UN in 1974, the apogee of his forty-year leadership. Palestinians who visit admit that the display and exhibits leave them feeling depressed. The story of past suffering, struggle and recognition is a painful contrast with what feels like a hopeless present.

'Balfour's chickens are coming home to roost,' was the conclusion of Hanan Ashrawi, the veteran member of the PLO Executive Committee.

> [The declaration] didn't create the State of Israel, but it set in motion a process by means of which Zionism was adopted internationally. It is an outcome of a colonial era and it belongs to that era in many ways – the European white man's burden of trying to reorganize the world as they saw fit, to distribute land, to create states. They defined us as the 'non-Jewish communities'. It's so patronizing, so racist.[1]

Mahmoud Abbas had recently demanded the British government apologize for its 'infamous' pledge to Lord Rothschild in 1917 – though that sounded more like a reflection of the prevailing despair than a matter of practical political significance.[2] It certainly mattered less than his call for British recognition of the State of Palestine: that was consistent with the ongoing campaign to internationalize his people's cause by seeking UN membership and wider legitimacy. Binyamin Netanyahu, always a far slicker performer than the now-octogenarian Palestinian president, responded with a sneer: 'Talk about living in the past!'[3] Viewed from Ramallah, interim capital of a Palestinian state that had yet to be born, the balance sheet of a century of conflict was unrelentingly skewed. 'Greater Israel', in Ashrawi's blunt formulation, was 'being imposed on historical Palestine.'

The decision that prompted the flurry of activity in the Muqataa was the vote, by sixty votes to fifty-two, by Israeli MPs to 'regularize' the status of Jewish 'outposts' built on private Palestinian land in the West Bank. It reflected the balance of power in the most right-wing parliament in the country's history, though it could be challenged by the Israeli High Court. It was a triumph for the settler lobby, emboldened by Donald Trump's stunning presidential victory in the US. Bezalel Smotrich, a crudely outspoken MP for Jewish Home, which initiated the legislation, thanked the American people for electing the billion-aire businessman and reality TV star, 'without whom the law would have probably not passed'. Israelis on the centre and left condemned a 'land grab'. The Labour Party leader, Isaac Herzog, warned of 'national suicide'. It meant the retroactive application of Israeli civil – not military – law in an area that was not part of Israel and whose residents could not vote. Up to fifty settlements could thus be given government recognition. Even Dan Meridor, a former Likud justice minister, called it 'evil and dangerous' and likely to lead to the prosecution of Israel by the International Criminal Court for breaching the Geneva Conventions. The view from the Muqataa was unequivocal. 'Such a law signals the final annexation of the West Bank,' Ashrawi declared. 'Despite being a captive people under occupation, we will resist such expansionism and oppression, and we will continue to pursue all diplomatic and legal channels to oppose Israeli violations and defend our people's right to self-determination, justice and freedom.'[34]

Ashrawi had been a highly articulate exponent of the Palestinian cause since the 1980s but she was far more effective abroad than at home, where, as an independent, she was not part of Fatah's inner circle. Israel's control of the occupied territories was complete, though there were frequent reminders that it was not cost-free. In the wake of the 2014 Gaza war and renewed tensions around the al-Aqsa mosque, four rabbis and a policeman were hacked to death in a West Jerusalem synagogue by two Palestinians from the eastern neigh-bourhood of Jebel Mukaber: pictures of bloody meat cleavers circulated afterwards on Arabic social media already saturated with atrocities perpetrated by Islamic State (ISIS) and the Syrian government. The fact that the killings were claimed by the secular PFLP did nothing to assuage concerns that religious extremism was becoming dangerously intertwined with nationalist rivalry. It reminded many of the 1994 massacre of Muslims by Baruch Goldstein in Hebron, albeit on a smaller scale – and the bloody events of 1929. In Jebel Mukaber, roads were closed off by concrete blocks and checkpoints set up at the entrances to other Arab districts of Jerusalem for the first time in years. Palestinian taxi drivers – always an accurate bell-wether of the current mood – refused to cross into Jewish areas of the city after dark.

It was a similar story in January 2017, when another Palestinian from the same neighbourhood drove his truck into a group of IDF officer cadets on the nearby Haas promenade, with its panoramic view of the Old City, scattering bodies before reversing and trying to ram them again until shots were fired and the driver was killed and the vehicle stopped. Four soldiers – three of them young women cadets – died instantly. The incident looked like the recent atrocities in Nice and Berlin, both claimed by ISIS. It was an ugly moment of fear, grief and hatred, all recorded on a nearby security camera. 'We bless the courageous and heroic truck operation in Jerusalem', Hamas tweeted. 'It comes within the context of the normal response to the crimes of the Israeli occupation.' Gazans handed out celebratory sweets under the Arabic hashtag #Intifadatruck. Netanyahu, visiting the scene, immediately described the perpetrator as a follower of ISIS, though no evidence was found to support that claim. Two of the dead soldiers, who were all in their early twenties, lived in West Bank settlements.[5]

RIGHT TURN

No direct Palestinian-Israeli talks had been held since John Kerry's final effort collapsed in April 2014. Barack Obama admitted the following summer that his administration had failed in its effort to help resolve the conflict. 'We worked very hard,' he said. 'But, frankly, the politics inside of Israel and the politics among the Palestinians as well made it very difficult.' The president's 2009 pledge to work 'actively and aggressively' to promote peace felt like ancient history and a wasted opportunity. It was hard to disagree with his conclusion that 'the politics of fear has been stronger than the politics of hope'[6] – though the shortcomings of the US role were also an important part of the story.

Horror grabbed the headlines again in July 2015 when an eighteen-month-old baby named Ali Dawabsheh and his parents were burned to death in Duma, near Nablus, after a petrol bomb was thrown into their home. Two Jews were later indicted, one for murder. This latest 'price-tag' attack came after a court ordered the demolition of unauthorized buildings in Beit El, the big settlement near Ramallah. Netanyahu condemned the incident and ordered the Shin Bet to work harder to combat Jewish extremists. The attack had echoes of the 'Jewish underground' of the 1980s but Israel's political atmosphere was now far more highly charged. Video footage showed Orthodox Jews at a wedding praising the attack, brandishing guns and knives and stabbing a photograph of the dead child. It was a disturbing parallel to images of Palestinians celebrating the killings of Israelis.[7]

Obama was right to say that the state of Israeli politics in the wake of the last Gaza war offered no hope for a revival of a moribund peace process. Palestinians were largely indifferent to the outcome of the March 2015 Knesset race. 'Time and time again, election after election after election has just brought something worse,' said Huneida Ghanem, director of Madar, the Ramallah-based Palestinian Forum for Israeli Studies.[8] The campaign was characterized by competition between the parties to strike hawkish and xenophobic anti-Arab poses, against the menacing background of the war in Syria and Hizbullah and Iranian activity on the Golan Heights. Likud videos showed ISIS fighters driving jeeps flying black flags into Israel. Netanyahu won his fourth term by campaigning for a hard line. To his right, Avigdor Lieberman of *Yisrael Beiteinu* called for the annexation of big West Bank settlements like Ariel and the 'transfer' of Arab towns inside Israel – such as Umm al-Fahm – to 'Palestine'. Arab parliamentary candidates were compared to poisonous weeds to be uprooted. On polling day Netanyahu used a Facebook video and the terminology of IDF mobilization orders to urge Jews to come out and vote because Arabs, organized by 'leftist groups', were arriving at polling stations 'in vast numbers' – a transparently racist statement which he later said he regretted after being rebuked by Obama for his 'divisive rhetoric'. It was, commented the *Haaretz* editor Aluf Benn, 'vintage Bibi: instilling fear and anxiety, retreating to outright racism against Israel's Arab citizens, portraying his opponents and critics as traitors, and standing up to the powers that be'.[9] Labour's Herzog was handicapped by an uncharismatic manner and a lacklustre performance. The coalition Netanyahu formed did not support the creation of a Palestinian state, however narrowly defined. And shortly afterwards he clarified that he no longer believed in one anyway, not even the minimalist, demilitarized version he had described in his Bar-Ilan address in 2009, though a few days later he claimed, unconvincingly, that he still did. Jewish Home called for the annexation of Area C of the West Bank, autonomy for the remainder of the territory and the transfer of the Gaza Strip to Egypt. Its strong performance meant that Naftali Bennett, the party leader, became minister of education and Ayelet Shaked minister of justice; both were known for their incendiary comments about Palestinians. 'In the two years since the last election, voters veered right when it came to their faith in the peace process and the future of the country as part of the Middle East', Nahum Barnea observed in *Yediot Aharonot*. 'In a sense, Israelis have gone back to living in splendid isolation, as they lived until 1967.'[10]

Domestic politics, as ever, determined the course of Israeli diplomacy. In February 2016 Netanyahu attended a secret summit meeting in Aqaba with King Abdullah of Jordan and Egypt's President Sisi, though without Abbas, in a last-gasp effort by Kerry to forge regional backing by friendly Arab regimes for a peace settlement that reportedly included recognition of Israel as a Jewish state. Netanyahu pleaded 'coalition difficulties' and objected to 'too detailed formulations'.[11] Shortly afterwards he began exploring the chances of forming a national unity government with Labour but dropped that option in May when he again veered to the right and appointed Lieberman as defence minister.

The previous incumbent in that post, the Likud's Moshe Yaalon, was no dove. He had been IDF chief of staff during the second *intifada* and had then overseen two wars in Gaza as defence minister. But he angered right-wingers with his comments about the case of Abdel-Fatah al-Sharif, a young Palestinian who had tried to stab an Israeli soldier in Hebron and was then shot dead at close range by another soldier as he lay incapacitated on the ground. The incident was filmed by a B'Tselem volunteer and the video went viral when it was posted online. The trial of Sergeant Elor Azaria for manslaughter – for what looked like a summary execution – prompted furious debate about the moral standards of the IDF and the reality of occupation and highlighted Israel's political divide. Yaalon condemned the killing as 'unethical' – though a majority of Jews supported the shooter.

Netanyahu condemned it too but telephoned Azaria's parents to assure them that their son would get a fair trial: he was eventually sentenced to eighteen months in prison.

Israel's shift to the right had been expressed in growing hostility to what was sometimes labelled the 'enemy within' – left-wing groups like Breaking the Silence, B'Tselem, *Gush Shalom* and supporters of BDS. *Im Tirtzu* (If You Will It*), which described itself as devoted to combating the de-legitimization of Israel, had wrongly claimed that the liberal, US-based New Israel Fund provided information to the Goldstone inquiry about the actions of the IDF in Gaza in 2008–9. It targeted left-wing academics and what it termed 'foreign agents' on the cultural scene, including the novelists Amos Oz and David Grossman[12] – triggering warnings about 'Israeli McCarthyism'. The Samaria Settlers Committee produced an animated video portraying the New Israel Fund and other groups as a money-grabbing, hook-nosed Jew betraying Israel in exchange for a handful of euro coins handed out by Nazi-sounding Germans.[13] In July 2016 the Knesset passed a law, tabled by Shaked, requiring greater transparency for NGOs funded by 'foreign government entities'. That was seen as an attempt to suppress dissent and scrutiny of the human rights abuses of the occupation and was condemned by the Obama administration and the EU. Shortly before the law was passed, in one poll, nearly 60 per cent of young Jews in their last two years at high school described themselves as right-wing, 23 per cent as centrists and 13 per cent as left-wing. But an overwhelming majority, 82 per cent, believed there was 'no chance' or 'barely a chance' for a peace agreement with the Palestinians.[14]

Polling among Palestinians provided a mirror image of that pessimism, with two-thirds believing that the two-state solution was no longer practical due to Jewish settlement construction, and 62 per cent in favour of abandoning the Oslo principles.[15] 'Rejecting the Oslo Accords fundamentally is not a rejection of peace, but a rejection of slavery and oppression that has persisted for decades', argued Alaa Tartir, a Palestinian intellectual who dismissed the PA as

---

* The name is taken from Theodor Herzl's famous saying about Zionism: 'If you will it, it is no legend.'

'unaccountable' and lacking popular legitimacy.[16] The curriculum for Israel's matriculation exams in history and civics avoided all reference to the occupation.[17] Polling showed that 72 per cent of Jews did not even consider the situation in the West Bank as occupation.[18] ' "There's no occupation" is the latest buzz, the offspring of Prime Minister Golda Meir's declaration that "there are no Palestinians", and just as ludicrous', the left-wing *Haaretz* writer Gideon Levy commented on the fiftieth anniversary of the 1967 war. 'When you claim that there is no occupation, or that there are no Palestinians, you effectively lose contact with reality in a way that can only be explained with recourse to terminology from the realm of pathology and mental health. And that's where we are.'[19] Ami Ayalon, who had been head of the Shin Bet in the 1990s, warned around the same time of the 'incremental tyranny' that was undermining Israel's democracy. Carmi Gillon, Ayalon's predecessor who resigned after Yitzhak Rabin's murder in 1995, said that the country was being 'driven by this occupation towards disaster'.[20]

INTIFADA OF KNIVES

In autumn 2015 people on both sides began talking about a third *intifada* after a spate of 'lone-wolf' attacks on Israelis, mostly in East Jerusalem and the West Bank. Knives, or screwdrivers and scissors, and sometimes crude, homemade guns called 'Carlos', were the chosen weapons – and many incidents ended with Palestinians being shot dead by Israelis, often at checkpoints. Few attackers were captured alive. The Azaria case was the best known of several in which there were suspicions about soldiers' behaviour, with human rights organizations accusing Israel of carrying out extrajudicial killings. Vehicle ramming attacks also took place. The old journalistic cliché about fear and loathing was all too appropriate – on both sides of the green line. One dark-skinned Jew made waves by wearing a T-shirt declaring: 'Don't worry, I'm a Yemeni.' The government called the attacks part of the PA's strategy of 'popular resistance' and blamed it for incitement, pointing to violent and anti-Semitic images on social media and the glorification of 'martyrs'. The UN also condemned

Palestinian incitement. But the Shin Bet's assessment was that the individuals involved had no organizational affiliation and that Abbas had in fact instructed his security forces to prevent violence as much as possible. In December a poll by the Palestinian Centre for Policy and Research found that 67 per cent of Palestinians supported knife attacks, while 31 per cent opposed them.[21]

By summer 2016 this wave – *habba* in Arabic – seemed to be petering out.[22] In nine months Palestinians killed 28 Israelis and 2 Americans while 200 Palestinians were killed, the majority in attacks on Israeli targets. Most were young men of the post-Oslo generation – part of the 55 per cent of West Bankers who were under the age of thirty – some of them reportedly suffering from mental health or social problems: the phenomenon was sometimes cynically called 'suicide by soldier'. Improved security co-ordination between Israel and the PA – once described by Abbas as 'sacred'[23] – helped reduce violence.[24] The number of Palestinian minors imprisoned for security-related offences rose from 170 in September 2015 to 438 in February 2016.[25] Abbas reported PA efforts to convince schoolchildren not to carry out attacks, drawing contemptuous reactions from Palestinians.[26] Israeli critics asked angrily why he had not ordered them sooner.[27] Palestinian spokesmen retorted that occupation without end and a right-wing Israeli government that included and appeased extremist settlers bred desperation – and that incitement worked both ways. The PLO began issuing its own 'monthly incitement report' cataloguing inflammatory comments by Israeli ministers and officials. 'Netanyahu has promoted a culture of fear of Arabs', complained Mehdi Abdel-Hadi of the PASSIA think-tank in East Jerusalem. 'A lot of it is about hatred and fear between the two societies. People on both sides say: "I don't trust you and I don't respect you. I fear you and I will stay away from you. And if you come into my space I will kill you." '[28]

The sense of hopelessness was sustained by the routine strangulation of everyday life, highlighted by media-savvy BDS activists with a #loveunderapartheid video campaign that showed a young man trying to meet his girlfriend but frustrated at every turn by Israeli checkpoints and the permit system required for Palestinian movement.[29] Political activity was paralysed too, the atmosphere fearful and authoritarian. Few saw any hope that the Fatah–Hamas rift would end despite occasional flurries of excitement about rapprochement. The impasse was blamed on a lack of will and the vested interests of those in power in both camps. Abbas privately described the Islamists as 'flies in a bottle' and said he was determined to keep them in it.[30] The president, who turned eighty-two in 2017, never named a deputy, surrounded himself with yes-men and sidelined rivals. Ahead of Fatah's seventh congress in late 2016, loyalists worked hard to see off a challenge to Abbas's leadership by Mohammed Dahlan, the Gaza-born former security chief who had been accused of corruption and misusing public funds, and who was supported by the UAE and Egypt.[31] Fatah's congress was held in the Muqataa – a striking reminder that there was no separation of powers between the PA and the president's political party. The congress, commented one expert, 'only intensified the aimless drift that characterises the Palestinian condition today'.[32] Nor was there any expectation that Abbas would overcome his habitual caution and improve his own credibility, let alone meet the increasingly insistent demand that he end security co-operation with Israel – potentially one of the Palestinians' strongest cards – never mind rip up Oslo, dissolve the PA and force the Israelis to reassume the burden of direct control of the West Bank.

The IDF and Shin Bet operated freely in Area A, which, according to the Oslo arrangements, was under exclusive Palestinian control. In reality, co-ordination consisted of Israeli instructions to PA forces to stay off the streets when an operation was under way.[33] Security cameras captured a raid on a Hebron hospital by Israeli soldiers wearing fake moustaches and beards or dressed as women, dragging away a wanted Palestinian in a wheelchair and shooting dead another man.[34] Art imitated life: the popular Israeli TV series *Fauda or Fawda* (Arabic for 'chaos'), broadcast globally on Netflix, dramatized the work of these undercover units, focusing in a grimly realistic way – the dialogue largely in colloquial Arabic – on the war on Hamas and others, facilitated by high-tech surveillance and intelligence. In hot spots like Jenin, youths stoned PA policemen once the Israelis had left, taunting them as collaborators. Hamas claimed its supporters were tortured in PA custody.[35] Journalists who criticized the PA on social media were detained and interrogated.[36]

In March 2017 demonstrations erupted in Ramallah after the Israelis tracked down and killed Basel al-Araj, a high-profile BDS activist who they claimed had been planning attacks and had previously been in PA custody, along with two others who were freed and then gaoled by the Israelis under the 'revolving door' principle. The IDF said al-Araj, a pharmacist, had been found in al-Bireh with an M16 rifle and a homemade 'Carlo' submachine gun and died in an exchange of fire. Palestinians said he had been 'executed'. The Shin Bet described al-Araj as 'connected to a local terror cell'. Supporters called him a 'martyr of the security co-ordination' and demanded the dissolution of the *Sulta* (the PA). The PA in turn accused 'mercenaries' and 'foreign agents' of sparking clashes to cause internal strife and called the protests 'cheap incitement'. The dead man's father was among those who were beaten by riot police.[37]

Incidents like that put the PA uncomfortably on the spot. Majid Faraj, head of Palestinian General Intelligence (*Mukhabarat*) and a confidant of Abbas, had pointed out before that the PA had foiled many armed attacks on Israelis but also warned that popular support was fading in the absence of any prospect for change. 'We in the security establishment witnessed three wars in Gaza, the continuation of Israeli crimes in the West Bank and almost daily Israeli invasions,' Faraj said in a rare interview. 'There's no hope for a political horizon . . . We have no state, but rather a state of settlers.'[38] The PLO's state-building project was frozen, with no strategy for the way ahead.

Hamas, meanwhile, chose a new leader in Gaza to replace Ismail Hanieh: Yahya al-Sinwar, from a family of 1948 refugees, was a hard-line figure in its military wing and had spent twenty-two years in Israeli prisons for killing collaborators before being released in the Shalit exchange. Other key Hamas men were assassinated in Gaza and even Tunisia. Three Gazans were tried and executed for one of these killings. At the same time the movement again displayed signs of pragmatism by discussing long-heralded changes to its 1988 charter. In the end the charter itself was not amended but a new document of 'general principles and policies' saw the replacement of anti-Semitic language by references to 'Zionist occupation' and the acceptance of a Palestinian state alongside Israel, though again without recognition of it.[39] It mirrored the evolution of the PLO's position in the

1970s and 1980s and paved the way for wider Palestinian consensus, but it convinced few Israelis that Hamas itself had become a potential partner for peace. The summer of 2017 marked a decade since the takeover of the Gaza Strip, still isolated and under siege. Hamas's slick online propaganda – lauding the Qassam Brigades' martyrs, boasting of its arsenal and cataloguing Israeli crimes – was in stark contrast to the unrelenting misery and hopelessness of everyday life.

In September 2014 some three hundred Gazans had reportedly drowned off Malta after leaving the Strip via tunnels to Egypt and sailing to Europe – a sad footnote to the huge number of Syrians fleeing their war-torn country.[40] In 2015 a UN report warned that Gaza would be unfit for human habitation by 2020. The electricity supply was disrupted, the water close to being undrinkable, unemployment soaring and construction efforts delayed.[41] Scores of young men risked their lives to jump the heavily guarded border fence to try to work illegally in Israel. Even a spell in prison – with a modest salary paid by the PA – was preferable to enforced idleness at home.[42] Occasional rocket salvoes by radical Salafi groups brought instant retaliation by IDF air strikes and tank fire. Following the 2014 war, rocket fire directed at Israel from the Strip dwindled to one or two missiles per month.[43] Israel appeared to understand that Hamas control, however unpalatable, was the most effective way to ensure quiet. But it could clearly not be guaranteed.

Elsewhere, Palestinian attacks of a more organized nature still took place. In June 2016 two cousins from the Hebron hills shot and killed four Israelis at a cafe in an upmarket shopping centre in the heart of Tel Aviv – symbolically just across the road from the ministry of defence compound. Ron Huldai, the city's Labour mayor, raised a troubling issue to which Netanyahu's government had no answer: 'We can't keep these people [the Palestinians] in a reality in which they are occupied and [expect] them to reach the conclusion that everything is all right and that they can continue living this way,' he said. Eli Ben Dahan, the deputy defence minister and a Jewish Home leader notorious for referring to Palestinians as 'animals',[44] retorted that 'the suggestion that terror attacks occur because of the occupation or because we haven't signed a peace deal is absurd'.

Israel's own actions, in the blinkered view of an ascendant right, were not a factor in unchanging Palestinian hostility.

Netanyahu's appointment of Lieberman to his government boosted his narrow majority and rendered the already slight chance of meaningful peace negotiations even more unlikely. Ehud Barak, the former Labour prime minister – exploring his chances of making a political comeback – made headlines when he warned that the government had been 'infected by budding fascism' and that Israel was on the way to becoming 'an apartheid state' unless it changed course. Ehud Olmert had made the same point in 2008. The A-word, rejected by the Netanyahu government and its supporters, had become a normal part of the country's polarized political discourse even if the parallels with the South African experience were not exact. It appeared increasingly in comment pieces and editorials in *Haaretz*, the lonely liberal voice of the Israeli media and the paper with the most comprehensive and sympathetic coverage of Palestinian affairs.[45] Language like that was rejected and attacked elsewhere, especially in the influential right-wing Hebrew free-sheet, *Yisrael Hayom*, owned by Netanyahu's American billionaire supporter Sheldon Adelson. Even the country's president, Reuven Rivlin, a Likud supporter of unusually liberal views, warned that the 2017 land 'regularization' law would make Israel 'look like an apartheid state', even though, he insisted, it was not one.[46] The neologism 'occupartheid' – which emphasized the specific nature of the Israeli case, especially the differences between the two sides of the now invisible green line and the dual system of military control and legal and spatial separation in the West Bank – was arguably a more accurate term.[47]

JOINING HANDS

Netanyahu's 2015 election victory had been accompanied by a striking achievement for Israel's Palestinian minority – by now one in five of the country's population – when MPs banded together to form a single bloc that became the third largest in the Knesset, with 13 of its 120 seats. The Joint List was created in response to a law, tabled by Lieberman, which raised the percentage of votes required for representation in parliament with the aim of pushing out the small and divided Arab parties. It had the opposite effect. Hadash, the Communist-dominated Democratic Front for Peace and Equality, championed Jewish-Arab co-existence. Balad was an Arab national-ist grouping founded by Azmi Bishara, who resigned his Knesset seat and moved to Qatar after being accused of spying for Hizbullah after the 2006 Lebanon war but dismissed what he called trumped-up charges. Conservative Islamists were represented along with the inde-pendent Ahmed Tibi, who had served as an adviser to Yasser Arafat and remained close to the PLO in Ramallah. The Joint List was led by a Haifa lawyer named Ayman Odeh. 'This has been the worst government in Israel in decades, not only because it killed 2,200 Palestinians in Gaza but because of its racist policies and because it has entrenched the occupation and increased the economic gap between Jews and Arabs in Israel,' Odeh declared. 'It has undermined democracy . . . and increased incitement against Arabs.'

Contact between Palestinian-Israelis and their kinfolk across the green line continued to intensify. Palestinian Israelis were exempt from the strict ban on Israeli citizens entering Area A (cities) of the West Bank – the subject of stern warnings on large red signs in Hebrew, Arabic and English at all crossing points – so that the mar-kets of Jenin and Nablus teemed at weekends with customers from Haifa, Nazareth and Galilee. Extensive commercial ties also existed. On some issues common political agendas were forged as well. Is-rael's demolition of Bedouin homes at Umm al-Hiran in the Negev – to make way for the establishment of a new exclusively Jewish settlement – looked identical to actions against Palestinians who had built without permission in Area C. Arab MPs accused the police of provoking violence when a policeman and demonstrator were killed. Homes demolished at Qalansawa, also in Israel, belonged to Arab families who had failed to obtain construction permits from the authorities: that operation was carried out just before Netanyahu (then facing criminal investigations for corruption) reluctantly bowed to a Supreme Court order to evacuate settlers from the 'unauthorized' West Bank outpost of Amona in the run-up to the passage of the 2017 land 'regularization' law. It was a sign of the times when Al-Haq, the Ramallah-based human rights group, announced plans to issue a joint report on house demolitions with Adalah, an Israeli organization based in Haifa. Palestinian Arabic media in the West Bank and Gaza referred routinely to areas inside Israel as 'occupied'.

Hard-line policies and the exclusionary and racist discourse used by Lieberman and other right-wingers reinforced the perception that there was no difference between Palestinians on either side of the green line. But Israeli-Arab citizens flatly rejected calls for the 'transfer' of border towns and villages to a future Palestinian state or demands for a 'loyalty oath' to the Jewish state. The so-called 'stand-tall' generation was more confident than any since 1948. The country's 1.6 million Arabs were poorer than Jewish citizens and faced discrimination in housing, land allocation, employment, education and services. But they lived much better lives than Palestinians in the West Bank and Gaza: fundamental freedoms, standards of living and job opportunities were all superior, especially for a young generation studying at Israeli universities in growing numbers – a phenomenon that drew fire from Jewish right-wingers. Still, in 2015 the government announced a five-year-development plan to narrow the gaps between the two communities. In 2016 Arabs made up 25 per cent of the first-year students at the Haifa Technion.[48] The 2017 film *In Between* provided an intriguing glimpse into the experiences of Palestinian-Israeli women living in Tel Aviv and torn between the conservative values of their families and the liberal lifestyle of the Jewish city.

On the negative side, senior public-sector jobs remained largely closed to Arabs, with a few token exceptions such as a High Court judge – who famously refused to sing *'Hatikvah'*, Israel's national anthem and expression of the Jewish soul's yearning for Zion – and a handful of diplomats. Druze, Bedouin and some Christians served in the IDF but the majority of other Arab citizens did not: a Greek Orthodox priest from Nazareth who encouraged members of his community to do so was condemned by Arab MPs. In 2016 just 2 per cent of Israeli policemen were Muslims.[49] Security considerations were invoked when the radical northern branch of the Islamic Movement was banned – against the advice of the Shin Bet – following an attempt to bar Haneen Zoabi of Balad from standing for the Knesset. When another Balad MP was accused of smuggling mobile phones into prisons to be used by Palestinian detainees, Lieberman denounced the Knesset bloc as a 'joint list of spies and traitors' and vowed to eject them not just from parliament but from the country.[50]

Brighter spots in Jewish-Arab relations included the growth of joint NGO coalitions – though mostly dealing with anti-Arab discrimination – and rising enrolment in a handful of bi-national schools where teaching was in Hebrew and Arabic, despite problems created by the education ministry and an arson attack on the Jerusalem branch of the pioneering network. The slogan posted outside the damaged building – 'We refuse to be enemies' – was defiant but optimistic.[51] Right-wing plans to revoke the status of Arabic as an official language alongside Hebrew were dropped, but road signage was still often inadequate or wrong. Arab citizens were usually bilingual while interest in Arabic among Jews remained limited, with 10 per cent saying they spoke or understood it well, but just 2.6 per cent able to read a newspaper and 1 per cent literature.[52] The majority of young Israeli Jews who studied advanced Arabic did so in IDF intelligence under the rubric of 'knowing the enemy'.

Comedy was one exception to this indifference: the primetime TV series *Avoda Aravit* (Arab Labour, with its idiomatic Hebrew meaning of shoddy work) by the Palestinian-Israeli writer Sayed Kashua introduced an Arab family to Jewish audiences for the first time. Kashua caused a stir in the tense summer of 2014 when the Gaza war was raging and he left his West Jerusalem home to move to the US, declaring: 'The lie I'd told my children about a future in which Arabs and Jews share the country equally was over.'[53] Kashua wrote in Hebrew, like the acclaimed novelist Anton Shammas, who had also emigrated in despair after the first *intifada*. Another exception was Arab food. Hummus and falafel had long been transformed into Israeli national dishes, generating Palestinian complaints about cultural and culinary appropriation: an 'Arab salad' of finely diced tomatoes, cucumbers, parsley, onions, lemon and olive oil, like an elegant Arab house, had an unequivocally positive ring to it.

Outside Hadash and small leftist groups, joint Arab–Jewish political activity remained rare and relations between the communities a highly sensitive issue. Mixed marriages were still unusual. Racist abuse of Arabs by Jews on Facebook and other social media, monitored by

Palestinian groups, was casual and rife, rising during periods of tension. Arab MPs, along with Mahmoud Abbas and Arab soccer teams, were regularly targeted. Fans of the Beitar Jerusalem football club were notorious for their anti-Arab chants. In the dry late autumn of 2016, when severe forest fires ravaged Haifa and other areas, there were accusations that Arabs had launched an 'arson *intifada*' – though no one was charged for having done so.

Shortly before that Ayman Odeh was criticized when he and other Arab MPs failed to attend the state funeral of Shimon Peres, Israel's former president, prime minister and foreign minister, who was widely hailed as a 'man of peace' when he died aged ninety-three. Eulogies to Peres, at home and abroad, emphasized the later, more dovish stage of his long career and tended to overlook his intimate involvement in defence and security and the promotion of the first West Bank settlements in the 1970s. 'I try to feel the historical pain of the Jewish people – the Holocaust, the pogroms,' Odeh explained. 'I'm asking Jews to feel my historical pain.'[54] Ahmed Tibi, who was renowned for his oratorical skills in Hebrew, honed a clever and quotable line about Israel's oft-declared wish to remain Jewish and democratic. 'This country is Jewish and democratic,' he said: 'Democratic towards Jews, and Jewish toward Arabs.'[55]

Epilogue

'The alternatives are simple and cruel. Either one people controls the other, dooming them both to eternal violence, or else a way must be found to live in a partnership based on shared sovereignty.'

Meron Benvenisti[1]

ONE STATE, TWO STATES, NO STATE SOLUTIONS

Ever since the late 1980s there had been broad agreement internationally that the Middle East's most enduring conflict could only be resolved by creating a Palestinian state alongside Israel – a return to the old idea of partition that had first been proposed by the British Peel Commission in 1937 and adopted by the UN a decade later. This always had opponents, including Palestinians who rejected the legitimacy of Zionism or a Jewish state, believed that partition ignored the *Nakba* and the right of return and saw an endless 'peace process' between vastly unequal parties as a smokescreen for continued Israeli expansion, entrenchment and control. It was also opposed by Israelis who claimed all of *Eretz-Yisrael* and rejected Palestinian independence, insisting it already existed in Jordan. The long failure of Oslo – whose interim arrangements never led to a final agreement – badly damaged the chances that a solution could be found. The numbers of people on both sides who backed two states were still substantial but shrinking. Polling in December 2016 showed support from 55 per cent of Israelis and 44 per cent of Palestinians, down from 59 per cent and 51 per cent six months earlier. In addition, however, support for a detailed permanent agreement, based on what had been on the table in previous rounds of negotiations, was lower than the support for the *principle* of a two-state solution.[2]

Oslo's last agreed stage, during Binyamin Netanyahu's first term as prime minister, had been the partial Israeli withdrawal from Hebron in 1997. Two decades since then, apart from Ariel Sharon's unilateral Gaza disengagement, the status quo was frozen. From the failure of the Camp David summit in 2000, the bloody interregnum of the second *intifada* and the halting revival of a peace process under Ehud Olmert and Mahmoud Abbas, to John Kerry's final effort in 2014, Jerusalem, refugees, settlements and borders remained the core issues. The single most significant change over the years was the number of Israelis living beyond the green line – 630,000 by 2016, close to 10 per cent of Israel's Jewish population, in some 230 settlements, whether 'authorized' by the government or not. Psychologically, the passage of time had eroded any sense, especially for Palestinians, that occupation was a temporary situation pending a peace agreement.

'In spite of the fact that the majority of the Jews claim to accept (in a very general and unspecified way) the notion of two states for two peoples as a kind of slogan . . . they do not accept a division on the basis of the 1967 lines and other conditions necessary in order to bring peace', the Israeli political scientist Daniel Bar-Tal concluded in 2014.[3] The concept had been emptied of content and lost all credibility, many believed. 'The "two states" conversation has been kidnapped by the Israeli centre-right after eviscerating the concept of statehood of any of its commonly associated connotations and implications', argued the Palestinian-Israeli philosopher Raef Zreik.[4]

Netanyahu, by 2017 Israel's longest-serving prime minister since David Ben-Gurion, never explained how a Palestinian state worthy of the name could be created. 'When Netanyahu is up against those who are more hawkish, he will say, "It will not happen on my watch",' observed Yossi Beilin, the Labour politician and architect of Oslo. 'When he speaks with those who are more moderate, he says, "I am ready to talk to the Palestinians, and I am committed to the idea of a two-state solution." '[5] The bottom line was that the Likud leader was not prepared to make the concessions needed to make such a solution possible. An undefined Palestinian 'state-minus . . . not exactly a state

with full authority', as Netanyahu put it, was the most he was prepared to consider.[6] Whatever that was, it meant demilitarization and
effective Israeli control of the area west of the Jordan. And that was
far from what any Palestinian leader, including the accommodating
Mahmoud Abbas, could accept. The West Bank and Gaza, after all,
as Abbas and others constantly reiterated, constituted just 22 per cent
of Mandatory Palestine, leaving Israel with 78 per cent.

'It is no longer necessary to ask whether the Israeli government
supports the two-state solution', commented the veteran journalist
Akiva Eldar.

> The answer is clear for all to see in the laws it passes and the edicts it
> imposes. The answer is to be found in the language it propagates and
> the funds it disburses. One state for two peoples – first-class citizens
> and second-class citizens – is gradually being established on the land
> between the Jordan River and the Mediterranean Sea. On Netanya-
> hu's watch, the term 'apartheid state' has gone from being a label to
> becoming substance.[7]

Nor did it seem likely that any future Israeli prime minister would
go far enough beyond Netanyahu's position to make a significant
difference.

Palestinian attitudes had also changed since the intoxicating David-
stands-up-to-Goliath empowerment of the first *intifada*, Yasser
Arafat's declaration of independence in 1988, the Madrid peace conference and the high hopes of the early post-Oslo years – but especially
since the al-Aqsa *intifada*, Israel's reoccupation of the West Bank and
the rise of Hamas. The Palestinian Authority's failure to obtain anything by negotiating with Israel and continuing security co-operation
while settlement activity increased had undermined its authority and
credibility. That boosted the appeal of armed resistance favoured
by the Islamists and others while simultaneously undermining the
nationalist quest for independent statehood *alongside* Israel. The
Sulta, in the words of one critic, was a 'failed project'.[8] In March
2015 49 per cent of Palestinians felt it had 'become a burden on the
Palestinian people'.[9]

Moreover, its failure was on constant and humiliating display.
Over the preceding decade the PA security sector had grown faster

than any other, by 2013 – when Salam Fayyad resigned as prime minister – employing 44 per cent of 145,000 civil servants and eating up 26 per cent of the entire budget.[10] In April 2017, when Israel announced the first brand-new West Bank settlement in twenty years – the grandly named Geulat Zion ('Redemption of Zion'), near Nablus, to rehouse settlers who had recently been evacuated from the 'illegal outpost' of Amona – the PLO expressed outrage: 'Netanyahu and his extremist, racist coalition government continue to persist with their systematic policies of settler colonialism, apartheid and ethnic cleansing, showing a total and blatant disregard for Palestinian human rights, independence and dignity', it protested.[11] The language was fierce and uncompromising. But it was still business as usual in terms of the PA's co-operation with Israel.

Even so, Abbas's pursuit of a strategy of international recognition was a clear admission that negotiations with Israel were unlikely to succeed. Independent Palestinian legal experts now opposed land swaps – discussed at Camp David and afterwards – which would allow Israel to keep its big settlement blocs and were deemed crucial to the implementation of any two-state deal.[12] And civil society activists argued that BDS was a far better strategy to end occupation even if it required a long-term effort. Campaigns to improve Palestinian self-reliance – including promoting organic *baladi* food and handicrafts by grass-roots organization – seemed more effective than conventional political activity. These combined *sumoud* with non-violent resistance.[13] Israel's nervousness about the boycott movement and the official efforts it devoted to fighting it – gathering intelligence about supporters, banning their entry into the country and mounting organized 'counter-delegitimization' campaigns – showed that it took this approach very seriously.[14]

BI-NATIONAL OR BUST?

The growing belief that a two-state solution was defunct, dead or dying, or simply not feasible, had led since the second *intifada* to intensifying discussion of the alternative: a single, bi-national state in which Jews, Muslims and Christians would enjoy equal rights irrespective of their ethnicity or religion. In early 2017, according to a joint Israeli–Palestinian poll, that was supported by 36 per cent of Palestinians and 19 per cent of Israeli Jews (but by 56 per cent of Israel's Arab citizens).[15]

Bi-nationalism had a respectable pedigree on the dovish wing of the Zionist movement in the 1920s and 1930s. *Brit Shalom*, Judah Magnes and *Hashomer Hatzair* (the predecessor of Mapam) had all argued that it was essential to secure Arab agreement to the Jewish presence in Palestine.[16] Internationally respected Jewish intellectuals like Martin Buber and Hannah Arendt concurred. But the idea had been marginal then and all but disappeared after the Holocaust and the watershed of 1948. In the light of the violent history of the conflict, bi-nationalism was an extremely radical aspiration. It would require Israel to give up its *raison d'être* as the nation state of the Jewish people, which it was unlikely to do voluntarily. Zionism was in its DNA. No Israeli government had recognized the right of return of Palestinian refugees while Jews had fretted endlessly about the 'demographic threat' posed by higher Arab birthrates both in Israel and the occupied territories. Scaremongering about this had been part of public discourse for years, but by 2014 there were indeed roughly equal numbers of Jews and Arabs – 6.3 million of each – living in the area of Mandatory Palestine. Demography, in this context, was synonymous with security.

In this spirit a group of two hundred senior former IDF officers and security officials, calling themselves Commanders for Peace and Security, returned to a familiar theme in 2015 and launched a campaign for 'separation at once' – complete with lurid graphics about a rapidly growing Palestinian population. Annexation of the West Bank, they stated, would begin with a Jewish majority of about 60 per cent, but within fifteen years the country would have an Arab majority.[17] Arguments like these inspired a sketch by the satirical TV show *Eretz Nehederet* (It's a Wonderful Country), which poked gentle fun at obsessive ethnic head-counting. It featured a Jewish man at Ben-Gurion Airport being informed in 2048 (the date presumably chosen for its historic anniversary) that he would not be allowed to fly out on holiday because his absence abroad would 'tip the demographic balance' and create an Arab majority between the

Mediterranean and the Jordan – the exactly deadlocked population figures recorded in columns flashing alarmingly on a giant digital screen. 'Jenin [in the West Bank] is lovely at this time of year,' says the passport control officer, consolingly. 'And it's ours.'[18]

Israeli right-wingers had their own variant of the one-state solution: annexation of part or all of the West Bank, with 'autonomy on steroids', in Naftali Bennett's catchy formulation, rather than citizenship for its Palestinian residents. President Reuven Rivlin occasionally called for Israeli annexation *with* citizenship for Palestinians – a striking variation on the traditional Zionist aspiration for more territory but with the minimum number of Arabs living on it. Rivlin had previously called for mass Jewish immigration in order to maintain a Jewish majority.[19] Gaza's fate was simply ignored, along with its now 2 million-strong population. In Israel, in any event, the idea was widely condemned. The risk was of sectarian or inter-communal strife, as experienced in Lebanon, the former Yugoslavia, or, more recently, in Syria. That kind of one-state solution 'could drag both peoples here into an endless civil war', *Haaretz* warned.[20] 'Marketing the one-state idea requires the systematic understatement of the ferocity of the conflict between Jews and Arabs, Palestinian and others', noted the Israeli Middle East scholar Asher Susser, making the case for what he called 'the two-state imperative'.[21] Other Israelis – scientists, artists and public intellectuals – and Diaspora Jews who agreed with that imperative, prepared for the jubilee of the 1967 war by setting up an organization they named SISO: Save Israel and Stop the Occupation.

Israeli-Jews who supported a single state were mostly confined to the tiny anti-Zionist left. The green line, they argued, was a temporary irrelevance. It was a nostalgic fixation for those who refused to recognize what Zionism had done to the Palestinians, long before the 'cursed blessing' of the 1967 victory had destroyed what they perceived as their 'little' or 'beautiful' country ('*Eretz Yisrael haktana/ hayafa*'). 'Liberal Israeli Zionists need the green line so as to render all that lies beyond it as temporary conquest', suggested Dan Rabinowitz and Khawla Abu-Baker in their study of the Palestinian minority. 'This exempts them from having to confront the historic legacy and lingering guilt associated with the military conquests and the ethnic cleansing Israel perpetrated in 1948.'[22]

Palestinian advocates of a one-state solution – the most prominent of them living in Western countries – used the language not of demographics, security and majorities but of universal human rights. Justice and equality required the replacement of the Zionist state (sustained in their view by racial discrimination and military occupation) by a shared democratic one of all its citizens. It was, they argued, the only way to address deeply rooted historical grievances and pave the way for reconciliation. Models included a confederation or unitary state, with examples taken from South Africa, Northern Ireland, Switzerland and Belgium. Supporters emphasized justice over viability. Their starting point was the illegitimacy not just of the 1967 occupation but the one that began with Israel's independence and the *Nakba* in 1948, the culmination of an *ongoing* settler-colonial project that had driven out, dispossessed and continued to oppress the native Palestinians. The way forward was to abandon Oslo and the 'defunct pseudo-state' that was the PA and demand full rights for 'all inhabitants ... between the river and the sea'.[23]

The one-state vision, however, was not accompanied by any coherent plan or time-frame. Critics on both sides found it wanting on both political and psychological grounds: in a single state Palestinians would have to live with a large Jewish population and accept the presence of Jewish settlements in the heart of densely populated Arab areas. Economic disparities between the two peoples were enormous: GDP per capita in Israel in 2015 was $37,700, in the West Bank $3,700 and in Gaza $1,700.[24] Without a massive redistribution of wealth and resources, gaps on that scale would condemn Palestinians to be a permanent underclass. One state was 'a slogan, not a programme', argued Bir Zeit University's Salim Tamari.[25] 'No one has articulated what people are talking about in coffee shops into a political programme', complained businessman Sam Bahour. The idea was born of frustration, not practical politics.[26] Israeli Jews who were prepared to consider the idea fretted about the issue of Jewish self-determination; Israel had, after all, been recognized internationally since 1948 and 75 per cent of its Jewish population had been born there and spoke Hebrew. Now that the 'settlers' had also become 'natives', and had no imperial 'mother country' to return to, that was an issue that could clearly not be ignored.[27] Yet details about constitutional and institutional arrangements for one state were conspicuously absent.

No one in the Palestinian leadership endorsed the idea. Nor did any joint Palestinian-Israeli effort promote it. What Ali Abunimah, a keen supporter, called a 'bold proposal'[28] was dismissed by many others as naïve, utopian and unattainable. Meron Benvenisti had described the choice succinctly: 'The alternatives are simple and cruel', he wrote. 'Either one people controls the other, dooming them both to eternal violence, or else a way must be found to live in a partnership based on shared sovereignty.'[29] Two states were accurately described as 'the least unachievable option'. But if that solution was now a 'delusion', obsolete or simply no longer possible, it did not mean there was any chance that a single state could be created by mutual agreement.[30]

The far more likely scenario for the foreseeable future was what was variously described as an irreversible one-state reality, condition or outcome, a 'no-state solution', or, in the words of Rashid Khalidi, 'an imposed reality of one-state'.[31] That meant the indefinite continuation of the status quo, maintained by force by Israel, and the subjugation of the Palestinians, still occupied, fragmented and dependent, even if somehow partially autonomous, with or without the PA's help. Nevertheless, perhaps, in decades to come – and in the absence of any other alternative – a struggle for equal rights for both peoples would make advances and create new and hitherto unimaginable opportunities for change.

TRUMP-PROOFING PEACE?

The future of Israeli–Palestinian relations attracted intense attention as the world held its breath for Donald Trump's inauguration as US president in January 2017. Trump's views delighted the Israeli right – especially his long-standing pledge to move the US embassy from Tel Aviv to Jerusalem, which breached the widely held view that the city's status had yet to be agreed. In addition, his choice of ambassador was his Jewish bankruptcy lawyer, David Friedman, with close links to the settler camp. Naftali Bennett, repeating his call for the annexation of part of the West Bank, hailed Trump's victory as marking the end of the Palestinian state.

But Barack Obama had a parting shot. On 23 December 2016, UN Resolution 2334 reaffirmed the commitment of the Security Council to a two-state solution and reiterated its condemnation of settlements as a 'flagrant violation' of international law.[32] The US had vetoed a similar resolution in February 2011 but this time it abstained – so the vote passed by fourteen votes to zero. The Israeli government was furious at this 'shameful' move, although it was made not long after Obama had authorized a ten-year, $38 billion military aid package to Israel. That was hardly a sign of a strategic rupture between the two countries despite the poor relations between president and prime minister, and was a vivid reminder of the contradiction at the heart of US policy.

John Kerry then attacked Netanyahu's government as 'the most rightwing in Israeli history, with an agenda driven by the most extreme elements' and warned that Israel could not remain a Jewish and democratic state if it continued to rule over millions of Palestinians against their will in a situation that was 'separate but unequal' – a phrase deliberately redolent of the American civil rights movement. Kerry's was an undiplomatic outburst of rare public candour and it was backed up by an unusually detailed account of what the status quo really meant: the fragmentation of the West Bank, the systematic denial of building permits for Palestinians in Area C, the crippling effect of Israeli checkpoints and the ruin and hopelessness of besieged Gaza waiting for the next war. 'Netanyahu lulls his public with the implicit notion that the two-state solution will wait until Israel deems the conditions ripe', commented one Bibi-watcher. 'Kerry illustrated that in reality it is almost already gone.'[33]

Opinions were divided as to the significance of Obama's eleventh-hour UN move. Palestinians generally saw it as a futile gesture that was too little and too late and motivated by frustration and perhaps guilt that the outgoing American president had so dismally failed to realize his own pledge to advance the peace process. Others saw it more positively as a cunning effort to 'Trump-proof' US Middle East policy by reiterating the only workable basis for Israeli–Palestinian agreement. 'Santa Obama delivered a wonderful Christmas present to Israel when the United States opted not to veto [the] United Nations security council vote condemning settlement policy', argued the Israeli commentator Amir Oren. 'The passage of the resolution won't result in the immediate dismantling of any West Bank settlements, but the world is beginning to come to the rescue and try to save Israel from itself.' Israeli ministers were not impressed by an effort whose altruism they refused to recognize. Shortly afterwards, when France (also deeply dismayed by Trump's victory) convened a one-day international conference on the Israel–Palestine conflict – though without the participation of the two protagonists – Avigdor Lieberman condemned 'a new Dreyfus trial'.

Netanyahu, relieved at Obama's departure, was all smiles when he met the new president in the White House in February 2017. Trump, simplistic and apparently ill-informed, pronounced himself indifferent as to what Israelis and Palestinians decided to do. 'I'm looking at two-state and one-state, and I like the one that both parties like,' he declared. In a few ill-chosen words he appeared to have jettisoned decades of US policy. In fact it was far from clear what he meant, especially as the American ambassador to the UN quickly reiterated continued backing for the traditional two-state approach. For some, the president was being creatively disruptive of preconceived ideas.[34] Ali Abunimah, editor of the *Electronic Intifada* and an influential advocate of a one-state solution, leaped on Trump's words, interpreting them – perhaps thinking wishfully – to mean that the two-state 'delusion' was now finally buried, and urged 'a rights-based national struggle' instead.[35] Yet how one state was to be achieved remained as unclear as ever. The big question, posed succinctly by Nadia Hijab of the al-Shabaka policy network, was this: 'If a sovereign Palestinian state in the occupied territory has not been possible, how can a democratic state of Israel/Palestine be achievable, one in which all citizens enjoy all human rights – individual and collective, political, social, and economic?'[36] Or, to take one or two crucial issues: how, in one state, would it be possible to reconcile Israel's granting of automatic citizenship to Jews under the Law of Return with the Palestinian demand for the right of refugees to return to their former homes? And how would land, so central to the history of the conflict, be fairly distributed? Israeli Jews found it difficult enough to live with an Arab minority of 20 per cent, it was pointed out; how would they manage with 50 per cent, never mind more? Shaul Arieli of Commanders for Peace and Security warned that one state would mean 'perpetual civil war, apartheid and socioeconomic implosion'. 'Would Israeli Arabs be allowed to volunteer for the army?' he asked plaintively. 'Would we let them have guns?'[37]

Hopes for any kind of positive change were still largely pinned on outside pressure on Israel. 'Without international intervention', predicted the PLO's Saeb Erakat, a veteran of long years of failed diplomacy, 'it will be very difficult to save the prospects of a sovereign and independent State of Palestine.'[38] Many liberal Israelis agreed. Unilateral annexation of more occupied territory would certainly generate resistance from Palestinians, perhaps a new *intifada*, and put at risk Israel's peace treaties with Egypt and Jordan – vital achievements in shrinking the circle of Arab hostility. European or wider international punitive measures might well also follow. UN Resolution 2334 had, after all, urged member states 'to distinguish, in their relevant dealings' between Israel and the occupied territories – a clear pointer to the possibility of imposing sanctions in the future, though not in the comprehensive way advocated by BDS. It was an unmistakable reminder that although the green line had disappeared from official Israeli discourse, it still mattered to Palestinians and others as an important relic of a now-distant past that could, perhaps, one day demarcate a more just future for two peoples doomed to live in the same land.

By 2017, the year that marked the centenary of the Balfour Declaration – that still-resounding act of a distant, European-dominated colonial era and a giant leap forward for the nascent Zionist project – much of the world 'viewed with favour' the establishment of an independent state for the Palestinian people alongside a secure and recognized Israel. For it to gain regional and international acceptance it would need to be on or close to the 1967 border – even though that had been all but erased over the preceding fifty years. Yet the prospect of an equitable two-state solution being agreed voluntarily by both sides was extremely dim. The impasse remained. Palestinians – divided, scattered, occupied and dispossessed, and by far the weaker of these unequal enemies and neighbours – faced a profoundly uncertain future. And because of that, in different ways, so did Israelis, despite their overwhelming advantages. Violence was never far away. No end to their conflict was in sight.

Acknowledgements

This book has had a very long gestation over more than four decades of living in, working and reporting from Israel and the occupied Palestinian territories. Many friends and colleagues, Palestinians, Israelis and others, have helped, tolerated, advised and inspired me, some of them sadly no longer alive. Several kindly read sections of this work as it progressed and made useful comments and suggestions. But I alone am responsible for its content and arguments – and of course for any errors. Grateful thanks are due to Mahdi Abdel-Hadi, Albert Aghazarian, Shlomo Abulafia, Nasser Atta, Xavier Abu Eid, Salman Abu Sitta, Gilbert Achcar, Hazem Balousha, Daphna Baram, Haim Baram, Nahum Barnea, Meron Benvenisti, Musa Budeiri, Neil Caplan, Brian Cheyette, Jonathan Cummings, Hillel Cohen, the late Ibrahim Dakkak, the late Peter David, Beshara Doumani, Vincent Fean, the late Elias Freij, Carmit Gai, Joel Greenberg, Rema Hammami, Akram Hanieh, Manuel Hassassian, Nadia Hijab, Shawan Jabarin, John Jenkins, Ahmad Samih Khalidi, Ghassan Khatib, Menachem Klein, Daoud Kuttab, Yvonne Lipman, Yehuda Litani, Alastair McPhail, Avishai Margalit, Yonatan Mendel, Richard Mindel, Benny Morris, Sara Ozacky-Lazar, Daniel Levy, Adel Manna, Dina Matar, Elias Nasrallah, Ori Nir, Sari Nusseibeh, Yoav Peled, Anshel Pfeffer, Yehoshua Porath, Peleg Radai, Charles Richards, David Richardson, Danny Rubinstein, Areej Sabbagh-Khouri, Anan Safadi, Hanna Siniora, Tom Segev, Eli Shaltiel, Greg Shapland, Avi Shlaim, Yoav Stern, Salim Tamari, Raymonda Tawil, Ahmed Tibi, Mandy Turner, Ahmed Youssef and Ziyad Abu Ziyad.

Thanks too to Laura Stickney, Simon Winder and Shoaib Rokadiya at Penguin Books and to Allison Malecha at Grove Atlantic; to my copy editor Charlotte Ridings; to my agents Felicity Bryan and George Lucas; my *Guardian* colleagues Peter Beaumont and Harriet Sherwood; and Toby Dodge, Robert Lowe and Sandra Sfeir of the Middle East Centre at the London School of Economics. And last but by no means least, my heartfelt thanks and love to Helen, without whom this project – and so much else besides – would simply not have been possible.

Notes

LANGUAGE MATTERS

1 Yusif Sayigh, *Arab Economist, Palestinian Patriot*, p. 190.

PREFACE

1 Edward Said, *The Question of Palestine*, p. 81.
2 Elia Etkin, The ingathering of (non-human) exiles: the creation of the Tel Aviv Zoological Garden animal collection, 1938–1948, *Journal of Israeli History* 35 (1), 2016.

INTRODUCTION

1 http://www.aljazeera.com/news/middleeast/2013/06/201362219549114 855.html.
2 https://www.youtube.com/watch?v=Aj-pyJF6ckU.
3 https://www.youtube.com/watch?v=OCCHsXCgaeA.
4 http://www.aljazeera.com/indepth/opinion/2012/11/201211211111787 8510.html.
5 http://www.palwatch.org/pages/news_archive.aspx?doc_id=7103.
6 http://www.zobbel.de/stamp/pna_2012.html.
7 https://www.facebook.com/NationalLibraryofIsrael/posts/13639110969 57444.
8 Paul L. Scham, The historical narratives of Israelis and Palestinians and the peacemaking process, *Israel Studies Forum* 21 (2), Winter 2006, pp. 58–84.
9 Nadim Rouhana, in Robert Rotberg (ed.), *Israeli and Palestinian Narratives*, p. 118.
10 Afif Safieh, *Independent*, 22 March 2015.

11 Nadera Shalhoub-Kevorkian and Sarah Ihmoud, Exiled at home: writing return and the Palestinian home, *Biography* 37 (2), Spring 2014, pp. 377–97.

12 Alan Cunningham, Palestine: the last days of the Mandate, *International Affairs* (Royal Institute of International Affairs) 24 (4), Oct. 1948, pp. 481–90.

13 Sami Adwan et al. (eds.), *Side By Side: Parallel Histories.*

14 Paul Scham et al., *Shared Histories*, pp. 44–6.

15 Adwan et al. (eds.), *Side By Side*, p. x.

16 Neil Caplan, *The Israel-Palestine Conflict*, pp. 241–4.

17 Walid Khalidi, *All That Remains.*

18 Yezid Sayigh, *Armed Struggle and the Search for a State.*

19 Rashid Khalidi, *The Iron Cage*, p. xxxiv.

20 Ari Shavit, *My Promised Land*, p. 108.

21 Neve Gordon, *Israel's Occupation*, pp. xvi–xvii.

22 Dina Matar, Whose 'ethnic cleansing'? Israel's appropriation of the Palestinian narrative. *Al-Shabaka*, 26 March 2017.

23 Scham, Historical narratives, op. cit.

24 Asher Susser, *Israel, Jordan and Palestine: The Two-State Imperative*, p. 219.

25 Avraham Sela and Alon Kadish, Israeli and Palestinian memories and historical narratives of the 1948 war – an overview, *Israel Studies* 21 (1), Spring 2016, pp. 1–25.

26 Ahmad Samih Khalidi, The Palestinians cannot be Zionists, *Foreign Policy*, 15 June 2011.

27 *Palestinian-Israeli Pulse*, 16 February 2017, http://www.pcpsr.org/en/node/678.

28 *Haaretz,* 17 February 2014.

1. 1917

1 *Jerusalem Post*, 9 December 1977; Tom Segev, *One Palestine, Complete*, pp. 52–3.

2 A. J. Sherman, *Mandate Memories*, p. 35.

3 Eitan Bar-Yosef, *The Holy Land in English Culture*, pp. 247–65.

4 Gudrun Kramer, *A History of Palestine*, p. 145.

5 Johann Büssow, *Hamidian Palestine*, p. 41.

6 Yehoshua Porath, *The Emergence of the Palestinian Arab National Movement*, pp. 7–8.

7 Rashid Khalidi, *Palestinian Identity*, pp. 150–58.

8   Arthur Koestler, *Promise and Fulfilment*, p. 4.
9   Mayir Verete, The Balfour Declaration and its makers, *Middle Eastern Studies* 6, 1970, pp. 48–76.
10 William M. Mathew, The Balfour Declaration and the Palestine Mandate, 1917–1923: British imperialist imperatives, *British Journal of Middle Eastern Studies* 40 (3), 2013, pp. 231–50.
11 Leonard Stein, *The Balfour Declaration*; Jonathan Schneer, *The Balfour Declaration*; Michael J. Cohen, Was the Balfour Declaration at risk in 1923? Zionism and British imperialism, *Journal of Israeli History* 29 (1), 2010.
12 George Antonius, *The Arab Awakening*, p. 395.
13 Chaim Weizmann, *Trial and Error*, p. 262.
14 Walter Laqueur, *The Road to War*, p. 15.
15 Verete, The Balfour Declaration, op. cit.
16 *Observer*, 8 December 2013; Walid Khalidi, SOAS lecture, London, 6 March 2014.
17 Schneer, *The Balfour Declaration*, p. 342.
18 Ronald Storrs, *Orientations*, p. 324.
19 Kristian Coates Ulrichsen, *The First World War in the Middle East*, p. 109.
20 Salim Tamari, http://www.palestine-studies.org/sites/default/files/jq-articles/30_tamari_1.pdf.
21 Storrs, *Orientations*, p. 347.
22 David Gilmour, *Curzon*, p. 482.
23 Khalidi, SOAS lecture, 6 March 2014.

2. 1882–1917

1   Shmuel Tolkowsky, in H. Sacher (ed.), *Zionism and the Jewish Future*, p. 155.
2   Menachem Klein, *Lives in Common*, p. 41.
3   Abigail Jacobson, *From Empire to Empire*, p. 86.
4   Mahmoud Yazbak, *Haifa in the Late Ottoman Period*, p. 217.
5   Derek Penslar, *Zionism and Technocracy*, pp. 18–19.
6   Ronald Florence, *Lawrence and Aaronsohn*, pp. 32–3.
7   Lawrence Oliphant, *Haifa: Or, Life in Modern Palestine*, p. 12.
8   David Kushner (ed.), *Palestine in the Late Ottoman Period*, p. 286.
9   Gershon Shafir, *Land, Labor and the Origins of the Israeli-Palestinian Conflict*, p. 187.
10 Adam M. Garfinkle, On the origin, meaning, use, and abuse of a phrase, *Middle East Studies* 27, October 1991, pp. 539–50.

11 Ami Ayalon, *Reading Palestine: Printing and Literacy, 1900–1948*, p. 16, cites literacy figures of 1–3 per cent in nineteenth-century Palestine.

12 Beshara B. Doumani, Rediscovering Ottoman Palestine: writing Palestinians into history, *Journal of Palestine Studies* 21 (2), Winter 1992, pp. 5–28.

13 Tolkowsky, in Sacher (ed.), *Zionism and the Jewish Future*, p. 140.

14 Yael Zerubavel, The desert and the settlement as symbolic landscapes in modern Israeli culture, in Julia Brauch et al. (eds.), *Jewish Topographies*, pp. 201–22.

15 Yehoshua Porath, *The Emergence of the Palestinian Arab National Movement*, p. 25.

16 Shafir, *Land, Labor*, p. 201.

17 Anita Shapira, *Land and Power*, p. 57.

18 Shafir, *Land, Labor*, p. 56.

19 Neville J. Mandel, *The Arabs and Zionism Before World War I*, p. 34.

20 Ben-Bassat, *Haaretz*, 4 November 2012.

21 Oliphant, *Haifa*, p. 288.

22 Mandel, *Arabs and Zionism*, p. 40.

23 Israel Cohen (ed.), *Zionist Work in Palestine*, pp. 164–5.

24 Alan Dowty, Much ado about little: Ahad Ha'am's 'Truth from Eretz Yisrael', Zionism, and the Arabs, *Israel Studies* 5 (2), Fall 2000, pp. 154–81.

25 David Goldberg, *To the Promised Land*, p. 39.

26 Mandel, *Arabs and Zionism*, p. 20.

27 Ilan Pappé, *The Rise and Fall of a Palestinian Dynasty*, p. 118.

28 Gudrun Kramer, *A History of Palestine*, p. 113.

29 David Hirst, *The Gun and the Olive Branch*, pp. 14–15; David Vital, *Zionism: The Formative Years*, p. 380.

30 Vital, *Zionism*, p. 381.

31 Theodor Herzl, *Old New Land (Altneuland)*, p. 42.

32 Gabriel Piterberg, *The Returns of Zionism*, p. 39.

33 Rashid Khalidi, *Palestinian Identity*, p. 104.

34 Michelle Campos, *Ottoman Brothers: Muslims, Christians, and Jews*, pp. 219–20.

35 Shapira, *Land and Power*, p. 51.

36 Dowty, Much ado about little, op. cit.

37 Gur Alroey, *An Unpromising Land*, p. 159.

38 Mark LeVine, *Overthrowing Geography*, p. 45.

39 Alroey, *Unpromising Land*, p. 169.

40 A. W. Kayyali, *Palestine: A Modern History*, p. 24.

41 Gil Eyal, *The Disenchantment of the Orient*, p. 33.
42 Anat Kidron, The Haifa Community Committee during World War I, in Eran Dolev et al. (eds.), *Palestine and World War I*, p. 245.
43 T. E. Lawrence, *The Letters of T. E. Lawrence*, p. 74.
44 Yaacov Ro'i, The Zionist attitude to the Arabs, 1908–1914, in Elie Kedourie and Sylvia G. Haim (eds.), *Palestine and Israel in the 19th and 20th Centuries*, p. 20.
45 Mustafa Kabha, *The Palestinian People*, p. 2.
46 Jonathan Gribetz, *Defining Neighbors*, p. 90.
47 Khalidi, *Palestinian Identity*, pp. 124–41; Emanuel Beška, Political opposition to Zionism in Palestine and Greater Syria: 1910–1911 as a turning point, *Jerusalem Quarterly* 59, 2014.
48 Yazbak, *Haifa*, pp. 221–2.
49 Michelle U. Campos, Between 'Beloved Ottomania' and 'The Land of Israel': the struggle over Ottomanism and Zionism among Palestine's Sephardi Jews, 1908–13, *International Journal of Middle East Studies* 37 (4), November 2005, pp. 461–83.
50 Gribetz, *Defining Neighbors*, p. 190; Goldberg, *Promised Land*, p. 163.
51 Jacob Norris, *Land of Progress*, p. 45.
52 Gribetz, *Defining Neighbors*, pp. 1–14.
53 Mandel, *Arabs and Zionism*, p. 106.
54 Yuval Ben-Bassat, Rural reactions to Zionist activity in Palestine before and after the Young Turk Revolution of 1908 as reflected in petitions to Istanbul, *Middle Eastern Studies* 49 (3), 2013, pp. 349–63.
55 Cohen (ed.), *Zionist Work*, pp. 172–3.
56 Kayyali, *Palestine*, p. 29.
57 Ro'i, Zionist attitude to the Arabs, p. 35, op. cit.
58 Tolkowsky, in Sacher (ed.), *Zionism*, p. 156.
59 Shapira, *Land and Power*, p. 64.
60 Shafir, *Land, Labor*, p. 87.
61 Ro'i, Zionist attitude to the Arabs, p. 47, op. cit.
62 Emile Marmorstein, European Jews in Muslim Palestine, in Kedourie and Haim (eds.), *Palestine and Israel in the 19th and 20th Centuries*, p. 10.
63 Shafir, *Land, Labor*, p. 141.
64 Yuval Ben-Bassat and Gur Alroey, The Zionist–Arab incident of Zarnuqa 1913: a chronicle and several methodological remarks, *Middle Eastern Studies* 52 (5), 2016, pp. 787–803.
65 Issam Khalidi, Palestine sports and scouts: factional politics and the Maccabiad in the 1930s, *Jerusalem Quarterly* 63/64, 2015.
66 Penslar, *Zionism and Technocracy*, p. 120.

67 Alroey, *Unpromising Land*, p. 116.
68 Shafir, *Land, Labor*, p. 203.
69 Yosef Gorny, *Zionism and the Arabs*, pp. 54–5.
70 23 February 1913 to Vera, Yehuda Reinharz, *Chaim Weizmann*, pp. 394–5.
71 Gorny, *Zionism*, p. 64.
72 Campos, *Ottoman Brothers*, p. 231.
73 Mandel, *Arabs and Zionism*, p. 229.
74 Mandel, *Arabs and Zionism*, p. 212.
75 *Filastin*, 29 April 1914; Kayyali, *Palestine*, p. 39.
76 Neil Caplan, *Palestine Jewry and the Arab Question*, p. 14.

3. 1917–1929

1 *Zionist Review*, July 1918.
2 Neil Caplan, *Palestine Jewry and the Arab Question*, p. 22.
3 Yehoshua Porath, *The Emergence of the Palestinian Arab National Movement*, p. 32.
4 Gudrun Kramer, *History of Palestine*, p. 158.
5 Geoffrey Furlonge, *Palestine is My Country*, pp. 35–64.
6 Chaim Weizmann, *Trial and Error*, p. 244.
7 Nakdimon Rogel, Weizmann's man in Damascus: Dr. Shlomo Felman's mission to Faisal's court, September 1919–July 1920, *Studies in Zionism* 4 (2), 1983.
8 Neil Caplan, Faisal Ibn Husain and the Zionists: a re-examination with documents, *International History Review* 5 (4), 1983, pp. 561–614.
9 Abba Eban, *My People*, p. 377.
10 Caplan, *Palestine Jewry*, p. 42; Tom Segev, *One Palestine, Complete*, p. 116.
11 *Zionist Review*, January 1920.
12 Haim Gerber, *Remembering and Imagining Palestine*, p. 97.
13 Ronald Storrs, *Orientations*, p. 428.
14 Storrs, *Orientations*, p. 398.
15 Anita Shapira, *Land and Power*, pp. 98–109.
16 Caplan, *Palestine Jewry*, p. 57.
17 Storrs, *Orientations*, p. 387.
18 Gerber, *Remembering and Imagining*, p. 96.
19 Porath, *Emergence*, p. 81.
20 Viscount Samuel, *Memoirs*, p. 154.
21 Ilan Pappé, *Rise and Fall of a Palestinian Dynasty*, p. 204.
22 Pappé, *Rise and Fall*, p. 206.

23 A. J. Sherman, *Mandate Memories*, p. 54.
24 Elie Kedourie, *The Chatham House Version*, p. 55.
25 Yoav Gelber, *Shorshei haHavatselet*, pp. 34–6.
26 Abigail Jacobson, *From Empire to Empire*, p. 165.
27 Hillel Cohen, *Army of Shadows*, p. 20.
28 Porath, *Emergence*, p. 68.
29 Gelber, *Shorshei haHavatselet*, p. 55.
30 Caplan, *Palestine Jewry*, p. 101.
31 Porath, *Emergence*, p. 68.
32 Neil Caplan, *The Israel-Palestine Conflict*, p. 11.
33 Porath, *Emergence*, p. 60.
34 Porath, *Emergence*, p. 133.
35 Yeruham Cohen, *Leor Hayom uvaMahshekh*, p. 10.
36 Caplan, *Palestine Jewry*, p. 94.
37 Simha Flapan, *Zionism and the Palestinians*, p. 61.
38 Weizmann, *Trial and Error*, p. 349.
39 David HaCohen, *Time to Tell*, p. 168.
40 Kedourie, *Chatham House Version*, p. 71.
41 Flapan, *Zionism and the Palestinians*, p. 62.
42 Meir Pa'il, *Min HaHaganah leTzva Haganah*, pp. 19–24.
43 The Iron Wall, *Razsviet*, 4 March 1923.
44 Haycraft Report, p. 50.
45 Haycraft Report, p. 50; Peel Report, p. 52.
46 W. F. Stirling, *Safety Last*, quoted in Walid Khalidi, *From Haven to Conquest*, pp. 233–4.
47 Weizmann, *Trial and Error*, pp. 372–4.
48 Yael Zerubavel, The desert and the settlement as symbolic landscapes in modern Israeli culture, in Julia Brauch et al. (eds.), *Jewish Topographies*, pp. 201–23.
49 Sharon Rotbard, *White City, Black City*, p. 89.
50 Mark LeVine, *Overthrowing Geography*, p. 119.
51 Rotbard, *White City, Black City*, p. 91.
52 Cohen, *Leor Hayom*, p. 10.
53 Sherman, *Mandate Memories*, p. 73.
54 Gur Alroey, *Unpromising Land*, p. 17.
55 Evyatar Friesel, Through a peculiar lens: Zionism and Palestine in British diaries, 1927–31, *Middle Eastern Studies* 29 (3), 1993, pp. 419–44.
56 Barbara J. Smith, *The Roots of Separatism*, p. 4.
57 Jacob Norris, *Land of Progress*, p. 85.
58 Caplan, *Palestine Jewry*, pp. 132, 198–9.

59 Elie Kedourie, Herbert Samuel and the government of Palestine, in *The Chatham House Version*, p. 59.

60 Kenneth Stein, *The Land Question in Palestine*, p. 59.

61 Yosef Gorny, *Zionism and the Arabs*, pp. 138–43.

62 Zachary Lockman, *Comrades and Enemies*, p. 44; Gelber, *Shorshei haHavatselet*, pp. 33–5.

63 Martin Gilbert, *Exile and Return*, p. 149.

64 Walter Laqueur, *A History of Zionism*, p. 251.

65 Roy Macleod, Balfour's mission to Palestine: science, strategy, and the inauguration of the Hebrew University in Jerusalem, *Minerva* 46 (1), 2008, pp. 53–76.

66 Nili Fox, Balfouriya: an American Zionist failure or secret success? *American Jewish History* 78 (4), 1989, pp. 497–512.

67 Pappé, *Rise and Fall*, p. 230.

68 Porath, *Emergence*, p. 213.

69 Stein, *Land Question*, p. 70; Ted Swedenburg, *Memories of Revolt*, pp. 98–9.

70 Donna Robinson Divine, *Politics and Society in Ottoman Palestine*, pp. 194–5.

71 Porath, *Emergence*, p. 253.

72 Weldon Matthews, *Confronting an Empire*, p. 65.

73 Hillel Cohen, *Tarpat*, pp. 133–4.

74 Porath, *Emergence*, p. 266.

75 Segev, *One Palestine*, p. 304; David Ben-Gurion, *Zichronot*, pp. 340–49.

76 Cohen, *Tarpat*, pp. 147–8.

77 Rana Barakat, The Jerusalem Fellah: popular politics in Mandate-era Palestine, *Journal of Palestine Studies* 46 (1), 2016, pp. 7–19.

78 Bernard Wasserstein, *The British in Palestine*, p. 237.

79 Shapira, *Land and Power*, p. 177.

80 Matthews, *Confronting an Empire*, p. 65.

81 Sami Adwan et al. (eds.), *Side By Side: Parallel Histories*, p. 63.

82 https://www.academia.edu/8567561/Calendars_martyrs_and_Palestinian _particularism_under_British_rule.

83 Segev, *One Palestine*, pp. 314–26.

84 Porath, *Emergence*, p. 272.

85 Shapira, *Land and Power*, p. 174.

86 Christopher Sykes, *Cross Roads*, p. 139.

87 Cohen, *Tarpat*, p. 163.

88 S. Y. Agnon, *Me-atzmi el atzmi*, p. 406.

89 Tom Segev, *1949: The First Israelis*, p. 67.

90 Gilbert, *Exile and Return*, p. 154.

91 Sykes, *Cross Roads*, p. 145.

92 Carly, Beckerman-Boys, The reversal of the Passfield White Paper, 1930–31: a reassessment, *Journal of Contemporary History* 51 (2), 2016, pp. 213–33.

93 Weizmann, *Trial and Error*, p. 415.

94 Hans Kohn, letter to Dr Feiwel, Jerusalem, 21 November 1929, cited in Martin Buber, *A Land of Two Peoples*.

95 Norman Bentwich, *For Zion's Sake: A Biography of Judah L. Magnes*, p. 178.

96 Michael Bar-Zohar, *Ben-Gurion*, p. 310.

97 Gerber, *Remembering and Imagining*, p. 34.

98 Jennifer Glynn (ed.), *Tidings from Zion*, p. 177.

99 Peel Report, p. 70.

100 Suzy Eban, *A Sense of Purpose*, pp. 47–8.

4. 1929–1936

1 *Filastin*, 2 November 1932.

2 Weldon Matthews, *Confronting an Empire*, p. 161.

3 Kenneth Stein, *The Land Question*, p. 215.

4 Mustafa Kabha, *The Palestinian Press*, pp. 114–18.

5 Raya Adler (Cohen), Mandatory land policy, tenancy and the Wadi al-Hawarith affair, 1929–1933, *Studies in Zionism: Politics, Society, Culture* 7 (2), 1986, pp. 233–57.

6 Matthews, *Confronting an Empire*, pp. 189–93.

7 Kabha, *Palestinian Press*, p. 135.

8 Matthews, *Confronting an Empire*, pp. 44–52.

9 Shai Lachman, Arab rebellion and terrorism in Palestine, 1929–1939: the case of Sheikh Izz al-Din al-Qassam and his movement, in Elie Kedourie and Sylvia G. Haim (eds.), *Zionism and Arabism in Palestine and Israel*, pp. 52–100.

10 Peel Report, p. 81.

11 Jacob Norris, *Land of Progress*, p. 170.

12 Haim Gerber, *Remembering and Imagining Palestine*, p. 125.

13 Yehoshua Porath, *Emergence of the Palestinian Arab National Movement*, p. 123.

14 Lachman, Arab rebellion, p. 53, op. cit.

15 Matthews, *Confronting an Empire*, p. 156.

16 Yoav Gelber, *Shorshei haHavatselet*, pp. 115–26.

17 David Ben-Gurion, *Zichronot*, p. 686.

18 Ian Black, *Zionism and the Arabs*, pp. 13–14.

19 Shabtai Teveth, *Retsah Arlosoroff.*

20 David Ben-Gurion, *My Talks with Arab Leaders*, p. 21.

21 Geoffrey Furlonge, *Palestine is My Country*, p. 104.

22 Neil Caplan, *Futile Diplomacy*, Vol. 2, pp. 189–92; Ben-Gurion, *My Talks*, pp. 14–21.

23 Black, *Zionism*, pp. 191–3.

24 Anita Shapira, *Ben-Gurion*, p. 94; Martin Kramer, *Sandbox*, 3 November 2015.

25 Porath, *Emergence*, pp. 132–3.

26 Gelber, *Shorshei haHavatselet*, pp. 106–7.

27 Mahmoud Yazbak, From poverty to revolt: economic factors in the outbreak of the 1936 rebellion in Palestine, *Middle Eastern Studies* 36 (3), 2000, pp. 97–105.

28 Nevill Barbour, *Nisi Dominus*, p. 133.

29 Ted Swedenburg, *Memories of Revolt*, pp. 29–30; Lachman, Arab rebellion, op. cit.

30 Gideon Shimoni, *The Zionist Ideology*, p. 380.

31 Gilbert Achcar, *The Arabs and the Holocaust,* p. 49.

32 Shimon Peres, *Battling for Peace*, p. 19.

5. 1936–1939

1 *Sefer Toldot haHaganah* (STH), Vol. 2, p. 632; Subhi Yassin, *Al-Thawra al-Arabiya al-Kubra fi Filastin*, p. 42; Gilbert Achcar, *The Arabs and the Holocaust*, p. 133.

2 Ian Black, *Zionism and the Arabs*, p. 17.

3 Mahmoud Yazbak, From poverty to revolt: economic factors in the outbreak of the 1936 rebellion in Palestine, *Middle Eastern Studies* 36 (3), 2000, pp. 93–113.

4 Zeina Ghandour, *A Discourse on Domination in Mandate Palestine*, p. 117.

5 Jacob Norris, Repression and rebellion: Britain's response to the Arab Revolt in Palestine of 1936–39, *Journal of Imperial and Commonwealth History* 36 (1), 2008.

6 Thomas Hodgkin, *Letters from Palestine*, 3 June 1936, p. 170.

7 *Filastin*, 12 July 1936, quoted in STH, Vol. 2, p. 639.

8 David Ben-Gurion, *My Talks with Arab Leaders*, p. 80.

9 Leila Parsons, *The Commander*, p. 120.

10 A. J. Sherman, *Mandate Memories*, p. 101.
11 Black, *Zionism*, p. 26.
12 Lord Melchett, *Thy Neighbour*, p. 225.
13 Black, *Zionism*, pp. 47–8.
14 Matthew Hughes, The banality of brutality: British armed forces and the repression of the Arab Revolt in Palestine, 1936–39, *English Historical Review* 124 (507), 2009, pp. 313–54.
15 Shabtai Teveth, *Ben-Gurion*; Mark LeVine, *Overthrowing Geography*, p. 104.
16 H. J. Simson, *British Rule and Rebellion*, p. 227.
17 Martin Gilbert, *Exile and Return*, p. 165.
18 Yehoshua Porath, *Emergence of the Palestinian Arab National Movement*, p. 212.
19 Neil Caplan, Faisal Ibn Husain and the Zionists: a re-examination with documents, *International History Review* 5 (4), 1983, pp. 561–614.
20 Peel Report, p. 123.
21 Rael Jean Isaac, *Israel Divided*, p. 33; *New Judaea*, August–Sept. 1937, p. 214.
22 Benny Morris (ed.), *Making Israel*, p. 16.
23 Black, *Zionism*, p. 90.
24 Ghandour, *Discourse on Domination*, pp. 166–74.
25 James Barr, *A Line in the Sand*, pp. 174–83.
26 Hughes, Banality, op. cit.
27 Mustafa Kabha, *The Palestinian People*, p. 77.
28 Hughes, Banality, op. cit.
29 William Quandt et al., *The Politics of Palestinian Nationalism*, p. 38.
30 Hughes, Banality, op. cit.
31 Matthew Hughes, The practice and theory of British counterinsurgency: the histories of the atrocities at the Palestinian villages of al-Bassa and Halhul, 1938–1939, *Small Wars & Insurgencies* 20 (3–4), 2009, pp. 528–50.
32 Norris, Repression and rebellion, op. cit.
33 Yusif Sayigh, *Arab Economist*, p. 158.
34 Itamar Radai, The rise and fall of the Palestinian-Arab middle class under the British Mandate, 1920–39, *Journal of Contemporary History*, 2016.
35 Ghandour, *Discourse on Domination*, p. 113.
36 Chaim Weizmann, *Trial and Error*, p. 484.
37 *Palestine Post*, 17 July 1938.
38 Black, *Zionism*, p. 380.

39 Elie Eliachar, *Lihiot im haPalestinaim*, p. 65.
40 Yoav Gelber, *Shorshei haHavatselet*, p. 184.
41 Hillel Cohen, *Tarpat*, p. 127.
42 Gelber, *Shorshei haHavatselet*, pp. 240–43.
43 Quandt et al., *Politics of Palestinian Nationalism*, p. 39.
44 Sayigh, *Arab Economist*, p. 160.
45 Cohen, *Tarpat*, pp. 143–4.
46 Weizmann, *Trial and Error*, p. 488; Hillel Cohen, *Army of Shadows*, pp. 143–4.
47 Matthew Hughes, Palestinian collaboration with the British: the peace bands and the Arab Revolt in Palestine, 1936–1939, *Journal of Contemporary History*, May 2015.
48 Haim Gerber, *Remembering and Imagining Palestine*, pp. 150–51.
49 Hughes, British counterinsurgency, op. cit.
50 Black, *Zionism*, pp. 390–98.
51 Anita Shapira, *Land and Power*, p. 253.
52 Sharon Rotbard, *White City, Black City*, p. 93.
53 Meir Pa'il, *Min HaHaganah leTzva Haganah*, p. 141.
54 Weizmann, *Trial and Error*, p. 489.
55 STH, Vol. 2, pt 2, p. 820; Anita Shapira, *Yigal Allon*, p. 96.
56 John Knight, Securing Zion? Policing in British Palestine, 1917–39, *European Review of History: Revue européenne d'histoire*, 2011.
57 STH, Vol. 2, pt 2, pp. 650, 800–802.
58 Sonia Nimr, in LeVine and Shafir (eds.), *Struggle and Survival*, pp. 141–56.
59 Gerber, *Remembering and Imagining*, p. 153.
60 Ted Swedenburg, *Memories of Revolt*, pp. 171–202.
61 Nasser Nashashibi, *Jerusalem's Other Voice*, p. 107.
62 Achcar, *Arabs and Holocaust*, p. 139.
63 Yezid Sayigh, *Armed Struggle*, p. 7.
64 Philip Mattar, *The Mufti of Jerusalem*, p. 151.
65 May Seikaly, *Haifa*, p. 250.
66 Yfaat Weiss, *A Confiscated Memory*, p. 67.
67 Simson, *British Rule*, p. 134.
68 Peel Report, p. 146.
69 Yonatan Mendel, *The Creation of Israeli Arabic*, p. 29.
70 Menachem Klein, *Lives in Common*, p. 74.
71 Tamir Goren, The struggle to save the national symbol: Jaffa Port from the Arab Revolt until the twilight of the British Mandate, *Middle Eastern Studies* 51 (6), 2015, pp. 863–82.
72 Weizmann, *Trial and Error*, p. 508.

6. 1939–1945

1 http://www.haaretz.com/news/features/this-day-in-jewish-history/
   1.545939.
2 Baruch Kimmerling and Joel Migdal, *The Palestinian People*, p. 138.
3 Joseph Nevo, The Arabs of Palestine 1947–48: military and political
   activity, *Middle Eastern Studies* 23 (1), 1987, pp. 3–38; Issa Khalaf,
   Politics in Palestine, p. 90.
4 Tom Segev, *The Seventh Million*, pp. 97–8.
5 *Guardian*, 15 February 1992.
6 Moshe Sharett, *Yoman Medini*, Vol. 5, p. 113.
7 Anita Shapira, *Yigal Allon*, p. 74.
8 Itamar Radai, *Palestinians in Jerusalem and Jaffa*, p. 133.
9 Hillel Cohen, *Army of Shadows*, p. 176.
10 Menachem Klein, *Lives in Common*, p. 74.
11 Countess Ranfurly, *To War with Whitaker*, p. 103.
12 Richard Crossman, *Palestine Mission*, p. 123.
13 Salim Tamari, *Jerusalem 1948*, p. 1.
14 Norman Rose, *A Senseless, Squalid War*, p. 58.
15 Chaim Weizmann, *Trial and Error*, pp. 529–30.
16 Ezra Danin, *Tzioni Bekol Tnai*, p. 157.
17 Walid Khalidi, The Arab perspective, in Louis and Stookey (eds.), *The
   End of the Palestine Mandate*, p. 107.
18 Anita Shapira, *Land and Power*, p. 283.
19 Shapira, *Land and Power*, pp. 308–10.
20 Noah Lucas, *Modern History*, p. 193.
21 Peel Report, p. 390.
22 Ian Black, *Zionism*, pp. 356–7; Yoav Gelber, The beginnings of the
   Israeli-Druze alliance, 1930–1948, *Cathedra* 60, 1991, pp. 141–81.
23 Nur Masalha, *Palestine Nakba*, p. 6; David Hirst, *The Gun and the
   Olive Branch*, p. 130.
24 Erskine Childers, The other exodus, *Spectator*, 12 May 1961, reprinted
   in Walter Laqueur (ed.), *The Israel–Arab Reader*, pp. 179–88.
25 Mordechai Bar-On, Cleansing history of its content: some critical
   comments on Ilan Pappé's *The Ethnic Cleansing of Palestine*, *Journal
   of Israeli History* 27 (2), 2008.
26 Yoav Gelber, *Shorshei haHavatselet*, pp. 510–27.
27 Ian Black and Benny Morris, *Israel's Secret Wars*, pp. 20–23.
28 Sarah Ozacky, The Haganah in Arab eyes, in Dani Hadari (ed.), *Homat
   Magen* pp. 303–42.

29 http://info.Palmah.org.il/show_item.asp?levelId=38612&itemId=5897 &itemType=0.
30 Meron Benvenisti, *Sacred Landscape*, p. 232.
31 Cohen, *Army of Shadows*, p. 188.
32 Hillel Cohen, *Tarpat*, p. 305.
33 Ari Shavit, *My Promised Land*, pp. 71–99.
34 Shapira, *Land and Power*, p. 311.
35 Shimon Peres, *Battling for Peace*, p. 47.
36 Benvenisti, *Sacred Landscape*, p. 71.
37 http://jerusalemquarterly.org/images/ArticlesPdf/JQ-52-Sela-Scouting_ Palestinian_Territory_1940-1948.pdf.
38 Salman Abu Sitta, *Mapping My Return*, p. 55.
39 Danin, *Tzioni Bekol Tnai*, pp. 217–18.
40 Hadara Lazar, *Out of Palestine*, p. 56.
41 Gelber, *Shorshei haHavatselet*, p. 300.
42 Cohen, *Army of Shadows*, p. 196.
43 T. R. Feiwel, *No Ease in Zion*, pp. 275–87.
44 Crossman, *Palestine Mission*, pp. 157–8.
45 Mustafa Kabha, *The Palestinian People*, p. 27.
46 Kabha, *Palestinian People*, p. 68.
47 Khalaf, *Politics in Palestine*, p. 91.

7. 1945–1949

1 S. Yizhar, *Khirbet Khiza*, p. 107.
2 Ilan Pappé, *The Ethnic Cleansing of Palestine*, p. 50; Saleh Abdel-Jawad, in Robert Rotberg (ed.), *Israeli and Palestinian Narratives of Conflict*; Benny Morris, *Righteous Victims*, pp. 89–90.
3 Said Aburish, *Children of Bethany*, p. 103.
4 David Horowitz, *State in the Making*, p. 102.
5 12 March 1947. Norman Rose, *A Senseless, Squalid War*.
6 Horowitz, *State in the Making*, p. 171.
7 Joseph Nevo, The Arabs of Palestine 1947–48: military and political activity, *Middle Eastern Studies* 23 (1), 1987, pp. 3–38.
8 Nevo, Arabs of Palestine.
9 Walid Khalidi, in Louis and Stookey (eds.), *The End of the Palestine Mandate*, p. 121.
10 http://zionism-israel.com/Letters_from_Jerusalem_1948.html.
11 Mustafa Kabha, *The Palestinian People*, p. 86.
12 Victor Kattan, *From Coexistence to Conquest*, p. 156.

13 Joseph Heller, in Elie Kedourie and Sylvia G. Haim (eds.), *Zionism and Arabism*, p. 147.
14 Richard Crossman, *Palestine Mission*, p. 141.
15 Benny Morris, *1948*, p. 81.
16 Uri Avnery, *1948*, pp. 4–5.
17 Salim Tamari, *Jerusalem 1948*, p. 98.
18 Gilbert Achcar, *The Arabs and the Holocaust*, p. 54.
19 Rashid Khalidi, *The Iron Cage*, pp. 22–30.
20 Aburish, *Children*, p. 94.
21 Hillel Cohen, *Army of Shadows*, p. 225.
22 Maurice Perlman, *The Mufti of Jerusalem*, pp. 24–33.
23 John Strawson, *Partitioning Palestine*, p. 74.
24 Nevo, Arabs of Palestine, op. cit.
25 Khalidi, *Iron Cage*, p. 125.
26 Walid Khalidi, *From Haven to Conquest*, p. 858.
27 Kabha, *Palestinian People*, p. 55.
28 Rose, *Senseless*, p. 58.
29 Christopher Sykes, *Cross Roads*, p. 402.
30 PASSIA, *100 Years*, p. 79.
31 Hisham Sharabi, *Embers and Ashes*, pp. 2–3.
32 Khalidi, in Louis and Stookey (eds.), *End of the Palestine Mandate*, p. 122.
33 Kabha, *Palestinian People*, pp. 100–101.
34 Leila Parsons, *The Commander*, pp. 157–8, 187–8.
35 Morris, *1948*, p. 93.
36 Itamar Radai, Jaffa, 1948: the fall of a city, *Journal of Israeli History* 30 (1), 2011, pp. 23–43.
37 Nevo, Arabs of Palestine, op. cit.; Cohen, *Army of Shadows*, pp. 232–3.
38 W. Roger Louis, Sir Alan Cunningham and the end of British rule in Palestine, *Journal of Imperial and Commonwealth History* 16 (3), 1988.
39 Nathan Krystall, The de-Arabization of West Jerusalem 1947–50, *Journal of Palestine Studies* 27 (2), 1998, pp. 5–22.
40 Ghada Karmi, *In Search of Fatima*, pp. 89–90.
41 Noam Chayut, *The Girl who Stole my Holocaust*, pp. 19–21.
42 Pappé, *Ethnic Cleansing*, p. 52.
43 Radai, Jaffa, 1948, op. cit.
44 Yoav Gelber, *Palestine 1948*, p. 75.
45 Nevo, Arabs of Palestine, p. 25, op. cit.
46 Itamar Radai, *Palestinians in Jerusalem and Jaffa*, p. 41.
47 Morris, *1948*, pp. 196–7.
48 Pappé, *Ethnic Cleansing*, p. 75.

49 Pappé, *Ethnic Cleansing.*

50 Walid Khalidi, Plan Dalet: master plan for the conquest of Palestine, *Journal of Palestine Studies* 18 (Special Issue: Palestine 1948), 1988, pp. 4–33.

51 Benny Morris, *The Birth of the Palestinian Refugee Problem*, p. 286.

52 Nur Masalha, *The Palestine Nakba*, p. 59.

53 Avi Shlaim, *Guardian*, 14 July 2014.

54 Avi Shlaim, *Collusion Across the Jordan*, p. 99.

55 Khalidi, in Louis and Stookey (eds.), *End of the Palestine Mandate*, p. 126.

56 Radai, *Palestinians*, p. 86.

57 Danny Rubinstein, The Last Battle. Unpublished manuscript.

58 Gelber, *Palestine*, p. 88.

59 Harry Levin quoted in Khalidi, *From Haven to Conquest*, pp. 767–70.

60 Cohen, *Army of Shadows*, p. 232.

61 Eric Silver, *Begin*, p. 89.

62 Radai, *Palestinians*, p. 87.

63 Benny Morris, *The Birth of the Palestinian Refugee Problem Revisited*, p. 237.

64 Sharif Kanaana and Nihad Zitawi, *Deir Yassin*. Monograph No. 4, Destroyed Palestinian Villages Documentation Project, Documentation Centre of Bir Zeit University, 1987, p. 55.

65 Tamari, *Jerusalem 1948*, p. 109.

66 Pappé, *Ethnic Cleansing*, p. 92.

67 Gelber, *Palestine*, p. 101.

68 Radai, *Palestinians*, p. 90.

69 Hadara Lazar, *Out of Palestine*, p. 255.

70 Gelber, *Palestine*, p. 109.

71 Mustafa Abbasi, The end of Arab Tiberias: the Arabs of Tiberias and the battle for the city in 1948, *Journal of Palestine Studies* 37 (3), 2008, pp. 6–29.

72 Morris, *1948*, p. 139.

73 http://moodle.technion.ac.il/file.php/2319/HAIFA_downtown2012/haifa_histories/out_3_.pdf.

74 Morris, *Refugee Problem Revisited*, pp. 309–10.

75 *Haaretz*, 26 May 2015.

76 Abu Iyad and Eric Rouleau, *My Home, My Land*, p. 23.

77 Beryl Cheal, Refugees in the Gaza Strip, December 1948–May 1950, *Journal of Palestine Studies* 18 (Special Issue: Palestine 1948), 1988, pp. 138–57, citing Paul Cossali and Clive Robson, *Stateless in Gaza*, 1986.

78 Mamdouh Nofal et al., Reflections on al-Nakba, *Journal of Palestine Studies* 28 (1), 1998, pp. 5–35.

79 Kattan, *Coexistence to Conquest*, p. 194.

80 Radai, Jaffa, 1948.

81 Mustafa Abbasi, The battle for Safad in the war of 1948: a revised study, *International Journal of Middle East Studies* 36 (1), 2004, pp. 21–47.

82 Mustafa Abbasi, The fall of Acre in the 1948 Palestine war, *Journal of Palestine Studies* 9 (4), 2010, pp. 6–27.

83 *Zochrot* interview, 12 July 2012.

84 Gelber, *Palestine*, pp. 114–15.

85 David Horowitz, *State in the Making*, p. 349.

86 Tom Segev, *Haaretz*, 21 October 2011.

87 Morris, *1948*, p. 187.

88 Gelber, *Palestine*, p. 137.

89 Muhammad Hallaj, Recollections of the Nakba through a teenager's eyes, *Journal of Palestine Studies* 38 (1), 2007–08.

90 Tamari, *Jerusalem 1948*, p. 266.

91 Sykes, *Cross Roads*, p. 405.

92 Musa Alami, The lesson of Palestine, *Middle East Journal* 3 (4), October 1949, pp. 373–405.

93 Kabha, *Palestinian People*, p. 110.

94 Pappé, *Ethnic Cleansing*, p. 132.

95 Morris, *1948*, p. 164.

96 Ilan Pappé, *Out of the Frame*, p. 73.

97 Kabha, *Palestinian People*, p. 118.

98 Adina Hoffman, *My Happiness*, pp. 113–16.

99 Sami Adwan et al., *Zoom In. Remembrances*, pp. 143–4.

100 Anita Shapira, *Yigal Allon*, p. 227.

101 Amos Ofer, testimony, *Zochrot*, 20 January 2016; Ari Shavit, *My Promised Land*, pp. 99–135.

102 Shapira, *Yigal Allon*, p. 229.

103 Yezid Sayigh, *Armed Struggle*, p. 71.

104 Dan Kurzman, *Soldier of Peace*, pp. 140–41.

105 Morris, *Refugee Problem Revisited*, pp. 181–232.

106 Efrat Ben-Zeev, *Remembering Palestine*, p. 84.

107 Abdel Bari Atwan, *A Country of Words*, p. 23.

108 S. Yizhar, *Khirbet Khiza*, p. 109.

109 Anita Shapira, Hirbet Hizah: between remembering and forgetting, in Benny Morris (ed.), *Making Israel*, pp. 81–123.

110 Uri Avnery, *Optimi*, p. 290.

111 Salman Abu Sitta, *Mapping My Return*, p. 90.
112 Morris, *1948*, p. 331.
113 Morris, *1948*, p. 346.
114 Kobi Peled, Oral testimonies, archival sources, and the 1948 Arab–Israeli war: a close look at the occupation of a Galilean village, *Journal of Israeli History* 33 (1), 2014, pp. 41–61; Ben-Zeev, *Remembering Palestine*, pp. 63–84.
115 Morris, *1948*, p. 406.
116 Bar-On, in Morris (ed.), *Making Israel*, p. 43.
117 Rosemarie M. Esber, *Under the Cover of War*, pp. 386–92.
118 Um Jabr Wishah, Palestinian voices: the 1948 war and its aftermath, *Journal of Palestine Studies* 35 (4), 2006, pp. 54–62.
119 Erskine Childers, The other exodus, *Spectator*, 12 May 1961.
120 Morris, *Refugee Problem Revisited*, p. 599.
121 *Al-Hamishmar*, 19 November 1948, quoted in Adel Manna, *Nakba and Survival*, p. 69.
122 Bar-On, in Morris (ed.), *Making Israel*, p. 43.

8. 1949–1953

1 Elias Sanbar, Out of place, out of time, *Mediterranean Historical Review* 16 (1), 2001.
2 Ian Lustick, *Arabs in the Jewish State*, p. 51.
3 Arif al-Arif, *Nakbat Bayt-al-Maqdis w'al Firdaus al-mafqoud*, p. 3.
4 Efrat Ben-Zeev, *Remembering Palestine*, p. 84.
5 Rosemary Sayigh, *The Palestinians*, p. 82.
6 Um Jabr Wishah, Palestinian voices: the 1948 war and its aftermath, *Journal of Palestine Studies* 35 (4), 2006, pp. 54–62.
7 Yoav Gelber, *Palestine 1948*, p. 267.
8 Beryl Cheal, Refugees in the Gaza Strip, December 1948–May 1950, *Journal of Palestine Studies* 18 (Special Issue: Palestine 1948), 1988, pp. 138–57.
9 Sami Adwan et al. (eds.), *Side By Side: Parallel Histories*, p. 153.
10 Mark LeVine and Gershon Shafir (eds.), *Struggle and Survival*, p. 185.
11 Tom Segev, *1949*, p. 29.
12 Quoted in Colin Shindler, *History of Modern Israel*, p. 50.
13 Benny Morris, *1948*, pp. 89–149.
14 Lodewijk van Oord, Face-lifting Palestine: early Western accounts of the Palestinian refugee problem, *History and Anthropology* 22 (1), 2011, pp. 19–35.

15 Progress Report of the United Nations Mediator on Palestine, 16 September 1948.
16 Meron Benvenisti, *Sacred Landscape*, p. 151.
17 Anita Shapira, Hirbet Hizah: between remembering and forgetting, in Benny Morris (ed.), *Making Israel*, p. 96.
18 Bar-On, in Morris (ed.), *Making Israel*, p. 43.
19 Avi Plascov, *Palestinian Refugees*, p. 73.
20 Nafez Nazaal, *The Palestinian Exodus from Galilee*, p. 69; Mark Tessler, *Israeli-Palestinian Conflict*, p. 282.
21 Gelber, *Palestine*, p. 267.
22 http://prrn.mcgill.ca/prrn/al-mawed.pdf.
23 Elias Nasrallah, *Shahadat ala al-Qarn al-Filastini al-Awal*, pp. 85-96.
24 Adel Manna, Nakba and survival, EUME Berliner Seminar, 9 November 2016.
25 Hillel Cohen, *Good Arabs*, p. 6.
26 Nadim N. Rouhana and Areej Sabbagh-Khoury (eds.), *The Palestinians in Israel*, p. 18.
27 Sarah Ozacky-Lazar, http://lib.cet.ac.il/pages/item.asp?item=13336.
28 Lustick, *Arabs*, p. 48.
29 Hannah Mermelstein, Overdue books: returning Palestine's 'Abandoned Property' of 1948, *Jerusalem Quarterly* 47, Autumn 2011.
30 Saleh Abdel-Jawad, in Robert Rotberg (ed.), *Israeli and Palestinian Narratives of Conflict*, p. 90.
31 Sabri Jiryis, *The Arabs in Israel*, p. 121.
32 Gelber, *Palestine*, p. 291.
33 Segev, *1949*, p. 67.
34 http://malam.cet.ac.il/ShowItem.aspx?ItemID=188f577d-0058-4e34-af a3-692e1cecco8e&lang=HEB.
35 http://zionism-israel.com/israel_news/2006/12/alexander-and-yiftah-zaid-end-of-legend.html.
36 Shira Robinson, *Citizen Strangers*, pp. 35-6.
37 Shammas, in Laurence J. Silberstein (ed.), *New Perspectives on Israeli History*, p. 218.
38 http://lib.cet.ac.il/pages/item.asp?item=13336.
39 Dan Rabinowitz and Khawla Abu-Baker, *Coffins*, pp. 51-2.
40 Moshe Shemesh, Palestinian society in the wake of the 1948 war: from social fragmentation to consolidation. *Israel Studies*, Spring 2004, pp. 86-100.
41 Abdel Bari Atwan, *A Country of Words*, p. 27.
42 Geoffrey Furlonge, *Palestine is My Country*, pp. 162-3.

43 Mamdouh Nofal et al., Reflections on al-Nakba, *Journal of Palestine Studies* 28 (1), 1998, pp. 5-35.
44 Adel H. Yahya, in Paul Scham et al., *Shared Histories*, p. 222.
45 Wishah, Palestinian voices, op. cit.
46 Plascov, *Palestinian Refugees*, p. 17.
47 Nofal et al., Reflections on al-Nakba.
48 Muhammad Hallaj, Recollections of the Nakba through a teenager's eyes, *Journal of Palestine Studies* 38 (1), 2007-08.
49 Benvenisti, *Sacred Landscape*, p. 141.
50 Shlomo Sand, *The Invention of the Land of Israel*, p. 260.
51 Menachem Klein, *Lives in Common*, p. 172.
52 Sharon Rotbard, *White City, Black City*, p. 114.
53 Noga Kadman, *Erased from Space*, p. 18; Benvenisti, *Sacred Landscape*, pp. 164-5.
54 Rebecca L. Torstrick, *Limits of Coexistence*, p. 175.
55 Walter Schwartz, *The Arabs in Israel*, p. 59.
56 Segev, *1949*, pp. 88-9.
57 Michael Roman and Alex Weingrod, *Living Together Separately*, p. 12.
58 Lustick, *Arabs*, p. 84.
59 Adina Hoffman, *My Happiness*, p. 241.
60 http://sfonline.barnard.edu/jewish/panel4_05.htm.
61 Jo Roberts, *Contested Land*, pp. 162-3.
62 A. B. Yehoshua, *Facing the Forests*, 1970.
63 Benvenisti, *Sacred Landscape*, p. 8.
64 Nur Masalha, *The Palestine Nakba*, p. 117.
65 Benvenisti, *Sacred Landscape*, pp. 271-306; entries in *Zochrot, Hikayat Balad, Omrim Yayshna Aretz.*
66 Charles S. Kamen, After the catastrophe II: the Arabs in Israel, 1948-51, *Middle Eastern Studies* 24 (1), 1988.
67 Rotbard, *White City*, p. 114.
68 Masalha, *Palestine Nakba*, pp. 88-119.
69 Benvenisti, *Sacred Landscape*, p. 14.
70 Segev, *1949*, p. 70.
71 Tamari, *Jerusalem 1948*, pp. 110-11.
72 Pinkerfeld testimony, *Zochrot*, 23 December 2012.
73 Noah Lucas, *Modern History*, p. 274.
74 Yfaat Weiss, *A Confiscated Memory*, p. 49.
75 Roberts, *Contested Land*, p. 49.
76 Michael Fischbach, *Records of Dispossession*, p. 74.
77 Shlomit Shaked, *Zochrot* interview, 23 October 2012.

78 Tamari, *Jerusalem 1948*, p. 1.

79 Robinson, *Citizen Strangers*, p. 10.

80 Yoav Gelber, Israel's policy towards its Arab minority, 1947–1950, *Israel Affairs* 19 (1), 2013, pp. 51–81.

81 Cohen, *Good Arabs*, p. 23.

82 Lucas, *Modern History*, p. 282.

83 Segev, *1949*, p. 66.

84 Cohen, *Good Arabs*, p. 40.

85 Kais M. Firro, The conscription of the Druze into the Israeli Army, in Rouhana and Sabbagh-Khoury (eds.), *The Palestinians in Israel*, p. 60.

86 Segev, *1949*, p. 66.

87 Gelber, Israel's policy, op. cit.

88 Lustick, *Arabs*, p. 203.

89 Atallah Mansour, *Waiting for the Dawn*, p. 36.

90 Michael Gorkin, *Days of Honey, Days of Onion*, p. 127.

91 Arnon Yehuda Dagani, The decline and fall of the Israeli military government, 1948–1966: a case of settler-colonial consolidation? *Settler Colonial Studies* 5, 2015.

92 Lustick, *Arabs*, p. 203.

93 Weitz to Sharett in May 1949: Kamen, After the catastrophe II.

94 *Observer*, 19 June 1950.

95 Adel Manna, *Nakba and Survival*, p. 184.

96 Gelber, Israel's policy, op. cit.

97 Morris, *1948*, pp. 257–71.

98 Quoted in Honaida Ghanim, Once upon a border: the secret lives of resistance. The case of the Palestinian village of Al-Marja, 1949–1967, *Biography* 37 (2), 2014.

9. 1953–1958

1 David Landau, *Arik*, pp. 25–7.

2 Eyal Kafkafi, The 'latent function' of the Qibya Raid: David Ben-Gurion's weapon against Pinchas Lavon, *Israel Affairs* 8 (3), 2002, pp. 118–33.

3 Mustafa Kabha, *The Palestinian People*, p. 191.

4 The 1953 Qibya Raid revisited: excerpts from Moshe Sharett's diaries, *Journal of Palestine Studies* 31 (4), 2002, pp. 77–98.

5 Benny Morris, *Israel's Border Wars*, pp. 135–7.

6 Jacob Tovy, *Israel and the Palestinian Refugee Issue*, p. 181.

7 Avi Shlaim, *Lion of Jordan*, pp. 69–74.

8   http://www.haaretz.com/weekend/week-s-end/doomed-to-fight-1.360698.

9   Uri Avnery, *Gush Shalom*, 12 April 2008.

10 Ian Black and Benny Morris, *Israel's Secret Wars*, p. 121.

11 Yezid Sayigh, *Armed Struggle*, p. 82.

12 Salman Abu Sitta, *Mapping My Return*, p. 111.

13 Guy Laron, The domestic sources of Israel's decision to launch the 1956 Sinai campaign, *British Journal of Middle Eastern Studies* 42 (2), 2015, pp. 200–218.

14 Black and Morris, *Israel's Secret Wars*, pp. 123–24.

15 Jean-Pierre Filiu, *Gaza: A History*, p. 93.

16 Nur Masalha, The 1956–57 occupation of the Gaza Strip: Israeli proposals to resettle the Palestinian refugees, *British Journal of Middle Eastern Studies* 23 (1), 1996, pp. 55–68.

17 *Haaretz*, 11 February 2010, http://www.haaretz.com/weekend/magazine/a-thin-black-line-1.263163.

18 Filiu, *Gaza*, pp. 96–9.

19 Sayigh, *Armed Struggle*, p. 65.

20 Ian Lustick, *Arabs in the Jewish State*, p. 86.

21 Shira Robinson, Local struggle, national struggle: Palestinian responses to the Kafr Qasim massacre and its aftermath, 1956–66, *International Journal of Middle East Studies* 35 (3), 2003.

22 http://www.timesofisrael.com/rivlin-to-address-ceremony-marking-kfar-kassem-massacre/; *Guardian*, 6 November 2015.

23 Hillel Frisch, *Israel's Security and Its Arab Citizens*, p. 20.

24 Lustick, *Arabs*, p. 67.

25 Walter Schwartz, *The Arabs in Israel*, p. 15.

26 Fawzi al-Asmar, *Lihiyot Aravi be-Yisrael*, p. 50.

27 Frisch, *Israel's Security*, p. 26.

28 Adel Manna, The Palestinian Nakba and its continuous repercussions, *Israel Studies* 18 (2), 2013.

29 Sami Adwan et al., *Zoom In. Remembrances*, p. 162.

30 Adina Hoffman, *My Happiness*, p. 144.

31 Camilla Suleiman, *Language and Identity*, p. 17.

32 Yusif Sayigh, *Arab Economist, Palestinian Patriot*, p. 243.

33 Interview, *Jerusalem Post*, 13 July 1979.

34 Adel Manna, *Nakba and Survival*, p. 10.

35 Michel Warschawski, *On the Border*, p. 31.

36 Julie Peteet, *Landscape of Hope and Despair*, pp. 111–16.

37 Fawaz Turki, *Soul in Exile*, p. 18.

38 Robert Fisk, *Pity the Nation*, p. 19.

39 A. L. Tibawi, Visions of the return, *Middle East Journal* 17 (5), 1963.

40 Beshara Doumani, Palestine versus the Palestinians? The iron laws and ironies of a people denied, *Journal of Palestine Studies* 36 (4), 2006–07.

41 Mahmoud Yazbak, The Nakba and the Palestinian silence, in Adwan et al., *Zoom In.*

42 Isabelle Humphries, Listening to the displaced narrative: politics, power and grassroots communication amongst Palestinians inside Israel, *Middle East Journal of Culture and Communication* 1, 2008, pp. 180–96.

43 Dina Matar, *What it Means*, p. 79.

44 Schwartz, *Arabs in Israel*, p. 88.

45 Geremy Forman, in Sandy Sufian and Mark LeVine (eds.), *Reapproaching Borders*, pp. 67–94.

46 Maha Nassar, The marginal as central: *Al-Jadid* and the development of a Palestinian public sphere, 1953–1970, *Middle East Journal of Culture and Communication* 3, 2010, pp. 333–51.

47 Al-Asmar, *Lihiyot Aravi be-Yisrael*, p. 64.

48 Degani, Jamal Zahalka, http://jewssansfrontieres.blogspot.co.il/2010/04/jamal-zahalka-on-ashkenaz.html.

49 Nissim Rejwan, *Outsider in the Promised Land*, pp. 65–6.

50 Suleiman, *Language and Identity*, p. 16.

51 Gil Eyal, *The Disenchantment of the Orient*, p. 157.

52 Ahmad H. Sa'di, Stifling surveillance: Israel's surveillance and control of the Palestinians during the military government era, *Jerusalem Quarterly* 68, Winter 2016.

53 Yonatan Mendel, *The Creation of Israeli Arabic*, pp. 59–83.

10. 1958–1967

1 Jewish Telegraphic Agency, 25 April 1958.

2 Walter Eytan, *The First Ten Years*, pp. 111–16.

3 http://www.hrc.utexas.edu/multimedia/video/2008/wallace/eban_abba_t.html, 12 April 1958; Asaf Siniver, *Abba Eban*, pp. 171–2.

4 Hillel Frisch, *Israel's Security*, pp. 24–5.

5 Aharon Shai, The fate of the abandoned Arab villages in Israel on the eve of the Six Days war and after (in Hebrew), *Cathedra* 105, September 2002.

6 Shalom Shalom ve'ain Shalom, 1961, A. Yisraeli.

7 Mustafa Abbas, The end of Arab Tiberias: the battle for the city in 1948, *Journal of Palestine Studies* 37 (3), 2008, pp. 6–29.

8 http://mfa.gov.il/MFA/ForeignPolicy/MFADocuments/Yearbook1/Pages/ 11%20Statement%20to%20the%20Special%20Political%20Committee %20of.aspx.

9 Shay Hazkani, *Haaretz*, 16 May 2013.

10 Shira Robinson, *Citizen Strangers*, p. 180.

11 Dan Rabinowitz, *Overlooking Nazareth*, p. 29.

12 David A. Wesley, *State Practices and Zionist Images*, p. 29.

13 Ian Lustick, *Arabs in the Jewish State*, p. 123.

14 Adina Hoffman, *My Happiness Bears No Relation to Happiness*, p. 281.

15 Walter Schwartz, *Arabs in Israel*, p. 16.

16 Hillel Cohen, *Good Arabs*, p. 142.

17 Ilan Pappé, *The Forgotten Palestinians*, p. 83.

18 Sabri Jiryis, *The Arabs in Israel*, pp. 138–9; Tamir Sorek, Palestinian nationalism has left the field: a shortened history of Arab soccer in Israel, *International Journal of Middle East Studies* 35, 2003, pp. 417–37.

19 Nissim Rejwan, *Outsider in the Promised Land*, p. 213.

20 Yezid Sayigh, *Armed Struggle*, p. 39.

21 Adel Manna, The Palestinian Nakba and its continuous repercussions, *Israel Studies* 18 (2), 2013, pp. 86–99.

22 Avi Plascov, *The Palestinian Refugees*, p. 29.

23 Fawaz Turki, *Disinherited*, p. 41.

24 Rejwan, *Outsider*, p. 22.

25 Sayigh, *Armed Struggle*, pp. 39–52.

26 Colin Shindler, *History of Modern Israel*, p. 52; UNRWA, 1956, supplement no. 14, p. 13.

27 http://www.foia.cia.gov/sites/default/files/document_conversions/14/esau-49.pdf, declassified 2007.

28 Danny Rubinstein, *The Mystery of Arafat*, p. 41.

29 Abu Iyad and Eric Rouleau, *My Home, My Land*, p. 20; Helena Cobban, *The Palestinian Liberation Organisation*, pp. 21–2.

30 Sayigh, *Armed Struggle*, p. 84.

31 Helga Baumgarten, The three faces/phases of Palestinian nationalism, 1948–2005, *Journal of Palestine Studies* 34 (4), 2005, pp. 25–48.

32 Erskine Childers, The other exodus, *Spectator*, 12 May 1961.

33 Ethel Mannin, *The Road to Beersheba*.

34 Sari Nusseibeh, *Once Upon a Country*, p. 67.

35 Efrat Ben-Zeev, *Remembering Palestine*, p. 91.

36 Arabic/English text in http://www.barghouti.com/poets/darwish/bit aqa.asp.

37 Edward Said, *The Question of Palestine*, p. 155.

38 Sayigh, *Armed Struggle*, p. 88.

39 Andrew Gowers and Tony Walker, *Behird the Myth*, p. 45.

40 Ami Gluska, *The Israeli Military*, pp. 68-9.

41 Omri Shefer-Raviv, From enemies to lovers: the Israeli public debates about the use of force in the West Bank, 1965-1969, *Cathedra* 163, April 2017.

42 William Quandt et al., *Politics of Palestinian Nationalism*, p. 159.

43 Avi Shlaim, *Iron Wall*, p. 230.

44 Shaul Mishal, *The PLO Under Arafat*, p. 4.

45 Cobban, *The Palestinian Liberation Organisation*, p. 29.

46 Said Aburish, *Arafat*, p. 57.

47 Avi Shlaim, *Lion of Jordan*, p. 205; Sayigh, *Armed Struggle*, p. 97.

48 Shaul Mishal, *West Bank, East Bank*, pp. 111, 120.

49 http://www.jewishvirtuallibrary.org/jsource/Peace/cover.html.

50 Shafiq al-Hout, *My Life in the PLO*, p. 53.

51 Rafi Sutton and Yitzhak Shoshan, *Anshei haSod veHester*, pp. 306-7.

52 Aburish, *Arafat*, p. 62.

53 http://www.palestine-studies.org/resources/special-focus/martyrdom-context-palestinian-national-struggle-o.

54 *Haaretz*, 15 January 1965, cited in Gluska, *Israeli Military*, p. 283.

55 Sayigh, *Armed Struggle*, p. 119.

56 Moshe Shemesh, *Arab Politics*, p. 94.

57 Cobban, *The Palestinian Liberation Organisation*, p. 34; http://blog.syracuse.com/opinion/2012/05/story_of_a_fathers_loss_of_hom.html.

58 Quandt et al., *Politics of Palestinian Nationalism*, p. 167.

59 Tom Segev, *1967*, p. 147.

60 Ian Black and Benny Morris, *Israel's Secret Wars*, pp. 237-8.

61 Michael Oren, *Six Days of War*, p. 32.

62 Shlaim, *Iron Wall*, p. 234.

63 Moshe Shemesh, The IDF raid on Samu: the turning point in Jordan's relations with Israel and the West Bank Palestinians, *Israel Studies* Spring 2002.

11. 1967

1 Meron Benvenisti, *Son of the Cypresses*, p. 232.

2 Avi Raz, *The Bride and the Dowry*, p. 7; Walter Laqueur, *The Road to War*, p. 295.

3 Randolph S. Churchill and Winston S. Churchill, *The Six Days War*, p. 195.

4 Guy Laron, *The Six-Day War*, pp. 107–17.
5 Michael Oren, *Six Days of War*, pp. 171–210.
6 Gershom Gorenberg, *Occupied Territories*, p. 37.
7 Edward Luttwak and Daniel Horowitz, *The Israeli Army*, p. 265.
8 Oren, *Six Days of War*, pp. 294–304.
9 Luttwak and Horowitz, *Israeli Army*, p. 213.
10 Laron, *Six-Day War*, p. 286.
11 Sadiq al-Azm, *Self-Criticism after the Defeat*.
12 Jonathan Cummings, *Israel's Public Diplomacy*, p. 55.
13 Abdullah Schleifer, *The Fall of Jerusalem*, p. 194.
14 David Hirst, *The Gun and the Olive Branch*, pp. 209–11; Joseph L. Ryan, The myth of annihilation and the six-day war, https://worldview.carnegiecouncil.org/archive/worldview/1973/09/2214.html.
15 Churchill and Churchill, *Six Days War*, p. 239.
16 Tom Segev, *1967*, p. 356.
17 Teddy Kollek, *For Jerusalem*, pp. 193–7.
18 Schleifer, *Fall of Jerusalem*, p. 205.
19 Shimon Peres, *Battling for Peace*, p. 107.
20 *Haaretz*, 31 December 1997.
21 Eitan Felner, *B'Tselem*, 1995.
22 *Haaretz*, 13 April 2017.
23 Michael Bar-Zohar, *Yaakov Herzog*, p. 299.
24 Menachem Klein, *Lives in Common*, p. 151.
25 Mark LeVine and Gershon Shafir (eds.), *Struggle and Survival*, p. 213.
26 http://www.sarahozacky.com/%D7%A6%D7%99%D7%95%D7%A0%D7%99-%D7%93%D7%A8%D7%9A/.
27 Yaron Ezrahi, *Rubber Bullets*, p. 55.
28 Michel Warschawski, *On the Border*, p. 13.
29 http://972mag.com/radio-ramallah-the-cultural-bridge-that-was/80661/.
30 Klein, *Lives in Common*, p. 141
31 Laqueur, *Road to War*, pp. 296–7.
32 *Davar*, 12 June 1967.
33 Yael Dayan, *Israel Journal: June, 1967*, pp. 109–11.
34 Michael Gadish, Jewish-Israeli identity in Naomi Shemer's songs: central values of the Jewish-Israeli imagined community, http://www.ugr.es/~estsemi/miscelanea/58/3.Gadish09.pdf.
35 https://www.youtube.com/watch?v=kubEFWFHbrA.
36 Laron, *Six-Day War*, p. 109.
37 Ian Lustick (ed.), *Palestinians under Israeli Rule*, p. 132.

38 Al-Haq, Where Villages Stood, Israel's Continuing Violations of International Law in Occupied Latroun, 1967–2007, December 2007; Raz, *Bride and the Dowry*, p. 324.

39 Oren, *Six Days of War*, p. 307.

40 Meron Benvenisti, *Sacred Landscape*, p. 327.

41 Raz, *Bride and the Dowry*, p. 110. See p. 114.

42 http://1967.walla.co.il/?w=/2066/1099788/@@/item/printer.

43 http://www.palestine-studies.org/sites/default/files/jps-articles/UNRWA%20Remembers%201967.pdf.

44 Avi Shlaim, *Lion of Jordan*, p. 254; Samir Mutawi, *Jordan in the 1967 War*, p. 171.

45 Peter Dodd and Halim Barakat, *River Without Bridges*, p. 40; Nur Masalha, *A Land Without a People*, p. 92; Nur Masalha, *The Politics of Denial*, p. 203.

46 Schleifer, *Fall of Jerusalem*, p. 207.

47 David Pryce-Jones, *The Face of Defeat*, p. 10.

48 Masalha, *Politics of Denial*, p. 203.

49 Mutawi, *Jordan*, p. 171.

50 Mustafa Kabha, *The Palestinian People*, p. 230.

51 *Haaretz*, 15 March 2017.

52 Sari Nusseibeh, *Once Upon a Country*, p. 98.

53 Pryce-Jones, *Face of Defeat*, p. 20.

54 *Shalom*, Gatekeepers, p. 28.

55 Schleifer, *Fall of Jerusalem*, pp. 213–14.

56 Raz, *Bride and the Dowry*, pp. 81–3.

57 Yezid Sayigh, *Armed Struggle*, p. 158.

58 Bassam Abu Sharif, *Arafat*, p. 14.

59 Segev, *1967*, p. 146.

60 Danny Rubinstein, *The Mystery of Arafat*, p. 55.

61 Kabha, *Palestinian People*, p. 226.

62 Musa Budeiri, Controlling the archive: captured Jordanian security files in the Israeli state archives, *Jerusalem Quarterly* 66, 2016.

63 Sayigh, *Armed Struggle*, p. 162.

64 http://www.palestine-studies.org/sites/default/files/jps-articles/jps.2007.37.1.88.pdf.

65 Sayigh, *Armed Struggle*, p. 162.

66 Shaul Mishal, *The PLO Under Arafat*, p. 9.

67 Moshe Dayan, *Story of My Life*, p. 405.

68 Sayigh, *Armed Struggle*, p. 172.

69 Kabha, *Palestinian People*, p. 234.

70 David Ronen, *Shnat Shabak*, p. 219.
71 Segev, *1967*, p. 469.
72 Shlaim, *Lion of Jordan*, p. 262.
73 Sayigh, *Armed Struggle*, p. 456.
74 Shlomo Gazit, *Hagezer ve haMakel*, pp. 178-9; B'Tselem, Collaborators in the Occupied Territories: Human Rights Abuses and Violations, January 1994, p. 11.
75 http://www.palestine-studies.org/sites/default/files/jps-articles/jps.2007.37.1.88.pdf.
76 Nusseibeh, *Country*, p. 97.
77 http://www.israeli-occupation.org/2013-05-07/musa-budeiri-always-with-the-oppressed-a-farewell-to-akiva-orr-1931-2013-humanist-radical-heretic/#sthash.TaTQITv2.dpu.
78 Atallah Mansour, *Waiting for the Dawn*, p. 115.
79 Gorenberg, *Occupied Territories*, p. 62.
80 Danna Piroyansky, From island to archipelago: the Sakakini house in Qatamon and its shifting ownerships throughout the twentieth century, *Middle Eastern Studies* 48 (6), 2012, pp. 855-77.
81 Danny Rubinstein, *The People of Nowhere*, p. 62.
82 *Jerusalem Post*, 30 June 1967.
83 Amos Oz, *In the Land of Israel*, pp. 175-6.
84 http://mosaicmagazine.com/observation/2016/08/conversations-with-the-palestinians-of-1967-has-anything-changed/.
85 Ilan Pappé, *Forgotten Palestinians*, p. 112.
86 Dan Rabinowitz and Khawla Abu-Baker, *Coffins*, p. 75.
87 Raja Shehadeh, *Language of War*, p. 21.
88 Mansour, *Waiting for Dawn*, p. 114.
89 Rafik Halabi, *The West Bank Story*, p. 55.
90 http://www.israeli-occupation.org/2013-05-07/musa-budeiri-always-with-the-oppressed-a-farewell-to-akiva-orr-1931-2013-humanist-radical-heretic/#sthash.TaTQITv2.dpuf.
91 Rubinstein, *People of Nowhere*, p. 62.
92 Mamdouh Nofal et al., Reflections on Al-Nakba, *Journal of Palestine Studies* 28 (1), 1998, pp. 5-35.
93 http://publishing.cdlib.org/ucpressebooks/view?docId=ft4489n8s2&chunk.id=ch11&toc.depth=100&toc.id=ch11&brand=ucpress;query=1967#1.
94 Dina Matar, *What it Means*, p. 143.
95 http://www.haaretz.com/print-edition/features/arab-town-both-israeli-and-palestinian-divided-by-shopping-1.410313.
96 Riyadh Kamel Kabha, *Shtay Gadot leWadi*, p. 55.

97 Assaf Peled, Descending the Khazooq: 'working through' the trauma of the Nakba in Emile Habibi's oeuvre, *Israel Studies* 21 (1), 2016, pp. 157–82.
98 Pappé, *Forgotten Palestinians*, pp. 113–14.
99 Shehadeh, *Language of War*, p. 21.
100 Raz, *Bride and the Dowry*, p. 39.
101 Baruch Kimmerling and Joel Migdal, *The Palestinian People*, p. 342.
102 Rael Jean Isaac, *Israel Divided*, p. 12.
103 Nissim Rejwan, *Outsider in the Promised Land*, p. 55.
104 Amos Elon, *A Blood-Dimmed Tide*, p. 31.
105 Gorenberg, *Occupied Territories*, p. 86.
106 Raz, *Bride and the Dowry*, p. 43.
107 Raz, *Bride and the Dowry*, p. 41.
108 Ami Gluska, *The Israeli Military*, p. 258.
109 Gorenberg, *Occupied Territories*, p. 51.
110 Anita Shapira, *Yigal Allon*, pp. 312–16.
111 Raz, *Bride and the Dowry*, p. 23.
112 Avi Shlaim, *The Iron Wall*, pp. 262–4.
113 Shlomo Ben-Ami, *Scars of War*, p. 125.
114 http://www.palestine-studies.org/sites/default/files/jps-articles/jps.2007.37.1.88.pdf.
115 Shabtai Teveth, *The Cursed Blessing*.
116 Reuven Pedatzur, *Nitzahon haMevucha*.
117 Benvenisti, *Son of the Cypresses*, p. 232.
118 Yeshayahu Leibowitz, *Judaism, Human Values*, pp. 225–6.
119 *Haaretz*, 21 July 1967.
120 *Haaretz*, 22 September 1967.
121 Nissim Rejwan, *Israel's Years of Bogus Grandeur*, p. xx.
122 http://www.nytimes.com/2015/01/26/world/disillusioned-by-war-israeli-soldiers-muted-in-1967-are-given-fuller-voice.html.
123 Matti Steinberg, *Omdim Legoralam*, p. 9.
124 Amos Oz, *My Michael*, p. 84; Jacqueline Rose http://www.theguardian.com/books/2008/may/10.

12. 1968–1972

1 Teddy Kollek, *For Jerusalem*, p. 223.
2 Eyal Weizman, *Hollow Land*, p. 25.
3 Kollek, *For Jerusalem*, p. 240.
4 Sari Nusseibeh, *Once Upon a Country*, p. 172.
5 PASSIA, *100 Years*.

6 Gershom Gorenberg, *Occupied Territories*, p. 101.
7 Avi Raz, *The Bride and the Dowry*, pp. 137–8; Shafiq al-Hout, *My Life in the PLO*, pp. 61–2.
8 Idith Zertal and Akiva Eldar, *Lords of the Land*, p. 15.
9 Gorenberg, *Occupied Territories*, p. 117.
10 http://www.haaretz.com/israel-news/.premium-1.733746?=&ts=_1470142 185577.
11 Gershom Gorenberg, *The Accidental Empire: Israel and the Birth of the Settlements*.
12 Raz, *Bride and the Dowry*, p. 267.
13 Meron Benvenisti, *Sacred Landscape*, p. 250.
14 Ian Black and Benny Morris, *Israel's Secret Wars*, p. 255.
15 Yaakov Peri, *HaBa leHorgekha*, pp. 47–53.
16 Abu Iyad and Eric Rouleau, *My Home, My Land*, p. 56.
17 Daniel Byman, *A High Price*, p. 40.
18 Raz, *Bride and the Dowry*, p. 224.
19 Said Aburish, *Arafat*, p. 83.
20 Andrew Gowers and Tony Walker, *Behind the Myth*, pp. 76–8.
21 Atallah Mansour, *Waiting for the Dawn*, p. 109.
22 Muhammad Muslih, Towards coexistence: an analysis of the resolutions of the Palestine National Council, *Journal of Palestine Studies* 19 (4), 1990, pp. 3–29.
23 *Time*, 13 December 1968.
24 *Free Palestine*, August 1969, quoted in Walter Laqueur (ed.), *Israel – Arab Reader*, pp. 445–51.
25 Neve Gordon, *Israel's Occupation*, p. 77.
26 Leila Farsakh, *Palestinian Labour Migration*, p. 209.
27 Joel Migdal (ed.), *Palestinian Society and Politics*, p. 195.
28 Gordon, *Israel's Occupation*, p. 66.
29 Aziz Shehadeh, *New Middle East* 35, August 1971.
30 George Bisharat, *Palestinian Lawyers and Israeli Rule*, p. 5.
31 Gordon, *Israel's Occupation*, p. 91.
32 Mansour, *Waiting for Dawn*, p. 117.
33 Migdal (ed.), *Palestinian Society*, p. 197.
34 Mustafa Kabha, *The Palestinian People*, p. 269.
35 *New Statesman*, 19 January 1979.
36 Yezid Sayigh, *Armed Struggle*, p. 287.
37 Weizman, *Hollow Land*, p. 70.
38 Kabha, *Palestinian People*, p. 247.
39 Ariel Sharon and David Chanoff, *Warrior*, p. 257.
40 Sayigh, *Armed Struggle*, p. 287.

41 Sharon and Chanoff, *Warrior*, pp. 248–58.
42 Jean-Pierre Filiu, *Gaza: A History*, p. 14.
43 *Haaretz*, 9 October 2002.
44 Geoffrey Aronson, *Israel, Palestinians, and the Intifada*, p. 25.
45 *Jerusalem Post*, 13 June 1973.
46 David Pryce-Jones, *Face of Defeat*, p. 115.
47 Uzi Benziman, *Sharon*, pp. 117–18.
48 Farsakh, *Palestinian Labour*, p. 209.
49 Kabha, *Palestinian People*, p. 240.
50 Gowers and Walker, *Behind the Myth*, pp. 92–116.
51 Shaul Mishal, *The PLO Under Arafat*, p. 15.
52 Kabha, *Palestinian People*, p. 245.
53 Avi Shlaim, *Lion of Jordan*, p. 335.
54 Black and Morris, *Israel's Secret Wars*, p. 258.
55 Nigel Ashton, *King Hussein of Jordan*, p. 157.
56 Shlaim, *Lion of Jordan*, p. 348.
57 Al-Hout, *My Life*, p. 103.
58 Leila Khaled, *My People Shall Live*, p. 21.
59 Hisham Sharabi, *Palestine Guerrillas*, pp. 31–2.
60 Sayigh, *Armed Struggle*, p. 307.
61 Black and Morris, *Israel's Secret Wars*, p. 258.
62 Byman, *A High Price*, p. 45.
63 Sayigh, *Armed Struggle*, p. 309.
64 Kabha, *Palestinian People*, p. 259.
65 David Gilmour, *Dispossessed*, pp. 159–60.
66 Kabha, *Palestinian People*, p. 260.
67 *Shooting the Witness: The Cartoons of Naji al-Ali*, London, 2008.
68 Salim Tamari, Normalcy and violence, the yearning for the ordinary in discourse of the Palestinian-Israeli conflict, *Journal of Palestine Studies* 42 (4), 2013, pp. 48–60.
69 *Maariv*, 13 June 1967.
70 *Sunday Times*, 15 June 1969.
71 *Maariv*, 9 September 1972.
72 Yaron Ezrahi, *Rubber Bullets*, p. 218.
73 Shlomo Ben-Ami, *Scars of War*, p. 132.

13. 1973–1977

1 Abraham Rabinovich, *The Yom Kippur War*, pp. 65–107.
2 Asaf Siniver (ed.), *The October 1973 War*, pp. 1–11.
3 Said Aburish, *Children of Bethany*, p. 223.

4 Shaul Mishal, *The PLO Under Arafat*, pp. 16–17; Shlomo Ben-Ami, *Scars of War*, p. 148.

5 Dan Schueftan, The Palestinian component in the Arab–Israeli conflict, in Alouph Hareven and Yehiam Padan (eds.), *Bayn Milhama le-Hesderim*, p. 83.

6 Yezid Sayigh, *Armed Struggle*, p. 332.

7 Muhammad Muslih, Towards coexistence: an analysis of the resolutions of the Palestine National Council, *Journal of Palestine Studies* 19 (4), 1990, pp. 3–29.

8 Mishal, *PLO Under Arafat*, p. 115.

9 Mark Tessler, *History of the Israeli-Palestinian Conflict*, p. 483; Nissim Rejwan, *Outsider in the Promised Land*, p. 141.

10 *Haaretz*, 2 November 1973.

11 *Maariv*, 23 November 1973.

12 *Haaretz*, 7 December 1973.

13 Ian Black and Benny Morris, *Israel's Secret Wars*, p. 345.

14 Weldon C. Matthews, The rise and demise of the left in West Bank politics: the case of the Palestine National Front, *Arab Studies Quarterly* Fall 1998.

15 Andrew Gowers and Tony Walker, *Behind the Myth*, p. 210.

16 Amos Oz, *In the Land of Israel*, p. 167.

17 Ilan Pappé, *Forgotten Palestinians*, p. 115.

18 Hillel Frisch, The PLO and the Arabs in Israel 1967–93: politicization or radicalization? *Nationalism and Ethnic Politics* 2 (3), 1996, pp. 446–64.

19 Riyadh Kamel Kabha, *Shtay Gadot leWadi*, pp. 82–6.

20 Pappé, *Forgotten Palestinians*, p. 131.

21 Shuli Dichter, *Mibaad Lekavanot Hatovot*, p. 94.

22 Ian Lustick, *Arabs in the Jewish State*, p. 256.

23 Salim Tamari, *Mountain Against the Sea*, p. 58.

24 Tamir Sorek, *Palestinian Commemoration in Israel*, p. 92.

25 Amos Elon, *The Israelis*, p. 12.

26 Eric Silver, *Begin*, p. 156.

27 Gershom Gorenberg, *Occupied Territories*, p. 295.

28 David Landau, *Arik*, p. 290.

29 Leila Farsakh, *Palestinian Labour Migration*, p. 50.

30 Geoffrey Aronson, *Israel, Palestinians, and the Intifada*, p. 70.

31 Aronson, *Israel*, p. 61.

32 Idith Zertal and Akiva Eldar, *Lords of the Land*, p. 205.

33 Eyal Weizman, *Hollow Land*, pp. 81–4.

34 David Shipler, *Arab and Jew*, p. 146.

35 nrg.il, 12 April 2011.

36 Raja Shehadeh, Negotiating self-government arrangements, *Journal of Palestine Studies* 21 (4), 1992, pp. 22–31.
37 Meron Benvenisti, The West Bank Data Base Project, 1986 Report, p. 46.
38 Meir Merhav, *Time* magazine, March 1980.
39 Tessler, *History*, pp. 520–23.
40 Salim Tamari, Building other people's homes: the Palestinian peasant's household and work in Israel, *Journal of Palestine Studies* 11, 10th Anniversary Issue: Palestinians under Occupation, 1981, pp. 31–66.
41 Juval Portugali, *Implicate Relations*, p. 2.

14. 1977–1981

1   Anwar Sadat in Knesset speech, November 1977.
2   http://www.archives.gov.il/NR/rdonlyres/AA5AB7B2-013B-40B7-9434-99B6C60C7C75/0/Egypt34.pdf.
3   Yitzhak Shamir, *Summing Up*, p. 101.
4   Andrew Gowers and Tony Walker, *Behind the Myth*, p. 229.
5   Yezid Sayigh, *Armed Struggle*, pp. 424–5.
6   Said Aburish, *Arafat*, p. 160.
7   Steven Spiegel, *The Other Arab-Israeli Conflict*, p. 344.
8   Eric Silver, *Begin*, p. 180.
9   David Landau, *Arik*, pp. 155–7.
10 Avi Shlaim, *The Iron Wall*, p. 368.
11 Sayigh, *Armed Struggle*, p. 426.
12 David Hirst, *Beware of Small States*, p. 118.
13 Silver, *Begin*, p. 191.
14 Mohamed Heikal, *Secret Channels*, p. 274.
15 A. D. Miller, *The Much Too Promised Land*, p. 176.
16 Mark Tessler, *History of the Israeli-Palestinian Conflict*, p. 514.
17 Silver, *Begin*, p. 203.
18 *Jerusalem Post*, 20 April 1979.
19 Sayigh, *Armed Struggle*, p. 479.
20 Dror Moreh, *Shomrei haSaf*, p. 29.
21 Landau, *Arik*, p. 280.
22 *New Statesman*, 1 December 1978.
23 Open Letter to the Prime Minister of Israel, Peace Now, March 1978.
24 Hagai Segal, *Dear Brothers*, p. 97.
25 Nahum Barnea, *Davar*, 9 May 1980. Quoted in Nahum Barnea, *Yorim ve Bochim*, p. 270.
26 Sayigh, *Armed Struggle*, p. 502.

27 Yehuda Litani, *Haaretz*, 30 November 1981.
28 Shaul Mishal, *Speaking Stones*, pp. 18–19.
29 Salim Tamari, In league with Zion: Israel's search for a native pillar, *Journal of Palestine Studies* 12 (4), 1983, pp. 41–56.
30 Hillel Cohen, Society–military relations in a state-in-the-making: Palestinian security agencies and the 'treason discourse' in the second intifada, *Armed Forces & Society* 38 (3), 2012, pp. 463–85.
31 Helena Cobban, *The Palestinian Liberation Organisation*, p. 118.
32 Raja Shehadeh, *The Third Way*, pp. 6–7.
33 *Jerusalem Post*, 4 May 1979.
34 *Sunday Times*, 19 June 1977.
35 Said Aburish, *Children of Bethany*, p. 220.
36 Michel Warschawski, *On the Border*, pp. 70–71.
37 George Bisharat, *Palestinian Lawyers and Israeli Rule*, p. 93.
38 PASSIA, *100 Years*, p. 169.
39 Cobban, *The Palestinian Liberation Organisation*, p. 116.
40 Idith Zertal and Akiva Eldar, *Lords of the Land*, p. 71.
41 Shamir, *Summing Up*, p. 131.

15. 1982–1987

1 Ze'ev Schiff and Ehud Yaari, *Israel's Lebanon War*, p. 43.
2 *Haaretz*, 22 February 2009.
3 Yoel Marcus, *Haaretz*, 26 March 1982.
4 Geoffrey Aronson, *Israel, Palestinians, and the Intifada*, p. 305.
5 Reuven Kaminer, *The Politics of Protest*, p. 36.
6 Yezid Sayigh, *Armed Struggle*, pp. 508–9.
7 *Guardian*, 7 March 1983.
8 Eric Silver, *Begin*, p. 223.
9 Shlomo Ben-Ami, *Scars of War*, p. 179.
10 Meir Pa'il, *New Outlook*, August–September 1982, http://www.slideshare.net/meirpail/ss-4109965.
11 PASSIA, *100 Years*, p. 170.
12 Hirsh Goodman, *Let Me Create a Paradise*, pp. 213–14; Robert Fisk, *Pity the Nation*.
13 PASSIA, *100 Years*, p. 170.
14 PASSIA, *100 Years*, p. 173.
15 Sayigh, *Armed Struggle*, p. 545.
16 Aronson, *Israel*, p. 306.
17 http://www.cfr.org/israel/reagan-plan-us-policy-peace-middle-east/p14140.

18 Schiff and Yaari, *Israel's Lebanon War*, p. 233.
19 http://www.nytimes.com/1982/09/03/world/israel-rejects-reagan-plan-for-palestinians-self-rule-terms-it-serious-danger.html?pagewanted=all.
20 Ben-Ami, *Scars of War*, p. 181.
21 Shaul Mishal, *Speaking Stones*, p. 19.
22 Salim Tamari, In league with Zion: Israel's search for a native pillar, *Journal of Palestine Studies* 12 (4), 1983, pp. 41–56.
23 *Guardian*, 9 August 1985.
24 Yitzhak Shamir, *Summing Up*, p. 165.
25 David Shipler, *Arab and Jew*, pp. 130–34.
26 Aronson, *Israel*, p. 312.
27 Shamir, *Summing Up*, p. 149.
28 *Washington Post*, 24 April 1984; Yehuda Litani, *Kol Hair*.
29 Salim Tamari, What the uprising means, in Zachary Lockman and Joel Beinin (eds.), *Intifada*, p. 131.
30 Baruch Kimmerling and Joel Migdal, *The Palestinian People*, p. 290.
31 UN statement, 5 December 1986.
32 *Guardian*, 21 May 1985.
33 Sayigh, *Armed Struggle*, p. 608.
34 F. Robert Hunter, *The Palestinian Uprising*, p. 26.
35 Law in the Service of Man, Torture and Intimidation in the West Bank: The Case of Al-Fara'a Prison, April 1984.
36 *Guardian*, 28 May 1987.
37 Laetitia Bucaille, *Growing up Palestinian*, p. 338.
38 Sahar Khalifeh, *Wild Thorns*, p. 49.
39 Michel Warschawski, *On the Border*, p. 69.
40 Samer Al-Saber, Permission to Perform: Palestinian Theatre in Jerusalem (1967–1993), University of Washington, 2013.
41 J. M. Winter, New life on the West Bank, *London Review of Books*, 7 January 1988.
42 Yoram Binur, *My Enemy, My Self*, p. 197.
43 Sara Roy, http://ialiis.birzeit.edu/fmru/userfiles/Gaza-Palestine-Out-of-the-Margins.pdf.
44 *Guardian*, 9 May 1985.
45 *Guardian*, 23 April 1985.
46 http://www.independent.co.uk/voices/comment/robert-fisk-how-achille-lauro-hijackers-were-seduced-by-high-life-8604519.html.
47 Andrew Gowers and Tony Walker, *Behind the Myth*, p. 330.
48 Avi Shlaim, *Lion of Jordan*, pp. 427–33.
49 *Guardian*, 23 November 1985.

50 *Guardian*, 4 March 1986.
51 *Haaretz*, 8 December 1986.
52 *Guardian*, 26 May 1987.
53 Julie Peteet, Male gender and rituals of resistance in the Palestinian 'intifada': a cultural politics of violence, *American Ethnologist* 21 (1), 1994, pp. 31–49.
54 *Guardian*, 26 May 1987.
55 Nahum Barnea, *Yorim ve Bochim*; Warschawski, *Border*, p. 135.

16. 1987

1 *Guardian*, 18 January 1989.
2 *Judea, Samaria and the Gaza District*, pp. 6–7.
3 *New York Review of Books*, http://www.nybooks.com/articles/archives/1988/jun/02/understanding-the-uprising/0.
4 Geoffrey Aronson, *Israel, Palestinians, and the Intifada*, p. 322.
5 F. Robert Hunter, *The Palestinian Uprising*, p. 37.
6 Aryeh Shalev, *The Intifada: Causes and Effects*, p. 19.
7 Mustafa Kabha, *The Palestinian People*, p. 316.
8 Salim Tamari, The Palestinian movement in transition: historical reversals and the uprising, *Journal of Palestine Studies* 20 (2), 1990–1991.
9 Don Peretz, *Intifada: Palestinian Uprising*, p. 37.
10 Shalev, *Intifada: Causes and Effects*, p. 33.
11 Muhammad Muslih, Towards coexistence: an analysis of the resolutions of the Palestine National Council, *Journal of Palestine Studies* 19 (4), 1990, pp. 3–29.
12 Amira Hass, *Drinking the Sea at Gaza*, p. 48.
13 Peretz, *Intifada*, p. 39.
14 Shalev, *Intifada: Causes and Effects*, p. 13.
15 Andrew Gowers and Tony Walker, *Behind the Myth*, pp. 356–8.
16 Yezid Sayigh, *Armed Struggle*, p. 614.
17 David Landau, *Arik*, pp. 240–41.
18 Hunter, *Palestinian Uprising*, p. 59.
19 *Guardian*, 19 December 1987.
20 Peretz, *Intifada*, p. 92; Shaul Mishal, *Speaking Stones*.
21 Mishal, *Speaking Stones*, pp. 148, 172.
22 *Guardian*, 12 February 1988.
23 Ze'ev Schiff and Ehud Yaari, *Intifada*, p. 171.
24 *Guardian*, 8 January 1988.
25 *Guardian*, 26 January 1988.

26 Peretz, *Intifada*, p. 86.
27 Anton Shammas, *New York Review of Books*, 31 March 1988.
28 Said Aburish, *Arafat*, p. 206.
29 *Guardian*, 30 January 1988; Kirsten Nakjavani Bookmiller and Robert J. Bookmiller, Palestinian radio and the intifada, *Journal of Palestine Studies* 19 (4), 1990, pp. 96–105.
30 Ted Swedenburg, *Memories of Revolt*, p. 173.
31 Swedenburg, *Memories of Revolt*, p. 172.
32 Zachary Lockman and Joel Beinin (eds.), *Intifada*, p. 35.
33 Ori Nir, *Ketem shel Anana Kala*, p. 97.
34 Mishal, *Speaking Stones*, p. 88.
35 *Guardian*, 26 January 1988.
36 Mishal, *Speaking Stones*, p. 133.
37 *Guardian*, 25 February 1988.
38 *Guardian*, 2 March 1988.
39 Mishal, *Speaking Stones*, p. 127.
40 Riyadh Kamel Kabha, *Shtay Gadot leWadi*, pp. 60–61.
41 Sayigh, *Armed Struggle*, p. 630.
42 Schiff and Yaari, *Intifada*, p. 228.
43 Aburish, *Arafat*, p. 203.
44 Ian Black and Benny Morris, *Israel's Secret Wars*, pp. 468–72.
45 Schiff and Yaari, *Intifada*, p. 164.
46 http://www.timesofisrael.com/israel-admits-to-top-secret-operation-that-killed-top-fatah-commander-abu-jihad-in-1988/.
47 Aburish, *Arafat*, p. 208.
48 http://www.aljazeera.com/news/2015/11/qa-middle-east-powerful-army-chasing-18 cows–151111094846819.html.
49 *Guardian*, 3 June 1988, 10 June 1988.
50 Nigel Ashton, *King Hussein of Jordan*, p. 250.
51 Gowers and Walker, *Behind the Myth*, pp. 381–91.
52 Bassam Abu Sharif, *Arafat and the Dream of Palestine*, pp. 163–8.
53 *Guardian*, 31 October 1988.
54 Sayigh, *Armed Struggle*, p. 623.
55 Shafiq al-Hout, *My Life in the PLO*, p. 232.
56 *Guardian*, 16 November 1988.
57 *Guardian*, 13 December 1988.
58 Sayigh, *Armed Struggle*, p. 624.
59 Al-Hout, *My Life*, p. 240.
60 Aburish, *Arafat*, p. 215.
61 *Guardian*, 14 December 1988.

62 *Guardian*, 25 January 1989.
63 Beverley Milton-Edwards and Stephen Farrell, *Hamas*, p. 10.
64 *Guardian*, 8 September 1988.
65 Jeroen Gunning, *Hamas in Politics*, pp. 33–4.
66 *Guardian*, 3 June 1986.
67 Milton-Edwards and Farrell, *Hamas*, pp. 42–51.
68 Schiff and Yaari, *Intifada*, p. 224.
69 *Guardian*, 26 October 1987.
70 Mouin Rabbani, Khalid Mishal: the making of a Palestinian Islamic leader, *Journal of Palestine Studies* 37 (3), 2007–2008.
71 Mishal, *Speaking Stones*, p. 202.
72 Mishal, *Speaking Stones*, p. 206.
73 http://avalon.law.yale.edu/20th_century/hamas.asp.
74 Sayigh, *Armed Struggle*, p. 631.
75 *Guardian*, 8 September 1988.

17. 1988–1990

1   Yehuda Amichai, Memorial Day for the War Dead.
2   *Guardian*, 20 January 1989.
3   Dennis Ross, *The Missing Peace*, p. 55.
4   *Guardian*, 17, 21 March 1989.
5   Don Peretz, *Intifada: Palestinian Uprising*, p. 99.
6   *Guardian*, 19 May 1989.
7   *Guardian*, 21–22 June 1989.
8   *Guardian*, 5, 6, 7 June 1989.
9   Arthur Neslen, *In Your Eyes a Sandstorm*, pp. 207–12.
10 Cate Malek and Mateo Hoke (eds.), *Palestine Speaks*, p. 165.
11 *Guardian*, 1 November 1989.
12 *Guardian*, 29 September 1989.
13 *Guardian*, 28 June 1990, 15 July 1989.
14 *Jerusalem Post*, 3 July 1992.
15 Neve Gordon, *Israel's Occupation*, p. 158.
16 B'Tselem, Violation of Human Rights in the Occupied Territories, 1990–1991, p. 12.
17 Peretz, *Intifada*, p. 151.
18 *Guardian*, 8 December 1989.
19 Zachary Lockman and Joel Beinin (eds.), *Intifada*, pp. 232–45.
20 Hillel Cohen, Palestinian armed struggle, Israel's peace camp, and the unique case of Fatah Jerusalem, *Israel Studies* 18 (1), 2013, pp. 101–23.

21 *Guardian*, 25 May 1988.
22 *Guardian*, 5 February 1990.
23 Peretz, *Intifada*, p. 159.
24 Michel Warschawski, *On the Border*, p. 128.
25 *New Left Review* 32, March–April 2005.
26 Sari Nusseibeh, *What is a Palestinian State Worth?* p. 205.
27 Yitzhak Shamir, *Summing Up*, pp. 180–82.

18. 1990–1991

1   Raja Shehadeh, *The Sealed Room*, p. 54.
2   Yitzhak Shamir, *Summing Up*, p. 207.
3   Yezid Sayigh, *Armed Struggle*, p. 639.
4   *Guardian*, 26 May 1990.
5   *Guardian*, 23 May 1990.
6   *Guardian*, 21 August 1990.
7   Amos Elon, *A Blood-Dimmed Tide*, p. 213.
8   *Guardian*, 30 August 1990.
9   Elon, *Blood-Dimmed Tide*, p. 192.
10 *Guardian*, 9, 10, 11, 12 October 1990.
11 *Guardian*, 27 October 1990.
12 *Guardian*, 3 November 1990.
13 *Guardian*, 12 October 1990.
14 Shehadeh, *Sealed Room*, p. 30.
15 *Guardian*, 8 December 1990.
16 Avi Shlaim, *Lion of Jordan*, pp. 497–501.
17 *Davar*, 30 January 1991.
18 *Guardian*, 23 January 1991.
19 Sari Nusseibeh, *Once Upon a Country*, pp. 321–5.
20 The Washington Report on Middle East Affairs 12 (4), 31 December 1993.
21 http://www.btselem.org/freedom_of_movement/closure.
22 Shehadeh, *Sealed Room*, p. 121.
23 *Guardian*, 16 February 1991.
24 *Guardian*, 11 March 1991.
25 Nusseibeh, *Country*, p. 339.
26 Shimon Peres, *Battling for Peace*, p. 316.
27 Said Aburish, *Arafat*, pp. 235–6.
28 Eytan Bentsur, *Making Peace*, p. 115.
29 *Guardian*, 16–17 April 1991.
30 George Bush and Brent Scowcroft, *A World Transformed*, p. 548.

31 A. D. Miller, *The Much Too Promised Land*, p. 229.
32 Bassam Abu Sharif, *Arafat and the Dream of Palestine*, pp. 221-3.
33 Yair Hirschfeld, *Track-Two Diplomacy*, p. 98.
34 Bentsur, *Making Peace*, p. 121.
35 Shamir, *Summing Up*, p. 241.
36 Shlomo Ben-Ami, *Scars of War*, p. 199.
37 Bentsur, *Making Peace*, p. 121.
38 Meron Benvenisti, *Intimate Enemies*, p. 153.
39 Peres, *Battling for Peace*, p. 317.

19. 1992-1994

1 A. D. Miller, *The Much Too Promised Land*, p. 232.
2 *Guardian*, 27 March 1992.
3 Mamdouh Nofal, Yasir Arafat, the political player: a mixed legacy, *Journal of Palestine Studies* 35 (2), 2006, pp. 23-37.
4 Ofira Seliktar, *Doomed to Failure*, p. 45.
5 *Guardian*, 21 January 1992.
6 *Jerusalem Post*, 4 May 1992.
7 *Guardian*, 27 June 1992.
8 Idith Zertal and Akiva Eldar, *Lords of the Land*, p. 135.
9 *Guardian*, 28 August 1992.
10 *Guardian*, 27 August 1992.
11 Sari Nusseibeh, *Once Upon a Country*, p. 359.
12 *Guardian*, 1 August 1992.
13 *Guardian*, 9 July 1992.
14 Shafiq al-Hout, *My Life in the PLO*, pp. 267-8.
15 Yezid Sayigh, *Armed Struggle*, p. 652.
16 Shimon Peres, *Battling for Peace*, p. 351.
17 Peres, *Battling for Peace*, p. 329.
18 http://www.haaretz.com/israel-news/.premium-1.701386.
19 *Independent*, 4 November 1993; Said Aburish, *Arafat*, p. 261.
20 *Yediot Aharonot*, 11 March 2013.
21 http://www.btselem.org/freedom_of_movement/closure.
22 *Maariv*, 10 March 1993.
23 Meron Benvenisti, *Intimate Enemies*, p. 180.
24 *Haaretz*, 11 June 1993.
25 *Haaretz*, 18 September 1998.
26 Yossi Beilin, *Touching Peace*, p. 90.
27 Ahmed Qurei, *From Oslo to Jerusalem*, p. 258.

28 *Guardian*, 30 August 1994.

29 Beilin, *Touching Peace*, p. 127.

30 Al-Hout, *My Life*, pp. 272–7; Mohamed Heikal, *Secret Channels*, p. 462.

31 Nusseibeh, *Country*, pp. 374–5.

32 Uri Savir, *The Process*, pp. 74–5.

33 Neve Gordon, *Israel's Occupation*, p. 170.

34 Baruch Kimmerling and Joel Migdal, *The Palestinian People*, pp. 358–9.

35 *Guardian*, 10 September 1993.

36 *Guardian*, 12 November 1993.

37 PASSIA, *100 Years*, p. 266.

38 Abba Eban, *Guardian*, 10 September 1993.

39 Yitzhak Shamir, *Summing Up*, p. 260.

40 Benvenisti, *Intimate Enemies*, p. 206.

41 PASSIA, *100 Years*, p. 263.

42 Mark Tessler, *History of the Israeli-Palestinian Conflict*, p. 76.

43 Aburish, *Arafat*, p. 256.

44 Hanan Ashrawi, *This Side of Peace*, p. 261.

45 *London Review of Books* 15 (20), 21 October 1993.

46 Seliktar, *Doomed to Failure*, p. 80.

47 Savir, *The Process*, p. 102.

48 Yaakov Peri, *HaBa leHorgekha*, pp. 257–9.

49 George Giacaman and Dag Jorund Lonning (eds.), *After Oslo*, p. 154.

50 David Shulman, *Dark Hope*, p. 6.

51 Amos Elon, *Blood-Dimmed Tide*, p. 267.

52 Amira Hass, *Drinking the Sea at Gaza*, p. 114.

53 Aburish, *Arafat*, p. 274.

54 Heikal, *Secret Channels*, p. 517; *Jerusalem Post*, 2 March 2014.

55 *Guardian*, 25 June 1994.

56 *New York Times*, 2 July 1994.

57 Graham Usher, *Palestine in Crisis*, p. 1.

58 http://www.nytimes.com/1994/07/14/world/israel-bars-palestinian-officials-from-gaza.html.

59 Benvenisti, *Intimate Enemies*, p. 225.

60 Nofal, *Yasir Arafat*.

61 *20 Years Since Oslo: Palestinian Perspectives*, p. 26.

62 Khalil Shikaki, The peace process, national reconstruction, and the transition to democracy in Palestine, *Journal of Palestine Studies* 25 (2), 1996, pp. 5–20.

63 *Guardian*, 21 November 1994.

20. 1995–1999

1 Nahum Barnea, quoted in *Guardian*, 9 September 1997.

2 Yuval Rabin interview, 16 June 2016.

3 Ahmed Qurei, *Beyond Oslo*, p. 4.

4 *20 Years Since Oslo: Palestinian Perspectives*, p. 27.

5 Uri Savir, *The Process*, p. 261.

6 David Horovitz, *A Little Too Close to God*, p. 19.

7 Dan Ephron, *Killing a King*, p. 182.

8 *Guardian*, 10 April 1995.

9 *Guardian*, 26 July 1995.

10 http://www.mfa.gov.il/mfa/foreignpolicy/peace/guide/pages/the%20israeli-palestinian%20interim%20agreement%20-%20annex%20i.aspx#article8.

11 Neve Gordon, *Israel's Occupation*, p. 177.

12 Khalil Shikaki, The peace process, national reconstruction, and the transition to democracy in Palestine, *Journal of Palestine Studies* 25 (2), 1996, pp. 5–20.

13 Sari Nusseibeh, *Once Upon a Country*, p. 395.

14 Idith Zertal and Akiva Eldar, *Lords of the Land*, p. 151.

15 *Guardian*, 11 October 1995.

16 Mourid Barghouti, *I Saw Ramallah*, p. 48.

17 Nabil Qassis, interview in *20 Years Since Oslo*.

18 Nusseibeh, *Country*, p. 392.

19 Menachem Klein, in *Palestine-Israel Journal* 14 (4), 2007: http://www.pij.org/details.php?id=1140.

20 Yossi Beilin, *Touching Peace*, p. 113.

21 Glenn Robinson, *Building a Palestinian State*, p. 181.

22 Said Aburish, *Arafat*, pp. 279–80.

23 Danny Rubinstein, *The Mystery of Arafat*, p. 126.

24 William B. Quandt, The urge for democracy, *Foreign Affairs* 73 (4), 1994, pp. 2–7.

25 Mamdouh Nofal, Yasir Arafat, the political player: a mixed legacy, *Journal of Palestine Studies* 35 (2), 2006, pp. 23–37.

26 Inge Amundsen and Basem Ezbidi, Clientelist politics: state formation and corruption in Palestine 1994–2000, Chr. Michelsen Institute (CMI Report R2002:17), 2002, p. 15.

27 *Guardian*, 12 November 1993.

28 Nusseibeh, *Country*, p. 376.

29 Yaakov Perry, *HaBa leHorgekha*, p. 261.

30 Maya Rosenfeld, *Confronting the Occupation*, p. 191.

31 Mustafa Barghouti interview, *New Left Review* 32, March–April 2005.
32 Tamara Cofman Wittes (ed.), *How Israelis and Palestinians Negotiate*, p. 51.
33 Shikaki, The peace process.
34 *Guardian*, 6 January 1996.
35 Aburish, *Arafat*, p. 295.
36 Jimmy Carter, *The Palestine Peace not Apartheid*, p. 146.
37 Nigel Parsons, *Politics of the Palestinian Authority*, p. 39; Ian Black, Fig leaf democracy, *Prospect*, 20 February 1996.
38 Dror Moreh, *Shomrei haSaf*, pp. 177–8.
39 *Guardian*, 5 March 1996.
40 Beverley Milton-Edwards and Stephen Farrell, *Hamas*, p. 219.
41 *Guardian*, 2 April 1996.
42 As'ad Ghanem, *The Palestinian Regime*, p. 126.
43 *Haaretz*, 17 August 2003.
44 Peter Weinberger, *Co-opting the PLO*, p. 137.
45 http://972mag.com/blame-peres-not-bennett-for-the-qana-massacre/101046/.
46 http://www.dayan.org/kap/images/stories/%20%20%205.pdf.
47 Savir, *The Process*, p. 308.
48 In a ruined country: how Yasir Arafat destroyed Palestine, *Atlantic* magazine, September 2005; Nofal, Yasir Arafat.
49 George Giacaman and Dag Jorund Lonning (eds.), *After Oslo*, pp. 212–26.
50 *Guardian*, 18 January 1997.
51 Robert Serry, *Endless Quest*, p. 59.
52 *Guardian*, 24 January 1997.
53 Qurei, *Beyond Oslo*, p. 21.
54 Graham Usher, *Dispatches from Palestine*, p. 138.
55 Nusseibeh, *Country*, p. 421.
56 Nahum Barnea, quoted in *Guardian*, 9 September 1997.
57 Paul McGeough, *Kill Khalid*, p. 126.
58 In a ruined country, *Atlantic* magazine, September 2005.
59 Ofira Seliktar, *Doomed to Failure*, p. 85.
60 Moreh, *Shomrei haSaf*, p. 223.
61 Brynjar Lia, *Building Arafat's Police*, pp. 297–8.
62 IISS, The Military Balance, 1998–1999, pp. 138–9.
63 *Guardian*, 21 April 1997.
64 Ghassan Khatib, *Palestinian Politics*, pp. 150–51.
65 Giacaman and Lonning (eds.), *After Oslo*, p. 221.
66 Lia, *Arafat's Police*, p. 347.

67 http://www.meforum.org/287/bio-sketch-faruq-qaddumi-the-plos-2.
68 Baruch Kimmerling and Joel Migdal, *The Palestinian People*, p. 367.
69 https://electronicintifada.net/content/cement-and-corruption/5123.
70 *Guardian*, 21 April 1997.
71 Cheryl Rubenberg, *The Palestinians*, p. 263.
72 Meirav Aharon-Gutman, 'The day the sun rises in the west' – ethnography of a peace process, *International Journal of Politics, Culture and Society* March 2009.
73 Qurei, *Beyond Oslo*, p. 67.
74 David Landau, *Arik*, p. 310.
75 Ghanem, *The Palestinian Regime*, p. ix.
76 Patrick Tyler, *Fortress Israel*, pp. 408–9.
77 A. D. Miller, *The Much Too Promised Land*, p. 310.
78 Jean-Pierre Filiu, *Gaza: A History*, p. 245.

21. 1999–2000

1 Akram Hanieh, The Camp David papers, *Journal of Palestine Studies* 30 (2), 2001, pp. 75–97.
2 Chapter 9, p. 152.
3 Darawsha, in Sarah Ozacky-Lazar and Yoav Stern (eds.), *Bnei Hamakom*, p. 84.
4 Gilad Sher, *Bemerhak Negia*, p. 24.
5 Ahmed Qurei, *Beyond Oslo*, p. 98.
6 Qurei, *Beyond Oslo*, p. 90.
7 A. D. Miller, *The Much Too Promised Land*, p. 284.
8 Shlomo Ben-Ami, *Scars of War*, pp. 241–4.
9 Sher, *Bemerhak Negia*, p. 65.
10 Qurei, *Beyond Oslo*, p. 114.
11 Yair Hirschfeld, *Track-Two Diplomacy*, p. 238.
12 Qurei, *Beyond Oslo*, p. 152.
13 Hanieh, Camp David papers.
14 Jeremy Pressman, Visions in collision: what happened at Camp David and Taba? *International Security* 28 (2), 2003, pp. 5–43.
15 Mark Tessler, *History of the Israeli-Palestinian Conflict*, pp. 802–3.
16 Charles Enderlin, *Shattered Dreams*, p. 223.
17 Qurei, *Beyond Oslo*, p. 151.
18 Raef Zreik, The Palestinian question: themes of justice and power, part I: the Palestinians of the occupied territories, *Journal of Palestine Studies* 32 (4), 2003, pp. 39–49.

19 Asher Susser, *Israel, Jordan and Palestine*, p. 47.
20 Benny Morris, *One State, Two States*, p. 173.
21 Qurei, *Beyond Oslo*, p. 246.
22 Hanieh, Camp David papers.
23 Miller, *Much Too Promised Land*, p. 305.
24 Pressman, Visions in collision.
25 Robert Malley and Hussein Agha, Camp David: the tragedy of errors, *New York Review of Books*, 9 August 2001.
26 *Guardian*, 9 September 2000.
27 David Landau, *Arik*, p. 347.
28 Dennis Ross, *The Missing Peace*, p. 728.
29 Ross, *Missing Peace*, p. 730.
30 Amira Hass, *Haaretz*, 1 October 2010; Hillel Cohen, Society–military relations in a state-in-the-making: Palestinian security agencies and the 'treason discourse' in the second intifada, *Armed Forces & Society* 38 (3), 2012, pp. 463–85.
31 Mamdouh Nofal, Yasir Arafat, the political player: a mixed legacy, *Journal of Palestine Studies* 35 (2), 2006, pp. 23–37.
32 http://news.bbc.co.uk/1/hi/world/middle_east/7083129.stm.
33 Azmi Bishara, Reflections on October 2000: a landmark in Jewish-Arab relations in Israel, *Journal of Palestine Studies* 30 (3), 2001, pp. 54–67.
34 Arij Sabbagh and Khouri Manhal, *Haaretz*, 30 September 2001.
35 *Washington Post*, 9 March 2000.
36 Ozacky-Lazar and Stern (eds.), *Bnei Hamakom*, pp. 84, 109.
37 Amira Hass, *Haaretz*, 1 October 2010.
38 Amira Hess, *Haaretz*, 20 November 2000.
39 Joshua Hammer, *A Season in Bethlehem*, p. 57.
40 Amos Harel and Avi Issacharoff, *Hamilhama Hasheviit*.
41 Cate Malek and Mateo Hoke (eds.), *Palestine Speaks*, p. 169.
42 Ross, *Missing Peace*, pp. 809–13.
43 Qurei, *Beyond Oslo*, pp. 294–5.
44 Susser, *Israel, Jordan and Palestine*, p. 58.
45 Ben-Ami, *Scars of War*, p. 276.
46 Qurei, *Beyond Oslo*, p. 322.

22. 2000–2002

1 Mitchell Report: http://eeas.europa.eu/archives/docs/mepp/docs/mitchell_report_2001_en.pdf.
2 *Guardian*, 7 February 2001.

3   *Guardian*, 8 February 2001.

4   Shlomo Ben-Ami, *Scars of War*, p. 252.

5   *Guardian*, 8 February 2001.

6   Nahum Barnea, quoted in *Guardian*, 15 June 2001.

7   David Landau, *Arik*, pp. 367–9.

8   *Guardian*, 30 April 2001.

9   PA TV (Fatah), 22 July 2009.

10 A. D. Miller, *The Much Too Promised Land*, p. 308.

11 Yezid Sayigh, Arafat and the anatomy of a revolt, *Survival* 43 (3), 2001.

12 Mitchell Report, pp. 4–5.

13 Ahmed Qurei, *Peace Negotiations in Palestine*, p. 46.

14 Neve Gordon, *Israel's Occupation*, p. 137.

15 *Newsweek*, 1 April 2002.

16 Lori Allen, Getting by the occupation: how violence became normal during the second Palestinian intifada, *Cultural Anthropology* 23 (3), 2008, pp. 453–87.

17 Qurei, *Peace Negotiations*, p. 48.

18 Bader Araj, in Mark LeVine and Gershon Shafir (eds.), *Struggle and Survival*, p. 378.

19 Mosab Hassan Yousef, *Son of Hamas*, p. 192.

20 Qurei, *Peace Negotiations*, p. 50.

21 Human Rights Watch, Erased in a Moment: Suicide Bombing Attacks against Israeli Civilians. October 2002, p. 39.

22 *Yediot Aharonot*, 1 September 2001, https://muse-jhu-edu.gate3.library.lse.ac.uk/article/492415/pdf/.

23 Emma Williams, *It's Easier to Reach Heaven*, p. 152.

24 Qurei, *Peace Negotiations*, p. 63.

25 *Yediot Aharonot*, 2 November 2001; Sara Roy, *Failing Peace*, p. 306.

26 Yair Hirschfeld, *Track-Two Diplomacy*, p. 277.

27 Dror Moreh, *Shomrei haSaf*, pp. 285–9.

28 http://www.jiis.org/.upload/the%20israeli%20palestinian%20violent%20confrontation%202000-2004.pdf.

29 *Haaretz*, 21 January 2002.

30 Amal Jamal, *The Palestinian National Movement*, p. 160.

31 Eyad El Sarraj, Suicide bombers: dignity, despair, and the need for hope, *Journal of Palestine Studies* 31 (4), 2001–2002.

32 Bader Araj, in LeVine and Shafir (eds.), *Struggle and Survival*, p. 380.

33 Ronen Bergman, *The Secret War with Iran*, pp. 269–71.

34 Sonia Nimr, in LeVine and Shafir (eds.), *Struggle and Survival*, pp. 141–2.

35 Ari Shavit, *Haaretz*, 10 March 2002.

36 Human Rights Watch, Erased in a Moment, p. 66.

37 Graham Usher, Facing defeat: the intifada two years on, *Journal of Palestine Studies* 32 (2), 2003, pp. 21–40.
38 Miller, *Much Too Promised Land*, p. 342.
39 *Observer*, 21 April 2002.
40 Gordon, *Israel's Occupation*, p. 204.
41 Nahum Barnea and Ariel Kastner, Backchannel: Bush, Sharon and the uses of unilateralism, Saban Center for Middle East Policy, Monograph Series 2 (December 2006), p. 24.
42 Baruch Kimmerling, *Politicide*, p. 163.
43 *New York Times*, 15 August 2002.
44 Kimmerling, *Politicide*, pp. 161–2.
45 Williams, *It's Easier to Reach Heaven*, pp. 208–9.
46 *Haaretz*, 5 March 2002.
47 Salim Tamari, Normalcy and violence: the yearning for the ordinary in discourse of the Palestinian-Israeli conflict, *Journal of Palestine Studies* 42 (4), 2013, pp. 48–60.
48 https://muse-jhu-edu.gate3.library.lse.ac.uk/article/492415/pdf, Rema Hammami, Musa Budeiri, *al-Quds*, 14 December 2001.
49 JMCC, Poll No. 45, 29–31 May, 1–2 June 2002, http://www.jmcc.org/publicpoll/results/2002/no45.htm.
50 Neil Lochery, *The View from the Fence*, p. 2.
51 *Haaretz*, 3 March 2002.
52 Al-Haq, The Annexation Wall and its Associated Regime, 2012.
53 https://www.ochaopt.org/documents/ocha_opt_barrier_update_july_2011_english.pdf.
54 Suad Amiry, *Sharon and my Mother-in-Law*, p. 188.
55 Leila Farsakh, Independence, cantons, or bantustans: whither the Palestinian state? *Middle East Journal* 59 (2), Changing Geopolitics, 2005, pp. 230–45.
56 World Bank, Stagnation or Revival, Israeli Disengagement and Palestinian Economic Prospects, December 2004, p. 6.
57 David Shulman, *Dark Hope*, p. 149.
58 *Haaretz*, 30 June 2002.
59 Ben-Ami, *Scars of War*, p. 303.
60 Landau, *Arik*, p. 401.

23. 2003–2006

1 Ariel Sharon at the UN General Assembly 15 September 2004.
2 Nahum Barnea and Ariel Kastner, Backchannel: Bush, Sharon and the

uses of unilateralism, Saban Center for Middle East Policy, Monograph Series 2 (December 2006), pp. 40–41.

3 Ahmed Qurei, *Peace Negotiations in Palestine*, p. 98.
4 Qurei, *Peace Negotiations*, pp. 104–7.
5 *Guardian*, 15 February 2003.
6 *Observer*, 12 October 2003.
7 *London Review of Books*, 6 November 2003.
8 Dror Moreh, *Shomrei haSaf*, p. 295.
9 Jean-Pierre Filiu, *Gaza: A History*, p. 264.
10 Ehud Yaari, *Times of Israel*, 30 July 2015.
11 http://www.jiis.org/.upload/the%20israeli%20palestinian%20violent%20confrontation%202000-2004.pdf.
12 *Guardian*, 24 February 2004.
13 *Haaretz*, 29 December 2003.
14 https://wikileaks.org/plusd/cables/04TELAVIV1452_a.html.
15 Sharif Hamadeh, *Adalah* newsletter 16, August 2005.
16 Qurei, *Peace Negotiations*, p. 219.
17 *Haaretz*, 6 October 2004.
18 Ari Shavit (ed.), *Partition: Disengagement and Beyond*, p. 103.
19 *Times of Israel*, 15 April 2012; Talia Sasson, Al pi Tehom, p. 87.
20 Filiu, *Gaza*, p. 273.
21 Nasser Abufarha, *The Making of a Human Bomb*, p. 127.
22 Beshara Doumani, Scenes from daily life: the view from Nablus, *Journal of Palestine Studies* 34 (1), 2004–2005.
23 Al Jazeera TV, 4 December 2013.
24 *London Review of Books*, 3 February 2005.
25 *Guardian*, 5 January 2005.
26 Wikileaks, US State Department cable, 1 April 2005.
27 Amira Hass, *Drinking the Sea at Gaza*, p. 7.
28 *Guardian*, 25 January 2011.
29 Mehdi Abdel-Hadi, bitterlemons.org, 4 April 2005.
30 Lisa Taraki, Enclave micropolis: the paradoxical case of Ramallah/al-Bireh, *Journal of Palestine Studies* 37 (4), 2008, pp. 6–20.
31 World Bank, West Bank and Gaza – Economic Update and Potential Outlook, 15 March 2006, p. 1; World Bank, The Impending Palestinian Fiscal Crisis, Potential Remedies, 7 May 2006, p. 7.
32 Arthur Neslen, *In Your Eyes a Sandstorm*, p. 145.
33 Emma Williams, *It's Easier to Reach Heaven*, pp. 249–50.
34 Ghada Karmi, *Return*, pp. 76–7.
35 Abufarha, *Making of a Human Bomb*, pp. 91–6.

36 https://www.hrw.org/world-report/2006/country-chapters/israel/palestine.

37 OCHA, Agreement on Movement and Access, November 2006.

38 Doumani, Scenes from daily life, op. cit.

39 World Bank, Movement and Access Restrictions in the West Bank, 9 May 2007.

40 Raja Shehadeh, In pursuit of my Ottoman uncle: reimagining the Middle East region as one, *Journal of Palestine Studies* 40 (4), 2011, pp. 82–93.

41 *Haaretz*, 4 January 2007.

42 *Haaretz*, 26 February 2015.

43 BDS: https://bdsmovement.net/what-is-bds.

44 Antony Loewenstein and Ahmed Moor (eds.), *After Zionism*, p. 19.

45 *Guardian*, 29 November 2004.

46 http://www.camera.org/index.asp?x_article=805&x_context=7.

47 Noam Chayut, *The Girl who Stole*, p. 192.

48 David Shulman, *Dark Hope*, p. 6.

49 *Guardian*, 24 January 2006.

50 Robert Serry, *Endless Quest*, p. 18.

51 Wikileaks, 13 January 2006.

52 International Crisis Group, Enter Hamas: The Challenges of Political Integration, 18 January 2006, https://www.crisisgroup.org/middle-east-north-africa/eastern-mediterranean/israelpalestine/enter-hamas-challenges-political-integration.

53 Serry, *Endless Quest*, p. 21.

54 De Soto Report, May 2007, http://image.guardian.co.uk/sys-files/Guardian/documents/2007/06/12/DeSotoReport.pdf.

55 *New York Times*, 25 January 2006.

56 http://english.al-akhbar.com/sites/default/files/The%20Prisoner's%20Document%20(June%202006)_0.pdf.

24. 2006–2009

1 Ehud Olmert, 17 July 2006.

2 Guardian, 9 July 2006; http://www.btselem.org/testimonies/200607 24_idf_missile_hits_a_horse_drawn_cart_killing_a_woman_and_her_grandchild.

3 http://www.brandeis.edu/crown/publications/meb/MEB12.pdf.

4 http://www.haaretz.com/lebanon-and-the-territories-no-resemblance-1.194494.

5 17 July, Knesset speech.

6 Nahum Barnea and Ariel Kastner, Backchannel: Bush, Sharon and the uses of unilateralism, Saban Center for Middle East Policy, Monograph Series 2 (December 2006).

7 http://www.brandeis.edu/crown/publications/meb/MEB10.pdf.

8 http://www.ochaopt.org/sites/default/files/GazaStripOCHA_sitrep_8 August06.pdf.

9 De Soto Report, May 2007, http://image.guardian.co.uk/sys-files/ Guardian/documents/2007/06/12/DeSotoReport.pdf.

10 John Deverell, Prospect, 27 August 2009.

11 Condoleezza Rice, No Higher Honor, p. 575.

12 http://www.vanityfair.com/news/2008/04/gaza200804.

13 De Soto Report.

14 Rice, No Higher Honor, p. 551.

15 Alan Johnston, Kidnapped, p. 27.

16 http://www.haaretz.com/israel-news/fatah-asked-israel-to-help-attack-hamas-during-gaza-coup-wikileaks-cable-shows-1.331654.

17 Guardian, 16 June 2007.

18 Rice, No Higher Honor, p. 581.

19 Alex Fishman, Yediot Aharonot, 27 June 2015.

20 Guardian, 15 June 2007.

21 Amos Elon, New York Review of Books, 14 February 2008.

22 Rice, No Higher Honor, pp. 600–605.

23 http://www.haaretz.com/news/the-full-text-of-olmert-abbas-speeches-at-the-annapolis-summit-1.234081.

24 http://www.haaretz.com/news/olmert-to-haaretz-two-state-solution-or-israel-is-done-for-1.2342010.

25 Fayyad interview, Guardian, 15 December 2008.

26 Karma Nabulsi, Guardian, 18 December 2007.

27 Haaretz, 9 September 2011.

28 Guardian, 3 March 2008.

29 Robert Serry, Endless Quest, p. 31.

30 Ghada Karmi, Introduction, in Clayton E. Swisher, The Palestine Papers, p. 10.

31 https://www.theguardian.com/world/palestine-papers.

32 Asher Susser, Israel, Jordan and Palestine, p. 67.

33 Rice, No Higher Honor, p. 653.

34 Jerusalem Post, 24 May 2013.

35 http://www.haaretz.com/haaretz-exclusive-olmert-s-plan-for-peace-with-the-palestinians-1.1970.

36 Guardian, 31 July 2008.

37 Rice, *No Higher Honor*, p. 724.
38 Mazal Mualem, *al-Monitor*, 4 November 2014.
39 Moshe Yaalon, Israel and the Palestinians: a new strategy, *Azure* 34, Autumn 2008.
40 *Times of Israel*, 19 November 2015.
41 George J. Mitchell and Alon Sachar, *A Path to Peace*, p. 109.
42 Wikileaks, US embassy, 29 August 2008.
43 *Yediot Aharonot*, 19 September 2008.
44 *Haaretz*, 28 December 2008.
45 *New York Times*, 28 December 2008.
46 *Guardian*, 9 January 2009.
47 Hisham Naffa, The Palestinians in Israel and Operation Cast Lead: a view from Haifa, *Journal of Palestine Studies* 38 (3), 2009.
48 Cate Malek and Mateo Hoke (eds.), *Palestine Speaks*, p. 45.
49 http://pchrgaza.org/en/?p=5260.
50 Izzeldin Abuelaish, *I Shall Not Hate*, pp. 179–80.
51 Rebecca L. Stein, Impossible witness: Israeli visuality, Palestinian testimony and the Gaza war, *Journal for Cultural Research* 16 (2–3), 2012, pp. 135–53.
52 Serry, *Endless Quest*, p. 37.
53 Rice, *No Higher Honor*, p. 726.
54 Congressional Research Service, US Security Assistance to the Palestinian Authority, Jim Zanotti, analyst in Middle Eastern affairs, 24 June 2009.
55 Yoram Cohen and Jeffrey White, Hamas in Combat: The Military Performance of the Palestinian Islamic Resistance Movement, Policy Focus #97, Washington Institute for Near East Policy, October 2009.

25. 2009–2014

1 Efraim Inbar and Eitan Shamir, 'Mowing the Grass': Israel's strategy for protracted intractable conflict, *Journal of Strategic Studies* 37 (1), 2014, pp. 65–90.
2 *Washington Post*, http://www.washingtonpost.com/wp-dyn/content/article/2009/01/22/AR2009012202550.html.
3 *Chicago Tribune*, 4 January 2009.
4 https://www.whitehouse.gov/the-press-office/remarks-president-cairo-university-6-04-09.
5 Josh Ruebner, *Shattered Hopes*, p. 65.

6   *Guardian*, 4 June 2009.

7   *Guardian*, 16 March 2009.

8   *The Economist*, 18 June 2009.

9   http://www.haaretz.com/news/full-text-of-netanyahu-s-foreign-policy-speech-at-bar-ilan-1.277922.

10 Raef Zreik, Why the Jewish state now? *Journal of Palestine Studies* 40 (3), 2011, pp. 23–37.

11 http://foreignpolicy.com/2011/05/25/should-the-palestinians-recognize-israel-as-a-jewish-state; https://www.washingtoninstitute.org/uploads/Documents/pubs/PolicyFocus108.pdf.

12 Interview, Ramallah, 7 February 2017.

13 *Independent*, 2 March 2009.

14 Congressional Research Service, US Security Assistance to the Palestinian Authority, Jim Zanotti, analyst in Middle Eastern affairs, 24 June 2009.

15 *Guardian*, 4 August 2009.

16 Al-Jazeera, October 2009.

17 George J. Mitchell and Alon Sachar, *A Path to Peace*, p. 158.

18 http://www.haaretz.com/news/netanyahu-declares-10-month-settlement-freeze-to-restart-peace-talks-1.3435.

19 *New York Times*, 4 May 2009.

20 Menachem Klein, Hamas in power, *Middle East Journal* 61 (3), 2007, pp. 442–59.

21 *Wall Street Journal*, 1 August 2007; *New Republic*, 26 March 2010.

22 *Guardian*, 6 December 2010.

23 Israel TV Channel 2, Hisul be'maagal sagur, 11 November 2015.

24 *The Economist*, 3 June 2010.

25 Gershon Shafir, *A Half Century of Occupation*, pp. 221–2.

26 *Guardian*, 29 June 2010.

27 Fayyad interview, Part I, 27 August and 1 September 2009, *Journal of Palestine Studies* 39 (1), 2009–2010.

28 Measures Taken by Israel in Support of Developing the Palestinian Economy, the Socio-Economic Structure, and the Security Reforms. Report of the Government of Israel to the Ad Hoc Liaison Committee (AHLC), Madrid, 13 April 2010.

29 Raja Shehadeh, *Occupation Diaries*, p. 43.

30 *Al-Shabaka*, 19 May 2014.

31 Lisa Taraki, Enclave micropolis: the paradoxical case of Ramallah/al-Bireh, *Journal of Palestine Studies* 37 (4), 2008, pp. 6–20.

32 Ruebner, *Shattered Hopes*, pp. 109–15.

33 *Guardian*, 17 July 2012.

34 *Haaretz*, 24 March 2011.

35 *Guardian*, 2 May 2014.

36 *Guardian*, 24 February 2011.

37 *The Economist*, 26 November 2011; Nicolas Pelham, Gaza's tunnel phenomenon: the unintended dynamics of Israel's siege, *Journal of Palestine Studies* 41 (4), 2012, pp. 6-31.

38 Husam Zumlot, quoted in Antony Loewenstein and Ahmed Moor (eds.), *After Zionism*, p. 48.

39 Ben Caspit, *Maariv*, 25 March 2013.

40 *Haaretz*, 15 March 2012.

41 Surat al-Fil, 105 v. 4.

42 Maan news agency, 3 July 2012.

43 *Haaretz*, 13 September 2012.

44 *Jerusalem Post*, 10 June 2013.

45 http://time.com/11458/israel-doubled-west-bank-settlement-construction-in-2013/.

46 https://972mag.com/in-bab-al-shams-palestinians-created-new-facts-on-the-ground/64732/, Abir Kopty, Heinrich Boll Foundation, Oslo.

47 https://peacenow.org/entry.php?id=10157#.WKVFsxJ970w.

48 *Guardian*, 3 March 2017; Maan news agency, 11 March 2017.

49 Ariel Handel et al., *Normalizing Occupation*, pp. 2-3.

50 Menachem Klein, *The Shift*, pp. 73-4.

51 *Haaretz*, 15 September 2010.

52 *Haaretz*, 10 June 2016.

53 Assaf Gavron, *The Hilltop*.

54 B'Tselem, Background on the Jordan Valley, 18 May 2011.

55 *Guardian*, 7 February 2014.

56 http://www.btselem.org/download/201007_by_hook_and_by_crook_eng.pdf.

57 Nahum Barnea, *Yediot Aharonot*, 18 March 2013.

58 *Guardian*, 28 April 2010.

59 Mandy Turner, Killing the zombie peace and building a new movement, *Mediterranean Politics* 21 (3), 2016, pp. 437-41.

60 Ian Lustick, *Guardian*, 22 February 2017.

61 Mitchell and Sachar, *Path to Peace*, p. 170.

62 Ir Amim, Jerusalem municipality budget analysis for 2013: share of investment in East Jerusalem, December 2014, http://www.ir-amim.org.il/sites/default/files/PL_Investment%20in%20East%20Jerusalem%20December%202014-2%2025%2015.pdf.

63 *New York Times*, 9 March 2010.
64 Michael Dumper, *Jerusalem Unbound*, p. 124.
65 Eliezer Yaari, *Me'ever le-Harei haHoshekh*.
66 'We are orphans here', *New York Times*, 1 December 2016.
67 Ibtisam Iskafi, Traveling through the 'borders' of the Israeli Interior Ministry and National Insurance, *Palestine-Israel Journal* 21 (4), 2016, pp. 57-9.
68 Ir Amim, Dangerous liaison: the dynamics of the rise of the Temple Movements and their implications, *Keshev*, 1 March 2013.
69 Natan Sharansky, *Haaretz*, 16 October 2003.
70 Ronen Bergman, *The Secret War with Iran*, pp. 3-40.
71 *Jerusalem Post*, 21 September 2016.
72 *Haaretz*, 3 April 2015.
73 *Haaretz*, 5 July 2014.
74 Robert Serry, *Endless Quest*, p. 133.
75 Ben Birnbaum and Amir Tibon, The explosive, inside story of how John Kerry built an Israel-Palestine peace plan – and watched it crumble, *New Republic*, 20 July 2014.
76 *Haaretz*, 4 August 2014.
77 *Guardian*, 21 February 2014.
78 *Haaretz*, 17 June 2014.
79 Surat al-Fil, 105 v. 5.
80 Atef Abu Saif, *The Drone Eats with Me*, p. 56.
81 *Haaretz*, 26 August 2014.
82 https://www.hrw.org/news/2014/08/03/qa-2014-hostilities-between-israel-and-hamas.
83 Abu Saif, *Drone*, pp. 12-34.
84 *Guardian*, 18 July 2014.
85 *Times of Israel*, 20 July 2014; al-Jazeera, http://www.aljazeera.com/indepth/opinion/2014/08/telegenically-dead-20148118231287o982.html.
86 *Times of Israel*, 29 July 2014.
87 Inbal Arnon, in Bashir Bashir and Azar Dakwar (eds.), *Rethinking the Politics of Israel and Palestine*, p. 34.
88 *New Statesman*, 22 July 2014.
89 *Al-Monitor*, 28 January 2015.
90 http://www.lrb.co.uk/v36/n15/mouin-rabbani/israel-mows-the-lawn.
91 See p. 399.
92 *New York Times*, 24 July 2014.
93 *Jerusalem Post*, 22 July 2014.

94 Assaf Sharon, Failure in Gaza, *New York Review of Books*, 25 September 2014.

26. 2015–2017

1 Interview, Ramallah, 7 February 2017.
2 *Guardian*, 27 July 2016.
3 http://www.reuters.com/article/us-un-assembly-israel-palestinians-id USKCN11S2CZ.
4 PLO statement, 6 February 2017.
5 *Times of Israel*, 8 January 2017.
6 http://english.alarabiya.net/en/webtv/reports/2015/05/15/U-S-President-Barack-Obama-in-an-exclusive-interview-with-Al-Arabiya.html.
7 *Haaretz*, 24 December 2015.
8 *Salon*, March 2015.
9 *Guardian*, 18 March 2015.
10 *Yediot Aharonot*, 13 March 2015.
11 *Haaretz*, 19 February 2017.
12 *Arutz Sheva*, 27 January 2016.
13 *Haaretz*, 15 February 2015.
14 *Haaretz*, 13 April 2016.
15 Palestinian Centre for Policy and Survey, 28 December 2016.
16 Alaa Tartir, Palestine-Israel: decolonization now, peace later, *Mediterranean Politics* 21 (3), 2016, pp. 457–60.
17 *Haaretz*, 7 February 2017.
18 http://www.peaceindex.org/files/Peace_Index_Data_April_2016-Eng%281%29.pdf.
19 *Haaretz*, 3 June 2017.
20 *Guardian*, 6 April 2017.
21 Maan news agency, 15–16 December 2016.
22 http://www.pcpsr.org/sites/default/files/poll%2060%20June%202016%20pressrelease%20English.pdf
23 *Times of Israel*, 28 May 2014.
24 *Times of Israel*, 31 March 2016.
25 *Haaretz*, 24 April 2016.
26 Mehdi Abdel-Hadi, *al-Rai al-Yawm*, 25 December 2016.
27 *Haaretz*, 6 April 2016.
28 *Guardian*, 5 November 2015.
29 http://www.loveunderapartheid.com/about.

30 Private information.
31 Omran Shroufi, *openDemocracy*, 17 January 2017.
32 Mouin Rabbani, *Jadaliya*, 6 December /2016, http://www.jadaliyya.com/pages/index/25621/fatah_the-disintegration-continues.
33 Alaa Tartir and Sabrien Amrov, After Gaza, What Price Palestine's Security Sector? Al-Shabaka, 8 October 2014.
34 *Times of Israel*, 13 November 2015.
35 AFP news agency, 7 July 2015.
36 Human Rights Watch, Palestine: crackdown on journalists, activists chilling effect on free expression, 29 August 2016.
37 Maan news agency, 6 March 2017; *Times of Israel*, 7 March 2017; Ynet, 13 March 2017.
38 *Defense News*, 18 January 2016.
39 Maan news agency, 3 April 2017; *New York Times*, 9 March 2017.
40 https://euobserver.com/justice/125652.
41 http://unctad.org/en/PublicationsLibrary/tdb62d3_en.pdf.
42 *Guardian*, 1 June 2016.
43 *Times of Israel*, 6 February 2017.
44 *Times of Israel*, 11 May 2015.
45 *Haaretz*, 29 October 2015.
46 *Haaretz*, 12 February 2017.
47 http://www.juancole.com/2014/05/occupartheid-isolating-degrading.html.
48 *Times of Israel*, 27 October 2016.
49 Ynet, 5 September 2016.
50 *Haaretz*, 18 December 2016.
51 *Haaretz*, 30 December 2014.
52 Command of Arabic amongst Israeli Jews, Van Leer Institute, 2015.
53 *Haaretz*, 4 July 2014.
54 *Haaretz*, 30 September 2016.
55 *Haaretz*, 22 December 2009.

EPILOGUE

1 Meron Benvenisti, The case for shared sovereignty, *The Nation*, 31 May 2007.
2 http://www.pcpsr.org/sites/default/files/Table%20of%20Findings_English%20Joint%20Poll%20Dec%202016_12Feb2017.pdf.
3 https://www.juancole.com/2014/05/occupartheid-isolating-degrading.html.

4 Bashir Bashir and Azar Dakwar (eds.), *Rethinking the Politics of Israel and Palestine*, p. 17.

5 *Washington Post*, 26 January 2017.

6 *Times of Israel*, 22 January 2017.

7 Akiva Eldar, *Al-Monitor*, 28 February 2017.

8 George Giacaman, Is a just and lasting peace possible? *Journal of Mediterranean Politics* 21 (3), 2016.

9 Reuters, 21 March 2015.

10 Alaa Tartir and Sabrien Amrov, After Gaza, What Price Palestine's Security Sector? Al-Shabaka, 8 October 2014.

11 PLO statement, 30 March 2017.

12 Al-Haq, Exploring the Legality of Land Swap Agreements under Occupation, 2011.

13 Muna Dajani and Lina Isma'il, Conscious Choices: A Guide to Ethical Consumerism in Palestine, April 2015.

14 *Haaretz*, 20 June 2016.

15 *Palestinian-Israeli Pulse*, 16 February /2017, http://www.pcpsr.org/en/node/678.

16 On Brit Shalom, see Chapter 3, p. 54.

17 *Haaretz*, 25 January 2017.

18 https://m.facebook.com/story.php?story_fbid=1183763391692005&id=739419262793089&_rdr.

19 *Haaretz*, 14 February 2017.

20 *Haaretz*, 16 February 2017.

21 Asher Susser, *Israel, Jordan and Palestine*, p. 126.

22 Dan Rabinowitz and Khawla Abu-Baker, *Coffins*, p. 12.

23 Alaa Tartir and Tareq Baconi, Al-Jazeera, 19 February 2017.

24 *The Economist*, 20–26 May 2017.

25 Salim Tamari, The dubious lure of binationalism, in Mahdi Abdul Hadi (ed.), *Palestinian-Israeli Impasse*.

26 *Los Angeles Times*, 29 December 2016.

27 Raef Zreik, When does a settler become a native? (With apologies to Mamdani), *Constellations* 23 (3), 2016.

28 Ali Abunimah, *One Country*.

29 Benvenisti, The case for shared sovereignty.

30 Padraig O'Malley, *The Two-State Delusion*, p. 302.

31 Rashid Khalidi, *Guardian*, 18 February 2017.

32 http://www.un.org/webcast/pdfs/SRES2334-2016.pdf.

33 http://www.al-monitor.com/pulse/originals/2017/02/israel-likud-benjamin-netanyahu-naftali-bennett-two-state.html.

34 Daniel Levy, *National Interest*, 6 March 2017.
35 Ali Abunimah, *Electronic Intifada*, 15 February 2017.
36 Nadia Hijab, *Guardian*, 22 February 2017.
37 Shaul Arieli, *Haaretz*, 25 January 2017.
38 *Christian Science Monitor*, 14 February 2017.

Selected Bibliography

Abdul Hadi, Mahdi (ed.), *Palestinian-Israeli Impasse: Exploring Alternative Solutions to the Palestine Israel Conflict*. Passia, 2005.

Abuelaish, Izzeldin, *I Shall Not Hate: A Gaza Doctor's Journey on the Road to Peace and Human Dignity*. Bloomsbury, 2011.

Abufarha, Nasser, *The Making of a Human Bomb: An Ethnography of Palestinian Resistance* (The Cultures and Practice of Violence). Duke University Press, 2009.

Abu Iyad and Eric Rouleau, *My Home, My Land: A Narrative of the Palestinian Struggle*. Times Books, 1981.

Abunimah, Ali, *One Country: A Bold Proposal to End the Israeli-Palestinian Impasse*. Picador, 2007.

Aburish, Said, *Arafat: From Defender to Dictator*. Bloomsbury, 1998.

Aburish, Said, *Children of Bethany*. Bloomsbury, 1998.

Abu Saif, Atef, *The Drone Eats with Me*. Comma Press, 2015.

Abu Sharif, Bassam, *Arafat and the Dream of Palestine: An Insider's Account*. Palgrave Macmillan, 2011.

Abu Sitta, Salman, *Mapping My Return*, American University in Cairo Press, 2016.

Achcar, Gilbert, *The Arabs and the Holocaust*. Saqi, 2010.

Adwan, Sami, Dan Bar-On and Eyal Naveh (eds.), *Side By Side: Parallel Histories of Israel–Palestine*. The New Press, 2012.

Adwan, Sami, Efrat Ben-Zeev, Menachem Klein, and others, *Zoom In: Palestinian Refugees of 1948, Remembrances*. Republic of Letters, 2011.

Agnon, Shmuel Yosef, *Me-atzmi el atzmi: Articles, Letters and Speeches*. Schocken, 1976.

Al-Arif, Arif, *Nakbat Bayt al-Maqdis w'al Firdaus al-mafqoud, 1947–1952* (The Catastrophe of Jerusalem and the Lost Paradise). Al-Maktaba al-Asriyya, Beirut, 1958–1960.

Al-Asmar, Fawzi, *Lihiyot Aravi be-Yisrael* (To be an Arab in Israel), Israel Shahak, 1975.

Al-Azm, Sadiq, *Self-Criticism after the Defeat*. Saqi, 2011.

Al-Hout, Shafiq, *My Life in the PLO: The Inside Story of the Palestinian Struggle*. Pluto Press, 2006.

Alroey, Gur, *An Unpromising Land: Jewish Migration to Palestine in the Early Twentieth Century*. Stanford University Press, 2014.

Amiry, Suad, *Sharon and my Mother-in-Law: Ramallah Diaries*. Granta, 2006.

Antonius, George, *The Arab Awakening: The Story of the Arab National Movement*. Hamish Hamilton, 1938.

Aronson, Geoffrey, *Israel, Palestinians, and the Intifada*. Kegan Paul International, 1990.

Ashrawi, Hanan, *This Side of Peace: A Personal Account*. Simon & Schuster, 1995.

Ashton, Nigel, *King Hussein of Jordan: A Political Life*. Yale University Press, 2008.

Atwan, Abdel Bari, *A Country of Words: A Palestinian Journey from the Refugee Camp to the Front Page*. Saqi, 2007.

Avnery, Uri, *1948: A Soldier's Tale*. Oneworld, 2008.

Avnery, Uri, *Optimi* (Optimist). Yedioth Books, 2016.

Ayalon, Ami, *Reading Palestine: Printing and Literacy, 1900–1948*. University of Texas Press, 2004.

Barbour, Nevill, *Nisi Dominus*. George G. Harrap & Co. Ltd., 1946.

Barghouti, Mourid, *I Saw Ramallah*. Bloomsbury, 2005.

Barnea, Nahum, *Yorim ve Bochim* (Shooting and Weeping). Zmora Bitan, 1981.

Barr, James, *A Line in the Sand: Britain, France and the Struggle that Shaped the Middle East*. Simon & Schuster, 2011.

Bar-Yosef, Eitan, *The Holy Land in English Culture*. Clarendon Press, 2005.

Bar-Zohar, Michael, *Ben-Gurion*. Weidenfeld & Nicolson, 1978.

Bar-Zohar, Michael, *Yaakov Herzog: A Biography*. Halban Publishers, 2005.

Bashir, Bashir and Azar Dakwar (eds.), *Rethinking the Politics of Israel and Palestine*. Bruno Kreisky Forum for International Dialogue, 2014.

Beilin, Yossi, *Touching Peace: From the Oslo Accord to a Final Agreement*. Weidenfeld & Nicolson, 1999.

Ben-Ami, Shlomo, *Scars of War, Wounds of Peace: The Israeli-Arab Tragedy*, Weidenfeld & Nicolson, 2005.

Ben-Gurion, David, *Zichronot* (Memoirs). Am Oved, 1971.

Ben-Gurion, David, *My Talks with Arab Leaders*. The Third Press, 1973.

Bentsur, Eytan, *Making Peace: A First-hand Account of the Arab-Israeli Peace Process*. Greenwood Publishing Group, 2001.

Bentwich, Norman, *For Zion's Sake: A Biography of Judah L. Magnes, First Chancellor and First President of the Hebrew University of Jerusalem*. Jewish Publication Society, 1954.

Benvenisti, Meron, *Intimate Enemies: Jews and Arabs in a Shared Land*. University of California Press, 1995.

Benvenisti, Meron, *Sacred Landscape: The Buried History of the Holy Land since 1948*. University of California Press, 2000.

Benvenisti, Meron, *Son of the Cypresses: Memories, Reflections, and Regrets from a Political Life*. University of California Press, 2007.

Ben-Zeev, Efrat, *Remembering Palestine in 1948: Beyond National Narratives*. Cambridge University Press, 2011.

Benziman, Uzi, *Sharon: An Israeli Caesar*. Adama Books, 1983.

Bergman, Ronen, *The Secret War with Iran*. Oneworld Publications, 2013.

Binur, Yoram, *My Enemy, My Self*. Doubleday, 1989.

Bisharat, George, *Palestinian Lawyers and Israeli Rule: Law and Disorder in the West Bank*. University of Texas Press, 2012.

Black, Ian, *Zionism and the Arabs, 1936–1939*. Routledge, 1986.

Black, Ian and Benny Morris, *Israel's Secret Wars*. Hamish Hamilton, 1991.

Brauch, Julia, Anna Lipphardt and Alexandra Nocke (eds.), *Jewish Topographies: Visions of Space, Traditions of Place*. Ashgate Publishing, 2008.

Buber, Martin, *A Land of Two Peoples*, ed. Paul Mendes-Flohr. University of Chicago Press, 2005.

Bucaille, Laetitia, *Growing up Palestinian: Israeli Occupation and the Intifada Generation*. Princeton University Press, 2006.

Bush, George and Brent Scowcroft, *A World Transformed*. Vintage Books, 1999.

Büssow, Johann, *Hamidian Palestine: Politics and Society in the District of Jerusalem, 1872–1908*. Brill, 2011.

Byman, Daniel, *A High Price: The Triumphs and Failures of Israeli Counterterrorism*. Oxford University Press, 2011.

Campos, Michelle, *Ottoman Brothers: Muslims, Christians, and Jews in Early Twentieth-Century Palestine*. Stanford University Press, 2011.

Caplan, Neil, *Palestine Jewry and the Arab Question, 1917–1925*. Frank Cass, 1978.

Caplan, Neil, *Futile Diplomacy, Volume 1: Early Arab-Zionist Negotiation Attempts, 1913–1931*. Frank Cass, 1983.

Caplan, Neil, *Futile Diplomacy, Volume 2: Arab-Zionist Negotiations and the End of the Mandate*. Frank Cass, 1986.

Caplan, Neil, *The Israel-Palestine Conflict: Contested Histories.* John Wiley & Sons, 2010.

Carter, Jimmy, *Palestine Peace not Apartheid.* Simon & Schuster, 2006.

Chayut, Noam, *The Girl who Stole my Holocaust.* Verso, 2013.

Churchill, Randolph S. and Winston S. Churchill, *The Six Days War.* Heinemann Books, 1967.

Cobban, Helena, *The Palestinian Liberation Organisation: People, Power and Politics.* Cambridge University Press, 1984.

Cohen, Hillel, *Army of Shadows: Palestinian Collaboration with Zionism, 1917–1948.* University of California Press, 2008.

Cohen, Hillel, *Good Arabs: The Israeli Security Agencies and the Israeli Arabs, 1948–1967.* University of California Press, 2010.

Cohen, Hillel, *Tarpat* (Year Zero of the Arab-Israeli Conflict). Keter, 2013.

Cohen, Israel (ed.), *Zionist Work in Palestine.* Unwin, 1911.

Cohen, Yeruham, *Leor Hayom uvaMahshekh* (By Day and Night). Hakibbutz Hameuchad, 1969.

Crossman, Richard, *Palestine Mission.* Harper & Brothers, 1947.

Cummings, Jonathan, *Israel's Public Diplomacy. The Problems of Hasbara, 1966–1975.* Rowman & Littlefield Publishers, 2016.

Danin, Ezra, *Tzioni Bekol Tnai* (A Zionist in All Conditions). Kiddum, 1987.

Dayan, Moshe, *Story of My Life.* William Morrow & Company, 1976.

Dayan, Yael, *Israel Journal: June, 1967.* McGraw-Hill, 1967.

Dichter Shuli, *Mibaad Lekavanot Hatovot* (On Tensions and Good Intentions). HaKibbutz haMeuchad, 2014.

Dinur, Benzion (ed.), *Sefer Toldot haHaganah* (History of the Haganah), Vol. 2. Maarachot, 1963.

Divine, Donna Robinson, *Politics and Society in Ottoman Palestine.* Lynne Rienner Publishers, 1994.

Dodd, Peter and Halim Barakat, *River Without Bridges: A Study of the Exodus of the 1967 Palestinian Arab Refugees.* Institute for Palestine Studies, 1969.

Dolev, Eran, Yigal Sheffy and Haim Goren (eds.), *Palestine and World War I: Grand Strategy, Military Tactics and Culture in War.* I. B. Tauris, 2014.

Dumper, Michael, *Jerusalem Unbound. Geography, History, and the Future of the Holy City.* Columbia University Press, 2014.

Eban, Abba, *My People.* Random House, 1968.

Eban, Suzy, *A Sense of Purpose.* Plunkett Lake Press, 2015.

Eliachar, Elie, *Lihiot im haPalestinaim* (Living with the Palestinians). Jerusalem Sephardi Jewish Community, 1975.

Elon, Amos, *The Israelis: Founders and Sons.* Adam Books, 1981.

Elon, Amos, *A Blood-Dimmed Tide: Dispatches from the Middle East*. Allen Lane, 1997.

Enderlin, Charles, *Shattered Dreams*. Other Press, 2003.

Ephron, Dan, *Killing a King: The Assassination of Yitzhak Rabin and the Remaking of Israel*. W. W. Norton, 2015.

Esber, Rosemarie M., *Under the Cover of War: The Zionist Expulsion of the Palestinians*. Arabicus Books & Media, 2009.

Eyal, Gil, *The Disenchantment of the Orient*. Stanford University Press, 2006.

Eytan, Walter, *The First Ten Years. A Diplomatic History of Israel*. Simon & Schuster, 1958.

Ezrahi, Yaron, *Rubber Bullets: Power and Conscience in Modern Israel*. Farrar, Straus & Giroux, 1997.

Farsakh, Leila, *Palestinian Labour Migration to Israel*. Routledge, 2005.

Feiwel, T. R., *No Ease in Zion*. Secker & Warburg, 1938.

Filiu, Jean-Pierre, *Gaza: A History*. Hurst, 2014.

Fischbach, Michael, *Records of Dispossession: Palestinian Refugee Property and the Arab-Israeli Conflict*. Columbia University Press, 2003.

Fisk, Robert, *Pity the Nation*. Oxford University Press, 1990.

Flapan, Simha, *Zionism and the Palestinians*. Croom Helm, 1979.

Florence, Ronald, *Lawrence and Aaronsohn: T. E. Lawrence, Aaron Aaronsohn, and the Seeds of the Arab-Israeli Conflict*. Viking, 2007.

Frisch, Hillel, *Israel's Security and Its Arab Citizens*. Cambridge University Press, 2011.

Furlonge, Geoffrey, *Palestine is My Country*. Praeger, 2008 [1969].

Gavron, Assaf, *The Hilltop*. Oneworld Publications, 2014.

Gazit, Shlomo, *Hagezer ve haMakel* (The Carrot and the Stick). Zmora Bitan, 1985.

Gelber, Yoav, *Shorshei haHavatselet* (Growing a Fleur-de-Lis: The Intelligence Services of the Jewish Yishuv in Palestine, 1918–1947). Misrad haBitahon, 1992.

Gelber, Yoav, *Palestine 1948: War, Escape and the Emergence of the Palestinian Refugee Problem*. Sussex University Press, 2006.

Gerber, Haim, *Remembering and Imagining Palestine*. Palgrave Macmillan, 2008.

Ghandour, Zeina, *A Discourse on Domination in Mandate Palestine*. Routledge-Cavendish, 2011.

Ghanem, As'ad, *The Palestinian Regime: 'A Partial Democracy'*. Sussex Academic Press, 2001.

Giacaman, George and Dag Jorund Lonning (eds.), *After Oslo: New Realities, Old Problems*. Pluto Press, 1998.

Gilbert, Martin, *Exile and Return.* Weidenfeld & Nicolson, 1978.

Gilmour, David, *Dispossessed: The Ordeal of the Palestinians, 1917–1980.* Sphere, 1982.

Gilmour, David, *Curzon.* Macmillan, 1995.

Gluska, Ami, *The Israeli Military and the Origins of the 1967 War.* Routledge, 2007.

Glynn, Jennifer (ed.), *Tidings from Zion: Helen Bentwich's Letters from Jerusalem, 1919–1931.* I. B. Tauris, 2000.

Goldberg, David J., *To the Promised Land: A History of Zionist Thought.* Penguin, 1996.

Goodman, Hirsh, *Let Me Create a Paradise, God Said to Himself.* Public Affairs, 2005.

Gordon, Neve, *Israel's Occupation.* University of California Press, 2008.

Gorenberg, Gershom, *Occupied Territories: The Untold Story of Israel's Settlements.* I. B. Tauris, 2007.

Gorkin, Michael, *Days of Honey, Days of Onion: The Story of a Palestinian Family in Israel.* University of California Press, 1991.

Gorny, Yosef, *Zionism and the Arabs, 1882–1948.* Oxford University Press, 1987.

Gowers, Andrew and Tony Walker, *Behind the Myth: Yasser Arafat and the Palestinian Revolution.* Corgi, 1991.

Gribetz, Jonathan, *Defining Neighbors: Religion, Race, and the Early Zionist-Arab Encounter.* Princeton University Press, 2014.

Grossman, David, *HaZman haTsahov* (Yellow Wind). HaKibbutz haMeuhad, 1987.

Gunning, Jeroen, *Hamas in Politics: Democracy, Religion, Violence.* Hurst, 2007.

HaCohen, David, *Time to Tell: An Israeli Life, 1898–1984.* Associated University Presses, 1985.

Hadari, Dani (ed.), *Homat Magen: Shemonim Shanah Leirgun haHaganah* (Defensive Shield, 80th Anniversary of the *Haganah*). Misrad haBiṭahon, 2002.

Halabi, Rafik, *The West Bank Story.* Harcourt Brace Jovanovich, 1982.

Hammer, Joshua, *A Season in Bethlehem.* Free Press, 2003.

Handel, Ariel, Marco Allegra and Erez Maggor, *Normalizing Occupation: The Politics of Everyday Life in the West Bank Settlements.* Indiana University Press, 2017.

Harel, Amos and Avi Issacharoff, *Hamilhama Hasheviit.* Yediot, 2004.

Hareven, Alouph and Yehiam Padan (eds.), *Bayn Milhama le-Hesderim* (The Arab-Israeli Conflict since 1973). Zmora, Bitan Modan, 1977.

Hass, Amira, *Drinking the Sea at Gaza*. Hamish Hamilton, 1999.

Haycraft Report. *Commission of Inquiry*, Colonial Office, HMSO, October 1921.

Heikal, Mohamed, *Secret Channels: The Inside Story of Arab-Israeli Peace Negotiations*. HarperCollins, 1996.

Herzl, Theodor, *Old New Land (Altneuland)*, trans. Lotta Levensohn. M. Weiner, 1987.

Hirschfeld, Yair, *Track-Two Diplomacy Toward an Israeli-Palestinian Solution, 1978–2014*. Johns Hopkins University Press, 2014.

Hirst, David, *The Gun and the Olive Branch: The Roots of Violence in the Middle East*. Faber & Faber, 1977.

Hirst, David, *Beware of Small States: Lebanon. Battleground of the Middle East*. Faber & Faber, 2010.

Hodgkin, Thomas, *Letters from Palestine, 1932–36*. Quartet, 1986.

Hoffman, Adina, *My Happiness Bears No Relation to Happiness: A Poet's Life in the Palestinian Century*. Yale University Press, 2009.

Horovitz, David, *A Little Too Close to God*. Knopf, 2000.

Horowitz, David, *State in the Making*. Knopf, 1953.

Hunter, F. Robert, *The Palestinian Uprising*. University of California Press, 1993.

Isaac, Rael Jean, *Israel Divided*. Johns Hopkins University Press, 1976.

Jacobson, Abigail, *From Empire to Empire: Jerusalem Between Ottoman and British Rule*. Syracuse University Press, 2011.

Jamal, Amal, *The Palestinian National Movement: Politics of Contention*. Indiana University Press, 2005.

Jiryis, Sabri, *The Arabs in Israel*. Institute for Palestine Studies, 1969.

Johnston, Alan, *Kidnapped and Other Despatches*. Profile Books, 2007.

Kabha, Mustafa, *The Palestinian Press as Shaper of Public Opinion, 1929–1939: Writing Up a Storm*. Vallentine Mitchell, 2007.

Kabha, Mustafa, *The Palestinian People: Seeking Sovereignty and State*. Lynne Rienner Publishers, 2013.

Kabha, Riyadh Kamel, *Shtay Gadot leWadi* (The Wadi has Two Banks: My Life Story). Hakibbutz haMeuhad, 2015.

Kadman, Noga, *Erased from Space and Consciousness: Israel and the Depopulated Palestinian Villages of 1948*. Indiana University Press, 2015.

Kaminer, Reuven, *The Politics of Protest: The Israeli Peace Movement and the Palestinian Intifada*. Sussex Academic Press, 1996.

Karmi, Ghada, *In Search of Fatima*. Verso, 2009.

Karmi, Ghada, *Return*. Verso, 2015.

Kattan, Victor, *From Coexistence to Conquest: International Law and the Origins of the Arab – Israeli Conflict, 1891–1949*. Pluto Press, 2009.

Kayyali, A. W., *Palestine: A Modern History*. Third World Centre for Research & Publishing, 1981.

Kedourie, Elie, *The Chatham House Version and Other Middle-Eastern Studies*. Weidenfeld & Nicolson, 1970.

Kedourie, Elie and Sylvia G. Haim (eds.), *Palestine and Israel in the 19th and 20th Centuries*. Frank Cass, 1982.

Kedourie, Elie and Sylvia G. Haim (eds.), *Zionism and Arabism in Palestine and Israel*. Frank Cass, 1982.

Khalaf, Issa, *Politics in Palestine: Arab Factionalism and Social Disintegration, 1939–1948*. State University of New York Press, 1991.

Khaled, Leila, *My People Shall Live*. NC Press, 1975.

Khalidi, Rashid, *Palestinian Identity: The Construction of Modern National Consciousness*. Columbia University Press, 1997.

Khalidi, Rashid, *The Iron Cage: The Story of the Palestinian Struggle for Statehood*. Beacon Press, 2006.

Khalidi, Walid, *From Haven to Conquest: Readings in Zionism and the Palestine Problem until 1948*. Institute for Palestine Studies, 1987.

Khalidi, Walid, *All That Remains: The Palestinian Villages Occupied and Depopulated by Israel in 1948*. Institute for Palestine Studies, 2006.

Khatib, Ghassan, *Palestinian Politics and the Middle East Peace Process*. Routledge, 2011.

Kimmerling, Baruch, *Politicide: Ariel Sharon's War Against the Palestinians*. Verso, 2003.

Kimmerling, Baruch and Joel Migdal, *The Palestinian People: A History*. Harvard University Press, 2003.

Klein, Menachem, *The Shift: Israel–Palestine from Border Struggle to Ethnic Conflict*. Hurst, 2010.

Klein, Menachem, *Lives in Common: Arabs and Jews in Jerusalem, Jaffa and Hebron*. Hurst, 2014.

Koestler, Arthur, *Promise and Fulfilment*. Macmillan, 1983.

Kollek, Teddy, *For Jerusalem*. Steimatzky, 1978.

Kramer, Gudrun, *A History of Palestine*. Princeton University Press, 2008.

Kurzman, Dan, *Soldier of Peace: Life of Yitzhak Rabin*. HarperCollins, 1999.

Kushner, David (ed.), *Palestine in the Late Ottoman Period*. Brill, 1986.

Landau, David, *Arik: The Life of Ariel Sharon*. Vintage Books, 2014.

Laqueur, Walter, *The Road to War: The Origin and Aftermath of the Arab-Israeli Conflict 1967–8*. Penguin, 1968.

Laqueur, Walter (ed.), *The Israel–Arab Reader: A Documentary History of the Middle East Conflict*, rev. edn. Pelican Books, 1970.

Laqueur, Walter, *A History of Zionism*. Schocken Books, 1972.

Laron, Guy, *The Six-Day War: The Breaking of the Middle East*. Yale University Press, 2017.

Lawrence, T. E., *The Letters of T. E. Lawrence*, ed. David Garnett. Cape, 1938.

Lazar, Hadara, *Out of Palestine*. Atlas, 2011.

Leibowitz, Yeshayahu, *Judaism, Human Values and the Jewish State*, ed. Eliezer Goldman. Harvard University Press, 1992.

LeVine, Mark, *Overthrowing Geography: Jaffa, Tel Aviv, and the Struggle for Palestine, 1880–1948*. University of California Press, 2005.

LeVine, Mark and Gershon Shafir (eds.), *Struggle and Survival in Palestine/Israel*. University of California Press, 2012.

Lia, Brynjar, *Building Arafat's Police: The Politics of International Police Assistance in the Palestinian Territories after the Oslo Agreement*. Ithaca Press, 2006.

Litani, Yehuda, *Cinderella Yerushalmit beMilano* (A Jerusalem Cinderella in Milano). Yentil, 2014.

Lochery, Neil, *The View from the Fence*. Continuum, 2005.

Lockman, Zachary, *Comrades and Enemies: Arab and Jewish Workers in Palestine, 1906–1948*. University of California Press, 1996.

Lockman, Zachary and Joel Beinin (eds.), *Intifada: The Palestinian Uprising Against Israeli Occupation*. South End Press, 1989.

Loewenstein, Antony and Ahmed Moor (eds.), *After Zionism: One State for Israel and Palestine*. Saqi, 2012.

Louis, W. Roger and Robert W. Stookey (eds.), *The End of the Palestine Mandate*. I. B. Tauris, 1986.

Lucas, Noah, *The Modern History of Israel*. Weidenfeld & Nicolson, 1974.

Lustick, Ian, *Arabs in the Jewish State*. University of Texas Press, 1980.

Lustick, Ian (ed.), *Palestinians under Israeli Rule*. Garland, 1994.

Luttwak, Edward N. and Daniel Horowitz, *The Israeli Army, 1948–1973*. University Press of America, 1983.

Malek, Cate and Mateo Hoke (eds.), *Palestine Speaks: Narratives of Lives under Occupation*. Verso, 2015.

Mandel, Neville J., *The Arabs and Zionism Before World War I*. University of California Press, 1992.

Manna, Adel, *Nakba and Survival: The Story of the Palestinians who Remained in Haifa and the Galilee, 1948–1956* (in Hebrew). Van Leer Institute Press and Hakibbutz Hameuchad, 2017.

Mannin, Ethel, *The Road to Beersheba*, Hutchinson, 1963.

Mansour, Atallah, *Waiting for the Dawn*. Martin Secker & Warburg, 1975.

Masalha, Nur, *A Land Without a People: Israel, Transfer and the Palestinians, 1949–96*. Faber & Faber, 1997.

Masalha, Nur, *The Politics of Denial: Israel and the Palestinian Refugee Problem*. Pluto Books, 2003.

Masalha, Nur, *The Palestine Nakba*. Zed Books, 2012.

Matar, Dina, *What it Means to be Palestinian: Stories of Palestinian Peoplehood*. I. B. Tauris, 2010.

Mattar, Philip, *The Mufti of Jerusalem: Al-Hajj Amin al-Husayni and the Palestinian National Movement*. Columbia University Press, 1988.

Matthews, Weldon, *Confronting an Empire, Constructing a Nation*. I. B. Tauris, 2006.

McGeough, Paul, *Kill Khalid*. Quartet, 2009.

Melchett, Lord, *Thy Neighbour*. Frederick Muller, 1936.

Mendel, Yonatan, *The Creation of Israeli Arabic*. Palgrave Macmillan, 2014.

Migdal, Joel (ed.), *Palestinian Society and Politics*, Princeton University Press, 1980.

Miller, A. D., *The Much Too Promised Land: America's Elusive Search for Arab-Israeli Peace*. Bantam Books, 2009.

Milton-Edwards, Beverley and Stephen Farrell, *Hamas*. Polity Press, 2010.

Mishal, Shaul, *West Bank, East Bank*. Yale University Press, 1978.

Mishal, Shaul, *The PLO Under Arafat*. Yale University Press, 1986.

Mishal, Shaul, *Speaking Stones: Communiqués from the Intifada Underground*. Syracuse University Press, 1994.

Mitchell, George J. and Alon Sachar, *A Path to Peace*. Simon & Schuster, 2016.

Moreh, Dror, *Shomrei haSaf* (The Gatekeepers). Yediot, 2014.

Morris, Benny, *The Birth of the Palestinian Refugee Problem, 1947–1949*. Cambridge University Press, 1987.

Morris, Benny, *1948 and After: Israel and the Palestinians*. Clarendon Press, 1990.

Morris, Benny, *Israel's Border Wars, 1949–1956*. Oxford University Press, 1997.

Morris, Benny, *Righteous Victims: A History of the Zionist-Arab Conflict, 1881–1999*. John Murray, 1999.

Morris, Benny, *The Birth of the Palestinian Refugee Problem Revisited*. Cambridge University Press, 2004.

Morris, Benny (ed.), *Making Israel*. University of Michigan Press, 2007.

Morris, Benny, *1948: The First Arab-Israeli War*, Yale University Press, 2008.

Morris, Benny, *One State, Two States: Resolving the Israel/Palestine Conflict*. Yale University Press, 2010.

Mutawi, Samir, *Jordan in the 1967 War*. Cambridge University Press, 1987.

Nashashibi, Nasser Eddin, *Jerusalem's Other Voice: Ragheb Nashashibi and Moderation in Palestinian Politics, 1920–1948*. Ithaca Press, 1990.

Nasrallah, Elias, *Shahadat ala al-Qarn al-Filastini al-Awal* (Testimonies of the First Palestinian Century). Dar al-Farabi, 2017.

Nazaal, Nafez, *The Palestinian Exodus from Galilee*. Institute for Palestine Studies, 1978.

Neslen, Arthur, *In Your Eyes a Sandstorm*. University of California Press, 2011.

Norris, Jacob, *Land of Progress: Palestine in the Age of Colonial Development, 1905–1948*. Oxford University Press, 2013.

Nusseibeh, Sari, *Once Upon a Country: A Palestinian Life*. Halban Publishers, 2007.

Nusseibeh, Sari, *What is a Palestinian State Worth?* Harvard University Press, 2011.

Oliphant, Lawrence, *Haifa: Or, Life in Modern Palestine*. Harper & Brothers, 1886.

O'Malley, Padraig, *The Two-State Delusion: Israel and Palestine – A Tale of Two Narratives*. Viking, 2015.

Oren, Michael B., *Six Days of War: June 1967 and the Making of the Modern Middle East*. Ballantine Press, 2002.

Oz, Amos, *In the Land of Israel*. Flamingo, 1983.

Ozacky-Lazar, Sarah and Yoav Stern (eds.), *Bnei Hamakom. Conversations with Arab Citizens in Israel*. Tami Steinitz Centre, 2016.

Pa'il, Meir, *Min HaHaganah leTzva Haganah* (The Emergence of Zahal). Zmora, Bitan, Modan, 1979.

Pappé, Ilan, *The Ethnic Cleansing of Palestine*. Oneworld, 2006.

Pappé, Ilan, *Out of the Frame: The Struggle for Academic Freedom in Israel*. Pluto Press, 2010.

Pappé, Ilan, *The Rise and Fall of a Palestinian Dynasty: The Husaynis, 1700–1948*. Saqi, 2010.

Pappé, Ilan, *The Forgotten Palestinians*. Yale University Press, 2012.

Parsons, Leila, *The Commander: Fawzi al-Qawuqji and the Fight for Arab Independence 1914–1948*. Saqi, 2016.

Parsons, Nigel, *The Politics of the Palestinian Authority from Oslo to al-Aqsa*. Routledge, 2005.

PASSIA, *100 Years of Palestinian History: A 20th Century Chronology.* PASSIA, 2001.

Peel Report. *Report of the Palestine Royal Commission.* HMSO, 1937.

Penslar, Derek, *Zionism and Technocracy: The Engineering of Jewish Settlement in Palestine.* Indiana University Press, 1991.

Peres, Shimon, *Battling for Peace.* Weidenfeld & Nicolson, 1995.

Peretz, Don, *Intifada: The Palestinian Uprising.* Westview, 1990.

Perlman, Maurice, *The Mufti of Jerusalem.* Victor Gollancz, 1947.

Perry, Yaakov, *HaBa leHorgekha* (Strike First). Keshet, 1999.

Peteet, Julie, *Landscape of Hope and Despair: Palestinian Refugee Camps.* University of Pennsylvania Press, 2005.

Piterberg, Gabriel, *The Returns of Zionism: Myths, Politics and Scholarship in Israel.* Verso, 2008.

Plascov, Avi, *The Palestinian Refugees in Jordan 1948–1957.* Frank Cass, 1981.

Porath, Yehoshua, *The Emergence of the Palestinian Arab National Movement, 1918–1929.* Frank Cass, 1974.

Porath, Yehoshua, *The Palestinian Arab National Movement 1929–1939: From Riots to Rebellion.* Frank Cass, 1977.

Portugali, Juval, *Implicate Relations: Society and Space in the Israeli-Palestinian Conflict.* Springer Netherlands, 1993.

Pryce-Jones, David, *The Face of Defeat.* Quartet, 1974.

Quandt, William, Paul Jabber and Ann Mosely Lesch, *The Politics of Palestinian Nationalism.* University of California Press, 1973.

Qurei, Ahmed (Abu Alaa), *From Oslo to Jerusalem: The Palestinian Story of the Secret Negotiations.* I. B. Tauris, 2006.

Qurei, Ahmed (Abu Alaa), *Beyond Oslo: The Struggle for Palestine.* I. B. Tauris, 2008.

Qurei, Ahmed (Abu Alaa), *Peace Negotiations in Palestine: From the Second Intifada to the Roadmap.* I. B. Tauris, 2015.

Rabinovich, Abraham, *The Yom Kippur War.* Random House, 2005.

Rabinowitz, Dan, *Overlooking Nazareth: The Ethnography of Exclusion in Galilee.* Cambridge University Press, 1997.

Rabinowitz, Dan and Khawla Abu-Baker, *Coffins on Our Shoulders: The Experience of the Palestinian Citizens of Israel.* University of California Press, 2005.

Radai, Itamar, *Palestinians in Jerusalem and Jaffa, 1948: A Tale of Two Cities.* Routledge, 2015.

Ranfurly, Countess, *To War with Whitaker: The Wartime Diaries of the Countess of Ranfurly, 1939–1945.* Mandarin, 1994.

Raz, Avi, *The Bride and the Dowry*. Yale University Press, 2012.

Reinharz, Yehuda, *Chaim Weizmann: The Making of a Statesman*. Oxford University Press, 1993.

Rejwan, Nissim, *Outsider in the Promised Land: An Iraqi Jew in Israel*. University of Texas Press, 2006.

Rejwan, Nissim, *Israel's Years of Bogus Grandeur: From the Six-Day War to the First Intifada*. University of Texas Press, 2010.

Rice, Condoleezza, *No Higher Honor*. Simon & Schuster, 2011.

Roberts, Jo, *Contested Land, Contested Memory. Israel's Jews and Arabs and the Ghosts of Catastrophe*. Dundurn, 2013.

Robinson, Glenn, *Building a Palestinian State: The Incomplete Revolution*. Indiana University Press, 1997.

Robinson, Shira, *Citizen Strangers: Palestinians and the Birth of Israel's Liberal Settler State*. Stanford University Press, 2013.

Roman, Michael and Alex Weingrod, *Living Together Separately: Arabs and Jews in Contemporary Jerusalem*. Princeton University Press, 2014.

Ronen, David, *Shnat Shabak* (The Year of Shabak). Israeli Ministry of Defence, 1989.

Rose, Norman, *A Senseless, Squalid War*. The Bodley Head, 2009.

Rosenfeld, Maya, *Confronting the Occupation: Work, Education, and Political Activism of Palestinian Families in a Refugee Camp*. Stanford University Press, 2004.

Ross, Dennis, *The Missing Peace*. Farrar, Straus & Giroux, 2005.

Rotbard, Sharon, *White City, Black City: Architecture and War in Tel Aviv and Jaffa*. Pluto Press, 2005.

Rotberg, Robert I. (ed.), *Israeli and Palestinian Narratives of Conflict: History's Double Helix*. Indiana University Press, 2006.

Rouhana, Nadim N. and Areej Sabbagh-Khoury (eds.), *The Palestinians in Israel: Readings in History, Politics and Society*. Mada al-Carmel–Arab Centre for Applied Social Research, 2011.

Roy, Sara, *Failing Peace: Gaza and the Palestinian-Israeli Conflict*. Pluto Press, 2007.

Rubenberg, Cheryl A., *The Palestinians: In Search of a Just Peace*. Lynne Rienner Publishers, 2003.

Rubinstein, Danny, *The People of Nowhere*. Three Rivers Press, 1993.

Rubinstein, Danny, *The Mystery of Arafat*. Steerforth Press, 1995.

Ruebner, Josh, *Shattered Hopes: Obama's Failure to Broker Israeli-Palestinian Peace*. Verso, 2013.

Sacher, H. (ed.), *Zionism and the Jewish Future*. John Murray, 1917.

Said, Edward, *The Question of Palestine*, Vintage, 1992 (1979).

Samuel, Viscount, *Memoirs*. The Cresset Press, 1945.

Sand, Shlomo, *The Invention of the Land of Israel*. Verso, 2012.

Savir, Uri, *The Process: 1,100 Days that Changed the Middle East*. Vintage, 1999.

Sayigh, Rosemary, *The Palestinians: From Peasants to Revolutionaries*. Zed Books, 2013.

Sayigh, Yezid, *Armed Struggle and the Search for a State: The Palestinian National Movement, 1949–1993*. Oxford University Press, 1997.

Sayigh, Yusif, *Arab Economist, Palestinian Patriot: A Fractured Life Story*, ed. Rosemary Sayigh. I. B. Tauris, 2015.

Scham, Paul, Walid Salem and Benjamin Pogrund, *Shared Histories: A Palestinian-Israeli Dialogue*. Left Coast Press, 2005.

Schiff, Ze'ev and Ehud Yaari, *Israel's Lebanon War*. Simon & Schuster, 1984.

Schiff, Ze'ev and Ehud Yaari, *Intifada: The Palestinian Uprising – Israel's Third Front*. Simon & Schuster, 1990.

Schleifer, Abdullah, *The Fall of Jerusalem*. Bertrand Russell Peace Foundation, 1972.

Schneer, Jonathan, *The Balfour Declaration*. Bloomsbury, 2010.

Schwarz, Walter, *The Arabs in Israel*. Faber & Faber, 1959.

Segal, Hagai, *Dear Brothers*. Beit Shamai Publications, 1988.

Segev, Tom, *The Seventh Million: The Israelis and the Holocaust*. Hill and Wang, 1994.

Segev, Tom, *1949: The First Israelis*. Henry Holt, 1998.

Segev, Tom, *One Palestine, Complete*. Little, Brown, 2000.

Segev, Tom, *1967: Israel, the War and the Year that Transformed the Middle East*. Little, Brown, 2007.

Seikaly, May, *Haifa: Transformation of an Arab Society, 1918–39*. I. B. Tauris, 2000.

Seliktar, Ofira, *Doomed to Failure: The Politics and Intelligence of the Oslo Peace Process*. Praeger, 2009.

Serry, Robert, *The Endless Quest for Israeli-Palestinian Peace: A Reflection from No Man's Land*. Palgrave Macmillan, 2017.

Shafir, Gershon, *Land, Labor and the Origins of the Israeli-Palestinian Conflict, 1882–1914*. University of California Press, 1996.

Shafir, Gershon, *A Half Century of Occupation: Israel, Palestine, and the World's Most Intractable Conflict*, University of California Press, 2017.

Shalev, Aryeh, *Intifada, Causes and Effects*. Westview Press, 1991.

Shamir, Yitzhak, *Summing Up*. Weidenfeld & Nicolson, 1994.

Shapira, Anita. *Land and Power: The Zionist Resort to Force, 1881–1948*. Oxford University Press, 1992.

Shapira, Anita, *Yigal Allon, Native Son: A Biography*. University of Pennsylvania Press, 2007.

Shapira, Anita, *Ben-Gurion: Father of Modern Israel*. Yale University Press, 2014.

Sharabi, Hisham, *Palestine Guerrillas: Their Credibility and Effectiveness*. Institute of Palestine Studies, 1970.

Sharabi, Hisham, *Embers and Ashes: Memoirs of an Arab Intellectual*. Olive Branch Press, 2008.

Sharett, Moshe, *Yoman Medini* (Political Diary), vols. I–V, *1936–1940*. Am Oved, 1968–74.

Sharon, Ariel and David Chanoff, *Warrior: An Autobiography*. Simon & Schuster, 2001.

Shavit, Ari (ed.), *Partition: Disengagement and Beyond* (in Hebrew). Keter, 2005.

Shavit, Ari, *My Promised Land: The Triumph and Tragedy of Israel*. Scribe, 2013.

Shehadeh, Raja, *The Third Way*. Quartet, 1982.

Shehadeh, Raja, *The Sealed Room*. Quartet, 1992.

Shehadeh, Raja, *Occupation Diaries*. Profile Books, 2012.

Shehadeh, Raja, *Language of War, Language of Peace*. Profile Books, 2015.

Shemesh, Moshe, *Arab Politics, Palestinian Nationalism and the Six Day War*. Sussex Academic Press, 2008.

Sher, Gilad, *Bemerhak Negia* (Just Beyond Reach): *The Israeli-Palestinian Peace Negotiations 1999–2001*. Miskal-Yediot, 2001.

Sherman, A. J., *Mandate Memories: British Lives in Palestine, 1918–1948*. Thames and Hudson, 1998.

Shimoni, Gideon, *The Zionist Ideology*. University Press of New England, 1995.

Shindler, Colin, *A History of Modern Israel*. Cambridge University Press, 2008.

Shipler, David, *Arab and Jew: Wounded Spirits in a Promised Land*. Bloomsbury, 1987.

Shlaim, Avi, *Collusion Across the Jordan: King Abdullah, the Zionist Movement and the Partition of Palestine*. Clarendon Press, 1988.

Shlaim, Avi, *The Iron Wall: Israel and the Arab World*. Allen Lane, 2000.

Shlaim, Avi, *Lion of Jordan*. Allen Lane, 2007.

Shulman, David, *Dark Hope: Working for Peace in Israel and Palestine*. University of Chicago Press, 2007.

Silberstein, Laurence J. (ed.), *New Perspectives on Israeli History*. New York University Press, 1991.

Silver, Eric, *Begin: A Biography*. Weidenfeld & Nicolson, 1984.

Simson, H. J., *British Rule and Rebellion*. William Blackwood & Sons, 1937.

Siniver, Asaf (ed.), *The October 1973 War: Politics, Diplomacy, Legacy*. Hurst, 2013.

Siniver, Asaf, *Abba Eban*. Overlook Duckworth, 2015.

Smith, Barbara J., *The Roots of Separatism in Palestine: British Economic Policy, 1920–1929*. Syracuse University Press, 1993.

Sorek, Tamir, *Palestinian Commemoration in Israel: Calendars, Monuments, and Martyrs*, Stanford University Press, 2015.

Spiegel, Steven L., *The Other Arab-Israeli Conflict: Making America's Middle East Policy, From Truman to Reagan*. University of Chicago Press, 1986.

Stein, Kenneth, *The Land Question in Palestine, 1917–1939*. The University of North Carolina Press, 1987.

Stein, Leonard, *The Balfour Declaration*. Valentine, Mitchell & Co., 1961.

Steinberg, Matti, *Omdim Legoralam: Hatodaa Haleumit Hapalestinit, 1967–2007* (Facing Their Fate: Palestinian National Consciousness, 1967–2007). Yediot, 2008.

Storrs, Ronald, *Orientations*. Ivor Nicholson & Watson, 1937.

Strawson, John, *Partitioning Palestine: Legal Fundamentalism in the Palestinian-Israeli Conflict*. Pluto Press, 2010.

Sufian, Sandy and Mark LeVine (eds.), *Reapproaching Borders: New Perspectives on the Study of Israel–Palestine*, Rowman & Littlefield Publishers, 2007.

Suleiman, Camilla, *Language and Identity in the Israel–Palestine Conflict: The Politics of Self-perception in the Middle East*. I. B. Tauris, 2011.

Susser, Asher, *Israel, Jordan and Palestine: The Two-State Imperative*. Brandeis University Press, 2012.

Sutton, Rafi and Yitzhak Shoshan, *Anshei haSod veHester* (Men of Secrets, Men of Mystery). Edanim, 1990.

Swedenburg, Ted, *Memories of Revolt: The 1936–39 Rebellion and the Palestinian National Past*. University of Minnesota Press, 1995.

Swisher, Clayton E., *The Palestine Papers: The End of the Road?* Hesperus, 2011.

Sykes, Christopher, *Cross Roads to Israel*. Collins, 1965.

Tamari, Salim, *Jerusalem 1948: The Arab Neighbourhoods and their Fate in the War*. Institute for Palestine Studies, 2002.

Tamari, Salim, *Mountain Against the Sea: Essays on Palestinian Society and Culture*. University of California Press, 2009.

Tessler, Mark, *A History of the Israeli-Palestinian Conflict*. Indiana University Press, 2009.

Teveth, Shabtai, *The Cursed Blessing*, Weidenfeld & Nicolson, 1969.

Teveth, Shabtai, *Retsah Arlosoroff*. Schocken, 1982.

Teveth, Shabtai, *Ben-Gurion and the Palestinian Arabs*. Oxford University Press, 1985.

Torstrick, Rebecca L., *The Limits of Coexistence: Identity Politics in Israel*. University of Michigan Press, 2000.

Tovy, Jacob, *Israel and the Palestinian Refugee Issue: The Formulation of a Policy, 1948–1956*. Routledge, 2014.

Turki, Fawaz, *Disinherited: Journal of a Palestinian Exile*. Monthly Review Press, 1972.

Turki, Fawaz, *Soul in Exile: Lives of a Palestinian Revolutionary*. Monthly Review Press, 1988.

20 Years Since Oslo: Palestinian Perspectives, Heinrich Böll Stiftung, 2013.

Tyler, Patrick, *Fortress Israel: The Inside Story of the Military Elite Who Run the Country – and Why They Can't Make Peace*. Farrar, Straus & Giroux, 2012.

Ulrichsen, Kristian Coates, *The First World War in the Middle East*. Hurst, 2014.

Usher, Graham, *Palestine in Crisis: The Struggle for Peace and Political Independence after Oslo*. Pluto Press, 1995.

Usher, Graham, *Dispatches from Palestine: The Rise and Fall of the Oslo Peace Process*. Pluto Press, 1999.

Vital, David, *Zionism: The Formative Years*. Clarendon Press, 1988.

Warschawski, Michel, *On the Border*. Pluto Press, 2002.

Wasserstein, Bernard, *The British in Palestine: The Mandatory Government and Arab-Jewish Conflict, 1917–1929*. Blackwell, 1991.

Weinberger, Peter Ezra, *Co-opting the PLO: A Critical Reconstruction of the Oslo Accords, 1993–1995*. Lexington Books, 2007.

Weiss, Yfaat, *A Confiscated Memory: Wadi Salib and Haifa's Lost Heritage*. Columbia University Press, 2011.

Weizman, Eyal, *Hollow Land: Israel's Architecture of Occupation*. Verso, 2007.

Weizmann, Chaim, *Trial and Error*. Hamish Hamilton, 1949.

Wesley, David A., *State Practices and Zionist Images: Shaping Development in Arab Towns in Israel*. Berghahn, 2006.

Williams, Emma, *It's Easier to Reach Heaven than the End of the Street*. Bloomsbury, 2007.

Wittes, Tamara Cofman (ed.), *How Israelis and Palestinians Negotiate: A Cross-Cultural Analysis of the Oslo Peace Process*, United States Institute of Peace, 2005.

Yaari, Eliezer, *Me'ever le-Harei haHoshekh* (Beyond the Mountains of Darkness). Albatross, 2015.

Yassin, Subhi, *Al-Thawra al-Arabiya al-Kubra fi Filastin* (The Great Arab Revolt in Palestine), Dar al-Kitab al-arabi, Cairo, 1967.

Yazbak, Mahmoud, *Haifa in the Late Ottoman Period, 1864–1914*. Brill, 1998.

Yizhar, S., *Khirbet Khiza*. Granta, 2011.

Yousef, Mosab Hassan, *Son of Hamas*, Authentic Media, 2010.

Zertal, Idith and Akiva Eldar, *Lords of the Land*. Nation Books, 2009.

Zochrot, *Hikayat Balad/Omrim Yayshna Aretz* (Story of a Land) (in Arabic and Hebrew). Zochrot/Pardes, 2012.

Index